HUMANITARIAN LAW OF ARMED CONFLICT
CHALLENGES AHEAD

This publication is an initiative of
The Netherlands' Red Cross Society and the
Department of Public International Law of the University of Leiden

T.M.C. ASSER INSTITUUT
THE HAGUE

Humanitarian Law of Armed Conflict Challenges Ahead

Essays in Honour of Frits Kalshoven

edited by
Astrid J.M. Delissen
Gerard J. Tanja

MARTINUS NIJHOFF PUBLISHERS
DORDRECHT/BOSTON/LONDON

T.M.C. Asser Instituut — Institute for Private and Public International Law, International Commercial Arbitration and European Law
20-22 Alexanderstraat 2514 JM The Hague, the Netherlands — tel. (0)70-3420300 — telex: 34273 asser nl, telefax: (0)70-3420359

Director: C.C.A. Voskuil

Senior Staff: M. Sumampouw (Private International Law), L.A.N.M. Barnhoorn (Public International Law), J.J.M. Tromm and A.E. Kellermann (Law of the European Communities), J.A. Swartzburg-Freedberg (International Commercial Arbitration), G.J. de Roode, Institute Manager (General Affairs), J.A. Wade (Legal Translations), M.H. Bastiaans (Publications), J.S. de Jongh (Library and Documentation).

The T.M.C. Asser Institute was founded in 1965 by the Dutch universities offering courses in international law to promote education and research in the fields of law covered by the departments of the Institute: Private International Law, Public International Law, including the Law of International Organisations, Law of the European Communities and International Commercial Arbitration. The Institute discharges this task by the establishment and management of documentation and research projects, in some instances in co-operation with non-Dutch or international organisations, by the dissemination of information deriving therefrom and by publication of monographs and series. In addition, the Institute participates in the editing of the Yearbook Commercial Arbitration and in the editing and publishing of, *inter alia*, the Netherlands International Law Review and the Netherlands Yearbook of International Law.

ISBN 0-7923-1335-6

Published by Martinus Nijhoff Publishers, P.O.Box 163, 3300 AD Dordrecht, The Netherlands. Kluwer Academic Publishers incorporates the publishing programmes of Martinus Nijhoff Publishers.

Distributors
for the United States and Canada: Kluwer Academic Publishers, 101 Philip Drive, Norwell, MA 02061, U.S.A.
for all other countries: Kluwer Academic Publishers Group, P.O.Box 322, 3300 AH Dordrecht, The Netherlands.

EDITORS' NOTE

Preparations for this *Liber Amicorum* started almost immediately after Frits Kalshoven retired from Leiden University in 1989 where he held the Chairs in Public International Law and in International Humanitarian Law Applicable in Armed Conflict.

Upon the initiative of the late Director-General of the Netherlands Red Cross Society, Chris Vogelzang, a four-member coordinating committee was established in order to supervise the necessary planning and preliminary activities. The other members of the committee were Peter Kooijmans, George Aldrich and Michel Veuthey.

Soon, however, Frits Kalshoven's retirement turned out to be merely administrative, as he continued to visit international conferences, to publish articles and -more often than before- to challenge his former colleagues at the University with intellectually stimulating discussions and with statements which were sometimes quite provocative on a wide variety of issues relating to international (humanitarian) law. It was then that the members of the coordinating committee and the editors found themselves confronted with a rather fundamental question: could you dedicate such a 'Collection of Essays' to a person who is still actively engaged in all kinds of research projects, who contributes in many respects to the further development of humanitarian law and who does not consider himself to be at the end, but to be at the beginning of a new period in his scientific and academic career? In other words: is it the right time to pay tribute to him? On the other hand, this situation offered the editors an opportunity to concentrate on a rather ambitious central theme, which looks to the future and which is in line with the former and present-day involvements and interests of Frits Kalshoven. The title of the Collection of Essays was thus born: international humanitarian law challenges. Unlike some other *Libri Amicorum*, this one would contain contributions based on the assumption that, although much has been achieved, a further codification and progressive development of the law is necessary and -perhaps even more important- feasible. The editors felt that in paying tribute to Frits Kalshoven such an approach would be most appreciated.

We have tried to reflect on those areas of international humanitarian law which have attracted Frits Kalshoven in particular during his career. Although we have tried to cover most issues relating to international humanitarian law to which Frits Kalshoven has always addressed himself, it proved virtually impossible to attempt complete coverage. Readers will, therefore, not find essays on conventional and chemical weapons; nor will they come across a contribution on protection of the environment in times of armed conflict. The editors apologize for these omissions, knowing as they do that Frits Kalshoven would certainly have welcomed essays focusing on such challenging aspects of humanitarian law, as may be concluded from his direct participation in the development of rules on the use of conventional weapons and his membership of a study group on the Protection of the Environment established by the Commission of the European Communities in 1983.

A further apology goes to those friends and colleagues of Frits Kalshoven who could not contribute; physical, technical and, above all, time constraints dictated our limitations and led to a somewhat rigorous editing policy.

The editors are indebted to the contributors to the book, including Jean Pictet and Jan van der Weel, who very generously agreed to follow the editors' somewhat demanding guidelines. It goes without saying that without the willingness of the contributors it would not have been possible to pay a proper *hommage* to Frits Kalshoven.

Apart from 34 essays, this *Liber Amicorum* contains a biographical note on Frits Kalshoven and his principal publications, a list of abbreviations (we tried to standardize recurring abbreviations as much as possible), a select bibliography and an index for easy reference.

We hope that with the publication of this Collection of Essays in honour of Frits Kalshoven, the importance of the implementation and further development of international humanitarian law will once more be brought to the fore, and that it will contribute to an increased observance of the law in the future.

In this respect the editors are convinced that, given the content and stimulating nature of the essays submitted, this *Liber Amicorum* will underline an essential aspect of the career of Frits Kalshoven: his emphasis on the need to instruct and educate those interested and involved in this branch of international law.

May 1991

CONTENTS

III   INTERNAL CONFLICTS AND INTERNAL STRIFE

ACKNOWLEDGMENTS

Undertaking the editing of this Collection of Essays was in many respects a
satisfying job; one of its pleasant aspects was that it concerned a *Liber
Amicorum* for our friend and teacher Frits Kalshoven, another that -despite
the sometimes tight time-schedules involved- we were always surrounded
by enthusiastic people who were willing to offer their help, advice and
spare time. They are too numerous to name individually, but particular
mention of Els Botje should be made for her invaluable help in making the
various contributions camera-ready and the ingrateful task of proof-
reading.

Our warm thanks go also to Marly van Houtum, Henri-Paul
Schreinemachers, Renet Gunning and Serv Wiemers, who assisted us
during the most important and critical stages of the editing. Ester Blanco
prepared the index; together with Marcel Brus she compiled the select
bibliography. Without their expertise the book would have been
incomplete. Generous assistance and indispensable material support was
provided by the Law Faculty of the University of Leiden. The devoted
help of Mieke Jacobs and all other secretaries of the Department of Public
International Law has always been an essential *point d'appui* for which we
are grateful.

Throughout the course of our editing, we had the privilege to work in
close cooperation with two international lawyers who, with their
encouragement and inspiring suggestions, contributed to the success of this
project. We owe a debt of thankfulness, therefore, to Professor George
Aldrich and Professor Peter Kooijmans for their valuable counsel and
support.

Above all, we feel indebted to Chris Vogelzang, the late Director-
General of the Netherlands Red Cross Society, for taking major initiatives
during the preparatory phases of the work which started in 1989.

A special word of appreciation goes to Michel Veuthey of the
International Committee of the Red Cross, Martine Meijer, head of the
section international humanitarian law of the Department of International
Affairs of the Netherlands Red Cross Society and Charlotte van Hall-
Siewertsz van Reesema, her predecessor with that Society.

Financial support for the publication of this Collection of Essays in
Honour of Frits Kalshoven has been granted by the Netherlands Red Cross
Society and also by the Gratama Foundation, the *Legatum Visserianum*, the

International Committee of the Red Cross and the Leiden University Foundation. We are indebted to these institutions which made this publication possible.

Finally, we would like to express our sincere gratitude to Marjolijn Bastiaans and to the Staff of the Publications Department of the T.M.C. Asser Instituut in The Hague for their critical remarks and useful comments while preparing the manuscript for publication.

Leiden/The Hague   Astrid J.M. Delissen
                                                    Gerard J. Tanja

PREFACE

When Mrs. Astrid Delissen, one of the editors of the *Liber Amicorum* dedicated to Professor Frits Kalshoven, asked me to write a preface to the book, I was happy to accept. Not only is Professor Kalshoven a friend and someone I hold in great esteem, but the Law Faculty of Leiden University, where he was a distinguished teacher for many years, once paid me the compliment of awarding me an honorary doctorate.

When I look at the list of eminent contributors to the book I see the family of specialists who for many years have given their best to the development and promotion of humanitarian law, in particular in the course of the memorable conferences held for that purpose. It gives me great pleasure that they have come together to pay tribute to one of their own, at a time when he has given up some of his official activities, while still pursuing his brilliant career. Who would ever guess that Professor Kalshoven has reached what is known somewhat inappropriately as retirement age? Rather, he is embarking on a new stage in his life, one which will be all the more fruitful because free of certain constraints.

I am convinced that this Collection of Essays, given the quality and number of the authors involved, will make a significant contribution to the understanding of international humanitarian law, the two mainsprings of which, as we all know, are the Hague and the Geneva Conventions. Our warmest thanks and congratulations go to the Committee which had this excellent idea.

Professor Kalshoven is one of a long line of Dutch legal scholars who, since Grotius, have enobled the study of law over the centuries and have greatly added to the fame of their country throughout the world. This is not the place to review his career but, having had the privilege of working with him during those years of concerted effort which gave birth to the Protocols Additional to the Geneva Conventions, I can attest to the decisive role he played in that undertaking, in particular as rapporteur. Indeed, his authority, his knowledge, his untiring work and his negotiating skills achieved wonders. The texts which are the tangible result of those meetings owe much to him.

At this point I should like to make a digression. The Additional Protocols are a momentous step forward in humanitarian law, especially as concerns protection of civilians against bombing and shelling. Some one hundred States have now ratified the Protocols, and yet several major powers have still not done so. Their reluctance, based on questionable arguments, may well compromise the efficacy of these two instruments which, while not perfect, are worthy of their predecessors and only too necessary. May the men and women who hold the fate of entire peoples in their hand bear this in mind and ponder, in their heart of hearts, their responsibility towards the international community.

Through his outstanding publications -I am thinking in particular of the landmark 'Belligerent Reprisals', for which I also had the honour of writing the preface- and his university teaching, Frits Kalshoven has also played a major role in disseminating knowledge of the humanitarian treaties, for it is obvious that these texts, which are fundamental to mankind's existence, will be applied only in so far as they are known, especially by civilian and military leaders. Finally, as legal adviser to the Netherlands Red Cross, which he has served with dedication, and as a delegate to many assemblies, Frits Kalshoven became involved with the International Red Cross Movement, in which he has countless friends.

The Collection of Essays is entitled: 'Challenges ahead'. An ambitious title, but an appropriate one; for the defenders of humanitarian law and human rights must, as the 21st century draws near, ask themselves a number of basic questions about the future of the law in a world undergoing such profound changes. Their reflections will certainly give them both cause for hope and reason to fear.

On the one hand, the past few years have seen democratic regimes put in place, usually without bloodshed, in different parts of the world where arbitrary behaviour and deceit were previously the rule. The conditions required for compliance with the law have thus been created. This is an almost miraculous turn of history.

On the other hand, we are witnessing a dangerous escalation of gratuitous violence and fanaticism. Is this the first sign of a new age of barbarism which will openly flout the law and even boast of its crimes?

Will the next century bring with it the much heralded Golden Age or the bloodshed predicted by Henry Dunant in his work *'L'avenir sanglant'*? I should not wish to hazard a guess.

In fact, the future will probably bring neither. I remain convinced that the ascendancy of law over might is, in a world threatened with annihilation, the best hope for the survival of our species. Remember, humanitarian law is in your hands. Make sure that it is strong and respected, that it is widely known, that it continues to save lives and to offer the oppressed a measure of the happiness that freedom brings.

JEAN PICTET

PREFACE

When I began to prepare to take over the presidency of the Netherlands Red Cross Society in 1986, I took up the study of international humanitarian law in depth. I may confess here that it was certainly not too soon for I already had many years of Red Cross service behind me. But that is often the way. I had been involved with national matters and international humanitarian law was not an immediate concern. I began with Professor Frits Kalshoven's slim volume entitled in Dutch 'Zwijgt het recht als de wapens spreken?' which was published in English as 'Constraints on the Waging of War'.

In the space of some 100 pages Frits Kalshoven succeeded in presenting to newcomers, such as myself at that time, a clear introduction to the subject. He belongs to that class of experts, one alas that is too rare, who can communicate a complex problem simply but without falling into the error of over-simplification and, consequently, of communicating error. I have often been able to benefit from that talent of his.

Thus, it is no surprise that, as far as possible, I have followed his teachings in his other publications, including his emeritus lecture at Leiden in 1989, in which he indicated the possibilities for the ICRC to work more closely with national societies in areas of conflict, both in the interest of the ICRC and that of the national society but primarily in the interest of those who are victims of armed conflicts. If the omens do not deceive us, such forms of cooperation should undoubtedly be given their chance in the near future.

There is no doubt that Frits Kalshoven may be regarded internationally as a leading expert in the field of international humanitarian law. His publications, both those already mentioned and innumerable others, testify to that conclusion. Yet he was more than that. At international conferences where differences of opinion threatened to obscure the right path, he was the one who was able to devise the formulas that led one back to the right path again. As advisor to the Netherlands Red Cross Society in his own field of expertise he has given valuable support to the work of the Dutch national society for many years.

Part of that work has been and remains the task of dissemination. What possibilities -and impossibilities- are concealed within that concept! Honesty compels one to admit that as far as the path of dissemination is concerned we are only just starting. Hesitant first steps are being taken within our own national society. Outside the society one has scarcely even begun. Here is a job to be done and the work of Frits Kalshoven can be used as one of the starting points for the task.

Naturally, Frits Kalshoven did not stand alone in all this. In fact, he did not actually stand for he occupied, reasonably comfortably, a professor's chair, namely, the extraordinary chair in international humanitarian law in the faculty of law at the University of Leiden. The initiative to found this chair was taken by the Netherlands Red Cross Society and led to the Royal Decree of 6 October 1975. The chair was held by Frits Kalshoven from that time until his retirement in 1989. I am certain that under his successors this chair will continue to occupy the place it deserves.

It is undeniably important, particularly in these times of actual and potential armed conflicts, for one to have the full set of legal instruments to hand in order at least to be able to avoid or diminish the worst consequences of any armed conflict.

Naturally, Frits Kalshoven would be one of the first with me to recognize the limitations of that law. The possibilities offered by the law in its entirety, whether public or private law, national or international law, can sometimes be frustrated by the shortcomings of man and the harsh realities of society. That applies equally to international humanitarian law. And yet: a small step can be won against such harsh realities each time the law is developed and propagated by practitioners of high quality. Without any shadow of doubt, Frits Kalshoven belongs in that category.

Here I wish to acknowledge the person without whom this book would never have been produced. It was the Director-General of the Netherlands Red Cross Society, Chris Vogelzang, who conceived the idea of publishing a Collection of essays on international humanitarian law in honour of Frits Kalshoven. He took the first steps to that end, together with the editors of the book. It is a matter of great regret that Chris Vogelzang was unable to witness the implementation of his idea, for he died on 11 February 1991.

I here express the wish that this book will achieve what its initiators intended: a growing interest in and a greater observance of international humanitarian law.

JAN J. VAN DER WEEL

BIOGRAPHICAL NOTE

and

PRINCIPAL PUBLICATIONS

of

FRITS KALSHOVEN

BIOGRAPHICAL NOTE OF FRITS KALSHOVEN

Frits Kalshoven was born on 29 January 1924 at The Hague, the Netherlands. He entered the Royal Dutch Navy in 1945 where he served as an officer until 1967. During this period, in 1954, he graduated from Leiden University and subsequently became an instructor in criminal and international law in the Royal Naval College. In 1967 Frits Kalshoven was appointed staff-member in the Department of Public International Law at Leiden University; in 1971 he received his doctor's degree *cum laude* for his dissertation on Belligerent Reprisals. From 1970 until 1985 he was Professor of Public International Law.

The Netherlands Red Cross Chair on International Humanitarian Law, in particular as applicable in Armed Conflicts was instituted in 1975: Frits Kalshoven was the first professor to hold this position, from which he retired in 1989. In this capacity, Frits Kalshoven was the person *par excellence* to advise the Netherlands Red Cross Society in legal matters on humanitarian issues. In addition, he was appointed on behalf of the Netherlands Government to take part in the Conference of the Red Cross Experts (The Hague, 1971; Vienna 1972) and the Conference of Government Experts (Geneva, 1971 and 1972). In 1974 he joined the Netherlands delegation to the Diplomatic Conference on the Reaffirmation and Development of International Law Applicable in Armed Conflicts (1974-1977). At this Conference he acted as the rapporteur of the Ad Hoc Committee on Conventional Weapons. As a consequence of these activities, Kalshoven was asked to become a rapporteur at the Luzern and Lugano Conferences, which were organized to prepare the 1980 UN Convention on Prohibitions or Restrictions on the Use of Certain Conventional Weapons Which May be Deemed to be Excessively Injurious or to Have Indiscriminate Effects.

In his capacity as legal advisor of the Netherlands Red Cross Society, Kalshoven organized various conferences on international humanitarian law issues, such as those on the Application of the Additional Protocols of 1977, on Guerilla and International Humanitarian Law and on Assistance to Victims of Armed Conflicts and Other Disasters.

As a member of the International Law Association he was actively engaged in committees like the Committee on Legal Problems of Extradition in Relation to Terrorist Offences. In 1985 Frits Kalshoven was asked to deliver a course on 'Arms, Armaments and International Law' at the Academy of International Law in The Hague. Together with Yves

Sandoz, he acted as Director of Studies of the 1986 session of the *Centre d'Etudes* of the Hague Academy of International Law on the Application of International Humanitarian Law.

Between 1971 and 1990, Frits Kalshoven was a Member of the Board of Editors of the Netherlands Yearbook of International Law.

He is a Honorary Professor of the International Institute of Humanitarian Law, San Remo and is a member of the Academic Commission for the Development of Humanitarian Law and Human Rights Law of that Institute.

Frits Kalshoven is a recipient of the 1971 Royal Shell Award for his work in the domain of humanitarian law. He was also awarded the Ciardi Award of the International Society for Military Law and the Law of War, for his thesis on Belligerent Reprisals (1973) and holds the *Kruis van Verdienste* (Cross of Merits) of The Netherlands Red Cross Society.

PRINCIPAL PUBLICATIONS OF FRITS KALSHOVEN

BOOKS AND OTHER MAIN WORKS

De Positie van de Niet-bezette Burgerbevolking in een Gewapend Conflict, in het Bijzonder met het Oog op de Massaal Werkende Strijdmiddelen (NBC-wapens) (The Position of the Non-occupied Population in an Armed Conflict, with Special Regard to Weapons of Mass Destruction (NBC Weapons)), preliminary report to the Netherlands Society of International Law, 61 Reports of the Society (1970).

Belligerent Reprisals, thesis, Leiden (1971).

Een Zaak van Leven of Dood (A Matter of Life and Death), inaugural lecture as Reader in Public International Law, University of Leiden (1971).

The Law of Warfare, A Summary of its Recent History and Trends in Development (1973).

Het Paradoxale Rode Kruis (The Paradoxical Red Cross), inaugural lecture as Professor of International Humanitarian Law, University of Leiden (1975).

Arms, Armaments and International Law, Hague Academy of International Law, 191 Recueil des Cours 187 (1985-II).

Constraints on the Waging of War (1987) [French edition to appear in 1991].

Impartiality and Neutrality in Humanitarian Law and Practice, farewell address as Professor of International Humanitarian Law, University of Leiden (1989); also in 29 International Review of the Red Cross 516 (1989).

AS EDITOR

The New Humanitarian Law in War and Conflict, Report of International Symposium organized by the Netherlands Red Cross on the Protocols of 1977 Additional to the Conventions of Geneva of 1949 (1978).

Essays on the Development of the International Legal Order, in Memory of Haro F. van Panhuys (with P.J. Kuyper and J.G. Lammers) (1980).

Assisting the Victims of Armed Conflict and Other Disasters (1989).

Implementation of International Humanitarian Law / Mise en oeuvre du Droit international humanitaire (with Y. Sandoz) (1989).

CONTRIBUTIONS AND ARTICLES

Criminal Jurisdiction over Military Persons in the Territory of a Friendly Foreign Power, 5 Nederlands Tijdschrift voor Internationaal Recht (Netherlands International Law Review) 165 (1958).

De Vrijlating van Krijgsgevangenen op Erewoord of Belofte (The Liberation of Prisoners of War on Parole or Promise), 56 Militair Rechtelijk Tijdschrift (Netherlands Military Law Review) 669 (1963).

Extradition and Handing Over for Military Offences: Practice in The Netherlands, 4 Recueils de la Société internationale de Droit pénal militaire et de Droit de la guerre 237 (1967).

Violations of the Humanitarian Conventions: Supervision and Sanctions, 18 Annales de droit international médical (1968).

Het Verdrag van Rome en het Nederlandse Militaire Tuchtrecht (The Treaty of Rome and Dutch Military Disciplinary Law), 61 Militair Rechtelijk Tijdschrift 409 (1968).

Nogmaals het Verdrag van Rome en het Nederlandse Militaire Tuchtrecht (Once again: the Treaty of Rome and Dutch Military Disciplinary Law), 62 Militair Rechtelijk Tijdschrift 65 (1969).

De Krijgsmacht en de Rechten van de Mens (The Armed Forces and Human Rights), 62 Militair Rechtelijk Tijdschrift 500 (1969).

Reaffirmation and Development of International Humanitarian Law Applicable in Armed Conflicts: The Conference of Government Experts, 24 May - 12 June 1971, 2 Netherlands Yearbook of International Law 68 (1971).

De Ontwikkeling van het Humanitaire Oorlogsrecht (The Development of Humanitarian Law Applicable in Armed Conflicts), 64 Militair Rechtelijk Tijdschrift 193 (1971).

Human Rights, the Law of Armed Conflict, and Reprisals, 1971 International Review of the Red Cross 183.

Reaffirmation and Development of International Humanitarian Law Applicable in Armed Conflicts: The Conference of Government Experts (Second Session), 3 May - 2 June 1972, 3 Netherlands Yearbook of International Law 18 (1972).

The Position of Guerrilla Fighters under the Law of War, 9 Revue de droit pénal militaire et de droit de la guerre 55 (1972).

Collective and Individual Responsibility for the Application of Humanitarian Rules in Armed Conflicts, Especially as Provided in Dutch Legislation, Norme Umanitarie e Istruzioni Militari 117 (1973).

Belligerent Reprisals, 12 Revue de droit pénal militaire et de droit de la guerre 265 (1973).

Reaffirmation and Development of International Humanitarian Law Applicable in Armed Conflicts: The First Session of the Diplomatic Conference, Geneva, 20 February - 29 March 1974, 5 Netherlands Yearbook of International Law 3 (1974).

International Law Tomorrow: General Conclusions, 25th Congress of the Association des auditeurs et anciens auditeurs de l'Académie de droit international de La Haye (Neuchâtel, 28 May - 2 June 1973), Proceedings published by the Faculty of Law and Economics of the University of Neuchâtel 111 (1974).

Consequences of the New Prospects for the Protection of Human Rights in Armed Conflicts and the Machinery of Supervision of Humanitarian Law, International Symposium on Humanitarian Law, Brussels 12 - 14 December 1974.

The Conference of Government Experts on the Use of Certain Conventional Weapons: Lucerne, 24 September - 18 October 1974, 6 Netherlands Yearbook International Law 77 (1975).

Applicability of Customary International Law in Non-international Armed Conflicts, A. Cassese, ed., Current Problems of International Law 267 (1975).

The Conference of Government Experts on the Use of Certain Conventional Weapons: Second Session, Lugano, 28 January - 26 February 1975, 7 Netherlands Yearbook of International Law 197 (1976).

Reaffirmation and Development of International Humanitarian Law Applicable in Armed Conflicts: The Diplomatic Conference, Geneva, 1974-1977, Part I: Combatants and Civilians, 8 Netherlands Yearbook of International Law 107 (1977).

Reprisals in the Diplomatic Conference on the Reaffirmation and Development of International Humanitarian Law Applicable in Armed Conflicts, R.J. Akkerman et al., eds., Declarations on Principles - A Quest for Universal Peace 195 (1977).

Reaffirmation and Development of International Humanitarian Law Applicable in Armed Conflicts: The Diplomatic Conference, Geneva, 1974-1977, Part II, 9 Netherlands Yearbook of International Law 107 (1978).

International Concern with Human Rights: Can It Be Effective?, 21 German Yearbook of International Law 119 (1978).

The Belligerent Reprisals in the Light of the 1977 Geneva Protocols, Report of European Seminar on Humanitarian Law 31 (1979).

The Netherlands and International Humanitarian Law Applicable in Armed Conflicts, H.F. van Panhuys et al., eds., 3 International Law in The Netherlands 289 (1980).

De Rechten van de Mens (Human Rights), H. Meijers ed., *Volkenrechtelijke Aspecten van Antilliaanse Onafhankelijkheid* (Aspects of International Law in Relation to Independence for the Antilles) 389 (1980).

Het Gebruik van Kernwapens en het Internationale Recht (The Use of Nuclear Weapons and International Law), 35 Internationale Spectator 471 (1981).

War, Laws of', Use of Force - War and Neutrality - Peace Treaties, 4 Encyclopaedia of Public International Law (1982).

Civilian Immunity and the Principle of Distinction, 31 The American University Law Review 855 (1982).

American Convention on Human Rights, II.E. International Organization and Integration (1982) Dir.II.E.1.f.

'Guerrilla' and 'Terrorism' in Internal Armed Conflict, 33 The American University Law Review 67 (1983).

Grotius: His Relevance to Present-day Law of Armed Conflict, Proceedings of the 77th Annual Meeting of the American Society of International Law 213 (1983).

The Soldier and His Golf Clubs, C. Swinarski, ed., Studies and Essays on International Humanitarian Law and Red Cross Principles, in Honour of Jean Pictet 369 (1984).

Guerilla and Humanitarian Law: An Introduction, Proceedings of the International Symposium of the Red Cross on Guerilla and International Humanitarian Law, Antwerp, February 2 and 3, 1984, at 23 (1984).

The Humanitarian Law of Armed Conflict: The Protocols of 1977 Additional to the Geneva Conventions of 1949, II.K International Organization and Integration (1984) Dir.*II.K.*2.1.

Guerriila en Mensenrechten (Guerrilla and Human Rights), 33 Ars Aequi 468 (1984).

Grotius' jus in bello with Special Reference to Ruses of War and Perfidy, A. Dufour et al., eds., Grotius et l'ordre juridique international 89 (1985).

Van Gewonden en Zieken, Bommen en Granaten (Of Wounded and Sick, Bombs and Grenades), 1985 Nederlands Juristen Blad (Netherlands Lawyers Review) 133.

Should the Laws of War Apply to Terrorists?, Proceedings of the 79th Annual Meeting of the American Society of International Law 114 (1985).

Wat is nu Eigenlijk Recht? Over Grensgeschillen en Andere Problemen van Volkenrecht (What does Law Really Mean? About Border Disputes and Other Problems of International Law), farewell address as Professor of Public International Law (1985, not published).

The Present State of Research Carried Out by the English-speaking Section of the Centre for Studies and Research, Hague Academy of International Law, The Application of Humanitarian Law (1986).

Conventionele Wapens in het Internationale Verdrags- en Gewoonterecht (Conventional Weapons in International Treaty Law and Customary Law), 79 Militair Rechtelijk Tijdschrift 29 (1986).

Humanitair Oorlogsrecht en de Bescherming van de Bevolking (Humanitarian Law and the Protection of the Population), 6 *Alert* 12 (1986).

Beheersing van Geweld via het Humanitaire Oorlogsrecht (Controlling Violence Through Humanitarian Law Applicable in Armed Conflicts), Maatschappij en Krijgsmacht (Society and the Armed Forces) 2 (1986).

Moyens de mise en oeuvre du droit international humanitaire: forces et faiblesses, Institut Français de Droit Humanitaire et des Droits de l'Homme, Le Droit International Humanitaire 65 (1987).

The Protocols of 1977 and the Netherlands Red Cross, 27 International Review of the Red Cross 305 (1987).

Extradition versus Asylum, International Institute of Air and Space Law, Aviation Security: How to Safeguard International Air Transport? Conference Proceedings 154 (1987).

Deportation, Internment and Repatriation of Dutch Civilians During and After the Second World War: International Legal Aspects, J.F.Ph. Hers, ed., Stress, Medical and Legal Analysis of Late Effects of World War II Suffering in The Netherlands 131 (1988).

1909 London Declaration Concerning the Laws of Naval War: Commentary, N. Ronzitti, ed., The Law of Naval Warfare 257 (1988).

Conventional Weaponry: The Law from St. Petersburg to Lucerne and Beyond, M.A. Meyer, ed., Armed Conflict and the New Law: Aspects of the 1977 Geneva Protocols and the 1981 Weapons Convention 251 (1989).

Instructions for the Armed Forces, 28 Revue de droit militaire et de droit de la guerre 315 (1989).

Der gegenwärtige Stand der Repressalienfrage (The Present State of Affairs with Respect to the Question of Reprisals), 2 Humanitäres Völkerrecht (International Humanitarian Law) 4 (1989).

The Conventional Weapons Convention: Underlying Legal Principles, 30 International Review of the Red Cross 510 (1990).

Belligerent Reprisals Revisited, 21 NYIL 43 (1990).

Forthcoming:

Noncombatant Persons: A Comment to Chapter 11 of the Commander's Handbook on the Law of Naval Operations (NWP 9), U.S. Naval War College (1991).

Maritime Aspects of the Gulf War: Dutch and Belgian Practice, De Guttry, ed.

The Gulf War and the Law of War: Prohibitions or Restrictions on Methods and Means of Warfare, H.H.G. Post, I.F. Dekker, eds., The Gulf War of 1980-1988. The Iran-Iraq War in International Legal Perspective.

ABBREVIATIONS

AG Rés./GA Res.	Assemblée Générale Résolution
AJIL	American Journal of International Law
Am. Univ. Law Review	American University Law Review
Am.U.J.Int.L.&Pol'y	American University Journal of International Law and Policy
ANC	African National Congress
Annual Digest	Annual Digest and Reports of International Law Cases
Ann. Français	Annuaire Français
ASIL	American Society of International Law
ASIL Proc.	Proceedings of the American Society of International Law
B.C. Int'l & Comp. L. Rev.	British Columbia International and Comparative Law Review
BYIL	British Yearbook of International Law
CDDH	Conférence Diplomatique sur la réaffirmation et le développement du droit humanitaire applicable dans les conflits armés
CDI/ILC	Commission du Droit International
CICR/ICRC	International Committee of the Red Cross
CIJ/ICJ	Court Internationale de Justice
Cmd.	UK Command Papers 1919-1956
CMD	Canadian Military Documents
CSCE	Conference on Security and Co-operation in Europe
Can. Y.b. Int'l Law	Canadian Yearbook of International Law
Denver J. Int'l Law and Politics	Denver Journal of International Law and Politics
DIH	Droit International Humanitaire
ECOSOC	Economic and Social Council of the United Nations
EEZ	Exclusive Economic Zone
EPIL	Encyclopaedia of Public International Law
FM	Field Manual
GA Res./AG Rés.	General Assembly Resolution
GB	Gesetzblatt

GYIL	German Yearbook of International Law
Hum.Rts. Quarterly	Human Rights Quarterly
HRQ	*Ibid.*
IAEA	International Atomic Energy Agency
ICAO	International Civil Aviation Organisation
ICJ/CIJ	International Court of Justice
ICLQ	International and Comparative Law Quarterly
ICRC/CICR	International Committee of the Red Cross
IDI	Institut de Droit International
ILA	International Law Association
ILC/CDI	International Law Commission
ILM	International Legal Materials
ILO	International Labour Organisation
ILR	International Law Reports
IMO	International Maritime Organisation
INF	Intermediate Range Nuclear Force
INTERTANKO	International Association of Independent Tank Owners
IRRC/RICR	International Review of the Red Cross
ITU	International Telecommunication Union
It.YIL	Italian Yearbook of International Law
JAG Journal	Judge Advocate General of the Navy Journal
Jap.Ann.Int.'Law	Japanese Annual of International Law
JDI	Journal de Droit International
LOSC	1982 Law of the Sea Convention
Loy.L.A. Int'l & Comp. L.J.	Loyola of Los Angeles International and Comparative Law Journal
MLR	Military Law Review
NATO/OTAN	North Atlantic Treaty Organisation
NGO/ONG	Non-Governmental Organisation
NILR	Netherlands International Law Review
NJW	Neue Juristische Wochenschrift
NPT/TNP	Non Proliferation Treaty
NLR	Natal Law Report
NSCSC	North Sea Continental Shelf Case
NWP	Naval Warfare Publication
NYIL	Netherlands Yearbook of International Law
OAU/OUA	Organisation of African Union

ODILA	Ocean Development and International Law
ONG/NGO	Organisation non-gouvernementale
ONU/UNO	Organisation des Nations Unies
Oregon L. Rev.	Oregon Law Review
OTAN/NATO	Organisation du Traité de l'Atlantique du Nord
OUA/OAU	Organisation de l'Union Africaine
PAC	Pan-Africanist Congress
PLO	Palestine Liberation Organisation
POW	Prisoner of War
RAF	Royal Air Force
RBDI	Revue Belge de Droit International
RCADI	Receuil des Cours de l'Académie de Droit International
Receuil des Cours	*Ibid.*
Rev. Int. Studies	Review of International Studies
Rev. Egypt. de Droit Int.	Revue Egypte de Droit International
RDPM	Revue de Droit Pénal Militaire et de Droit de Guerre
RGDIP	Revue Générale de Droit International Public
RIAA	Reports of International Arbitral Awards
RICR/IRRC	International Review of the Red Cross
SALT I, II	Strategic Arms Limitation Talks I, II
SC Res.	Security Council Resolution
SDN	Société des Nations
SIPRI Yearbook	Stockholm International Peace Research Institute Yearbook
SWAPO	South West Africa People's Organisation
TIAS	Treaties and Other International Acts Series (United States)
TNP/NPT	Traité sur la non-prolifération des armes nucléaires
UCLA Pacific Basin Law Journal	University of California Los Angeles Pacific Basin Law Journal
UNCLOS III	Third United Nations Conference on the Law of the Sea
UNDRO	Office of the United Nations Disaster Relief Co-ordinator

UNESCO	United Nations Educational, Scientific and Cultural Organisation
UN GAOR	United Nations General Assembly Official Records
UNHCR	United Nations High Commissioner for Refugees
UNICEF	United Nations (International) Children's (Emergency) Fund
UNIDIR	United Nations Institute for Disarmament Research
UNO/ONU	United Nations Organisation
UNTS	United Nations Treaty Series
UNWCC	United Nations War Crimes Commission
USAF	United States Air Force
UST	United States Treaties
Vand. J. Transnat'l L.	Vanderbilt Journal of Transnational Law
Virg. J. Int. Law	Virginia Journal of International Law
VJIL	*Ibid.*
WCR	War Commission Reports
Yb.ILC	Yearbook of the International Law Commission
YJIL	Yale Journal of International Law
ZaöRV	Zeitschrift für ausländisches öffentliches Recht und Völkerrecht

I

HUMANITARIAN LAW IN GENERAL

THE RESTRAINT OF WAR IN HISTORICAL AND PHILOSOPHICAL PERSPECTIVE *

GEOFFREY BEST

1.   THE DEVELOPMENT OF THE IDEA TO CONTROL WAR

Such a title and a theme have something paradoxical and far-fetched about them. Restraint of *war*, of all things? *Restraint*, in this of all centuries? To some extent, we are treading the boards of a theatre of illusions. But this is not surprising. The cause may not lie wholly in the subject. It may indeed be true that our century, not least because it has discovered so many ways of inventing and diffusing illusions, is one that has become particularly

---

*   This essay is an elaborated and updated version of the keynote address delivered by the author at the Conference on Restraint of War, The Royal Military College of Canada, 1986.

prone to them; even, dependent upon them. That at any rate is how its character is often interpreted; an interpretation helpful to my own approach to the subject, which conceives of it as part of the general history of our age and of our civilization. Approaching it thus, we find ourselves wedged between two lynx-eyed (though otherwise ill-matched) observers of our recent times. Orwell was driven by the barrages of lies laid down by all parties over the Spanish Civil War to exclaim: 'the very concept of objective truth is fading out of the world'; and Mailer discovered a more pleasing aspect of the same phenomenon in Marilyn Monroe: 'she dramatises one cardinal peculiarity of existence in this century; the lie, when well embodied, seems to offer more purchase upon existence than the truth.'[1]

Let us turn at once from the more fanciful to the most unfanciful aspects of the subject: its historiography and vocabulary. One of our classic modern texts is titled *The Great Illusion*. One of our path-finding historical studies was titled *The Disarmament Illusion*. One of the acutest observers of the disarmament conferences of the twenties enunciated a truth which seems to remain valid: 'all disarmament conferences are armament conferences.'[2] After which it is no pain to mark *en passant* the easy terms on which we have become accustomed to live with other slippery meanings in the neighbourhood; with aggression called defence, and 'weapons (which are) defensive if you possess them or hope to possess them, offensive if not'; and peace activists presented -in some countries, punished- as war-mongers, and 'civil' and 'military' 'become two sides of the same coin', and war-making presented as the persuit of peace, and war disguised as 'armed conflict', and the law of war re-clothed as 'international humanitarian law', and desolation called pacification.[3] Euphemism in description of war is as old as war itself, but this chameleon flux of meanings in our discourse on the control and conduct of war seems something new, as if our century can no longer see these things clearly, or know how to make sense of them.

If our situation in these respects is more confused and confusing than it ever was before, there is no lack of explanations why it should have

---

1   G. Orwell, *Looking back on the Spanish War* (1942), Part 4, as appended to the Penguin edition of *Homage to Catalonia* 235 (1966); N. Mailer cit. by L. Hudson in The Times Literary Supplement of 24 January 1975.

2   N. Angell, The Great Illusion (1910). Also N. Angell, Europe's Optical Illusion (1909); M. Tate, The Disarmament Illusion (1942); S. de Madariaga, Disarmament 88, 192 (1929).

3   'Defensive/Offensive Weapons', in M. Wight, Power Politics 210 (1979). 'Civil/military ...', in M. Pearton, The Knowledgable State. Diplomacy, War and Technology since 1930, 279 (1982).

become so. Meanwhile the historian cannot help noticing that the particular problem being addressed here, the idea of the control of war, is as old as war itself. Indeed, by what I take to be our best definition of war, it is integral to the idea of war itself, though neither more nor less so than recognition that war has in it some intrinsic resistance to control. Howard embraces the paradox at the very beginning of the book he edited, in 1979, on *Restraints on War*. There, as in other notable places, he stands by Clausewitz. But where does Clausewitz stand? Clausewitz speaks with two voices: on the one hand, stigmatising the notion of controlling war as leading to 'logical absurdity'; on the other, actually writing about the conduct of war as if it were susceptible of control.[4] All the best contemporary commentators on Clausewitz -Aron, Gallie, Paret, and Howard himself- find it possible to explain the two voices as echoes of an ambiguous belief that war, although peculiarly difficult to control, was in principle (in *political* principle) controllable and that in many circumstances (as a practical soldier and politician, Clausewitz understood his contemporary circumstances very well) it could be controlled. The ancient idea could retain credibility because circumstances continued to support it, and so long as that was the case Clausewitz could retain his pre-eminence as the arch-philosopher of war. But what if circumstances should have changed to an extent that makes the idea, at least in part, incredible? Howard himself goes on to acknowledge that post-1945 circumstances have done precisely that, making it possible that war is not so much the continuation of politics, but their bankruptcy.

Ambiguity and contradiction are not singular to Clausewitz. They mark in general the whole of our Europe-based philosophy of war, which is founded in the reconciliation of the principles of military necessity and humanitarian concern. Its story can be read as the record of a never-ending dialectic between an idea (an idea itself tense with contradictions) and circumstances (cultural, ideological, political, or whatever) which are sometimes conducive to it but sometimes so discouraging as to bring even the boldest hearts to the brink of despair. And yet they have never all despaired altogether, any more than believing men have ever, even in darkest times, abandoned the hope of salvation. The idea of controlling and restraining war has survived and is alive and well in the world today, although by no means as alive and well as it was one or two centuries ago. The following part of this essay will address the question whether there is

---

4   M. Howard, Restraints in War: Studies in the Limitation of Armed Conflict 1, 3 (1979).

little or much to be brought forward into our present calculations from the accounts of earlier ages.

The fact that the idea of controlling war goes back time out of mind is neither surprising nor, from our point of view, of much interest. One presumes that it developed alongside our species' distinctive capacity for thought, reflection, self, consciousness, or just *consciousness*, as it seemed to Hardy, in one of his grimmest poems:

'A time there was - as one may guess,
And as, indeed, earth's testimonies tell -
Before the birth of consciousness,
When all went well
(...)
If something ceased, no tongue bewailed,
If something winced and waned, no heart was wrung:
If brightness dimmed, and dark prevailed,
No sense was stung.

But the disease of feeling germed,
And primal rightness took the tinct of wrong ....'[5]

So killing became differentiated, and one kind was called murder; war was perfected, but it could bring an uneasy conscience. The will to brotherhood and harmony existed but was at odds with the will to competitiveness and aggression.

'In the beginning Cain slew Abel and Romulus slew Remus .... The tale spoke clearly: whatever brotherhood human being may be capable of has grown out of fratricide, whatever political organization man may have achieved has its origin in crime. The conviction, in the beginning was a crime -for which the phrase 'state of nature' is only a theoretically purified paraphrase- has carried through the centuries no less evident plausibility for the state of human affairs than the first sentence of St John, 'In the beginning was the word', has possessed for the affairs of Salvation.'[6]

5   T. Hardy, *Before Life and After*, in Collected Poems 260 (1930).
6   H. Arendt, On Revolution 10-11 (1963).

2.   EARLY PLANS FOR A PEACEFUL ORDER

Abhorrence of war and with it the making of plans for its abolition, prevention, or limitation is an old-age aspect of man's confused and ambivalent thinking about war; an aspect which for the most part fitted snugly within those streams of religious and political thought classified under the heads of Utopias, Pacifism, and the Perfectability of Man. Indeed, it must be admitted that a particular European sub-set of plans for the establishment of a peaceful international order -from Dante and Marsilius of Padua through Dubois, Cruce, Sully, Penn, Saint-Pierre, and Rousseau to Kant- have often been and still often are presented as heartening precedents of some particular value, demonstrating, it may be supposed, that the twentieth century's endeavours in this direction have more solid foundations than simply utopian aspiration. A more cautious and sceptical view is taken by Hinsley. Dealing with these writers in the early pages of his celebrated book *Power and the Pursuit of Peace*, he writes: 'Even if these early plans had any relevance to practicability when they were formulated, which was rarely so, they would still have no relevance to modern situations'.[7] The circumstances in which they were produced, were so different from those of our nineteenth and twentieth centuries that after all they remain floating, from *our* point of view, in the spacious firmament of bright and attractive ideas which do credit to the moral standing of our species without doing much to improve its mortal condition.

But from all those earlier centuries of thought and planning about the control of war, there is one unbroken stream whose relevance to practicability was never doubted, whose particular and unique idea was rooted in circumstances where it directly made sense: the idea of restraint and self-respect in the conduct of war. These ideas have turned up in most civilizations and societies. Keeping now to its appearances within our own Mediterranean-and-Atlantic civilization, one notes how commentators through the centuries of its most decided development, the fifteenth to the nineteenth, differed as to its evaluation. Did it do more good than harm, or could it do more harm than good? Was it to be regarded as the *best* (in the way of control) man could ever achieve in a wicked (war-devoted) world, or was it to be regarded as a temporary *better* in the world from which (war-devoted) wickedness might in the end be banished? This division of

---

7   F.H. Hinsley, Power and the Persuit of Peace: Theory and Practice in the History of Relations between States 13-14 (1963).

opinion still exists and matters mightily. Commentators of the more
sceptical sort, particularly if any part of their mind was fixed on the
ultimate abolition of war, argued that the valorous and dedicated warriors,
the military chieftains and heroes in whom people and nations could
discover exemplary virtue, were given a needless gloss of glamour. If a
man could only attain maximum virtue by fighting in war -which is
certainly what the warrior and knightly ethics have maintained in all
countries where they have flourished- then the retention of war among the
institutions of mankind became a matter of some ethical significance. The
abolition of war, by the same token, would be seen as a sadly mixed
blessing.

3.   THE INFLUENCE OF WAR IN SOCIETY

Everyone knows what the elder Von Moltke thought about 'perpetual
peace' on the occasion when Bluntschli, desirous of selling him the latest
model code of war law, dangled that further objective before him: 'a
dream, and not even an attractive dream', he replied. Von Moltke's
opinion, as is generally accepted, was representative of his professional
caste and his ruling class in that intensely militarized society and
imperialistic-cum-nationalistic culture which burst like a boil in the Great
War. But was he not to some extent representative also of something
larger, more intractable - something to which nations at large are liable as
well as individuals? It seems to me a rather forbidding fact, which students
of war and peace ignore at their peril, that through the greater part of
history as we know it, popular national literature, folklore and mythology
find more nourishment in war than peace. Nation-building has generally
rested upon this preference, and where nation-building is still going on,
still does. That succesful wars ('happy wars'!) can be built into the
treasuries of national culture is easy enough to understand. What seems
less easy and in itself perhaps more odd, is that the less succesful and less
happy wars can be accommodated too, even if only by prodigies of
selective recollection. And this phenomenon necessarily has its effect on
the ways people at large respond to plans for the control of war, by
determining the mentality with which they approach such. One aspect of
this collective mentality was shrewdly commentated on by Bergson:

> '... it is strange to see how soon the sufferings of war are forgotten in time
> of peace. It is asserted that woman is provided with a special psychological
> mechanism which causes her to forget the pains of childbirth; a too

complete recollection might prevent her from having another child. Some mechanism of the same order really seems to be operative in favour of the horrors of war, especially among young nations ....'[8]

Whether Bergson did well or not to pin this characteristic especially on young nations, need not be determined here. But in those years, young and old nations were prone to the same military enthusiasms, gorging on the same diet of militarized history. Here was another source of that more optimistic reading of war which -not just in national cultures but within the minds of individuals too- accompanied the more pessimistic readings which history and philosophy also made available: another of those contradictions, those encounters of opposites, which mark our subject, and upon which my argument much relies.

4.   WAR-CONTROLLING ENDEAVOURS: 1860-1914

During the nineteenth and early twentieth centuries this optimistic reading of war achieved very wide acceptance. At the same time the development of international organization and of public international law were being read as elements of that overall progress in the condition of mankind which the majority of inhabitants of the imperial powers took for granted. And the realm of war was one of those over which Progress was believed to beam. Not that everybody measured the beams the same way. For the men and women active in various branches of the Peace Movement (we refer to societies in which women were insisting on contributing to public debate, and war was one of the subjects on which they felt they had most to contribute) progress showed in the laying of foundations for demilitarization, disarmament, and the non-violent resolution of inter-State conflicts. For men untouched (except counter-productively) by the Peace Movement and wedded still to the cult of war, Progress showed in the applications of science and industry which might make wars more intense and lethal but would, they believed, make them decisive and short (A maxim dear to such war-embracers between the 1860s and 1914 was: 'short sharp wars are the most humane'.). For people in between, to whom the Peace people appeared impractical and the War people insensitive, Progress showed most persuasively in the development of international law and 'the public conscience'; a law and an ethic which would work together

---

8   H. Bergson, The Two Sources of Morality and Religion 246 (1935).

to impose humanitarian restraints and prohibitions on the conduct of war and to keep it, they supposed, relatively cool.

So much of a war-controlling kind was proposed to be done between 1815 and 1914, and enough actually was done, for the record of those years to serve as a kind of compendium of ideas and illustrations covering all branches of our subject. The ideas for the most part were far from new but they were activated now in circumstances sufficiently like those of our own times to justify our regarding them as a trial run for what was to come later.

4.1   Disarmament

Disarmament, for a start: the jewel in the peace-lover's crown; what results had been derived from experimentation in the field of Disarmament (generously defined, as men then defined it, to include Arms Control) before the World War I? Disarmament proposals of one sort or another were put forward by Russia in 1816, 1859, and 1899; by France in 1863 and 1877; Britain in 1866, 1870, and 1890; Denmark in 1893. Nothing like them had been heard of before. None of them got anywhere. Each of course has its own particular explanation, grounded in the political circumstance of the time and the proposer's sense of occasion. One may however dare to offer some general explanations without greatly endangering historical truth.

The spirit of the age was receptive to such schemes, and not through the medium of public opinion alone. Some of those schemes were floated in the normal confidentiality of top-level diplomatic discourse; whatever interests the proposers had at heart, they did not always include mass popularity or the satisfaction of pressure groups. Something in the spirit of the age was encouraging to the idea of disarmament and it is not difficult to see what it was. Besides the rampant nationalism and imperialism and pure bellicism which excited the minds of men from the cottage to the throne, there were also certain preferences for peace and revulsions from war which waxed in attractiveness as the century wore on. There is no reason to suppose that Tsar Nicholas II was not in some part of his mind serious about peace and disarmament after his talks with De Bloch. Nor can we suppose that he, of *all* Heads of State, was influenced by considerations which might weigh heavily on statesmen under the eyes of representative institutions and a free press. Humanitarianism (there is no better word for it, awkward though it may be) was all the rage from the sixties; the 'peace movement' was noisy and prestigious enough from the eighties to demand some acknowledgement; and popular sensibility to the seamy side of war was easily enough aroused for politicians to wish to save their countries from looking inhumane. Already by the close of the Crimean War a British statesman could be found contemplating the popularity to be gained from a grand humanitarian gesture. Pressure in that same direction was so strong by the close of the century that even the German Kaiser and his courtiers, whose public language made normally the least concessions towards humanitarianism (which they regarded as weakly sentimental), did not feel able to stand before the world at The Hague assembled as enemies of 'peace and disarmament'. Disarmament, humanitarianism, and so on had a firm lodging in the altruistic, progressive side of the later-nineteenth century mind, no matter how oddly they consisted with some of the other lodgers.

Disarmament had other attractions too, of a more prudential and self-serving nature. Armaments and armed forces cost money. Wars that paid for themselves had always been exceptional. By the later nineteenth century, the costs of military preparedness were becoming fearsome, and *part* of the public mind (obviously not the 'We want eight and we won't wait!' part) was interested in reducing them. Every Government felt the pressures of military expenditure, and could imagine the pleasure of release from them. The German Government in 1899 made a big thing of denying that it felt any such pressure. It proclaimed that the German people were perfectly happy to pay for all the armaments their country's security required. But this was putting a bold face on a risky business. Part of the German people was in fact audibly distressed under such a load, and even the German Government within its own war-planning walls was soon admitting that military demands outstripped financial supply. As for the less prosperous and confident countries, their theoretical interest in disarmament was intense. But the burden of armaments was a hook off which the more prosperous, locked into military rivalry with others of the same kind, could not get themselves. Yet more and more they wished to seem anxious to do so.

With what measure of self-delusion, we may wonder? Some measure of self-delusion seems necessary to explain, for example, two of the most striking phenomena in this field: first, the British belief that all other countries must admire and welcome the Pax Britannica as much as Britain itself did; and second, the apparent belief of a succession of Russian proposers of disarmament that they would look like something other than eagles in dove's feathers. But that, of course, is exactly how they looked on the very first occasion, and the pattern has remained unchanged ever since.

What Alexander proposed in 1816 was 'a simultaneous reduction in the armed forces of all kinds which the powers have brought into being to preserve the safety and independence of their peoples'. The proposal was weakened (observed Martin Wight): '... by Russia's being the only power that had not, since the return of peace, reduced her own forces'. In a tactful and practical reply, Castlereagh pointed out the difficulties, which remained constant until partially modified by the pressure of nuclear weapons:

> 'It is impossible not to perceive that the settlement of a scale of force for so many powers, under such different circumstances as to their relative means, frontiers, positions and faculties for rearming, presents a very complicated question for negotiation; that the means of preserving a system, if once created, are not without their difficulties, liable as all States are to partial necessities for an increase of force; and it is further to be considered that on this, as on many subjects of a jealous character, in attempting to do too much, difficulties are rather brought into view than made to disappear.'[9]

4.2   Arbitration

If disarmament, broadly understood, was one of the principal war-controlling endeavours of the nineteenth century, another was arbitration (although it was admittedly stretching things a bit, to include among ways of controlling war a way of avoiding it). Some elements of the peace movement favoured the one, some the other, but almost always they went hand in hand: *disarmament*, to reduce the ability to fight wars and to remove the pressures and inducements thereto; *arbitration*, to resolve international conflicts by peaceful and rational means instead of by violent and uncontrollable means. Like disarmament, the idea of it could be traced back ever so far into the years before Christ. Unlike disarmament, it could boast a respectable history of modest practical achievements through many ages and phases of civilisation. In this history of intermittent limited success, the nineteenth century neatly fitted. By the close of the century one of the peace movement's most aptly-named historians, Fried, was able to cite these impressive figures: from 1844 to 1860, 25 arbitration treaties; 1861 to 1880, 54; 1881 to 1900, 111. In all, 212 arbitral awards made in the course of the century, and all of them, he claimed, 'carried out in good

---

9   Wight, loc. cit. n. 3, at 267-268.

faith'.[10] After 1900, the rage for arbitration only grew fiercer in the heydays of The Hague and Geneva; the rising line of its continuing development swept its recorders, helpless with self-congratulation, off the top of the graph.

And yet, from our disillusioned point of view, as from that of any serious historian of international relations, all those figures of treaties, awards and settlements add up to very little. It was a chronicle of small beer: either the settlement of disputes between small States, often under the admonitory eye of a regional hegemonist (as was especially likely to be the case among Members of the Pan-American Union); or the settlement of disputes in which even great and normally touchy powers could find nothing affecting their vital interests, honour or prestige; or, in the only few cases which catch a realist's eye, disputes which great powers could have got heated about but which one or other of the parties decided to cool down. Sometimes, the parties felt so close, or had as allies come so close to each other, that they were not going to let even serious disputes sour their relationship. The only reason for great powers' acceptances of arbitration over potentially explosive issues was temporary convenience; as for instance when Russia accepted it after its Baltic fleet *en route* to disaster in the Far East sank several British trawlers in October 1904 off the Dogger Bank in the North Sea, and when France and Germany in 1908 decided not to let a police incident in Casablanca turn into a *casus belli*. The moral was clear. Arbitral procedures, whether *ad hoc* or by bilateral treaty, could work wonders when the parties wished them to or when friendly neighbourhood hegemonists wished them to do so. Otherwise they were likely to be so much good-looking, fine-sounding, humanitarian-heartwarming waste paper.

4.3 The laws and customs of war

Disarmament and arbitration were both major preoccupations of The Hague Conferences of 1899 and 1907. But before dwelling on them it is necessary to wheel back fifty years or so to pick up the other half of the war-controlling story, which also proved to be big at The Hague: the laws and customs of war. These had origins as ancient and basic as the ideas of disarmament, arbitration, and so on, and had over the ages achieved a

---

10 Fried's figures as given in G. Schwarzenberger, Power Politics 216-217 (1941). As for all that 'good faith', one notes in W.E. Hall, International Law (8th ed.) at 425n, that the United States rejected in 1831 an Award given against it in a boundary dispute with the United Kingdom.

firmer foothold than them in the war practices of mankind. This had not been done without sacrifice. In its historic origins, the law of war meant what law had to say about going to war in the first place as well as what it said about how to conduct a war once you were in it: in those still convenient Roman terms, the *jus ad bellum* as well as the *jus in bello*. By the eighteenth century, in Europe anyway, the *jus ad bellum* had ceased to be of more than speculative interest to the jurists, political theorists, and conscientious soldiers upon whose combined efforts the development and refinement of the law of war depended. Wars engaged in by sovereign rulers had become accepted as *ipso facto* legitimate exercises of their proper (most writers would still have said god-given) functions within the States-system - and this was calmly accepted! The law of war therefore came to mean simply the laws and customs governing the conduct of hostilities between civilized States; and the *jus ad bellum's* concerns about the rights and wrongs of wars were left aside, to be picked up in due course by the other stream of war-controlling thought we have had in view: that concerned with world order and the prevention of war. For those thinkers the *jus ad bellum's* concerns were so basic, and its ways of thinking so congenial, that their digestion of it was thorough to the point of total absorption; concealing from peace-writers who took the *jus ad bellum's* concerns for granted the intimacy of its original relations with the *jus in bello* (which, if they realized it, they might not much have liked). It is worth mentioning the parenthesis that there has been since the last few decades, a reconciliation of those long-divorced partners. International political scientists (*e.g.* McDougal, Falk, and Bull) as commonly include the *jus in bello* within their all-embracing purview as do law of war writers like Johnson and O'Brien include the *jus ad bellum*. The *jus ad bellum* has come out of the closet; looking at the use now made of it by ideologically-inflamed parties, some would say, it has done so with a vengeance.

So, in the years before The Hague, when only the *jus in bello* was involved, the law of war underwent a colossal development. Before the sixties it could enjoy only the status of *customary* law; which might mean much to men of honour in decent, self-respecting armed forces, but might mean less elsewhere, and in any case left a lot open to argument. Now a series of treaties wrote out the main parts of the law of war in a fashion which looks piecemeal but which had in fact behind it the invisible hand of humanitarian realism, happier in its work here than in the more ambitious war-controlling endeavours which were sketched above (so largely do these piecemeal efforts cohere that I shall telescope them and present their results as if they belonged more together than was historically the case).

4.3.1   The principle of necessity

Preliminary to everything else in the law of war was, and is, a basic
definition of how far the state of war entitles men to go; war by definition
being politically purposeful and not the indulgence of uncontrolled
violence; an exercise of necessary violence and of that alone. Not until
1977 (and then only indirectly) did any multilateral treaty get near offering
such a definition.[11] Turning therefore to definitions offered by men who
have closely studied the subject, we get guidance from, for example,
Napoleon: 'My guiding maxim has always been that every injury inflicted,
even though it may be within the rules, is excusable only insofar as it is
absolutely necessary; anything beyond that is simply criminal'.[12] The
admirable Lieber, whose draft 'Instructions' for the Union armies in 1863
is the Adam and Eve of all subsequent law of war manuals, including this
definition:

> 'Military necessity (...) consists in the necessity of those measures which
> are indispensible for securing the ends of the war, and which are lawful
> according to the modern law and usages of war. It admits of all direct
> destruction of life or limb of armed enemies, and of other persons whose
> destruction is incidentally unavoidable (...) and of such deception as does
> not involve the breaking of good faith either positively pledged, regarding
> agreements entered into during the war, or supposed by the modern law of
> war to exist. Men who take up arms against one another in public war do
> not cease on this account to be moral beings, responsible to one another
> and to God.
> Military necessity does not admit of cruelty - that is, the inflicting of
> suffering for the sake of suffering or for revenge, nor of maiming or
> wounding except in fight, nor of torture and, in general, military necessity

---

11 It seems reasonable to identify something of this sort in Article 52(2) of Protocol I Additional
   to the Geneva Conventions:
   'Attacks shall be limited strictly to military objectives. In so far as objects are concerned,
   military objectives are limited to those objects which by their nature, location, purpose or use
   make an effective contribution to military action and whose total or partial destruction, capture
   or neutralization, in the circumstances ruling at the time, offers a definite military advantage.'
   Definitions like this have long been familiar in military and legal literature, but never before
   has one appeared in a treaty text.
12 My translation of Napoleon as cited by M. Huber, *Die kriegsrechtlichen Verträge und die
   Kriegsraison* (The Laws and Customs of War in Relation to Military Necessity), in 7
   Zeitschrift für Völkerrecht 353 (1913).

does not include any act of hostility which makes the return to peace unnecessarily difficult.'[13]

And there are two contemporary American ones, descendants of Lieber's just a century later. O'Brien's, carefully phrased:

'Military necessity consists in all measures immediately indispensible and proportionate to a legitimate military end, provided they are not prohibited by the laws of war or the natural law, when taken on the decision of a responsible commander, subject to judicial review.'[14]

Not unlike it, though with a de-controlling twist in its tail, is the briefer version in the USAF Law of War Manual:

'Military necessity (...) justifies measures of regulated force not forbidden by international law which are indispensible for securing the prompt submission of the enemy, with the least possible expenditures of economic and human resources.'[15]

So much the reflective war-maker will understand at the outset; the violence that the state of belligerence authorizes him to use has limits and purpose. The law of war will help him understand what those limits are (so far as they are not purely political). Some have become more precisely expressed than others but rock-like behind and beneath them all is the general principle stated in the Preamble to The Hague Convention containing the 1907 Regulations:

---

13 F. Lieber's *Instructions* as repr. in D. Schindler, J. Toman, eds., The Laws of Armed Conflict, 2nd ed., 2-3 (1981). Also R.S. Hartigan, Lieber's Code and the Law of War (1983).

14 W.V. O'Brien, *The Law of War, Command Responsibility and Vietnam*, 60 Georgetown Law Journal 616 (1972).

15 Department of the Air Force, *The Conduct of Armed Conflict and Air Operations* (Air Force Pamphlet) 110-131 (1976). The preceding paragraph, 1-2(f), offers this Lieber-like definition of the 'Functions of the Law of Armed Conflict':
'The law of armed conflict is essentially inspired by the humanitarian desire of civilised nations to diminish the effects of conflicts. It protects both combatants and non-combatants from unnecessary suffering, and safeguards the fundamental rights of civilians, POWs, and the wounded and sick. The law also attempts to prevent degeneration of conflicts into savagery and brutality, thereby facilitating the restoration of peace and the friendly nations which must, at some point, inevitably accompany of follow the conclusion of hostilities. It has been said to represent in some measure minimum standards of civilization.'

'In cases not included in the Regulations (...), inhabitants and belligerents (*i.e.*, civilians and combatants) remain under the protection and the rule of the principles of law of nations, as they result from the usages established among civilized peoples, from the laws of humanity, and the dictates of the public conscience.'[16]

4.3.2 *Limitations of means and methods*

Let us now turn to the more precise formulations as expressed in the series of multilateral treaties mentioned above. First, following naturally from the general principle just stated: '... the right of belligerents to adopt means of injuring the enemy is not unlimited'. So says Article 22 of The Hague Regulations. Limitation means first and foremost discrimination: discrimination between combatants and others (whether civilians or combatants rendered *hors de combat*). This idea had been hardening in the heads of decent warriors for several centuries and was no doubt firm customary law before it received positive formulation in the 1860s. The first Geneva Convention in 1864 cast a protective cover of 'neutrality' (as it boldly called it) over one specific catagory of unthreatening enemies: sick and wounded soldiers, a category to which sick and wounded sailors, prisoners of war, and at last civilians too would in course of time be added.[17] Civilians, as such were not to be specifically singled out until 1949 (arguably, because of their protection so far as military necessity permitted was felt to be self-evident) but their relatively protected status was inferred in the argument of the other treaty landmark of the 1860s, the strangely under-known Declaration of St. Petersburg of 1868. Its main business was the prohibition, for the first such time, of a weapon considered to cause unnecessary or superfuous suffering. It introduced that business however by a rehearsal of certain principles, which were understood to be declaratory of customary law and which in fact embody, however obliquely, the principle of discrimination:

---

16 The particular interest of this passage (commonly referred to, after its proposer at the 1899 Hague Conference, as the 'Martens Clause') lies in its definition of the ethical substratum of international humanitarian law. Nothing like it had hitherto been said in any (part of any) multilateral treaty. It has been repeated in the major humanitarian treaties since then, in language almost unchanging: see the four 1949 Geneva Conventions, Articles 63/62/142/158, and Additional Protocol I, 1977, Article 1(2).

17 The Principles of the 1864 Geneva Conventions were adapted to maritime warfare by the tenth of The Hague Conventions of 1907; the 1864 Convention having itself been updated in 1906. Prisoners of war were added in 1929.

'Considering that the progress of civilization should have the effect of alleviating as much as possible the calamities of war;
That the only legitimate object which States should endeavour to accomplish during war is to weaken the military forces of the enemy;
That for this purpose it is sufficient to disable the greatest possible number of men;
That this object would be exceeded by the employment of arms which uselessly aggravate the sufferings of men, or render their death inevitable;
That the employment of such arms would, therefore, be contrary to the laws of humanity; (...).'

What followed was the prohibition of 'any projectile of a weight below 400 grammes, which is either explosive or charged with fulminating or inflammable substances'. To this Declaration, seventeen States' signatures were set on December 11, 1868; all European except for Brazil, Persia, and (unless it was to be counted as European) Turkey. In itself it was not much - just the banning of a new weapon, the use of which directly against the human body was felt by the majority military opinion at the time to be needlessly nasty; but it set going a process of scrutinizing particular weapons and uses of them with which we are familiar still under such titles as CBW, unrestricted submarine warfare, city bombing, napalm, fragmentation bombs, unmapped minefields, and the great and awful nuclear question itself.

4.4   'The Peace Conferences'

Some of those prohibitions were included in The Hague Land War Regulations. Their continuing importance ought to keep us mindful, if nothing else does, of the singular significance of those Conferences held at The Hague in 1899 and 1907. Both Conferences were known as Peace Conferences but it was only the 1899 one that grappled with the roots of the problem, so far as that was one of armaments, armed strengths, and an arms race running beyond control. Disarmament had a much more tenuous place on the agenda for 1907, where it was only briefly touched upon. In 1899, it was the heart of the matter, a strident call on the diplomatic resourcefulness of the participants and source of excitement to the peace movement's observers, a vocal vanguard of whom moved into the city for the Conference's duration, rejoicing to regard it as 'the Parliament of Peace'. With their relentless lobbying and acclamation as an ever-present reminder of the interest the self-styled civilized world was focussing upon them, the delegates in charge of negotiating had to move cautiously. But for those who watched what they did rather than what they said, the direction of their movement was never in doubt; it was towards rejection of every disarmament proposal that did not promise to leave their own countries in a relatively improved position *vis-à-vis* the rest; which meant, of course, that since every country hoped that the others would be as slow to notice its own self-interest as it was quick to notice the self-interest of others, no progress was made towards disarmament at all. The conference ended with no more than this uncontroversial declaration, that 'the limitation of military expenses, which presently weigh heavy on the world, is much to be desired for the sake of both material and moral development of humankind'.

The Hague Peace Conferences are not to be sneered at. They made the first steps down many war-controlling roads which are still being travelled on (and repeatedly repaired) in our own times. They did enough to cause one of our best writers on international organization to describe their achievement as 'a distinctive "Hague System" (...) interrupted all too soon by the outbreak of World War I'.[18] Some of the thirteen Conventions instituted in 1907 remain basic to our contemporary law of war, peace, and neutrality. The Land War Regulations together with their updating of the Geneva Conventions were a landmark of humanitarian law.[19] But the Conferences' failure was almost complete in respect of their announced purposes of disarmament and arms control; and our own continuing failures in the same lines enable us to behold with some compassion their going through the same disappointments and disillusionments that their successors have gone through ever since. Even the material circumstances of those Conferences have a familiar air. Enthusiasts on the spot produced (in 1899 anyway) a special newspaper which must be the ancestor of the *Disarmament Times* produced by an NGO-Committee at the UN. Public opinion -at least, a noteworthy part of it- hung on its doings and expected something to come out of it. 'The whole world' was there in 1907, so far as it could be; the Members of the Pan-American Union came over *en bloc*, determined to speak for themselves; Japan, China, Siam and Persia spoke for Asia. There was of course no more question at that date of anyone from the Arab world or black Africa being there than there was of anyone from Australia or Canada. A few were *not* there in 1899 who

---

18 I.L. Claude Jr., Swords into Plowshares: The Problems and Progress of International Organization, 4th ed., 28-29 (1971).
19 The Regulations are appended to the Fourth of the 1907 Conventions, in a form scarcely changed from their first appearance, appended to the Second Convention of 1899. The two sets are conveniently printed side by side, in Schindler, Toman, eds., op. cit. n. 13, at 57-87.

might have been if weighty insiders had not objected, as the British did to Transvaal and the Dutch to the Holy See.

The Hague Conferences were recognizably of our own era. No major power gave away anything that could be of use to it; no weapon was banned if any major power had serious need of it; they were legislating on the brink of unforeseeable technical developments (for example, submarines and aeroplanes) that would nullify or render inapplicable their measures; and their failures and hedgings were obscured from public view in the 'meaningless resolutions' and happy 'cobwebs of words' with which statesmen and diplomats were learning how to protect their flanks in the dawn of Wilsonian international relations.[20]

The 1907 Peace Conference was not in fact quite as open to public scrutiny as great diplomatic conferences have been since 1919 (*a fortiori*, since 1945), but in being a lot more open than any such occasion had ever been before, it marked yet again its pivotal character, with the nineteenth and earlier centuries receding into the furthest distance on the farther side of it and, on this side of it, so many of our century's ways of conducting international affairs.

There are, however, some important exceptions. In respect particularly of the control of war, how many of our century's ideas about it are new? I do not mean the vocabulary in which they have to be expressed to deal with weaponry which is forever developing and situations which never cease to change. But the ends pursued do not change; arms control is arms control, whether the arms are quick-firing field guns of fifteen inch, battleships, poison gas or Pershing missiles. Disarmament simply aims to get rid of the deadly stuff, whatever it is. And national security perceptions have the same material considerations to work on, an unchanging single purpose to secure. No *idea* is new in this lexicon; the only novelty is perhaps (I keep being told this, but after many years have ceased to believe it) the passion, sense of urgency, and determination with which the ideas are held. That determination and sense of urgency have their home, I suggest, not only in the body of ideas themselves but among the circumstances which tip them into debate and define its limits.

---

20 'Meaningless Resolutions', in N. Rich, Friedrich von Holstein 2, 603 (1965). 'Happy cobwebs of words', in the ('secret') Subsidiary Report Submitted to the Secretary of State by the leader of the United States Delegation to the 1947 Government Experts Conference, Geneva (1947). See United States National Archives, Diplomatic Section, 514.2 Geneva 8/2647, (R.G. 59 Box 2467).

5. POST WORLD WAR II CIRCUMSTANSES

The UNO is a post-1945 circumstance which makes a big mark. Its predecessor the League of Nations also made a mark for a few years but it did not last. The control of war by one means or another was the League's *raison d'être*, and the more that *raison d'être* was frustrated, the lower the League sank towards its tragic, humiliating grave. The case of the UN is quite different. Disarmament, not initially one of its main purposes, early became one in proportion with the evaporation of optimism as to its peace-keeping capabilities. Because too much was not hoped for too long, failure to achieve much in the war-controlling line has not been too disappointing. But apart from that, the UN just simply *is there* and is in many ways *useful*. It is the world's central mart and exchange for the transaction of much international business. It has sunk roots, as the League never did. Although one might argue that endless talk cannot actually do much good for arms control and other means of controlling war, one can just as well argue that the important issues are better talked about too much than not talked about at all.

To refer to the UN is to refer to the Third World, Non-Aligned and Socialist States who for nearly thirty years have been able to manage majorities in the General Assembly when they have so wished, and whose polemical preoccupations have somewhat lowered the Organization's character and status for many of us. What part has the control of war in that endless war of words? It can be said that it has some part. Hardly a week passes but the UN's information bulletins report the concerns of the great majority of its members about the conduct of wars actual or prospective, about military occupations, civil strifes and the plight of refugees from war and persecution on every continent. How much does this ceaseless and selective vigilance signify? Humanitarian law provides a well-stocked magazine for vilification; no grand idea of our age has more often been advanced to justify intervention than defence or vindication of human rights; human rights and humanitarian law are sometimes ardently pressed on others by parties which themselves notoriously abuse them. The humbug element in all this is nauseating but at least the subject is kept alive, and even infamous States may sooner or later get hoist on their own humanitarian petards.

Often advanced as a novel circumstance in discussions like this is 'the military-industrial complex'. But, under whatsoever terms we know it, is of course a determinant feature of the politics of 'advanced' countries in our own time and has transformed the ways in which questions of war and peace and of treading viable ways between them are understood and settled. The military-industrial complex is a modern phenomenon but not quite as modern as Eisenhower's coining of the term at the end of his Presidency might lead one to suppose. Two scholars who command respect have had to make up their minds about this, and they both plump for the last decades of the nineteenth century; McNeill invites us to see its beginning in Britain in the mid-eighties, Pearton remarks that however many years it had been developing since the fifties, it was clearly there by 1890. Pearton also argues powerfully for World War I, not World War II, as the one when our twentieth century's characteristic experience of war fully matured.[21] Not so much may be new since the World War II as we supposed.

What *is* unquestionably new since then, however, is the question of nuclear weapons. But there are limits to the newness of the terms of the debate which we conduct about them. As *deterrents* they are not new. Quester and others have reminded us how the theory of deterrence goes back quite openly to the original justifications offered by Trenchard for his strategic-bombing-oriented independent RAF in the twenties, and Steinberg even invited us to go twenty years further back still, to find its *debut* in Tirpitz's battlefleet.[22] What States can do with nuclear weapons *is* new; but deciding whether to do it or not, however, invokes no new ideas, runs into no new difficulty - unless it relates to a raising of the alleged primacy of scientific and technical factors to a new height. Scientific and technical factors are commonly supposed to amount to a sort of 'imperative' to which other factors must yield, an ace of trumps which can always sweep the board. Clearly the scientific and technical questions introduced by nuclear weaponry are enormously complicated and if there *is* a technological imperative, I suppose it could be more imperious here than elsewhere. The question is whether such an imperative exists. Is it not rather the case, that 'imperative' only means that no one has hit upon or devised an alternative course of action or has bothered to investigate one? In the words of Pearton:

21 W.H. McNeill, The Pursuit of Power. Technology, Armed Force, and Society since A.D. 1000, Chapter 8 (1983); anticipated in *The Industrialization of War*, (6th M. Wight Lecture, 1980), 8 Review of International Studies 203-213 (1982); also Pearton, loc. cit. n. 3, at 49.

22 G.H. Quester, Deterrence before Hiroshima. The Airpower Background to Modern Strategy (1966); J. Steinberg, Yesterday's Deterrent: Tirpitz and the Birth of the German Battle Fleet (1965).

'The (alleged) imperatives of policy, so far from being compulsions, are *choices* (though the language of necessity is frequently used by those who retrospectively want to justify choices which have turned out badly).'[23]

The idea that war, and ways of fighting war, are matters of choice, of *will*, is not at all new!

6.   1945-1980: THE PROTECTION OF CIVILIANS

To return from the realm of MX and SDI to that of humanitarian law is quite a leap but is necessary in order to return to the prime actor in these complicated affairs - the human being, whose choice or will is adduced by national policy-makers to support this and that proposal for or against the control of war. We must return to him because his mental confusion, even schizophrenia, regarding these matters may since World War II have become increased in certain surprising and unfortunate ways. I suggest, twentieth century man is in no fundamental respects different from nineteenth or any earlier century man in perceiving war with mixed or divided mind; at once attracted and repelled, excited and appalled, exalted and ashamed. It might have been expected that the advent of mass-destructive nuclear weapons would produce a dramatic and widespread change of the public mind, but such change does not seem to have gone far beyond the memberships of the anti-nuclear and peace movements. Meanwhile, a partial explanation of why it has not, may be found in one of the circumstances which is new since 1945 and which, ironically, ought to have had precisely the opposite effect.

I refer to the development since then of the international law of war, under its new name, the international humanitarian law of armed conflicts. What has happened to this old faithful means of controlling war by legal prohibitions and restraints has brought with it some potential for deception, much power of illusion. The signs were already there to be read before 1914 by people with their wits about them. If *that* half century's development of the law of war was 'progress', so after all were the bomber and the machine-gun. Not every sage soldier believed that short sharp wars were the most humane, or that wars could be kept short either. It is clear now that those disbelievers were right.

---

23 Pearton, loc. cit. n. 3, at 255.

The law of war has since then, between 1945 and 1980, gone through a second phase of 'reaffirmation and development'; and it is much more concerned than it had ever been before with the protection of 'civilians'.[24] That indeed might be thought to have become its main business -reasonably enough, considering how the ratio of civilian to military losses has risen in the wars of our century, and how frightful civilian sufferings often are- and that must be its chief attraction to the civilian mind. It offers -within the legal meaning of the technical term- 'protection'; which is likely to encourage the civilian to think he can be protected from the horrors of war and to feel indignant when he is not.

I shall conclude with two questions. In the first place: is this offer of protection realistic? Secondly: does the civilian deserve it?

As to the first question, I merely note that most of the important restraints proposed in the big 1977 updating have attached to them some such qualification as, 'military necessities permitting'; that the effective 1972 'Christmas bombings' of places in North Vietnam (*operation Linebacker II*) conformed quite closely with the letter of 1977 law; that the civilian is *not* likely to benefit from its permission to guerillas (so long as in other respects they observe the law) to look like civilians unless they are actually deployed for action; and that in any case, once the dread cycle of reprisals and retaliations starts, not all the restraining legal language in the world is likely to moderate it.

But as to the question - whether the civilian deserves all this protection, which may in any case be illusory I have to confess I am curiously worried. To admit this gives no joy at all to one who has given the last fifteen years to studying this legal side of the history of war; who has been more inspired by a member of the ICRC, the late Boissier, than by anyone else ever; and who has been proud to help the ICRC and his own national Red Cross with the work of publicizing the latest 'improved' version of international humanitarian law.[25] But it has to be said that the 1977 Additional Protocols have adopted a drastically reductionist solution to the age-old problem of determining who, in any given situation of armed conflict, is a proper object of attack and who is not. They have drawn a

---

24 'Reaffirmation' and 'development' were the key words adopted by the ICRC for the phase of updating of international humanitarian law which culminated in the two Additional Protocols of 1977; Protocols which by no means all States have ratified or are likely to ratify.

25 P. Boisser's two books deserve to be better known: L'Epée et la balance (1953), and De Solférino à Tsoushima. Histoire du comité international de la Croix-Rouge (1963). Something of the man himself may be learned from the book of essays published by the Institut Henry Dunant after his tragically early death: 'Pierre Boissier 1920-1974' (1977).

restrictive definition of combatants and declared that all other persons (including guerrillas off combatant duty) are 'civilians'. That makes for many difficulties of a military order, with which critics of the Protocols continue to be much occupied.[26] But the difficulty to which I must draw attention is more in the socio-political sphere. It must not be forgotten that the adult human being, in times of peace and in the most developed and democratic countries is also the citizen or subject who does so much to decide whether war shall occur, and if so, what it shall be like. He -and I mean she as well, for what evidence is there that states*women* are less capable of bellicosity than states*men*?- is the same person who has, by my analysis, such an inconstant and divided mind when it comes to urgent, exciting matters of public violence and who is still so capable (as when Sir Robert Walpole observed them at the same game 240 years ago) of ringing the bells one day, wringing the hands the next. That war, the so-called War of Jenkins' Ear, was a petty one, fought far away, and personally unexperienced by Britons unless their shares or ships went down. My own country's South Atlantic war, which elicited from much of the British public war enthusiasm of classic imperial cut, was in its remoteness and minuteness rather comparable. But revolutionary and counter-insurgency wars and civil wars and anarchies in the Third World are different; so in the Second and First Worlds are (or would be) wars between Medium- and Superpowers. What, other than costly and risky deterrence, can stop or prevent them except peoples' realization and well-imagined understanding of what war, if it comes to them, must mean, and how little is gentle-sounding humanitarian law actually to be able to protect them?

7.   CONCLUSION

Control of war, like charity (to which it is related) begins at home. This was foreseen in 1899 itself by Britain's law-of-war expert, Cambridge University's Professor John Westlake. The hot-headed peace publicist Stead asked him (and many others) if they had any message for him to transmit to The Hague and the world. Westlake had no illusions. Whatever might be achieved at the conference, it could not save men from themselves. He responded thus:

---

26 The most recent and by any standards the most weighty of such criticism is that by W.H. Parks, *Air War and the Law of War*, 32 Air Force Law Review 1-225 (1990). This huge article covers very much more legal, historical and political ground that its title suggests.

'Let every individual citizen do his best to keep the claims of his own country within just limits, and to advocate on each occasion, even after that, a disposition not to insist on the last farthing, and arbitration when possible. Let every individual State do its best to prevent injustice between its neighbours, either on entering on a war or in the terms of peace by which a war may be concluded, by not shrinking from expressing an opinion or from supporting that opinion by the needful pressure.

If its citizens have not the courage and States have not the unselfishness for this, no machinery will help the case. If they have, machinery will not be wanted or will be arranged easily so far as wanted.'[27]

Westlake did not live to see World War I. Oliver Stewart did and fought in it as an airman. He reviewed Jones' history of *The War in the Air* in 1936, the year of Guernica and Shanghai; a year by when the shape of things to come was clear enough to those with eyes to see. In a sentence which has haunted me ever since I first came across it, he stripped from the idea of controlling war the last illusion:

'If (strategic bombing) involves certain things which have hitherto been regarded as outside the rules of warfare, two comments are possible: either that civilized nations ought not to make war on each other, or, alternatively, if they do they must put up with the kind of war they themselves invent.'[28]

Only equal inventiveness in the control of war and in the control of themselves seems likely to save them.

---

27 Repr. in *War against War! A Chronicle of the International Crusade of Peace*, 13 January 1899.
28 Repr. in 81 Journal of the Royal United Services Institute 95-101 (1936).

PERTINENCE ET PERMANENCE DU DROIT INTERNATIONAL HUMANITAIRE

YVES SANDOZ

1.   PERTINENCE DU DROIT INTERNATIONAL HUMANITAIRE

1.1   Place du DIH dans l'ordre juridique international

Presque tout au long de son histoire, le droit international humanitaire (DIH) a été remis en question dans son principe même. Humaniser la guerre, n'est-ce pas la rendre plus acceptable?[1] La plus simple manière de répliquer à cette question, à laquelle tout enseignant en DIH a été maintes fois confronté, est d'en poser une autre, dont la réponse est évidente: peut-on donner un exemple où la motivation véritable de ceux qui

---

1 En ce sens, *cf.*, J. Pictet, Le droit humanitaire et la protection des victimes de la guerre (1973).

déclenchaient une guerre était de voir les souffrances qu'elle allait provoquer atténuées par le droit humanitaire?

Mais d'éthique, le dialogue s'est aussi transposé sur le plan juridique quand le droit international a restreint la possibilité de recourir à la guerre dans le Pacte de de la SDN,[2] puis l'a mise hors la loi dans la Charte des Nations Unies.[3] Après l'adoption de cette dernière, le DIH avait peine à trouver une place logique dans l'ordre juridique international. Le refus de la Commission du Droit International de l'ONU de se saisir du dossier du DIH, peu après l'adoption de la Charte, reste symptomatique à cet égard.[4]

Certes, une contre-argumentation était possible même sur le plan de la logique du système international mis en place par l'ONU: d'une part, en admettant le droit à la légitime défense,[5] la Charte n'exclut pas la possibilité d'une guerre internationale, d'autre part, les conflits armés non internationaux ne sont pas couverts par l'interdiction du recours à la force.[6]

Mais c'est surtout le bon sens et la conscience que l'ONU n'avait pu se donner les moyens de son ambition d'imposer la paix dans le Monde,[7] qui ont conduit les Etats à réaffirmer la nécessité de renforcer et développer le DIH en adoptant les quatre Conventions de Genève du 12 août 1949.

1.2   Efficacité du DIH

Si la contestation du principe même du DIH relève aujourd'hui surtout d'un public relativement peu averti, la mise en question de son efficacité est en revanche courante au sein même des milieux spécialisés dans le domaine du droit international. Et il est vrai que l'ambition d'obtenir le respect du DIH ne sera jamais entièrement satisfaite.

1.2.1   *'Environnement naturel' du DIH*

Cela provient, tout d'abord, du fait que même si le droit humanitaire était parfaitement respecté, une guerre reste une guerre et qu'il est loin le temps

---

2   *Cf.*, Pacte de la Société des Nations, Articles 12, 15.
3   *Cf.*, Charte des Nations Unies, Article 2(4).
4   *Cf.*, Annuaire de la Commission du Droit International (CDI), 1949, comptes rendus analytiques et documents de la première session.
5   *Cf.*, Charte des Nations Unies, Article 51.
6   *Ibid.*, Article 2(7).
7   Notamment du fait du non aboutissement des négociations engagées sur la base de l'Article 43 pour fixer les effectifs des forces mises à la disposition du Conseil de Sécurité pour contribuer au maintien de la paix et de la sécurité internationales.

où l'on parlait avec nostalgie des 'guerres fraîches et joyeuses'.[8] Les guerres sont toujours des tragédies et notre monde de la communication, en mettant leurs horreurs sous nos yeux, ne laisse planer aucun doute à cet égard. On ne peut donc jamais vraiment se réjouir de la bonne application du droit humanitaire, vu son environnement tragique.

1.2.2   Les 'Accidents' dans l'application du DIH

En deuxième lieu, il faut admettre que le DIH ne sera jamais parfaitement respecté. Des accidents de la circulation se produisent malgré le code de la route, des crimes malgré les codes pénaux. Comment espérer qu'il n'y aura pas 'd'accidents' dans la tension de combats et de la guerre en général? Le problème, qui est général mais particulièrement évident dans le cadre du DIH, est que l'on parle surtout de ce droit quand il est violé. Or, que des prisonniers de guerre qui devraient être rapatriés ne le soient pas est certes un échec. Mais qu'ils n'aient pas été simplement massacrés, qu'ils soient correctement nourris et logés, qu'ils puissent correspondre avec leur famille sont, malgré cela, des succès non négligeables: l'histoire nous apprend que cela n'a pas toujours été le cas. Par ailleurs, si l'on se scandalise à juste titre de l'emploi d'armes chimiques, par exemple, comment connaître les méthodes et moyens que des militaires ont renoncé à utiliser par souci de respecter les normes humanitaires?

Bref, l'apport du DIH, insuffisamment apparent, est certainement sous-estimé et cela d'autant plus que ceux-là même qui sont chargés de veiller à son application se doivent de mettre l'accent sur ses violations et sur l'insuffisance de cette application.[9]

1.3   Les améliorations possibles

Il a paru nécessaire de relever les aspects positifs du DIH pour éviter que le constat de ses échecs n'entraîne une remise en cause d'acquis réels.

Il ne s'agit cependant pas de tomber dans la complaisance: on ne saurait considérer comme inéluctables des manquements trop nombreux au respect du DIH et il est nécessaire de réfléchir sans cesse aux moyens de remédier à cette situation.

---

8   *Cf.*, G. Bouthoul, Traité de polémologie 89-90 (1970).

9   On relèvera notamment à cet égard les appels lancés par le président du CICR lors des deux dernières Conférences internationales de la Croix-Rouge et du Croissant-Rouge, respectivement à Manille en 1981 et à Genève en 1986. *Cf.*, XXIV Conférence internationale de la Croix-Rouge (1981); XXV Conférence internationale de la Croix-Rouge (1986).

1.3.1   L'éducation (diffusion du DIH)

Le premier de ces moyens est évidemment l'éducation. Celle des soldats, d'abord, puisque c'est entre leurs mains, au bout de leur fusil, que repose le sort de ceux que le DIH a pour but de protéger. Mais aussi celle des peuples, dont la volonté finit toujours par infléchir le cours des choses; celle des étudiants, desquels émergeront les dirigeants; celle des médias, dont le pouvoir ne cesse de croître; celle des enfants, dont l'avenir dépend.

Cette tâche est immense, ambitieuse, coûteuse, et ses effets difficilement mesurables. Elle est, en outre, indissolublement liée à d'autres facteurs: l'enseignement du DIH doit s'insérer dans le cadre général de l'éducation et il n'y a pas d'éducation possible sans développement. Elle est, enfin, un devoir des Etats,[10] ignoré trop souvent, et un pari pour le Comité international de la Croix-Rouge (CICR), qui cherche à mobiliser à cette fin l'ensemble du Mouvement de la Croix-Rouge et du Croissant-Rouge. Pari audacieux parce qu'il prétend renverser les barrières des langues, des cultures, des ethnies, de l'ignorance ... avec des moyens dérisoires et la seule force de la conviction que le message du droit humanitaire est intégré dans toute grande culture, enfoui dans chaque homme;[11] pari contesté parce qu'il est toujours difficile de penser à long terme quand l'urgence immédiate de la souffrance mobilise les énergies; mais pari indispensable tant il est vrai que le respect de l'action de protection et d'assistance, symbolisée si souvent par l'emblème de la croix rouge ou celui du croissant rouge, passe par la compréhension de cette action et de ces symboles.

1.3.2   Le respect du droit international

Dire que le respect du droit international est un facteur d'amélioration du respect du DIH paraît aller de soi. Il n'est cependant pas inutile de le rappeler[12] tant il est vrai que les Gouvernements ont souvent tendance à considérer le DIH comme des préceptes moraux ou, en tout cas, à ignorer

---

10   Cf., Articles 47, 48, 127, 144 commun aux quatres Conventions de Genève du 12 août 1949; Article 83 du Protocole additionnel I de 1977; Article 19 du Protocole additionnel II de 1977.

11   Plusieurs études ont cherché à identifier les racines du DIH dans les grandes cultures. On notera en particulier les ouvrages suivants:
M.A. Boisard, L'humanitarisme de l'Islam (1979); E. Bello, African Customary humanitarian law (1980); J.G. Lossier, Les civilisations et le service du prochain (1958); J. Pictet, Les principes du droit international humanitaire (1966).

12   Voir notamment, à ce sujet, C. Swinarski, Introducción al derecho internacional humanitario (Introduction to International Humanitarian Law) 72 (1984).

dans la pratique le caractère obligatoire de ce droit. Cette attitude est évidemment confortée par le mépris non sanctionné que certains dirigeants affichent pour le droit international en général au nom, abusivement invoqué, de la souveraineté nationale. Un renforcement de l'ordre juridique international fondé sur le droit et la sanction de ses violations ne peut donc que servir la cause du DIH.[13]

1.3.3   *Le renforcement des agents de mise en oeuvre du DIH*

L'acceptation par le DIH d'agents chargés de contrôler son application sur le territoire des Parties en conflit est un acquis remarquable. La 'fantaisie' d'avoir inclus dans ce système un organisme privé tel que le CICR s'avère d'une importance déterminante. Les Etats, pourtant, ne sont, par nature, guère fantaisistes et c'est l'évidente utilité d'une telle Institution qui, au fil des ans, les a conduits à lui reconnaître notamment l'étrange pouvoir d'imposer aux Etats en guerre ses visites aux prisonniers de guerre et aux internés civils.

Certes, les Etats ont prévu principalement un autre système de contrôle sur place, celui des Puissances protectrices, plus conforme à la logique des relations internationales, qui reposent sur les rapports des Etats entre eux ou avec des Organisations internationales dont ils sont membres.

Mais ce système n'a pas fonctionné dans la pratique[14] alors que le CICR peut assurer une présence dans presque toutes les situations conflictuelles. Il faut en voir la raison principale dans l'inévitable politisation d'organes internationaux: les Etats ont, par essence, des intérêts politiques et économiques dont ils ne peuvent faire abstraction et qui joueraient un rôle, sinon sur leur manière de remplir le mandat de Puissance protectrice, du moins sur leur acceptabilité par les deux Parties en conflit; quant aux organisations internationales, l'expérience montre bien qu'elles ne peuvent se dégager totalement des pressions politiques et financières exercées sur elles par leurs membres.

Le CICR présente l'avantage d'être dégagé de ces pressions et de ne pas avoir à négocier *en son sein* la manière d'aborder les Etats en vue de fixer les modalités de son travail ou l'attitude pratique qu'il doit adopter face aux difficultés ou succès rencontrés dans sa mission. Il est plus

---

13 On saluera positivement, en ce sens, la décision de l'Assemblée générale de l'ONU de proclamer une Décennie des Nations Unies pour le Droit International. *Cf.*, AG Rés. 44/23, 17 novembre 1989.

14 A ce sujet, *cf.*, G. Abi-Saab, *The Implementation of humanitarian law*, dans A. Cassese, réd., The New Humanitarian Law of Armed Conflict 310-346 (1979).

prévisible, plus souple, et aussi plus fragile, qu'une organisation internationale intergouvernementale. Et c'est pour ces raisons qu'il est plus acceptable.

Quand on prétend le renforcer, il faut donc bien réfléchir à ces éléments et le CICR lui-même doit comprendre qu'il s'agit avant tout de préserver son acceptabilité, que le privilège rare dont il jouit sur la scène internationale n'est jamais acquis et que seules la neutralité, la rigueur, l'honnêteté et une certaine modération sur la place publique lui permettront de le conserver.

Certes, il n'est pas en mesure d'accomplir toutes ses tâches et il faut réfléchir aux moyens d'améliorer cette situation. Mais il faut le faire avec discernement, sans perdre de vue les clés, ci-dessus évoquées, d'un succès tout de même important. L'internationalisation, la médiatisation à outrance de son action, le mandat impératif donné par un organe politique ne seraient que des pseudo-remèdes qui tueraient l'organisation. C'est au contraire la démonstration, si difficile aujourd'hui, que son action humanitaire est détachée de tout jugement politique qui reste, avec une pression générale et nécessaire sur l'exigence de respecter les normes humanitaires fondamentales, l'élément déterminant pour permettre son action. Tant il est vrai que l'objectif n'est pas de plaire au monde mais d'atteindre les victimes où elles se trouvent et, pour ce faire, de convaincre ceux qui les détiennent.

Il existe cependant d'autres agents qui peuvent concourir à une amélioration de l'application du droit international humanitaire. Le renforcement d'un système d'établissement des faits semblerait notamment particulièrement opportun.

Rien n'est plus délicat que les faits quand ils sont controversés. C'est pour cette raison que le CICR s'est fixé pour règle de ne pas procéder lui-même à des enquêtes à cet effet,[15] comprenant bien que la seule parade d'un Etat accusé de mentir serait de mettre en question l'honnêteté de l'accusateur et, suite logique, de récuser le CICR pour l'ensemble de son action.

Cette tâche d'établissement des faits doit donc être confiée à d'autres organismes et, à cet égard, des missions d'enquêtes ponctuelles demandées par le Secrétaire général des Nations Unies ont joué un rôle positif.[16]

---

15 *Cf.*, à ce sujet *Les démarches du CICR en cas de violations du droit international humanitaire*, Revue Internationale de la Croix-Rouge (1981).
16 *Cf.*, M. Ermacora, Rapport sur la situation des droits de l'homme en Afghanistan, Doc. ONU E/CN.4/1986/24; Rapport de la mission envoyée par le Secrétaire Général pour enquêter sur les allégations concernant l'utilisation d'armes chimiques dans le conflit entre la République

Mais on peut surtout concevoir un certain espoir du fait de la création prochaine de la Commission d'établissement des faits prévue par le Protocole I de 1977.[17] Quoique obligatoire seulement pour la petite minorité d'Etats ayant reconnu sa compétence automatique, cette Commission aura l'avantage d'exister et d'être à disposition d'autres Etats. Mais, ici aussi, c'est la crédibilité qu'elle réussira à acquérir de par la qualité de ses membres et de ses premières enquêtes qui sera déterminante quant à l'ampleur de son rôle.

2. PERMANENCE DU DROIT INTERNATIONAL HUMANITAIRE

2.1 Les éléments permanents

L'objectif et la construction du droit international humanitaire sont restés les mêmes qu'à son origine.

En ce qui concerne l'objectif, c'est celui de préserver la vie et l'intégrité des victimes de la guerre. Cela reste donc un objectif limité puisqu'il ne prétend ni toucher aux causes de la guerre, ni étendre son champ à des personnes requérant protection et assistance pour des causes non liées à la guerre.

Quant à la construction, elle reste fondée sur la neutralisation de la victime, la neutralité de l'aide et l'identification des agents portant secours par un emblème reconnu.

2.2 Les facteurs d'évolution

Le maintien jusqu'à aujourd'hui de l'objectif et de la construction originels du système ne doit pas nous cacher cependant l'importance des facteurs d'évolution. Plus, même, il faut aujourd'hui honnêtement se demander si ces facteurs d'évolution ne sont pas de nature à remettre en cause ces objectifs et cette construction.

---

d'Iran et l'Iraq, Doc. ONU S/19823, 25 avril 1988; Rapport de la mission envoyée par le Secrétaire Général pour enquêter sur les allégations concernant l'utilisation d'armes chimiques dans le conflit entre la République Islamique d'Iran et l'Iraq, Doc. ONU S/18852, 8 mai 1987. Voir aussi Doc. ONU S/16627; S/16750 et Corr.1; S/169210.

17 L'Article 90 du Protocole additionnel I de 1977 prévoit la constitution de la Commission dès que 20 Etats Parties au Protocole auront reconnu sa compétence. Or 19 Etats ont actuellement fait une déclaration dans ce sens.

Il est certes difficile d'identifier précisément les facteurs d'évolution à prendre en compte d'autant plus que la plupart d'entre eux sont interdépendants. Nous essayons néanmoins d'en déterminer trois principaux: l'évolution technique, l'évolution de la notion de guerre et l'évolution de la nature des conflits.

2.2.1   *L'évolution technique*

Il y a moins de différence qualitative entre les armes utilisées à l'âge de la pierre et celles utilisées en 1864 qu'entre celles-ci et les moyens actuels. D'armes de champs de bataille, on est passé à des armes planétaires. Cette terrible puissance a considérablement modifié les enjeux de la guerre. Les bombardements massifs de la deuxième guerre mondiale en sont le plus frappant exemple. Les moyens ou méthodes de destruction massive, du fait de leur caractère aveugle ou indiscriminé, remettent en cause la neutralisation des victimes, de même que l'identification et la protection de ceux qui sont chargés de leur porter secours.

Cette terrifiante puissance peut avoir valeur dissuasive et éviter des guerres par ce qu'on a appelé 'l'équilibre de la terreur', mais il est très difficile d'imaginer qu'on renonce à son utilisation si elle est propre à procurer un avantage déterminant, une fois la guerre engagée.

Certes, la plupart des guerres se déroulent au moyen d'armements conventionnels, dans des régions où l'avancée technologique n'a pas encore pris pied. Certes aussi, le développement des techniques de signalisation, notamment par moyens visuels, accoustiques ou radar, permet d'identifier les personnes et biens à protéger à grande distance.[18]

Mais si l'on peut admettre que l'existence d'armes telles que la bombe nucléaire réduit le risque de conflits planétaires, on doit aussi indiquer sans ambiguïté que le DIH n'offrirait pas de solution acceptable si de tels moyens venaient à être utilisés. De nouveaux enjeux apparaissent, par ailleurs, tels que la défense de la planète et de l'espèce humaine, qui ont une dimension dépassant à l'évidence le cadre primitif du DIH.

---

18 P. Eberlin, *La modernisation de la signalisation protectrice et les communications des unités et moyens de transport sanitaires*, dans C. Swinarski, réd., Etudes et essais sur le droit international humanitaire et sur les principes de la Croix-Rouge en l'honneur de Jean Pictet 47-55 (1984).

2.2.2   *L'évolution de la notion de guerre*

L'évolution du droit international vers la reconnaissance d'Etats aux frontières inviolables, inscrite dans la Charte des Nations Unies[19] et qui s'est développée avec la décolonisation et la reconnaissance du droit des peuples à disposer d'eux-mêmes, a entraîné une évolution parallèle du concept de guerre. Il y a certes encore des questions territoriales non réglées, mais la notion de territoires sans maître n'est plus de mise, ni la liberté de conquérir des territoires par la force.

Par ailleurs, la reconnaissance par les Etats de l'obligation d'appliquer certaines règles humanitaires lors des conflits armés non internationaux a conduit à l'émergence d'un droit humanitaire à deux vitesses.

Nous n'épiloguerons pas sur le caractère positif de ces évolutions sur un plan général, mais il faut bien reconnaître qu'elles ont eu le fâcheux 'effet secondaire' de politiser le droit international humanitaire. D'une part, la mise à l'écart de la guerre comme moyen admis de modeler la carte du monde rend plus délicate la reconnaissance d'un état de guerre internationale puisqu'il implique la culpabilité 'originelle' de l'un au moins des belligérants. D'autre part, la transposition aux conflits internes de la systématique du DIH impliquant que les parties au conflit sont titulaires de droits et devoirs identiques provoque fréquemment des réticences de la part des Gouvernements. Ils craignent, en reconnaissant l'applicabilité du DIH, de donner un statut international aux rebelles qu'ils combattent, même si juridiquement cette égalité est strictement confinée au plan du DIH, et de dramatiser une situation dont ils veulent généralement minimiser la gravité.

L'applicabilité du DIH ne va plus de soi et c'est même souvent le problème le plus délicat à résoudre. Dès lors, la souplesse des critères d'intervention du CICR a pris une grande importance à cet égard. D'une intervention en tant que substitut reconnu d'une Puissance protectrice à celle fondée sur son droit de proposer ses services même en dehors de situations de conflits armés,[20] le CICR peut jouer plusieurs rôles et donne ainsi parfois aux Etats la possibilité de bénéficier de ses services en gardant un certain flou sur la base de son action et, par là-même, sur la nature de la situation.

---

19 *Cf.*, notamment Article 2(1,4) de la Charte des Nations Unies.

20 *Cf.*, Articles 10, 10, 10, 11 et Articles 9, 9, 9, 10 commun aux quatre Conventions de Genève du 12 août 1949; Article 5, Protocole additionnel I de 1977; Article 5(2,d), (3) des Statuts du Mouvement international de la Croix-Rouge et du Croissant-Rouge.

2.2.3 *L'évolution de la nature des conflits*

Les guerres traditionnelles étaient le fait du Prince et avaient pour objet la conquête territoriale. Aujourd'hui, la majorité des guerres proviennent de troubles internes non maîtrisables ayant leur racine dans la misère, le sous-développement ou des confrontations ethniques qui, souvent, débordent des frontières. Dans de nombreux cas, les Gouvernements paraissent entraînés dans la guerre davantage qu'ils n'y conduisent leur peuple, dans une dynamique qui paraît échapper à tout contrôle.

En ce qui concerne l'application du DIH, les conflits qui se développent spontanément sur le lit de la misère posent des problèmes particulièrement aigus sur le plan du respect de l'action humanitaire comme sur celui de sa définition.

Sur le plan du respect du droit humanitaire, les difficultés ont principalement trois causes: d'abord le message du DIH rencontre bien peu d'écho chez des gens pour qui la seule loi est celle de la survie, dans un monde sans espoir; ensuite il est extrêmement difficile de transmettre un tel message en dehors d'un système d'éducation quelque peu structuré; enfin les engagements pris au niveau des autorités n'ont que peu de suites au niveau de ceux qui utilisent la force, vu le caractère anarchique de l'emploi de celle-ci dans ce type de conflits.

Quant à la définition de l'action humanitaire et de ses objectifs, elle est rendue très ardue par l'environnement général dans lequel elle se déroule. Comment identifier les victimes de la guerre quand une grande partie de la population est sous-alimentée et quand les maladies infectieuses se répandent du fait de cette malnutrition, conjuguée à une pénurie de personnel soignant et de médicaments? La guerre, en réalité, en les aggravant, met le doigt sur des situations tragiques de manière endémique.

3.   CONCLUSIONS

Comme l'a dit Frits Kalshoven dans son remarquable ouvrage sur le DIH, celui-ci, plutôt qu'une fin en soi, constitue un moyen de préserver l'humanité face à la réalité de la guerre.[21]

En élargissant les catégories de victimes des conflits à l'ensemble de la population civile dans des guerres qui ectent de vastes territoires et n'épargnent pas les villes, puis en déplaçant leur axe principal vers le sud,

---

21 F. Kalshoven, Constraints on the Waging of War 159 (1987).

dans des pays où le sous-développement cause des ravages, les guerres rendent la poursuite de cet objectif particulièrement ardue.

Depuis 1949, suite à la tragédie de la deuxième guerre mondiale, le DIH a reconnu la nécessité de protéger la population civile en tant que telle.[22] Dans la pratique, c'est surtout depuis la guerre de sécession du Biafra que le CICR, comprenant qu'il ne pouvait se contenter de veiller au bon traitement de quelques prisonniers internés quand des populations entières souffraient dramatiquement des effets de la guerre, a pris la décision de se lancer dans des vastes actions d'assistance alimentaire.[23] Or ces actions posent d'énormes problèmes quant au choix prioritaire des bénéficiaires et au contrôle des distributions, sans parler des questions logistiques et de sécurité. En outre, si le conflit du Nigéria-Biafra a eu une durée relativement limitée, d'autres conflits, comme celui de l'Angola, ont mis en évidence, du fait même de leur durée, des problèmes supplémentaires. Quand on s'occupe pendant plusieurs années des blessures et des maladies de populations vulnérables, comment ne pas envisager des actions préventives, telles que les vaccinations, ou dans les domaines de l'hygiène et de la 'sanitation'? Quand on sait que chaque année, à des périodes que l'on peut prévoir, l'insuffisance des récoltes nécessitera l'apport massif d'aide alimentaire, pourqoi ne pas fournir des semences et des outils aux agriculteurs qui en manquent? Quand on connaît les maladies qui affectent régulièrement le bétail de populations dont c'est la principale ressource, pourquoi faudrait-il renoncer à vacciner ce bétail?

Mais quand Henry Dunant a conçu le droit humanitaire en pensant aux blessures des soldats sur le champ de bataille, pouvait-il prévoir que ses successeurs seraient amenés à vacciner des vaches? Ces actions s'inscrivent-elles vraiment dans la même logique?

En étendant le champ des victimes qu'ils atteignent et en augmentant leur durée, les conflits armés contraignent l'action humanitaire d'urgence à s'étendre dans les zones générales de la santé publique, du développement, des droits de l'homme. Ses agents se trouvent dès lors confrontés à des missions d'une ampleur si grande qu'elles leur imposent des choix: il s'agit de préciser les tâches qu'ils peuvent accomplir dans des zones où le DIH se recoupe avec le droit du développement ou celui des droits de l'homme. Un des principaux défis auquel l'humanité doit faire face ces prochaines années, dans le domaine du DIH, pour reprendre le thème général du

---

22 La IVè Convention de Genève du 12 août 1949 est en effet consacrée à la protection de la population civile.

23 Sur l'action du CICR dans ce conflit, *cf.*, notamment T. Hentsch, Face au blocus: La Croix-Rouge internationale dans le Nigéria en guerre (1967-1970) 307 (1973).

présent ouvrage, est donc celui d'assurer la mise en oeuvre des normes protégeant la population civile. A cet effet, la coordination entre les organismes engagés dans l'aide humanitaire s'impose, au sein et en dehors du Mouvement de la Croix-Rouge et du Croissant-Rouge. Il faut faire appel à d'autres ressources, bien plus considérables, pour prendre à la racine les problèmes mis à nu par les conflits armés davantage que provoqués par ceux-ci. Mais, d'une part, l'intervention de ces organismes peut être rendue difficile du fait des problèmes politiques, logistiques et de sécurité engendrés par le conflit armé, d'autre part, bien souvent, les ressources nécessaires ne sont tout simplement pas disponibles.

Pour une organisation comme le CICR, le dilemme peut devenir cruel s'il s'agit soit de renoncer à accomplir l'ensemble de la mission qui lui est confiée en sélectionnant les situations où il doit intervenir ou, dans ces situations, les victimes dont il doit s'occuper, soit de s'engager dans des actions d'une ampleur disproportionnée à sa taille et à ses moyens.

Certes, il n'y a pas de réponse simple à ces questions. A l'évidence, une institution dont la vocation et les forces vives sont humanitaires ne peut imposer des choix inhumains, tels que celui de s'occuper d'un enfant ayant sauté sur une mine et pas d'un enfant affamé. Mais, à l'évidence aussi, dans un monde où les conflits armés nourrissent la misère autant qu'ils se nourrissent d'elle, le CICR, même en s'appuyant sur l'ensemble du grand Mouvement de la Croix-Rouge et du Croissant-Rouge, ne saurait suffire à la tâche: l'aide humanitaire d'urgence ne peut suppléer au développement.

En conclusion, nous dirons que le message de 1864 reste donc plus pertinent que jamais et que le DIH garde sa logique originelle: la prolifération de conflits armés doit même engendrer une mobilisation humanitaire accrue des ressources humaines et financières.

Mais les problèmes rencontrés dans les conflits actuels rendent difficile une approche fondée sur le seul DIH, qui doit s'intégrer dans une réflexion plus générale. Ces conflits doivent aussi -et peut-être surtout- être un signal d'alarme. Il ne suffit pas de mobiliser les foules pour envoyer massivement de l'aide à des enfants dont elles ont croisé le regard insoutenable dans les postes de télévision. L'aide d'urgence ne saurait devenir un alibi pour renoncer à s'attaquer à la racine des véritables problèmes du sous-développement et de la croissance démographique. Sinon, le cercle vicieux de la misère et des conflits armés se développera dans une dynamique que personne ne pourra plus maîtriser.

Témoins de cette évolution, les organismes spécialisés dans l'aide d'urgence ont aussi le devoir de le dire.

QUELQUES CONSIDERATIONS GENERALES SUR L'EVOLUTION DU DROIT INTERNATIONAL HUMANITAIRE

RENÉ-JEAN WILHELM

1.   INTRODUCTION: L'IMPACT PARTICULIEREMENT GRAND
        DE CERTAINES GUERRES SUR LA CODIFICATION DU
        DROIT HUMANITAIRE (DIH)

Tout le long de la paroi, appelée le 'Mur du temps', qui entoure la salle
centrale du Musée international de la Croix-Rouge à Genève, s'inscrivent,
année après année, les noms des guerres et des catastrophes naturelles qui
n'ont cessé d'ensanglanter le monde de 1863 à 1988, avec en regard les
créations successives des Sociétés nationales de la Croix-Rouge et du
Croissant-Rouge. Cette liste impressionnante doit sans doute montrer aussi
que les efforts des hommes pour mettre un frein ou un terme à la violence
armée restent primordiaux. Parmi ces efforts figurent ceux qui tendent a
supprimer la guerre et ceux, dont nous nous occupons dans cet essai, qui
s'efforcent d'en restreindre les maux, notamment en fixant des limitations
d'ordre juridique à l'arbitraire des belligérants, les uns et les autres étant
nécessaires et complémentaires.

Si cette liste, en raison de son étendue, met toutes ces guerres sur le
même pied, pour celui qui s'occupe de l'évolution du droit international
humanitaire (DIH) applicable dans les conflits armés (et nous nous
bornerons désormais à parler simplement de droit international
humanitaire),[1] il est indéniable que dans la codification de cette partie du
droit international, certaines guerres ont eu un impact beaucoup plus grand
que d'autres, un impact parfois décisif.

Si l'on fait abstraction de la Guerre d'Italie de 1859 et de la bataille de
Solférino en particulier, et de leur influence sur la première codification
réussie dans le domaine considéré, à savoir la Convention de Genève de
1864, quelle qu'ait été l'importance de la guerre civile américaine pour les
lois de Lieber, quelle qu'ait été l'influence des conflits de la fin du XIXe
siècle et du conflit russo-japonais de 1905 dans l'élaboration des
Convention de La Haye de 1899 et 1907 consacrées aux lois de la guerre
sur terre et sur mer, quelle qu'ait été, plus près de nous, l'importance
capitale des deux grandes guerres mondiales pour la révision et l'extension
des Conventions de Genève, il nous paraît que les deux conflits armés les

---

1   Sans entrer dans des problèmes de définitions, indiquons que cette expression englobe, pour
    nous, les Conventions pertinentes de La Haye, y compris celles sur la protection des biens
    culturels (1954), tout le droit de Genève, Convention de 1949 et Protocoles additionnels de
    1977, ainsi que les instruments d'ordre humanitaire relatifs aux armes (Déclaration de Saint-
    Pétersbourg de 1868, Protocole de Genève de 1925 et Convention des Nations Unies du 10
    octobre 1980). Elle n'englobe pas, à notre avis, les Droits de l'Homme dont l'applicabilité en
    cas de conflit armé soulève des problèmes complexes.

plus marquants dans l'évolution du DIH sont ceuz qui ont jalonné à 100 ans de distance environ les étapes les plus fondamentales de la codification de ce droit, fondamentales en ce sens que lors de ces étapes on a visé à fixer des limitations humanitaires aussi bien à la conduite des hostilités, à l'emploi des armes, qu'au traitement des personnes et des biens hors de combat. Nous voulons parler de la Guerre franco-prussienne de 1870 et de son impact sur la Déclaration de Bruxelles de 1874, et de la deuxième Guerre du Vietnam et de ses effets sur l'élaboration des Protocoles additionnels aux Conventions de Genève de 1949, adoptés en 1977 (qui seront désormais désignés simplement par l'expression les Protocoles additionnels).

Nous allons essayer de mettre en parallèle ces deux processus de codification du DIH, en dégageant certaines de leurs caractéristiques, en notant les oppositions et les similitudes, afin de mieux marquer l'évolution considérable de ce droit de l'une à l'autre étape. Ce sera là l'objet des parties 2 et 4 de cette étude. Une troisième partie traitera brièvement de l'évolution du DIH à la suite des deux Guerres Mondiales, caractérisée notamment par les Conventions de Genève de 1929 et de 1949. Enfin, dans une cinquième et une sixième partie, nous formulerons quelques considérations générales sur les Protocoles additionnels à la lumière des conflits qui ont eu lieu depuis lors.

Compte tenu de l'espace disponible, l'ampleur du sujet choisi nous oblige à donner à ces considérations un caractère parfois trop schématique; nous éviterons aussi d'expliciter des notions qui nous semblent bien connues. Seuls peuvent justifier ce type de considérations, qui sont plus d'ordre historico ou politico-juridique que de droit pur, une longue expérience au service du Comité de la Croix-Rouge (abrégé désormais CICR) et du DIH, ainsi que le recul des ans - expérience au cours de laquelle les entretiens avec le Professeur Kalshoven que le présent ouvrage doit honorer ont constitué des moments heureux et enrichissants.

2.   LA GUERRE DE 1870 ET LA DECLARATION DE
       BRUXELLES

Pour toute une série de raisons, la Guerre franco-prussienne de 1870, qui se double en France d'une terrible guerre civile, est celle du XIXe siècle, depuis les guerres de la Révolution française et napoléoniennes, qui a eu le

plus de retentissement dans l'opinion publique d'alors[2] et qui a mis le plus
à rude épreuve les lois de la guerre admises alors par la communauté
internationale, entraînant entre les Gouvernements français et prussien de
violentes protestations de violation.

2.1   L'origine et les éléments caractéristiques de la Déclaration de Bruxelles

Quelles qu'aient été les raisons profondes[3] à l'origine de l'initiative du
Gouvernement russe de convoquer la Conférence de Bruxelles de 1874, il
est indéniable que le désir de restreindre les souffrances constatées lors de
la Guerre de 1870, par une clarification des lois de la guerre, a été à la
base des travaux de cette conférence. Celle-ci, notons-le, va porter
d'emblée sur la plus grande partie des problèmes dont le DIH va se
préoccuper jusqu'à nos jours: à savoir la conduite des hostilités, les
bombardements en particulier, la limitation dans l'emploi des armes, le
problème de l'occupation celui du statut du combattant régulier, le
traitement des prisoniers de guerre et celui des blessés et malades. Seules
pour le moment les questions relatives à la guerre maritime ne sont pas
touchées.

Mettre en relief la Déclaration de Bruxelles ne diminue en rien
l'importance capitale des Conférences de La Haye de 1899 et 1907 et des
Conventions qui en sont issues. Si nous le faisons, c'est dans la perspective
qui est la nôtre: le lien étroit entre la guerre et le développement du droit
humanitaire. Les Conférences de La Haye, appelées 'Conférences de la
paix', ont été convoquées principalement pour d'autres raisons sous la
poussée des aspirations et de mouvements pour le désarmement et pour la
paix. A défaut d'aboutir, sur le plan du désarmement, ce que les
chancelleries prévoyaient, ces conférences, et notamment celle de 1899, se
sont repliées, pour ainsi dire, sur la codification des lois de la querre, en
reprenant la plus grande partie des règles de Bruxelles.

Essayons de dégager quelques traits caractéristiques de la codification
de Bruxelles - ce qui permettra de mieux saisir la nouveauté considérable

---

2   Dans le conte 'La Marseillaise', extrait de Morbacka (Souvenirs d'enfance), le grand écrivain
    suédois Selma Lagerlöf évoque l'impression terrible (elle avait alors 11 ans) qu'elle ressentait
    à l'idée du bombardement de Paris de 1870. S. Lagerlöf, Cent et un contes 279 (1956).
3   Voir G. Best, Humanity in Warfare, The Modern History of the International Law of Armed
    Conflicts 346, n. 44 (1980). Dans cette note, après avoir relevé la part extraordinaire jouée
    par la Russie dans l'élaboration du droit de la guerre entre 1815 et 1914, l'auteur ajoute: 'I
    regret that I am in no position to explain it'. Espérons que l'ouverture plus large, maintenant,
    des archives historiques russes permettra de l'expliquer.

et fondamentale que représente la codification qui est à l'autre bout de la chaîne, à savoir les Protocoles additionnels.

Un premier élément à relever est l'absence, dans cette oeuvre de codification, de la principale puissance industrielle, commerciale et navale de l'époque, à savoir la Grande-Bretagne. En dépit d'opinions d'internationalistes anglais favorables à la codification des lois de la guerre,[4] le Gouvernement britannique se montra dès le début hostile à la Conférence de Bruxelles et, s'il y fut finalement représenté par un observateur, c'était pour s'assurer que les débats ne portaient en tout cas pas sur les questions maritimes.[5] Cette non-participation va contribuer puissamment, avec les réserves de petites Puissances, à l'échec de la Conférence. (L'évolution politique du monde à la fin du XIXe siècle dissipera, il est vrai, les craintes de la Grande-Bretagne, qui acceptera à La Haye l'extension des travaux à la guerre sur mer, et celles des petits Etats).

Pendant assez longtemps, et dans de nombreux milieux, la Déclaration de Bruxelles, et notamment le projet russe, qui était à la base des travaux, ont été considérés comme la codification des droits, dirions-nous dans la terminologie moderne, de l'agresseur; on les a dénoncés comme le 'code de l'invasion'.[6] On y a vu -certains petits Etats notamment- une atteinte aux droits inprescriptibles de la défense nationale, une codification favorisant les droits du fort au préjudice du faible,[7] sentiment qui n'était pas étranger au souvenir de la Guerre franco-prussienne.

Un autre trait à relever, et sur lequel il n'est guère besoin d'insister, est le caractère homogène et restreint de la communauté internationale d'alors. Elle est essentiellement européenne. Les Etats-Unis ne se sont pas encore joints à ces travaux. Ils le feront, avec la Turquie et des puissances asiatiques, aux conférences de La Haye. De 15 Etats représentés à Bruxelles, ils seront 26 à La Haye, mais les lois que la communauté internationale se donne ne doivent s'appliquer qu'aux 'nations civilisées' et non dans leur rapport avec les peuples à coloniser. Ce caractère fermé, de club fermé, se manifeste précisément dans la *clausula si omnes*.

Cette communauté se caractérise aussi par son acceptation du *jus ad bellum*. Best cite surtout, à l'appui de ce sentiment, l'opinion de militaires allemands.[8] Mais cette idée du *jus ad bellum* est sans doute plus répandue,

---

4   F. de Martens, La paix et la guerre 93-97 (1901).
5   *Ibid.*, pp. 106-109.
6   *Ibid.*, p. 100.
7   *Ibid.*, p. 113.
8   Best, op. cit. n. 3, pp. 144-147.

et la course aux armements qui s'amplifie dans le dernier quart du XIXe siècle en est un reflet.

Relevons aussi un autre trait de la codification de Bruxelles. Même non ratifiée, elle va servir de modèle. Elle va inspirer les manuels militaires nationaux; elle sera à la base de traités théoriques publiés sur le droit de la guerre, et notamment du Manuel d'Oxford; elle fait autorité dans des conflits internationaux surgis après 1874.

2.2   L'attitude du CICR à l'égard de cette Déclaration

Quelle est l'attitude du CICR lors de la codification de Bruxelles? Elle est déterminée par quatre préoccupations constantes que nous pourrons suivre maintenant dans l'évolution du droit international humanitaire. Les deux premières se maintiendront jusqu'aux Protocoles additionnels; les deux autres se modifieront par la volonté du CICR ou en raison des circonstances. Ces quatre 'constantes' sont les suivantes.

Travailler sans cesse, sur la base des expériences faites au cours de conflits armés, à l'amélioration des règles du droit international protégeant les victimes réelles ou, par la suite, potentielles, et cela avec le concours des sociétés nationales de la Croix-Rouge et d'experts, en vue d'une conférence diplomatique convoquée par le Gouvernement suisse.

Eviter, dans ce travail, les risques d'une remise en question fondamentale des règles de protection mûrement admises par accord entre les Puissances, ou une régression par rapport à ces règles. Ainsi, déjà avant Bruxelles, tirant les leçons de la Guerre prusso-autrichienne quant à l'application de la Convention de Genève, puis celles, désastreuses, de la guerre de 1870, le CICR avait envisagé la révision de cette Convention et l'extension de ses principes à la guerre maritime, par des 'Articles additionnels'. Mais à l'annonce de la réunion de Bruxelles, et en présence du projet russe qui, sur les blessés et malades, contenait quelques articles jugés par le Comité en retrait, le CICR va prendre une attitude plus que réservée.

La troisième constante, qui se renforce de Bruxelles à La Haye, est que les dispositions sur les blessés et malades, bref ce qu'on appelle 'le droit de Genève', ne doivent pas voisiner avec celles qui touchent à la conduite des hostilités et aux moyens de combat. 'Elles sont d'une autre essence, elles doivent demeurer distinctes, dans un traité séparé'.[9]

---

9   P. Boissier, Histoire du Comité international de la Croix-Rouge 493 (1963).

Enfin, quatrième constante, c'est le souci du CICR que les heurts des intérêts nationaux sur des dispositions très controversées ne viennent donner aux délibérations un tour polémique nuisible à l'élaboration des règles humanitaires. Comme le précise Pictet dans le Commentaire des Protocoles additionnels publiés par le CICR:

'... en restant fidèle à la voie traditionelle qui avait rendu possible jusqu'ici l'élaboration des Conventions de Genève le recours au CICR pour la phase préparatoire, puis au Gouvernement suisse pour convoquer la conférence on créerait, cette fois encore, les conditions les plus propices au succès; en maintenant l'entreprise sur un terrain neutre, on espérait éviter, en partie du moins, la politisation des débats.'[10]

Par cette attitude, le CICR va obtenir de la Conférence de Bruxelles que la Déclaration de 1874 renvoie, en ce qui concerne les blessés et les malades, à la Convention de Genève. De même, son représentant à la Conférence de La Haye de 1899 obtiendra le même type de renvoi. Cette conférence émettra tout de même le voeu que la Convention de Genève soit révisée à bref délai. Ce voeu sera exaucé par une conférence réunie en 1906 par le Gouvernement suisse et cette révision se fera dans des conditions propres à rassurer le CICR quant à ses quatre préoccupations constantes.

Le courant de La Haye va pourtant se mêler à celui de Genève: la Conférence de La Haye de 1899 adoptera une Convention pour l'adaptation à la guerre maritime des principes de la première Convention de Genève et cette Convention maritime sera à son tour, à La Haye en 1907, revue à la lumière de la Convention de Genève révisée en 1906. Mais les constantes que nous venons de dégager dans l'attitude du CICR sont en quelque sorte respectées: il s'agit d'adapter à la guerre sur mer les principes de 1864; ceux-ci ne sont donc pas fondamentalement touchés. Cette adaptation prend corps dans une convention séparée de celle qui traite de la conduite des hostilités. Enfin, comme le relève à juste titre Boissier,[11] 'quelques-uns des ténors des réunions de La Haye sont non seulement des diplomates, mais aussi des hommes de Croix-Rouge'; ils ont suivi les travaux de l'organisation, ce qui facilite le débat et en évite singulièrement la politisation.

---

10 J. Pictet, *Introduction générale*, in CICR, Commentaire des Protocoles additionnels du 8 juin 1977 aux Conventions de Genève du 12 août 1949, p. XXX (1986).
11 Boissier, op. cit. n. 9, p. 494.

3.   L'IMPACT DES GUERRES MONDIALES SUR
      L'EVOLUTION DU DIH

3.1   Les éléments de continuité avec le DIH antérieur

On sera peut-être surpris de notre propos: si grande que soit l'extension de
la protection et des garanties offertes aux personnes que protègent les
Conventions de Genève de 1929 et même de 1949, ces Conventions, soit
dans leur processus d'élaboration, soit dans leur matière même, ne vont
pas apporter des changements absolument fondamentaux par rapport à ce
que nous avons dégagé dans le paragraphe précédent, à l'exception des
cinq points que nous examinerons plus loin.

La Croix-Rouge, notons-le, n'est pas à l'origine des règles de la
Déclaration de Bruxelles relatives au traitement des prisonniers de guerre.
Cependant le rôle important que l'organisation va progressivement jouer en
faveur des militaires capturés amène le CICR -en vertu de la première
constante de son attitude (*supra* 2.2) et à la lumière de l'expérience
considérable acquise notamment entre 1914 et 1918- à estimer que ces
victimes hors de combat peuvent être assimilées aux militaires blessés et
malades, et qu'il est fondé à s'efforcer d'améliorer et de développer les
règles qui les protègent, faisant ainsi rentrer dans le droit de Genève cette
partie du droit de La Haye.

D'où, selon la voie traditionnelle, la convocation par le Gouvernement
suisse de la Conférence diplomatique de 1929, qui révise la Ière
Convention de Genève et élabore ce qu'on appellera le 'Code des
prisonniers de guerre'.

Cet effort pour améliorer le DIH se réalise au moment même où le
mouvement visant à restreindre le recours à la guerre, par la création
notamment de la Société des Nations, trouve une sorte d'apogée dans le
Pacte Briand-Kellogg de 1928, qui entre en vigueur trois jours avant la
Conférence diplomatique de 1929. N'y a-t-il pas incompatibilité entre ces
deux courants? Max Huber ne le pense pas et dira en particulier: 'Aussi
longtemps que les Etats n'ont pas déposé les armes, la Convention de
Genève n'est pas sans objets.'[12]

Pourtant des voix autorisées et officielles estimeront alors vraiment
contraire aux aspirations pacifiques l'idée partagée par le CICR et d'autres
personnalités de la Croix-Rouge, selon laquelle l'expérience des conflits

---

12   A. Durand, Histoire du comité international de la Croix-Rouge, De Sarajevo à Hiroshima 206
     (1978).

montre qu'il convient de développer aussi les règles de protection pour les civils contenues dans le droit de La Haye. La montée des périls de guerre allait donner à cette idée toute sa force et toute son ampleur, mais trop tard: au moment où elle allait se réaliser par la voie traditionelle, la Deuxième Guerre Mondiale éclatait. Mais retenons surtout ce point: la codification de 1929 s'effectue donc tout à fait en marge de l'organisation internationale d'alors.

On a dit qu'avec les quatre Conventions de Genève de 1949, l'approche est totalement différente des celle des Conventions de 1929 et que l'influence des Droits de l'Homme, notamment, se fait fortement sentir sur le DIH issu de la Conférence diplomatique de 1949.[13] N'est-ce pas avoir une vue rétrospective de ces Conventions? Elles représentent, elles aussi, les leçons que l'on veut tirer, le plus tôt possible, des terribles expériences de la Deuxième Guerre Mondiale et notamment des persécutions nazies. Mais cette entreprise se situe également en marge des Nations Unies; l'emprise de la Déclaration des Droits de l'Homme, toute récente, n'est nullement évidente, et cela même dans l'Article 3, comme le montre bien l'étude de Rosemary Abi-Saab.[14] D'ailleurs, dans la composition des délégations à la Conférence diplomatique de 1949 se reflète une majorité de représentants ayant l'expérience acquise pendant la guerre d'activités liées au sort des victimes.

Quant à la matière normative de protection, elle est certes considérablement étendue dans l'intérêt des victimes, mais elle ne rompt pas, sous réserve des cinq points mentionnés ci-dessous, avec le droit de La Haye, la coutume ou la pratique des Etats. Il en est ainsi par exemple du système des Puissances protectrices ou des sanctions pénales. Sur cinq points cependant, il y a une rupture importante, voire fondamentale, avec ce qui a été vu précédemment.

3.2   Les éléments de rupture

D'abord la *clausula si omnes* est abandonnée déjà en 1929. Ce qui revient à dire que l'on tient compte également de l'extension de la communauté internationale. Pourtant, c'est encore une communauté limitée, dominée par l'Occident et l'Amérique latine: 50 Etats en 1929 et 59 en 1949 signent

---

13 K. Obradovic, *Les Protocoles de 1977 dix ans après: bilan et perspectives pour l'avenir*, dans Colloque sur les Protocoles de 1977 additionnels aux Conventions de 1949: Dix ans après 12-15 (1987).

14 R. Abi-Saab, *Droit humanitaire et conflits internes, Origines et évolution de la réglementation internationale* 51-73 (1986).

l'Acte final de la Conférence diplomatique. L'Union soviétique, contrairement à 1929, participe en 1949 avec les autres pays socialistes de l'Europe de l'Est à la Conférence, et la conception marxiste-léniniste de la lutte de classes ne se fera guère sentir dans les débats et n'entraînera pas leur politisation car, comme le relève à juste titre Best: 'The Soviet Government perceived that it [the international law of war] contained valuable humanitarian substance of universal value ...'.[15] Seul signe marquant de cette conception, la réserve -qui a tant occupé et préoccupé notre collègue Pilloud- par laquelle l'Union soviétique et ses alliés entendaient priver du statut de prisonnier de guerre les militaires poursuivis et condamnés pour infractions graves.[16]

Après l'abandon de la *clause si omnes* qui donne un caractère objectif aux règles des Conventions de Genève, ce caractère est encore renforcé par l'obligation faite aux Etats parties, dans les Conventions de 1929, de les respecter 'en toutes circonstances', c'est-à-dire indépendamment de la conduite de la Partie adverse au conflit. Cette notion est reprise et approfondie en 1949 et dans le Protocole additionnel I, de sorte, selon Condorelli, '... qu'il est justifié d'affirmer que le droit international humanitaire tout entier pivote sur la répudiation du principe de la réciprocité'[17] - même si, hélas, cette répudiation est loin d'être réalisée dans les faits.

Autre exception: l'extension des règles de protection aux personnes civiles en temps de guerre par l'établissement de la IVe Convention de Genève, dont les travaux préparatoires remontaient déjà à 1934. Pour les civils *internés*, l'assimilation *mutatis mutandis* aux prisonniers de guerre ne posait pas de problème de principe. En revanche, l'extension de la protection aux civils en territoire occupé en posait un de fondamental pour le CICR: avec l'accord du Gouvernement de La Haye, il reprenait dans ses travaux une partie du droit de La Haye, mais, selon une expression de Max Huber: 'on entrait dans une lutte corps à corps avec la guerre elle-même puisqu'il ne s'agissait plus seulement d'atténuer des souffrances mais

---

15 Best, op. cit. n. 3, p. 307.

16 C. Pilloud, *Les réserves aux Conventions de Genève de 1949*, Revue internationale de la Croix-Rouge 202-214 (1976).

17 L. Condorelli, *Le droit international humanitaire en tant qu'atelier d'expérimentation juridique*, dans W. Haller, A. Kölz, G. Müller, D. Thürer, réd., Im Dienst an der Gemeinschaft, Festschrift für Dietrich Schindler zum 65. Geburtstag (Au service de la communauté, Mélanges offerts en l'honeur du Professeur Dietrich Schindler pour son 65e anniversaire) 197 (1989).

de faire tarir les sources dont elles découlent':[18] à moins d'être internés, la plupart des civils ne sont pas hors d'état de nuire et les mesures prises en leur faveur peuvent être une sérieuse entrave à la conduite de la guerre. Ainsi le CICR consentait à pénétrer dans un domaine dont il s'était gardé jusque-là. L'interdiction absolue d'attaquer les hôpitaux civils, contenue dans la IVe Convention, constituait, elle aussi, plus qu'on ne l'a vu alors, une limitation certaine à la guerre aérienne, comme nous l'avons montré par ailleurs.[19]

Autre exception importante et rupture par rapport à la coutume: l'interdiction des représailles, pour les prisonniers de guerre et les blessés et malades déjà en 1929, puis les personnes civiles protégées en 1949 - interdiction qui prendra dans les Protocoles additionnels une extension telle que bien des internationalistes s'interrogent sur son opportunité.[20]

Enfin, l'Article 3 commun aux quatre Conventions qui, pour la première fois, introduit dans le droit international des garanties d'ordre humanitaire en cas de conflit interne. Les préoccupations antérieures à ce sujet de sociétés de droit international, comme de la Croix-Rouge, considérablement renforcées par les événement de la Guerre civile espagnole, ont été, à notre avis, un moteur plus décisif pour l'établissement de cet article que la Déclaration des droits de l'homme.

Enfin, un autre impact marquant de la première guerre doit être signalé, impact qui se situe, lui, dans le domaine de l'emploi des armes: le Protocole de Genève de 1925. Quelles qu'aient été l'attention et les préoccupations de la Croix-Rouge à l'égard des armes visées par ce Protocole, notamment des gaz, avant comme après sa conclusion, l'éboration de ce dernier intervient dans un cadre entièrement étranger à l'organisation humanitaire et selon un processus qui, sur un plan tout à fait limité, peut rappeler celui du droit de La Haye: dans le cadre des travaux du désarmement de la Société des Nations, et toujours en attendant en vain d'aboutir dans ce domaine, les participants se replient sur une interdiction d'arme dont la guerre a montré la nécessité.

---

18 Cité dans l'Introduction au *Commentaire des Conventions de Genève du 12 août 1949 publié sous la direction de Jean Pictet*, La Convention de Genève IV relative à la protection des personnes civiles en temps de guerre, CICR 9 (1956).

19 R.-J. Wilhelm, *Les Conventions de Genève et la guerre aérienne*, Revue internationale de la Croix-Rouge 10-42 (1952).

20 Voir les débats sur les représailles in Américan Society of International Law, Proceedings of the 74th Annual Meeting, Washington April 17-19, pp. 196-212 (1980), et C.J. Greenwood, *Reprisals and Reciprocity in the New Law of Armed Conflict*, dans M.A. Meyer, réd., Armed Conflict and the New Law: Aspects of the 1977 Geneva Protocols and the 1981 Weapons Convention, British Institute of International and Comparative Law 227-250 (1989).

4.   LA GUERRE DU VIETNAM ET LES AUTRES
      CIRCONSTANCES AYANT CONTRIBUE A L'ELABORATION
      DES PROTOCOLES ADDITIONNELS DE 1977

4.1   **Les effets de la 2ème guerre du Vietnam sur l'élaboration des
       Protocoles**

Comme l'a relevé justement l'ambassadeur Aldrich, le succès de la
codification ayant abouti aux Protocoles additionnels 'reflected a special
confluence of events, experiences and perceived opportunities'.[21] Dans ce
concours de circonstances, la deuxième Guerre du Vietnam, disons surtout
à partir de l'engagement américain 1964-1973, a constitué un élément
déterminant sur le plan politico-juridique avec les conséquences que nous
allons examiner ci-dessous. Elément déterminant mais qui n'est pas le seul,
et c'est pourquoi nous allons aussi plus loin tenir compte des autres
circonstances qui ont favorisé la codification de 1977 et les conditions dans
lesquelles elle s'est opérée à la Conférence diplomatique sur la
réaffirmation et le développement du droit international humanitaire
applicable dans les conflits armés, Genève 1974-1977 (abrégée désormais
par 'la Conférence diplomatique (1974-1977)').
    Voyons d'abord les conséquences de la Guerre du Vietnam. Sans entrer
dans la question de savoir si les moyens employés au Vietnam par les
armées des Etats-Unis étaient ou non contraires au DIH existant alors, il
est indéniable, à mesure que les bombardements américains s'intensifiaient
sans aboutir au résultat annoncé, que l'opinion publique mondiale, et
notamment occidentale, sous l'effet également de l'essor des mass-médias
et notamment de la télévision, a été de plus en plus sensible à ces
bombardements et qu'elle y a vu de plus en plus des attaques
indiscriminées. Ainsi, sans parler des effets de cette guerre aux Etats-Unis
même, l'image de cette grande nation s'est détériorée dans l'opinion
mondiale. C'est donc le mérite des autorités politiques américaines d'alors,
et notamment de Kissinger, de l'avoir compris et d'avoir voulu, par toute
une série de mesures, mettre un terme à l'engagement des Etats-Unis au
Vietnam, ainsi que restaurer cette image et donner le sentiment d'une
nation aspirant à la paix.[22] Dans le cadre de cette politique, la première

---

21 G.H. Aldrich, *Some reflections on the origins of the 1977 Geneva Protocols*, dans C.
    Swinarski, réd., Etudes et essais sur le droit international humanitaire et sur les principes de la
    Croix-Rouge en l'honneur de Jean Pictet 129 (1984).
22 Voir H. Kissinger, White House Years (1979), notamment à partir de la Partie III (1970-1971:
    From Turmoil to Hope).

Puissance mondiale, contrairement donc à l'attitude de la Grande-Bretagne en 1874, a adopté -et c'est là le fait capital- une attitude positive à l'égard de la réaffirmation des règles relatives à la conduite des hostilités et du renforcement des Conventions de Genève qui se sont esquissés à ce moment-là - constatation qui ne diminue en rien l'intérêt humanitaire que les Autorités américaines ont aussi pu voir dans cette réaffirmation. Attitude non seulement positive, mais constructive, en déléguant notamment à la Conférence diplomatique qui s'est ouverte en 1974 et aux réunions préparatoires d'experts de 1971 et 1972, des personnalités de renommée internationale dont l'autorité s'est imposée au point que la délégation américaine s'est vu confier des postes clés dans des commissions parmi les plus importantes.

L'issue de la Guerre du Vietnam a aussi incontestablement renforcé le courant disons tiers-mondiste et les vues favorables aux mouvements de libération nationale, aux luttes que mènent ces mouvements contre leur anciens maîtres, et aux demandes formulées dans de nombreuses résolutions des Nations Unies, notamment depuis la Guerre d'Algérie, de voir ces guerres de libération assimilées à des conflits internationaux. Ces vues vont trouver leur consécration dans une des disposition du Protocole additionel I, une disposition des plus controversées, il est vrai.

Les conséquences de la Guerre du Vietnam se font également sentir sur plusieurs plans dans le domaine juridique. Ainsi, en ce qui concerne le caractère illicite des attaques qui ne sont pas dirigées contre des objectifs militaires, on a pu relever que l'attitude de la doctrine, encore assez flottante après 1945, avait semble-t-il connu en 1970 un tournant décisif,[23] dans le sens des efforts du CICR afin que la distinction fondamentale entre civils et militaires soit réaffirmée dans tous les aspects de la conduite des hostilités. C'est qu'à ce moment-là l'efficacité militaire des bombardement conventionnels à caractère indiscriminé, notamment au Vietnam, est, depuis un certain temps, de plus en plus mise en doute. Ce sentiment est renforcé par le connaissance des résultats, trop longtemps ignorés, des commissions d'enquête américaines sur l'efficacité relative de certains bombardement alliés sur les fronts occidentaux de la Deuxième Guerre Mondiale. Ces sentiments n'ont pu qu'accentuer cette évolution de la doctrine vers les règles codifiées par le Protocole additionnel I.

Autre conséquence sur le plan juridique: la question du statut des combattants de la guérilla, qui n'avait pour ainsi dire pas évolué depuis

---

23 L. Doswald-Beck, *The Value of the 1977 Geneva Protocols for the Protection of Civilians*, dans Meyer, réd., op. cit. n. 20, p. 151.

1874, va trouver dans le Protocole I une solution que les expériences de la Guerre du Vietnam, et les conversations entre délégués vietnamiens et américains à la Conférence diplomatique (1971-1977) vont faciliter, une solution qui représente sans doute un pas en avant, si controversée soit-elle.

Autre conséquence d'ordre juridique: les préoccupations très vives des autorités et de l'opinion publique amércaines quant au sort des prisonniers de guerre américains au Vietnam. Ni le CICR ni aucune Puissance protectrice n'ont accès à ces prisoniers et ne peuvent exercer à leur égard les fonctions prévues par la IIIe Convention de 1949. Ces autorités sont ainsi amenées à s'interroger sur l'efficacité des mécanismes de mise en oeuvre des Conventions de Genève, et à souhaiter que la codification qui est envisagée examine cette question et améliore ces mécanismes.

Autre conséquence importante: selon Best, après la Conférence internationale des Droits de l'homme (Téhéran, 1968), convoquée sous l'égide de l'ONU, le droit de La Haye comme celui de Genève était mûr pour une révision. Ce que les belligérants entendaient faire, sous-entendu dans la conduite des hostilités, ne pouvait plus être tenu séparé du traitement proposé pour les victimes 'as ICRC practice, with the historical structuring of the international law of war on its side, had hitherto presumed'.[24] Le *hitherto* (jusqu'ici) devrait être remplacé par *in the past* (autrefois). Car, et c'est là le point intéressant et capital, si -ainsi que nous l'avons dit à propos de la Déclaration de Bruxelles- le CICR ne veut pas mêler droit de Genève et droit de La Haye, cette attitude va progressivement évoluer de façon complète. D'abord en 1949, comme nous l'avons vu, avec la reprise des problèmes relatifs aux territoires occupés. Puis, et surtout, à propos des limitations d'ordre humanitaire à réaffirmer quant à la guerre aérienne, ce dont il s'était soucié dès l'entre-deux-guerres, le CICR devient de plus en plus conscient du lien qui existe entre ces limitations et l'application des Conventions de Genève: La Haye et Genève ne peuvent plus être séparés. Il le dit déjà en 1956 dans le commentaire du Projet de Règles soumis à la XIXe Conférence internationale de la Croix-Rouge, et la Guerre du Vietnam le renforce dans cette conviction et le pousse encore plus fortement à prendre les mesures nécessaires pour réaffirmer ces limitations.[25] La conscience de ce lien l'a

---

24 Best, op. cit. n. 3, p. 319.
25 *Le CICR rappelle que les Conventions de Genève risqueraient de rester inopérantes si les belligérants ne rencontraient aucune limitation dans le choix des moyens et méthodes de combat*, Commentaire du Projet de Règles limitant les risques courus par la population civile en temps de guerre 17 (1956) - *Le CICR a été amené à se rendre compte ... qu'il n'est plus*

même amené à accepter, à la demande de la Conférence diplomatique (1974-1977), d'organiser à deux reprises des Conférences d'experts gouvernementaux, en 1974 et 1976, sur la question des armes conventionnelles propres à causer des maux superplus ou à avoir des effets indiscriminés - travaux repris par les Nations Unies pour aboutir à la Convention du 10 octobre 1980 sur l'interdiction ou la limitation de certaines armes classiques.[26]

4.2 Des autres circonstances ayant contribué à l'élaboration des Protocoles

A côté de la Guerre du Vietnam, élément déterminant pour la codification de 1974-1977, d'autres circonstances, parfois parallèles, ont exercé une influence dans le même sens, et nous allons souligner celles qui nous paraissent les plus importantes.

Tout d'abord, l'intérêt pour un renforcement des mécanismes de mise en oeuvre des Conventions de 1949 n'a pas été seulement le fait des autorités américaines. Il s'est trouvé aussi constituer une préoccupation des pays arabes, en raison du conflit avec Israël, qui après la Guerre de 1967 est devenu Puissance occupante sans reconnaître l'applicabilité des Conventions de Genève, mettant ainsi en échec le système des Puissances protectrices. Ce renforcement va devenir une préoccupation constante du monde arabe, renforcée par la Guerre de 1973, et il n'est pas étonnant qu'un des cosignataires du projet de la Résolution de la Conférence de Téhéran sur le 'Respect des droits de l'homme en période de conflit armé' ait été précisément la République Arabe Unie.[27]

Un autre conflit marquant de la décennie qui précède la Conférence diplomatique de 1974 est la Guerre civile au Nigéria (1967-1970), conflit marquant non seulement par le fait qu'il ne s'agit pas, cette fois-ci, d'une guerre de libération, mais d'une véritable guerre civile dans l'Etat le plus peuplé d'Afrique. Phénomène marquant aussi par l'impact médiatique que les parties à ce conflit s'efforcent de donner à leur cause, notamment auprès de l'opinion occidentale. L'impact de ce conflit et les problèmes

---

possible de maintenir - ainsi qu'on le pensait autrefois - une distinction nette entre ces deux domaines du droit applicable aux conflits armés: les belligérants considèrent forcément ce droit comme un tout, Réaffirmation et Développement des lois et coutumes applicables dans les conflit armés, Rapport du CICR à la XXIe Conférence internationale de la Croix-Rouge 8 (1969).

26 Voir F. Kalshoven, *Conventional Weaponry: The Law from St. Petersburg to Lucerne and Beyond*, dans Meyer, op. cit. n. 20, p. 254 *et seq.*

27 Résolution A/Conf. 32/C 2/L 45 de 5 mai 1968.

particulièrement difficiles de secours qui se posent à la Croix-Rouge montrent l'insuffisance des règles de l'Article 3, si précieux qu'ait été ce dernier. Cette insuffisance est ressentie encore plus fortement par de nombreux milieux, dont le CICR qui avait déjà auparavant réuni des experts sur les problèmes de conflits internes.

Autre élément d'une grande importance: l'intérêt manifesté par les Nation Unies pour l'application du DIH et pour les compléments à y apporter, intérêt qui -indépendamment des demandes antérieures relatives aux guerres de libération- s'est exprimé d'une façon marquante et globale à la Conférence internationale des Droit de l'homme de Téhéran et s'est traduit ensuite par une série de résolutions adoptées durant plusieurs années (de 1969 à 1977) par l'Assemblée générale de l'ONU sous le même titre 'Respect des droits de l'homme en période de conflit armé'.[28] Comment s'en étonner? Les Nations Unies, et notamment leur Assemblée générale, ne sont-elles pas devenues le forum, la caisse de résonance où s'expriment les aspirations et les préoccupations du monde, et notamment des nouveaux Etats? Cette extension considérable de la communauté internationale, qui s'accomplit à partir des années 60, se reflète précisément à l'Assemblée générale de l'ONU. La Croix-Rouge a fait tout son possible pour que les Etats nouveaux deviennent parties aux Conventions de Genève, mais c'est avant tout aux Nations Unies beaucoup plus qu'aux conférences internationales de l'organisation humanitaire, que ces nouveaux Etats, par la force des choses, se font représenter. En outre, comme le relève Best,[29] ce forum est aussi celui de beaucoup d'organisations non gouvernementales (des NGO) qui se préoccupent également de la protection de la personne humaine en temps de guerre.

Ainsi, phénomène à souligner, alors que jusque-là, comme nous l'avons montré, les travaux pour le développement du DIH, notamment en 1929 et en 1949, se sont poursuivis en marge, en quelque sorte, de la SDN ou de l'ONU, brusquement il est vrai, le Secrétaire général des Nations Unies d'une part et le CICR d'autre part sont appelés, le premier par la Conférence de Téhéran et le second par les conférences internationale de la Croix-Rouge, à oeuvrer pour le développement du DIH. On se tromperait cependant en pensant que l'intérêt de l'ONU pour ce développement va prendre le CICR au dépourvu: dans son mémoire aux gouvernements des Etats parties aux Conventions de Genève, du 19 mai 1967, donc *un an avant la Conférence de Téhéran* -mémoire destiné à leur transmettre la

28 Voir la liste et les références de ces résolutions dans Bibliography of International Humanitarian Law Applicable in Armed Conflicts 137-138 (1987).
29 Best, op. cit. n. 3, p. 318.

résolution adoptée à Vienne en 1965 par la Conférence internationale de la Croix-Rouge et qui proclamait quatre principes essentiels de protection des populations civiles- le CICR demandait à ces gouvernements de consacrer ces normes dans un instrument adéquat de droit international et, en attendant, de marquer sans délai la valeur qu'ils attachaient à ces principes 'par toute manifestation officielle appropriée, telle qu'une résolution de l'Assemblée générale des Etats Unies'.[30] Comme on le voit, le CICR lui-même jugeait opportun de recourir aux Nations Unies pour donner dès que possible la force nécessaire à ces principes.[31] Pour la suite des travaux, et notamment les travaux préparatoires de la Conférences diplomatique (1974-1977), la communauté internationale a finalement choisi, pour les raisons évoquées plus loin, la solution disons traditionnelle: des travaux placés sous l'égide du CICR et suivis d'une conférence diplomatique convoquée par le Gouvernement suisse. Mais, élément entièrement nouveau, ces travaux préparatoires, notamment les réunions d'experts gouvernementaux de 1971 et 1972, et ceux de la Conférence diplomatique (1974-1977) se sont poursuivis non seulement en liaison étroite avec le représentant du Secrétaire général de l'ONU, mais sous le regard attentif de l'Assemblée générale des Nations Unies.

Autre élément d'importance: alors que jusqu'en 1949 le développement du DIH s'est opéré dans une communauté relativement *homogène* et restreinte, et que même en 1949, comme nous l'avons relevé, ne se fait pas encore sentir le changement radical qui va intervenir progressivement dans cette communauté, au contraire, la nouvelle codification du droit applicable dans les conflits armés aura lieu dans une communauté internationale en pleine extension et fondamentalement *hétérogène*. Même si on peut alors distinguer trois groupes, selon le professeur Cassese,[32] cette distinction est toute relative, à manier avec prudence et avec le temps deviendra de plus en plus relative. Or, ce que le CICR constate, c'est que ces nouveaux Etats, même s'ils adhèrent aux Conventions de Genève de 1949, ne deviennent *pas* parties aux Conventions de La Haye sur le droit de la guerre ni au Protocole de Genève de 1925, en dépit de l'invitation que la Conférence de Téhéran de 1968 leur adresse à ce sujet. Le droit de La

---

30 CICR, Mémoire du 19 mai 1967: *Protection des populations civiles contre les dangers de la guerre indiscriminée*, Revue internationale de la Croix-Rouge 264-265 (1967).
31 L'Assemblée générale des Nations Unies, par sa résolution adoptée à l'unanimité A/Res/2444 (XXIII) le 19 décembre 1968, a consacré les trois premiers de ces principes. Ne peut-on pas considérer que ces principes ont ainsi pris une valeur de droit coutumier pour les conflits armés de toute nature?
32 A. Cassese, Le droit international dans un monde divisé 98 (1986).

Haye et les règles principales de 1949 peuvent certes être regardés comme du droit coutumier s'imposant à tous, mais pour ces nouveaux Etats, qui ont le sentiment, par les résolutions des Nations Unies, de participer à la formation d'un droit international nouveau, les règles de La Haye et même de Genève ne risquent-elles pas d'être considérées comme une sorte de *res inter alios acta*? Cette constatation (pas d'adhésion aux Conventions de La Haye) et la conscience de ce risque n'ont fait que renforcer le CICR dans la conviction de l'urgence de réaffirmer et développer le DIH *afin d'y associer tous ces nouveaux Etats*. Si ces derniers n'ont joué qu'un rôle très limité dans les réunions d'experts gouvernementaux de 1971 et 1972, leur participation a été beaucoup plus étendue, beaucoup plus active à la Conférence diplomatique (1974-1977), peut-être aussi en raison de la tournure politico-juridique qu'elle a prise. Un des plus grands mérites des Protocoles additionnels de 1977, peut-être le plus grand, est d'avoir associé la nouvelle communauté internationale, si hétérogène et disparate soit-elle, à la formation des règles des Protocoles, et ainsi indirectement à la réaffirmation des principes des Conventions de Genève.

4.3 De certaines conditions particulières dans lesquelles cette élaboration s'est effectuée

A ces circonstances qui ont poussé à la codification du DIH entre 1974 et 1977, nous voudrions ajouter deux observations d'ordre général quant aux conditions dans lesquelles elle s'est opérée, pour mieux marquer la grande différence qui la distingue des codifications antérieures.

Nous avons vu l'importance prise par le tiers monde dans la communauté internationale et le poids politique dont il jouit, souvent appuyé par le groupe des Etats socialistes, dans les débats et résolutions de l'Assemblée générale des Nations Unies. Nous avons vu que l'évolution de la Guerre du Vietnam renforce en un sens cette situation. Un autre événement vient encore augmenter l'importance du tiers monde au début de la Conférence diplomatique. En effet, à la suite de la Guerre israélo-arabe de 1973, le monde occidental subit durement le choc pétrolier. Cette nouvelle puissance du tiers monde, ou plutôt sa confiance dans une nouvelle puissance, se traduit notamment, aux Nations Unies, précisément au printemps 1974, par une Résolution proclamant un 'nouvel ordre économique international'[33] - résolution dont les résultats ultérieurs

---

33 Résolution 3201 du 1er mai 1974 de l'Assemblée générale.

montreront que ce sentiment de puissance ne correspond pas à la réalité des forces en présence dans le monde.

C'est donc dans ce climat disons de 'relative faiblesse des puissances occidentales' qu'ont lieu les deux premières sessions de la Conférence diplomatique (1974-1977). Est-ce à dire que la codification qui en résulte traduit ces circonstances particulières du moment? Ce serait trahir la réalité. A l'exception de quatre domaines où ces circonstances se sont vraiment fait sentir (à savoir la question des guerres de libération nationale, son influence sur la réduction du Protocole II, la question des mercenaires, et la mention de l'apartheid à l'Article 85 du Protocole I[34]) les rapports de force en présence ont plutôt amené un certain équilibre entre les grandes Puissances militaires et les Etats moyens ou petits, ce qui a évité, le plus souvent, des solutions forcées obtenues par des votes, et ce qui a entraîné la recherche parfois très longue de solutions acceptables de part et d'autre. On ne peut plus dire de cette codification, comme on l'a dit de celle de Bruxelles, qu'elle est le 'code de l'invasion', le code du plus fort.

Pour donner suite à ces aspirations quant au dévelopement du DIH, la communauté internationale a donc finalement donné sa préférence à la 'voie traditionnelle' (travaux préparatoires menés par le CICR et suivis d'une Conférence diplomatique convoquée par la Suisse). Ce choix s'explique sans doute en raison de l'expérience du CICR et de l'état déjà avancé de ses travaux dans plusieurs domaines. mais certains gouvernements, surtout du côté occidental, ont partagé l'idée rappelée plus haut par Pictet, que cette voie éviterait autant que possible la politisation des débats et, comme l'a relevé l'ambassadeur Aldrich, *'polemics were frequently avoided or muted in ways that simply would not have happened in a United Nations conference'*.[35]

---

34 Les Puissances 'occidentales' ont elles finalement renoncé à s'opposer à ces dispositions dans l'idée que leur libellé rendrait leur application pratique peu vraisemblable et que, comme le dit G. Aldrich de l'Article 1(4) du Protocole I: 'In effect, the provision is a dead letter', *Progressive Development of the Laws of War: A Reply to Criticisms of the 1977 Geneva Protocol I*, 26 VJIL 703 (1986). Ou bien faut-il plutôt dire de cette disposition, comme de celle sur les mercenaires, selon H.A. Wilson:

'If the conflicts in South Africa and Israel are resolved, Article 1(4) will not necessarily fade away, although many hope it will. Its subjective character make it a prime target for flexible interpretation based on the exigencies of the moment'.

H. Wilson, International Law and the Use of Force by National Liberation Movement 168 (1988).

35 Aldrich, loc. cit. n. 21, p. 135.

En réalité, contrairement aux précédentes conférences diplomatiques convoquées par le Gouvernement suisse dans le domaine du DIH, et comme on pouvait normalement s'y attendre compte tenu du développement et du caractère de la communauté internationale, l'élaboration des Protocoles additionnels s'est réalisée dans une conférence fortement politisée, principalement en séances plénières et durant les sessions de 1974 et 1975, en raison notamment du problème de l'invitation des mouvements de libération et surtout de celle du Gouvernement révolutionnaire provisoire de la République du Vietnam du Sud - cette dernière question s'étant résolue d'elle-même dès 1976 par le sort des armes au Vietnam! Best écrit, à propos des Protocoles additionnels: '*it must by now be clear that the debate about the law of war had become thoroughly politicized by the time it underwent its latest reconstruction, the debate between 1968 and 1977*'.[36] Peirce, dans son étude sur le système des Puissances protectrices, relève que si les controverses politiques se sont suffisamment apaisées pour permettre à la conférence de terminer ses travaux en 1977, elles ont néanmoins eu '*a significant impact on the debates and the final results. In a very real sense, the Protocols represent a contemporary political consensus defining the limits of modernization of humanitarian law*'.[37]

Certes, si l'on songe à certaines Assemblées générales de l'ONU, où la polémique fait rage et où les discours de prestige et de caractère purement politique se succèdent, la Conférence diplomatique (1974-1977) était bien éloignée, pour la plus grande partie, et surtout dans son travail dans les commissions et le comité de rédaction, de cette politisation-là. Mais si l'on considère sa procédure, ses méthodes de décision, le rôle des groupes régionaux, elle ne se distinguait plus du tout fondamentalement des conférences de codification du droit convoquées sous l'égide des Nations Unies: ces dernières aussi, quel que soit leur degré de politisation, savent souvent, par la qualité de la préparation, par celle des réprésentants, et par le caractère approfondi des discussions souvent en petits groupes, arriver à des compromis propres à satisfaire les intérêts nationaux en même temps que la solidarité internationale, que ce soit par exemple dans le Convention de Vienne de 1969 sur le droit des traités, dans la troisième Convention de 1982 sur le droit de la mer, ou dans la Déclaration de 1970 relative aux principe du droit international touchant les relations amicales et la coopération entre les Etats conformément à la Charte des Nations Unies.

---

36 Best, op. cit. n. 3, p. 315.
37 G.A.B. Peirce, *Humanitarian protection for the victims of war: The System of Protecting Powers and the role of the ICRC*, 90 Military Law Review 133 (1980).

Peut-être en définitive -outre le rôle joué par le CICR dans la préparation des projets, dans la présentation et l'explication de ces textes durant la Conférences, outre les moyens exceptionnels mis à la disposition du Comité de rédaction- la présence d'un membre du Gouvernement suisse à la tête de la conférence, son autorité naturelle, sa présidence active et sa volonté d'aboutir, qu'il a su communiquer à l'ensemble des délégations, ont-elles finalement distingué la Conférence diplomatique (1974-1977) des conférences qui se réunissent sous l'égide des Nations Unies.

5. LES PROTOCOLES A LA LUMIERE DES GUERRES RECENTES (DE 1977 A 1990)

Si les guerres, et notamment celles que nous avons examinées, ont eu un effet indéniable sur la codification du DIH, elles en ont également pour juger dans quelle mesure ce droit est profondément accepté et intégré par la communauté internationale car, comme le relève Best, une reconnaissance formelle des Conventions de Genève de 1949, par exemple par une sorte de *lip-service*, est une chose, et une acceptation significative et véritable (meaningful) en est une autre, '*and evasion is, given the present poor state of world law and order, easy and commonplace*'.[38] Même restée à l'état de simple déclaration, celle de Bruxelles a reçu, comme nous l'avons montré, une certaine consécration dans la pratique des Etats, et cela dans le dernier quart de siècle qui a suivi son adoption.

5.1 Questions relatives à leur valeur juridique actuelle

Qu'en est-il à cet égard des Protocoles additionnels? A l'exception du conflit interne du Salvador, les conflits armés qui se sont poursuivis ont mis aux prises des Etats qui n'étaient pas encore liés par les Protocoles. Néanmoins, les attitudes adoptées, notamment à l'égard des Conventions de Genève, et les déclarations faites à propos de la conduite des hostilités, constituent des indices utiles quant à cette acceptation véritable ou, tout au moins, quant aux chances de cette dernière. Si le conflit des îles Falkland-Malouines a été plutôt un motif de satisfaction -bien qu'il ait soulevé peu de questions concernant les Protocoles additionnels- les autres conflits en revanche ont représenté plutôt des sujets de préoccupation. Le temps qui s'est écoulé depuis 1977 est sans doute trop court pour tirer déjà, quant à

---

38 Best, *Preface*, dans Meyer, réd., op. cit. n. 20, p. VI.

cette acceptation véritable, des conclusions de la pratique des Etats - pratique qui est une des trois conditions, selon le professeur Greenwood, qui se réfère à l'arrêt de la Cour internationale de Justice dans l'Affaire du plateau continental de la mer du Nord, pour déterminer si une règle nouvelle contenue dans une traité est devenue coutumière et oblige toutes les parties à un conflit.[39]

Si le recul du temps n'est pas suffisant pour porter des jugements hâtifs sur cette pratique ou sur les Protocoles additionnels eux-mêmes, il nous permet tout au moins de formuler les quelques observations générales suivantes.

Dans la communauté internationale actuelle qui a écarté le *jus ad bellum* de son système juridique, on ne saurait admettre que les conflits armés servent d'indices principaux de la pratique étatique: la situation est bien différente d'une codification de règles valables pour le temps de paix. Cette pratique pourra donc se dégager aussi d'une série d'autre éléments, dont les manuels d'instruction militaire constitueront une donnée importante, ainsi que les déclarations officielles faites également par des Etats non engagés dans des conflits ou des résolutions des Nations Unies.

Le nombre d'adhésions aux Protocoles additionnels ou de ratifications n'est-il pas un élément déterminant? Même avec l'évolution récente et heureuse de la part des pays de l'Europe de l'Est, il n'en reste pas moins que quelques-unes des grandes Puissances militaires ou moyennes du globe ne sont pas encore formellement liés par les Protocoles. Ne serait-il pas peu judicieux, dans ces conditions, de donner l'impression que le nombre maintenant élevé des Etats parties aux Protocoles additionnels est un signe décisif de leur acceptation véritable par la communauté internationale?

Le caractère forcément hétérogène de cette communauté et le fait aussi que plusieurs de ses nouveaux membres viennent d'accéder à la notion d'Etat avec tout ce qu'elle implique dans la formation des structures administratives et politique ne devrait pas, semble-t-il, faire attribuer aux luttes parfois si féroces et si sanglantes qui surgissent entre communautés humaines encore mal rattachées entre elles par cette notion, une signification plus importante qu'elle n'est dans ce que l'on appelle la pratique des Etats.

Mais, diront certains, les Protocoles additionnels ne font en grande partie que consacrer du droit coutumier, qui lie *ipso facto* tous les membres de la communauté internationale. Cela est incontestable pour une

---

39 C.J. Greenwood, *L'application des Protocoles additionnels et leur impact sur le droit international général en matière humanitaire*, dans: Colloque sur les Protocoles additionnels, op. cit. n. 13, p. 18.

série de règles. Cependant dans bien des cas, comme le relève à juste titre Greenwood,[40] les dispositions des Protocoles additionnels impliquent un mélange de codifications et de développement qui rend difficile de déterminer leurs effets sur le droit coutumier. Certains internationalistes ont essayé, en nous prévenant des précautions à prendre dans ce domaine, de dresser la liste, pour les principales dispositions, de ce qui est déjà du droit coutumier, de ce qui ne l'est pas, et de ce que l'on peut appeler un droit coutumier en émergence.[41] Cette façon de faire n'est pas sans danger, car il peut y avoir divergence d'opinions sur cette liste. Il suffit de considérer les divergences qui existent sur la question des guerres de libération.[42] Comme le relève Gasser, conseiller juridique au CICR, il n'appartient pas à cette institution de se prononcer sur les différentes interprétations données et il faut plutôt souhaiter que les gouvernements règlent ces questions par consultations mutuelles.[43] L'opération consistant à déterminer ce qui est droit coutumier et ce qui ne l'est pas n'est donc pas sans danger.

Cependant, on peut dire avec Greenwood que quelle que soit la valeur juridique attribuée aux règles des Protocoles additionnels, ceux-ci, et notamment le Protocole I, auront probablement un impact indirect même pour les Etats non formellements liés et que ces derniers devront, dans une certaine mesure, en tenir compte.[44] Cette situation aura d'autant plus de chance de se réaliser que ce nouveau droit, à l'exception des règles dont le caractère coutumier est unanimement admis, ne sera pas présenté comme ayant en grande partie déjà ce caractère, mais comme le reflet d'aspirations de la communauté internationale qu'on ne saurait plus de nos jours ignorer totalement.

Ce qui est certain en revanche, c'est que la condamnation du *jus ad bellum* n'est plus seulement, de nos jours, l'objet des prohibitions de la Charte de l'ONU, mais elle est de plus en plus ressentie, par les peuples libres du moins, comme une donnée impérieuse de la survie de la communauté internationale. Par conséquent, celui ou ceux qui, par fanatisme idéologique, religieux ou autre, se croient tenus de recourir à la guerre, savent qu'ils prennent des risques d'autant plus grands. Ils seront

---

40 *Ibid.*, p. 17.
41 A. Cassese, *The Geneva Protocols of 1977 on the Humanitarian Law of Armed Conflict and Customary International Law*, 3 UCLA Pacific Basin Law Journal 57-118 (1984).
42 *Ibid.*, p. 71; Greenwood, loc. cit. n. 39, p. 21.
43 H.-P. Gasser, *Some Legal Issues Concerning Ratification of the 1977 Geneva Protocols*, dans Meyer, réd., op. cit. n. 20, p. 86.
44 Greenwood, loc. cit. n. 39, p. 14.

plus poussés à mener des actions rapides et violentes sans s'embarrasser d'aucunes limitations, y compris hélas d'ordre humanitaire. Contre de telles entreprises, la diffusion préalable du DIH, qui reste indispensable, n'aura guère d'effets.

Faut-il, dans cette perspective, considérer que le Protocole I en lui-même est un frein indirect à l'agression et un rempart contre l'emploi de la force en subordonnant, comme le pense le professeur Obradovic, les nécessités militaires aux exigences humanitaires, aux impératifs des droits de l'homme, au point que ce Protocole favoriserait visiblement la partie qui se défendrait sur son territoire.[45] N'est-il pas dangereux de suivre ce raisonnement trop loin, car si on se place vraiment dans le cadre de la Charte de l'ONU et des droits de l'homme, on ne doit pas oublier que celle-ci, précisément pour défendre ces derniers, envisage, certes comme recours extrême, le recours à la force dans le cadre des mesure de légitime défense individuelle ou collective - recours à la force qui peut s'étendre au territoire de l'agresseur? Il faut plutôt reconnaître que les limitations sans doute beaucoup plus nombreuses et plus explicites qui résultent du Protocole I s'imposent non pas pour décourager l'agresseur, mais traduisent les besoins plus grands de solidarité et de respect de la personne humaine qu'exige l'évolution de la société internationale. Mais pour le gouvernement qui prend le grand risque de recourir à la guerre, le Protocole I ne sera sans doute guère un frein véritable.

5.2   Le problème du contrôle subsiste

Si ce nouveau droit ne saurait vraiment constituer un frein, il est l'expression, assurément, surtout le Protocole I, d'un droit international par certains aspects très évolué. Bien que les analogies entre droit interne et droit international soient souvent trompeuses, on peut toutefois remarquer qu'un droit évolué présuppose des mécanismes appropriés pour la mise en oeuvre de ce droit, et notamment pour la constation des manquements au droit. Or n'y a-t-il pas déséquilibre, pour les Protocoles, entre les normes parfois développées de comportement et la faiblesse des solutions trouvées pour la mise en oeuvre et la constatation des infractions, au point qu'un internationaliste a pu dire: '*Even with the procedural addition of Article 5(3), the process by which a protecting power is*

---

45 Obradovic, loc. cit. n. 13, p. 27.

appointed has changed little from the time of the Franco-Prussian War over a century ago'.[46]

Cela est d'autant plus préoccupant que si, d'un côté on a considérablement développé, dans le Protocole I, les règles relatives à la conduite des hostilités, d'un autre côté, les débats de la Conférence diplomatique (1974-1977) ont montré que les Puissances protectrices ou leurs substituts n'entendaient guère aller au-delà de leur fonction traditionnelle, qui est de se s'occuper surtout des manquements au *traitement* des victimes. Et l'on ne peut guère actuellement fonder trop d'espoir sur la Commission internationale d'établissement des faits, prévue à l'Article 90 du même Protocole. On a dit que le droit de la guerre doit être compréhensible et applicable au cours même du combat et non après coup devant des tribunaux.[47] Mais il est indéniable qu'en raison de la complexité du nouveau droit -qui impose, certes, d'être rendu facilement accessible aux militaire et aux civils concernés par des instructions apropriées-[48] bien des combattants, s'ils doivent fort heureusement garder un statut ou un traitement de prisonniers de guerre en tombant aux mains de l'ennemi, risquent fort d'être jugés pour des infractions alléguées aux règles relatives à la conduite des hostilités. Qui interviendra, par exemple, pour dire, à la décharge du prisonnier inculpé, que telle ou telle attaque n'était pas illicite?

Le CICR a pu exercer une activité d'aide judiciaire utile pour les prisonniers de guerre allemands en France, mais cela s'est passé *après* la fin de la guerre et non dans la tension et la haine du conflit. A défaut d'un fonctionnement des Puissance protectrice, le recours au CICR, soit comme substitut, soit même comme organisme purement humanitaire, finit par être considéré comme une solution normale. Mais n'y a-t-il pas là un risque et un danger? D'une part pour le CICR lui-même: en acceptant, plus ou moins à son corps défendant, d'être en fait, sinon en droit, le substitut de la Puissance protectrice, ne court-il pas le risque assez grand de se voir reprocher, après coup, une inaction à l'égard de certaines violations, par des personnes ou des milieux qui oublient les limites que connaît l'activité du CICR? D'autre part, n'y a-t-il pas aussi le danger de voir la communauté internationale se résigner au déséquilibre que nous avons

---

46 Peirce, loc. cit. n. 37, p. 155. Voir aussi Best, op. cit. n. 3, p. 323; A. Martin, *Le contrôle de l'application du droit international humanitaire, Réflexions sur l'établissement d'un contrôle international obligatoire,* dans Condorelli, loc. cit. n. 17, pp. 255-282.

47 H. McCoubrey, *Jurisprudential Aspects of the Modern Law of Armed Conflicts,* dans Meyer, réd., op. cit. n. 20, p. 40.

48 H.-P. Gasser, *An appeal for ratification by the United States,* 81 AJIL 923-924 (1987).

mentionné plus haut, quelles que soient les difficultés d'aller plus loin que les solutions trouvée lors de la Conférence diplomatique (1974-1977)?

Les expériences décevantes, semble-t-il, que le CICR a faites dans le conflit Iran-Iraq sur la base d'une interprétation large de l'Article 1 du Protocole I[49] ne devraient pas décourager d'essayer de donner à cette interprétation, éventuellement en liaison avec l'Article 89 de ce Protocole, un caractère plus organique, plus structuré, et cela dès le temps de paix. Car en cas de conflit localisé, la préoccupation des Puissances non engagées dans le conflit sera tournée principalement vers la possibilité de contenir l'explosion de la violence et d'y mettre un terme.

6.   CONCLUSIONS

6.1   L'impact de la 'Guerre du Golfe' et le Protocole I

Les pages qui précèdent, conçues au cours de l'été 1990, ont été terminée alors que l'invasion du Koweit par l'Irak venait d'étendre brutalement une ombre nouvelle sur le respect du DIH et sur celui du droit international tout court. Pour répondre aux voeux des éditeurs de ces Mélanges ainsi qu'à l'objet même de ces derniers, qui visent le futur du DIH, nous ajoutons ces conclusions alors que le défaite récente des armées irakiennes rétablit un ordre conforme aux résolutions des Nations Unies.

Le conflit armé international qui vient de s'achever, de courte durée comparé à d'autres, mais d'une grande intensité, également par ses répercussions psychologiques étendues, aura, lui aussi, un impact certain sur le DIH, mais qui sera sans doute bien différent de ceux que nous avons mis en évidence dans les parties précédentes. Ce conflit armé ne sera probablement pas le moteur de l'élaboration de règles nouvelles du droit humanitaire (sans pour autant exclure ce processus dans des domaines limités, tels les développements nécessaires quant à la signalisation des établissements et transports sanitaires ou l'extension possible de la Convention du 10 octobre 1980 à d'autres armes classiques). La 'Guerre du Golfe' ne sera-t-elle pas bien plutôt, dans les années à venir, un *révélateur* quant à la mise en oeuvre et aux possibilités d'application du Protocole additionnel I de 1977 et, en particulier, de ses dispositions sur la conduite des hostilités et sur la protection des populations civiles?

---

49 Voir Y. Sandoz, *Appel du CICR dans le cadre du conflit entre l'Iraq et l'Iran*, XXIX Annuaire français de droit international 161-173 (1983); I. Vichniac, Croix-Rouge, les stratèges de la bonne conscience 19-25 (1988).

Certes, comme dans le conflit des îles Falkland-Malouines, ce Protocole n'était pas juridiquement applicable, les principaux adversaires n'étant pas encore liés par lui - et pour les membres de la 'coalition' Parties au Protocole (telles la Syrie ou l'Arabie saoudite) l'attitude de l'Irak n'ayant pas, à notre connaissance, entraîné pour eux l'application résultant de l'Article 96(2), 2ème phrase. Mais cette fois-ci, contrairement au conflit anglo-argentin, les hostilités dirigées principalement sur des objectifs à terre dans des régions parfois fortement peuplées ont mis largement en cause les règles relatives à la protection des populations civiles. Ainsi, à la lumière des expériences faites dans cette guerre, expériences dont tous les aspects sont encore loin d'être connus, notamment en ce qui concerne le territoire irakien, une réflexion va s'engager chez les membres de la communauté internationale, sur le Protocole I, sur ses règles fondamentales, et aussi sur la Convention du 10 octobre 1980 qui le complète.

Les gouvernements des Etats non liés par le Protocole additionnel I ou par la Convention du 10 octobre 1980 (en tout ou partie) seront vraisemblablement amenés, même si l'examen interne du processus de ratification ou d'adhésion était déjà fortement avancé à la veille du conflit du Golfe, à reprendre cet examen. Pour les Etats déjà liés, la réflexion portera sans doute plutôt sur l'interprétation à conférer à certaines dispositions des instruments précités et, dans la diffusion aux militaires, sur les réponses à donner aux questions qu'ils ne manqueront pas de poser.

Si le Protocole additionnel I n'était pas applicable dans le conflit considéré, pour les raisons indiquées ci-dessus, bien que certains membres de la coalition aient été liés par lui, on peut imaginer une nouvelle situation d'action collective de sécurité impliquant la force armée et dans laquelle ce Protocole serait applicable pour certains membres de la coalition sans l'être pour les autres. L'éventualité d'une telle situation commande que s'instaure entre les gouvernements intéressés une réflexion sur les normes devant au minimum être observées par tous.

Un domaine qui appelera aussi une réflexion particulière est celui des mécanismes visant à renforcer la mise en oeuvre du DIH, telle la répression des violations graves, et surtout le problème du contrôle, dont nous avons montré précédemment les difficultés dans certaines situations - difficultées qu'est venu illustrer le cas du 'bunker' de Bagdad considéré comme une objectif militaire par un des adversaires et, par l'autre, comme un abri destiné aux civils. Et cette réflexion ne concernera pas seulement le Protocole additionnel I ou la Convention du 10 octobre 1980, mais aussi les autres règles du droit humanitaire qui étaient applicables, dont notamment les Conventions de Genève de 1949.

6.2   Perspectives limitées pour le Protocole II

Enfin, quelles perspectives pour le Protocole additionnel II dans les années à venir? Ce Protocole a connu également, l'an dernier, une sorte de révélateur, resté en partie masqué, il est vrai, par l'attention portée principalement sur la crise du Golfe. En effet, si des conflits armés non internationaux se sont poursuivis, hélas, sans interruption depuis l'élaboration du Protocole II dans des pays non liés par lui et guères prêts à l'accepter, on peut admettre en revanche qu'au *Liberia*, Partie à cet instrument, les conditions de son application, prévues par l'Article premier, étaient réunies. Pourtant, les atrocités commises de part et d'autre, les atteintes portées aux non-combattants et les obstacles rencontrés par le CICR pour exercer un minimum d'activité humanitaire ont confirmé la tendance qui se dégage des autres conflits armés d'ordre interne: la difficulté, en raison de la tension et de la haine existant entre factions rivales, de voir reconnues par les Parties au conflit l'existence de conditions de fait semblables à celles qu'implique l'application du Protocole II, et aussi le risque que court le CICR ou tout autre organisme d'aide humanitaire, en invoquant l'existence de ces conditions, même pour un Etat lié par ce Protocole, de compromettre ses possibilités d'aide aux victimes.

La base juridique applicable dans les conflits internes, même pour les Etats liés par le Protocole considéré, risque fort, par conséquent, de rester encore longtemps l'Article 3 des Conventions de Genève de 1949. Il est alors essentiel que la communauté internationale et, en particulier, les gouvernements propres à exercer une influence sur l'une ou l'autre des Parties au conflit s'efforcent, à défaut de pouvoir mettre une terme aux hostilités par des voies pacifiques, de convaincre les belligérants qu'il est dans leur intérêt de respecter fidèlement les règles de l'Article 3 et aussi de s'inspirer, dans le traitement des ennemis et la conduite des hostilités, encore d'autre normes humanitaires, telles que celles du Protocole II ou celles dégagées par l'Institut international de droit humanitaire de San Remo, lors de sa XIVe Table Ronde en septembre 1989.[50] De telles démarches auront sans doute plus de chances de réussite si ces normes sont présentées non comme ayant un caractère impératif, mais comme représentant les aspirations de la communauté internationale.

---

50   Voir Revue internationale de la Croix-Rouge 415-442 (1990).

L'ACTION HUMANITAIRE

RENÉ J. DUPUY

1.   INTRODUCTION

Dans l'univers des souverainetés, la souffrance des hommes est une affaire d'Etat. Eux seuls ont le droit de s'en préoccuper. Le droit, non le devoir. Et chacun pour lui-même. Le quadrillage étatique place le malheur d'un peuple sous le monopole de son gouvernement. Jaloux de cette gestion, il répugne souvent à informer le monde du sinistre, naturel ou accidentel, survenu chez lui ou n'en donne qu'une image tronqueé, cache la pauvreté de ses moyens de secours, de crainte que d'autres Etats ne viennent proposer une assistance suspectée par lui de camoufler des volontés d'ingérence. Et dans ce sanctuaire, clôturé de frontières, des innocents sont sacrifiés à la prévalance de l'Etat souverain.

Envoyer des secours, parachuter des médicaments ou des vivres sans l'accord des autorités du pays éprouvé, serait commettre un délit international. L'injure faite à l'Etat serait plus intolérable que les épreuves endurées par son peuple. L'objet du droit des gens, dans son rêve classique, est de garantir les droits de l'Etat. Non les droits de l'homme.

Sans doute les souverainetés ont-elles souffert d'effectives violations à l'ère de l'expansion coloniale, alors que les dangers que des troubles intérieurs faisaient peser sur des étrangers, suscitaient la pénétration armée de leurs Etats. Cela s'appelait 'l'intervention d'humanité'. On faisait ainsi référence à l'inspiration humanitaire d'une ingérence qui se voulait excusable. La Guerre de Boxers, en 1900, conduite par des forces internationales pour libérer les colonies étrangères assiégées dans Pékin, constitue une des illustrations les plus connues parmi des précédents qui s'échelonnent jusqu'aux opérations américaine à la Grenade en 1982, et française à Kolvésy en 1979. Reconnues valables par la pratique et la doctrine de maîtres incontestés comme Huber lorsqu'elles répondaient à une nécessité, elles ont toujours encouru la méfiance des chancelleries et laissé, outre-mer, les souvenirs humiliants attachés à la diplomatie de la canonnière. On touche ici à la carence majeure de la communauté internationale: l'absence d'une police, puissante et impartiale, chargée de maintenir ou de rétablir l'ordre public entre Etats ou sur leurs territoires respectifs. Mais toute police est dans les mains d'un pouvoir. Organisée au-dessus des Etats, elle supposerait un gouvernement mondial. Telle quelle, l'assistance humanitaire, avec ses insuffisances et ses équivoques, est condamnée à rester le seul recours des victimes. Le génie d'Henri Dunant, au soir de Solférino, fut d'avoir imaginé l'intervention d'une organisation privée dont l'autorité morale garantirait l'impartialité. L'idée lui en venait, au cours d'une guerre, événement que le droit international qualifie de procédure conduite par des Etats souverains. Mais le Comité international de la Croix-Rouge réussit à faire accepter son assistance au cours des guerres civiles. Ainsi, est né le droit humanitaire. Il s'établissait à une époque où les droits de l'homme n'étaient point reconnus dans l'ordre international. Aussi ses utilisateurs et commentateurs veillaient-ils à lui donner un autre fondement. Pour faire admettre son intervention par des soveraicetés sourcilleuses, la Croix-Rouge sentait bien qu'invoquer les droits de l'homme eût laissé à penser qu'ils étaient méconnus dans le pays où elle souhaitait être reçue. C'eût été se référer à un argument de tonalité juridique, alors que proposer une assistance humanitaire s'adresse à un sentiment de compassion. La prudence de la Croix-Rouge, jugée parfois excessive, lui a permis d'acquérir une autorité morale qui condamne l'Etat qui refuse son assistance, à encourir la désapprobation de l'opinion publique. Son attention à conduire ses opérations à l'écart de toute ingérence politique ou militaire, nécessite une identification facile, authentifiée par l'emblème.

Une longue pratique a fini par ériger le comportement du CICR en modèle juridique. C'est à lui que se réfère la Cour Internationale de Justice en 1986 pour définir les conditions de licéité de l'assistance humanitaire (affaire des activités militaires et paramilitaires au Nicaragua). Répond-il encore aux épreuves imposées à l'humanité? En fait, les manifestations de la solidarité internationale s'inspirent du sentiment humanitaire plus que de la prise en compte des victimes d'une catastrophe naturelle ou d'un conflit armé, en leur qualité de membre de l'humanité. C'est dire que les secours n'échappent pas à une discrimination inspirée par des mobiles intéressés, soit par la recherche de la publicité dispensée par les médias soit par la mise en oeuvre de projets politiques.

Cependant, même si elle n'est pas conduite pour l'humanité, l'assistance lui profite indirectement. Elle trouve dans la communauté des Nations diverses institutions qui s'animent à l'annonce d'un cataclysme. C'est le cas de plusieurs des Institutions du système des Nations Unies, comme l'Organisation Mondiale de la Santé, le Programme Alimentaire Mondial, le Haut Commissariat pour les Réfugiés, le Fonds International de Secours à l'Enfance. Il faut aussi compter avec des organisations non gouvernementales. La multiplicité d'organismes de secours est de nature à entraîner des double-emplois inutiles et dispendieux. Elle requiert la mise en place d'une coordination des efforts. Dans ce but, les Nations Unies ont élaboré, depuis 1971, un programme de secours en cas de catastrophes, dans le cadre duquel a été institué un Bureau de Coordination des Secours, l'UNDRO, dont la tâche essentielle est la surveillance permanente des risques de survenance des sinistres et des situations d'urgence. Le fait que ce Bureau n'ait pas été érigé en Institution spécialisée et la modestie de son budget démontrent l'inhibition relative de l'organisation internationale, par le souci de ménager les souverainetés. Au coeur d'un désastre, elles émergent des décombres, refusent de demander des secours étrangers. On mesure les limites de la démarche classique des relations internationales fondée sur la seule recherche des arrangements entre Etats. Mais voici que se dessinent l'idée d'un droit de la personne à obtenir une assistance et le droit de l'humanité à voir soigner ses plaies.

2.   LE DROIT HUMANITAIRE ET LES DROITS DE L'HOMME

Le XXe siècle aura banalisé le tragique. Après deux Guerres Mondiales, le foisonnement des communications amoncelle les nouvelles de catastrophes naturelles, naguère moins promptes à parvenir, celles des sinistres causés par des technologies mal maîtrisées, le tout sur un fond de conflit armé, entremêlant les belligérances: guerres interétatiques, civiles, transnationales, subnationales, culturelles, raciales, révolutionnaires, de conquête ou de libération, idéologique ou religieuse. Autant de démentis à la formule de Giraudoux: 'La paix est l'intervalle entre deux guerres'. Cet entrelacs d'affrontements concommittants, signe de l'intégration planétaire de l'humanité, a sans doute été encouragé par la Guerre Froide mais il ne semble pas que le rapprochement Est/Ouest suffise à y mettre fin. Tous ces conflits n'étaient pas suscités par les Super-puissances; elles étaient parfois poussées à y prendre certains engagements alors que leur origine était imputable à des facteurs locaux ou régionaux. Il faut encore compter avec l'instabilité du Tiers-Monde qui semble devoir s'ajouter à celle produite par le nationalisme et le désordre économique sévissant dans nombre de pays qui devraient leur hibernation à la férule soviétique. Le malheur aura toujours droit de cité en ce monde et l'assistance à ses détresses restera un devoir impérieux. A condition que le droit en permette l'exécution. Evolution que seule rend possible la conscience de la nouveauté du monde. Certes, les souverainetés y flamboient toujours. Même sous les décombres, elles se veulent intouchables. Mais la médiatisation universelle faisant de chacun le témoin des épreuves des autres, il est inadmissible qu'en dépit des moyens que la technique met dans les mains des sauveteurs, ceux-ci soient ralentis ou arrêtés par les entraves frontalières. Tant il est vrai qu'aujourd'hui encore la terre est peuplée d'étrangers. Elle ne deviendrait leur patrie que si la solidarité submergeait les frontières. Alors le droit des gens mériterait le nom de 'droit cosmopolite' que lui donnait Kant. Il y tend de plus en plus cependant. L'homme est parvenu à s'évader de l'enclos étatique et à faire déclarer ses droits et libertés au-dessus des Etats.

Apparus en même temps au XVIe siècle, la souveraineté et les droits de l'homme se sont jusqu'en 1948 affrontés dans l'arène nationale. La Déclaration Universelle votée par les Nations Unies a inauguré l'adoption d'une série d'instruments internationaux, à l'échelle mondiale et régionale, apportant des garanties au respect de la personne. Ils ont atteint une efficacité, non négligeable dans l'ordre des Nations Unies, très remarquable dans le cadre du Conseil de l'Europe où deux organes, la Commission et la Cour des Droit de l'Homme, ont accumulé une jurisprudence fort riche. On doit toutefois observer que ces conquêtes de l'humanisme juridique apparaissaient toujours comme des concessions octroyées par les Etats. Ils y étaient contraints pour se laver des crimes accumulés dans un temps où Sardanapale désormais dispose d'ordinateurs.

Mais, si la protection internationale de la personne reçoit ainsi des garanties de caractère judiciaire ou para-judiciaire, assiste-t-on parallèlement à une certaine ouverture des barrières souveraines devant des équipes de secours, demandant l'accès aux victimes des catastrophes naturelles ou technologiques, de luttes armées d'autant plus impitoyables qu'elles s'affirment guerres justes?

Le signe premier de cette évolution apparaît dans la disparition progressive de la distinction traditionnelle du droit humanitaire et des droits de l'homme. L'émergence de ces derniers à l'ordre international, dans la proximité généralisée des peuples, permet auhourd'hui de fonder l'assistance humanitaire sur le droit à la vie, comme sur celui de ne pas subir des traitements inhumains ou dégradants. Rapprochement qu'annonçait le principe fondamental donné par le CICR à l'action humanitaire: 'prévenir et alléger en toutes circonstances les souffrances des hommes'. Et tout aussi bien la 'norme d'inviolabilité' qui reconnaît au non combattant le droit au respect de son intégrité physique et morale. Comment soutenir que le droit humanitaire a d'autres objectifs que la sauvegarde de l'homme alors qu'il prohibe les représailles collectives, nul ne pouvant être tenu responsable pour des actes qu'il n'a pas commis et que, dans la mise en oeuvre des secours, il impose une égalité de traitement, écartant par définition toute discrimination de sexe, de race, de nationalité, de langue, de classe sociale, d'opinion politique, philosophique ou religieuse? De fait, les Nations Unies et le CICR lui-même affirment la convergence de l'assistance humanitaire et de l'action pour les droits de l'homme. On ne craint plus maintenant de la clamer à la face des gouvernants. La diversification des formes de conflits et des guerres sans frontières a pour effet de réduire les distinctions formelles qui, naguère encore, semblaient structures de l'esprit: l'interne et l'international, le combattant et le non-combattant, le national et l'étranger, les conflits et les sinistres naturels, pour ne laisser paraître que la détresse des hommes. L'invocation des droits de l'homme devient alors irrésistible.

Elle est le fait d'ONG. Médecins du monde, Médecins sans frontières se donnent pour mission, selon le mot de l'un d'eux, d''exporter de l'être': non seulement de l'avoir, mis à la disposition des autorités locales, mais des soins donnés par eux-mêmes à des personnes. Ainsi se réalise l'ingérence dont ils revendiquent le devoir. Nul ne saurait s'y opposer.

3.   LE DROIT DE TOUS A L'ASSISTANCE DE TOUS

Dans une conférence réunie à Paris en janvier 1987 par Kouchner et Bettati, le médecin et le juriste ont montré que ces aventuriers du secours campent dans un ordre juridique international qui ne leur consent aucune personnalité de droit et, partant, aucune protection.[1] Ils ont pris le parti d'intervenir sur un terrain de conflits ou de catastrophes, sans attendre une invitation des Etats. A l'écoute seulement des cris des victimes. Ils ont forgé une morale: celle de l'extrême urgence. Dans la jungle des nations où ce mot n'est jamais prononcé, sauf à passer pour idéalistes qui n'en verraient ni les calculs, ni les haines, ni le meurtre, ils exportent de l'amour. Sans passeports, ni visas, lorsque ce produit paraît trop suspect aux autorités frontalières.

Cette audace leur a valu de cruels déboires: captivités, jugements sommaires prononcés par des tribunaux grotesques, mais impitoyables. L'assistance humanitaire ne peut se borner au témoignage. Son efficacité requiert un statut protecteur.

> 'Le malheur des hommes ne doit jamais être un reste muet de la politique. Il fonde un droit absolu à se lever et à s'adresser à ceux qui détiennent le pouvoir.'

Exhortation de Foucault que les médecins de détresse entendent mettre en pratique. Sur quel fondement établir la double et universelle reconnaissance du droit des victimes et du droit des secouristes sinon sur la solidarité, tenue pour le ferment de l'humanité, justifiant à la fois le droit à l'invoquer et le devoir de la vivre? Que signifie l'universalité des droits de l'homme si elle n'appelle une ouverture sur tous les lieux où des hommes endurent les affres de la détresse, alors que désormais le prochain est le peuple de la terre? Dans une telle vision globale, chacun est habilité à intervenir et, s'il a pris comme médecin cet engagement, est tenu de le faire.

On observera que ces normes métajuridiques ne peuvent prétendre à la consécration de la positivité au mépris de la souveraineté étatique, donnée majeure de la communauté des nations. De fait, c'est à elle que s'en prennent, dans ce domaine des catastrophes naturelles -moins sensible que celui des conflits armés- les résolutions votées par diverses sociétés de pensée et d'action. Leur insistance a trouvé quelque écho à l'Assemblée générale des Nations Unies.

Dans un symposium tenu à Copenhague en 1986, à la suite de Tchernobyl, l'Académie Internationale des Droits de l'Homme demande l'engagement des Etats victimes à accepter l'assistance humanitaire sans soumettre celle-ci à des restrictions autres que celles nécessaires à la

---

1 Cette Conférence a fait l'objet d'un livre: M. Bettari, B. Kouchner, Le devoir d'ingérence (1987).

sécurité ou à l'ordre public. Pour la Conférence de Paris de Médecins du Monde de 1978, l'assistance doit être donnée dans un dessein strictement humanitaire et désintéressé, sans discrimination entre les victimes. Ces précautions destinées à apprivoiser les Etats sont d'autant plus explicables que certains médecins ont voulu assortir leur mission du témoignage porté sur les entraves que leur opposaient les gouvernements ou, dans les conflits armés, sur les causes soutenues par les belligérants. Sans doute la défense des droits de l'homme appelle-t-elle le ministère de la parole. Parler pour alerter les consciences ou se taire pour être admis à apporter ses soins? Action clandestine ou diplomatique? On n'empêchera jamais les médecins de l'ombre de s'infiltrer à travers les interdits; mais, lorsque l'Etat en fléchit la rigueur pour tolérer l'action humanitaire, force est d'admettre qu'elle exclura toute ingérence politique. Dans l'avancée de l'imaginaire vers le réel, le 21 novembre 1988 a valeur de fondation. A l'initiative de la France, l'Assemblée générale des Nations Unies a adopté par consensus (c'est-à-dire sans opposition) une résolution qui, lorsque des catastrophes naturelles 'et situations d'urgence du même ordre' commandent une assistance rapide et efficace de la communauté internationale, (sauf à méconnaître la vie et la dignité de l'homme), affirme la nécessité du libre accès aux victimes.[2] Sans doute ce texte n'a-t-il que la portée d'une recommandation, mais en affirmant qu'aucune entrave ne doit être opposée par l'Etat touché ou par ses voisins à l'arrivée des secours et en les invitant à la faciliter, la résolution ouvre la voie aux 'organisations internationales non gouvernementales agissant dans un but strictement humanitaire'. La signification révolutionnaire de ces principes s'est affirmée: au moment même où ils étaient proclamés, se produisait en Arménie un séisme qui détruisit une partie du pays. L'Union Soviétique qui avait montré une sérieuse réticence à donner des informations sur le désastre de Tchernobyl et à accueillir des secours, adopta une attitude toute différente, faisant savoir au gouvernement français qu'elle ouvrait ses frontières aux sauveteurs venus, même sans visas, des pays occidentaux. Secours qui furent importants. Que la dialectique de la *perestroïka* explique ce retournement ne réduit pas la valeur du précédent. Car il a valeur de signe. Celui d'une transformation en cours de la vision des droits de l'homme.

---

2 Résolution de l'Assemblée générale des Nations Unies, A/C3/43/L.38/Rev. 1, 16 novembre 1988.

4. L'ANTHROPOLOGIE MOLECULAIRE

Dans la perspective individualiste originelle, les droits de l'homme étaient propres à chacun. Celui qui en invoquait la violation devait démontrer qu'il en était lui-même victime. Il en est toujours ainsi notamment devant une juridiction interne ou une instance internationale du type de la Commission ou de la Cour de Justice Européenne des Droits de l'Homme. En revanche, dans le plan de l'humanité, l'homme tient ses droits de sa qualité de membre de celle-ci. De ce fait, toute méconnaissance de ces droits fait grief à tous.

Cette analyse prend place aujourd'hui dans l'imaginaire juridique. Une compagnie aussi prestigieuse que l'Institut du Droit International qui, depuis 1872, groupe des juristes éminents, universitaires et practiciens, recrutés par cooptation, et prépare des projets de conventions a adopté, lors de sa session de 1989, à Saint Jacques de Compostelle une résolution s'inspirant de cette conception.[3] Pour ce texte 'l'obligation pour les Etats d'assurer le respect' des droits de l'homme leur incombe 'vis-à-vis de la communauté internationale dans son ensemble'. Il en résulte que 'tout Etat a un intérêt juridique à la protection de ses droits'. 'Cette obligation implique au surplus un devoir de solidarité entre tous les Etats en vue d'assurer le plus rapidement possible une protection universelle et efficace des droits de l'homme'.

Il est aussi précisé qu'aucun Etat ne peut se soustraire à sa responsabilité internationale en invoquant sa souveraineté. Elle ne saurait tenir les droits de l'homme en l'état. Il en résulte que sont admissibles des mesures diplomatiques, économiques pour le contraindre à les respecter. Seul l'usage de la force demeure écarté.

On ne saurait rejeter plus nettement la conception étriquée du droit classique qui limite à chaque victime le droit de se plaindre. On fait de celui-ci une *actio popularis*: on fonde un ordre public international dont la personne est le centre. Sans doute, l'Institut parle-t-il de 'communauté internationale dans son ensemble', (formule prélevée dans le vocabulaire des Nations Unies) et non d'humanité. Cette démarche, conçue dans les rapports entre Etats, s'en approche cependant. La résolution fait référence aux 'organisations humanitaires impartiales' de secours alimentaires et sanitaires, précisant que leur offre d'assistance comme celle des Etats, 'ne saurait être considérée comme une intervention illicite dans les affaires

---

3 63-99 Annuaire de l'Institut de droit international, Session de Saint Jacques de Compostelle 285-291.

intérieures' du pays touché par l'épreuve. La logique devrait conduire à situer pleinement la défense des droits de l'homme dans la défense des droits de l'humanité.

5.   CONCLUSION

Le droit humanitaire ne doit plus se limiter à réguler les opérations d'assistance conduites par des organisations privées. Il semble que la voie la plus réaliste serait d'élaborer une convention-cadre de portée générale. Elle énoncerait des principes d'action ne comportant pas d'obligations détaillées mais qui seraient complétés par des accords bilatéraux, régionaux, adaptés aux besoins spécifiques des Etats signataires. Ainsi les principes généraux de coopération, définis au nom de l'humanité, trouveraient progressivement leur concrétisation dans des cas particuliers. Des précédents seraient créés et, petit à petit, les Etats traditionnellement réticents finiraient par se rallier à un système d'assistance dont les garanties auraient démontré leur valeur. Par cette croissance normative, se trouverait consacré le droit des individus et des collectivités à recevoir une assistance fondée sur leur qualité de membre d'une humanité solidaire.

Pour rester réaliste, il faudrait concevoir un régime qui prendrait en compte la réalité de la structure de la Communauté internationale, établie sur le quadrillage étatique du monde, mais qui s'efforcerait de le dépasser au nom de la transcendance de l'humanité. Deux séries de règles devraient répondre à ce double souci: celui qui pousse à sauvegarder les intérêts légitimes de l'Etat victime et celui de la mise en oeuvre d'une solidarité qui n'est rien d'autre que l'action de l'humanité au secours des siens.

5.1   Les règles qui poussent à sauvegarder les intérêts légitimes de l'Etat victim

Toute catastrophe infligée par la nature frappe le territoire d'un Etat. Lors même qu'elle brise le mât où flottait son drapeau, il reste souverain. Dans ces conditions force est de reconnaître à ses autorités le rôle premier dans l'organisation des opérations de secours. S'il est vrai qu'elles ne sauraient abuser de leur pouvoir, au risque de sacrifier les droits des victimes à l'assistance humanitaire, il est normal que, dans la mesure du possible, elles assument un rôle directeur. Il devrait se manifester à trois moments.

a) Lors de l'accès des secours sur le territoire de l'Etat victime, la Convention reconnaîtrait à ses autorités le droit de vérifier la qualité des agents de secours, spécialement de ceux émanant d'organisations non gouvernementales dont l'identification doit révéler qu'il s'agit de personnes qualifiées pour participer utilement à des opérations d'assistance humanitaire. Certains Etats s'inquiètent de la possible intervention de certains nombres des équipes de secours sur des terrains politiques les conduisant à porter des jugements sur les régimes du pays dans lequel ils entendent apporter leur aide aux victimes. En fait, ce problème se pose surtout pour l'assistance humanitaire, en cas de conflit armé intérieur ou de guerre civile. Il ne revêt pas la même acuité lorsqu'il s'agit de catastrophes naturelles. C'est pourquoi la Convention ne devrait s'appliquer qu'à celles-ci et, de toutes façons, disposer que l'assistance ne doit avoir qu'un caractère humanitaire, écartant toute action politique.

b) L'Etat d'accueil des secours doit pouvoir superviser leur organisation et leur déroulement, et notamment aménager la coopération entre l'action des organismes d'assistance, étatiques ou privés, avec ses propres autorités. L'Etat victime doit d'ailleurs assurer la sûreté des personnels de secours, la protection des locaux, de leurs biens et matériels.

c) La détermination de la fin de la période dite de catastrophe doit intervenir à la suite d'un accord entre l'Etat victime et les Nations Unies représentées par le coordinateur. Si la conclusion d'une Convention préalable à toute catastrophe a pour objet d'éviter que l'Etat qui reçoit les secours n'y mette fin de façon unilatérale et discrétionnaire, il est normale qu'il puisse demander au coordinateur de considérer que la période critique est terminée. A cet égard, et pour faciliter l'adhésion des Etats à une telle convention, on pourrait prévoir que celle-ci ne concerne que 'l'assistance humanitaire d'urgence', formule qui reconnaîtrait à l'Etat victime une plus grande marge d'appréciation. L'intérêt essentiel de la communauté des hommes est, en effet, que la Convention envisagée s'applique au plus grand nombre possible d'Etats.

5.2   L'action de l'humanité au secours des siens

La reconnaissance universelle d'un droit des victimes de catastrophes naturelles à recevoir des secours se fonde, on l'a vu, tant sur le concept de droit de l'homme que sur le droit de l'humanité à son intégrité. La Convention envisagée devrait affirmer le devoir des Etats, sur la base de l'obligation de coopération mise à leur charge par la Charte des Nations Unies, de s'engager à faciliter l'assistance humanitaire. Obligation qui devrait peser non seulement sur l'Etat où s'est produit la catastrophe, mais également sur tous les membres de la Communauté internationale: les Etats de transit sur le territoire desquels l'assistance est acheminée, les Etats, même lointains, susceptibles d'apporter une aide efficace, enfin ce devoir s'appliquerait aussi aux personnes privées agissant par l'intermédiaire d'organisations non-gouvernementales reconnues.

Le cri de l'homme en détresse qui justifie l'assistance est le cri de l'humanité. Droits de l'homme et droits de l'humanité sont alors en conjonction. L'homme en détresse n'est pas une victime isolée. Il est le membre d'un corps. L'humanité communie à la souffrance de l'homme.

II

THE 1977 ADDITIONAL PROTOCOLS:
WHERE DO WE STAND TODAY

NEGOTIATING THE 1977 ADDITIONAL PROTOCOLS: WAS IT A WASTE OF TIME?

HANS-PETER GASSER

1.   INTRODUCTION

The two Protocols Additional to the Geneva Conventions, adopted on 8 June 1977 in Geneva by a Diplomatic Conference especially convened for the purpose of reaffirming and developing international humanitarian law, were registered with the Secretariat of the United Nations and published in vol. 1,125 of the UNTS, entries nos. 17.512 and 17.513.[1] It is difficult not to be perplexed by the idea that the two laboriously negotiated

---

1   Protocol Additional to the Geneva Conventions of 12 August 1949, and relating to the Protection of Victims of International Armed Conflicts, (Protocol I) and Protocol Additional to the Geneva Conventions of 12 August 1949 and relating to the Protection of Victims of Non-International Armed Conflicts (Protocol II). See Final Act of the Diplomatic Conference on the Reaffirmation and Development of International Humanitarian Law Applicable in Armed Conflicts, Geneva (1974-1977). For the text see also XVI ILM 1391, 1442 (1977); D. Schindler, J. Toman, eds., The Laws of Armed Conflicts, 2nd ed., 621, 689 (1988).

Protocols might ultimately be mere entries in vol. 1,125, just after Treaty no. 17.511. For the Registrar that is precisely what they are. But are they also more than that?

With these few lines written in honour of Professor Kalshoven, one of those able and diligent workers who hammered out the Protocols, we intend to consider whether it was really worthwhile, whether the two Protocols have indeed become more than mere entries in the UNTS. We shall do so by trying to identify some of the effects the Protocols have already had in practice.

2.   THE 1977 ADDITIONAL PROTOCOLS: A SHORT REMINDER

To begin with, the part played by the Protocols in modernizing and strengthening international humanitarian law (also known as the international law of armed conflicts, or the law of war) will be briefly recalled.

Protocol I deals with humanitarian law applicable in international armed conflict. In the first place, it reaffirms the fundamental principle that the right of parties to an armed conflict to choose methods and means of combat is not unlimited and codifies several specific prohibitions. Protocol I also reaffirms the principle that a distinction must be made at all times between civilians and combatants and between civilian objects and military objectives, and that consequently the civilian population as such, as well as individual civilians, shall not be the object of attack. That general injunction is made operative by several specific prohibitions and orders which are all designed to safeguard the civilian population while taking into account the exigencies of warfare. By modernizing essential parts of the 'Hague Law' on the conduct of hostilities, Protocol I includes rules which should effectively cope with the dangers of modern warfare.

Furthermore, Protocol I updates rules on a broad range of issues which have long been the concern of the 'Law of Geneva'. For instance, military and civilian medical services henceforward benefit from the same legal regime which, incidentally, has also been improved by Protocol I. New rules should enable medical aircraft to operate in safety, even in combat zones. Rules for the identification of medical personnel and means of transport (on land, at sea and in the air) create the necessary conditions for effective action in favour of the wounded, be they combatants or civilians. Also, for the first time parties to an armed conflict are now under an obligation to search for missing persons. A new definition of the requirements for combatant status, which, in very narrow circumstances, allow for recourse to methods of guerrilla warfare, has brought an acceptable solution to an age-old issue, without, however, putting to rest all controversies. Finally, in response to developments which took place outside the purview of humanitarian law, Protocol I submits wars of national liberation to the law of international armed conflicts.

The Diplomatic Conference did not succeed, however, in substantially strengthening the mechanism for ensuring compliance with humanitarian law applicable in international armed conflicts.

Protocol II, on the other hand, is a short text which develops humanitarian law for non-international armed conflicts. Building upon Article 3 common to the four Geneva Conventions of 12 August 1949, Protocol II sets new limits to the horrors of war in internal conflicts. Without breaking new ground its fifteen substantive articles make the law more specific. The essential principles of common Article 3 are thus developed into specific obligations, thereby becoming better suited to the requirements of humanitarian action. Some of the new rules highlight the close relationship between protection through humanitarian law in internal conflicts and the law on human rights. Protocol II lacks an international mechanism to ensure respect, by both sides, for their obligations. However, the right of the ICRC 'to offer its services to the parties to an (internal armed) conflict', as codified by the Conventions' common Article 3, has been reaffirmed by the Diplomatic Conference through an unanimous expression of political will.

At the time of writing, 99 States are bound by Protocol I and 89 States by Protocol II.[2] In view of the delicate matters covered by these treaties, and taking into account their bearing on defence and internal security, this result is encouraging. Many more States will undoubtedly ratify the two Protocols in the near future. Both Protocols are well on the way to becoming universally accepted law, on a par with the Geneva Conventions.

3.   EEFECTS ON THE PRACTICE OF STATES

So much for the content and present status of the 1977 Protocols. What are their effects on the practice of States today, almost fourteen years after their adoption by the Diplomatic Conference? After a reminder of the self-evident -that a treaty creates obligations for the States which are bound by

---

2   Status as of 31 January 1991.

that treaty- we intend to explore some other less obvious effects on the
behaviour of States.

3.1   A source of treaty law

As international treaties, the Protocols create rights and obligations for
those States which have consented to be bound by them (or by one of
them), through ratification or accession. They are a source of international
law *inter partes*, *i.e.*, of treaty law. A certain number of their provisions,
in particular of Protocol I, accordingly require action after ratification:
measures have to be taken at the national level in peacetime already to
ensure their implementation as treaty obligations.

It is not the purpose of these comments to analyse in detail the
obligations created by the two Protocols. That is the task of the already
abundant literature on the Protocols, in particular of the Commentaries.[3]
We are more interested in pinpointing the *effects* of the Protocols as treaty
law, *i.e.*, as obligations between parties to such treaties, on the actual
practice of parties to armed conflicts.

Up to now, *Protocol I* has not become applicable to any armed conflict
between States, as no such conflict between two States Party to that
Protocol has arisen since its adoption in 1977. As Protocol I has not been
tested on the battlefield, there is no way of judging it on the basis of
practical experience. *Protocol II* is another matter. Arguably, it is or was
applicable to the conflicts in El Salvador and in the southern parts of the
Philippines. Although its applicability has not been recognized in either
situation by official statements, the two Governments seem (or seemed) to
be aware, to say the least, of their obligations under that treaty. However,
the time is not yet ripe for an analysis of the actual impact of Protocol II
on internal armed onflicts.

There is a further difficulty in evaluating the effects of Protocol II on
the behaviour of parties to an internal armed conflict. As we have already
seen, Protocol II essentially develops existing norms, in particular the
generally worded obligations of common Article 3. It is a matter of
conjecture whether a party to such an internal armed conflict has in mind
common Article 3, human rights law (customary or written) or the specific
obligations codified by Protocol II when it decides on a specific course of

---

3   M. Bothe, K.J. Partsch, W.A. Solf, eds., New Rules for Victims of Armed Conflicts (1982);
     Y. Sandoz, C. Swinarski, B. Zimmerman, eds., Commentary on the Additional Protocols of 8
     June 1977 to the Geneva Conventions of 12 August 1949 (1987).

action. The question may be interesting for scholarly debate, but is irrelevant for humanitarian policy in practice.

3.2 Clarifying customary law

It is commonly agreed that major parts of both Protocols are not completely new law but, to a varying extent, give expression to customary law. In particular, many Articles of Protocol I have firm roots in pre-existing general principles of law or in customary law.[4]

The 'hard core' of the *law on non-international armed conflict* as codified by common Article 3 of the 1949 Conventions is part of customary law. That is not controversial. It is also accepted that these rules are binding not only for the Government side but also for insurgent parties to such a conflict. Protocol II goes several steps further than Article 3 and codifies some essential rules of human rights law. Arguably, these human rights rules are part of customary law. The merit of Protocol II is not so much to have created completely new humanitarian obligations (which it did not), but to have considerably strengthened the protection of basic human rights in situations of internal armed conflict. In that sense, Protocol II has clarified existing customary law relating to the protection of individual persons in civil wars. There is little doubt that Protocol II, as a treaty, will serve to facilitate the interpretation of customary law in situations where, for lack of ratification by the State concerned, Protocol II itself is not applicable.

The case of *Protocol I* is even more evident: a considerable number of its provisions are in some way linked to customary law and only a minority of articles break absolutely new ground. This is true in particular of its *Part III (Methods and Means of Warfare, Combatant and Prisoner-of-War Status)* and *Part IV (Civilian Population)*. Much of the law contained therein is firmly embedded in the 'Hague Law', which itself is considered to be customary law. But Protocol I gives new expression to old ideas and thereby clarifies the content of generally accepted obligations.

As examples we may recall the 'principle of distinction' with its concomitant 'prohibition of attacks against the civilian population as such or against individual civilians'. That general prohibition has been elaborated and made more specific by a number of articles in Part IV. Several other rules also clarify existing customary law -such as the

---

4   See, in particular, the discussion of the customary law elements in the Protocols by T. Meron, *Human Rights and Humanitarian Norms as Customary Law* (1989), with many references.

prohibition of indiscriminate attacks or of attacks on civilian objects-whereas others codify existing rules and simultaneously develop their content. Turning to a different domain covered by Protocol I, we may argue that the new rules prohibiting perfidy are also a mere clarification of customary law, as is the obligation to safeguard an enemy who is *hors de combat*. It is not the purpose of this essay to contribute to the ongoing search for the line to be drawn between those articles which codify customary law and the rules creating new obligations.[5] However, irrespective of the outcome of that debate we may draw two conclusions:

a) The process of negotiating the two Protocols has revived interest in customary law relating to armed conflict. The Diplomatic Conference has taken customary law relating to the conduct of hostilities out of its previous oblivion. Through the process of codification customary law rules have again been given the importance that is due to them.

b) The two Protocols of 1977 have an influence on customary law rules, probably quite an extensive one. Today, no governmental agency, no drafter of a manual on the law of warfare or academic writer can deal with customary rules relating to the law of war without (wittingly or unwittingly) referring to their codification by the Protocols, all the more so as these texts are of course not the product of an independent scholar but of government representatives. That fact gives them added legitimacy, even in the absence of ratification. It is not the least of their merits that the diplomats, lawyers and military experts, by giving shape to vague customary rules, made those rules operational and did so moreover for all States, whether they are bound by the Protocols or not.

3.3   Contributing to the formation of customary law

Whereas we are on safe ground with our thesis that the Protocols give shape to existing but vaguely worded customary law rules, it is of course much harder to plead 'affirmative action', *i.e.*, demonstrate the actual part they play in creating new rules of customary law.

Within the scope of this essay we cannot broach the difficult topic of how customary law is formed. Suffice it to say that in the domains covered

---

5   *Ibid.*. See also, A. Cassese, *The Geneva Protocols of 1977 on the Humanitarian Law of Armed Conflict and Customary International Law*, 3 UCLA Pac. Basin LJ 55-118 (1984); Panel on Customary Law and Additional Protocol I to the Geneva Conventions for Protection of War Victims, 81 ASIL Proc. 26-43 (1987).

by the two Protocols, *i.e.*, the use of force between States or within the territory of a State, it is not easy to induce a State to comply with obligations which, by refusing to ratify them as treaty law, it has in effect declined to accept. Careful scrutiny of a controversial provision by legal proceedings, usually after the event, is often precluded by the way humanitarian law works. That law is indeed to be understood as the sum of commands or orders whose main effect is to prevent things from happening. Only rules whose binding force is largely unquestioned and which have the necessary support of States can claim authority in the harsh reality of the battlefield. The mere acceptance of a rule by a Diplomatic Conference is not sufficient evidence for the acceptance, by a State, of a new obligation, even though its representatives may have voted in favour or may have joined in the consensus for accepting that rule.

There is no doubt, however, that the two new treaties will be conducive to the *formation of customary law*, perhaps by bringing about a slow change in an existing rule of customary law. The process of merely giving expression to an existing norm is in any case closely related in practice to the process of developing that rule. To make an educated guess we can postulate, *e.g.* that the new rules on the protection of the environment and the new legal regime for civil defence may, without major difficulty, become customary law.

In conclusion, it is too early to judge the effects of the Protocols on the state of customary law. There is little doubt, however, that they will have such effects. They are a potential legal gold-mine, ready to be explored and exploited. If another Nuremberg Tribunal had to ascertain right now the content of customary law relating to the conduct of hostilities, it is hardly far-fetched to say that the Court would extensively consult the Protocols. The eminent judges would not have an easy task.

3.4   Providing guidelines for state practice

The consistent behaviour of States may be explained not only by the relevant authorities' conviction that they *ought* to act in a specific way (legal obligation) but also by a mere statement of facts: they simply *do* act that way. A form of behaviour has thus become an accepted practice followed by States. In other words, rules of treaty law can influence the behaviour of States, without any normative claim, by the mere fact of being perceived as useful and reasonable, as an adequate and acceptable solution for a controversial issue.

As Protocol I has not yet faced the challenge of being applied to an armed conflict, it might seem a little premature to claim that it influences the behaviour of States. However, those of its obligations which come into effect in peacetime have to be observed by the Parties to the treaty after ratification. Such rules may also have an influence on those States which are not bound by that treaty.

For lack of evidence it is hard to prove that other rules of Protocol I have already been the object of State practice. It would seem, however, that, *e.g.* the new techniques for the identification of medical aircraft -in practice medical helicopters- have already been used by armed forces. Thus, radar identification seems to have been established by tacit agreement between the armed forces in the South Atlantic conflict to identify helicopters on medical missions. Furthermore, when in the aftermath of its intervention in Panama (December 1989) the United States' armed forces gave members of Panama's forces, whether captured in uniform or not, the benefit of prisoner-of-war treatment, it is hard not to look at the new definition of combatant status given in Protocol I. Indeed, Article 44 -and in particular its paragraph 3- makes new law for the (previously insoluble) problem of 'irregulars', *i.e.*, of members of armed forces or associated groups (militias, resistance movements, etc.) who do not behave in the same way as ordinary combatants but nevertheless identify themselves as members of such armed forces. The United States' 'generous' or 'liberal' approach in granting POW privileges to persons irrespective of their having been captured in uniform or not is in line with Protocol I and its Article 44.

An even more elusive task is to show how the Protocols might affect future State practice. However, as the use of armed forces is planned in advance to a very high degree, future State practice is actually largely predetermined by present decisions: planning, preparing, issuing instructions, training, etc. Another practical example may prove the point. In its explanations to the American public after the air-raid on Tripoli (1986), the United States Government took great care to show that every effort had been made to spare civilians from the effects of the bombing of military objectives in order to reduce otherwise unavoidable losses among the civilian population to an absolute minimum. It seemed to the present author that, while listening to the announcement, he recognized words and phrases which echoed those of Protocol I, Articles 51 and 52, on the protection of the civilian population. This is an interesting example of the way rules are being assimilated outside the purview of a legal obligation (the United States is not bound by Protocol I as treaty law).

4.   ON SOME SIDE-EFFECTS OF THE PROTOCOLS

We have sought to demonstrate the influence of both Protocols on the law and on State practice; we now intend to explore some effects of a different nature. The thrust of the analysis is no longer on the effects produced by the Protocols as treaties in international law. Instead we shall enquire whether *the mere fact that the Diplomatic Conference of 1974-1977 took place* has left any real mark. In other words: we want to know whether the two Protocols are the sole legacy of the Diplomatic Conference -as treaties nos. 17.512 and 17.513 in the UNTS- or whether the Conference has also left us something more. Similarly, we wonder whether the existence of the two Protocols has had some effect on States and on their perception of the standing of humanitarian law.

Let us first recall that after the adoption of the Protocols on 8 June 1977 the administrations of all States present at the Conference[6] had to come to terms with these new treaties. And some of them have still not yet finished doing so. Behind the abstract notion of 'administration' there are the men and women who work with these texts, as legal advisers in the diplomatic service, as officers in the General Staff or as military lawyers. The Protocols -no different from other legal texts- must have some effects on those who deal with them by influencing and changing their perception of humanitarian law. To put it in a different way, assuming that no State had actually ratified the Protocols, would the 'humanitarian world of today' be the same, for instance, as in 1970 when the experts' discussions on the ICRC Draft began?

The following comments attempt to show that the answer to this question is a clear no. The world is no longer the same! The standing of humanitarian law has been considerably enhanced by the Diplomatic Conference and by the subsequent period of preparing the Protocols for decision on the national level.

4.1   Creating a body of experts in humanitarian law

Divided into four annual sessions the Diplomatic Conference convened in all for about nine months, not including the preparatory meetings of experts. During that time around sevenhundred representatives of more than a hundred Governments dealt with a topic -humanitarian law- that

---

6   Representatives of 126 States were present at the First Session and 102 States signed the Final Act. Two liberation movements also participated in the work of the Conference.

only few of them were familiar with at the outset of the Conference. At the end of it they *had* a thorough knowledge of the subject matter. The Conference provided excellent training for many diplomats, military lawyers, staff officers and others associated with the negotiations.

In addition to the persons directly involved in the work in Geneva, there were the officers back home in the capitals who prepared the instructions and saw to the necessary follow-up before, during and after the sessions.

Several delegations decided, furthermore, to associate university professors with the work of the Conference. Kalshoven belongs to that group of delegates, who rendered outstanding service to the cause of humanitarian law.

At the end of the Diplomatic Conference, on 8 June 1977, the number of experts in humanitarian law was therefore incomparably higher than a few years earlier. This side-effect of the Protocols' drafting is particularly important for countries of the Third World, most of which were confronted with that particular subject matter for the first time in their history. It is impossible today to visit the capital of any country anywhere in the world without meeting at least one expert on humanitarian law, in Government or university. Many are actually lecturing on the subject, which means that humanitarian law is now part of the *curriculum* at a great number of universities. It is of course true that at the end of the Diplomatic Conference not everybody continued to work in the same field; many delegates, in particular members of the diplomatic staff, were assigned to other tasks. But they kept their acquired knowledge and many maintained their interest in humanitarian law. Others joined their ranks after 1977, namely those who had to take over the task of preparing the Protocols for governmental decision. Furthermore, every second year the UN General Assembly debates the state of ratifications of and accessions to the 1977 Protocols.[7] That agenda item obliges at least the members of the Sixth Committee of the UN to update their knowledge of humanitarian law.

4.2   Heightening awareness of the relevance of humanitarian law

Nobody would deny that humanitarian law is much better known today than it was twenty years ago. There is more being written about subjects

---

7   GA Res. 43/161 of 9 December 1988 and preceeding resolutions. The Parliamentary Assembly of the Council of Europe, the Council of Ministers of the Organization of African Unity (OAU) and the ICRC (1977, 1981 and 1986) also adopted resolutions recommending ratification of the Protocols.

relating to humanitarian law than ever before. In many universities it has now found the place it deserves in the teaching of international law. The armed forces have been increasingly exposed to humanitarian law. Decision-makers, and those who advise them, can no longer plead ignorance of its precepts. This heightened awareness can be attributed to the continuing discussions on the 1977 Protocols. It is yet another side-effect of the Diplomatic Conference. Other developments, such as the increased public coverage of the ICRC's activities, do of course also play a part. But the initiating effect of the Protocols cannot be underestimated.

4.3   Familiarizing the armed forces with humanitarian law

A greater awareness of humanitarian law means a larger number of experts on the subject; the armed forces should acknowledge the effects of such a development. They certainly do. Never before has there been such interest in humanitarian law matters among members of the armed forces. One of its tangible results are the manuals on respect for humanitarian law which take into account the new law of 1977, some of them despite the fact that the Protocols have not yet been ratified by the State concerned. This development testifies to the 'non-legal' effects of the two Protocols better than any long discourse could do. We know, moreover, that the text of the Protocols can be found today on the desk of every military lawyer.

In short, there is no longer any informed debate on a matter relating to humanitarian law without reference to the Protocols. This holds true also for military circles. The new awareness appears not only to have produced new and better manuals and instruction material but also to have changed the armed forces' approach to humanitarian law. As an officer once put it, when referring to these developments in the last few years: '... from a rather esoteric subject humanitarian law has changed into a very practical matter.' That result alone justifies much of the arduous work of negotiating the Protocols.

For obvious reasons it remains a matter of speculation whether this new approach has also reached through to the minds of decision-makers and those who execute their decisions, *i.e.* of those who are actually instrumental in ensuring respect for the law. Various testimonies lead us to believe that this is the case. There seems to be a generalized new awareness, not only among members of armed forces, of the obligations arising out of international humanitarian law.

5.   CONCLUDING OBSERVATIONS

These few remarks do not claim to be more than a preliminary examination
of an exciting question, namely, what effects have the 1977 Protocols
produced other than those inherent in any law-making text? The answer is,
in short, that those men and women, lawyers and staff officers, diplomats
and law teachers who patiently negotiated and finally adopted the two
Protocols in the name of their Governments have decisively influenced the
standing of humanitarian law in the modern world. In particular, they have
given soldiers, officials and politicians a heightened awareness of the
importance of humanitarian concerns in the conduct of military operations.
*They have conclusively shown that humanitarian law is possible also in the
new circumstances of the late twentieth century.*

The ultimate test for humanitarian law is its capacity to prevent
suffering and destruction, to prevent unacceptable violations of human
dignity and, eventually, to prevent war from becoming a terrible reality.
We are convinced that the Protocols, through their mere existence, help to
achieve that end.

CUSTOMARY LAW STATUS OF THE 1977 GENEVA PROTOCOLS

CHRISTOPHER GREENWOOD

1.   INTRODUCTION

It is a great pleasure to contribute an essay on the 1977 Geneva Protocols to this collection of essays in honour of Frits Kalshoven. In his writings about the Protocols,[1] Professor Kalshoven has done so much to explain their meaning, effect and impact upon the general law that anyone interested in this subject owes him a considerable debt. The present writer, who came to the study of this subject for the first time in the year in which the Protocols were adopted, has derived such invaluable assistance from

---

1   See F. Kalshoven, *Reaffirmation and Development of Humanitarian Law Applicable in Armed Conflicts*, 8 NYIL 107 (1977) and 9 NYIL 107 (1978); F. Kalshoven, Constraints on the Waging of War (1987); F. Kalshoven, *Arms, Armaments and International law*, 191 Recueil des Cours, II, 187 (1985).

those works over the years that he is particularly delighted to have this opportunity to express his gratitude.

Although the relationship between the 1977 Protocols and customary international law has already received widespread attention,[2] several considerations make a further examination of this subject important in the context of the overall theme of the challenges for humanitarian law in the 1990's. First, most of the discussion hitherto has turned on the extent to which provisions of the two Protocols were declaratory of international law as it stood at the time they were adopted. Thirteen years later it is necessary to ask whether any provisions which were wholly or partly innovative in 1977 have come to be regarded as stating rules of general application. Secondly, while the period 1988-1990 has seen a remarkable increase in the number of States becoming Party to the Protocols,[3] it is now clear that the Protocols are not going to achieve the near universal participation enjoyed by the 1949 Geneva Conventions, at least in the immediate future. Nor is there any indication that states are generally willing to apply the Protocols on a voluntary basis, irrespective of the formal applicability of their provisions, in the way that the 1949 Conventions were frequently applied in conflicts during the decade after their adoption.[4]

It is, however, the international response to Iraq's invasion of Kuwait which has caused the whole question of the customary law status of the Protocols -and particularly Protocol I- to assume an immediate practical importance. Since Iraq is not a Party to Protocol I, the Protocol does not apply to the hostilities between Iraq and the allied forces which, at the time of writing, were engaged in conflict with Iraq. It thus becomes particularly important to determine which of its provisions should be regarded as authoritative statements of customary international law. The importance of this task is magnified by the fact that the forces involved in the hostilities

---

2   T. Meron, Human Rights and Humanitarian Norms as Customary International Law 62-78 (1989); L.R. Penna, *Customary International Law and Protocol I*, in C. Swinarski, ed., Studies and Essays on International Humanitarian Law and Red Cross Principles 201 (1984); A. Cassese, *The Geneva Protocols of 1977 on the Humanitarian Law of Armed Conflict and Customary International Law*, 3 UCLA Pacific Basin Law Journal 55 (1984) and *A Workshop on Customary International Law and the 1977 Protocols*, 2 Am. U.J. Int. L. & Pol'y. 415 (1987). The customary law status of provisions of the Protocol is also the subject of frequent comment in M. Bothe, K.J. Partsch, W.A. Solf, eds., New Rules for Victims of Armed Conflicts (1982).

3   On 1 January 1991, 99 States were Parties to Protocol I and 89 States to Protocol II.

4   *E.g.* the Korean War and Suez conflict.

with Iraq are drawn from a large number of States[5] and are operating under the authority of the UN Security Council.[6] While the United States, which has contributed the overwhelming majority of the forces involved, has decided not to ratify Protocol I, and the United Kingdom has yet to make a decision, other States deploying forces in the Gulf are Parties to the Protocol and have presumably incorporated the standards of Protocol I into their military training. In these circumstances, there is clearly a need for some common understanding regarding which provisions of the Protocol lay down rules of general application. It is evident that the proclaimed policy of the allies regarding targetting and aerial bombardment has been drawn up with these considerations in mind. Statements by allied commanders and heads of government have already made clear that the principles of distinction and proportionality set out in Protocol I are regarded by the allied States as declaratory of custom. On the other hand, it seems that Article 56, which prohibits most attacks against nuclear gererating stations, is not deemed to have attained that status.

When the United States decided in 1987 not to ratify Protocol I it announced its intention of consulting its allies with a view to determining which provisions of the Protocol were generally acceptable.[7] This initiative had not, however, led to any published results by the end of 1990. Moreover, it did not distinguish between those provisions of Protocol I which stated rules of customary international law and those which the United States regarded as 'positive innovations'. While such an approach avoids some of the difficulties inherent in any attempts to determine the exact status of each provision in the Protocol and focusses attention upon the substantive merits of each provision,[8] there are dangers in blurring the distinction between those provisions which state rules of customary law and must therefore be observed as a matter of legal obligation and those which contain rules that States may wish to observe as a matter of policy.

This essay will not attempt to consider the policy question of whether particular innovations introduced by the Protocols represent positive developments or not but will discuss only the customary law status of the Protocols. To do so, it is first necessary to determine the test to be applied. Part 2 of this essay will therefore examine the relationship

---

5   More than twenty States have deployed ground, air or naval forces to the Gulf.

6   SC Res. 678 of 29 November 1990.

7   See M. Matheson in panel on *Customary Law and Additional Protocol I*, 81 ASIL Proc. 26 (1987) and in the workshop, loc. cit. n. 2, at 419.

8   Matheson in the workshop, loc. cit. n. 2, at 422.

between treaties and customary law in general. Part 3 will briefly review the practice in international armed conflicts since 1977 to see what light that sheds upon the attitudes of States towards the status of Protocol I. In Part 4 there will be an examination of the provisions of Protocol I which deal with the conduct of hostilities[9] and are thus of the greatest comtemporary relevance. The controversial provisions regarding wars of 'national liberation' will be considered in Part 5, while Part 6 will briefly examine the status of Protocol II on internal armed conflicts.

2.   TREATIES AND CUSTOMARY INTERNATIONAL LAW

It is generally assumed that the provisions of a multilateral treaty are to be treated as authoritative statements of customary international law in two cases:

a) when they codify principles which already form part of customary international law prior to the conclusion of the treaty; and
b) when, although they go beyond the existing customary law, the principles which they lay down come to be accepted as generally applicable and thus become part of a new customary international law.

The first of these categories requires little discussion. It should, nevertheless, be remembered that even when a treaty provision is 'merely codificatory', the adoption of that provision may nevertheless have an important effect. In the first place, it serves to confirm the customary rule and remove doubts which may have existed about its continued existence. This was a particularly important feature of Protocol I and, indeed, one of the main purposes of the Diplomatic Conference, for many of the customary principles codified in the Protocol had been violated on such a massive scale during World War II and many of the post-1945 conflicts that their continued validity was questioned. Moreover, most of these principles were the product of a much smaller world community and their reaffirmation by a conference in which the newly independent States participated fully had considerable political significance. For example, the principle that the rules of humanitarian law apply equally to both sides in a conflict had been challenged by North Vietnam during the Vietnam War and was in danger of being eroded by the growth of a modern 'just war'

---

9   Articles 35-60.

school of thought, particularly in relation to wars of national liberation. The preamble to Protocol I and the provisions of Article 96(3) make clear that humanitarian law continues to apply equally to both sides in an international conflict.

Secondly, the codification of a hitherto unwritten rule will almost invariably affect the content of that rule. In selecting words to codify a customary principle, those responsible for the draft are generally forced to try to resolve the ambiguities about the scope and content of that rule and their choice may have the effect of creating new ambiguities. Attention in the future will focus upon the text so that the scope of the customary rule will tend to become a matter of textual interpretation.[10] As will be seen in Part 4, many of the provisions of Protocol I regarding the protection of civilians from the effects of hostilities have codified for the first time principles of customary law in ways which have had profound effects upon those rules.

The way in which treaty provisions which cannot be regarded as codificatory may come to affect customary law requires closer attention. In the *North Sea Continental Shelf Cases* (NSCSC)[11] the ICJ laid down three requirements which had to be met if a treaty provision which was substantially innovative was to be deemed to have become binding as part of the general law:

a) the provision must be of a norm-creating character;
b) State practice, particularly that of the States whose interests are most specially affected, must indicate a widespread acceptance of the principle; and
c) that practice must be based upon *opinio iuris*.

The Court warned, moreover, that such a result was 'not lightly to be regarded as having been attained'[12] and held that it had not occurred in the case of the provision of the Geneva Convention on the Continental Shelf, 1958, which lay at the heart of the NSCSC. This test suggests that an innovative provision in a treaty can only be regarded as having passed into custom if there is convincing evidence of widespread State practice

---

10 See, *e.g.*, The Decision of the Arbitral Tribunal for the Agreement on German External Debts, in *Kingdom of Belgium and Others* v. *Federal Republic of Germany*, 59 ILR 494 (1980).

11 *Federal Republic of Germany* v. *Denmark, Federal Republic of Germany* v. *Netherlands*, 3 ICJ Rep. (1969).

12 § 71 of the Judgment.

applying the principle enshrined in that provision in circumstances where the treaty itself was not applicable and the States concerned appear to have treated the principle as binding in customary law.

Nevertheless, in the *Nicaragua Case*[13] the Court, while quoting with approval its earlier judgment in the NSCSC, adopted in practice a far less rigorous approach, holding that numerous provisions in multilateral conventions -including common Articles 1 and 3 of the 1949 Conventions- had become part of customary law although the Judgment contains no examination of the State practice upon which such conclusions should have been based if the approach in the NSCSC had indeed been followed.[14] Nor is the *Nicaragua* judgment unique in adopting such a cavalier approach. The International Military Tribunal at Nuremberg assumed, without explanation, that the provisions of the Hague Regulations on Land Warfare, 1907, had become part of customary international law by 1939.[15] Even more striking is the readiness with which the United States Military Tribunal in *United States* v. *Von Leeb* (the *High Command Case*) was prepared to accept that many provisions of the Geneva Convention of Prisoners of War, 1929, had passed into customary law before the outbreak of war between Germany and the Soviet Union in 1941.[16]

This suggests two refinements to the test in the NSCSC. First, where a treaty provision is merely a detailed application of a more general principle which is already well established in customary law, the passage of the detailed provision into custom may more easily be assumed. Baxter has suggested that the provisions of humanitarian treaties may more readily be accepted as having entered into customary law than those of other multilateral agreements:

'... on the ground that each new wave of such treaties builds upon the past conventions, so that each detailed rule of the Geneva Conventions for the Protection of War Victims is nothing more than an implementation of a more general standard already laid down in an earlier convention, such as the Regulations annexed to Convention No. IV of The Hague.'[17]

---

13 *Military and Paramilitary Activities in and Against Nicaragua*, ICJ Rep. 1986, at 114 (112-115).
14 For criticism of the Court's approach, see Meron, op. cit. n. 2, at 25-37 and J. Charney, *Customary International Law in the Nicaragua Judgment on the Merits*, 1 Hague Yearbook of International Law 16 (1988).
15 *Trial of the Major German War Criminals*, Cmd. 6964, 65 (1946).
16 11 Trials of War Criminals, Nuremberg Military Tribunals 462 (1948).
17 R.R. Baxter, *Multilateral Treaties as Evidence of Customary International Law*, 41 BYIL 286 (1965-1966).

Secondly, in examining the State practice as required by the NSCSC test, it should be remembered that the adoption of the treaty text is itself an important piece of State practice which in some cases may be sufficient to bring about a change in the customary law.[18] If abused, this approach runs the risk of obliterating the distinction between conventional and customary law and of ignoring the often delicate 'package deal' nature of treaty negotiations. Nevertheless, it is suggested that it is acceptable -and is, indeed, applied in practice- in cases where the treaty provision concerned commands general acceptance (amongst the international community as a whole) not merely as part of a treaty package but as the statement of a rule of general application.[19]

Even with these refinements, the application of the NSCSC test to the provisions of the 1977 Protocols present problems. It is clear that one of the factors which is in practice of great importance in establishing the customary law status of treaty provisions is the existence of decisions of the ICJ or another authoritative international tribunal. Once such a tribunal has decided that a particular provision has become part of customary law, its customary law status tends to be assumed in subsequent discussion.[20] Thus, a series of decisions of the ICJ is generally regarded as having settled the status of some of the most important provisions of the Vienna Convention on the Law of Treaties, 1969.[21] No such decisions exist regarding the 1977 Protocols. Indeed, international decisions are rare in respect of any of the humanitarian law treaties, the war crimes cases quoted above being the exception rather than the rule. Nor is State practice easy either to discover (given the secrecy which generally surrounds the wartime activities of States) or to evaluate (since the nature of armed conflict means that the gulf between principle and practice is likely to be particularly marked).

---

18 The judgment in the NSCSC admits this possibility, ICJ Rep. 1969, loc. cit. n. 11, at 42.

19 For a more far-reaching view of the role of treaties in shaping customary law, see Cassese, loc. cit. n. 2, at 65-68.

20 Meron, op. cit. n. 2, at 43.

21 *Namibia Opinion* ICJ Rep., 1971, at 47; *Fisheries Jurisdiction Case*, ICJ Rep., 1973, at 18; *Jurisdiction of the ICAO Council*, ICJ Rep., 1972, at 67.

3.   PRACTICE REGARDING INTERNATIONAL ARMED
         CONFLICTS

3.1   The Iran-Iraq War

State practice during the numerous armed conflicts since 1977 sheds
relatively little light upon the status of the provisions of Protocol I. There
has been no conflict in which the Protocol has been formally applicable
and few in which any serious official reference has been made to its
provisions.[22] It is, however, instructive briefly to examine the Iran-Iraq
War as the longest conflict of the period and one in which reference was
made to the Protocol on numerous occasions both by the parties and by the
United Nations and the ICRC.

Most of the references to the Protocol concerned those provisions which
reaffirmed the traditional prohibition on attacks against the civilian population and which, for the most part,[23] reflected the pre-1977 customary
international law. Thus, Iran accused Iraq of violating the principles
enshrined in Articles 48, 51, 53, 54, 57 and 59.[24] Similarly, in a letter to
the Security Council in 1984, Iraq accused Iran of using centres of civilian
population to shield troop concentrations, contrary to Article 28 of the
Fourth Convention and continued: '[t]his prohibition was reaffirmed clearly
in Protocol I, signed at Geneva in 1977. Article 58, paragraph (b), states
the necessity of avoiding the establishment of military targets in or near
densely populated areas'.[25] However, in view of the widespread disregard
for the law during the hostilities, it is difficult to attach much significance
to these references to the Protocol, which appear to have been made
largely for propaganda reasons.

SC Resolution 540 referred to the 1949 Conventions but not to the
Protocol. Nevertheless, the call for the 'immediate cessation of all military
operations against civilian targets, including cities and residential areas'[26]
seems to have been based more upon provisions of the Protocol than
Convention IV. In addition, the ICRC made several public appeals to the

---

22 Although there are extensive unofficial references to the Protocol in relation to the Israeli
    invasion of Lebanon in 1982. See S. MacBride, ed., *Israel in Lebanon*, Report of the
    International Commission to enquire into reported violations of International Law by Israel
    during its invasion of the Lebanon (1983).
23 See part 4.
24 See P. Tavernier, *La Guerre du Golfe: Quelques Aspects de l'application du Droit des Conflits
    Armés et du Droit Humanitaire*, 30 Ann. Français 43 (1984).
25 UN Doc. S/16649 of 28 June 1984.
26 SC Res. 540 of 31 October 1983, § 2. See also SC Res. 598 of 20 July 1987.

Parties to respect the principles of humanitarian law, particularly with regard to the protection of the civilian population. These appeals frequently echoed the language of the Protocol and sometimes made express references to its provisions.[27]

The references to the Protocols sometimes went beyond those provisions which codified the pre-1977 customary law. Thus, the ICRC, in a public appeal in 1983, stated that 'civilians must not be the object of attack, nor of reprisals' and urged the Parties 'to respect these basic humanitarian rules everywhere and at all times'.[28] The status of the prohibition on reprisals against civilian targets will be considered in Part 4 but its claim to customary law status is controversial. Similarly, the provisions of Article 35(3) and Article 55 on methods and means of combat likely to cause long-term, widespread and severe environmental damage, also considered innovative in 1977, were referred to by Iran in complaints about Iraqi attacks on oil facilities.[29] On the other hand, it must be borne in mind that both States continued to attack civilian targets and to justify their actions as reprisals throughout the conflict, while each attacked environmentally sensitive targets when it had the capacity to do so.

Another novel provision of Protocol I which was quoted in the context of the Iran-Iraq War was Article 77(2) which required the Parties to 'take all feasible measures in order that children who have not attained the age of fifteen years do not take a direct part in hostilities' and to refrain from recruiting them into their armed forces. This provision was seen as filling a lacuna in the protection of children by international humanitarian law[30] and it is difficult to perceive it as codificatory of existing customary law, although it built upon other provisions of humanitarian law and human rights law for the protection of children. Nevertheless, both the ICRC and the UN Commission on Human Rights relied upon Article 77(2) in the Iran-Iraq War. It was one of a number of texts invoked by the Human Rights Commission in a resolution calling upon Iran to cease the use of child soldiers,[31] while in 1983 the ICRC expressed consternation that children were being recruited to fight in the Iran-Iraq War and, after referring to Article 77, noted that '[t]hese provisions were adopted by the

---

27 See *e.g.*, ICRC Annual Report, 67 (1985); ICRC Annual Report 78 (1988).
28 ICRC Annual Report 58 (1983).
29 See also SC Res. 540 of 31 October 1983.
30 Bothe, Partsch and Solf, op. cit. n. 2, at 475; H. Mann, *International Law and the Child Soldier*, 36 ICLQ 32 (1987).
31 GA Res. 1984/39; E/CN.4/1984/SR.51; see also Mann, loc. cit. n. 30, at 53.

Diplomatic Conference ... in order to lay down clearly in international humanitarian law a universal moral rule of extraordinary importance'.[32]

On the other hand, a UN Report on the Iran-Iraq War, commenting on a dispute about the status of mercenaries, took the position that Article 47 of Protocol I, which provides that mercenaries are not lawful combatants, was an innovation which could not 'be invoked by States which have not ratified the First Protocol'.[33]

3.2   Military manuals and other State practice

More instructive, perhaps, is State practice of another kind, in the form of military manuals and statements made outside the context of an armed conflict. Thus, the United States clearly acknowledged the customary law status of some of the basic principles for the protection of civilians when it amended its Field Manual, shortly before the adoption of the Protocols, to incorporate language taken directly from Protocol I. The amended Paragraph 40 of the Field Manual included a definition of military objectives which is clearly based upon Article 52(2) of Protocol I: 'Military objectives -*i.e.*, combatants, and those objects which by their nature, location, purpose, or use make an effective contribution to military action and whose total or partial destruction, capture or neutralization, in the circumstances ruling at the time, offers a definite military advantage- are permissible objects of attack'.[34]

It is also significant that Paragraph 41, which dealt with the proportionality test, was amended to incorporate the language of Article 51(5,b) as well as the core of the precautions in attack provisions of Article 57. These amendments, which were made long before the question of United States ratification of the Protocol became an issue, are particularly important, because they give a clear indication that the United States regarded these provisions as stating rules of customary international law.

Since the United States decided not to ratify Protocol I, there have been a number of other pronouncements from officials and agencies of the Government indicating the United States attitude towards the status of provisions of Protocol I. The Annotated Supplement to the new edition of the United States Naval Commander's Handbook also treats the principle that civilians are not legitimate targets, the proportionality test as expressed

---

32 ICRC Annual Report 58 (1983).
33 UN Doc. S/16962 (1985) of 19 February 1985, at 59.
34 United States Department of the Army, *Field Manual*, FM 27-10 (1956), Change No. 1 (15 July 1976).

in Article 51(5,b) and the definition of a military objective in Article 52(2) as part of customary law. Although the text itself defines a military objective in terms which differ somewhat from those of Article 52(2), the accompanying note states that 'this variation of the definition in Additional Protocol I Article 52(2) is not intended to alter its meaning and is accepted by the United States as declarative of the customary rule'.[35] The Handbook also describes Articles 35(1, 2), 52(1) (except insofar as it deals with reprisals), 54(2) and 57(2) and (4) as declaratory of custom.[36]

To these publications may be added the statements made by United States officials after the announcement that the United States would not ratify Protocol I.[37] They are evidence that, in addition to the provisions listed above, the United States regards Articles 37 (perfidy), 40 (refusal of quarter), 42 (on persons parachuting from a disabled aircraft), 59 (non-defended localities), 60 (demilitarized zones), 73 (refugees), 75 (fundamental guarantees) and 79 (journalists) as declaratory of custom. The statements also show that the United States regards a number of other provisions, such as Article 54(1), which prohibits the starvation of civilians as a method of warfare, as desirable innovations which should become customary law. On the other hand, the Naval Commander's Handbook and the other statements make clear that the United States does not accept that some of the more controversial provisions of the Protocol, in particular, the treatment of wars of national liberation, the relaxation of the requirements for combatant status, the prohibition of reprisals against any kind of civilian target and the special rules for dams, dykes and nuclear electrical generating stations in Article 56, have acquired or should acquire customary law status.

---

35 United States Department of the Navy, *Annotated Supplement to the Commander's Handbook on the Law of Naval Operations*, NWP 9, (rev A), (1989). The annotations to the Handbook, unlike the text of the Handbook, do not have official status. They are, however, a good indication of the attitude of the United States to the provisions of the Protocol cited therein.

36 *Ibid.*, Chapter 8, n. 9.

37 See the contributions by Matheson and Carnahan in panel on *Customary Law and Additional Protocol I*, loc. cit. n. 7., at 26.

4.   PROVISIONS OF PROTOCOL I RELATING TO THE
       CONDUCT OF HOSTILITIES

Space does not permit an analysis of the status of each provision of
Protocol I. The present section will, therefore, be confined to an
assessment of the provisions which have the most direct impact upon the
conduct of hostilities, *i.e.*, those where the Protocol combines elements of
both 'Hague Law' and 'Geneva Law'. It has been in respect of these
provisions that controversy regarding the impact of the Protocol on the
customary law has been greatest. They are, moreover, the provisions in
respect of which problems of 'inter-operability', within a multi-national
force are most likely to arise and are thus of particular interest in relation
to the Kuwait crisis.[38]

4.1   Methods and means of warfare (Articles 35-42)

The main provisions in this section of the Protocol are a reaffirmation of
long established provisions of customary law. Thus, Article 35(1) reaffirms
the rule that 'the right of the parties to the conflict to choose the methods
or means of warfare is not unlimited', while Article 35(2) confirms the
prohibition of weapons and methods of warfare 'of a nature to cause
superfluous injury or unnecessary suffering'. Although these provisions are
largely a repetition of Articles 22 and 23(e) of the Hague Regulations,
1907, they clarify the law in two small but significant respects. First, the
debate amongst anglophonic international lawyers over whether the phrase
'maux superflus' in the authentic French text of Article 23(e) of the Hague
Regulations should be translated as 'superfluous injury' or 'unnecessary
suffering'[39] was finally laid to rest by the adoption of both terms in the
English text of Article 35(2). Secondly, and more importantly, Article 35
makes clear that the principles which it reaffirms apply not only to the
choice of weapons but also to the way in which weapons are employed
(*i.e.*, to the *methods* as well as the *means* of warfare). Article 35(3), which
prohibits the employment of: '... methods or means of warfare which are
intended, or may be expected, to cause widespread, long-term and severe
damage to the natural environment', is more contentious and, unlike the
rest of Article 35, was not based upon the provisions of earlier treaties.
Nor could it be said that State practice prior to 1977 provided much

---

38 See Part I.
39 For an account of the course of this debate, see Kalshoven, *Arms, Armaments and
   International Law*, loc. cit. n. 1, at 244.

support for the existence of such a rule. Although the Article was adopted by consensus, the Federal Republic of Germany stated that it participated in that consensus on the understanding that Article 35(3) introduced a new rule.[40] Subsequent United States statements regarding Article 35(3) and Article 55 take the same position.[41] If, as is suggested, Article 35(3) was an innovation in 1977, there is little or no subsequent practice which might have had the effect of incorporating the principle stated therein into customary law. Nevertheless, while there is likely to be continuing controversy about the extent of the principle contained in Article 35(3), the core of that principle may well reflect an emerging norm of international law.

The requirement in Article 36 that States examine new and proposed weapons to determine whether their use would comply with the law of armed conflict is a novelty but one which is uncontroversial and, in any event, follows logically from the obligations of Artricle 35(1).[42]

Articles 37 (perfidy) and 38 (improper use of recognized emblems) are also largely codificatory. The only substantial (and uncontroversial) innovation in each case is the introduction of a prohibition of the improper use of the emblems or uniforms of the United Nations. It is clear from the records of the Diplomatic Conference that this new prohibition applies only in respect of UN peacekeeping operations and not in cases, such as Korea, where forces authorized to display the UN flag and emblems are engaged in combat.[43] Article 39(2), which provides that 'it is prohibited to make use of the flags or military emblems, insignia or uniforms of adverse Parties while engaging in attacks *or in order to shield, favour, protect or impede military operations* [emphasis added]', goes beyond the generally understood customary international law, since the italicised words are contrary to the approach adopted in the *Case of Skorzeny*.[44] That case was generally considered (although the matter was not entirely free from doubt) as authority for the proposition that the use of enemy uniforms etc. was forbidden only during an attack. For that reason, Article 39(2) has attracted some controversy[45] and should not be regarded as declaratory of customary law.

---

40 VI, Off. Rec. CDDH 115, Geneva 1974-1977.

41 See Matheson in the Workshop, loc. cit. n. 2, at 424.

42 Assessments of the kind required by Article 36 are already carried out by a number of States. See, *e.g. Commander's Handbook*, op. cit. n. 35, Chapter 9, n. 1.

43 See C. Pilloud *et al., Commentary on the Additional Protocols* § 1560 (1987).

44 9 WCR 90.

45 See Matheson in the Workshop, loc. cit. n. 2, at 425.

There is no controversy, however, regarding the status of Articles 40 (prohibiting refusal of quarter) and 41(1, 2) (concerning the safeguard of an enemy rendered *hors de combat*). Article 41(3), which provides that where prisoners of war have been taken in unusual conditions which prevent their evacuation as required in the Third Convention, 'they shall be released and all feasible precautions taken to ensure their safety', is not quite in the same category. Insofar as it makes clear that commando units and raiding parties or guerrillas cannot use their inability to treat prisoners as required by the Convention as a justification for killing them, it reaffirms an important principle of customary law.[46] The customary law did not, however, indicate what should be done with prisoners in such cases and Article 41(3) introduces a welcome element of flexibility in this respect. As such, it is an innovative provision but one which is fully in accord with general humanitarian principles and reflects the best (though sadly not the invariable) practice under the customary law.[47]

Article 42 (prohibiting attacks on persons parachuting from a disabled aircraft) was the subject of heated debate at the Conference. Although it merely stated a rule already found in a number of national manuals[48] and the Draft Hague Rules on Aerial Warfare, 1923[49] a number of States maintained that the immunity of aircrew from attack should apply only when they would land in territory where they could be made prisoner and argued that the customary rule supported that position. This view was decisively rejected at the Diplomatic Conference and the adoption of the unqualified prohibition contained in Article 42 should be seen as a reaffirmation of a customary rule prohibiting attacks upon persons parachuting from an aircraft in distress irrespective of where those persons might land. Both the United States and the ICRC Commentary on the Protocols have taken that position.

46　See, *e.g.* United States *Field Manual*, op. cit. n. 34, at § 85 and the United Kingdom *Manual of Military Law*, Part III, § 137 (1958).

47　C. Pilloud *et al.*, loc. cit. n. 43, § 1629.

48　See, *e.g.* United States *Field Manual*, loc. cit. n. 34, § 30; United Kingdom *Manual of Military Law*, loc. cit. n. 46, § 119; France *Règlement de discipline générale dans les armées*, Article 34(2); C. Pilloud *et al.*, loc. cit. n. 43, § 1637 *et seq.*.

49　Article 20.

4.2   Combatant and prisoner of war status (Articles 43-47)

The rules regarding entitlement to combatant and prisoner of war status were already the subject of detailed provisions in the Hague regulations and the Third Geneva Convention. Articles 43-47 of Protocol I depart from the earlier agreements in several important respects, some of which have proved highly controversial.

Article 43 restates existing principles, except that it removes the threshold distinction, found in both Article 1 of the Hague Regulations and Article 4 of the Third Convention, between the regular armed forces and volunteer groups, militias and resistance movements. Article 43 starts from the presumption that the criteria for determining entitlement to combatant and prisoner of war status and the effects of failing to meet any one of these criteria are the same for members of both groups. This was a change in respect of the pre-1977 law but appears to be uncontroversial and is likely to be absorbed into customary international law quite quickly.

The same cannot be said of Article 44. Article 44(3) introduces two major changes into the law. While the first sentence restates the customary law requirement that combatants distinguish themselves from the civilian population, it differs from customary international law regarding how that should be done. Whereas the Hague Regulations and Article 4(A,2) of the Third Convention stipulated that irregular combatants should wear a fixed, distinctive sign and carry arms openly, the Protocol merely states that they must distinguish themselves from the civilian population without specifying how this must be done. This change was relatively uncontroversial and may be expected to pass into customary law without difficulty. The rule laid down in the first sentence was, however, qualified by the compromise text embodied in the second sentence of Article 44(3), which provides that, where it is impossible for a combatant to distinguish himself as required, he may nevertheless retain his status as a combatant provided that he carries arms openly in the situations specified in the sentence. This was one of the most controversial provisions inserted in the Protocol and has been identified by the Untied States as a major reason for its decision not to ratify Protocol I. Since it departs markedly from the pre-1977 law it cannot be regarded as part of customary law and the strengh of opposition to it means that it will not pass easily into custom.

Of the other provisions in this part of the Protocol, Article 45 is an innovation but one which is unlikely to attract opposition and should easily become part of the customary law. Article 46 (on spies) is declaratory of the exisiting law (and mirrors the provisions of Articles 29-31 of the Hague Regulations) except for Paragraph 3, which contains an element of novelty. Article 47 (on mercenaries) is wholly new and its status as an innovation not yet regarded as a reflection of customary law was confirmed during the Iran-Iraq War.[50]

4.3   Protection of civilians from the effects of hostilities (Articles 48-60)

The most important feature of the Protocol's provisions on the civilian population is that they reaffirm and, in some respects, elaborate two customary principles of fundamental importance:

a) the principle of *distinction*:
   'the Parties to the conflict shall at all times distinguish between the civilian population and combatants and between civilian objects and military objectives and accordingly shall direct their operations only against military objectives' (Article 48).

b) the principle of *proportionality*, which prohibits even an attack upon a military objective:
   'which may be expected to cause incidental loss of civilian life, injury to civilians, damage to civilian objects or a combination thereof, which would be excessive in relation to the concrete and direct military advantage anticipated' (Article 51(5,b)).

The customary law status of the principle of distinction was never seriously questioned but its reaffirmation in the Protocol was timely in view of the extent to which it had been violated during World War II and subsequent conflicts. Those violations have not ceased since 1977[51] but no State has denied the binding character of the basic prohibition.[52] The Protocol also clarifies the principle in a number of important respects. First, Article 52(2) gives a definition of 'military objective' which, for all its faults, is generally regarded as an improvement on the earlier, looser attempts at definition.[53] Secondly, the Protocol makes clear that the principle of

---

50 See text accompanying n. 33.
51 See *Respect for International Humanitarian Law*, Report of the ICRC to the 25th International Conference of the Red Cross (1987).
52 See, *e.g.* the practice during the Iran-Iraq War discussed in Paragraph 3.1 *supra*.
53 See, however, the criticism of this definition by A. Randelzhofer, *Civilian Objects*, in R. Berhardt, ed., 3 Encyclopaedia of Public International Law (1982).

distinction applies to all types of conflict, including guerrilla warfare.[54] Finally, the Protocol spells out in greater detail some of the implications of the principle of distinction in provisions such as Article 51(2) prohibiting terror attacks and 51(7) prohibiting the use of civilians as a human shield for military operations.[55] These provisions clearly enjoy customary law status.

The principle of proportionality was also part of the pre-1977 law, although it is expressed in the Protocol in more precise language than that used hitherto. This has led some commentators to question the extent to which the expression of this principle in Article 51(5,b) and Article 57 can be regarded as posessing customary law status.[56] Nevertheless, the representative of the United Kingdom seems to have reflected the general view when he described what became Article 51(5,b) as: 'a useful codification of a concept that was rapidly becoming accepted by all States as an important principle of international law relating to armed conflict'.[57] In addition, as seen in Part 3, the formula employed in Article 51(5,b) has been adopted in the United States Field Manual and the Naval Commander's Handbook. It is suggested, therefore, that Article 51(5,b) should be treated as an authoritative statement of the modern customary rule.

In some respects, however, the Protocol did go beyond the existing law in detailing what were seen as some of the implications of the principles of distinction and proportionality. While the prohibition of indiscriminate attacks in Article 51(4) is part of customary law, the elaboration of what constitutes an indiscriminate attack in that paragraph and in Article 51(5,a) probably constituted a refinement of the customary law, albeit a desirable one. Articles 50(1) and 52(3) create a presumption of civilian status in respect of persons and certain categories of objects. Again, this is a highly desirable development which, as Kalshoven has pointed out, should, if faithfully applied, put an end to the practice of 'shoot first and question later'.[58] Although it is inherent in the principle of distinction that there is a duty to take reasonable steps to determine whether or not a person or object is a legitimate target, it is questionable whether the pre-1977 law

---

54 See H.-P. Gasser, *Prohibition of Terrorist Acts in International Humanitarian Law*, International Review of the Red Cross 200 (1986).
55 See Paragraph 3.1 *supra*.
56 See Meron, op. cit. n. 2 at 65, n. 178.
57 VI Off. Rec. 164 (1974-1977).
58 F. Kalshoven, *Reaffirmation and Development of Humanitarian Laws Applicable in Armed Conflicts*, 9 NYIL 112 (1978).

went so far as to prescribe a presumption of civilian status. Nevertheless, these provisions are, for the most part, likely to command general acceptance.

Article 53 (cultural objects) largely repeats the existing law. Article 54(1), which prohibits 'starvation of civilians as a method of warfare' repudiates a practice which has long been regarded as legitimate. However, the traditional approach that starvation of the civilian population was to be regarded as a legitimate form of siege warfare was something of an anomaly in view of the principle that civilians are not legitimate targets in their own right. Article 54(1) may, therefore, be regarded as the articulation of a basic humanitarian principle. Since it was uncontroversial, it is arguable that it has already become part of customary international law. The US Naval Commander's Handbook takes the view that Article 54(2) states a rule of customary law and that Article 54(1) represents a positive development which should mature into customary law.[59] Article 54 represents a blend of customary law and innovative provisions which are not easy to disentangle but most of it is likely to become part of customary law with little difficulty if it does not already have that status.

Article 55 (protection of the natural environment) is closely linked to Article 35(3) and should be regarded as having the same status.[60] Article 56, which confers special protection on dams, dykes and nuclear electrical generating stations over and above that provided by the general principles of distinction and proportionality, was an entirely innovative provision. There were no customary rules specifically dealing with this question before 1977 and there is insufficient evidence in the records of the Diplomatic Conference or in subsequent practice to sustain a suggestion that the provisions of Article 56 have become part of customary law.[61] Although the provision is clearly intended to enhance the protection of the civilian population, insofar as it goes beyond the protection afforded by the general principles it has proved controversial and has been rejected by the United States.[62]

Articles 51 to 56 also prohibit any reprisals against the persons and objects protected by them. These prohibitions of reprisals aroused considerable controversy at the Diplomatic Conference. While some states maintained that some or all of them were declaratory of customary law, this view was vigorously denied by others. Military manuals and the

---

59 Op. cit. n. 35, Chapter 8, n. 19.
60 See text accompanying n. 40-41.
61 See Cassese, loc. cit. n. 2, at 94.
62 See *e.g.* Matheson in Workshop, loc. cit. n. 2, at 427 and A. Sofaer, *ibid.* at 468.

literature on the subject prior to 1977[63] suggest that the reprisals provisions should be seen as innovative.[64] Practice since 1977 tends to reinforce this conclusion. In spite of their invocation of some of the provisions of the Protocol regarding the protection of civilians, both Iran and Iraq sought to justify attacks upon civilian targets as reprisals. The United States has expressly rejected the reprisals provisions and its Naval Commander's Handbook states that reprisals against civilians and civilian objects (other than those protected by the Fourth Convention) remain lawful under customary international law.[65] There is some evidence that other States view such reprisals as legitimate in the last resort, at least in response to attacks which are themselves violations of Articles 51 to 56.[66]

The provisions of Articles 57 and 58 of Protocol I, which prescribe certain precautionary measures in attack and defence, are based on customary international law but go beyond it in certain respects. Article 57 imposes obligations upon those who have authority in respect of ordering or cancelling an attack and, except perhaps for Paragraph 3 (which is a novel provision but one which follows logically from the general principles enunciated in the Article) reflects customary law. Article 58 extends and develops customary law in a way likely to gain acceptance and thus to be absorbed into custom with little difficulty.

Article 59, which deals with the immunity from attack of undefended localities, reaffirms the principle in Article 25 of the Hague Regulations and provides detailed rules to give effect to that principle. Article 59(5) and Article 60 (which creates a separate regime for demilitarized zones) depend for their operation on the agreement of the Parties to the conflict and are innovative although it is open to any States, irrespective of whether they are Parties to the Protocol, to take them as a reference point.

5.   WARS OF NATIONAL LIBERATION

The controversy caused by this issue at the first session of the Conference is well known. Some of the proponents of Article 1(4) have argued that it does no more than recognize the effects of developments in customary law

---

63 See United States *Field Manual*, op. cit. n. 34, § 497 and United Kingdom *Manual of Military Law*, op. cit. n. 46, §§ 642-649 and F. Kalshoven, Belligerent Reprisals 361 (1971).

64 Cassese, loc. cit. n. 2, at 102; C.J. Greenwood, *The Twilight of the Law of Belligerent Reprisals*, 20 NYIL 35-69 (1989).

65 Op. cit. n. 35, chapter 6, n. 33. Also, Sofaer in Workshop, loc. cit. n. 2, at 469.

66 See, *e.g.* the statement made by Italy on ratification, Int. Rev. of the Red Cross 114 (1986).

which had already taken place by 1974.[67] Other commentators see it as an undesirable innovation[68] and it has been expressly rejected by the United States,[69] as well as being the subject of restrictive declarations made by a number of States.[70] A third group of commentators deny that the provision has any status in customary law and conclude that since the States most likely to be affected by it will not become Parties to the Protocol, 'in effect, the provision is a dead letter'.[71] At first glance, practice since 1977 appears to support this third view. The States most likely to be affected by Article 1(4) have not become Parties to the Protocol and the Governments of South Africa and Israel have strenuously resisted any suggestion that the provision reflects customary rules which bind them in their relations with the ANC, SWAPO or the PLO.[72] No declaration under Article 96(3) has successfully been deposited. Despite Abi-Saab's argument that the provision merely reflected the fact that wars of national liberation were already treated as a matter of international rather than domestic concern, the considerable body of opposition in State practice to treating such conflicts, for the purposes of the *ius in bello*, as though they were conflicts between States suggests that Article 1(4) went well beyond customary law as it stood in 1974 and has not met the criteria for being absorbed into customary law since its inclusion in Protocol I.

6.   THE STATUS OF PROTOCOL II

Unlike Protocol I, Protocol II on internal armed conflicts was drafted against the background of a customary law which contained few relevant provisions. Indeed, some States argued that there was no customary law regarding the conduct of internal armed conflicts and it was that sentiment which helped to ensure that the version of the Martens Clause which appears in the preamble to Protocol II contains no reference to principles

---

67 G. Abi-Saab, *Wars of National Liberation in the Geneva Conventions and Protocols*, 165 Recueil des Cours, IV, 371-372 (1979); Cassese, loc. cit. n. 2, at 68-71.
68 See, *e.g.* G.I.A.D. Draper, *Wars of National Liberation and War Criminality*, in M. Howard, ed., Restraints in War (1979).
69 See *e.g.* the hostile attitude of the Administration in the President's Message to the Senate regarding the Protocols. Repr. in XXVI ILM 561 (1987).
70 See *e.g.* the Declarations made on signature by the United Kingdom. Repr. in A. Roberts, R. Guelff, Documents on the Laws of War 467-468 (1989).
71 G. Aldrich, *Progressive Development of the Laws of War: A Reply to Criticisms of 1977 Protocol I*, 26 Vir. Jnl. Int. Law 703 (1986).
72 But see C. Murray, *The 1977 Protocols and Conflict in South Africa*, 33 ICLQ 462 (1984).

of international law (in sharp distinction to the version in Article 1(2) of Protocol I). That, together with the hostile attitude of many States towards the whole of Protocol II, has led some commentators to argue that none of the provisions of the Protocol can be regarded as reflecting customary law.[73]

Such a position is too extreme. In places Protocol II does no more than restate principles already contained in common Article 3 of the Geneva Conventions. Other provisions of the Protocol do no more than cloak the bare bones of Article 3 with a moderate amount of flesh. Thus, Article 4(1) and (2) of the Protocol are really just an elaboration of the general duty of humane treatment imposed by common Article 3(1). Similarly, Article 6(2), which deals with due process guarantees, is an elaboration of common Article 3(1,d). In the one case in which the Protocol has so far been applied, the civil war in El Salvador, the Government of El Salvador has avoided taking a position on whether the Protocol is formally applicable by stating that its provisions developed and completed the basic minimum provisions of common Article 3.[74] It is highly likely that pragmatic use of the Protocol's provisions will be made as an aid to implementing the broad principles of common Article 3, as well as provisions in human rights agreements.

Nevertheless, it is difficult to avoid the conclusion that most of Protocol II has to be regarded as confined to treaty law in the absence of more substantial State practice evidencing an acceptance of its provisions into customary law.

---

73 See J.E. Bond in Workshop, loc. cit. n. 2, at 472. For a more cautious approach, see Cassese, loc. cit. n. 2, at 104-112.

74 See, *Informe de la Fuerza Armada de El Salvador (FAES) sobre el respeto y la vigencia de las normas del Derecho Internacional Humanitario durante el periodo de Septiembre de 1986 a Agosto de 1987* (Report of the Armed Forces of El Salvador regarding the respect and the validity of the norms of International Humanitarian Law during the period of September 1986 till August 1987), submitted by the Government of El Salvador to the Special Representative of the Commission on Human Rights. See also R. Hammer, Developing a Humanitarian Awareness (1987). The ICRC, on the other hand, has consistently maintained that Protocol II applies *de iure* to the conflict in El Salvador, ICRC Annual Report 39 (1989). I am most grateful to Mrs. C. Pellandini of the Legal Division of the ICRC for drawing my attention to some of these references.

7.   CONCLUSIONS

It is clear that to arrive at an assessment of the status of the principal provisions of Protocols I and II is no easy task. The drafting history reveals that many provisions involved a subtle mixture of codification and development. Practice since 1977 is, to say the least, an uncertain guide. Yet the task is an important one and, so long as many of the major military powers are not Parties to Protocol I, a very practical one. The theme of this volume is to examine the challenges for humanitarian law in the last decade of the twentieth century. In many respects the biggest of those challenges is to make what was traditionally known as 'Hague Law' work. To stand any chance of doing that, it is necessary to have a clear understanding of what that law requires. Unless and until the Protocols achieve the same degree of acceptance as the Geneva Conventions, that will require a close examination of customary international law as it stands now after the adoption of the Protocols.

That is not to say that those provisions which do not have the status of customary international law will be devoid of impact in conflicts where the Protocols are not formally applicable. Such provisions may well be important as a convenient point of reference or an indication of the political expectations of parties to the conflict or the international community as a whole. As time passes, many of them will become part of the customary law or will influence it in various ways. Yet the combatant is entitled to ask the humanitarian lawyer 'what are the rules that apply today?'. That is a question which can only be answered -and a challenge which can only be met- by an examination of customary law.

THE 1977 ADDITIONAL PROTOCOLS AND GENERAL INTERNATIONAL LAW: SOME PRELIMINARY REFLEXIONS

GEORGES ABI-SAAB

1.   INTRODUCTION

It was at the Conference of Government Experts on the Reaffirmation and Development of Humanitarian Law Applicable in Armed Conflicts (1971-1972) that I first met Frits Kalshoven, after having just read and appreciated his 'Belligerent Reprisals'.[1] Since then I have come to know him better and appreciate even more his knowledge, expertise and sense of humour.

The Conference of Government Experts was a significant moment in the process that culminated in the adoption in 1977 of the two Protocols Additional to the Geneva Conventions. Thirteen years after their adoption by the Diplomatic Conference, however, the Protocols have yet to command as wide an acceptance as the Conventions they are intended to supplement.

This state of affairs, as well as the sense of crisis it generated at one point, but no longer, are largely attributed to the refusal by the United

---

1   F. Kalshoven, Belligerent Reprisals (1971).

States Government to ratify Protocol I (and its attempt under the Reagan Administration even to discredit it)[2] and the impact of this hostile attitude on allies and adversaries alike.

It is in this context that custom has been increasingly referred to. Indeed, in his letter of transmittal of Protocol II to the Senate for its advice and consent to ratification, President Reagan, after stating his reasons for discarding Protocol I, adds:

'... we can reject Protocol I as a reference for humanitarian law, and at the same time devise an alternative reference for the positive provisions of Protocol I that could be of real humanitarian benefit if generally observed by the parties to international armed conflicts. We are therefore in the process of consulting with our allies to develop appropriate methods for incorporating these positive provisions into the rules that govern our military operations, *as customary international law* (emphasis added).'[3]

The question raised here of the relationship between general multilateral codification conventions dealing with humanitarian law and custom is not new. It suffices to recall the famous 'Martens Clause' which figures in the Preamble of the 1899 Hague Convention (and most subsequent humanitarian law instruments):

'Until a more complete code of the laws of war is issued, the High Contracting Parties think it right to declare that in cases not included in the Regulations adopted by them, populations and belligerents remain under the protection and empire of the principles of international law, as they result from the usages established between civilized nations, from the laws of humanity and the requirements of the public conscience.'[4]

One could also mention the famous finding by the Nuremberg International Military Tribunal that, by 1939, the Hague Regulations had

---

2   See for example the very strong language used by President Reagan in *Message from the President of the United States Transmitting the Protocol II Additional to the Geneva Conventions ...,* US Senate, 29 January 1987, 100th Congress, 1st Session. According to the President: '... we must not, and need not, give recognition and protection to terrorist groups as a price of progress in humanitarian law.' *Ibid.,* at IV. In the same vein, Secretary of State Shultz who, referring to Protocol I, speaks of 'a debasement of our values, and of humanitarian law itself'. *Ibid.,* at X.

3   *Ibid.,* at IV.

4   Repr. in D. Schindler, J. Toman, eds., The Laws of Armed Conflict; A Collection of Conventions, Resolutions and Documents 64 (1981).

passed into custom and thus become binding on parties and non-parties alike.[5]

But what is new in the United States invocation of custom in connexion with Protocol I is its reductionist or destructive intent. Its purpose is not to preserve what is left out of the codification convention (as does the Martens Clause), nor to extend its application beyond its conventional limits (as did the Nuremberg Tribunal), but to pick and choose from what is already included therein those provisions which suit its purposes, while scuttling the rest. In other words, it seeks to undo what has already been agreed upon at the stages of negotiation and signature of the Protocol (which it did sign), and to unpack a 'package deal' which was reached after lengthy and laborious negotiations and at the cost of great concessions on all sides, but mainly to the United States.

Custom is thus solicited by those who want to scuttle the Protocols or reduce them to their own desired minimum, as it can be by those who would like to extend their reach beyond the conventional community.

In view of the exaggerations and distortions that such contentious reference to custom can and has given rise to, all this essay proposes to do is to bring the debate on the relationship between the Protocols and general international law (I prefer 'general international law' to 'custom' in this context for reasons which will become apparent) within reasonable legal bounds, permitting a realistic assessment of the place and prospects of the Protocols in international humanitarian law.

To that end, and proceeding by successive approximations, I would like to make four remarks by way of theoretical or technical clarification.

2.   THE PROSPECTS OF THE PROTOCOLS AS TREATIES

My first remark, and point of departure, concerns the performance and prospects of the Protocols (particularly Protocol I) *qua* treaties. For the larger the conventional community, the more the treaty approximates the status of general international law.

In this respect, the Protocols are leading a normal life cycle as general multilateral conventions (*traités-lois*) in our present-day and increasingly

---

5   *Judgement of the International Military Tribunal for the Trial of Major War Criminals*, HMSO (1946), Cmd. 6964, at 64. This finding neutralized the limiting effect of the 'general participiation' or *si omnes* clause figuring in the Conventions. See also *Judgement of the International Military Tribunal for the Far East of 1948, UN War Crimes Commission*, 15 Law Reports of Trials of War Criminals 15 (1949).

complex international community. While by no means spectacular, the pace of ratifications and accessions is not much worse or different from that of most similar law-making conventions, including the Geneva Conventions themselves for that matter, if one allows for the changing context.[6] States take their time in such matters; their decision-making process can be multipolar and laborious; their attention can be absorbed by more urgent and competing needs.

In a Colloquium convened by the Faculty of Law of the University of Geneva in June 1987 to celebrate the tenth anniversary of the adoption of the Protocols, and which I had the pleasure of attending with Professor Kalshoven, one or the participants declared that in the calculus of international relations, sometimes one and one may add up to a hundred, while a hundred minus two may yield a nought; the two in both cases being the Superpowers. In my concluding remarks as chairman of that session on 'Future prospects', I responded to the argument in the following terms:

'I am not convinced of the veracity of this calculus in this specific context. It is too deterministic. For even if both the US and the USSR keep away, there will still remain a possibility for the Protocols to apply. Let me explain how, by drawing an analogy with the 'nuclear reservation'. The real import of this reservation is that those who make it declare that they will apply the rules in conventional wars, but not when it comes to nuclear deterrence, i.e., the possibility of nuclear retaliation. The same logic can be applied at one remove. We can imagine that in wars between the Superpowers, the Protocols will not apply; but that they do in wars between smaller States.

The US and the USSR are of course very powerful. They may try, but I do not think that they are necessarily able to impose the rules of the game on all the others, particularly if they do not act in unison. Now, if one of the Superpowers joins the Protocols, the conventional community will still be imperfect, but it becomes workable at a much higher level of effectiveness. We should not consider the fate of the Protocols as an all or nothing proposition. There are many possible scenarios. For example, the US has not ratified the Human Rights Covenants, but the system is working. It may not be very efficient, and perhaps it is not very good; but

---

6   For an extremely interesting and extensive comparative study of this aspect, see R. Abi-Saab, *Le degré d'acceptation des Protocoles de 1977 après 10 ans: ratifications, adhésions, réserves, décisions de ne pas en devenir partie*, Report, University of Geneva, Colloquium on Les Protocoles de Genève de 1977 additionnels aux Conventions de 1949: dix ans après (1987).

it has impregnated the body politic of the international community. And who knows, the US may end up joining after all, as they did with the 1925 Protocol fifty years later.

The very existence of such legal instruments progressively structures the international legal environment. However light and imperceptible their imprint may be at the beginning, they can end up imposing themselves as legal facts of international life even on the highest and mightiest.[7]

In the meantime, *i.e.*, since 1987, we have witnessed the realization of one of the above-mentioned scenarios, though overtaken and improved upon by the quickening pace of change in the international environment. First, the front of the United States allies started to crumble as they ratified the Protocols one after the other, though with some reservations or interpretative declarations.[8] More important still was the ratification of the Protocols by the Soviet Union in 1989 without any reservation or interpretative declaration, quickly followed by its (now former) Warsaw Pact allies. Ratifications and accessions by Third World States are steadily forthcoming, though not at a very accelerated pace, and with some noticeable absences.

These developments put paid to the prior malaise and sense of crisis and concern about the prospects of the Protocols as general multilateral conventions *à vocation universelle*. But they have not disposed of the question of the relationship between the protocols and general international law as long as the Protocols do not approximate the near universal level of acceptance of the Geneva Conventions, which nobody questions that they express general international law.

3.   THE MAIN CONTRIBUTION OF THE PROTOCOLS:
     REAFFIRMING PRE-EXISTING LAW

This brings me to my second remark which is that quantitively speaking, the greatest contribution of the Protocols is not in introducing new rules, but in specifying the meaning and import of the general principles and provisions of the Conventions -and to a lesser extent the Hague Regulations- in the conditions of present-day warfare. Most of the provisions of the Protocols fall into this category.

---

7   The proceedings of the Colloquium (supra n. 6) have not yet been published.
8   See Abi-Saab, loc. cit. n. 6, at 29-42.

This is a very important contribution (comparable to that of judicial decisions). Through fleshing out and thickening the texture of existing rules and principles it makes for their more effective implementation and reduces the margin of interpretative controversies. Viewed from the angle of the theory of sources, however, it is not considered as normatively creative. This means that there is no need at all to invoke custom or general international law is this context which formally involves the mere interpretation of pre-existing law.

Even the most contested provisions of Protocol I can be considered (and have been put forward well before the adoption of the Protocol) as interpretations of the 1949 Conventions, including Article 1(4) and Article 96(3) on wars of national liberation,[9] Article 44 on the status of prisoner of war in guerrilla warfare,[10] and the Articles concerning aerial bombardments in Part IV on civilian population (in relation to the law of The Hague, particularly the rule of discrimination).

It is true that while certain general principles or rules can be generally accepted, controversy may arise at a certain level of specification regarding their content and implications. But this argument can in no way be accepted where the specification in question derives by necessary implication from the accepted general principle (as for example the rules concerning the protection of the civilians against aerial bombardments in Protocol I). It would amount, in such a case, to introducing an exception or a limitation to the already accepted principle or rule via a so-called 'interpretation', and repudiating totally or partially an existing obligation. The fact that these necessary implications figure in a convention to which the State in question is not a party does not make them any less binding on that State, as are the principles or rules from which they derive.

Moreover, if the principle or the rule is considered as a norm of general international law, there is no way of preventing States, international organizations, NGO's and municipal and international tribunals from invoking the codification convention as the proper interpretation of that norm even against a State which is not party to that convention. This is precisely what the ICJ did in the *Nicaragua Case*[11] where it was barred by the United States reservations from applying the

---

9 See G. Abi-Saab, *Wars of National Liberation and the Laws of War*, 3 Annales d'Etudes Internationales 93-117 (1972).

10 See, for example, some of the suggestions by D. Bindschedler-Robert, A Reconsideration of the Law of Armed Conflict; the Law of Armed Conflict 52 *et seq.* (1969).

11 Military and Paramilitary Activities in and against Nicaragua (*Nicaragua* v. *United States of America*), ICJ Reports 1986, at 14.

multilateral treaties binding on the parties *in casu*, but used them extensively all the same to interpret the principles of general international law to which they give expression.[12]

4. THE DEVELOPMENT COMPONENT: TOWARDS GENERAL INTERNATONAL LAW

Even where there is a normative increment, *i.e.*, where the Protocols introduce new law, we have to keep in mind that they belong to a special category of treaties, the law-making multilateral conventions (*traités-lois*), and more particularly and significantly to a sub-species of this category which has, to use the language of the ICJ, 'a purely humanitarian and civilizing purpose'.[13]

This explains their special technical and substantive characteristics (*e.g.* the absolute and *erga omnes* character of their obligations);[14] but above all it makes for their universal vocation and explains the general tendency to consider them as having a particular propensity to 'generalize', *i.e.*, to pass into general international law, and to view this contingency as a normal stage or the normal outcome of their development. It has sometimes been suggested[15] -on the basis of the findings of the post-war International Military Tribunals-[16] that there is a presumption to that effect, whether rebuttable (Tokyo) or irrebuttable (Nuremberg).

To explain such a tendency (whether we consider it a legal presumption or a mere predisposition), and root it in international law, one does not necessarily have to call on custom and go through the stringent operation of proving the existence of its two elements in relation to each and every provision of the Protocol. Indeed the ICJ has operated a significant and useful shift in the *Nicaragua Case*,[17] by referring not so much to custom but to general international law. In fact what one tries to achieve through

---

12 *Cf.*, R. Abi-Saab, *The 'General Principles' of Humanitarian Law according to the International Court of Justice*, International Review of the Red Cross 367-375 (1987).

13 Advisory Opinion Concerning Reservations to the Convention on Genocide, ICJ Reports 1951, at 23.

14 *Cf.*, G. Abi-Saab, *The Specificities of Humanitarian Law*, in C. Swinarski, ed., Studies and Essays on International Humanitarian Law and Red Cross Principles in Honour of Jean Pictet 266-273 (1984).

15 See R. Baxter, *Multilateral Treaties as Evidence of Customary International Law*, 41 BYIL 299 (1965-1966).

16 See also *supra* n. 5.

17 Loc. cit. n. 11.

an exercise such as the reaffirmation and development of humanitarian law is to launch rules into the orbit of general international law. Up to now we knew (or recognized) only one vector or process capable of achieving this result: custom. But there is no reason why such a result cannot be reached by other means or vectors, such as successive treaties; as is indeed the pattern of development of humanitarian legal norms which evolve from convention to convention, each updating and perfecting the former in response to changing conditions and in the light of experience.[18]

As time passes and the circle of formal participants widens, the new updated instrument as a normative whole -and not some of its isolated provisions here and there- (with the possible exception of those establishing new institutional and procedural arrangements), ends up structuring expectations and the legal environment as the only standard of reference; whence *opinio juris* if you like. But to me, there are no two feelings of legal obligation: one by way of treaty, the other by way of custom. Either there is a generalized feeling that one is legally bound or not.

Indeed, there is no logical reason why such a generalized feeling should only emerge from a number of precedents considered sufficient to establish the existence of a general custom, and not from a treaty accepted by a large (and growing) number of States, in any case larger than those involved in the above-mentioned precedents (leaving aside for the moment the case of possible objectors).

5.   THEORETICAL MISCONCEPTIONS AND CLARIFICATIONS

If we want, nevertheless, to call on custom, it is necessary to dispel some current theoretical misconceptions which are used, without much fear of contradiction, to depict the passage of the Protocols into general international law either as an insuperable task or as a simple matter of wilful choice, depending on one's likes and dislikes of the provisions in question.

5.1   The crystallizing effect of codification treaties

One such fallacy is the oft-repeated assertion that the customary components of the Protocols are limited to those rules which existed as such before the elaboration of the Protocols.

---

18 See G. Abi-Saab, loc. cit. n. 14, at 273-277.

The fallacy of this assertion lies in its partial character, in the artificiality of the 'before' and 'after' approach. For things may happen 'during' or in between. In other words, it does not see or allow for the impact of the process of negotiating the Protocols on customary rules regardless of the outcome of the negotiations, *i.e.*, even outside the Protocols as such. The ICJ envisaged such a possibility in its famous Judgement in the *North Sea Continental Shelf Cases* of 1969,[19] where it considered that a codification treaty can affect custom in three different ways: it can have a 'declaratory effect' of pre-existing custom; a 'crystallizing effect', whereby the process of negotiation, formulation and adoption of the Convention in itself brings to maturity customary rules that were still in process of formation; or a 'generating effect' of new customary rule along the line of its provisions.[20]

Thus one should not only look backwards to what existed before the Protocols. One has to look at the situation during and at the end of the negotiations, as well as beyond it, in order to identify what might have become customary law in the meantime as a direct or indirect result of the process of codification and progressive development. UNCLOS III provides us with telling examples in this respect, such as the institution of the Exclusive Economic Zone (EEZ).

5.2   Practice and motivations

Another such fallacy concerns the way to gauge or prove *opinio juris*. It has been suggested, for example, that those who ratify or accede to the Protocols, because they think that the occasion will never arise for the Protocols to apply to them, but only to others, as well as those who invoke the provisions of the Protocols against others but contest them when they are invoked against themselves, are not significant and should not be counted for the purposes of assessing the existence of a generalized *opinio juris*.

That States harbour such motivations and act in such a manner may well be true; in which case it would be selfish, and self-serving behaviour. But it is also *rational* behaviour. No law would have any chance of

---

19 ICJ Reports 1969, §§ 61-62, at 38.

20 The triptych is that of Judge Jimenez de Arechaga, former President of the ICJ, in his general course at The Hague: *International Law in the Past Third of a Century*, I RCADI 14-22 (1978). See also G. Abi-Saab, *La coutume dans tous ses états, ou le dilemme du développement du droit international général dans un monde éclaté*, in International Law at the Time of its Codification: Essays in Honour of Roberto Ago 53-65 (1987).

emerging if we assume that it can exist only by going against the grain of human nature and self interest, *i.e.*, only if States act in total abnegation.

What counts is that a State has openly taken position or revealed a sense of legal obligation, regardless of the underlying motivation, which in any case remains a matter of conjecture. Even the hypocritical and self-interested behaviour of States, including the samples just mentioned, forms part of the stuff of which customary law is made, if we consider custom, as we should, as an interactive and cumulative process which works itself out in time or along a time schedule (and not merely at a given point of time), and which takes hold through the recurrence and reversibility of situations over time.

For example, country A invokes a rule against country B in a given situation. Subsequently, after a short or a long while, it may find itself in a situation where the shoe is on the other foot, where country C is invoking the same rule against it. Country A cannot then say: '... this is not a customary rule binding on me', because it has already invoked it as such against State B. This is the 'widening circle' effect of custom, as it emerges through such interactions. Thus, even a self-serving position can contribute to law or custom creation; because it is self-serving in a specific context, but can have a legal significance which transcends that context, whatever the motivation of the actor at the time.

5.3   The case of the persistent objector

If a widespread or generalized (rather than unanimous) practice and *opinio juris* suffice to establish the existence of a general rule of customary law, this does not take into account the case of the 'persistent objector'.

Much is made of this vague theory, to the effect that a State which cannot prevent a customary rule from emerging, can at least -by its continued resistance- keep itself out of its ambit. And this on the basis of a single dictum of the ICJ in the *Norwegian Fisheries Case*,[21] which has been stretched out of context and out of all proportion. This is no place for undertaking a detailed critical analysis of this theory. It suffices for the purposes of our subject to make a few clarifications. First, a fundamental distinction has to be made between special and general or universal custom. Special custom (whether bilateral, regional or otherwise) ulitmately rests on consent, and can thus easily accommodate a phenomenon like the 'persistent objector'; but not so universal custom.

---

21 ICJ Reports 1951, at 131.

One has also to distinguish the special context in which the Court's dictum was formulated, that of territorial delimitations, where as a result of the interplay of such legal institutions as effeciveness and acquiescence, historic waters, historic title, etc., every case is almost a special case, or has its own special legal regime in which consent (or lack of it) plays a crucial role. This is a very special and different context from that of general international law, as of general law-making conventions, with their manifest legislative intent, particularly when it comes to rules relating to community interests, as is the case of humanitarian law.

In this latter context the persistent objector can only be a transient phenomenon. Either it succeeds in preventing the rule from emerging and asserting itself as part of general international law or, if the rule prevails, it is swept away by it; a process which is perfectly illustrated by the resistance to the concept of *jus cogens* in the sixties. And I submit that the same can be said of the resistance to the Protocols today.

5.4　The dangers of unpackaging

My fourth and concluding remark about custom is not by way of clarification but by way of warning; warning against the dangers of excessive eclecticism and voluntarism, and also of contradiction.

It has been contended that all a State that rejects the Protocols has to do is to look at them and decide what is acceptable to it and what is not. The former is customary and applicable even outside the conventional community, but the rest is not.[22] This justification of the 'pick and choose' attitude of States refusing formally to accede to the Protocols -an attitude which by the way perfectly illustrates the self-serving behaviour of States mentioned above- is both technically doubtful and extremely dangerous on legal policy grounds.

---

22 See the quotation from President Reagen's letter of transmittal of Protocol II to Congress. Loc. cit. n. 3. An interesting aspect of this attitude is the conviction it reveals on the part of its holders that they can 'will' those provisions they like into legal existence separate from the Protocols as custom, whether they fulfil the requirements at present of not. This is said explicitly in Secretary of State Schultz's letter, loc. cit. n. 2, at X. Also by the Deputy Legal Adviser of the State Department, M. Matheson, in a workshop at the American University, College of Law in 1987, where he declared: '... in our discussions with our allies to date we have not attempted to reach an agreement on which rules are presently customary law, but instead have focussed on which principles are in our common interest and therefore should be observed and in due course recognized as customary law, whether they are presently part of that law or not.' Repr. in 2 American University Journal of International Law and Policy 422 (1987).

The provisions of the Protocols are not a mere assemblage of norms haphazardly put together. They were produced through a complex process of careful drafting and lengthy negotiations, whose outcome was reached and had to be accepted as a whole, as a package deal. It would be too easy (and this is why it can be as easily dismissed) for those States which kept themselves outside the conventional community to invoke aspects of this integrated legal regulation against the members of the conventional community when it suits their purposes, while refusing to abide by those other apects which do not suit them, using custom as a technical smoke screen. In fact, the interaction of such 'package deals' (the whole, and not the individual components) with custom, as revealed in recent studies such as those of Jennings, Caminos and Molitor,[23] is much more complex and subtle than the above-mentioned simplistic argument would lead us to believe.

Moreover, even if it were technically sound (which, in my submission, it is not), this argument is very dangerous in practice. For can one 'pick and choose' from the Protocols without opening Pandora's box? 'Unpackaging' is a very risky business, because it may end up with the proverbial baby going down with what some consider the bathwater. Once it starts, no one knows beforehand where the process can or will stop; and the erosion effect can go very far indeed.

There is no objective reason for such a pessimistic perspective, however. At the threshold of the hundredth ratification (or accession) of the first (slightly less for the second), the Protocols have gone well beyond the critical stage of their existence as general law-making Conventions; and by the same token along the path of general international law.

---

23 R.Y. Jennings, *Law-Making and Package Deal*, in D. Bardonnet, *et al.*, eds., Mélanges offerts à Paul Reuter 347 (1981); H. Caminos, M. Molitor, *Progressive Development of International Law and the Package Deal*, 79 AJIL 871 (1985).

WHY THE UNITED STATES OF AMERICA SHOULD RATIFY ADDITIONAL PROTOCOL I *

GEORGE H. ALDRICH

1.   Introduction

2.   Importance of the Protocol

3.   Application of the Protocol to wars of national liberation

4.   The status of irregular combatants

5.   Reservations and understandings

6.   Conclusion

1.   INTRODUCTION

Additional Protocol I[1] to the Geneva Conventions of 1949[2] was adopted in 1977 after four years of negotiations in which the Delegation of the

---

* Parts of this essay have appeared in a different form in the American Journal of International Law, 85 AJIL 1 et seq. (1991).

1   For the text of Protocol I Additional to the Geneva Conventions of 12 August 1949, and Relating to the Protection of Victims of International Armed Conflicts, see Diplomatic Conference on the Reaffirmation and Development of International Humanitarian Law Applicable in Armed Conflicts, Final Act (1977), repr. in XVI ILM 1391 (1977); D. Schindler, J. Toman, eds., The Laws of Armed Conflict 551 (1981); A. Roberts, R. Guelff, eds., Documents on the Laws of War 389 (1989). Useful commentaries on the Protocol are found in M. Bothe, K.J. Partsch, W.A. Solf, eds., New Rules for Victims of Armed Conflicts (1982). Also Y. Sandoz, et al., eds., Commentary on the Additional Protocols (1987).

2   Convention for the Amelioration of the Condition of the Wounded and Sick in Armed Forces in the Field, 12 August 1949, 6 UST 3114, TIAS No. 3362, 75 UNTS 31 Geneva Convention I; Convention for the Amelioration of the Condition of the Wounded, Sick and Shipwrecked Members of Armed Forces at Sea, 12 August 1949, 6 UST 3217, TIAS No. 3363, 75 UNTS 85 Geneva Convention II; Convention Relative to the Treatment of Prisoners of War, 12 August 1949, 6 UST 3316, TIAS No. 3364, 75 UNTS 135 Geneva Convention III; Convention Relative to the Protection of Civilian Persons in Time of War, 12 August 1949, 6 UST 3516, TIAS No. 3365, 75 UNTS 287 Geneva Convention IV.

United States was an active participant. I know, because I was the chairman of that delegation. The general satisfaction of the delegation with the Protocol was clear. During the final plenary session of the Diplomatic Conference, I stated the following on behalf of my Government:

> 'The United States welcomes the adoption of Protocol I. We are satisfied that this Protocol represents a major advance in international humanitarian law, an advance of which this Conference can be proud. We hope that it will be signed and ratified by all the States represented in this Conference.'[3]

This statement represented not only my own views or even those of the Department of State; those views were shared fully by the representatives of the Department of Defense. The Office of the Secretary of Defense and the Joint Chiefs of Staff approved our position papers for each annual session of the Diplomatic Conference. Military officers, led by Major General Prugh and Major General Reed, who represented the United States in Committees I and III respectively, played key negotiating roles. Moreover, the United States Delegation as a whole concurred in the conclusions of our report to the Secretary of State that the Conference had 'succeeded beyond our expectations in codifying and developing the law applicable in armed conflict.'[4]

The United States signed both Protocols on 12 December 1977, the day they were opened for signature. With respect to Protocol I, the United States stated two understandings at the time of signature:

a) It is the understanding of the United States of America that the rules established by this protocol were not intended to have any effect on and do not regulate or prohibit the use of nuclear weapons.

b) It is the understanding of the United States of America that the phrase 'military deployment preceding the launching of an attack' in Article 44(3) means any movement towards a place from which an attack is to be launched.[5]

---

3 Statement made in the final plenary session on the adoption of the two Protocols (9 June 1977), repr. in Report of the United States Delegation to the Diplomatic Conference on the Reaffirmation and Development of International Humanitarian Law Applicable in Armed Conflicts, App. D. (8 September 1977).

4 *Ibid.*, at 28.

5 Repr. in Department of the Army Pamphlet 27-1-1, at 138 (1979); Roberts, Guelff, op. cit. n. 1, at 468.

For several years after signature of the Protocol, further consideration was given, both within the United States Government and among Members of the North Atlantic Treaty Organisation (NATO) consulting in Brussels, to the formulation of certain other appropriate understandings or reservations to be made at the time of ratification. Most of these were uncontroversial. The only contentious issue at that time within the United States Government was whether we should reserve certain rights of reprisal that would otherwise be prohibited by the Protocol. When I left Washington in May 1981, the ultimate submission of Protocol I to the Senate for advice and consent to ratification seemed merely a matter of time. It also seemed entirely probable that, like the 1949 Geneva Conventions, Protocol I would eventually achieve nearly universal acceptance.

In the event, acceptance by States other than the United States has proceeded at a reasonable pace, although it is still too soon to be certain that Protocol I will obtain as many Parties as the 1949 Conventions. By July 1990 there were ninety-seven Parties to Protocol I.[6] Included among these are two permanent Members of the UN Security Council -China and the Soviet Union- and nine Members of the NATO: Belgium, Denmark, Greece, Iceland, Italy, Luxembourg, the Netherlands, Norway, and Spain. Moreover, it is my understanding that two other major Powers, Great Britain and Germany have begun the process of ratification. On the other hand, France ratified Protocol II, but not Protocol I, in large part, I believe, because of objections to Protocol I's prohibitions of reprisal, an issue to be addressed *infra*.

In the United States, the Reagan Administration turned against Protocol I. In January 1987, President Reagan informed the Senate that he would

---

6   Algeria, Angola, Antigua and Barbuda, Argentina, Austria, Bahamas, Bahrain, Bangladesh, Barbados, Belgium, Belize, Benin, Byelorussian SSR, Bolivia, Botswana, Bulgaria, Burkina Faso, Cameroon, Central African Republic, China, Comoros, Congo, Costa Rica, Cuba, Cyprus, Czechoslovakia, Democratic People's Republic of Korea, Denmark, Ecuador, El Salvador, Equatorial Guinea, Finland, Gabon, Gambia, Ghana, Greece, Guatemala, Guinea, Guinea-Bissau, Guyana, Holy See, Hungary, Iceland, Italy, Ivory Coast, Jamaica, Jordan, Kuwait, Laos, Liberia, Libyan Arab Jamahiriya, Liechtenstein, Luxembourg, Mali, Malta, Mauritania, Mauritius, Mexico, Mozambique, Namibia (represented by the Council for Namibia), the Netherlands, New Zealand, Niger, Nigeria, Norway, Oman, Qatar, Peru, Republic of Korea, Romania, Rwanda, Saint Christopher and Nevis, Saint Lucia, Saint Vincent and the Grenadines, Solomon Islands, Saudi Arabia, Senegal, Seychelles, Sierra Leone, Soviet Union, Spain, Suriname, Sweden, Switzerland, Syria, Tanzania, Togo, Tunisia, Ukrainian SSR, United Arab Emirates, Uruguay, Vanuatu, Vietnam, Western Samoa, Yemen, Yugoslavia, Zaire. ICRC, 1977 Protocols Additional to the Geneva Conventions of 12 August 1949; Ratifications and Accessions 20 July 1990.

not submit the Protocol to the Senate for its advice and consent to ratification. While he recognized that the Protocol contained many useful provisions, he nevertheless described it as 'fundamentally and irreconcilably flawed'.[7] The principal flaw asserted by the President was that the Protocol would give aid and comfort to terrorists. He said:

> 'But we cannot allow other nations of the world, however numerous, to impose upon us and our allies and friends an unacceptable and thoroughly distasteful price for joining a convention drawn to advance the laws of war. In fact, we must not, and need not, give recognition and protection to terrorist groups as a price for progress in humanitarian law.'[8]

In my view, the negative judgment on the Protocol rendered by the Reagan Administration was itself fundamentally flawed, and I remain confident that either the present American Administration or a successor will reconsider the Protocol and decide to accept it. As a contribution toward such favorable reconsideration, I offer the following comments.

2. IMPORTANCE OF THE PROTOCOL

The Protocol is, without any doubt, the most important treaty codifying and developing international humanitarian law applicable in armed conflicts since the four Geneva Conventions of 1949, and it is the first such Treaty since 1907 to deal with methods and means of warfare and the protection of the civilian population from the effects of warfare. In my view, the following are important treaty provisions that significantly advance or prudently codify the law:

- the fifth paragraph of the Preamble, which states that the provisions of the 1949 Conventions and the Protocol 'must be fully applied in all circumstances to all persons who are protected by those instruments, without any adverse distinction based on the nature or origin of the

---

7 Letter of Transmittal from President Reagan, Protocol II Additional to the 1949 Geneva Conventions, and Relating to the Protection of Victims of Non-international Armed Conflicts, S. Treaty Doc. No. 2, 100th Cong., 1st Sess., at III (1987). Repr. in 81 AJIL 910 (1987).
8 *Ibid.*, at IV.

armed conflict or on the causes espoused by or attributed to the Parties to the conflict';[9]

- the provision of Article 3 stating that the application of the Conventions and of the Protocol shall continue in occupied territory until the termination of the occupation, a provision that amends the more limited provision of Article 6 of Convention IV;[10]

- the provisions of Article 5 which significantly improve the prospects for appointment of protecting powers or substitutes, in particular by requiring each Party to a conflict to respond within two weeks to a request by the International Committee of the Red Cross (ICRC) for a list of five acceptable protecting powers and by obligating those Parties to accept an offer by the ICRC to act as a substitute;[11]

- the provisions of Articles 8-19 which expand the protections accorded wounded, sick, and shipwrecked persons and medical personnel, units and transports; and the provisions of Article 20 prohibiting reprisals against the persons and objects protected by those articles;

- the provisions of Articles 24-31 which greatly expand the protection from attack of medical aircraft, which protection under the 1949 Conventions was virtually non-existent;[12]

- the provisions of Articles 32-34 which are designed to improve the accounting for missing and dead persons and to protect the remains of dead persons and facilitate their return at the end of the conflict;[13]

---

9   This was an important provision from the American perspective in view of the refusal by both North Korea in the nineteen fifties and by North Vietnam in the nineteen sixties and senventies to treat captured American military personnel as prisoners of war and their efforts to justify such refusal by alleging that the United States was an aggressor.

10 Article 6 of Geneva Convention IV, *supra* n. 2, provides that the application of the Convention shall cease one year after the close of military operations but that a number of specified provisions of the Convention will continue to apply for the duration of the occupation. See A. Roberts, *Prolonged Military Occupation: The Israeli-Occupied Territories Since 1967*, 84 AJIL 44, 55 (1990).

11 While a State cannot effectively be compelled against its will to accept a Protecting Power or to permit the delegates of such a Power to scrutinize its compliance with the law in territory under its control, Article 5 will at least make it more difficult and politically costly for a Party to the Protocol to refuse to accept a Protecting Power or substitute in the future.

12 See Geneva Convention I, loc. cit. n. 2, Article 36.

13 The United States proposed these provisions as a result of its experience in the Vietnam War.

- the provisions of Article 36 requiring a Party that develops a new weapon to 'determine whether its employment would, in some or all circumstances,' be prohibited by any rule of international law applicable to that Party;

- the provisions of Article 40 prohibiting a Party from refusing to grant quarter, that is, refusing to take prisoners, or threatening to do so;

- the provisions of Article 41 safeguarding persons who are *hors de combat* and requiring release of prisoners of war in circumstances where their evacuation is impossible;

- the provisions of Article 42 protecting from attack persons parachuting from an aircraft in distress;

- the clarification in Article 44(2) that violations of the laws of war may not be used as an excuse to deprive captured combatants of their right to protection as prisoners of war, with the sole exception, in paragraphs 3 and 4, of irregular combatants who fail to comply with the minimum requirements prescribed in paragraph 3 of carrying arms openly;[14]

- the clear statement in Article 48 of the principle of distinction between combatants and military objectives on the one hand and the civilian population and civilian objects on the other;

- the provisions of Article 51 prohibiting (i) acts or threats of violence the primary purpose of which is to spread terror among the civilian population, (ii) indiscriminate attacks, including target area bombardment of cities, towns, or villages and those attacks that violate the rule of proportionality, and (iii) the direction of the movement of civilians in order to use them to shield military objectives from attacks;

- the definition of which objects can be military objectives in Article 52;

- the prohibition of the use of starvation of civilians as a method of warfare in Article 54(1);

---

14 Both North Korea and North Vietnam alleged that American pilots, in particular, had committed war crimes and used that allegation as a justification for denying them prisoner of war treatment.

- the precautionary measures prescribed by Article 56 intended to prevent, where possible, the release of dangerous forces (water and radiation) contained by dams, dikes, and nuclear power stations;

- the fundamental guarantees of humane treatment required by Article 75 to be accorded to any persons who are in the power of a Party to the conflict and who do not benefit from more favorable treatment, including that Party's own nationals; and

- the permanent International Fact-Finding Commission established by Article 90 to enquire into allegations of grave breaches or other serious violations of the 1949 Conventions and the Protocol and to facilitate, through its good offices, compliance with the law. The potential importance of the Commission has been greatly increased by the recent, surprising acceptance of its competence by the Soviet Union. As of September 1990, there were nineteen such acceptances.[15] When there are twenty, the Commission is to be formed. In my view, it should be an important objective for the United States to ratify the Protocol, accept the competence of the Commission, and persuade as many other States as possible to do likewise.

In view of the importance of these contributions to the law -an importance which, with a very few exceptions, even the Reagan Administration did not deny- one would have thought that the Protocol's defects would have to be very serious indeed -and not curable by means of reservations or understandings- if they were to justify rejection of the Protocol. And so they were seen by an Administration that willfully distorted the meaning of several articles in order to declare the Protocol unacceptable. While the Administration made reference in passing to objections to certain provisions by the Joint Chiefs of Staff, it is clear that political and ideological considerations were determinative. Let us examine these considerations.

---

15 Sweden, Finland, Norway, Switzerland, Denmark, Austria, Uruguay, Italy, Belgium, Iceland, the Netherlands, New Zealand, Malta, Spain, Liechtenstein, Algeria, Soviet Union, Byelorussian SSR, and Ukranian SSR.

3.   APPLICATION OF THE PROTOCOL TO WARS OF
      NATIONAL LIBERATION

The most complete public explanation of the arguments made against the
Protocol within the Reagan Administration is set forth in a brief essay
entitled The Rationale for the United States Decision by the Legal Adviser
of the State Department, Sofaer, that appeared in 1988 in the American
Journal of International Law.[16] It is clear from that article, which is
consistent with the formal transmittal documents sent to the Senate in
1987, that the decisive factor in the Administration's decision was Article
1(4) of the Protocol, which deals with wars of national liberation.

Article 1 of the Protocol provides, in paragraph 3, that the Protocol,
which supplements the 1949 Geneva Conventions, 'shall apply in the
situations referred to in Article 2 common to those Conventions', that is,
to all armed conflicts between two or more of the Parties to the
Conventions. In Article 1(4), the Protocol adds the following:

'The situations referred to in the preceding paragraph include armed
conflicts in which peoples are fighting against colonial domination and alien
occupation and against racist regimes in the exercise of their right of self-
determination, as enshrined in the Charter of the United Nations and the
Declaration on Principles of International Law concerning Friendly
Relations and Co-operation among States in accordance with the Charter of
the United Nations.'

The Reagan Administration argued that this provision is harmful
because it makes wars of national liberation international (rather than
internal) armed conflicts on the basis of the perceived 'just' nature of those
conflicts, because it would grant those fighting for such movements
immunity from prosecution for belligerent acts, and because treating as
soldiers members of groups like the PLO that often use terrorist tactics
undesirably enhances their stature 'to the detriment of the civilized world
community'.[17]

Certainly it is true that most Western States, including the United
States, reacted negatively at the Diplomatic Conference when paragraph 4

---

16   82 AJIL 784 (1988).
17   *Ibid.*, at 786. Similar points are made in remarks prepared by the Legal Adviser for delivery
     to a Workshop on International Humanitarian Law at the Washington College of Law,
     American University, Washington, D.C., on 22 January 1987. The text of those remarks is
     published in 2 Am.U.J.Int'l L.& Pol'y 415, 460 (1987).

was first adopted in committee, primarily out of concern either that it could import into humanitarian law the dangerous concept of the just war and might lead to provisions limiting protections of the law to those engaged in 'just wars', or that it could be construed to justify external intervention in such wars. In the end, however, we were successful in our efforts to include in the Preamble to the Protocol two key provisions, noted *supra*, which obviate these risks: a provision that requires the protections accorded by the Geneva Conventions and the Protocol to be fully applied 'without any adverse distinction based on the nature or origin of the armed conflict or on the causes espoused by or attributed to the Parties to the conflict' and a provision that nothing in the Protocol 'can be construed as legitimizing or authorizing any act of aggression or any other use of force inconsistent with the Charter of the United Nations'.[18] Moreover, the Conference also adopted Article 96(3) which provides as follows:

'The authority representing a people engaged against a High Contracting Party in an armed conflict of the type referred to in Article 1(4) may undertake to apply the Conventions and this Protocol in relation to that conflict by means of a unilateral declaration addressed to the depositary. Such declaration shall, upon its receipt by the depositary, have in relation to that conflict the following effects:

a) the Conventions and this Protocol are brought into force for the said authority as a Party to the conflict with immediate effect;

b) the said authority assumes the same rights and obligations as those which have been assumed by a High Contracting Party to the Conventions and this Protocol; and

c) the Conventions and this Protocol are equally binding upon all Parties to the conflict.'

As a result of this provision, in the absence of such a declaration, the Conventions and Protocol have by their terms no application to wars of national liberation. Members of the armed forces of a national liberation movement do not therefore enjoy the protections of those treaties unless the movement formally accepts all the obligations of the Conventions and the Protocol in the same way as the State Parties. Few, if any, liberation

---

18 Also Article 4, which provides:
'The application of the Conventions and of this Protocol, as well as the conclusion of the agreements provided for therein, shall not affect the legal status of the Parties to the conflict. Neither the occupation of a territory nor the application of the Conventions and this Protocol shall affect the legal status of the territory in question.'

movements could expect to be in a position to carry out such obligations unless and until they were about to succeed in becoming the Government of the State. In any event, members of the armed forces of liberation movements are not granted protections simply because they may be deemed to be fighting for a just cause; the Protocol and the Conventions must apply equally to both sides if they are to apply to the conflict at all.

Article 1(4) was designed by its sponsors with certain conflicts in mind, specifically those in Palestine and southern Africa and was drafted in terms fashioned to exclude its application to civil wars within existing States. That is why it uses derogatory terms like 'colonial domination', 'alien occupation', and 'racist regimes'; indeed, the use of these terms goes far to ensure that the provision will never be applied.[19] First, the language by itself may deter the main target States from acceding to the Protocol so long as liberation struggles persist in territory under their control. Second, if a State Party to the Protocol should find itself suppressing a rebellion, it is not likely to agree that it is a 'colonial' power or is engaged in 'alien occupation' or is a 'racist regime'; and, if it does not agree that it fits within one of those categories, the provision simply will not be applied. Third, liberation movements are unlikely to file declarations under Article 96, in which case the State involved need not address the question at all. In all the years since the signing of Protocol I, not a single declaration has been filed under Article 96.[20]

In sum, Article 1(4) poses no threat to the United States or its NATO allies and needs no reservation. If it were feasible to apply the Geneva Conventions and Protocol I to the armed conflicts to which that provision is intended to apply, compliance with these treaties could bring significant humanitarian benefits. Such application and compliance have not been

---

19 Solf also points out that the reference in paragraph 4 to the UN Declaration on Friendly Relations was intended to give an additional basis for States other than South Africa, Rhodesia, and Israel to deny that any armed conflict they might face was a war of national liberation. W.A. Solf, *A Response to Douglas J. Feith's Law in the Service of Terror - The Strange Case of the Additional Protocol*, 20 Akron L. Rev. 261 (1986).

20 On 3 December 1980, the ANC made a 'Declaration' to the ICRC limited to an intention to respect the 'general principles of humanitarian law applicable in armed conflicts'. The Declaration was annexed to a letter from the Chairman of the UN Special Committee against Apartheid to the Secretary General, UN Doc. A/35/710 (1980). The Declaration did not refer specifically to Article 1(4) or to Article 96, but referred to the Geneva Conventions and Protocol in the following terms:
'Wherever practically possible, the African National Congress of South Africa will endeavour to respect the rules of the four Geneva Conventions of 1949 for the victims of armed conflicts and the 1977 Additional Protocol I relating to the protection of victims of international armed conflicts.'

feasible and seem unlikely to become feasible for a multitude of reasons, both political and practical. In effect, the provision is a dead letter.

One may easily understand the political reasons why Israel and South Africa are unwilling at present to accede to Protocol I, but it does not follow that the United States should feel compelled to go so far in support as to join them in rejecting the Protocol because of Article 1(4).

4.   THE STATUS OF IRREGULAR COMBATANTS

The Reagan Administration argued further that the problems it saw in the wars of national liberation provision were compounded by Article 44 of the Protocol insofar as it relates to members of irregular military groups. In particular, it alleged that, by eliminating the pre-existing requirements that irregulars must have at all times a 'fixed distinctive sign recognizable at a distance' and that the irregular group as such must conduct its operations in accordance with the laws and customs of war, the Article increases the risks to the civilian population.[21] On the contrary, the Article is a serious and thoughtful attempt to *improve* the protection of the civilian population in occupied territory. To understand it, we must start with the legal situation as it existed before the Protocol.

The 1949 Geneva Convention Relative to the Treatment of Prisoners of War established four requirements that had to be met by irregular armed forces for their members to be entitled, if captured, to be treated as prisoners of war:

a) that of being commanded by a person responsible for his subordinates;
b) that of having a fixed distinctive sign recognizable at a distance;
c) that of carrying arms openly;
d) that of conducting their operations in accordance with the laws and customs of war.[22]

It requires no great knowledge of history or of the realities of military resistance activities in occupied territory to recognize that only rarely can all of these requirements be met. Except perhaps for irregular units in isolated, mountainous areas, such as parts of Yugoslavia or the French Alps during World War II, irregular armed forces in occupied territory

---

21 Letter of Transmittal, loc. cit. n. 7, at IV.
22 Geneva Convention III, loc. cit. n. 2, Article 4(A,2).

cannot possibly comply with the second of these conditions and hope to survive. Moreover, the fourth condition serves as a convenient excuse for an occupying power to treat *all* captured irregulars as terrorists because *some* may have committed war crimes. The predictable result of the conditions set forth in the 1949 Convention, unfortunately demonstrated by history, is that irregulars will make *no* effort to comply with those conditions, that *all* civilians consequently become suspect in the eyes of the occupying power, and that the civilian population will suffer as a result.[23] Although the Geneva Diplomatic Conference could not be certain that it would be possible to revise the requirements in a way that would offer irregulars adequate inducements to comply with the law, thereby achieving a real increase in the protection of the civilian population, it could not responsibly have avoided trying.

The solution found by the Conference begins with Article 43, which treats as combatants all members of the armed forces, groups and units of a Party to the conflict, including irregulars, provided that they are 'under a command responsible to that Party for the conduct of its subordinates.' The Article further provides that: 'Such armed forces shall be subject to an internal disciplinary system which, *inter alia*, shall enforce compliance with the rules of international law applicable in armed conflict'. It is clear, I believe, that the absence of either the required command link to a Party to the conflict or the internal disciplinary system to enforce compliance with the law would justify a refusal to consider the force, group, or unit in question as covered by Article 43.[24] This would also justify a consequent refusal to accord the personnel of such a unit the right to be combatants or, if captured, to be prisoners of war.

Having defined combatants in Article 43, the Protocol proceeds in Article 44(1) to state that all captured combatants are prisoners of war. As noted *supra*, paragraph 2 provides that although all combatants are obligated to comply with the laws of war, violations of those laws shall not deprive a combatant of his status as a combatant or of his right to be prisoner of war. This provision is one that the United States was most anxious to obtain because of our own experience in Korea and Vietnam, where all our personnel captured by the enemy were denied POW treatment by specious allegations of war crimes. Criminal responsibility for war crimes is and should be individual, based on proof of individual guilt

---

23 See, Bothe, Partsch, Solf, eds., op. cit. n. 1, at 244; J. Stone, *Legal Controls of International Conflict* 566 (1954); G.H. Aldrich, *New Life for the Laws of War*, 75 AJIL 764, 768-70 (1981).

24 *Accord*, ICRC Commentary, loc. cit. n. 1, §§ 1672-1675.

established before an appropriate tribunal, not collective, based on allegations of group responsibility. If an irregular unit is under a command responsible to a Party to the conflict and has an internal disciplinary system that enforces compliance with the laws of war, why should it be treated differently in this regard from a regular unit?

Paragraphs 3 and 4 of Article 44 deal with the requirement of carrying arms openly. They need to be read carefully:

> '3. In order to promote the protection of the civilian population from the effects of hostilities, combatants are obliged to distinguish themselves from the civilian population while they are engaged in an attack or in a military operation preparatory to an attack. Recognizing, however, that there are situations in armed conflicts where, owing to the nature of the hostilities an armed combatant cannot so distinguish himself, he shall retain his status as a combatant, provided that, in such situations, he carries his arms openly:
> a) during each military engagement, and
> b) during such time as he is visible to the adversary while he is engaged in a military deployment preceding the launching of an attack in which he is to participate.
>
> Acts which comply with the requirements of this paragraph shall not be considered as perfidious within the meaning of Article 37, paragraph 1(c).
>
> 4. A combatant who falls into the power of an adverse Party while failing to meet the requirements set forth in the second sentence of paragraph 3 shall forfeit his right to be a prisoner of war, but he shall, nevertheless, be given protections equivalent in all respects to those accorded to prisoners of war by the Third Convention and by this Protocol. This protection includes protections equivalent to those accorded to prisoners of war by the Third Convention in the case where such a person is tried and punished for any offenses he has committed.

The first sentence of paragraph 3 states the general rule and requires combatants to distinguish themselves from the civilian population at all times during attacks and during military operations preparatory to an attack. Any combatant who fails to do so is subject to punishment - not by loss of POW status, but by criminal sanctions for violating the rule.[25] What is not required is that an irregular must distinguish himself at all times. This provision recognizes the reality that some irregulars in

---

25 States should, of course, ensure that this offense is made criminal under their law if it is not already criminal, and that appropriate penalties are provided.

occupied territory will, of necessity, be part-time soldiers - bakers by day and soldiers by night. It represents the judgment of the Geneva Conference, in which the US Delegation joined, that it makes sense to encourage part-time combatants to comply with the rule of distinction during attacks and military operations preparatory to attack by recognizing their combatant status and POW rights if they do so and by subjecting them to criminal penalties if they fail to do so. Admittedly, the phrase 'military operation preparatory to an attack' is imprecise and will have to be interpreted in practice in the light of concrete factual situations, but it is the irregular who runs the risk that flows from such lack of precision, not his adversaries. It will be the captor who has to decide whether to prosecute a captured irregular for violation of that first sentence of paragraph 3, and it will be the military courts of the captor that will have to decide whether anyone prosecuted is guilty of a violation.

The second sentence of paragraph 3 and paragraph 4 carry further the possible sanctions for an irregular combatant's failure to distinguish himself from the civilian population. These provisions recognize that a failure to carry arms openly can, in certain circumstances, create such serious risks for the civilian population that this failure must be discouraged by greater sanctions - the loss of combatant and prisoner of war status and the consequent punishment of the individual as a common criminal.[26] The circumstances in which these greater sanctions may be imposed for a failure of distinction are the following: first, if the situation is not one 'where, owing to the nature of the hostilities' he 'cannot' so distinguish himself; second, if he fails to carry his arms openly during a 'military engagement'; or third, if he fails to carry his arms openly 'during such time as he is visible to the adversary while he is engaged in a military deployment preceding the launching of an attack'. Insofar as each of the quoted situations is ambiguous, the protection accorded by this Article to irregulars may be less than it seems, because it is the captor Power and its tribunals that will have to interpret it.

Moreover, it is open to any State, when it becomes a Party to Protocol I, to make its acceptance subject to understandings, as well as

---

26 Solf points out that irregulars who fail to meet the minimum standards of paragraph 4 and thus forfeit their rights to POW status are vulnerable, not only to trial as common criminals, but also for breaches of the law of armed conflict, for example, perfidy, as prohibited by Article 37 of the Protocol. Solf, loc. cit. n. 19, at 279.

reservations.[27] I would expect that a number of States, including the United States, might wish to express their understanding of at least some of these terms in Article 44. As noted above, the United States expressed its understanding of the phrase 'military deployment preceding the launching of an attack' at the time of signature of the Protocol. As the principal drafter of Article 44, I have always believed that the only circumstances in which the nature of the hostilities prevents compliance with the basic rule of distinction are hostilities between irregular armed forces and the forces of an occupying power within occupied territory (and, of course, the analogous situation in wars of national liberation in the unlikely event the Protocol were ever applied to such a war). Appropriate understandings on that point have already been made by several States upon ratification, including Italy, Belgium, and New Zealand.

Only experience in future armed conflicts will determine whether Protocol I has succeeded in its efforts to give irregular armed forces adequate inducements to distinguish themselves from the civilian population, thereby improving the protection accorded in practice to the civilian population. It certainly offers more hope in this regard than the demonstrably unworkable conditions of Article 4(A,2) of the 1949 Geneva Convention on the Protection of Prisoners of War.

Finally, it should be obvious that neither the provisions of Article 1(4) nor of Article 44, nor of the two in combination provide any solace or support for terrorists. Failure by a combatant to distinguish himself from the civilian population throughout his military operations is a punishable offense. Terrorist acts, whether they are attacks on civilians, the taking of hostages, or disguised, perfidious attacks on military personnel, are all punishable crimes, whether committed by combatants or by non-combatants and whether the perpetrator is entitled to POW status or not. Assertions that ratification of Protocol I would give aid to or enhance the status of the PLO or of any terrorist group are errant nonsense.

---

27 The Diplomatic Conference considered, but ultimately decided to reject, an article that would have prohibited reservations to certain specified provisions. Being unable to agree on the non-reservable provisions, the Conference recognized that, pursuant to Article 19 of the Vienna Convention on the Law of Treaties, a reservation would be permissible unless it were 'incompatible with the object and purpose of the treaty'. See Bothe, Partsch, Solf, eds., op. cit. n. 1, at 570-572.

5.   RESERVATIONS AND UNDERSTANDINGS

I would not want to give the impression that there are no defects in the Protocol. Any effort to negotiate a legal text in a forum in which more than one hundred countries are represented is almost certain to result in some troubling provisions and ambiguities. Protocol I is no exception, but its defects are curable by means of reservations and understandings.

The only provisions of the Protocol that I believe may warrant a reservation are the various prohibitions of reprisal found in Articles 51-56.[28] Effectively, the sum of these provisions prohibits reprisals against virtually everyone and everything except the enemy's armed forces. And how, one may ask, can a State take reprisals against the enemy's armed forces whom it is in any event trying to kill or capture? The only answer I have heard to that question is that the Party could use otherwise prohibited weapons of warfare. That scarcely seems to be a useful or desirable reprisal except, of course, in the situation where the reprisal is itself taken in response to the use by the enemy of prohibited weapons.

While the right to use illegal weapons in reprisal against the use of such weapons is an important right to maintain in order to deter or stop the use of such weapons, I suggest that it may not be the only reprisal measure that should be permitted. What is a State to do, for example, if its enemy adopts a practice of refusing quarter or of systematically slaughtering part or all of the population in occupied territory? Can the victim State content itself with threats to try the responsible persons for war crimes should it prevail and be in a position to do so? I very much doubt it. I believe the victim State in those admittedly extreme circumstances would be compelled to threaten belligerent reprisals of some kind, and, if the threat failed to stop the enemy's practice, then to take reprisal action, regardless of the law. If I am correct, then States should seriously consider making a reservation to at least one of the prohibitions of reprisal set forth in Protocol I in the event of serious and systematic war crimes.[29] Such a

---

28 Reprisals are prohibited against civilians and the civilian population (Article 51), civilian objects (Article 52), certain cultural objects and places of worship (Article 53), objects indispensable to the survival of the civilian population (Article 54), the natural environment (Article 55), and dams, dikes, and nuclear power stations (Article 56).

29 Thusfar, States have not done so. France decided not to ratify the Protocol in part, I believe, because of its objections to those prohibitions of reprisal. Italy has made a declaration that is ambiguous but certainly relates to the reprisal issue. To date, no other Party has referred to the reprisal issue, but I believe the United States will feel the need to do so when it reaches the point -as I am confident it will- of accepting the Protocol. I would expect that Article 51 prohibiting reprisals against the civilian population would be the most likely subject of a

reservation should, of course, be so framed as to respect the traditional conditions of a lawful belligerent reprisal, that is, that prior warning has been given and has failed to stop the unlawful acts, that the decision to resort to reprisal is taken at a responsible political level, that the reprisal action is not disproportionate to the unlawful acts against which it is taken, and that the reprisal ends as soon as the unlawful acts by the enemy cease. A State that accepts the competence of the International Fact-Finding Commission established by Article 90 of Protocol I should also condition its reservation by first according the Commission a reasonable time to investigate the alleged unlawful acts by its enemy in any case where its enemy also accepts the competence of the Commission. In my view, such a reservation by a State that accepts the competence of the Fact-Finding Commission should not be seen as an impermissible reservation, that is, one contrary to the object and purpose of the Protocol.[30] Whether a reservation of a right of reprisal by a State that does not accept in advance the competence of the Commission would be a permissible reservation is a more difficult question.

During the negotiations of Protocol I, the representatives of the United States made a number of statements of their understanding of the text. These included:

a) that the rules established by the Protocol were not intended to have any effect on and do not regulate or prohibit the use of nuclear weapons;
b) that the situations in which combatants could not distinguish themselves throughout their military operations, as stated in Article 44(3) could exist only in the exceptional circumstances of territory occupied by an adversary or in those armed conflicts described in Article 1(4);
c) that the phrase 'military deployment preceding the launching of an attack' in Article 44(3) means any movement towards a place from which an attack is to be launched;
d) that a specific area of land may be a military objective if, because of its location or other reasons specified in Article 52, its total or partial destruction, capture, or neutralization, in the circumstances ruling at the time offers definite military advantage;

---

reservation.

30 See Article 19 of the 1969 Vienna Convention on the Law of Treaties. Opened for signature 23 May 1969, UN Doc. A/Conf. 39/27. The Convention entered into force on 27 January 1980. Repr. in VIII ILM 679 (1969).

e) that the first sentence of Article 52(2) prohibits only such attacks as may be directed against non-military objectives and does not deal with the question of collateral damage;

f) that, if the cultural objects and places of worship protected by Article 53 are used in support of the military effort, they lose the special protection of that Article;

g) that, in relation to Articles 51-58, commanders and others responsible for planning, deciding upon, or executing attacks necessarily have to reach decisions on the basis of their assessment of the information from all sources which is available to them at the relevant time; and

h) that the reference in Articles 51 and 57 to 'military advantage' means the advantage anticipated from the attack considered as a whole and not only from isolated or particular parts of that attack.[31]

These statements of understanding are examples of the kinds of statements that could be made by the United States as part of its ratification of the Protocol. Such statements of understanding are useful means of reassuring those in the United States who fear that the ambiguities in the Protocol may ultimately be interpreted in ways contrary to the understanding of the United States at the time of ratification. Most of these understandings have already been stated upon ratification by one or more of the Members of the NATO.

6.   CONCLUSION

Protocol I is an important part of the fabric of international humanitarian law applicable in armed conflicts, and it represents, for the most part, an international consensus - a consensus that the United States played a major role in creating. Its rejection by the Reagan Administration should not prevent a successor Administration from recognizing that its ratification is in the interest of the United States. The recent ratification by the Soviet Union and its astonishing acceptance of the competence of the International Fact-Finding Commission should, at a minimum, inspire an early reconsideration by the United States of its position.

---

31 Report of the United States Delegation, loc. cit. n. 3, App. C.

SIEGE WARFARE AND THE STARVATION OF CIVILIANS

YORAM DINSTEIN

1.   INTRODUCTION

Siege warfare is conducted by encircling an enemy military concentration, a strategic fortress or any other location defended by the enemy, cutting it off from channels of support and supply. Since time immemorial, siege warfare has constituted one of the principal methods employed by belligerents in the course of hostilities. Siege scenes have been found in Egyptian tombs as early as the third millennium B.C.[1] One of the most celebrated sieges described in the Bible is that of the city of Jerusalem, which (in 586 B.C.) fell to the Babylonian King Nebuchadnezzar after a year and a half of investment ending with starvation.[2] The Bible also includes a prohibition of cutting down food-yielding trees in the course of a siege.[3]

The essence of siege warfare lies in an attempt to capture the invested location through starvation and thirst. A besieged army, although entrenched in a militarily impregnable fortress, can be driven to surrender by the paucity of foodstuffs and drinking water *per se*. Even when siege warfare cannot be consummated without bombardments and assaults,[4] the

---

1   See 1(2) The Cambridge Ancient History 358-360 (3rd ed. 1971).

2   2 Kings 25, 1-3.

3   20 Deuteronomy 19-20.

4   Since this paper is devoted to the subject of starvation of civilians, we shall not examine rules of international law governing bombardments and assaults in siege warfare. These rules are exemplified by Article 27 of the Hague Regulations Annexed to the Hague

stamina of the besieged forces is likely to decline considerably owing to insufficient nutrition.

When siege warfare is conducted against a military stronghold, enemy combatants may be the only ones suffering from its effects. But frequently there is a substantial civilian population in the surrounded area. This is especially the case when a siege is laid to a defended town. While actual resistance to the investing force may be offered solely by the military garrison manning the fortifications, the civilian inhabitants of the town (possibly joined by refugees from the adjacent countryside) will naturally share in the privations of the siege. The suffering of civilians in a prolonged siege may be immense, as demonstrated by the experience of Leningrad which was invested for almost three years during World War II.[5]

The legality of siege warfare has not been contested in classical international law: 'The propriety of attempting to reduce it [a besieged place] by starvation is not questioned'.[6] This has been the rule even in those instances in which most of the victims of starvation resulting from the siege were civilians rather than combatants. By way of illustration, customary international law permits the diversion of the channel of a river supplying drinking water to the besieged.[7]

When shortages of food and water in an invested town become intolerable, and no relief is in sight, civilians will usually try to escape. Generally speaking, the military authorities of the besieged area will 'be in favour of evacuating civilians so as to avoid feeding "useless mouths"'.[8] Conversely, the besieging force may be disinclined to permit the evacuation of civilians, lest it ease the drain on the limited resources of the invested town. The customary rule is that 'it is lawful, though an extreme measure, to drive them back so as to hasten the surrender'.[9]

This rule was confirmed by an American Military Tribunal, in the 'Subsequent Proceedings' at Nuremberg, in the *High Command Case*. The principal defendant in this trial, Field Marshal von Leeb, had issued during

---

Convention Respecting the Laws and Customs of War on Land (No. II of 1899 and No. IV of 1907). D. Schindler, J. Toman, eds., The Laws of Armed Conflicts 63, 84 (3rd ed. 1988).

5   See H.E. Salisbury, The Siege of Leningrad (1969).

6   C.C. Hyde, International Law Chiefly as Interpreted and Applied by the United States 1803 (2nd ed. 1945); L. Nurick, *The Distinction between Combatant and Noncombatant in the Law of War*, 39 AJIL 680, 686 (1945).

7   See L. Oppenheim, in H. Lauterpacht, ed., 2 International Law 419 (7th ed. 1952).

8   E. Rosenblad, International Humanitarian Law of Armed Conflict 109 (1979).

9   Hyde, op. cit. n. 6, at 1803; Nurick, loc. cit. n. 6, at 686.

the siege of Leningrad an order to the German artillery to fire on Russian civilians attempting to flee through the German lines.[10] In its Judgement of 1948, the Tribunal held that von Leeb's order was not unlawful, adding: 'We might wish the law were otherwise but we must administer it as we find it'.[11]

2.   SIEGE WARFARE AND THE FOURTH GENEVA CONVENTION

The Fourth Geneva Convention (of 1949) Relative to the Protection of Civilian Persons in Time of War, deals with siege warfare in a very peripheral way. Article 17 proclaims:

> 'The Parties to the conflict shall endeavour to conclude local agreements for the removal from besieged or encircled areas, of wounded, sick, infirm, and aged persons, children and maternity cases, and for the passage of ministers of all religions, medical personnel and medical equipment on their way to such areas.'[12]

Clearly, only limited categories of civilians benefit from this stipulation and, moreover, '... [t]he words "The Parties to the conflict shall endeavour" show that under the Convention evacuation is not compulsory': Article 17 merely amounts to a strong recommendation to belligerents to conclude an agreement effecting the removal of those listed.[13]

Article 23 of the Fourth Geneva Convention deals generally with consignments of medical supplies, food and clothing to civilians of a different nationality (including enemy civilians).[14] The text mandates the 'free passage of all consignments of medical and hospital stores' for exclusively civilian use, as well as 'essential foodstuffs, clothing and tonics intended for children under fifteen, expectant mothers and maternity

---

10 High Command Case (*U.S.A.* v. *von Leeb et al.*, 1948), 11 *Trials of War Criminals before the Nuremberg Military Tribunals under Control Council Law No. 10*, at 462, 563 (1950).

11 *Ibid.*

12 Schindler, Toman, eds., op. cit. n. 4, at 495, 507.

13 See O.M. Uhler, H. Coursier, eds., Commentary, IV Geneva Convention 138-139 (1958).

14 Schindler, Toman, eds., op. cit. n. 4, at 508-509.

cases', subject to prescribed conditions.[15] Unlike the previous provision, Article 23 makes no reference to besieged areas. In fact, it was primarily designed to regulate blockades in maritime warfare.[16] But even if Article 23 is applicable to sieges in land warfare, it is noteworthy that there is no requirement to allow supply of essential foodstuffs to the civilian population in general, as distinct from certain groups deemed particularly 'vulnerable.'[17]

3.   ADDITIONAL PROTOCOL I

It is thus clear that, to all intents and purposes, the freedom of action of the besieging force is hardly curtailed in the Fourth Geneva Convention. The legal position is radically changed, however, in Protocol I (of 1977) Additional to the Geneva Conventions of 12 August 1949, and Relating to the Protection of Victims of International Armed Conflicts.[18] Of course, it is necessary to bear in mind that, unlike the Geneva Conventions, which (with more than 160 Contracting Parties) are almost universally binding today, Protocol I has so far been ratified or acceded to by less than 100 States and most of the major powers are not among them.[19] The United States, for one, has already tendered formal notice that it is not going to ratify the Protocol.[20] Still, insofar as Contracting Parties to the Protocol are concerned, a new legal regime has come into force.

The cardinal rule is promulgated in Article 54(1) of the Protocol: 'Starvation of civilians as a method of warfare is prohibited'.[21]

Although there is no specific reference here to siege warfare, the clear implication is that the plight of civilians deprived of nourishment in an invested town can no longer be utilized by the other side as a legitimate means to win a war. Yet, what is the concrete duty incumbent on the besieging army? Standing by itself, Article 54(1) might be construed only as an undertaking to allow enemy civilians to cross the lines of the

---

15 *Ibid.*
16 See Uhler, Coursier, eds., op. cit. n. 13, at 181.
17 E. Rosenblad, *Starvation as a Method of Warfare - Conditions for Regulation by Convention*, 7 International Lawyer 252, 261-262 (1973).
18 Schindler, Toman, eds., op. cit. n. 4, at 621.
19 For a list of the Parties to the Protocol, at the beginning of 1990, see 30 International Review of the Red Cross 66-69 (1990).
20 Message from the President of the United States of America, repr. in XXVI ILM 561, 562 (1987).
21 Schindler, Toman, eds., op. cit. n. 4, at 652.

besieging force without let or hindrance. Consistent with such an interpretation, the duty devolving on the besieging force would be discharged once the civilians are offered an opportunity to depart from the invested town.

Any degree of flexibility in the meaning of Article 54(1) is eliminated when the text is read in conjunction with subsequent paragraphs. Article 54(2) pronounces unequivocally:

'It is prohibited to attack, destroy, remove or render useless objects indispensable to the survival of the civilian population, such as foodstuffs, agricultural areas for the production of foodstuffs, crops, livestock, drinking water installations and supplies and irrigation works, for the specific purpose of denying them for their sustenance value to the civilian population or to the adverse Party, whatever the motive, whether in order to starve out civilians, to cause them to move away, or for any other motive.'[22]

Article 54(3) qualifies the injunction in the following way:

'The prohibitions in paragraph 2 shall not apply to such of the objects covered by it as are used by an adverse Party:
a) as sustenance solely for the members of its armed forces; or
b) if not as sustenance, then in direct support of military action, provided, however, that in no event shall actions against these objects be taken which may be expected to leave the civilian population with such inadequate food or water as to cause its starvation or force its movement.'[23]

Article 54(4) forbids recourse to reprisals in this context, and Article 54(5) permits derogation from the prohibitions contained in paragraph 2 only by a Party to the conflict in defense of its national territory against invasion (within that part of the national territory which is under its own control) where required by imperative military necessity.[24]

The salient point elucidated in Article 52(2) *et seq.* is the legality of a 'scorched earth' policy. Such a policy was employed as a screening tactic during large scale retreats in the course of World War II.[25] The Protocol

---

22 *Ibid.*, at 652-653.
23 *Ibid.*, at 653.
24 *Ibid.*
25 See J. Stone, ed., Legal Controls of International Conflict 558-559, n. 71 (1959).

permits recourse to 'scorched earth' measures only when the area affected belongs to the belligerent Party and is under its control (in contradistinction to enemy territory or even part of the national territory which is under the enemy's control).[26] Subject to that single exception, it is clear that the destruction of foodstuffs indispensable to the survival of the civilian population is strictly forbidden by the Protocol. Although siege warfare is not specifically mentioned, it cannot be excluded from the scope of the strictures laid down in Article 54(2) *et seq.* in the light of their sweeping language.

It follows that a siege laid to a defended town (uninhabited by civilians) must be differentiated from one encircling a military fortress. In the latter case, since only the sustenance of members of the enemy armed forces is at stake, starvation is a legitimate method of warfare, and it is permissible to destroy systematically all foodstuffs which can be of use to the besieged. By contrast, in the former case, inasmuch as civilians are directly affected, starvation and destruction of foodstuffs are interdicted. In conformity with the Protocol:

> 'A food supply needed by the civilian population does not lose its protection simply because it is also used by the armed forces and may technically qualify as a military objective. It has to be used exclusively by them to lose its immunity.'[27]

If that is not enough, Article 70 of the Protocol[28] -which obligates Parties to the conflict to allow the unimpeded passage of relief consignments to civilians (subject to certain controls)- apparently applies also to besieged locations.[29]

This analysis leads to a far-reaching conclusion. If the destruction of foodstuffs sustaining the civilian population in a besieged town is excluded, how can a siege be a siege? To be fully effective, siege warfare must posit the deprivation of nourishment from the besieged. If no such deprivation is permitted, a siege becomes devoid of its central hallmark. What we are actually told by the framers of the Protocol, then, is that 'a true siege

---

26 See Y. Sandoz *et al.*, eds., Commentary on the Additional Protocols of 8 June 1977 to the Geneva Conventions of 12 August 1949, 658-659 (1987).

27 H. Blix, Means and Methods of Combat. International Dimensions of Humanitarian Law 135, 143 (1988).

28 Schindler, Toman, eds., op. cit. n. 4, at 663.

29 See W.A. Solf, *Siege*, in R. Bernhardt, ed., 4 Encyclopaedia of Public International Law 226-227 (1982).

would no longer be feasible' if civilians are affected.[30] In short, siege warfare 'in the old meaning and function of the term' is prohibited.[31]

The broad injunction against sieges affecting civilians is untenable in practice, since no other method of warfare has been devised to bring about the capture of a defended town with a tenacious garrison and formidable fortifications. This is not to say that the complete freedom of action vouchsafed to a besieging force by customary international law is entirely justified. Compelling humanitarian considerations demand that, if civilians attempt to evacuate an invested town, they must not be precluded by the besieging force from crossing the lines. Any countervailing military advantages pale by comparison. However, if the civilians in a besieged town are allowed to leave the encircled area yet choose to stay *in situ*, what legitimate claim do they have for special protection from the hardships of starvation? Similarly, if the civilians are coerced to stay where they are by edict of the military commander of the garrison of the besieged town, why should the other belligerent be barred from destroying the foodstuffs sustaining them? A refusal by the military commander to allow civilians to evacuate the town is liable to be based on a desire to use their presence as a shield, a ruse specifically proscribed by Article 28 of the Fourth Geneva Convention,[32] as well as Article 51(7) of the Protocol.[33] Why should the besieging force be required to raise a siege or avoid hermetically sealing the enveloped town when it is offering civilians a safety valve?

The Protocol completely fails to take into account the inherent nature of siege warfare in which starvation of those within the invested location is not an end but a means. It is important to bear in mind that a siege does not generate starvation for the purpose of killing civilians with hunger, but only in order to cause the encircled town to surrender.[34] The starvation continues only as long as that town continues to defend itself. Once it surrenders, foodstuffs must certainly be made available again to all civilians (as well as to prisoners of war). Article 54 disregards the temporary and functional purpose of siege warfare by enunciating

---

30 G.B. Roberts, *The New Rules for Waging War: The Case against Ratification of Additional Protocol I*, 26 VJIL 109, 153 (1985-1986).

31 I. Detter de Lupis, The Law of War 253 (1987).

32 Schindler, Toman, eds., op. cit. n. 4, at 511.

33 *Ibid.*, at 651-652.

34 See G.A. Mudge, *Starvation as a Means of Warfare*, 4 International Lawyer 228, 246 (1969-1970).

categorically that the motive underlying the starvation of civilians is irrelevant.

This disregard for the transitory nature of siege warfare is compounded by the direct ban in Article 54(2) on using starvation as a method of forcing civilians to move away. Had it not been for this clause, it might have been arguable that siege warfare (with the attendant starvation) is legitimate, provided that an offer is made by the besieging force to allow civilians to depart from the encircled town. However, since such an offer amounts to an attempt to employ starvation as a means of removing civilians from their place of habitation (if only temporarily), it is proscribed by Article 54.

4.   CONCLUSION

In its totality, whether or not the framers of the Protocol had that intention,[35] Article 54 rules out as a permissible *modus operandi* siege warfare affecting civilians. It remains to be seen whether future wars will confirm in practice this major normative modification of the *jus in bello*.[36] We believe that an absolute prohibition of starvation of civilians in siege warfare is unjustifiable as well as utopian. It is hard to imagine that a method of warfare resorted to since time immemorial will be discontinued in the absence of an effective military alternative for reducing invulnerable enemy positions. Siege warfare is only one of several instances in which the Protocol reveals a manifest gap between law and reality.[37] This is exceedingly regrettable. If international humanitarian law is to leave its imprint on future armed conflicts, it cannot afford to ignore military imperatives.

---

35 Although Article 54 (originally numbered 48) 'was the subject of prolonged discussion and considerable amendment', there is no indication that the issue of siege warfare was addressed by the drafters. For two summations of the *travaux préparatoires*, see Report of Committee III (2nd Session, 1975, Doc. CDDH/215/Rev. 1), 15 Official Records of the Diplomatic Conference on the Reaffirmation and Development of International Humanitarian Law Applicable in Armed Conflicts (Geneva, 1974-1977) 259, 278-280; Report of the Working Group to Committee III (Doc. CDDH /III/264/Rev. 1), *ibid.*, at 347, 348-350.

36 Protocol I has not been applied in the war with Iraq in 1991.

37 See Y. Dinstein, *The New Geneva Protocols: A Step Forward or Backward?*, 33 Yb. of World Affairs 265-278 (1979).

LEGAL PROTECTION OF CHILD-COMBATANTS AFTER THE PROTOCOLS: REAFFIRMATION, DEVELOPMENT OR A STEP BACKWARDS? *

Astrid J.M. Delissen

1.   Introduction

2.   Reaffirmation

3.   Attempts towards a further development

4.   Concluding observations

1.   INTRODUCTION

One of the further innovations of the Law of Geneva which we can find in the 1977 Additional Protocols, concerns those provisions in the Articles on the protection of children (Article 77, of Protocol I and Article 4, of Protocol II) which deal with participation of children in armed conflict.

These provisions aim to restrain the practices of the parties to so many modern armed conflicts to use children in one way or another as participants in hostilities. These practices became frequent notably after World War II. Specific protection against participation of children in military activities was not provided for in the Geneva Conventions of 1949.

A good ten years after the adoption of the Protocols, yet another instrument, dealing with the matter of child-soldiers, saw the light. This was not an instrument within the domain of the humanitarian law of armed conflict, but a human rights convention entirely devoted to the rights of children: the Convention on the Rights of the Child, adopted by the UN General Assembly in November 1989 (from now on: the Convention).[1]

---

*   The author wishes to express her gratitude to Judge G.H. Aldrich for his counsel during the preparation of this paper.

1   Convention on the Rights of the Child, GA Res. 44/25 of 20 November 1989, 44 UN GAOR Supp. (no. 49), at 166; UN Doc. A/34/46 (1990).

A provision on the participation of children in hostilities found its place in Article 38 of the Convention. In effect, a subject-matter provided for in the 1977 Protocols as an addition to the Law of Geneva, was within a short period of time, being dealt with again. Does this fact also imply a new development in the sphere of the Geneva Law *after* the Protocols? This essay, a tribute from a student who is privileged to have Frits Kalshoven as her outstanding teacher of humanitarian law, will look into this question. For the following reasons, it seems a question of interest.

Firstly, the 1977 Additional Protocols do not put unconditional obligations on parties to a conflict with respect to prohibiting child-participation in hostilities. According to Article 77(2) of Protocol I parties to an international conflict shall only:

> '... take all feasible measures in order that children who have not attained the age of fifteen years do not take a direct part in hostilities and, in particular, they shall refrain from recruiting them into their armed forces. In recruiting among those persons who have attained the age of fifteen years but who have not attained the age of eighteen years, the Parties to the conflict shall endeavour to give priority to those who are oldest.'[2]

For three reasons this is a weak provision from the point of view of child-protection: it fails to protect children who are older than fifteen years; only feasible measures (instead of all necessary measures) must be taken in order to prevent children from taking a direct part in hostilities, and there is no ban on so-called indirect child-participation.

As we can learn from the Official Records of the Diplomatic Conference on the Reaffirmation and Development of International Humanitarian Law applicable in Armed Conflict (CDDH), the text of Paragraph 2 is the result of a compromise reached among the Conference delegations.

This compromise consists of placing a flat ban on the recruitment of children, while omitting any absolute prohibition on voluntary participation by children, as this was felt to be unrealistic, particularly in occupied territories and in wars of national liberation.[3]

Also, differing ideas on the age limit (only few delegates were in favor of raising the limit to eighteen years) were brought together in the last sentence of Paragraph 2. The wording of Article 77(2) of Protocol I

---

2   D. Schindler, J. Toman, eds., *The Laws of Armed Conflicts* 667 (1988).
3   Official Records of the CDDH (1978); Doc. CDDH/III/391, XV, at 517.

therefore certainly leaves room for an extension of the protection of children in armed conflict.

In the second place, the repugnant, frequent use of children in many armed conflicts after the conclusion of the Additional Protocols, gives reason for continuing critical examination of the problem of child-combatants. In this respect, one of the relevant questions certainly concerns the appropriateness of the humanitarian law standards, reached in 1977.

Both these standards and the worries about the innumerable child-victims of today's military conflicts were clearly on the minds of many of those involved in the drafting of Article 38 of the Convention. The wording of this provision on child-combatants became one of the most controversial issues of the draft-convention, which not only caused lengthy debates in the Working Group on a Draft Convention on the Rights of the Child (from now on: Working Group)[4] but even beyond that stage, from the final deliberations in the UN Commission on Human Rights until adoption of the Convention by the UN General Assembly. The controversy was one between advocates and opponents of the upgrading of the level of child-protection in comparison to the existing humanitarian law standards. Did the drafting finally result in a further development of what had been achieved in 1977, or should such a development still rank among the humanitarian law challenges ahead of us?

The answer depends to a great extent on how the provisions of the Protocols are being interpreted. This matter of interpretation, which played a role in the debates on Article 38, is of interest when we want to determine whether this Article can be seen as a mere reaffirmation, a further development, or even a step backwards of the earlier provisions on child-combatants.

2.   REAFFIRMATION

The first question to be answered is whether the Working Group intended a reaffirmation of the existing humanitarian law standards, or opted for a totally new approach.

A provision on protection of the child in armed conflict did not form part of the initial Draft for a Convention on the Rights of the Child, which was presented in 1980.[5] By 1983, during consultations among non-

---

4   This Working Group was established by the UN Commission on Human Rights at its Thirty-fifth Session, 35 UN ESCOR Supp. (no. 6), at 60; UN Doc. E/CN/4/1347 (1979).

5   The so-called 'Revised' Polish Draft, 36 UN ESCOR; UN Doc. E/CN/4/1349 (1980).

governmental organisations (NGO's) concerned with the draft of a child-convention, this was for the first time identified as an omission. Accordingly the NGO's prepared a text for a new draft article and submitted it to the Working Group.[6]

The suggestion was taken up by the Netherlands delegate to the Working Group, who presented a proposal for a draft article on protection of the child during armed conflict at the 1985 Meeting of the Working Group. The proposal was supported by the delegations of Belgium, Finland, Peru, Senegal and Sweden. The text of this proposal (to be reffered to as 'the proposal of 1985'), which was discussed during the 1986 Meeting of the Working Group, was as follows:

'1. States Parties to the present Convention undertake to respect and to ensure respect for rules of international humanitarian law applicable in armed conflicts which are relevant to children.

2. In order to implement these obligations States Parties to the present Convention shall, in conformity with the relevant rules of international humanitarian law, refrain in particular from recruiting children into the armed forces and shall take all feasible measures to ensure that children do not take part in hostilities.'[7]

Most striking in this proposal was the absence of an age-limit. However, the reference in Paragraph 2 to '... the relevant rules of international humanitarian law ...' could have been understood as implying that States Parties would nevertheless be bound by the age-limit of fifteen years, set in the Additional Protocols. However, during the debate several delegates expressed their preference for adding a reference to age. It was the only point in the discussion where mention was made of the relevant rules in the Additional Protocols. The delegate of the ICRC pointed out that the age level of fifteen was established in the Protocols. Although some delegates disagreed with such a low age limit (they were in favor of upgrading it to eighteen years), a majority supported reference to the age of fifteen.[8]

One important proposal which related to the standard of protection reached in 1977, was not accepted by the Working Group. The representative of the United Kingdom proposed to replace the word

---

6   See Rädda Barnen, Report on Child Victims of Armed Conflict (NGO Forum, Rome, 28 April 1984), at 32.

7   For the text of this, and some other proposals, see UN Doc. E/CN/4/1986/39, at 27-28.

8   *Ibid.*, at 28-29.

'recruiting' in Paragraph 2 by the word 'conscripting'.[9] The adoption of this suggestion would have implied that voluntary enlistment of children into the armed forces (in contrast to compulsory military service) would have been allowed. That would have been a weakening of the 1977 standard. According to the Head of the USA Delegation to the CDDH, Ambassador G.H. Aldrich, who was the Rapporteur of Committee III of the Conference, and the Chairman of the Working Group in which the text of Article 77 of Protocol I was prepared, the flat ban on the recruitment of children in that Article, includes a ban on the enrolment of children in the armed forces, even when the children volunteer.[10] For this reason Ambassador Aldrich is of the opinion that the Commentary of the ICRC on the interpretation of the word 'recruitment' in Article 77(2) is misleading. The ICRC Commentary states that (in contrast to the text of Article 68 -on the protection of children- of the ICRC Draft Additional Protocol)[11] the obligation to refuse the voluntary enrolment of children is no longer explicitly mentioned in Article 77 of Protocol I.[12] However, according to Dutli, the word 'recruitment' in Article 77(2) '... covers both compulsory and voluntary enrolment, which means that the Parties must also refrain from enrolling children under fifteen years of age who volunteer to join the armed forces.'[13] Mann seems to be of the opinion that the deletion by the Working Group of Committee III of the ban on accepting the voluntary enrolment of children, which was included in the ICRC-Draft, has the consequence that: '... parties are permitted to allow children to volunteer ...'.[14]

It is important to strictly distinguish between the flat ban on recruitment (including voluntary enrolment) in Article 77(2) and the more flexible

---

9   *Ibid.*, § 130, at 28.
10 Aldrich made this statement during the Asser Institute Colloquium on the Gulf War of 23 November 1990. See G.H. Aldrich, *Comments on Professor Paul Tavernier's Paper 'Combatants and Non-Combatants'*, in H.H.G. Post, I.F. Dekker, eds., The Gulf War of 1980-1988, the Iran-Iraq War in International Legal Perspective (Forthcoming).
11 According to Article 68(2):
    'The Parties to the conflict shall take all necessary measures in order that children aged under fifteen years shall not take any part in hostilities and, in particular, they shall refrain from recruiting them in their armed forces or accepting their voluntary enrolment.'
    Draft Additional Protocols to the Geneva Convention of 12 August 1949, ICRC Commentary 86 (1973).
12 See Y. Sandoz, C. Swinarsky, B. Zimmerman, eds., Commentary on the Additional Protocols of 8 June 1977 to the Geneva Convention of 12 August 1949, at 900 (1987).
13 M.T. Dutli, *Captured Child Combatants*, 278 International Review of the Red Cross 424 (1990).
14 H. Mann, *International Law and the Child Soldier*, 36 ICLQ 47-48 (1987).

restriction that Parties to the conflict shall take all feasible measures to prevent children from taking a direct part in hostilities during an armed conflict. According to the Chairman of the Working Group, in his later statement, parties to the conflict may not be able, in all circumstances, to prevent completely the latter type of participation. On the other hand, the Working Group of Committee III did not intend to authorize the enrolment of children in the armed forces, which it is always feasible for Parties to prohibit.[15]

It is submitted (although somewhat prematurely, but we shall return to it) that the initial Working Group debate in 1986 has not been heavily influenced by the earlier humanitarian law standards. And although the proposal of 1985 could give the impression that it provides a higher standard, nothing in the debate indicates that this was the purpose of the parties involved. The final text as adopted in 1986 shows more similarity to Article 77 of Protocol I than the proposal of 1985 in that it merely puts a ban on *direct* participation in hostilities.[16] However, as with the latter it fails to oblige parties to endeavour to give priority to the oldest persons while recruiting among the group of persons between fifteen and eighteen years; an obligation that *is* included in Article 77(2).

3.   ATTEMPTS TOWARDS A FURTHER DEVELOPMENT

The NGO proposal for an article on child-protection in armed conflict submitted to the Working Group in 1984 would, if adopted, certainly have been a further development of the existing humanitarian law standards. That article showed a preference for imposing unconditional obligations on States. According to its paragraph 1: 'The States Parties to the present convention shall refrain from recruiting children into the armed forces and shall take all measures to ensure that children do not take part in hostilities'. However, after 1986 it became definitely clear that (to many people's regret) the debates in the Working Group of that year had not been thoroughly inspired by ideas on furtherance of the legal protection for children in this field.

---

15 See G.H. Aldrich, loc. cit. n. 10.
16 The text adopted in 1986 is the following:
   'States Parties to the present Convention shall take all feasible measures to ensure that no child takes a direct part in hostilities and they shall refrain in particular from recruiting any child who has not attained the age of fifteen years into their armed forces.'
   UN Doc. E/CN.4/1986/39, § 140, at 30.

At the end of 1986 two developments took place in other fora which would influence the views of the participants in the Working Group on the text they had adopted in their meeting of that year.

One of these developments concerned the adoption of a resolution by the International Conference of the Red Cross of October 1986 on protection of children in armed conflicts, which stressed that the protection accorded by the Convention on the Rights of the Child: '... should be at least the same as that accorded by the Geneva Conventions and the two Additional Protocols'.[17]

Another initiative was the adoption, by the General Assembly of the UN, of a resolution in the field of human rights. By this resolution the General Assembly urged Member States, when developing new international human rights standards 'to pay due regard in this work to the established international legal framework', so as to ensure that such standards do not go below the level of existing provisions of human rights and humanitarian law.[18]

In the next meeting of the Working Group, in 1987, some participants were of the opinion that the implementation of these two resolutions necessitated a reopening of the discussion on the Draft Article on protection of the child in armed conflict (which meanwhile had been adopted as Article 20 of the Draft-Convention).

In this connection, specific mention was made of the standards of the Additional Protocols of 1977. Amongst others, the observer for the Netherlands stated that:

'... Article 20 should be reviewed at a later stage, for the protection given to children in armed conflicts should at least be the same as that which they enjoyed under the Geneva Conventions and their Additional Protocols.'[19]

The requests for a review of Article 20 indeed resulted in a reopening of the debate, in which the question on the need for an even better protection for children than the one supplied in the Protocols, was a fundamental one. It was made clear from that debate, which took place in 1988, that the fact that Article 20 in some aspects undermined existing humanitarian law

---

17 XXVth International Conference of the Red Cross, Resolution IX on Protection of Children in Armed Conflicts, UN Doc. E/CN.4/1987/WG.1/WP.4, at 4-5.

18 Par. 2 of GA Res. 41/120 of 4 December 1986: Setting international standards in the field of human rights.

19 UN Doc. E/CN/4/1987/25, § 165, at 42.

standards, had remained unnoticed in the meeting of 1986.[20] A Swedish amendment to Article 20 functioned as an initiative to balance this Article with the corresponding provision of Protocol I, *and* as an attempt to adopt, in the Convention on the Rights of the Child, an even higher standard than the one codified in that humanitarian law instrument. The wording of the Swedish amendment is as follows:

'States Parties to the present Convention shall take all necessary measures to ensure that persons who have not attained the age of eighteen years do not take part in hostilities and they shall refrain from recruiting into their armed forces persons below the age of fifteen years. In recruiting among those persons who have attained the age of fifteen years but who have not attained the age of eighteen years, the States Parties to the present Convention shall endeavour to give priority to those who are oldest.'[21]

In the first sentence, the term 'necessary measures' replaces the term 'feasible measures'; this is a genuine improvement as it gives priority to the protection of the child instead of to the success of military operations.[22]

In the second place, by deleting the word 'direct' in the phrase 'take direct part in hostilities', this amendment prohibits not only the direct participation in hostilities by children, such as firing at enemy soldiers or blowing up a bridge, but also indirect activities in which young children are often involved.[23] Examples of the latter are acts in relation with direct participation such as transmission of military information and transport of

---

20 According to one of the delegates, this neglect may have been caused by the fact that: '[f]ew of us were present when Article 20 was originally discussed'. (Observed during the debate on Article 20 in the first reading of the Draft Convention on the Rights of the Child, on 5 February 1988).

21 UN Doc. E/CN.4.1988/WG.1/WP.19.

22 At the CDDH, the word 'feasible' was interpreted by a number of delegations as: '... that which is practicable or practically possible, taking into account all circumstances at the time, including those relevant to the success of military operations.' See M. Bothe, K.J. Partsch, W.A. Solf, eds., New Rules for Victims of Armed Conflict 373 (1982).

23 The examples of acts of direct participation are given by Kalshoven; he describes a person who takes a direct part in hostilities as someone who: 'performs warlike acts, which by their nature or purpose are designed to strike enemy combatants or matériel ...'. F. Kalshoven, Constraints on the Waging of War 91 (1987). On the meaning of the word 'directly' in this context see also: ICRC Documentation presented to the first session of the Conference of Government Experts, III Protection of the Civilian Population against Dangers of Hostilities 28 (1971).

war material.[24] Finally, a major advancement is made in the Swedish amendment by the change of the age-limit from fifteen into eighteen years. This proposal was in line with the awareness of '... the presence of far too many adolescents aged between fifteen and eighteen on the battlefield'.[25] The last sentence of the Swedish amendment is meant to balance Article 20 with the text of Article 77 of Protocol I, by obliging States who select adolescents for recruitment, to choose the oldest.

It can easily be seen that an upgrading of the age-limit to eighteen years would effect the standard of protection. However, it seems less obvious to conclude *a priori* that the same meaning can be given to the deletion of the words 'directly' and 'feasible' in the Swedish amendment. It was stressed during the discussions on Article 20 in 1988 that the effect of such deletions would not upgrade, but simply balance the provision on children in armed conflict of the Draft Convention with the standard of the Additional Protocols. This assumption was based on the interpretation of the text of the provision on child-combatants in Article 4(3) of Additional Protocol II, which is applicable in non-international armed conflicts. In contradistinction to Article 77 of Protocol I, this Article gives rather unconditional obligations with regard to the protection of the child, by providing that: 'Children who have not attained the age of fifteen years shall neither be recruited in the armed forces or groups nor allowed to take part in hostilities'.[26] May we infer from the wording of this paragraph that the delegations of the CDDH meant to impose stricter rules for the protection of children in internal armed conflicts than in international wars? As Mann points out, the *travaux préparatoires* of the CDDH are silent on this matter.[27] In his opinion, the states participating in the Diplomatic Conference intended indeed to impose a stricter standard on parties involved in an internal armed conflict. According to Mann, the underlying reasons can be found in the concern of many of the States present at the CDDH (particularly among the developing States): 'with not weakening their hand in dealing with internal difficulties'[28] as well as in the fact that:

---

24 For these and other examples see: ICRC, Draft Additional Protocols to the Geneva Conventions of August 12, 1949, Commentary 87 (1973).

25 As observed by F. Krill, *A Controversial Article on Children in Armed Conflicts*, 12 Dissemination Magazine of the ICRC 11 (August 1989).

26 Article 4(3,c) of Additional Protocol II of 1977, Schindler and Toman loc. cit. n. 2 at 693.

27 H. Mann, loc. cit. n. 14, at 50.

28 *Ibid.*, at 49, note 70.

'...it was widely presumed during the Conference that local 'rebel' groups were better placed to recruit young children to participate in the conflict for an extended period of time.'[29]

Mann concludes from this that:

'In returning to a stronger prohibition for internal armed conflicts in comparison with that adopted for international conflicts, the participating States were intending to make it more difficult ... for the dissident groups within their territory to achieve this perceived military advantage.'[30]

The explanation by Aldrich on the difference in the comparable texts of Protocols I and II differs from the one made by Mann. He indicates that the different text of Protocol II was adopted at the very last stage of the Diplomatic Conference, in its final Plenary Sessions, where the text that became Article 4(3,c) was presented: '...at the very last moment by Judge Hussain of Pakistan as part of a drastically reduced Protocol II and without any explanation of the change in this provision'. The initiative by Judge Hussain was made: 'in order to save Protocol II from likely rejection by the many developing nations that believed the draft Protocol went much to far, particularly in according international status to rebellious or separatist groups.'[31] Shortly before the final PlenarSessions, Committee III had adopted a text for Protocol II which still was identical in wording to the text of Article 77(2) of Protocol I.[32] An intention to opt for a substantially different wording in Protocol II can certainly not be deduced from the adoption of this Article by Committee III. Nor can such a conclusion easily be drawn from the adoption of Article 4(3,c) in the Plenary Session. On that last event, Aldrich comments in the following way:

'I do not know if anyone noticed the change in the text on children combatants; certainly no one commented on it. In all probability, the revision was designed by Judge Hussain simply to avoid any reference to "Parties to the conflict", a phrase he excised from all articles of Protocol II in order to eliminate any suggestion that a rebellious Party was being recognized as having rights under the Protocol.'[33]

---

29 *Ibid.*, at 50.
30 *Ibid.*.
31 See G.H. Aldrich, loc. cit. n. 10.
32 Meeting of Committee III, 10 May 1977 CDDH/III/380.
33 See G.H. Aldrich, loc. cit. n. 10.

From the drafting history of Article 4(3,c) of Protocol II we can conclude that most probably it was not the intention and the purpose of the delegations at the CDDH to adopt a provision on child-combatants in Protocol II which differs substantially from the one in Protocol I, in that it provides for stricter rules to be observed for the protection of children in internal conflicts. The assumption that Protocol II provides a higher standard of protection to children can only be derived from the literal wording of Article 4(3,c) of Protocol II, or, in the words of the Vienna Convention on the Law of Treaties from: '... the ordinary meaning to be given to the terms of the treaty ...'[34]. However, in order to examine whether a difference exists in the standards of protection provided by the Protocols, it seems more appropriate to have recourse to the preparatory work of Protocol II and the circumstances of its conclusion. Returning to the question whether the Swedish amendment of Article 20 of the Draft Convention on the rights of the child was in every sense an upgrading of the provisions on child-combatants in the Protocols, it is submitted that this was indeed the case. As a consequence, adoption of this amendment by the Working Group in Article 20 of the Draft Convention would constitute a further development of the standards of the Protocols.

4. CONCLUDING OBSERVATIONS

During the debate on the Draft Convention in second reading the Working Group finally failed to succeed in reaching consensus on any amendments aimed at upgrading the level of protection.[35] However, this failure was not due to a total lack of willingness. Many delegations stressed their preference for a revision of Article 20 in line with the Swedish amendment. When, after a rather confused discussion, the final text of Article 20 was adopted,[36] some delegations even emphasized that they could not go along in the consensus.[37]

---

34 Vienna Convention on the Law of Treaties, Article 31(1).
35 Debate of 8 December 1988.
36 The final text of the relevant paragraphs reads:
   '2. States Parties shall take all feasible measures to ensure that persons who have not attained the age of 15 do not take direct part in hostilities.
   3. States Parties shall refrain from recruiting any person who has not attained the age of 15 into their armed forces. In recruiting among those persons who have attained the age of 15 but who have not attained the age of 18 years, States Parties shall endeavour to give priority to those who are the oldest.'
37 UN Doc.E/CN.4/1989/48, § 612, at 114.

In a later stage, after adoption of the Draft Convention by the Working Group and by the UN Commission on Human Rights, again some attempts were undertaken to strengthen the relevant text of Article 20.[38] The delegation of the ICRC proposed to delete Article 38(2) and (3).[39] This proposal would result in an article on children in armed conflict consisting only of the first paragraph of Article 38, which reads:

'States Parties undertake to respect and to ensure respect for rules of international humanitarian law applicable to them in armed conflicts which are relevant to the child.'

In the opinion of the ICRC, mere reference to existing standards would be an improvement in comparison to the text of Article 38(2) and (3). From this assumption by the ICRC delegation we can conclude that the standard of Article 38 was seen as a step backwards from the provision of Protocol II. Here again the interpretation of the wording of Article 4(3,c) of Protocol II is at stake. It is conclusive for determining whether Article 38, which remained unchanged after all[40], should be seen as a step backwards or not. The present author submits that the text of Article 38(2) and (3) would only have been a step backwards if the Working Group had failed to adopt that part of the Swedish amendment which balanced Draft Article 20 with the text of Article 77 of Protocol I.[41]

However, setting aside a possible difference on the interpretation of the existing standards on child combatants, we must conclude that the need for an upgrading of the level of protection in this field certainly remains a challenge ahead.

---

38 Draft Article 20(2) and (3) finally became Article 38(2) and (3) of the Convention.

39 *and* Article 38(4) which reads:
    'In accordance with their obligations under international humanitarian law to protect the civilian population in armed conflicts, States Parties shall take all feasible measures to ensure protection and care of children who are affected by an armed conflict.'
    The wording of this provision was seen as a step backwards in comparison to the Geneva Conventions of 1949, which lay down absolute obligations in this field instead of referring to 'feasible measures'.

40 Discussion on Article 38 in the Third Committee of the General Assembly did not lead to changes in this provision.

41 This part of the amendment reads:
    'In recruiting among those persons who have attained the age of 15 years but who have not attained the age of 18 years, States Parties shall endeavour to give priority to those who are oldest.'

FROM REPRISALS TO INDIVIDUAL PENAL RESPONSIBILITY

STANISLAW E. NAHLIK

1.   INTRODUCTION

As soon as I had been approached to contribute to the Collection of Essays in honour of Professor Kalshoven, I knew that I was doomed to write something about reprisals. For it so happened that it was this particular subject which linked us on several occasions.

When, in the early seventies, I had first to deal with the problem of reprisals and started to collect the essential bibliography on the subject, the monograph which impressed me more than any other was the book by Frits Kalshoven on Belligerent Reprisals, published in Leyden in 1971. It was an exhaustive, very well documented and -what is much rarer in a scientific book- extremely well-written and hence a *readable* book. After having analysed all aspects of the problem on a rich historical basis, the author pronounces himself against any recourse to reprisals. He says *inter alia* that any situation 'where a belligerent reprisal seems permissible presents the belligerent with an opportunity to violate a rule of the law of war with impunity'. He therefore thinks that an absolute prohibition of reprisals would be the most plausible solution since 'the balance of the merits and demerits of belligerent reprisals has now become so entirely negative as no longer to allow their being regarded as even moderately effective sanction of the laws of war'.[1]

I confess that, greatly under the influence of that categorical statement, I myself also became a fervent adversary of the very idea of reprisals.

2.   REPRISALS AT THE DIPLOMATIC CONFERENCE

Then, all of a sudden, our paths crossed. We were both called by our respective governments to participate in the Diplomatic Conference on Humanitarian Law,[2] convened by the Swiss Federal Government at the request of the ICRC,[3] at Geneva, for one session only, to be held in February 1974. But the organizers proved to be too optimistic. So many controversial problems arose at the Conference that, instead of one, it had to hold four sessions ending its work only in June 1977 by the adoption of two Protocols, meant as 'Additional to the Geneva Conventions of 12 August 1949', I: relating to the protection of victims of international armed conflicts, II: of those of *non*-international armed conflicts.[4]

After the work of the Conference had been divided, to my mind not always logically, among three Main Committees,[5] Frits Kalshoven and I found ourselves in two different committees: Kalshoven in Committee III which had to deal mainly with the protection of civilians and with some questions concerning actual combat - questions which, incidentally, transgressed the traditional framework of the 'Geneva Law' by passing into areas which formerly would have been considered as pertaining rather to the 'Hague Law'.[6] I, on the other hand, found myself entrusted with the chairmanship of Committee II which comprised all questions regarding the protection of the sick, wounded and shipwrecked. So our respective tasks

---

1   F. Kalshoven, Belligerent Reprisals 367-377 (1971).
2   From the first letters of the French title of the Conference, it has been generally referred to as CDDH (Conférence Diplomatique sur le Droit Humanitaire) and all its documents are quoted with numbers preceded by these four letters.
3   In a similar way, this Committee has been generally referred to as CICR (Comité International de la Croix-Rouge).
4   The titles of the Protocols are so long and cumbersome that they have been generally referred to as 'Protocol I' and 'Protocol II', respectively. In this essay, we shall only deal with Protocol I.
5   The fourth, simply called the '*Ad hoc* Committee', was added somewhat later.
6   In the Annuaire Français de Droit International 9 *et seq.*, (1978), I published the article 'Droit dit de Genève et droit dit de La Haye'. In this article I was trying to argue that this dichotomy has become outdated. I think that Kalshoven is very close to the same view.

were seemingly not very near one another. However, the problem of reprisals arose in both our Committees.

2.1 Committee II

In Committee II, whose tasks were perhaps simpler, we dealt with the problem, after some discussion but with no opposition, in one short general Article 20, stating unequivocally that 'Reprisals against the persons and objects protected by this Part are prohibited'. So here my position, greatly based on the influence of Kalshoven's 1971 monograph, could be integrally applied.

2.2 Committee III

The position of the problem in Committee III was much more difficult, due in particular to the varied nature of the problems alloted to it. There was no question of prohibiting reprisals in provisions dealing specifically with combat situations. On the other hand, this question played a major role in the discussions and decisions of Committee III concerning the protection of civilian population and civilian objects.

The legal protection of civilian populations was a comparatively new problem. Older Conventions, especially those signed at The Hague in 1899 and 1907, seemed to be inspired by the noble ideas of the Age of Enlightenment that war should be limited to combat between armed forces of belligerent States in which civilians as a rule would not be involved and thus not particularly endangered. Only unprecedented atrocities committed against civilians in World War II, especially under occupation, induced the ICRC to include in the programme of the 1949 Geneva Conference a special Convention, the Fourth, on the protection of civilians. However, that important Convention was somewhat limited in scope. There were certain rules in Part II of a general character. But the main body of the Convention applied to persons 'who, at a given moment and in any manner whatsoever', found themselves in the hands of the adverse party (Article 4(1)). It meant in practice civilians sent to concentration or labour camps or, at the very best, merely interned.

The CDDH was meant to enhance this field of application by stipulating that belligerents 'shall at all times distinguish between the civilian population and combatants', that the 'civilian population comprises all persons who are civilians' and that the Protocol would apply in all circumstances, to protect both the whole civilian population and individual civilians. The Protocol also said that, in case of doubt, the civilian status

of a person should be presumed (Articles 48, 50(1,2) and 51(1) Protocol
I). The protection granted to civilians was thus considerably enlarged.

These rules did not encounter serious opposition, including the
important provision, contained in Article 51(6), that 'Attacks against the
civilian population or civilians by way of reprisals are prohibited'.

The prohibition of reprisals against civilian objects would seem to be a
logical corollary to the prohibition of reprisals against civilian persons.
However, at the CDDH, the amendments aiming at the inclusion of such a
prohibition did not fare so well. Several delegates, mostly of the Western
groups, had serious doubts about its feasibility. The spokesman for the
opponents, the representative of France, was afraid that such a general
prohibition of reprisals against civilian objects was likely to limit the right
of legitimate self-defence and persisted in expounding that view even at the
plenary stage of the CDDH. Nevertheless, already in Committee III, the
principle, in the final text of the Protocol constituting its Article 52(1)
clause 1, 'Civilian objects shall not be the object of attack or reprisals',
had been adopted - mainly after the relevant amendment had been
presented, in the name of the whole group of its sponsors, by Professor
Kalshoven. He very convincingly said *inter alia* that:

> 'there should be either no prohibition at all but simply general restrictions,
> or else outright prohibition .... In fact, reprisals could rarely be confined to
> civilian *objects* alone and the infliction of the suffering on the civilian
> population would be virtually inevitable.'[7]

There was less opposition to prohibiting reprisals in provisions dealing
with certain specified groups of civilian objects, mentioned here in order of
their appearance in the text of Protocol I, namely, cultural objects and
places of worship, objects indispensable to the survival of the civilian
population, natural environment, works and installations containing
dangerous forces (Articles 53, 54, 55 and 56, respectively).

All these discussions and decisions were completed before the end of
the second session of the Conference, *i.e.*, in 1975. They have been
excellently analysed and reported in the article published by Professor
Kalshoven in mid-1977.[8] So there is no need to add here anything else on
this subject.

---

7   Doc. CDDH/III/SR.14, § 26.
8   Reprisals in the CDDH, see R.J. Akkerman, P.J. van Krieken, Ch.O. Pannenberg, eds.,
     Declarations on Principles - A Quest for Universal Peace 195 *et seq.* (1977).

2.3 The problem of a general prohibition of reprisals

But soon a new problem emerged: whether to insert in the text of Protocol I, or not, a *general* clause concerning reprisals. To this effect, two proposals, hardly to be referred to as 'amendments', were submitted to the Conference: one, by the Polish delegation, to prohibit reprisals against *any* persons and objects protected by the Protocol; two, by France, to admit reprisals, under certain conditions, in certain circumstances. The contents of these two amendments were thus mutually exclusive of one another. It was necessary to adopt either the first or the second, or ... none at all.

The first of these amendments, which will be referred to as 'New Article 70 bis', escaped the attention of Professor Kalshoven. Although, dated 1 October 1974, it had been submitted to the CDDH between sessions I and II, probably because it came to be discussed only during the IVth session while Kalshoven's article obviously recounts the story of first three sessions only.

As the two proposals related to matters which had already been discussed and decided, although only in part, in either Committees II or III, there arose a rather difficult procedural question: how could either of the two conflicting proposals -especially the French one- supersede decisions already taken in Committees II and III. To reopen the problem a two-thirds majority would have been required. The Polish and French proposals were submitted, rather ingeniously, to Committee I which, until then, had on its agenda nothing relating to reprisals. Committee I would have been required to include the new proposal, either the French, or the Polish one, in Part V of Protocol I which had to deal with the 'execution' of the Protocol. However, not having superior standing to the other two Committees, it would have found itself in a rather awkward position when taking a decision contrary to the already adopted decisions of two other Committees. There emerged the suggestion of calling into existence a joint body in which all three Committees would be represented. But the General Committee of the Conference was unwilling to create one more body and decided that the whole problem would pass into the competence of Committee I. The question of what would happen if indeed Committee I were to adopt a solution contrary to those already adopted either by one or both other Committees, was left unanswered.

The presentation of the French proposal was intended to add to the Protocol a new Article: 74 bis, discussion of which played an important role in the meetings of Committee I at the third session of the CDDH. Professor Kalshoven's article recounts its story with full knowledge of what happened, so here also there is no need to repeat it. Suffice it to say that, carefully avoiding the word 'reprisals', the French proposal was trying to establish a whole system of 'certain measures ... designed to repress the breaches -committed by the adverse party- and induce compliance with the Protocol, but which would otherwise be prohibited by the Protocol'. Such measures could be taken only if 'serious, manifest and deliberate breaches of its obligations' were being committed by the adverse party without paying any attention to 'other efforts to induce it to comply with the law'. The decision to resort to such measures would be taken 'at the highest level of government', the adverse party would have to be warned in advance about resorting to them, and they would have to cease as soon as they have achieved their objective. The principle of proportionality would also have to be observed. In view of the reservation contained in the French proposal that the measures concerned should not involve any actions prohibited by the Geneva Conventions of 1949, it would seem that only measures transgressing such prohibitions as appeared in Protocol I would be permissible.

Although the term 'reprisals' had not been used, everybody was aware that the euphemistic expression 'certain measures' was indeed tantamount to reprisals. Therefore, the whole discussion centred around the dilemma: would it be better to retain the prohibition of reprisals in articles where such a decision had already been taken either in Committee II or III, leaving all other possible cases to customary law, or to make the possible recourse to reprisals, under whatever name, subject to codification, setting precise conditions under which one could resort to them. Many speakers, mostly from the Western group, were for this second solution seeing in the French proposal a 'courageous attempt' to codify what until recently seemed to be uncodifiable. Others, among them all the countries of what was at that time referred to as the Eastern bloc, but also some from the West, were against any such possibility. Their representatives expressed the view that reprisals, however named, unavoidably lead to counter-reprisals and that eventually one would face an unending series of atrocities in which, of course, strong countries would always have the upper hand over their weaker adversaries. It was also to be feared that in practice it would prove extremely difficult to observe the principle of proportionality. Moreover, the main objection against reprisals, expressed since the first authors who had criticized the concept, commencing with the 16th century Spanish Dominican, Francisco de Vitoria, was that reprisals, although theoretically directed against States, would in practice hit innocent citizens. To show the typical approach of the opponents to the French proposals, I shall quote here a short fragment of the speech held on the subject by Mgr. Luoni, representative of the Holy See:

'Indeed, to admit that a party to a conflict could in certain more or less defined cases have recourse to reprisals would sanction the idea that that lamentable practice was legitimate and would change it from a deplorable *de facto* practice to one regulated by law .... It was, however, unthinkable from the legal standpoint that any means which were themselves a violation of humanitarian law could be codified!'[9]

So many speakers opposed the French proposal that, when the time came to present the Polish one, Kakolecki, who at that juncture represented Poland in Committee I, limited himself to saying that he considered all those who had spoken against the French proposal as automatically supporting the Polish one.[10]

But the really interesting, rather heated, discussion on both the merits and defects of the French and the Polish proposals took place during the fourth session of the CDDH, held in 1977, mostly not in the full meetings of Committee I, but rather in the special Working Group B which devoted three days to it: 19, 20 and 21 April 1977. That part of the Conference's work on the problem of reprisals was obviously not yet known to Professor Kalshoven when he wrote the afore-mentioned article. On the other hand, I happened to be the principal speaker for Poland at the meetings of that special Working Group and, as meetings of Working Groups are not officially recorded, I had to base myself merely on my personal notes and recollections. Since I recorded them in two articles, one in French,[11] another in English,[12] there is no need to repeat here my argument nor the arguments of those who were supporting the Polish proposal. Suffice it to say that they were advocating the insertion in Protocol I of a general prohibition of reprisals against any persons or objects protected by that Protocol, and militating against the introduction and codification of reprisals under whatever name and under whatever circumstances. Instead of repeating what I may have said at that juncture, I have simply quoted above the enunciation of the representative of the Holy See.

Since, after three days of debate, it became obvious that none of the two conflicting proposals could count on the necessary majority and that there was no way of reconciling them and working out some kind of

---

9 Document CDDH/I/SR.48, §§ 32, 37.
10 *Ibid.*, § 53.
11 S.E. Nahlik, *Le Problème des Représailles à la Lumière des Travaux de la CDDH*, 1 Revue Générale de Droit International Public 130 *et seq.* (1978).
12 S.E. Nahlik, *Belligerent Reprisals as seen in the Light of the DCHL ...*, in Changing Rules for Changing Forms of Warfare. Law and Contemporary Problems, Duke University School of Law, Durham (1978).

compromise formula, when the matter came back to the meeting of the full Committee I, both the French and the Polish delegates said that they were withdrawing their proposals. And so the story of the problem of reprisals at the CDDH ended.

3.   RETHINKING REPRISALS AFTER 1977

In August 1979, at an international seminar on humanitarian law, organized by the Jagellonian University in Cracow, Kalshoven was entrusted with a report on belligerent reprisals which he prepared and delivered admirably. One could hardly have expected that he would succeed in giving a masterful synthesis of everything that an average jurist should know about reprisals on ... thirteen pages. It is a rare example of brevity, clarity and indeed of an uncanny faculty to comprise so much, not omitting any essential aspect, in such a concise study![13]

He was now less categorical than in his 1971 monograph. The real question is simply this -says Kalshoven towards the end of his Cracow report- will the prohibitions of reprisals against the civilian population and civilian objects be able to stand up against the forces urging belligerents to retaliate against the enemy civilian population, or will they fail to do so? Apparently, Kalshoven is of the opinion that the prohibition will probably have the same effect as other legal rules, that is, that of restraining the actors in some cases but not in all.

I can now subscribe to nearly every statement by Kalshoven. Upon reflection, I am now inclined to think that the Polish proposal submitted to the CDDH went indeed somewhat too far as, for other reasons, so too did the French one. I think that the international law of today tends to get dangerously *over*codified. It is better to leave some situations uncodified. It would indeed be awkward if a country retaliating against the violation of law by the adverse party could say that it does so by virtue of a concrete provision of a treaty or protocol on ... humanitarian law. Let it rather invoke some customary rule or general principle like the state of emergency or military necessity. Therefore, I could subscribe even today to the last sentence of Kalshoven's Cracow report: 'A complete prohibition of reprisals in this sensitive field of the law of warfare, recourse to

---

13 F. Kalshoven, *The Belligerent Reprisals in the Light of the 1977 Geneva Protocol*, European Seminar on Humanitarian Law 31 *et seq.*, CICR, ed., (1979).

reprisals represents a less severe measure than the unmitigated operation of the principle of reciprocity'.

Let me give just one instance to show how difficult it may be, in some circumstances, to refrain from resorting to reprisals. During World War II, when in Summer and Autumn of 1940, the *Luftwaffe* started bombing London and other British towns, the British population, whenever Churchill appeared in public, shouted unanimously: 'Pay it back to them!' And so indeed the Royal Air Force did, after it had reached the necessary strength. Could it have been otherwise?

It does not mean of course that, all of a sudden, I have become a partisan of reprisals. I only think that it may sometimes prove to be a lesser of two evils. But it does not change its many deficiencies: that reprisals are apt to hit the innocent and that it usually is extremely difficult to keep them within the limits of proportionality, as well as to avoid counter-reprisals.

4.   THE PROBLEM OF THE PENAL RESPONSIBILITY OF INDIVIDUALS

What is the answer? Would it provide a remedy or, let us be explicit, another, perhaps somewhat better solution, to punish directly those responsible for having violated a rule of the law of war?

The first endeavour to specify such violations is to be found in Article 6 of the Charter of the International Military Tribunal, annexed to the London Agreement between the four major Allied Powers, signed in London on 8 August 1948. In that famous provision, the distinction has been established between three kinds of international crimes, namely: crimes against peace, war crimes in the proper sense of the term, and crimes against humanity. Everything that includes warfare as such belongs, of course, to the second group. The relevant provision gives, however, only a few examples of such crimes leaving the rest to the further development of international law.

4.1   On the national level

Such further development in our field has indeed taken place, namely: first, in the 1949 Geneva Conventions on the Protection of the Victims of War;[14] later, in Protocol I of 1977.[15]

Already in the 1949 Convention, we find a fairly comprehensive list of grave breaches of the Convention concerned, a list considerably extended and described in more detail in Protocol I so that it now covers violations of all the essential provisions of acts concerned. A significant provision of Protocol I adds that all grave breaches either of the Conventions or of the Protocol 'shall be regarded as war crimes'[16] which institutes an interesting link between the 'Geneva law' and the afore-mentioned Charter of the International Military Tribunal, generally referred to as the 'Nuremberg Tribunal'. So there is now no lack of provisions which can be considered as constituting in our field the *material* penal law.

But what about the *procedural* penal law in this respect? Here the question seems to be far more difficult.

The 1949 Conventions -we take here as an example Article 146 of the Fourth Convention, but analogous provisions are to be found in three other Conventions as well- provide:

'The High Contracting Parties undertake to enact any legislations necessary to provide effective penal sanctions for persons committing, or ordering to be committed, any of the grave breaches of the present Convention defined in the following Article:
    Each High Contracting Party shall be under the obligation to search for persons alleged to have committed, or to have ordered to be committed, such grave breaches, and shall bring such persons, regardless of their nationality, before its own courts. It may also, if it prefers, hand such persons over for trial to another High Contracting Party concerned, provided such High Contracting Party has made out a *prima facie* case.'

In principle, these provisions seem to constitute an important step forward since they are guided by the old Roman precept *aut punire, aut*

---

14 Convention I for the Amelioration of the Condition of the Wounded and Sick in Armed Forces in the Field, Articles 49-54; Convention II for the Amelioration of the Condition of Wounded, Sick and Shipwrecked Members of Armed Forces at Sea, Articles 50-53; Convention III relative to the Treatment of Prisoners of War, Articles 129-132; Convention IV relative to the Protection of Civilian Persons in Time of War, Articles 146-149.

15 Protocol I, adopted at Geneva on 10 June 1977, Articles 85-91.

16 Article 86(5) Protocol I.

dedere. It is particularly important that they establish the jurisdiction of every country over persons of whatever nationality. On the other hand, however, they leave everything in the field of the domestic jurisdiction of States. So, in practice, the individual concerned may find himself in the hands of either his own country, or of the adverse party to the conflict concerned, or of a third State. In the last case, the individual *perhaps* would be tried, in the second, *certainly* so. But in the first case? The chances that he would be tried with sufficient severity by the courts of his own country would seem to be rather meagre. And the possibility of extradition would probably be limited to the mutual relations between the party adverse to the country of the guilty person and a third State. One can hardly expect that his own country, should such a case occur, would extradite him abroad. Rather it would try him itself and inflict upon him, if at all, a mild punishment.

4.2   On the international level

But what about the possible interference of an international body? This has been provided for only in an auxiliary character, and at an early stage of proceedings, namely in the establishment of facts should the parties differ as to their appreciation.

The 1949 Conventions provide -in Article 149 of the Fourth Convention- for the institution of 'an enquiry', at the request of one of the Parties and with their mutual agreement. Should they be unable to reach such agreement the Parties should choose an umpire 'who will decide upon the procedure to be followed'. This provision can be regarded as a typical *lex imperfecta* since the Conventions do not provide for any remedy in case of the Parties not being able to agree upon the choice of an umpire

Protocol I of 1977 went a step further since, in Article 90, it provided for the institution of the 'International Fact-Finding Commission', a permanent body of fifteen Members which, however, would be called into existence only after at least twenty Parties to the Protocol had agreed to create it. In such case, the representatives of these Parties only would be called to proceed to the election of the Members of the Commission. So far, we are nearing that minimum number of twenty States. Nevertheless, quite a number of States, when ratifying the Protocol or acceding to it, do not accept the Fact-Finding Commission. So it is difficult to predict today when the Commission is going to be created and what the practical value of its activities would be. Even in the best of cases, however, it will play only an auxiliary role, the actual trial of those involved being left in the hands of a domestic jurisdiction.

Of course, it would be much more desirable, at least from the point of view of an internationalist, to see in perspective the possibility of creating an international penal tribunal with the competence of trying individuals of whatever nationality accused of having violated a rule of the law of war. The Nuremberg Tribunal is hardly, in this respect, a laudable precedent since it was created merely by the victorious Powers to try citizens of a defeated State. A really noteworthy tribunal would be one composed of citizens of *all* groups of States, something based indeed on the example of the existing International Court of Justice or some of the bodies functioning in the frame of European organizations. Perhaps a similar mode of electing the Commission's members could be envisaged as the one applied to the election of the Judges of the International Court of Justice, General Assembly *and* the Security Council of the United Nations. But of course a Convention to that effect would first need to be concluded. Is such a goal likely to be attained in the near future? A couple of years ago, this would have seemed practically impossible. But now, given the pace at which the rapprochement between the so-called West and the so-called East is progressing, one cannot exclude such a possibility. It would be the fulfilment of an internationalist's dream and it certainly is a challenge ahead.

THE SYSTEM OF REPRESSION OF BREACHES OF
ADDITIONAL PROTOCOL I

JULIAN J.E. SCHUTTE

1.   INTRODUCTION

Entrusting the enforcement of humanitarian law in armed conflict, *i.e.*, the laws and customs governing this branch of public international law, largely to penal law can be attributed to a decreasing confidence in other implementation mechanisms, rather than to the demonstrated efficiency of penal law. The diminishing acceptability of reprisals as a means of law enforcement during the negotiations on the 1977 Protocols Additional to the Geneva Conventions on the Protection of War Victims of 1949 has been the subject of a number of publications.[1] The role of state responsibility for violations of the rules of public international law has never been elaborated through binding international regulations. Moreover, the functioning of a system of Protecting Powers, another instrument ensuring compliance with obligations under the Conventions and Protocol I, can be assured only if such Powers are actually appointed and allowed to

---

1   See F. Kalshoven, *The Belligerent Reprisals in the Light of the 1977 Geneva Protocols*, 1979 European Seminar on Humanitarian Law, ICRC, 31 (1988). S.E. Nahlik, *Belligerent Reprisals as Seen in the Light of the Diplomatic Conference on Humanitarian Law, Geneva, 1974-1977*, 42 Law and Contemporary Problems 2, 36 (1978).

operate efficiently. Alas, history shows too many instances of non-fulfilment of these basic conditions.

Since, as appears from the elaboration of the provisions on penal enforcement in Protocol I, strong emphasis is laid on this method of implementation, the question arises whether the instruments of criminal law, including those of international criminal law, provide sufficient possibilities for action in cases of violations of international norms.

This question has to be kept in mind when reading this essay. The reader should be aware that on the one hand enforcement through penal law of violations of norms of public international law is indispensable, but that on the other, given the way in which this instrument of enforcement has been elaborated in the Geneva Conventions[2] and Protocol I,[3] in practice its role is bound to remain limited. Over-emphasizing the importance of penal law enforcement for violations of the laws and customs of war bears the risk of over-estimating its potential and thus affecting its credibility.

2.   GRAVE BREACHES OF THE GENEVA CONVENTIONS

The Geneva Conventions of 1949 on the protection of the victims of war all contain a similar provision, including the obligation for the Contracting Parties to enact legislation to provide effective penal sanctions for persons committing, or ordering, any of the so-called grave breaches of the Conventions.[4] Moreover, the same provisions of the four Conventions oblige Contracting Parties to search for persons alleged to have committed, or to have ordered, such grave breaches and to bring such persons before their courts, or, if they prefer, to hand them over for trial to another Contracting Party, provided a *prima facie* case is made out.

Apart from this, each Contracting Party is under the obligation to take the necessary measures for the suppression of all breaches other than grave breaches. Such suppression, however, need not exclusively be effected through the application of criminal law.

---

2   For the text of the Geneva Conventions see D. Schindler, J. Toman, *eds., The Laws of Armed Conflict, A Collection of Conventions, Resolutions and Other Documents* 289-517 (1973).

3   For the text of Protocol I see *Commentary on the Additional Protocols to the Geneva Conventions,* ICRC (1987).

4   Articles 49/I, 50/II, 129/III and 146/IV.

The Geneva Conventions all contain a similar provision defining the notion of grave breaches under each of the Conventions,[5] as follows:

a) wilful killing;
b) torture or inhuman treatment, including biological experiments;
c) wilfully causing great suffering or serious injury to body or health;
d) extensive destruction and appropriation of property, not justified by military necessity and carried out unlawfully and wantonly;
e) compelling a prisoner of war or other protected person to serve in the forces of the hostile Power;
f) wilfully depriving a prisoner of war or other protected person of the rights of fair and regular trial prescribed in the Third or Fourth Convention;
g) unlawful deportation or transfer of a protected person;
h) unlawful confinement of a protected person;
i) taking of hostages.

Such conduct amounts to grave breaches under the Conventions only if it has been directed against persons or objects which are qualified by the Conventions as 'protected' persons or objects. This implies a clear restriction, for the Conventions attach 'protected' status only to persons and objects which are in the hands of an adversary and, in the case of combatants, no longer actively engaged in hostilities.

This may not appear in so many words in the First and Second Conventions. The First Convention defines protected persons as the wounded and sick belonging to any of the categories listed in Article 13 as well as medical personnel referred to in Articles 24 and 26. The protected objects are those covered by the Articles 19 and 35. The Second Convention defines protected persons as the wounded, sick and shipwrecked belonging to any of the categories listed in Article 13 as well as personnel referred to in Articles 36 and 37. The protected objects under that Convention are hospital ships mentioned in Articles 22, 24, 25 and 27. In each of the two Conventions the relationship between protected person or protected object and the fact of having fallen into the hands of the enemy is explicitly mentioned.[6]

This relationship appears unmistakably in the Third and Fourth Conventions. A prisoner of war of course has this status only while taken

---

5   Articles 50/I, 51/II, 130/III and 147/IV.
6   See Articles 35/I and 37/II.

prisoner by the enemy. In the Fourth Convention only members of the civilian population in occupied territory qualify as protected persons *vis-à-vis* the occupying Power.

It is true that the latter Convention in its Part II also contains provisions on the general protection of populations, *i.e.*, covering the whole of the population, and not just the part in occupied territory, but nowhere in Part II is it stated that the civilian population as a whole and as such is to be protected. What is crucial is whether the Conventions specifically consider certain categories of persons and objects as persons or objects 'which shall be respected and protected'. Only thus qualified, may such persons or objects become the 'victim' of violations of provisions of the Conventions, which, in serious cases, may amount to 'grave breaches'.

We shall discuss later in this essay the extent to which Protocol I, in particular Article 85, has followed the same methodology. Before doing so, it seems appropriate to consider further the kinds of substantive conduct which constitute grave breaches under the four Conventions.

It is to be noted first that whether conduct 'unlawful' or incompatible with specific provisions of the Conventions, can only be interpreted in conjunction with other norms of international law, which may draw the line between what is to be considered licit or illicit. Thus there would be 'unlawful deportation or transfer of a protected person' within the meaning of the Fourth Convention only to the extent that such conduct took place in violation of the provisions of Article 49 of that Convention. It is already much less clear in what cases there is 'unlawful confinement' of a protected person under the same Convention. In particular it remains unclear whether there is unlawful confinement only in cases where legal authority to order or apply confinement is lacking or has been misused, or also in cases where the detaining Power is withholding rights to which the detainee, who has otherwise been detained on legitimate grounds, is entitled.

It is also not immediately clear which provisions the Conventions are referring to, when qualifying as grave breaches the extensive destruction and appropriation of protected property committed 'unlawfully and wantonly'. The wording of this provision has apparently been inspired by Article 6(2,b) of the Charter of the International Military Tribunal, adopted as an Annex to the Agreement of London of 8 August 1945, which in its definition of 'war crimes', referred to as 'the violations of the laws and customs of war', includes: '... wanton destruction of cities, towns or villages, or devastation not justified by military necessity.' This description finds its predecessor in Article 23(g) of the Regulations Respecting the Laws and Customs of War on Land, which prohibits destruction or seizure of the enemy's property, 'unless such destruction or seizure be imperatively demanded by the necessities of war.'[7]

At first sight it looks somewhat surprising to find prohibitions derived from combat law, the so-called 'Hague law of warfare', being incorporated in the Geneva Conventions, since property or objects specifically protected under the First and Second Convention may under no circumstance be made the object of an attack. The same is true for property which has been specifically qualified as 'protected objects' under the Fourth Convention.[8] Thus it seems awkward that only cases of 'excessive destruction, not justified by military necessity and carried out wantonly' of such property would amount to a grave breach.

Otherwise the only point of reference in the Fourth Convention is Article 53, which generally prohibits the destruction by the Occupying Power of real or personal property not belonging to that Power, except where such destruction is rendered absolutely necessary by military operations. In the context of this Article the qualification as a grave breach of cases where such destruction becomes 'extensive' and is carried out 'wantonly' appears to be appropriate.

It has to be added, however, that Article 53 concerns only destruction of property and not its unlawful appropriation. Here the only relevant point of reference in the Fourth Convention seems to be Article 33(2) prohibiting pillage against protected persons.

The rights of a protected person to fair and regular trial are described in the Third Convention in Articles 84, 99, 105 and 106 and in the Fourth Convention in Articles 66, 70, 71, 72 and 73.

As far as prisoners of war are concerned those rights include the right in principle to be tried by a military court or at least by a court 'which offers the essential guarantees of independence and impartiality as generally recognized, and in particular, the procedure which affords the accused the rights and means of defence provided for in Article 105'. Article 99 contains the rule *nulla poena sine praevia lege* as well as the *nemo tenetur* rule and the right to legal assistance. This is further elaborated in the important Article 105/III. This Article enumerates basic guarantees for an adequate defence and the communication of the particulars of any charge made against the prisoner of war. In principle trials are to be held in the presence of representatives of Protecting Powers, although hearings in camera are not prohibited. The right of

---

7   See Schindler, Toman, op. cit. n. 2, at 77.
8   See *inter alia* Articles 18, 21 and 22/IV.

appeal or application for pardon against a sentence has to be made available.

The rights of the civilian population in occupied territory *vis-à-vis* the Occupying Power are of a similar nature. Non-political, military tribunals only are qualified to sit in trial in occupied territory. This reflects on the one hand the idea that an occupation is to be temporary by its nature and is not to provide the Occupying Power a right of annexation, or a territorial expansion of its sovereignty as embodied in its civil judicature. On the other hand, it assumes that military courts are able to offer all fundamental guarantees for a fair and equitable administration of justice.

The *nulla poena* rule has also been provided for, while courts of the Occupying Power have jurisdiction only with respect to offences committed after the beginning of the occupation. Moreover, the rights to legal assistance and to enjoy sufficient opportunity to prepare one's defence have been elaborated in more detail than in the Third Convention. Here too, representatives of Protecting Powers are entitled to attend the trials, although again hearings in camera are not precluded. Rights to appeal or petition for a pardon must be ensured.

One may question whether, even if all fundamental procedural rules under the Third or Fourth Convention have been observed in respect of a protected person, there may still be room for arguing that he has not enjoyed 'the rights of fair and regular trial' to an extent which amounts to a grave breach of the relevant Convention. This seems unlikely, since the provisions of these two Conventions which define grave breaches explicitly refer to what has been prescribed by the Conventions and the relevant articles do not refer to general principles of law. This, as we will discuss later on, is somewhat different under Article 85(4,e) of Protocol I.

At first sight the prohibition against compelling protected persons, in particular prisoners of war and civilians in occupied territory, to serve in the forces of a hostile Power, seems to be a clear and unambiguous provision. However, it may not always be easy to draw a clearcut line between licit coercion of protected persons who are detained or who are present in occupied territory, to perform labour, including labour for the benefit of the hostile Power, and illicit enlistment in, or employment for that purpose by, that Power's forces. The fact that the relevant provision of the Conventions refers just to 'forces' and not to 'armed forces' seems to imply that other institutions empowered to use force or violence, such as police forces, para-military forces or citizen militias, may be covered. The dividing line may be found by resorting to Articles 50/III and 40/IV, which enumerate the kinds of labour to which protected persons may be subjected by a hostile Power.

What remain as grave breaches under the Conventions are types of conduct which are considered as such without further qualification. It is, however, uncertain whether they are described and interpreted in the same way under the national laws and legal practices of the Parties to the Conventions. Some of these types of conduct have been made the subject of subsequent specific international Conventions, which have elaborated their legal description.

This is the case for instance with the taking of hostages, which constitutes a grave breach under the Fourth Convention. This type of conduct has been defined in the International Convention Against the Taking of Hostages of 19 December 1979. Article 1 of that Convention reads as follows:

'Any person who seizes or detains and threatens to kill, to injure or to continue to detain another person (hereinafter referred to as the "hostage") in order to compel a third party, namely a State, an international intergovernmental organisation, a natural or juridical person, or a group of persons, to do or abstain from doing any act as an explicit or implicit condition for the release of the hostage, commits the offence of taking of hostages ("hostage-taking") within the meaning of this Convention.'

The second paragraph adds to this:

'Any person who:
(a)   attempts to commit an act of hostage-taking, or
(b)   participates as an accomplice of anyone who commits or attempts to commit an act of hostage-taking likewise commits an offence for the purpose of this Convention.'

Something similar applies to the offence of 'torture', qualified as a grave breach under all four Conventions. Torture is defined in the Convention Against Torture and Other Cruel, Inhuman or Degrading Treatment or Punishment of 10 December 1984 in the following terms:

'For the purpose of this Convention, the term "torture" means any act by which severe pain or suffering, whether physical or mental, is intentionally inflicted on a person for such purposes as obtaining from him or a third person information or a confession, punishing him for an act he or a third person has committed or is suspected of having committed, or intimidating him or a third person, or for any reason based on discrimination of any kind, when such pain or suffering is inflicted by or at the instigation of or with the consent or acquiescence of a public official or other person acting in an official capacity. It does not include pain or suffering arising only from, or inherent in or incidental to lawful sanctions.'

What is remarkable is that the Geneva Conventions put torture on an equal footing with 'inhuman treatment' as grave breaches. As an example of the latter, reference is made to biological experiments. It has to be assumed that this includes the 'medical or scientific experiments not necessitated by the medical (dental or hospital) treatment' to which the Articles 13/III and 32/IV refer. This is remarkable since the Convention Against Torture does make a distinction between torture on the one hand and other inhuman and degrading treatment on the other. As far as the latter types of conduct are concerned the Convention does not create the same obligations under international law as for torture, particularly as concerns the obligation to establish universal criminal jurisdiction, the qualification of these offences as extraditable offences, the non-applicability of a defence based on superior orders, the obligation of non-refoulement etc..[9] Whereas the Geneva Conventions do not differentiate between torture and other inhuman treatment, it follows that the latter type of conduct, when committed in time of international armed conflict against protected persons, is also subject to the universal criminal jurisdiction of the Parties to the Conventions and is an offence for which extradition in the form of handing over of alleged offenders is to be available.

The notion of biological experiments was further elaborated when Protocol I was negotiated, in particular in Article 11. This should give national legislatures and courts a sufficient basis for its application.

It is more difficult to judge when circumstances have indeed amounted to a situation of 'inhuman treatment' constituting a grave breach of the Conventions. For criminal responsibility to be warranted, it has to be apparent that deliberate human behaviour has been conducive to the inhumanity of the treatment concerned. There has to be evidence that such treatment was unnecessary, that is, that it could have been prevented without any serious risk for the offender. The application of corporate punishment constitutes an appropriate example.

Specific cases of inhuman treatment are those where persons are wilfully subjected to great suffering or serious injury to body or health. Here again a certain margin of appreciation is bound to exist in assessing whether in a specific case the suffering has been sufficiently great or the

---

9   See Article 16 of the Convention Against Torture and Other Cruel, Inhuman or Degrading Treatment or Punishment.

injury sufficiently serious to make the conduct concerned amount to a grave breach.

This seems anyway to be the case where injury has resulted in permanent disablement or where suffering has lead to chronic traumatic consequences, but does not exclude the application of the Conventional provisions in cases of less serious results, particularly where it can be established that the offender intended to inflict very serious suffering or injury.

Finally, the offence the Conventions list as the first of the grave breaches is wilful killing. Wilful killing constitutes a grave breach when persons, having the status of protected persons are deliberately killed by someone who has the obligation to respect that status. This implies that the offender knew that his victims were protected persons and that it was his intention to kill such persons in that capacity. It is not necessary, however, to establish that such killing was done with other specific motives such as premeditation or with malice, or under specific circumstances such as the abuse of power or confidence. Such additional requirements should not be inferred from the use of the term 'murder' in Article 32/IV.

One might argue that according to the terms of the Conventions, wilful killing amounts to a grave breach only when there is more than one victim. Taken literally, the Conventions suppose that grave breaches are 'acts, committed against persons protected by the Conventions.' Such an interpretation, however, is untenable, since it would be at variance with the other formulations used in the Articles concerned, which refer to 'compelling a protected person to serve in the forces of a hostile Power' or 'wilfully depriving a protected person of the rights of fair and regular trial.'

3.   GRAVE BREACHES OF PROTOCOL I

3.1   Traditional patterns of Geneva Law

Turning to Protocol I, what do its provisions on the repression of breaches of the Protocol actually add to the system of penal law enforcement as embodied in the four Conventions? The key provision is Article 85 of the Protocol. Its negotiating history has been described extensively

elsewhere;[10] we will confine ourselves here to considering the structure
and content of the Article, in which a number of additional 'grave
breaches' are defined. But first of all the Article makes clear that the
system of the four Conventions for the suppression of both ordinary
breaches and grave breaches likewise applies to the suppression of ordinary
and grave breaches of the Protocol. This means that, with respect to grave
breaches of the Protocol, Contracting Parties have to enact legislation
necessary to provide effective penal sanctions for persons committing, or
ordering such offences. Moreover, they have to establish the necessary
criminal jurisdiction, *i.e.*, universal jurisdiction, allowing the courts of
each Contracting Party to take cognizance of grave breaches, irrespective
of where and by whom they may have been committed. Moreover,
provisions must be made for handing over persons who are suspected of
having committed such grave breaches to other Contracting Parties.

As far as breaches, which are not grave, are concerned, each Party is
also under an obligation to take measures for their suppression, even if this
need not imply resort to penal law in all cases. Other means of
enforcement, such as disciplinary law, may be appropriate.

Paragraph 2 of Article 85 of Protocol I states that conduct which is
considered to constitute grave breaches under the four Conventions -the
scope of which has been analysed in the previous part- shall also constitute
grave breaches of the Protocol, if committed against persons or objects
belonging to categories qualifying as 'protected persons' and 'protected
objects' under the Protocol.

As far as persons are concerned, this applies to those who, by virtue of
the broader terms of Article 44 of the Protocol, compared to those of
Article 4 of the Third Convention, are entitled to prisoner of war status.
Another category of protected persons under the Protocol are those who
must be treated as prisoners of war according to Article 45, as long as
their status has not been finally determined. A third category comprises
refugees and stateless persons who, by virtue of Article 73 of the Protocol
are in all circumstances protected persons within the meaning of Parts I
and III of the Fourth Convention. This includes persons who fled from the
Occupying Power prior to the occupation and were already officially
recognized as refugees at that time by the Occupied Power. Thus the
general condition that persons qualify as 'protected persons' only if they
have fallen in the hands of the adverse or hostile Power, may imply for

---

10 See J. de Breucker, *La répression des infractions graves aux dispositions du premier Protocole
additionnel aux quatre Conventions de Genève du 12 août 1949*, XVI Revue de Droit Pénal
Militaire et de Droit de la Guerre 495 (1977).

such persons that they qualify as such *vis-à-vis* the authorities or forces of the State of their own nationality.[11]

Yet another category of persons are those wounded, sick and shipwrecked who are not considered as 'protected persons' under the First and Second Conventions. This does not concern persons who are already covered by the terms of Articles 13/I and 13/II, *i.e.*, persons who are entitled to protection as prisoners of war, but covers wounded, sick and shipwrecked civilians not entitled to treatment as prisoners of war, as well as those who find themselves shipwrecked (including the victims of forced landings of aircraft) in waters other than the sea. Such persons are considered as 'protected persons' only if they belong to the adverse Party and provided they continue to refrain from hostilities. If the latter condition is not met, the wilful killing of such a person cannot amount to a grave breach under the Protocol.

The description of 'medical or religious personnel' and 'medical units or medical transports' is also somewhat broader in the Protocol than in the First and Second Conventions. For instance under the Protocol they include the medical and religious personnel attached to civil defence organizations. Also these persons and units or transports are qualified as 'protected' only towards the adverse Party and any grave breaches committed against them by the adverse Party produce the legal consequences following from the four Conventions and Article 85(1) of the Protocol.

3.2   The incorporation of Hague Law

The conclusion so far is that Article 85(2) of Protocol I does not depart from the premises of the Conventions for qualifying conduct as grave breaches. The basic condition that this is the case only if persons or objects, explicitly defined as 'protected', have fallen into the hands of, or are in the power of, the adverse Party and therefore in a position of increased vulnerability.

The drafters of the Protocol had to face the question, however, whether violations of provisions of the Protocol which are traditionally ranged under that part of the laws of war commonly referred to as 'Hague Law', should be submitted to the system of penal law enforcement of the Geneva law? In particular should this include violations of provisions pertaining to

---

11 See J.J.E. Schutte, *The Applicability of the Geneva Conventions on the Protection of War Victims and Protocol I to the Relation Between a Contracting Party and Its Own Nationals*, 33 Österreichische Zeitschrift für öffentliches Recht und Völkerrecht 29 (1982).

the general protection of civilians and the civilian population as such (even
outside occupied territory) against hostilities and their effects, as well as
the protection of civilian objects indispensable to the survival of the
civilian population or whose destruction is likely to have catastrophic,
uncontrollable consequences?

It was observed that the Conventions which are part of The Hague Law
had never contained specific provisions on individual criminal
responsibility for violations of any of their rules.

It should, however, not be inferred from this that public international
law rejects any individual criminal responsibility for any such violations.
In fact it has been accepted and explicitly stated in the London Agreement
of 8 August 1945 and the Annexed Charter of the International Military
Tribunal, established at Nuremberg for the trial and punishment of the
major war criminals of the European Axis, and it has been reaffirmed in
GA Res. 95(I) 11 December 1946 and in the Principles of International
Law recognized in the Charter of the Nuremberg Tribunal and in the
Judgment of the Tribunal, adopted in 1950 by the ILC.[12]

The description in these documents of war crimes for which the
existence of individual criminal responsibility was assumed was as follows:

'Violations of the laws and customs of war. Such violations shall include,
but not be limited to,
(i)   murder, ill-treatment or deportation to slave labour or for any other
        purpose of civilian population of or in occupied territory,
(ii)   murder, ill-treatment of prisoners of war or persons on the seas,
(iii)   killing of hostages,
(iv)   plunder of public or private property,
(v)   wanton destruction of cities, towns or villages, or devastation not
        justified by military necessity.'

The types of conduct referred to under (i), (ii) and (iii) must be deemed to
be covered by the scope of application of the four Geneva Conventions of
1949. To some extent the same is true for the type of conduct referred to
under (iv), in so far as the acts occur within occupied territory.[13] The
prohibition of this kind of conduct, and certainly the kind of conduct
referred to under (v), finds its source in Articles 28 and 25 respectively, of
the Regulations Concerning the Laws and Customs of War on Land,
Annexed to the Hague Conventions of 1899 and 1907 on the Laws and

---

12 See Schindler, Toman, op. cit. n. 2, at 689-702.
13 See Articles 33/IV and 53 read together with 147/IV.

Customs of War on Land. Those Regulations, however, have not been further elaborated in written public international law since World War II in the way in which the Geneva Conventions of 1949 have elaborated other parts of the laws and customs of war.

The single exception is to be found in the Hague Convention of 14 May 1954 on the Protection of Cultural Property in the Event of Armed Conflict,[14] which constitutes an elaboration of the principle contained in Article 27 of The Hague Regulations. This Convention, though concluded at the Hague, nevertheless shows a number of features in common with the Geneva law of 1949. In this connection reference may be made to Article 28 of the 1954 Hague Convention, obliging Contracting Parties to take, within their ordinary criminal jurisdiction, all necessary steps to prosecute and impose penal or disciplinary sanctions upon those persons, of whatever nationality, who commit or order a 'breach' of that Convention.

The step taken in 1954 was followed in 1977 in Article 85 of Protocol I, where -initially in conformity with the principles of the Charter of the Nuremberg Tribunal- certain serious violations of provisions of the Protocol concerning the general protection of the civilian population against effects of hostilities and concerning methods and means of warfare are qualified as grave breaches of the Protocol, with all the consequences of penal law. Those grave breaches are listed in Article 85(3). They deserve a closer look.

3.3   The details of Article 85(3)

The opening sentence of paragraph 3 refers first to the fourth paragraph of Article 11. That paragraph departs from the corresponding provisions of the 1949 Conventions in qualifying as grave breaches certain kinds of conduct against persons who are in the power of a Party other than the Party to which they belong, *irrespective* of their status, that is, whether they are protected persons or not. The conduct itself, as described in Article 11(1) of the Protocol may be considered as a definition of 'inhuman treatment' or of 'wilfully causing serious injury to body or health'.

For the remaining types of conduct, listed under (a) to (f), to constitute grave breaches, it is necessary that they be performed wilfully, in violation of the relevant provisions of the Protocol, and with certain specific consequences. The last condition implies that attempts to commit these acts cannot amount to grave breaches. One might question whether the required

---

14 See Schindler, Toman, op. cit. n. 2, at 525-564.

intent, expressed by the word 'wilfully', implies that intent must also be directed at producing the specific consequences, *i.e.*, causing death or serious injury to body or health. Such a conclusion seems in general to go too far. It seems sufficient that the conduct concerned, *i.e.*, making certain items the object of an attack, be performed wilfully in the sense that the perpetrator knows the character of the item under attack.

In two instances, however, -those referred to under (b) and (c)- the perpetrator must know that his conduct will have certain consequences, namely excessive loss of life or injury to civilians or excessive damage to civilian objects, or both. The required knowledge may be construed as 'conditional intent' by applying a standard of 'wilful blindness' or the criterion that the offender has willingly and knowingly accepted the risk that his acts might have such consequences.

Making the civilian population or individual civilians the object of attack is prohibited in Article 51(2) of the Protocol. The concept of 'attack' is defined in Article 49(1). It does not matter whether the acts of violence were committed for offensive or defensive purposes.

One may wonder who may be held accountable for the type of conduct described by the words 'launching an attack' or 'making someone or something the object of attack'. It is arguable that the responsibility for 'launching an attack', as this term is used in subparagraphs (b) and (c) of paragraph 3, lies with the commanding officer who ordered the attack, or perhaps, with anyone having authority to determine which objectives are to be attacked. Such responsibility would not fall on persons merely charged with the execution of the order.

The terms 'making the object of attack' -see subparagraphs (a), (d) and (e) of paragraph 3 as well as subparagraph (d) of paragraph 4- appear to allow for a wider interpretation and to include in appropriate cases a responsibility for those who are engaged in the execution of attacks, and for everyone taking part in hostilities.

It follows from Article 50 who are to be considered as civilians and what is to be considered as civilian population. It has to be inferred *a contrario* from subparagraph (a), that making civilian objects the object of attacks, even in cases where this causes death or serious injury to body or health of civilians, does *not* constitute a grave breach, unless such attacks are covered by the terms of subparagraphs (b), (c) or (d).

Acts described in subparagraph (b) cover attacks, which are not aimed against the civilian population, but which are carried out in an indiscriminate way, that is without making distinctions between specific military objectives and civilian objects, while knowing that this will cause excessive losses among the civilian population or excessive damage to civilian objects. The norm violated is Article 51(5,b) of the Protocol.

It is virtually impossible to tell *in abstracto* under what circumstances losses are excessive or disproportionate. It seems possible to assess this only in a concrete case submitted to judicial decision based on the proportionality, or rather serious disproportionality, between the actual number of victims made among the civilian population and the direct military advantage anticipated beforehand. For the act to be qualified as a grave breach there should be sufficient evidence to assume that the author 'launching' the attack actually understood beforehand, or at least accepted the calculated risk, that the attack would cause disproportionate losses to the civilian population or disproportionate damage to civilian objects.

The norm underlying the grave breaches described in subparagraph (c) of paragraph 3 is set out in Article 56 of the Protocol. It has to be assumed that 'works and installations containing dangerous forces' are those enumerated in Article 56, that is dams, dykes and nuclear electrical generation stations. That Article can hardly be understood other than as a specification of the general principle contained in Article 51. The norm that dams, dykes and nuclear generation stations shall not be made the object of attack if such attack may cause severe, that is, disproportionate, losses among the civilian population follows from that principle. It is simply recognized that this is often (though not always) likely to be the case for such objects. That in addition Article 56 provides that such objects may under such circumstances not be attacked even where they are military objectives, looks somewhat awkward in view of Article 52, which already prohibits in general terms making civilian objects the object of attacks or reprisals. The fact that Article 56(3) goes on to reaffirm the rule of proportionality in cases of attacks made against dams, dykes or nuclear generation stations performing functions supportive to military operations, is just a reaffirmation of this general principle.

One might thus conclude that subparagraph (c) of Article 85(3) does not substantially add anything to subparagraph (b).

Subparagraph (d), as well as subparagraph (d) of paragraph 4 (to be addressed in paragraph 3.4) provide the only examples of cases where attacks directed against objects may amount to grave breaches. Under paragraph 3 it remains necessary that such an attack produces victims, albeit not to a disproportionate extent, whereas this is not necessary for the grave breaches contemplated in paragraph 4.

The definition of 'non-defended localities' or 'demilitarized zones' is given in the Articles 59 and 60 respectively of the Protocol. It concerns places and zones in respect of which it is established between the Parties to the conflict, either by virtue of the exchange of declarations referred to in Article 60 or of express agreements contemplated in Article 60, that they have such status. If there is to be a grave breach under this provision, it has to be established that the person who made a non-defended locality or a demilitarized zone the object of attack or who was involved in its execution, actually knew that such localities or zones had this particular status and had not lost it in the meantime.

Article 41 of the Protocol protects the person *'hors de combat'*. These are persons who have not yet obtained the status of 'protected person' within the meaning of the Third or Fourth Convention or Article 45 of the Protocol, since they have not yet fallen 'in the hands of' the adverse Party, but who would be entitled to that status, once this is the case. From that moment any wilful act of violence against them causing their death or serious injury would constitute a grave breach under the terms of the Conventions and Article 85(2) of the Protocol. It is therefore perfectly understandable that the wilful killing or injuring of persons *hors de combat* has also been made a grave breach, since this shows that any acts performed with a view to depriving persons of their right to acquire the status of protected persons are to be taken as seriously as the violation of the basic rights to which persons having that status are entitled.

The prohibition of perfidy, in particular by misusing internationally recognized emblems intended to provide clear identification to persons and objects subject to special protection under international law, had already been embodied in the Regulations Respecting the Laws and Customs of War on Land in their Article 23(f). Abuse of the distinctive signs recognized by the Conventions themselves has been prohibited in Articles 54/I and 45/II, although the violation of these Articles has not been made into a grave breach. This has been done in the Protocol, in cases where such abuse amounts to perfidy as described in Article 37 and causes death or serious injury to body or health. Moreover the provision covers perfidious abuse of other protective signs created or recognized by the Protocol. One may observe that Article 85(3,e) only mentions 'emblems' and 'signs', whereas Article 38 also makes reference to 'signals'. The negotiating history of Article 85 does not show an intent to exclude the perfidious abuse of protective signals from the Article. It should therefore be taken for granted that such abuse may also constitute a grave breach of the Protocol.

3.4 The details of Article 85(4)

Article 85(4) is different from paragraph 3 where the conduct described in that paragraph is less clearly connected with specific rules or norms created or set out in the four Conventions or the Protocol. And yet the opening sentence again requires that if such conduct is to constitute a grave breach it shall be performed in violation of the Conventions and the Protocol. It is, however, not always necessary that such conduct be qualified by certain effects produced by it.

The conduct described in subparagraph (a) is already largely covered by what has been defined as a grave breach under Article 147/IV, read in conjunction with Article 49/IV. The latter Article in its final paragraph prohibits an Occupying Power deporting or transfering parts of its own civilian population into the territory it occupies. Since its own population does not have the status of 'protected persons' under the Fourth Convention, Article 147 is not applicable to this situation. So in this respect Article 85(4,a) extends the existing scope of grave breaches under the Fourth Convention. This extension has obviously been inspired by opponents of the settlement policies of the Israeli Governments with respect to territories occupied by Israel since the Six-Day War of 1967.

Subparagraph (b) in its turn has been inspired by experiences of delays in the repatriation of prisoners of war after the armed conflict between India and Pakistan in 1971, from which the independent State of Bangladesh emerged. Strictly speaking the notion of 'repatriation' is used in the Conventions only in relation to prisoners of war, and in particular in Articles 118-119/III and 109-110/III. As far as civilians having the status of protected persons are concerned, Article 35/IV offers them only the right to be allowed to leave the territory of the hostile Power. This does not, however, imply the right to be repatriated to the territory of their own State. Thus subparagraph (b) seems to have no substantive meaning as far as the reference to civilians is concerned. When assessing whether there has been 'unjustifiable' delay in the repatriation of prisoners of war one has to take account of the fact that such prisoners may have expressed the wish not to be repatriated at all or at least not immediately.

When considering the kind of practices qualified as grave breaches by virtue of subparagraph (c), one has to concede that here the drafters of the Protocol have completely departed from the traditional approach. This consisted in finding, when defining grave breaches, a certain connection with specific rules or norms set out in the Conventions or the Protocol. In fact the term '*apartheid*' has nowhere been used in any of those instruments, nor has the notion of 'practices of *apartheid*' been defined.

Moreover, in its description of a grave breach, subparagraph (c) does not relate the status of protected person to the victim of the practices concerned. Whenever specific international instruments against *apartheid* refer to this phenomenon as a crime -*e.g.* in the International Convention on the Suppression and Punishment of the Crime of Apartheid[15]- it is considered to consitute a 'crime against humanity'. Now if Article 85(5) of the Protocol has any meaning, this must be that grave breaches are not to be ranged in the class of 'crimes against humanity' but in the class of 'war crimes'.

It is therefore to be concluded that subparagraph (c) of paragraph 4 is legally relevant only in cases where the kind of conduct to which it refers would qualify as 'torture or inhuman treatment against protected persons' and thus constitute a grave breach of the Conventions and the Protocol.

Obviously subparagraph (d) is intended to link up with the provisions of Article 53. Given the quite general formulation of that Article it has to be appreciated that the drafters have tried, for purposes of defining behaviour appropriately qualifying as a grave breach, to introduce some specific elements. The two provisions are identical as far as the description of the nature of the protected objects are concerned. These are 'historic monuments, works of art or places of worship which constitute the cultural or spiritual heritage of peoples'.

If there is to be a grave breach these kinds of objects have to be involved and the four following conditions must be met:
a) that they are 'clearly recognized';
b) that they are given special protection by special arrangement, for example within the framework of a competent international organization;
c) that they are not used in support of the military effort; and
d) that they are not located in the immediate proximity of military objectives.

Apart from that, the act should have resulted in 'extensive destruction' of the object concerned.

This description raises many questions which are only partially answered by referring to other international instruments,[16] even if such instruments are not binding upon the parties to the conflict. It appears as though the provision has been drafted with only immovable property in

---

15 Convention adopted by the UN in GA Res. 3068 (XXVIII) of 30 November 1973.
16 Schindler, Toman, op. cit. n. 2, at 525-564.

mind, although movable property has not been explicitly excluded. A specific reference to transport of works of art is lacking.

Whereas Article 53 prohibits 'acts of hostility' against cultural and religious property Article 85(4,d) uses the terms 'making the object of attack' which seems to have a more specific and narrower meaning.

It is not clear how to interpret the words 'clearly recognized', or whether this implies that the specific character of the objects concerned has to appear from distinctive signs or features, or whether it may be just a matter of subjective appreciation. It is also not clear whether the special arrangement from which the objects derive their protection has to be one which equally binds the two Parties to the conflict and whether the person responsible for the attack should have been aware of the existence and validity of such an arrangement.

Despite the undoubtedly good intentions of the drafters of this text, one cannot but ask oneself whether it really adds much of substance to the grave breach consisting of 'the extensive destruction and appropriation of protected property, not justified by military necessity and carried out unlawfully and wantonly' as covered by Article 147/IV, perhaps completed by the grave breaches covered by the terms of Article 85(3,b) of the Protocol.

What is it subparagraph (e) adds to the provisions of the Articles 130 of Convention III and 147 of Convention IV, where this subparagraph refers only to the rights of fair trial of persons who have the status of 'protected persons'? The answer has to be found in Article 75(3) and (4) of the Protocol, which according to Article 72 pertains *inter alia* to Parts I and III of the Fourth Convention. It is uncertain whether Article 75 applies also to prisoners of war. An argument against this is the fact that the Article forms part of Part IV of the Protocol, which deals only with the civilian population. An argument in favour is the fact that Article 75(1) refers in very general terms to 'persons who are in the power of a Party to the conflict and who do not benefit from more favourable treatment under the Conventions.' Anyway it should be pointed out that Article 75 contains a more elaborate interpretation of the notion of 'fair trial' than the relevant provisions of both the Third and the Fourth Conventions.

Thus Article 75 explicitly refers to the principles of *lex mitior*, the *presumptio innocentiae*, the right to be present during the trial, of *nemo tenetur*, of *ne bis in idem* and the right to have the judgment pronounced publicly. These principles are not mentioned in so many words in the Third and Fourth Conventions.

The fact that in a given case one of the guarantees of Article 75(4) has not been observed in respect of a protected person need not by itself imply that a grave breach of the Protocol has been committed. This would be the case only if the failure to observe one or more of those guarantees in the course of the proceedings would lead to the conclusion that the procedure taken in its entirety has not been fair and regular.

In such a case there would be individual criminal responsibility *vis-à-vis* all Parties to the Protocol for the very persons who seriously failed in the exercise of their own professional responsibilities as judges and prosecutors in criminal cases. A further reflection of the juridical and practical consequences of this last statement might be a suitable subject in itself for a separate essay. It would go beyond the agreed limits of the present one.

4.   FINAL OBSERVATION

One concluding observation can be offered with respect to Article 85(5). Here I can be brief, in contrast to many other authors who have devoted lengthy speculation to this provision:[17] in my view this paragraph is legally meaningless.

Protocol I is in force now for more than ten years but may not have been applicable to many of the armed conflicts which took place over this period. To the knowledge of the present author there have not been any reports on applications of its system of repression of breaches. It is therefore hard to tell whether this system is able to contribute in any fashion to the enforcement of the rules of international humanitarian law. Let us hope that the next decade shall not produce many opportunities to put this method of implementation of international legal norms to the test. I venture that this mechanism was not created in the first place to be operative and effective, but rather to embody a Code of ethical rules which the community of civilised nations has agreed to declare to remain valid under all circumstances, and whose violations it qualified by the most depreciative term available: crime.

---

17 See G. Doucet, *La qualification des infractions graves au droit international humanitaire*, in
    F. Kalshoven, Y. Sandoz, eds., Implementation of International Law 79 (1989).

THE SUPPRESSION OF WAR CRIMES
UNDER ADDITIONAL PROTOCOL I

CHRISTINE VAN DEN WYNGAERT

1. Introduction

2. The new grave breaches under Protocol I

3. The penal control system under the Protocol

4. The implementation of the grave breaches provisions in domestic law

5. The international control mechanism based on the rule *aut dedere aut judicare*

6. Conclusion

1. INTRODUCTION

In his book on belligerent reprisals, Kalshoven believed that a total prohibition of belligerent reprisals would, in the end, be 'the only tenable proposition'.[1] When he wrote this, in the early seventies, belligerent reprisals were only prohibited under the 'law of Geneva', not under the 'law of The Hague'. In this respect, the explicit prohibition of reprisals against civilian targets in Article 51(6) of Protocol I (1977)[2] was a substantial step in the direction of what Kalshoven hoped the international community would eventually achieve.

However, while making this statement, Kalshoven at the same time warned that, in order for this prohibition to be effective, there should be other means to ensure that the laws of war will be respected:

---

1 F. Kalshoven, Belligerent Reprisals 375 (1971).
2 Protocol Additional to the Geneva Conventions of 12 August 1949, and Relating to the Protection of Victims of International Armed Conflicts (Protocol I) of 8 June 1977.

'... the power of belligerents to resort to belligerent reprisals can only be effectively abolished to the extent that other adequate means take over their function of law enforcement.'[3]

The question therefore is whether these 'other adequate means' have been realised. One of the 'other means' *par excellence* is the enforcement of the laws of war through the criminal law, through the prosecution and punishment of those responsible for the violation of the laws of war. This essay, written *en hommage* to the great Kalshoven, will briefly explore whether, in compensation for the quasi-abolition of legitimate belligerent reprisals, Protocol I has made a substantial contribution to the development of these 'other means'.

2.   THE NEW GRAVE BREACHES UNDER PROTOCOL I

Protocol I has considerably expanded the category of crimes that are considered to be 'grave breaches'. Under the Conventions of 1949, this category only included infringements of the 'law of Geneva', *i.e.*, the provisions for the protection of those who do not (or do not any longer) take part in hostilities, including the wounded and sick, prisoners of war and protected civilians.[4]

Protocol I not only adds new grave breaches to this category,[5] but introduces a new category of grave breaches, namely those referring to violations of the 'law of The Hague', *i.e.*, of the rules that regulate the conduct of hostilities as such. It is impossible to give an adequate summary of all these new grave breaches, which are contained in Article 85(3,4) of the Protocol. From the long enumeration, the following examples can be quoted:

---

3   Kalshoven, op. cit. n. 1.

4   Convention for the Amelioration of the Condition of the Wounded and Sick in Armed Forces in the Field, Article 50, 75 UNTS 31 (1950); Convention for the Amelioration of the Condition of Wounded, Sick and Shipwrecked Members of Armed Forces at Sea, Article 51, 75 UNTS 85 (1950); Convention Relative to the Treatment of Prisoners of War, Article 130, 75 UNTS 135 (1950); Convention Relative to the Protection of Civilian Persons in Time of War, Article 147, 75 UNTS 287 (1950).

5   See for example Article 11(4) (protecting the physical or mental health and integrity of persons in the power of the adverse party by prohibiting, *inter alia*, physical mutilations and medical or scientific experiments) and Article 85(2) (extending the applicable scope of the grave breaches under the 1949 Conventions to new categories of protected persons).

'Making the civilian population or individual civilians the object of an attack; launching an indiscriminate attack; making non-defended localities and demilitarised zones the object of an attack; making a person the object of an attack, knowing that he is *hors de combat*; the perfidious use of the Red Cross emblem; the transplantation by the Occupying Power of parts of its own civilian population into the territory it occupies; the unjustifiable delay in the return of prisoners; making clearly recognized historical monuments, works of art or places of worship which constitute the cultural or spiritual heritage of peoples and to which special protection has been given by a special arrangement, the object of an attack.'

These provisions are not new in the sense that they create new prohibitions: most of them refer to conduct that was already prohibited under the Hague Conventions of 1899 and 1907[6] and had been declared a war crime under the Nuremberg Charter.[7] What *is* new, however, is that, by declaring the conduct to be a 'grave breach', the Protocol has brought it under the international control mechanism based on the principle *aut dedere aut judicare*.[8] This means that States are now obliged to enact domestic legislation criminalizing the conduct described above and providing for the possibility either to extradite or to prosecute persons who are suspected or convicted of grave breaches.

3. THE PENAL CONTROL SYSTEM UNDER THE PROTOCOL

In order for the criminal law to be an adequate 'other means' to ensure that the laws of war are respected, it should, quite obviously, be enforceable and enforced. The question therefore is whether the Protocol, while creating new grave breaches, has also provided legal machinery to ensure that violations can, in practice, be suppressed. Only then can the Protocol,

---

6 Hague Conventions on Land Warfare, Articles 22-28, especially Articles 22 and 25 (Convention II with respect to the Laws and Customs of War on Land, 29 July 1899; Convention IV respecting the Laws and Customs on Land, 18 October 1907).

7 Agreement for the Prosecution and Punishment of Major War Criminals of the European Axis, London, 8 August 1945 (Nuremberg-Charter), Article 6(b). See also the Principles of International Law recognized in the Charter of the Nuremberg Tribunal and in the Judgment of the Tribunal (Nuremberg-Principles). Geneva, 29 June 1950, UN Doc A/1316 (1950).

8 The duty either to extradite or to prosecute is only applicable to grave breaches, not to the other violations of the Conventions and the Protocol. For example, violations of Article 3, common to the four Geneva Conventions of 1949 and relating to non-international conflicts, are not 'grave breaches' and thus beyond the scope of the international control mechanism based on the principle *aut dedere aut judicare*.

while nearly outlawing belligerent reprisals, be said to have offered the 'other means' insisted upon by Kalshoven.[9]

In contrast with its broad formulation of new grave breaches, the Protocol contains very few provisions relating to the penal enforcement of these grave breaches: it simply adopts the control mechanism set forth in the four Red Cross Conventions of 1949,[10] which is based on the above-mentioned principle *aut dedere aut judicare*.[11] However, in doing so, it fails to develop and refine the system further or to take into account the difficulties that had arisen from the practical application of the principle in the 25 years during which the Red Cross Conventions had already been in force.

These difficulties are concentrated in two areas: first, the development of domestic legislation for the implementation of the Conventions, and second the loopholes in the international co-operation system built on the principle *aut dedere aut judicare*.

4.　　THE IMPLEMENTATION OF THE GRAVE BREACHES PROVISIONS IN DOMESTIC LAW

It is sometimes argued that the implementation of the grave breaches provisions in domestic criminal law is superfluous because most grave breaches are already criminal acts under domestic penal statutes. While this may be true for many of the 'grave' breaches, it is not true for *all* grave breaches. For example, the perfidious use of the Red Cross emblem,[12] or the deprivation of a person of his fair trial rights under Article 75 of the Protocol[13] are, most probably, not criminal offences under the domestic legislation of most States.

Another problem may arise from the fact that, even in cases where grave breaches are covered by existing domestic legislation, the sanctions may not be adequate. For example, under Belgian law, it makes no difference whether the defendant has maimed two or two thousand prisoners of war, as far as the sanction is concerned: the general sentencing provision on this point in the penal code provides a ceiling of

9　*Supra*, n. 2.
10　Articles 49-50, 129, 146 of the four Conventions.
11　Article 85(1) of Protocol I.
12　Article 85(3,f) of Protocol I.
13　Article 85(4,e) of Protocol I.

two times the maximum sentence provided for the offence,[14] *i.e.*, depending on the circumstances, 2 x 6 months, 2 years or 5 years.[15] It is therefore appropriate for States to enact the necessary domestic legislation in order to ensure that grave breaches can be adequately suppressed.

This, however, is not the only problem as far as domestic law is concerned. In addition to the problem of lacunae in the national criminal legislation, another, perhaps even more important lacuna often exists: the uncertainty about the applicability of general justifications and excuses under domestic law to grave breaches of the Geneva Conventions and Protocol I. To put it in the language of criminal lawyers: the difficulties do not lie only in the 'special part' of the criminal law, but also in the 'general part'.

Concerning this general part, the question that still keeps arising today, although it was clearly answered by the Nuremberg Tribunal, is whether justifications and excuses under domestic criminal law can be applied to international crimes. The most traditional defences to be used in war crimes trials are *superior orders* and *necessity*. Although there seems to be a wide agreement among scholars, both with respect to superior orders[16] and to necessity,[17] that these defences cannot justify grave breaches of the Geneva Conventions or Protocol I, confusion seems to subsist among practitioners, and what is worse, in education programmes for the military.

From the (very few) war crimes trials that have taken place outside the context of World War II,[18] it appears that the defendants, although they

---

14 Article 60 of the Belgian Penal Code (1867).
15 Articles 398-400 of the Belgian Penal Code.
16 See generally Y. Dinstein, The Defense of Superior Orders in International Law (1965); E. Müller-Rappard, L'ordre supérieur militaire et la responsabilité pénale du subordonné (1965). See also A. Andries, *L'obéissance militaire et le droit international public*, Xe Journées d'études juridiques Jean Dabin 449 (1982); N. Keijzer, *Oorlogsmisdrijven en het Beroep op Wettelijk Voorschrift of Hoger Bevel: Artikel 10(1) van de Wet Oorlogsstrafrecht*, 73 Militair Rechtelijk Tijdschrift (War Crimes and the Defences of Legal Authorisation and Superior Orders: Article 10(1) of the War Crimes Statute) 344 (1980); J. Verhaegen, L'ordre illégal et son exécutant devant les juridictions pénales, 97 Journal des tribunaux 449 (1982).
17 Kalshoven, op. cit. n. 1., at 366; E. Castrèn, The Present Law of War and Neutrality 66 (1954); E. David, *'L'excuse de l'ordre supérieur et l'etat de nécessité'*, XIV Revue belge de droit international 612 (1978-1979); J. Verhaegen, *'L'activité militaire en période de crise'*, XXX Revue belge de droit international 312 (1984-1984).
18 The best-known case is that of Lt. Calley in the United States, who was prosecuted for his involvement in the massacre of My Lai. Text in L. Friedman, ed., The Laws of War. A Documentary History 1703 (1972). See also J. Rubin, *Legal Aspects of the My Lai Incident*, Oregon L. Rev. 171 (1971). In Belgium, there were two cases: the *Weise Case*, involving a sergeant who had killed an unarmed old woman during the crisis of Stanleyville in 1964, Court Martial of Brussels, 18 May 1966, Court of Appeal, 14 July 1966, reported by A.

often realized that they had engaged in forbidden conduct, mistakenly assumed that they were justified either by superior orders or by necessity. Lower courts have in certain instances accepted the argument, thus indicating that even professional lawyers are not well enough informed about the law on these points.[19]

It is therefore highly regrettable that the Protocol has not explicitly addressed these issues. The provision excluding the defence of superior orders, which was incorporated in the draft version of Protocol I,[20] was eventually deleted. No explicit provision relating to the defence of necessity was included.[21]

5. THE INTERNATIONAL CONTROL MECHANISM BASED ON THE RULE *AUT DEDERE AUT JUDICARE*

War crimes are one of the classic examples of international crimes for which an 'international control mechanism' is said to exist: the four Conventions of 1949 and Protocol I provide for the duty either to extradite or to prosecute suspected or convicted war criminals. On closer scrutiny, however, the system hardly seems to work. Problems exist on two levels, both with respect to extradition (*aut dedere*) and with respect to

Andries, 'La répression nationale des infractions graves au droit humanitaire - aspects criminologiques', XI Congress International Society of Military Law and the Laws of War, (1988), 1-2 Revue internationale de droit pénal militaire et du droit de la guerre 1990 (in print). See also the *Paratroopers Case*, involving a number of recruits who, during a simulation exercise, had tortured their captured 'prisoners of war', Court Martial of Liège, 20 November 1971. See also J. Verhaegen, *Savoir où porter le fer. A propos de la condamnation de six para-commandos*, 88 Journal des Tribunaux 137 (1973) and J. De Wolf, *A propos de la condamnation de six para-commandos. Ibid.*, at 186.

19 A Belgian example is the *Case of Schramme & Rodrique*. The facts occurred during the Congo-crisis in the sixties: Schramme ordered one of his mercenaries, Rodrique, to kill Quintin, an envoy of Mobutu. The case against Rodrique was originally discontinued, because the Court of Appeal of Brussels had held that the crime committed by Rodrique was justified by superior orders; in the opinion of the Court, Rodrique could not have believed that the order was illegal, Court of Appeal of Brussels (Chamber of Indictment), 29 June 1982, vacated by Supreme Court, 12 January 1983, 48 Rechtskundig Weekblad 667 (1984-1985)).

20 Article 77 of the Draft, discussed by B. De Schutter and C. Eliaerts, De Bescherming van het Individu in Moderne Conflictsituaties (The Protection of the Individual in Modern Conflict Situations) 165 (1974).

21 *Cf.*, The Convention Against Torture and Other Cruel, Inhuman or Degrading Treatment or Punishment, adopted by the General Assembly of the UN in 1984 (Annex to GA Resolution 39/46 of 10 December 1984). Article 2(2) of this Convention explicitly excludes necessity and superior orders (Article 2(3)) as justifications for torture.

prosecution (*aut judicare*). Here too, Protocol I has failed to remedy the problems.

With respect to extradition, the difficulties have arisen from the fact that, despite the circumstance that they created the obligation for States to extradite, the 1949 Red Cross Conventions have not dealt with the problem of the applicability of the traditional exceptions to extradition, such as, *inter alia*, the nationality exception, the political offence exception, statutory limitations, or the requirement of a treaty.

In the extradition cases involving war criminals after World War II, these exceptions have blocked the majority of the extradition requests, to the extent that it hardly seems exaggerated to say that, apart from the extraditions that have taken place right after the war in the framework of the UN War Crimes Commission, extradition of war criminals has been the exception rather than the rule.[22]

Protocol I has done nothing to cope with this problem. For example, while the draft excluded grave breaches from the political offence exception,[23] this provision was not maintained in the final text. The Protocol did not even adopt the standard formula used in nearly all international criminal law Conventions since the Hague Convention on Hijacking in the early seventies, filling the loopholes that may arise from the treaty-requirement in extradition cases.[24] Although the draft version of the Protocol had copied this formula,[25] it was deleted in the final text.

In theory, the deficiencies of the extradition system should be compensated by the other part of the international duty either to extradite or to prosecute, namely the prosecution of alleged war criminals. The provision on universal jurisdiction, contained in all four Geneva Conventions[26] and incorporated by the Protocol[27] should, theoretically,

---

22 See, particularly with respect to the political offence exception, C. van den Wyngaert, The Political Offence Exception to Extradition. The Delicate Problem of Balancing the Rights of the Individual and the International Public Order 142 (1980).

23 Article 78 of the Draft made the grave breaches extraditable, whatever the motive for which they were committed. See De Schutter, Eliaerts, op. cit. n. 20, at 165.

24 See for example conventions on aviation terrorism (Article 7 of the Hague Convention for the Suppression of Unlawful Seizure of Aircraft, 16 December 1970, 860 UNTS 105 (1973); Article 8 of the Montreal Convention for the Suppression of Unlawful Acts against the Safety of Civil Aviation, 23 September 1971, 974 UNTS 564 (1975), and Article 8 of the 1984 Convention on the Suppression of Torture.

25 Article 78 of the Draft provided this standard formula. According to this article, grave breaches would be automatically included as extraditable offences in existing and future extradition agreements. See De Schutter, Eliaerts, op. cit. n. 20, at 165.

26 Articles 49-50, 129-130 of the four Conventions.

27 Article 85(1) of Protocol I.

oblige States to prosecute those offenders whose extradition has been denied.

Here too, the system does not seem to have led to the desired results. One of the reasons is of a technical nature, deriving from the fact that many States have not enacted appropriate domestic legislation in order to allow them to prosecute war criminals.[28]

Another technical explanation for the fact that the *aut judicare* alternative is difficult to apply in practice, originates from difficulties in establishing the facts against a defendant whose extradition has been denied. In most cases, the evidence will be in the State which sought extradition, which makes it difficult for the State which denied extradition to try the case. These problems can be resolved by a system of mutual assistance in criminal matters. Here, Protocol I has included a provision obliging the Contracting Parties:

'... to afford one another the greatest measure of assistance in connection with criminal proceedings brought in respect of grave breaches of the Conventions or of this Protocol.'[29]

This obligation, however, is much too vague to be really operative. It is predicated on either the existence or the future conclusion of bilateral or multilateral conventions on mutual assistance in criminal matters. The question remains whether this assumption is realistic.

But apart from these technical problems, there are also political reasons explaining why the system based on the principle *aut dedere aut judicare* has never really worked. The formula is based on the ideal of a homogeneous international community with shared values, at least on the subject of the supression of war crimes. In practice, such a community does not exist, nor has it ever existed, not even with respect to the atrocities committed during World War II. For example, it is common knowledge today that after that War, while States were paying lip-service to the principle that war criminals should be brought to justice, many Nazi war-criminals were recruited by the intelligence services of 'western' States, and deliberately sheltered from prosecution and punishment.

---

28 In their replies to the questionnaire circulated in preparation of the XIth Congress of the International Society of Military Law and the Law of War (Edinburg, 1988), most national reporters answered that no national implementation legislation had been adopted. *Cf.*, A. Andries, loc. cit. n. 18.

29 Article 88 of Protocol I. Also Article 89 of Protocol I.

In addition, States having refused extradition for technical reasons (nationality exception, absence of a treaty, etc.) were often politically reluctant to prosecute the offenders themselves. Prosecutions, if undertaken, often resulted in acquittals based on an incorrect application of domestic justifications. For example, the Belgian war criminal Verbeelen, who was sentenced to death in Belgium after the war, found shelter in Austria where he died in peace in 1990: his extradition was refused because he had meanwhile become an Austrian national; he was prosecuted but acquitted on the defence of superior orders.[30]

6.   CONCLUSION

While it has nearly outlawed reprisals as a means of ensuring compliance with the laws of war, Protocol I does not seem to have compensated this with a reinforcement of the penal control system. Penal law therefore does not seem to be the 'other adequate means' taking over the function of law enforcement, in the sense meant by Kalshoven as quoted in the beginning of this essay.

The question, however, remains, if, apart from what the Protocol has or should have realized, it can be expected that criminal law will function as a tool of law enforcement *vis-à-vis* the adversary. Maybe this is asking too much from the criminal law. During hostilities, such enforcement will be very difficult, and restricted to those captured adversaries who have been so unfortunate as to fall into the hands of the other party. After the hostilities have ended, much will depend on the outcome of the conflict. History shows no example of systematic prosecution and punishment of war criminals on both sides of a conflict. Even one-sided prosecutions by the victors, of the war criminals among the vanquished are exceptional. As time progresses, the uniqueness of the Nuremberg and Tokyo precedents becomes all the more evident.

It may therefore be asked whether the more important function of the criminal law in an armed conflict is not law enforcement *vis-à-vis* the States own nationals. This is an -often forgotten- part of the penal enforcement of grave breaches. Whereas it is debatable whether criminal law in general has a deterrent effect on potential law-breakers, there seem to be good reasons to assume that, with respect to war criminals, it can have such an effect. The defendants in the (admittedly very small sample

---

30 De Standaard, 3 and 5 September 1990.

of) war crimes trials in the era after World War II[31] were not social outcasts or marginal people, but in general 'respectable' persons who were higly esteemed by their superiors. As such, unlike ordinary criminals, they did not belong to the category persons in need of beeing 'resocialized'. On the contrary, they were, in many instances, rather 'over-socialised', in that they were willing to do anything that was in the interest of their country.[32] As was observed above, they often mistakenly assumed that their behaviour could be justified under domestic law. It is submitted that if potential offenders were better informed concerning the illegality of certain acts and the non-applicability of the defences of necessity and superior orders, many war crimes could be avoided. The slaughter of My Lai, the killing of an unarmed civilian in Stanleyville and the torturing of 'prisoners of war' during an army exercise in Belgium in the early seventies[33] might have been avoided if the persons concerned had been better informed about their duties under international humanitarian law.

Precisely because of the fact that domestic legislation is often obscure in this respect, it is highly regrettable that Protocol I has not explicitly dealt with all these issues.

---

31 See *supra* n. 18.
32 Andries, loc. cit. n. 18.
33 *Supra*, n. 18.

III

INTERNAL CONFLICTS
AND
INTERNAL STRIFE

HUMANITARIAN LAW AND INTERNAL CONFLICTS: THE EVOLUTION OF LEGAL CONCERN

ROSEMARY ABI-SAAB

1.   Introduction

2.   Historical background

3.   The legal regulation today
3.1   Scope of application
3.2   Content of protection
3.3   Implementation

4.   Unresolved problems

1.   INTRODUCTION

The laws of armed conflicts[1] are based on a fundamental -though truly artificial- distinction between international and non-international armed conflicts. This distinction, which is deeply entrenched in the 1949 Geneva Conventions on the Protection of War Victims, has been maintained and even confirmed with the adoption, in 1977, of two Additional Protocols to these Conventions, Protocol I applying solely to international armed conflicts, and Protocol II to non-international armed conflicts.

This could appear as a purely legalistic distinction if it did not entail a fundamental distinction in the content and scope of protection for war victims in these two admittedly different situations.

It is interesting to note in this context, however, that none of the Declarations or Conventions on the laws of armed conflicts adopted prior to 1949 contained a specific provision on the scope of application of these

---

1   This terminology, though of a somewhat larger scope, is in our opinion more appropriate than the now current one of 'international humanitarian law', which has found its way particularly in ICRC documents and the 1974-1977 Diplomatic Conference, as it refers to rules governing the conduct of hostilities. In the following text, however, the term 'humanitarian law' will sometimes be used by way of commodity.

instruments. The Geneva Conventions of 1949 introduced for the first time, in common Articles 2 and 3, a distinction in their scope of application and the rather imprecise concept of 'non-international armed conflicts'.

Tracing the evolution of humanitarian legal regulation, particularly as it came to apply to internal conflicts, could help us to understand the realities behind such a distinction and the ways and means of improving the protection of war victims in all situations of armed violence.

2.   HISTORICAL BACKGROUND

The very first codification of what was then called 'the laws and customs of war' was attempted by Lieber, at the time of the American Civil War, in 1860-1863. The 'Lieber Code', as it came to be known, was to serve as a field manual for the use of Federal troops engaged in the Civil War.[2] But its impact was much greater, as most of the military manuals that were prepared around the same time in other countries, particularly in Europe, were influenced by this American model.[3]

Unfortunately, although the Lieber Code was considered at the time as a major step in the codification of the laws and customs of war in general, and although Lieber himself saw it as a codificaton of general application, those in Europe who shared the same feeling of urgency for such a codification, saw the Lieber Code as closely associated only with the experiences of the American Civil War. In other words, it was seen as a Code that could apply only in similar cases of civil war.

When we consider humanitarian law today and the efforts being made with great pains to extend its applicability to all situations and all forms of conflicts, it is highly paradoxical to recall that the Lieber Code was at the time taken as an example of how the laws and customs of war should be codified to apply to inter-State wars, in view of the great similarities between civil and inter-State wars.[4] Nowadays, the situation is precisely the reverse: we still emphasize the similarities of international and non-

---

2   F. Lieber, Instructions for the Government of Armies of the United States in the Field. Rev. ed. (1863).

3   Particularly in the Netherlands, France, Russia, Turkey.

4   See La Convention de La Haye Concernant les Lois et Coutumes de la Guerre sur Terre, d'après les Textes et Documents des Conférences de Bruxelles de 1874 et de La Haye de 1899 et 1907, at 72.

international armed conflicts, but in order to maintain the applicability of existing humanitarian law to internal conflicts as well.

Civil wars were not completely forgotten by classical international law. Indeed, the laws of war applied to civil wars in case of recognition of belligerency; that is to say if a Government, facing rebellion on its territory, declared its willingness to apply the laws of war to the rebels. But, as long as recognition of belligerency in favour of rebel groups fighting the central authority was purely a consensual act on the part of the central Government, it had very little chance of occurring. And indeed, practical cases of recognition of belligerency were extremely rare, while this procedure was the only one available, in classical international law, to give full effect to the laws of war in internal conflicts.[5]

Attempts were made in theory to make recognition of belligerency compulsory for Governments if certain conditions were fulfilled; but they did not have much effect in practice. The theory of recognition of insurgency, which was developed later on, had the same purpose: imposing on Governments the obligation to apply at least some of the principles of the laws of war in cases of internal conflicts.

These theories of recognition of belligerency, voluntary or compulsory, and of recognition of insurgency, which were the essential pillars of the application of the law of war to internal conflicts, are now almost totally forgotten and rarely mentioned in contemporary international law.

The question of the protection of victims, however, is all the more acute in internal conflicts, where Governments will find it very difficult, from a political point of view, to accept outside intervention by humanitarian institutions in favour of their own nationals fighting the central authority. Indeed, this opposition between sovereignty and humanity is permanent in situations of internal conflicts.

The ICRC and national Red Cross societies have made every effort, on an essentially *ad hoc* basis, to bring humanitarian assistance in the numerous cases of insurrections that occured in the late nineteenth and early twentieth centuries in Eastern Europe, the Balkans or Spain, not to speak of the Western Hemisphere.[6] If humanitarian action was possible, to some extent, without any specific legal grounds, it was thought that some

---

5 See for example the recognition of belligerency by America of Spanish colonies in their War of Independence (1815); or in the Greek War of Independence (1821-1829) by Great Britain.

6 For a detailed and historical account of humanitarian assistance, see J. Moreillon, *Le CICR et la protection des détenus politiques* (1973).

form of legal regulation would, however, better impose on Governments the obligation to agree to such actions.

And here again, the initiatiative came from America, more specifically from the American Red Cross, which submitted the first project of this kind to the International Red Cross Conference, meeting in 1912 in Washington.[7] But it was not until 1921, that a Resolution was adopted to this end by a subsequent Red Cross Conference.[8] This resolution confers on Red Cross societies not only the right but also the duty to offer their services in situations of civil wars or other internal disturbances; it also imposes on the ICRC the duty to intervene in cases of civil wars.[9]

Up to 1949, the 1921 Red Cross resolution and the Statutes of the ICRC, as revised in 1928, were the only legal titles on which the ICRC could base its action in situations of internal conflicts.

In view of the numerous conflicts that occurred in various parts of the world and of the difficulties that the ICRC met with in these situations, it became evident that such a legal title should be included in the Geneva Conventions themselves.

The 1949 revision of the Geneva Conventions was a very fundamental one. And as far as internal conflicts are concerned, it was for the first time that a minimum of legal regulation became formally applicable to situations of internal conflicts, that had not been up to then explicitly included in the field of application of humanitarian law. But it was also the first time that unequal treatment, a fundamentally unequal legal protection of victims of armed conflicts, was affirmed by a legal text.

This double standard of protection implied in itself an essential question, which appeared not to be too difficult at first to resolve, but which has now become very problematic, namely that of the legal definition or legal classification of the various situations.

As with all classifications, there are some situations that fit without too much difficulty within the qualification of 'non-international armed conflicts'. But the problem lies with the limiting cases, which are more and more frequent, at the two ends of the spectrum. If the aim of humanitarian law is the protection of all victims, and if this protection is governed by such legal qualifications, some fundamental questions arise: at what point does a non-international armed conflict cross the threshold or the 'ceiling' of the category and qualify as international for the purposes of

---

7   Ninth International Conference of the Red Cross, Washington, 1912.
8   See Tenth International Conference of the Red Cross, Geneva, 1921.
9   *Ibid.*, 1921, Annexes, at 217.

humanitarian protection? At what point could a situation of internal unrest cross the threshold of the category of non-international armed conflict?

From the time when common Article 3 was first discussed in the 1949 Diplomatic Conference, until today, we see the shift of the pendulum between those who wanted to extend the definition contained in this Article as widely as possible to cover all situations, and those who wanted to confine it within very restrictive limits. These might be cases of civil wars in the classical sense of the term, that is to say armed conflicts of very high intensity, where rebels exert effective control over part of the territory; typical examples being the Spanish Civil War or the Nigerian Civil War. There was a shift of the pendulum too between the content of the protection and the extent of the definition: for the majority of Governments who participated in the Diplomatic Conferences of 1949 and 1974-1977, only a limited protection could be accepted in the case of an extended definition, whereas, if the point of departure was a restricted definition, a wider protection could be envisaged.

The 1949 common Article 3 has served its purposes if only because it brought internal conflicts formally within the ambit of the Geneva Convention and of humanitarian law in general. It had, however, serious limitations that could only be surmounted by an extensive and somewhat bold and forwardlooking interpretation.[10]

Subsequent developments in internal conflicts that occurred in the nineteen sixties and seventies brought out more clearly the inadequacies of the content and scope of application of common Article 3 in the context of contemporary conflicts. First, their frequency, their intensity and duration, due mainly to the outside intervention which occurs in most cases of internal conflicts, make them increasingly similar to international wars. This alone would call for an extension of the content of the protection, particularly as concerns the status of combatants and its corollary, the status and treatment of prisoners, and as concerns restraints on belligerents in their methods of combat, in order to protect civilian populations.

Secondly, the very frequent occurrence of what is called in ICRC and humanitarian law terminology 'internal disturbances and tensions', made it necessary for those concerned with the protection of victims, to try to seek formal adoption of an extensive interpretation of the scope of application of the existing regulation, in other words of common Article 3.

---

10 For a study of common Article 3 and its legislative history, see R. Abi-Saab, *Droit humanitaire et conflits internes. Origines et évolution de la réglementation internationale* (1986).

These are some of the developments that were aimed at by the 1974-1977 Diplomatic Conference. Several approaches were possible in addressing these problems. The first was that the Conference, which has been convened to supplement and update the Geneva Conventions, adopt one single Additional Protocol. This proposition had been formally put forward by Norway, but was, however, rejected.[11]

If the fundamental distinction between international and non-international armed conflicts was maintained, together with a fundamentally unequal protection, the second avenue open to the Conference to improve the protection of victims was to extract as many types of situations as possible from the category of 'non-international conflicts' and bring them under the umbrella of the protection provided for international armed conflicts. This move was attempted for those conflicts already recognized as 'international' by the international community, namely the struggle for self-determination: the principle of self-determination of peoples being one of the fundamental UN principles.[12] This development proved, however, to be very controversial; and its humanitarian intent, namely the protection of victims and the imposition of restraints on all belligerents, has not been perceived by many Governments, of whom some advanced this as one of the reasons not to ratify Protocol I.[13]

The third approach open to the Diplomatic Conference was to supplement the content of the protection applying to internal conflicts as defined by common Article 3 of the Geneva Conventions. This is the approach which has been followed in the ICRC draft submitted to the Conference. This attempt failed, however, on two levels. First, the definition of internal armed conflicts finally adopted by the Conference is much more restrictive than that of common Article 3. Second, in spite of this restrictive definition, most of the developments contained in the ICRC Draft as far as the content of the combatants protection is concerned, particularly the status of combatants and prisoners, and the restraints on belligerents, were not adopted by the Conference.[14]

---

11 ICRC, *Conference of Government Experts on the Reaffirmation and Development of Humanitarian Law Applicable in Armed Conflicts*. Report on the Work of the Conference (First Session, annex) 70 (1971).

12 See G. Abi-Saab, *Wars of National Liberation in the Geneva Conventions and Protocols*, 65 RCADI 333-445 (1979).

13 *Message from the President of the United States Transmitting the Protocol II Additional to the Geneva Conventions*, US Senate, 100th Congress, 1st Session (1987).

14 See in general, R. Abi-Saab, op. cit. n. 10.

3.   THE LEGAL REGULATION TODAY

Conventional legal regulation applying today to internal conflicts is thus composed of common Article 3 of the Geneva Conventions, together with Protocol II Additional to these Conventions. To these should be added the ICRC right of initiative as deriving from its Statutes and confirmed by the Geneva Conventions.[15]

One of the characteristics of the progressive development of humanitarian law, which is the outcome of a long process of evolution, is a succession of treaties, each trying to improve on the preceding one; each new instrument has a cumulative or supplemental effect in relation to what preceded it. This pattern is expressly recognized in the Preambles of most of these treaties. Thus, the Preamble to Protocol II recalls that:

> '... the humanitarian principles enshrined in Article 3 common to the Geneva ... constitute the foundation of respect for the human person in cases of armed conflicts not of an international character ....'

The simultaneous validity and autonomous application of common Article 3 and Protocol II are in effect essential and were explicitly specified in the original ICRC Draft.[16] The fundamental importance of the simultaneous validity of these two instruments will be better understood when we look into the question of their respective scope of application, in other words the question of the definition of non-international armed conflicts in these two instruments will be better understood when we look into the question of their respective scope of application in other words the question of the definition of non-international armed conflicts in these two instruments.

3.1   Scope of application

Common Article 3, according to the Geneva Conventions, is applicable 'in case of *armed* conflict *not of an international character* occurring *in the territory* of one of the High Contracting Parties ...' (emphasis added). This very vague formulation leaves ample room for interpretation, particularly of the terms 'armed' conflict and 'non-international' character: what should be the nature of hostilities, should there be hostilities only between Government forces and rebel forces, should these rebel forces exercise

---

15 Geneva Conventions I-IV, Articles 9(I-III) and 10(IV).
16 ICRC Draft Protocol II, Preamble.

territorial control? What does non-international really mean in practice, what is the situation in case of foreign intervention?

In other words, common Article 3 had not formulated the objective conditions of, nor the objective criteria for, its application. This vague formulation, which was considered at the time as one of the major defects of Article 3, is now considered, however, as one of its main advantages, in the sense that it does not formally exclude a broad interpretation. This is particularly so when we compare it with the field of application of Protocol II, as defined in its Article 1.

Indeed, Protocol II has a much more restrictive approach to internal conflicts and even formally excludes some situations that, with a broad interpretation, could be included in the scope of application of Article 3. It stipulates that it shall apply 'to all armed conflicts which are not covered by Article 1 (of Protocol I)'; in other words, it shall not apply to international armed conflicts. If it had stopped at that, it would have covered a very wide spectrum of situations. But this spectrum is progressively narrowed by the following subsequent qualifications: it shall apply to conflicts 'which take place in the territory of a High Contracting Party' (the same formulation as common Article 3), but 'between its armed forces and dissident armed forces or other organized groups' (which is a more restrictive formulation, because it would for example exclude conflicts between two or more rebel groups, not involving Governments forces); these dissident forces should be 'under responsible command' and 'exercise such control over a part of its territory as to enable them to carry out sustained and concerted military operations and to implement this Protocol'. These conditions are very restrictive indeed in the context of contemporary situations. It would for example be very difficult for a rebel movement to reach effective control until the situation was one characterized as civil war, in the classical sense of the term; in other words, a conflict of high intensity, which is not the case in most internal conflicts. These would thus be excluded from the new legal regulation.

The other serious limitation in the definition of internal conflicts in Protocol II comes from the last words in the second paragraph of Article 1, a provision which was accepted almost inadvertently by the Diplomatic Conference:

'This Protocol shall not apply to situations of internal disturbances and tensions ... as not being armed conflicts.'

These last words were added to the original ICRC Draft proposed to the Conference, and they were even seen and intended by their sponsors as an attempt to impose a restrictive interpretation of the scope of application of common Article 3 itself.[17]

In view of these various limitations on the scope of application of the Protocol, the continuous validity of common Article 3, or its autonomy in relation to Protocol II, is of the utmost importance. This autonomy is explicitly provided for in Article 1 of Protocol II, which specifies that it: '... develops and supplements Article 3 ... without modifying its existing conditions of applications ....'

3.2   Content of protection

In its operative part, common Article 3 explictly provides for the application, in cases of non-international armed conflict, of a few fundamental humanitarian principles, related basically to the protection of the human rights and physical integrity of individuals in any circumstances: prohibition of torture, of murder, of mutilations, of cruel treatment, prohibition of the taking of hostages, *etc.*.

Such acts are prohibited only with respect to persons not taking part in the hostilities, or who have laid down their arms, or who are *hors de combat*. In other words, the fundamental difference from the protection provided by the Geneva Conventions in general, is that this Article provides no specific regulation applicable to combatants (neither rights nor obligations), nor to prisoners; particularly, it provides no immunity from punishment, including capital punishment, for the mere participation in the conflict.

It is true that the Article recommends that, beyond these express provisions of Article 3, which apply as a minimum in all cases of non-international armed conflicts, the parties to a conflict should endeavour to apply 'by means of special agreements, all or part of the other provisions' of the Conventions. This possibility, however, has very rarely been formally used in practice for obvious reasons - the conclusion of a formal agreement, at the time of an armed conflict, between the Government and rebel forces being highly problematic.[18]

But in all internal conflicts that occurred since the adoption of the Geneva Conventions and their common Article 3, in 1949, the ICRC has not limited its action to what the Article expressly provides. And in many

---

17 See R. Abi-Saab, op. cit. n. 10, at 145-148.
18 Cuba (1958) and Angola (1975) are the rare examples where special agreements have been concluded for the exchange of prisoners. See, on this question, Ch. Zorgbibe, *Pour une réaffirmation du droit humanitaire des conflicts armés internes*, 97 JDI 666 (1970).

cases it succeeded in convincing the parties to respect and apply much more specific rules of humanitarian law, particularly as regards combatants and prisoners.[19]

In view of the very frequent occurrence of internal conflicts, particularly since the nineteen sixties, and their increased intensity, the aim of the ICRC and the International Red Cross Conferences, has been to bring the international community to accept a new updating of the Geneva Conventions that would, among other developments, formally provide a protection *similar* to the one applicable to international conflicts, particularly as concerns the protection of prisoners and the restraints to be imposed on belligerents, in the case of internal conflicts.

Such a proposal was submitted to the 1974-1977 Diplomatic Conference in the form of the ICRC Draft of Protocol II Additional to the Geneva Conventions.[20] However, aiming for a protection too similar to the one applicable in the case of international conflicts was not perhaps the best point of departure. It could be qualified as a 'law of war approach' to internal conflicts by contrast to a human rights approach. It implied the applicability of most of the fundamental humanitarian law principles to situations that are considered by the Governments concerned as falling within their exclusive domestic jurisdiction, that of the maintenance of law and order. Moreover, Governments would find it particularly difficult to admit that they were faced, on their territory, with conflicts similar to war situations. This largely explains why the original ICRC Draft was drastically reduced by the Diplomatic Conference to a very pale reflection of what it had been intended to be. Moreover, for many Third World countries, particularly African countries, their main concern was with wars of national liberation, that had been already included in the category of international conflicts. They had not the same concern for other internal conflicts.

As far as the content of the protection is concerned, the main provisions that were rejected by the Conference are precisely those that the ICRC considered most essential: the status of combatants, the treatment of prisoners of war and the regulation of means and methods of warfare in the context of the protection of civilian populations, although some of these restraints have been introduced in the context of the general protection of the civilian population.[21]

---

19 See in general, ICRC Annual Reports.
20 ICRC Draft Protocol.
21 Particularly in Part IV.

This is not to say, however, that the Protocol has brought no improvement to pre-existing regulation. It would be very tedious to examine here in detail, Article by Article, the additions to common Article 3 introduced by the Protocol relating to the content of the protection. In many cases, these additions are not new in themselves, but appear more as a detailed interpretation of existing rules, particularly as concerns fundamental guarantees, and they do not go much beyond what had been provided in very general terms by common Article 3.

The main impact of Protocol II comes first of all from the few Articles on the protection of civilian population and civilian objects, in Part IV. Whereas no provision of this sort appeared in common Article 3, some restraints are imposed on all belligerents by these Articles, which prohibit, for example, attacks on civilians; starvation as a method of combat; destruction of goods indispensable for the survival of the population; attacks on installations such as dams, dykes, etc., containing dangerous forces; the prohibition of forced movements of populations is also a major contribution of Protocol II.[22]

A second important addition in Protocol II are the Articles on the protection of medical and sanitary personnel, medical units and transports. Such provisions were considered as essential by the ICRC in the fulfilment of its duties.[23] Yet another contribution of the Protocol is the prohibition of collective punishment and of the order that there shall be no survivors.[24]

The two long Articles 5 and 6 on the treatment of detained persons can be seen as a detailed interpretation of the general provisions contained in common Article 3. They can be seen also as approaching prisoner of war treatment (not status, however) for detained persons, with the important omission of immunity from capital punishment for mere participation in the conflict.

In short, it can be said that although the final text adopted by the Diplomatic Conference is far from the original ICRC draft as far as the content of the protection is concerned, it has nevertheless provided some important developments. But one should not forget, however, the very restrictive scope of application of the Protocol. In the circumstances where it can apply, namely in cases of conflicts of high intensity, *i.e.*, civil wars, a much wider protection should have been adopted. Under classical

---

22 Articles 13-17.
23 Articles 9-11.
24 Articles 4(1) and 4(2).

international law, civil wars, in case of recognition of belligerency, would
call for the protection of the laws of war in their entirety.

3.3   Implementation

As with the Geneva Conventions in general, the question of the
implementation of Protocol II is very problematic. Apart from the ICRC's
right of initiative deriving from its Statutes, common Article 3 of the
Geneva Conventions provides that, in case of non-international armed
conflicts, 'an impartial humanitarian body, such as the ICRC, may offer its
services to the Parties to the conflict'. Obviously, this provision does not
impose a duty on the ICRC to offer its services in such situations, nor does
it impose on the parties to the conflict an obligation to accept them if they
are offered.

A similar provision was introduced in the ICRC draft of Protocol II,
with the difference that it specified that the ICRC could offer its services
'to co-operate in the observance of the provisions' of the Protocol.[25] In
other words, it specifically classified the services offered as pertaining to
'scrutiny' or 'control' of application of the Protocol in the context of non-
international armed conflicts. This was seen by some delegations at the
Diplomatic Conference as an unacceptable instrusion in the internal affairs
of the Governments concerned.[26]

This draft article was rejected by the Conference which did not even
retain a reference to the offer of services of the ICRC in such situations, as
mentioned in common Article 3. This is one more reason why the
simultaneous validity and autonomous applicability of common Article 3 is
important for the protection of victims.

4.   UNRESOLVED PROBLEMS

It now remains to examine whether the existing regulation, namely
common Article 3 and Protocol II, are sufficient in themselves to provide a
basis for the protection of victims in contemporary internal conflicts.

If we proceed from the distinction between international and non-
international armed conflicts, one of the first difficulties comes from the
fact that, in most cases, contemporary conflicts do not correspond to the

---

25 ICRC Draft Article 39.
26 See R. Abi-Saab, op. cit. n. 10, at 185-187.

criteria and conditions of the existing legal regulation, particularly the condition of effective territorial control adopted in Protocol II. At the same time, increased external intervention1
 in most internal conflicts, make for the obsolescence of this classical distinction.

A second difficulty is that the nature of military equipment engaged in most of these conflicts, as well as military tactics, make them more similar to wars in the classical sense of the term.[27]

Civilian populations are exposed to the dangers of hostilities just as they are in international conflicts and should be protected by restraints imposed on all the belligerents. Combatants taken prisoners by any of the belligerents should be afforded a treatment different than mere criminals. Humanitarian institutions, such as the ICRC, should be able to bring relief and protection to all victims.

At the other end of the scale, situations classified by humanitarian law as internal disturbances and tensions, and not involving resort to armed forces in the normal sense of the term, are more and more frequent, but are not formally covered by existing legal regulation and even formally excluded from the scope of application of Protocol II. Such situations raise nonetheless humanitarian problems that would justify the action of independent humanitarian organizations such as the ICRC, particularly as concerns the protection of detained persons, generally called 'political detainees'. And indeed the ICRC systematically offers its services as soon as such situations arise, but on a purely *ad hoc* basis and subject to the consent of the authorities concerned.

For all these reasons, the cumulative resort to different sources of applicable law is useful in establishing rights and duties applicable in all circumstances for the protection of victims.

In its Preamble, Protocol II, after recalling the permanent validity in internal conflicts of the humanitarian principles contained in common Article 3 of the Geneva Conventions, also recalls that 'the international instruments relating to human rights offer a basic protection to the human person', and that, 'in cases not covered by the law in force, the human person remains under the protection of the principles of humanity and the dictates of the public conscience'.[28]

---

27 See H.P. Gasser, *Armed Conflict within the Territory of a State*, in W. Haller, A. Kölz, G. Müller, D. Thürer, eds., Im Dienst an der Gemeinschaft, Festschrift für D. Schindler zum 65. Geburtstag 225 (1989).
28 Martens Clause.

It is the first time that a humanitarian Convention has refered specifically to international instruments relating to human rights. These are primarily to instruments adopted by the UN, in other words the Universal Declaration of Human Rights and the two Covenants, the Covenant on Civil and Political Rights being particularly relevant in this case. They also include the more specific instruments, such as the Genocide Convention, the Convention on Racial Discrimination, the Convention on Torture. Regional human rights instruments should also be taken into consideration here.

If humanitarian law instruments apply only in situations of armed conflicts, human rights instruments apply in all circumstances, and in the case of armed conflicts they apply concurrently with humanitarian law. However, the Covenant on Civil and Political Rights, in Article 4, allows the suspension of all but a few fundamental and non-derogable rights 'in time of public emergency which threatens the life of the nation'. In other words, in situations of armed conflicts, which will in most cases be declared situations of emergency, only the hard core of fundamental human rights remains guaranteed: the right to life, the prohibition of torture, of slavery, the right to freedom of conscience and religion and the principle of non-retroactivity of penal law. Most of these fundamental rights, as well as those proclaimed by the Universal Declaration of Human Rights and attaching to the human person, are included in Protocol II and, in more general terms, in common Article 3.

The specific contribution of human rights instruments to the content of humanitarian law is therefore not very significant. Their relevance is much greater, however, as far as the general obligations of States are concerned. Even if Governments question the applicability of common Article 3 and Protocol II to specific situations of non-international armed conflicts, they are nonetheless bound by some fundamental principles of humanity, such as those proclaimed by the Universal Declaration of Human Rights and other human rights instruments, where they are applicable and for those States who have ratified them. They are also bound by the Martens Clause, to which Protocol II also refers in its Preamble, and which is a principle of customary law.[29]

We can even say that the Geneva Conventions and the Protocols are not much more than the detailed and specific elaboration of these fundamental principles of humanity in the context of war. This is precisely the line of

---

29 See in general T. Meron, Human Rights and Humanitarian Norms as Customary Law (1989).

argument that the ICJ has adopted in its Judgement in the *Nicaragua Case*, where it expressed itself in detail on the customary nature of the 'general principles' of humanitarian law.[30]

The essential purpose of this approach is to ensure respect in all circumstances for the general principles of humanity, which are binding, whether or not the States concerned are Parties to the Conventions and Protocols and whether or not there are any doubts as to the applicability of these instruments in certain circumstances.

The question which arises here is how to determine what these principles are and to see how they can be distilled from the existing body of rules without reducing its content exclusively to these principles. The Court identified these 'fundamental principles' with the rules set forth in common Article 3 of the Geneva Conventions, and it established a direct linkage between these principles and the Conventions as a whole, by considering the latter to be only the expression, 'and in certain respects the development', of these principles; the difference between these principles and the Conventions lying only in the degree of specificity of the Conventions.[31]

In this Judgement, the Court has thus resolved one of the major problems relating to the basis of obligation of humanitarian law, by affirming that the fundamental general principles of humanitarian law (common Article 3, in the opinion of the Court) belong to the body of general international law in other words, that they apply in all circumstances, for the better protection of the victims.

This approach is not based on the legal classification of armed conflicts, in other words on the distinction between international and non-international armed conflicts; it is not based either on the content of the protection, as the 'fundamental principles' that apply regardless of the situation, vary only in their measure of specificity.

For such an approach to find its way into the practice and the *opinio juris* of the international community, will be one of the most crucial challenges for the next decade.

---

30 ICJ Reports 1986, at 14.

31 R. Abi-Saab, *The 'General Principles' of Humanitarian Law According to the International Court of Justice*, International Review for the Red Cross 367-375 (1987).

IN THE SHADOWLAND BETWEEN CIVIL WAR AND CIVIL STRIFE: SOME REFLECTIONS ON THE STANDARD-SETTING PROCESS

PETER H. KOOIJMANS

1.   INTRODUCTION

International humanitarian law and international human rights law have much in common, nevertheless their roots are completely different. What they have in common is their focus on respect for human values and for the dignity of the human person. But the angle from which this common object of concern is approached is intrinsically and basically different. The origins of humanitarian law lie in inter-state relations, while those of human rights law lie in the relations between the Government and the governed within the State. Humanitarian law intends to alleviate human suffering which is the direct result of armed conflict, and armed conflict, until recently was seen as armed conflict between States. Human rights law (at least in its modern sense) originated with the development of constitutional law; it only became internationalized when during World War II it was realized that the protection of the basic rights of the human person could not be left to the State, since this State, although intended to be the guarantor of these rights, is also in the position to be their main violator.[1] The internationalization of human rights thus has as its goal a strenthening of the legal protection enjoyed by a citizen against his own State.

It is only in the period since World War II that these two branches of human values-oriented law really touched upon each other, and internal conflict was the meeting-place. The post-war era was characterized not so much by inter-state armed conflicts in the traditional sense of the word as by conflicts which started as internal conflicts and sometimes received an international dimension by rather strong involvement of foreign powers but nevertheless remained localized within the border of one State. For this reason it is only logical that humanitarian law extended its concern to this type of conflict as well: human values are as much threatened by internal conflicts as they are by genuine inter-state conflicts.

Since, however, an internal conflict is situated within the border of one State it is also covered by human rights law. Basically that law concerns the relationship between the Government and its (rebellious) subjects, albeit under rather abnormal conditions. Internal conflict may cover a wide variety of situations, from riots to full-fledged civil war, but in all its ramifications it is a true shadowland which is situated between humanitarian law and human rights law. Since both are focused on the preservation of human dignity, their fields of interest converge. Both have tried to develop rules for this shadowland, to bring it under control and to preserve the values they have in common. But the sad truth is that until now both have failed in this effort. The shadowland between civil war and civil strife thus far has successfully eluded adequate regulation. In one of his books Meron states that:

'ideally there should be a continuum of norms protecting human rights in all situations, from international armed conflicts at one end of the spectrum to situations of non-armed internal conflict at the other. In every situation, there should either be a convergence of humanitarian and human rights norms, or one of these two systems of protection should clearly apply.'[2]

In view of the fact that until now it has been impossible to bring the shadowland under control the question seems justified: does the convergence of the field of interest of both human values-oriented branches

---

1 C. Tomuschat, *Human Rights in a World-Wide Framework. Some Current Issues*, 45 ZaöRV 560 (1985).

2 Th. Meron, Human Rights in Internal Strife: Their International Protection 3 (1987).

of law automatically lead to a convergence of the legal systems and therefore to a convergence of the rules? Or is a continuum of norms impossible because of their different origins and, consequently, their different characters? If that would be the case, an ultimate solution can only be found in Meron's second alternative, *viz.* by bringing it firmly under the application of only one of the systems of protection. By approaching the shadowland from two sides in order to explore its crevices and unravel its secrets, we ourselves may increase the number of shadows and therefore make its surface more untraceable.

In order to have an effective set of rules two conditions should be met:
a) it should be clear in which situations the rules are applicable; and
b) the substance of the applicable rules should be adequate for the realization of the underlying values.

It is the first question which has bedevilled the humanitarian law approach, whereas the second one has seriously hampered the human rights law approach.

2. THE HUMANITARIAN LAW APPROACH

The first clear reference to internal armed conflict in international humanitarian law is to be found in common Article 3 of the four Geneva Conventions of 1949. Its scope of application is formulated rather loosely: 'In the case of an armed conflict not of an international character occurring in the territory of one of the High Contracting Parties, each Party to the conflict shall be bound to apply as a minimum ...' (follow some substantive rules).

Common Article 3 -rightly called the 'humanitarian convention in miniature'- evokes, however, more questions than it answers. First it should be noted that no definition is given of what is to be understood by an 'armed conflict not of an international character'. Although the lower threshold seems to be the mutual use of armed force, no indication is given of the intensity of this armed force necessary to make the provision applicable.[3] This makes a satisfactory answer to the next question all the more urgent: Who is competent to decide whether common Article 3 is

---

3   F. Kalshoven, *'Guerilla' and 'Terrorism' in Internal Armed Conflict*, 33 American University Law Review 68 (1983). According to Kalshoven:
'While the term "armed conflict" was left undefined in common article 3 ... it was widely understood to exclude situations of political unrest accompanied by nothing more than sporadic acts of violence.'

applicable? It is here that the difference in character between common Article 3 and the traditional rules of humanitarian law leaps to the eye. With regard to the latter, common Article 2 says that 'the convention(s) shall apply to all cases of declared war or any other armed conflict which may arise between two or more of the High Contracting Parties even if a state of war is not recognized by one of them'. The applicability is objectively determined -the use of armed force- and the basis of obligation is the contractual relationship between the parties to the conflict. In the case of common Article 3, however, the basis of obligation is a contractual relation between one party to the conflict and other States Parties to the convention, whereas the other party to the conflict is considered to be bound by the relevant rules although it has no status in international law. Whereas the traditional rules of conventional humanitarian law become automatically applicable if there is a use of force, common Article 3 by implication must be *declared* applicable, either by the Contracting Party which is almost always also a party to the conflict or by the other Contracting Parties. The second alternative, however, seems to be ruled out -in the absense of a specific authorization to those other Contracting Parties, which does not exist- by the principle of non-interference, as the conflict occurs within the territory of another State. The only alternative left is that the Contracting Party, in whose territory the conflict occurs must declare common Article 3 applicable. Although in theory the conclusion drawn by a Commission of Experts convened by the ICRC in 1962, *viz.* that the decision whether common Article 3 is legally applicable 'should rest on objective conditions and not be the result of a discretionary appreciation by States Parties to the Geneva Conventions' must be called sound, these objective conditions have never been agreed upon and, consequently, the discretion of the State Party seems to remain the decisive element.

This State Party will, however, not easily be inclined to declare Article 3 applicable for various reasons. In spite of the fact that Article 3 states that its application shall not affect the legal status of the Parties to the conflict, an explicit statement by the State, that there are two parties to an armed conflict, equally bound to comply with certain international rules, will nearly invariably be interpreted as a raising of the status of the opponent.[4] Moreover, the State Party will not be in a position to ensure that the other party to the conflict will also comply with the applicable rules and that will make it less willing to accept restraints for its own

---

4   See also Meron, op. cit. n. 2, at 38.

conduct. This willingness may increase if the conflict is a protracted one and approaches a full-fledged civil war, but will nearly invariably be absent if the Government is of the (often ill-based) opinion that it can quell the insurgency rather speedily.[5]

These difficulties are not solved if one shares the position taken by the International Court of Justice that common Article 3 is a rule of customary law since 'it reflects elementary considerations of humanity and constitutes the minimum yardstick for all kinds of armed conflict, whether international or non-international'.[6]

Apart from the fact that Judge Jennings in his Dissenting Opinion, not without reason, called this finding of the Court 'a matter not free from difficulty',[7] the fact remains that, even if common Article 3 must be considered to be customary law (which would not solve the problem of the contractual basis of obligation since the other party to the conflict has no formal international legal personality) the applicability of this customary rule in practice will still be left to the discretion of one of the parties to the conflict. A legal system under which the beneficiaries of the rules (*i.e.*, persons taking no active part in the hostilities) are completely dependent for the exercise of their 'rights' on the discretion of one of the parties to the conflict, can hardly be called an effective system.

It has been said that common Article 3 has the merit that it enables the International Committee of the Red Cross (ICRC) to play a role in internal armed conflicts, since it authorizes an impartial humanitarian body to offer its services to the parties. Theoretically this may be true, but two comments must be made: first, that the parties to the conflict are under no obligation to accept the offer, and secondly that in actual practice the ICRC, when offering its services to Governments, rarely relies on the legal character of the conflict.[8]

---

5   For a list of cases where Common Article 3 was declared or implicitly understood to be applicable, see D. Forsythe, *Legal Management of Internal War: The 1977 Protocol on Non-International Armed Conflicts*, 72 AJIL 275 (1978).

6   ICJ Reports 1986, § 218, at 114.

7   *Ibid.*, at 537. See also T. Meron, Human Rights and Humanitarian Norms as Customary Law 35 (1989). According to Meron:
    'The norms specified in Article 3 have an undisputable humanitarian character, but elementary considerations of humanity may not necessarily have attained the status of already crystallized customary law.'

8   See, *e.g.*, H.-P. Gasser, *International Non-International Armed Conflicts: Case Studies of Afghanistan, Kampuchea, and Lebanon*, 31 American University Law Review 911, 922-933 (1982). See also J. Moreillon as quoted in Meron, op. cit. n. 2, at 115,116. According to Moreillon:

The adoption of two Protocols to the 1949 Geneva Conventions in 1977 may truly be called a landmark in the development of international humanitarian law; for the subject under discussion, however, the situation became, if anything, more obfuscated. First of all, a number of armed conflicts which hitherto had been considered as internal conflicts were lifted to the international level. Article 1(4) of Protocol I states that the term 'international conflicts' also includes 'armed conflicts in which peoples are fighting against colonial domination and alien occupation and against racist regimes in the exercise of their right of self-determination as enshrined in the Charter of the United Nations'. By authorizing movements engaged in such fights (usually called national liberation movements) to deposit a unilateral statement with the Swiss Government (the depositary of the Protocols) declaring their intent to be bound by the Protocols and the Geneva Conventions, their status in international law is 'upgraded'; they have been granted a limited treaty-making capacity and therefore, international legal personality.

To a certain extent this was a confirmation of the position these liberation movements already enjoyed in the context of the United Nations and, therefore, in itself not very revolutionary; by obtaining observer-status with the United Nations their fight for self-determination had already been 'internationalized'. The applicability of the rules of international conflict (*i.e.*, of the Conventions of 1949 and Protocol I), is, however, not only dependent upon the deposit of the declaration with the depository by the liberation movement, but also upon the ratification of the Protocol by the State concerned: Article 96(3) explicitly requires that the war is against a High Contracting Party. It is, therefore, very easy for the Government concerned to evade the applicability of the Protocol by not ratifying it,[9] or, if it has done so, by denying that the situation is covered by the criteria of Article 1(4). It is, therefore, again left to the discretion of one of the

---

'I feel relatively confident that if we were to approach any of these governments and tell them: you must let us see these people (in places of detention) because they are covered by Protocol II or Article 3, they would be more reluctant to let us in than if we approach them by saying: we offer our humanitarian services on the basis of our internationally recognized right of humanitarian initiative, you are not obliged to accept it.'

9   Neither Israel nor South-Africa has ratified Protocol I, although Article 1(4) was drafted to benefit the PLO, respectively the ANC and PAC. Neither did these liberation movements deposit the declaration of Article 96(3), although the ANC and PLO declared their intent to abide by the laws of armed conflicts to the extent possible. After the State of Palestine had been proclaimed in November 1988, the PLO requested, in June 1989, that Palestine become a Party to the Geneva Conventions.

parties to the conflict to determine the applicability of the rules of humanitarian law.

Protocol II deals with all armed conflicts not covered by Article 1 of Protocol I, consequently with all other non-international armed conflicts. Originally, its scope of application had been envisioned as virtually the same as that of common Article 3; the Protocol, therefore, was to be an expansion and development of the rather vague guidelines prescribed by that Article. In the draft submitted by the ICRC a lower threshold was indicated by the provision that the Protocol 'shall not apply to situations of internal disturbances and tensions, *inter alia*, riots, isolated and sporadic acts of violence and other acts of a similar nature'. During the Conference the threshold was considerably raised. Article 1 as it stands now requires that the dissident armed forces are under responsible command and exercise such control over a part of the territory (of the High Contracting Party) as to enable them to carry out sustained and concerted military operations and to implement the Protocol. Although the threshold is put rather high, Article 1 seems to have the advantage that the criteria for its applicability are much more objective than the ones determining the applicability of Article 3. Forsythe, however, rightly points out that, although it seems clear that material conditions activate the law, *ad hoc* governmental assent seems to be necessary for the application of the law by the government forces.[10] Thus, in spite of the increased objectivity of the criteria for the applicability of the provisions of the Protocol, their operational value is still dependent upon the decision of one of the parties to the conflict. Although a number of internal armed conflicts seem to have met the conditions of Article 1 of Protocol II, in none of those cases was the Government concerned willing to recognize its applicability.[11] A number of insurgent movements have notified the ICRC that they intend to abide by the laws of armed conflict as far as possible,[12] although Protocol II has no provision comparable to that of Article 96(3) of Protocol I. In none of those cases, have the Governments concerned reacted to such notifications by declaring that they consider Protocol II applicable. In another case, that of the Philippines after the ousting of President Marcos, the authorities did not seem averse to considering common Article 3 and Protocol II applicable; in December 1988 a Draft Code was adopted by a Conference, in which various parties and non-governmental organizations

---

10 Forsythe, loc. cit. n. 5, at 285.

11 See Meron, op. cit. n. 2, at 48.

12 R.S. Myren, *Applying International Laws of War to Non-international Armed Conflicts: Past Attempts, Future Strategies*, 37 NILR 353, n. 34 (1990).

participated, requiring combatants to abide by Protocol II. In this case, however, it was one of the insurgent movements which hesitated to accept the Draft Code.[13] After cease-fire talks broke down in 1989, a 'total war strategy' (euphemistically called 'total approach strategy') against the insurgents was launched by the Government. During a visit the present author paid to the Philippines in October 1990 in his capacity as UN Special Rapporteur on Questions Relevant to Torture, the armed forces admitted that conditions 'short of war' indeed prevailed in certain areas and that, therefore, Protocol II, to which the Philippines is a Party, could be applicable.[14] It was not made clear what prevents the authorities from officially declaring that it should be applied but there may be a mixture of motives: uncertainty about the position of the main insurgent movement, the leftist New People's Army, with regard to the application of Protocol II, fear for political loss of prestige if it is implicitly admitted that part of the territory is under control of the insurgents (the authorities prefer to speak of 'insurgent-affected' regions), unwillingness to upgrade the status of the insurgent, a position which was easier to take when prospects for cease-fire talks were still favourable. In the meantime, it is the local population which is the main victim of an armed conflict to which none of the rules of humanitarian law seems to be applied.

3.   PROVISIONAL EVALUATION OF THE HUMANITARIAN LAW APPROACH

I have given this example on purpose in order to show how extremely untraceable the shadowland between civil war and civil strife is if we approach it from the view-point of humanitarian law.[15] Formally, there seem to be four rather distinct situations, each with their own legal regime. First, there are the 'wars of liberation' in the sense of Article 1(4) of Protocol I. In principle, all humanitarian laws regulating an international armed conflict are applicable provided the State Party to the conflict is Party to the Protocol and the other party to the conflict has deposited the declaration of Article 96(3). The basis of obligation, therefore, is quasi-contractual and obligations are reciprocal. This type of 'internal conflict' seems to correspond with the basic characteristics of humanitarian law.

---

13 *Ibid.*, at 369.
14 See UN Doc. E/CN.4/1991/17, § 266.
15 See also W.M. Reisman, J. Silk, *Which Law Applies to the Afghan Conflict?*, 82 AJIL 459 *et seq.* (1988).

Secondly, we have the internal armed conflicts which cannot be called wars of liberation in the sense just mentioned but which meet the fairly objective criteria of Article 1 of Protocol II. In this case the basis of obligation of the State Party to the conflict is contractual, but not *vis-à-vis* the other party to the conflict. In fact, Protocol II does not even mention the other party to the conflict.[16] Does that mean that the obligations of the State Party to the conflict are unilateral, irrespective of the position of the other party? Quite correctly Kalshoven draws attention to the fact that Article 1(1) makes it a condition for application of Protocol I that the armed groups of the 'adverse party' exercise such control over a part of the territory of the State 'as to enable them ... to implement this Protocol' which seems to presuppose an obligation to do so.[17] Reciprocity of obligations, therefore, seems to be an in-built element for the applicability of Protocol II. Third, we have situations which do not meet the requirements of Article 1(1) of Protocol II but which are clearly above the threshold of Article 1(2), *viz.* internal disturbances and tensions. Such situations necessarily remain covered by common Article 3.[18] Here the basis of obligation between the parties to the conflict neither is contractual nor seems it to be reciprocal. Finally, we have situations which are not considered to constitute an armed conflict and therefore are below the threshold of common Article 3. Seemingly such situations (which may be labelled 'internal disturbances and tensions') are covered by the 'slimmed down' de Martens Clause mentioned in the Preamble of Protocol II, *viz.* by the 'principles of humanity and the dictates of the public conscience'.

The shadowland between civil war and civil strife seems to be mapped out quite neatly; nevertheless, even a bird's eye view of actual State practice teaches us that the dividing-lines between the various sectors are extremely blurred. The explanation is simple: the decision to activate the rules governing each sector is left to one of the parties to the conflict which has a direct and immediate interest of its own in not making that decision. The weakness of the whole system is that, unlike the regime for international armed conflicts, there is no objective machinery to make authoritative characterizations as to which situation occurs and which

---

16 F. Kalshoven, Constraints on the Waging of War 138 (1987). Kalshoven explains this 'utter silence' by the 'fear of many Governments that the mere reference to an adverse party might in concrete instances be interpreted as a form of recognition'.

17 *Ibid.*, at 139.

18 Kalshoven correctly refers to Article 1(1) of Protocol II which explicitly states that the Protocol develops and supplements Article 3 *without modifying its existing conditions of application* (emphasis added, PHK).

regime consequently should apply if the material conditions have been fulfilled. On first sight this may be ascribed to the complete absence of a supervising or monitoring system like the one embodied in the Geneva Conventions in the case of international armed conflicts. The rather meagre role given to humanitarian organizations like the Red Cross in common Article 3 and in Article 18 of Protocol II can hardly be compared to the functions of the Protecting Powers or the ICRC in the case of international armed conflicts.

I strongly feel, however, that the reluctance of States to allow for a more convincing implementation system has deeper roots and is closely connected with the reciprocity character which is so typical for international humanitarian law. Kalshoven is right in pointing out that Protocol II is based upon the presupposition that both parties to the conflict are obliged to apply its provisions. But that does not answer the question what the legal basis for that presupposition is.

Meron opines that it is *desirable* (italics mine, PHK) that Article 3 should be construed as imposing direct obligations on the forces fighting the Government, but his wording seems to indicate that he himself doubts whether this is already *lex lata*. It cannot be denied that international law can directly confer rights and obligations on individuals since nowadays the fact that they have a limited international personality is generally recognized. But can international law confer obligations upon an 'adverse party' (and that is the basic philosophy of international humanitarian law) without vesting it at the same time with some form of legal international personality?

Are the rather reassuring words in common Article 3 that its application shall not affect the legal status of the parties to the conflict sufficient to prevent that effect? Meron continues by saying that the imposition of direct obligations on forces fighting the Government should not be understood as conferring on them a different legal status and should not be used by a Government as a pretext for refusal to apply the duties stated in Article 3. Are Governments reluctant to declare applicable common Article 3 and/or Protocol II because they fear the *political* recognition of dissident groups or because they fear their *legal* recognition? If they fear the latter these fears will not be allayed by Meron's reminder that, according to the International Court of Justice, '[t]he subjects of law in any legal system are not necessarily identical in their nature or in the extent of their rights',[19] since what they want to avoid at all costs is that such groups will be

---

19 Meron, op. cit. n. 2, at 39, 40.

considered as subjects of international law in their own right for any purpose and to any extent.

4. THE HUMAN RIGHTS LAW APPROACH

Before going further into this question, let us first approach the shadowland between civil war and civil strife from the view-point of human rights law. Immediately the landscape seems to become more recognizable, since irrespective of the intensity or the stage of the conflict we find ourselves within the jurisdiction of a State. And nowadays it is a generally recognized principle of customary law that each State has to protect the essential human rights of all those who find themselves within its jurisdiction. This principle is implicit in the famous *obiter dictum* of the ICJ in the Barcelona Traction Case in which it classifies under the obligations *erga omnes* the rules concerning the basic rights of the human person.[20] This does not mean that all human rights as they appear in the catalogue formed by the Universal Declaration and the various human rights treaties belong to customary law;[21] for the moment it suffices to state that each and every State is under an obligation to guarantee to all those within its jurisdiction the enjoyment of certain rights, irrespective of whether that State has become a party to a human rights convention. This obligation is a unilateral one; in most constitutional systems the fundamental freedoms of the individual are qualified as rights he has *vis-à-vis* the State; the basis of obligation for the State is not a contractual one (the construction of the social contract which lies at the base of the concept of human rights has always been seen as a hypothetical one) nor is it based upon reciprocity; if the individual does not comply with the norms established by the State for the general well-being he may be punished, but even then his fundamental rights have to be respected. When human rights passed into international law to better ensure their protection they were, as in constitutional law, formulated as rights of the individual *vis-à-vis* his own State. What was peculiar about this internationalization of human rights is that a State became accountable to the international community and to other States for the non-compliance with his obligations towards his own subjects. In particular, if a State is a Party to a human rights treaty this accountability towards the other State Parties is clearly visible in the

---

20 ICJ Rep. 1970, § 34, at 32.
21 See for the passage of human rights norms into customary law, T. Meron, op. cit. n. 7, at 79 *et seq.*.

right of state-complaint. In such cases the basis of this *accountability* is contractual and reciprocal, but I strongly feel that this does not change the original basis of the 'obligation to respect' since this obligation is owed to the individual and remains a unilateral one. Consequently, it is the relationship of State-subject (in the sense of subject to its jurisdiction) which determines the applicability of human rights law and not any material conditions.

A provisional conclusion, therefore, may be drawn: human rights law answers more satisfactorily the first condition for an effective legal system, mentioned in the introductory paragraph: *viz.* that it should be clear in which situations the rules are applicable. With human rights law that is the case whenever there is a relationship of State-subject.

Now we have to see whether also the second condition is met, *viz.* that the substance of the applicable rules is adequate for the realization of the underlying values. It is exactly here that we find the weak spot of human rights law when we look at the shadowland between civil war and civil strife.

We have seen that in most national systems human rights are constitutional or constitution-based rights. In practice we have seen that during periods of serious civil unrest or insurgency the constitution or at least these constitutional guarantees were suspended and rendered inoperative. Evidently this reflects the idea that the preservation of public order prevails over the rights of the individual, since if public order collapses, respect for human rights will come to naught anyhow. Undoubtedly there is logic and truth in this reasoning; on the other hand it should be realized that in those circumstances the individual is exposed to authorities whose power is no longer bridled by the constitution and who feel threatened by forces from within, *i.e.*, by part of those individuals whose fundamental rights they are expected to protect. We are, therefore, confronted with a paradoxial situation: at the very same moment that the existence of the community which forms the basis of the State is threatened, the fundamental rights of the individual are at peril to a much greater extent than they are in normal times;[22] nevertheless the exercise of

---

22 Meron, op. cit. n. 2, at 51. According to Meron: 'Experience shows that it is in times of emergency, when the life of the nation is threatened, that cruel abuse of human rights are at their worst.'

those rights is suspended 'with the aim of rectifying the situation, and indeed protecting the most fundamental rights'.[23]

This paradox also passed into international law when human rights became a matter of international concern after World War II. All general human rights conventions, whether universal or regional (with the exception of the 1981 African Charter on Human and People's Rights) contain derogation clauses which may be put into effect in times of emergency 'in order to enable states, when confronted with such situations, to loosen the stranglehold of their obligations without running the risk of their membership of the community of States parties being called in question'.[24]

States which wish to make use of these derogatory powers can do so only under certain procedural and substantive conditions. Of the latter the most important for our subject is that there are certain rights which cannot be derogated under any circumstances. Although the list of these non-derogable rights is not identical in the relevant general conventions (the UN Covenant on Civil and Political Rights and the European and the American Conventions), four of them are listed in all three: the right to life, the prohibition of torture, the prohibition of slavery and the prohibition of retroactive penal measures. These rights, therefore, have to be respected and guaranteed under all circumstances to all persons within the derogating State's jurisdiction, including those who are seen by the authorities as the 'adverse party'.

In her important study on states of emergency submitted to the UN Subcommission on Prevention of Discrimination and Protection of Minorities, Questiaux draws a highly interesting conclusion:

'[T]he idea of a basic minimum, from which no derogation is possible, is present in a sufficient number of instruments to justify our approaching the matter by reference to a general principle of law recognized in practice by the international community, which could, moreover, regard it as a peremptory norm of international law within the meaning of Article 53 of the 1969 Vienna Convention on the Law of Treaties .... It therefore seems to us that the peremptory nature of the principle of non-derogation should

---

23 N. Questiaux, *Study of the Implications for Human Rights of Recent Developments Concerning Situations Known as States of Siege or Emergency*, UN Doc. E/CN.4/Sub. 2/1982/15, § 23, at 8.
24 *Ibid.*, § 37, at 11.

be binding on every State, whether or not it is a party and irrespective of the gravity of the circumstances.'[25]

The fact that there is a set of basic human rights to which each and every person is entitled under all circumstances and that this now seems to be generally recognized is in itself of inestimable importance for the realization of the values to which both humanitarian law and human rights law are committed. But at the same time it has to be admitted that there is an unacceptably deep gap between the professed legal theory and actual practice. Partly this is due to the semi-organized character of international society where a system of communal sanctions against a violator of the law is lacking; as important is the fact that one basic human right is conspicuously absent from the list of non-derogable rights, *viz.* the right to a fair trial. A common feature under states of emergency are arbitrary deprivations of liberty, whether they result in enforced or involuntary disappearances, incommunicado detention or administrative detention. In her report Questiaux draws attention to the fact that usually in such cases there is no place for judicial review, not even in the form of direct intervention through recourse to *habeas corpus*. This results in a total absence of guarantees, a situation which is conducive to the violation of those very rights which have been declared inalienable. The present author has stressed this point in all his reports on Questions Relevant to Torture and has called incommunicado detention the torturer's bosom-friend.[26]

Questiaux is right in concluding that '[f]ailure to respect the right to a fair trial generally accounts for the most frequent violations' (of the non-derogable rights). Of vital importance is her next remark: Although it has to be admitted 'that international law in no way prohibits derogation from that right ...., the restrictions established should not modify that right to the point of making it non-existent'.[27] Governments should never restrict derogable rights in such a way that the enjoyment of non-derogable rights by the individual becomes futile.

The provisions of the human rights treaties and, consequently, also the customary rules on states of emergency, fall short of what is needed to realize the values they pretend to guarantee.[28] A favourable exception in this respect is the American Convention which in Article 27(2) forbids

---

25 *Ibid.*, § 68, at 19.
26 UN Doc. E/CN.4/1991/17, § 291.
27 Questiaux, loc. cit. n. 23, § 181-193, at 40-42.
28 See on the insufficiency of the treaty provisions also Meron, op. cit. n. 2, at 50 *et seq.*.

suspension of the judicial guarantees essential for the protection of such (non-derogable) rights.

In 1988 the General Assembly adopted the so-called Body of Principles for the Protection of All Persons under Any Form of Detention or Imprisonment.[29] Now it is interesting to note that the scope of this instrument is extremely broad: 'These principles apply for the protection of all persons under *any* form of detention or imprisonment' (including therefore administrative detention). Principle 4 states that 'any form of detention or imprisonment and all measures affecting the human rights of a person under any form of detention or imprisonment shall be ordered by, or be subject to, the effective control of a judicial or other authority' ('other' to be understood as 'independent from the arresting authority') and Principle 11 gives the detainee the right to be heard *promptly* by such a judicial or other authority.

The most remarkable element, however, is that there is no reference to times of public emergency which would allow for derogation from these Principles. This is not the result of an oversight since an earlier Draft contained such an exception clause. May the fact that the General Assembly adopted this resolution by consensus and that it was drafted by its legal (sixth) Committee be seen as an indication that there is an emergent *opinio iuris* that the right to a fair trial, including the principle of *habeas corpus*, belongs to the core human rights and therefore must be deemed to be inalienable and non-derogable? That certainly would be a highly essential strengthening of the safety-net constructed to safeguard the basic human values. Even taking into account the fact that the Body of Principles is not a binding instrument, in my opinion one does not go too far in saying that it may be seen as an authoritative present-day interpretation of the relevant provisions of the Covenant on Civil and Political Rights, adopted by that same General Assembly twenty-two years earlier.

5.   PROVISIONAL EVALUATION OF THE HUMAN RIGHTS LAW APPROACH

The human rights law approach is attractive because of its simplicity. The State is under a (national but also international) obligation to respect and guarantee the basic human rights of all those who are subject to its

---

29   GA Res. 43/173 of 9 December 1988.

jurisdiction. No Government can evade that obligation by labeling certain groups of such subjects as 'enemies of the people'. If such dissident groups refuse to obey the law they are subject to the criminal jurisdiction of the State. The exercise of this jurisdiction finds its constraints in the rights of the individual. Just as the basis of the State's 'obligation to respect' is unilateral, so the basis of the individual's 'obligation to abide by the law' is unilateral. Failure on the one side can never be a justification for failure on the other side.

This essentially coherent set-up, however, becomes fragile as soon as the stability of the internal order is at stake. If authority itself is at stake because it is seriously challenged by (part of) the subjects, positive human rights law tips the balance in that confrontation in favour of the Government by authorizing it to suspend most of the rights of the individual. Although international human rights law has put some constraints on the Government by excepting from that authorization certain inalienable rights, the way in which this has been done can hardly be called well-considered. Some rights have been singled out which are indeed basic for man and his dignity, but what was overlooked is that the various human rights are not isolated specimens, which can be set apart in a laboratory, but that the enjoyment of each of them is completely dependent on the rule of law; and the rule of law is a complicated and highly interwoven fabric.

The conclusion, therefore, must be that in the shadowland between civil war and civil strife, human rights law has failed to meet the second of the conditions for an effective legal system, *viz.* that the substance of the applicable rules should be adequate for the realization of the underlying values.

6.   COMPARISON OF THE HUMANITARIAN LAW APPROACH AND THE HUMAN RIGHTS LAW APPROACH

In referring to emergency situations resulting from a serious political crisis, Questiaux in her study distinguishes between four different hypotheses: a) international armed conflicts; b) wars of national liberation; c) non-international armed conflicts; d) situations of internal disorder or internal tension. In doing so, she follows closely the categories established in international humanitarian law, a) being covered by the Geneva Conventions and Protocol I; b) being assimilated to a) by means of Article 1(4) of Protocol I; c) being covered by Protocol II and common Article 3; and d) being still a vacuum in international humanitarian law. She continues by saying that the first two hypotheses, and, under certain conditions, the third constitute the area of application *par excellence* of the humanitarian law of war. And then follows a highly remarkable statement: 'They will therefore not come directly within the scope of the study'. She justifies this choice (for it is a choice) by her terms of reference which implied that 'situations of war in the terms of humanitarian law are not envisaged'. She seems, however, not entirely convinced of the rationality of that decision from the view-point of human rights law for she recognizes that 'humanitarian law is considered by a significant section of opinion as a branch of the international law of human rights, with the result that the latter, by its very basis, would cover the four hypotheses mentioned above'.[30]

Of course, it would not be very useful to split up the shadowland between civil war and civil strife in seperate sectors and to allor them either to humanitarian law or to human rights law. Why would the scope of application of human rights law end with the non-sporadic use of arms within the State?

In this respect it is not without interest that two endeavours have been made to cover also the still-vacant area of internal disturbances and tensions with humanitarian norms. I refer to the Code of Conduct in the Event of Internal Disturbances and Tensions, drafted by Gasser and to the Draft Model Declaration on Internal Strife by Meron.[31] The approach taken by Gasser is much more cautious than that of Meron. Gasser's first concern is not the state of the law, but it is purely humanitarian in the sense of 'helping mankind'. His position can best be summarized by the following quotation: 'The humanitarian approach focuses on the actual situation of the victims which it strives to assist and protect, and not on redressing a legal wrong or on restoring the rule of law'.[32] His aim is to bring together a number of existing rules that will meet the specific requirements of internal disturbances and tensions, and he continues: 'The Code does not propose new rules, but it simply *recalls rules* generally considered as being part of customary law or appearing to express general legal principles'. He calls his code first and foremost didactic in character and addresses himself also to persons unconnected with the authorities.[33]

---

30 Questiaux, loc. cit. n. 23, § 28-30, at 9.
31 Both the Draft Code of Conduct (prepared by H.P. Gasser) and the Draft Model Declaration (prepared by T. Meron) have been published in IRRC 38-58, 59-76 (1988).
32 *Ibid.*, at 41 (Gasser).
33 *Ibid.*, at 46.

Meron's Model Declaration is much more legalistic in character. It clearly is his intention to fill a vacuum: the declaration must contain 'an irreducible and non-derogable core of human and humanitarian norms that must be applied in situations of internal strife and violence'. Why? Because humanitarian law is not applicable in cases of internal strife falling below the threshold of common Article 3 and human rights law is either not applicable because the states concerned have not ratified the conventions or is ineffective because of the frequency of *de facto* or *de jure* derogations and because of the 'grave inadequacy of non-derogable rights relevant to situations of violent internal strife'.[34] Most illustrative of his intention is the following quotation: '[The declaration] should represent to denizens of a country suffering internal strife what the Universal Declaration of Human Rights represents to persons living in conditions of tranquillity'.[35]

I feel that with these different approaches by Gasser and Meron we have reached the most crucial issue. Meron states that in the shadowland human rights law is either inapplicable or gravely inadequate and that, consequently, there is a legal vacuum; Gasser maintains that 'internal disturbances and tensions *automatically* (italics mine, PHK) fall within the scope of international human rights law'.[36]

It is certainly no coincidence that common Article 3 contains some of the rights which were later formulated as non-derogable rights under the human rights conventions. The Geneva Conventions were adopted one year after the General Assembly had proclaimed the Universal Declaration of Human Rights. The Universal Declaration had no binding force; in common Article 3 binding force was given to those provisions of the Declaration which were considered to be essential under all circumstances, in peace as well as in times of armed conflict, for the preservation of human life and integrity (Articles 1, 5 and 11). To this extent common Article 3 can be called the first international legislation on human rights law.[37] On the other hand it also reflects the character of humanitarian law since it only guarantees these rights to persons taking no active part in the hostilities and not to combatants, although these are formally subject to the jurisdiction of the Contracting State and enjoy the article's protection as

---

34 *Ibid.*, at 60 (Meron).
35 T. Meron, *Towards a Humanitarian Declaration on Internal Strife*, 79 AJIL 864 (1984).
36 Gasser, loc. cit. n. 31, at 49.
37 Myren, loc. cit. n. 12, at 349. According to Myren:
   'Human rights (which apply at all times) have often influenced humanitarian law (which applies only to situations of armed conflicts), and common article 3 offers a prime illustration of such influence. These provisions mirror those of the Universal Declaration which was negotiated at the same time.'

soon as they are placed *hors de combat*. In its substance, therefore, common Article 3 is human rights law, in its presentation it is humanitarian law.

Protocol II to the Geneva Conventions is different since it is a mixture of human rights law and of humanitarian provisions. Although it does not contain many rules on methods and means of combat, the provisions of Parts I, III and IV are germane to situations of armed conflict. Part II, however, for the greater part, contains genuine human rights law.[38] The personal scope of application of these provisions, on the other hand, is typical for humanitarian law. Although the adverse party is not mentioned throughout the Protocol, protection is only guaranteed to 'all persons who do not take part or who have ceased to take part in hostilities' (Article 4(1), first sentence; Article 2(1) refers to 'persons *affected* by an armed conflict as defined in Article 1'). Strangely enough, the only protection given to combatants can be found in the same article that excludes them from the protection of the Protocol, *viz.* that it is prohibited to order that there shall be no survivors (Article 4(1), last sentence).[39]

Here we are confronted with a strange situation. In so far as it does not repeat them, Part II of Protocol II can be said to extend the scope of the provisions on non-derogable rights of the human rights conventions. In particular Article 6 guaranteeing the right to a fair trial, is of prime importance.

Beneficial as as this may be, it has the curious effect that for a Party to Protocol II the right to a fair trial is a non-derogable right whenever an internal conflict has reached the stage where Protocol II should be declared applicable, whereas it lacks the non-derogable character during conflicts which are below the threshold of Protocol II. Moreover, since Protocol II is understood to bind both parties to the conflict, any insurgent or rebellion group is expected to apply the same human rights provisions,[40] whereas according to human rights law the obligation to protect and guarantee such basic human rights is a unilateral one for the Government only. In the case of Protocol II this dual obligation to a certain extent is understandable since the adverse party exercises factual control over part of the territory, but in cases below this threshold such a reciprocity of human rights obligations would certainly create serious problems.

---

38 Kalshoven, op. cit. n. 16, at 139. In the opinion of Kalshoven: '... quite a few provisions in the Protocol have been taken almost verbatim from existing human rights conventions ....'
39 *Ibid.*, at 140.
40 For the difficulties an adverse party will have in meeting such human right requirements, see, Forsythe, loc. cit. n. 5, at 289-290.

What about the shadowland's third province: internal disturbances and tensions? In preparing his model declaration, Meron concluded that it should be applicable to the entire population. Quite correctly he says that 'in a low-intensity conflict, the traditional distinctions, such as between combatants and civilians ... may not be meaningful and, moreover, may be abused by Governments so as to circumvent the objects and purposes of the declaration'. More relevant, however, seems to be his other argument in favor of a broad applicability, *viz.* the non-derogable provisions of the human rights instruments: 'It would ... be inconceivable that all persons could benefit from such non-derogable provisions under applicable human rights instruments, but not under the declaration'.[41] But basically, the same argument holds true for situations covered by common Article 3 and Protocol II.

It would be a strange situation indeed if the State could exclude the adverse party from the protection it is obliged to give under the non-derogable provisions of the human rights instruments to all its subjects, by opting for the regime of common Article 3 and/or Protocol II. Conversely, it would be illogical that in a situation where the material conditions of Article 3 and/or Protocol II are met but their regime has not been declared applicable by the Government, this Government would be bound by the regime for internal disturbances and tensions which has a broader personal scope than the proper regime, specifically drawn up for that situation.

The difficulty is that, although in principle no gap between the field of applicability of the different regimes of humanitarian law should be possible, in actual fact the choice to decide which regime is applicable or not to decide at all is at the Government's discretion; unlike in international armed conflicts objective criteria activating the applicable regime play a much less decisive role in internal conflicts. As far as human rights are concerned, this is irreconcilable with the basic characteristic of human rights law, *viz.* that it is a comprehensive and self-contained system: as long as a person is subject to a State's jurisdiction (and jurisdiction is a formal concept) he is entitled to respect for his human rights (under a state of emergency that means the non-derogable rights) and the State is under an obligation to respect and guarantee these rights.

The second element in humanitarian law which seems to be at odds with human rights law is the concept of reciprocity. Partsch rightly has drawn attention to the fact that the proposition that also the adverse party is bound by the rules for non-international conflicts can only be made by

---

41 Meron, loc. cit. n. 35, at 863.

means of a rather hazardous construction, *viz.* that the ratification by the Contracting State of the Geneva Conventions (common Article 3) or Protocol II not only binds the ratifying State, but also the adverse party.[42]

This may already be true for the rules of humanitarian law proper but with regard to its provisions on human rights such a construction is totally superfluous and may even be harmful, since it may lead to confusion in spite of the prohibition of reprisals.

Human rights law places unilateral obligations on the State. When an individual or a group of individuals violates the human rights of its co-citizens, this forms a criminal act under national law or may be even a crime under international law, *e.g.*, a crime against humanity. The concept of reciprocity which is so typical for humanitarian law, creates confusion where human rights are concerned;[43] the fact that the adverse party does not respect the basic human rights of others may be used -and is often used- as a (seemingly convincingly) argument for the Government's lack of respect for the basic human rights of its disobedient subjects. But as the Government may continuously broaden the circle of disobedient citizens, even respect for the non-derogable rights will gradually evaporate.

7.   CONCLUDING REMARKS

We started this exploration of the shadowland between civil war and civil strife with Meron's proposition that in every situation there should either be a convergence of humanitarian and human rights norms, or one of these two systems of protection should clearly apply. I feel that now the stage has been reached that this question can be answered. First of all, one should keep in mind that humanitarian law for non-international armed conflict forms a *mixtum compositum*. Partly it contains rules which are typical for situations of armed conflict (care for the wounded and sick, protection of medical duties, ways and means of combat). Such rules should remain the domain of humanitarian law. Partly, however, it contains provisions on human rights and the lower on the ladder of violence the situation is the more so. It will be clear from what I have said

---

42 K.J. Partsch, *Regeln für den Aufstand* (Rules for Insurgency), Neue Zeitschrift für Wehrrecht 3 (1989).

43 In the Philippines, where neither common article 3 nor Protocol II has been declared applicable, the Armed Forces regularly lodge complaints about human rights violations by the rebel forces with the independent Human Rights Commission, whereas the proper place to file them is the public prosecutor's office.

before that in my opinion such rules do not belong to humanitarian law proper. If such rules are presented as humanitarian law norms, confusion may be the result whereas in the shadowland between civil war and civil strife it is clarity what is most needed since confusion contributes to normless behaviour. When the application of a certain regime of humanitarian law, containing also human rights norms, is rejected out of fear that this will raise the status of the adverse party, the human rights prevailing under that regime may be withheld whereas they have no direct relevance to that regime since they must be respected anyhow.

One sometimes does get the impression that standard-setting in the field of humanitarian law is used as a means to expand the catalogue of non-derogable human rights. Such an expansion is highly desirable, starting with the right to a fair trial, but the proper way to do so is the conclusion of additional protocols to the human rights instruments. The European human rights system has shown how effective such an 'incremental system' can work.

It would, therefore, be preferable that humanitarian law, when dealing with internal conflicts, would remind Governments of their obligations under human rights law instead of presenting such norms as independent norms of humanitarian law. I, therefore, prefer Gasser's approach to that of Meron. Both Gasser's Code of Conduct and Meron's Model Declaration contain nearly exclusively norms of human rights law. Whereas Gasser's approach is mainly didactic and moral by recalling rules which are already in force for Governments and appealing to non-governmental parties to act with moderation,[44] Meron's document pretends to have a legislative character: 'Because the applicability of humanitarian law is often denied, and the non-derogable human rights protections are inadequate and frequently ignored, there is a dire scarcity of governing norms'.[45] If human rights law is inadequate, it should be improved through its own procedures for standard-setting and not by an instrument which intends to establish a continuum from the highest step to the lowest step on the ladder of a legal system originally designed for armed conflict between States and, therefore, substantially different in character from human rights law.

In conclusion, I feel that the shadowland between civil war and civil strife is in need of both humanitarian law and human rights law and, that, consequently, not one of the two systems can apply exclusively. An essential condition, however, is that the difference between the two

---

44 Gasser, loc. cit. n. 31, at 46-47.
45 Meron, loc. cit. n. 2, at 153.

systems is clearly distinguished in order to prevent a deleterious confusion. To that extent it can be said that there is a convergence of humanitarian and human rights norms, but it should be realized that this convergence does not imply confluence. It is precisely this assumed confluence that may hamper the effectiveness of both systems. In exploring the shadowland between civil war and civil strife one should constantly be guided by Professor Norgaard's sound counsel: 'The influence of theory and theoretical conceptions upon the creation of new rules of international law may not be overlooked as confusion in theory and concepts may lead to less adequate rules'.[46]

---

46 C.A. Norgaard, The Position of the Individual in International Law 1 (1962).

INTERNAL STRIFE: APPLICABLE NORMS AND A PROPOSED INSTRUMENT *

THEODOR MERON

1.   INTRODUCTION

The tragedy of internal strife[1] is unfolding in a large and growing number of countries throughout the world. UN bodies, governmental agencies, non-governmental organizations and of course, the International Committee

---

*   Th. Meron wishes to express his gratitude to Filomen D'Agostino and Max E. Greenberg Research Fund of New York University Law School for its support of this study.

1   For a definition of internal disturbance (internal strife) by the ICRC see T. Meron, Human Rights in Internal Strife: Their International Protection (Hersch Lauterpacht Memorial Lectures, Cambridge) 76 (1987). For a discussion of pathology of internal strife, see *ibid.*, at 71-104.

of the Red Cross (ICRC) have studied the situations in many of these countries. On the basis of their reports, it would be possible to describe the symptoms of internal strife in particular countries. However, this essay focuses on the general features of internal strife without reference to specific countries, since accounts of the situation in any one country inevitably prompt debate over factual allegations. Such debate would distract us from our task of developing an understanding of the nature of internal strife and suggesting the necessary remedies.

Internal strife frequently involves an aggregate of violent acts and human rights abuses which are interrelated rather than isolated phenomena. Despite the salutary efforts of the ICRC, the United Nations, and such non-governmental organizations as the Human Rights Watch and Amnesty International to humanize the behaviour of the principal actors in situations of internal strife, gross abuses of human dignity continue unabated. A systemic relationship often exists between various types of abuses, so that a given practice will create an environment in which other abuses are almost certain to occur. This essay focuses on the most serious and the most frequent of these abuses.

In preparing this essay, I have drawn on my published writings[2] regarding the increasingly common calamity of internal strife and on the working paper presented, on my own responsibility, to the ICRC in April 1984. In these writings I attempted to demonstrate the need to draft a declaration containing an irreducible and non-derogable core of human rights and humanitarian norms that must be applied in situations of internal strife and violence. Such normative progress should accompany efforts to strengthen the implementation of extant human rights and humanitarian norms. In addition, I explained both the conceptual context and the practical urgency of such an initiative, particularly for situations which can be regarded as a public emergency but as falling below thresholds of applicability of humanitarian instruments.

During the last few years, situations of internal strife have resulted in an escalating loss of human life and increasingly grave violations of human dignity. Although international efforts to promulgate a declaration on internal strife have not been successful as yet, the 1988 publication of a special issue of the International Review of the Red Cross on 'Internal

---

2   T. Meron, *On the Inadequate Reach of Humanitarian and Human Rights Law and the Need for a New Instrument*, 77 AJIL 589 (1983); T. Meron, *Towards a Humanitarian Declaration on Internal Strife*, 78 AJIL 859 (1984); Meron, op. cit. n. 1; *Draft Model Declaration on Internal Strife*, 3 Nordic Journal on Human Rights 12 (1987); T. Meron, *Draft Model Declaration on Internal Strife*, 262 Int'l Rev. Red Cross 29 (1988).

Disturbances and Tensions'[3] demonstrates the continuing importance of humanizing internal strife.

A declaration on this subject rather than a formally binding instrument would stand a much better chance of adoption. Public opinion, Governments and international governmental and non-governmental organizations would encourage respect for the defined minimum standards of conduct. Hopefully it would affect the practice of Governments and other actors involved in situations of internal strife and shape rules of customary international law.[4]

2.   RESERVATIONS AS TO THE DESIRABILITY OF THE ADOPTION OF A DECLARATION

A number of reservations have been raised. I shall first consider and try to comment on these reservations and then outline the content of the minimum core of the declaration.

Various observers, and particularly participants in the Geneva Diplomatic Conference, which culminated with the adoption of the two Additional Protocols of 1977, have raised some doubts as to the prospects of attempting, at the present time, to develop rules of humanitarian law. Naturally, the truncation of Protocol II during the Diplomatic Conference[5] in which it was adopted made them pessimistic about the prospects for further development of international humanitarian law. Without minimizing the difficulties, I feel that repeated efforts, against great odds, have always characterized the incremental growth of enlightened norms of humanitarian law. Moreover, the situation since 1977 has changed considerably. If in the seventies the struggle for national liberation in the Portuguese colonies together with the situation in South Africa and the occupation of the West Bank and Gaza, dominated international attention, internal violence is now among the greatest concerns of Governments and human rights

---

3   262 Int'l Rev. Red Cross (1988).

4   Regarding the role of declarations in the development of international human rights law, see Meron, loc. cit. n. 1, at 141; T. Meron, Human Rights and Humanitarian Norms as Customary Law 82-84 (1989). Support for such a declaration was expressed by the Report of the Independent Commission on International Humanitarian Issues: Winning the Human Race 73, 74 (1988).

5   Y. Sandoz, C. Swinarski, B. Zimmermann, eds., ICRC, Commentary on the Additional Protocols of 8 June 1977 to the Geneva Conventions of 12 August 1949, 1319-1336 (1987); M. Bothe, K. Partsch, W.A. Solf, eds., New Rules for Victims of Armed Conflicts 604-617 (1982).

organizations. These situations of protracted acts of political violence are characterized by substantial violations of human dignity.

Some observers have expressed the belief that the very absence of an instrument relating to internal strife has made Governments less concerned about possible intrusions upon their sovereignty and, thus, has made it easier for the ICRC to obtain access to detainees in countries involved in internal strife. The fact that in many cases the ICRC has been refused access to places of detention, and even altogether to the countries concerned, casts some doubts on the view espoused by these observers. However, even if it were true that the ICRC would sometimes benefit from the absence of a declaration, it must be remembered that the ICRC is only one of the important actors. Other actors, such as third Governments and such non-governmental organizations as the Human Rights Watch could effectively use a declaration on internal strife in trying to persuade Governments to abide by international standards and to focus public opinion.

Some human rights experts have followed a different approach. Characteristically, they are reluctant to admit that international human rights instruments, such as the International Covenant on Civil and Political Rights, leave unsettled some important norms. They appear to believe that these instruments provide, either explicitly or implicitly, all the necessary norms and, that even if they do not, such norms can be developed through expansive interpretation and the rapid growth of customary law. They emphasize the need for improving implementation procedures and hope that through such improvement, *e.g.* further regulating the declaration of states of emergency, and derogations on grounds of national emergencies, most of the normative difficulties can be resolved and abuses eliminated.

Of course, the failure to respect the existing law accounts for many, perhaps most, of the difficulties encountered. And, to be sure, experience accumulated over the years has shown that the means for scrutinizing states of emergency and derogations are in need of refinement. Nevertheless, improved implementation alone will not provide an adequate substitute for the absence of certain norms, particularly non-derogable norms which are essential for the protection of human lives and human dignity in situations of internal violence.

Professor Higgins has recently criticized the tendency to focus exclusively on implementation:

'... there is a widely held view that the past forty years has seen an unparalleled elaboration of a multitude of human rights norms, and that what is now required is not a further expansion of the list of human rights but rather their enforcement. It is to the implementation of these rights, rather than to the enlargement of the list, that in the view of many attention should now be directed.

I believe this to be an oversimplified approach, because it assumes that there are two basic, and very different, activities - the articulation of human rights and their implementation. My own view is that there is rather a seamless web, and that the identification and invocation of human rights is a necessary integral element in implementation ....

Obviously a human right cannot be implemented until it has been identified and articulated ....'[6]

I agree with Professor Higgins. It is, of course, true that enlightened interpretations of human rights' instruments and practices can speed up the evolution of moral rules into customary law. However, basing protection of human dignity in internal strife on customary law presents many difficulties. Unfortunately, examples of States observing essential humanitarian rules in situations of internal strife are scarce. As a result, the scarcity of the required practice and of normative international declarations addressing such norms, specifically for situations of internal strife, makes the proof of customary law difficult. It is hard to persuade the actors involved in situations of internal strife about the content and the binding character of unwritten rules.

Moreover, one of the difficulties with regard to the usefulness in situations of internal strife of such human rights instruments as the International Covenant on Civil and Political Rights (Political Covenant) is that the obligations which it states are addressed primarily to Governments (vertical applicability). Unless some obligations are addressed also to the groups fighting the Governments, and to the groups which are fighting each other, Governments are unlikely to accept a declaration on internal strife. The prospects for humanizing internal strife are greatly improved if the obligation to abide by essential humanitarian principles is addressed to the opposition as well as to the Government in such a way that the duties are reasonably balanced and the norms of behaviour are not unduly favourable to either side. Whether a particular obligation should be addressed exclusively to the Government or also to groups opposing the Government should depend on the content of the obligation. For example, only Governments and organizations possessing advanced elements of state-

---

6   R. Higgins, *Some Thoughts on the Implementation of Human Rights*, 89/1 UN Bulletin of Human Rights 60 (1990).

like structure can realistically implement judicial guarantees, while all
parties should uphold the duty to respect principles of humanity and such
prohibitions as those against torture or taking hostages.

Some situations of internal strife involve more complex conflicts in
which, regardless of the role played by the *de jure* Government of the
State, two or more ethnic or religious groups are involved in acts of
violence against each other (horizontal applicability).[7] The declaration on
internal strife should contain an appropriate statement of the policy that
humanitarian obligations and norms protecting individual safety and human
dignity apply as broadly as possible.

Such a declaration, or declarations, if available, would help generate
and shape customary law. It is often assumed that customary law develops
spontaneously. However, its advancement can be accelerated, directed and
shaped through deliberate actions, such as the adoption of normative
declarations. A declaration on internal strife would provide a clear focal
point for moral pressure to respect humanitarian rules.

3.   STATE OF NECESSITY

Another difficulty with the existing legal climate stems from the fact that in
situations not governed by the derogation clauses of human rights
instruments, deviation from customary law rules arguably may be justified
by invoking exceptions recognized by general international law. In other
words, even where a case can be made for a new norm of customary
human rights, that norm might be displaced on grounds of emergency in
situations of internal strife. I propose to elaborate on this proposition.

Customary law rules providing exceptions to the normally applicable
obligations of States, such as those based on *force majeure*, state of
necessity and self-defence, may preclude the wrongfulness of an act which
does not conform to a State's international obligations.[8] The ILC
explained that:

'... the term state of necessity ... denote[s] the situation of a State whose
sole means of safeguarding an essential interest threatened by a grave and

---

7   See generally Meron, op. cit. n. 4, at 162-171.
8   Draft Articles 31-34 of ILC's Draft Articles on State Responsibility (Part One), (1980), II Yb.
    of the ILC 33 (1980); UN Doc. A/CN.4/SER.A/1980/Add.1, (Part 2), (1981).

imminent peril is to adopt conduct not in conformity with what is required of it by an international obligation to another State.'[9]

Because States often invoke 'necessity' to justify deviations or derogations from the conduct required by human rights and humanitarian norms law, the applicability of this exception to these obligations requires close scrutiny.

It is now generally accepted that humanitarian instruments, having been adopted to govern situations of armed conflict,[10] are not subject to derogations on such grounds as public emergency except in the rather narrow context of Article 5 of the Fourth Geneva Convention[11] and Article 45(3) of Protocol I.[12] These provisions parallel the limitation clauses of human rights instruments. Imperative military concerns, military necessity or security reasons are mentioned, for example, in Articles 49(2), 64(1) or 78(1) of the Fourth Geneva Convention, which grant States certain additional freedoms only when such freedoms are explicitly stated in the treaties concerned.[13] Invoking other necessity-related exceptions derived from customary law would clash with the purpose of humanitarian instruments. The principles both of effectiveness and of *expressio unius est exclusio alterius* preclude any other interpretation.[14]

This conception of humanitarian instruments is strongly supported by the ILC's *Commentary* on Draft Article 33 on the state of necessity.[15]

---

9   *Ibid.*, at 34.

10 Meron, op. cit. n. 1, at 156.

11 Convention for the Amelioration of the Condition of the Wounded and Sick in Armed Forces in the Field (First Geneva Convention), 12 August l949, 6 UST 3114, TIAS No. 3362, 75 UNTS 31; Convention for the Amelioration of the Condition of the Wounded, Sick, and Shipwrecked Members of Armed Forces at Sea (Second Geneva Convention), 12 August 1949, 6 UST 3217, TIAS No. 3363, 75 UNTS 85; Geneva Convention Relative to the Treatment of Prisoners of War (Third Geneva Convention), 12 August l949, 6 UST 3316, TIAS No. 3364, 75 UNTS 135; Convention Relative to the Protection of Civilian Persons in Time of War (Fourth Geneva Convention), 12 August l949, 6 UST 3516, TIAS No. 3365, 75 UNTS 287.

12 Protocol Additional to the Geneva Conventions of 12 August 1949, and Relating to the Protection of Victims of International Armed Conflicts (Protocol I) 16 ILM 1391 (1977).

13 Meron, op. cit. n. 1, at 15.

14 Special Rapporteur R. Ago argued that the international law of war was not necessarily 'an absolutely closed area as regards any possible application of "state of necessity" as a circumstance precluding the wrongfulness of conduct...'. R. Ago, Addendum to the Eighth Report on State Responsibility, UN Doc. A/CN.4/318/Add.5-7, Yb. of the ILC, I, 37 (1980). The ILC's *Commentary* did not follow Professor Ago's position on this question.

15 Article 33 of the ILC's Draft Articles on State Responsibility (Part One) reads as follows: 1. A state of necessity may not be invoked by a State as a ground for precluding the wrongfulness of an act of that State not in conformity with an international obligation of the

The ILC has adduced several reasons why a situation of necessity cannot excuse a State from compliance with rules of humanitarian law which, in order to attenuate the rigors of war, limit the belligerents' choice of means and methods for conducting hostilities.[16] First, some humanitarian law rules constitute norms of *jus cogens* and are thus non-derogable. Second, even in regard to non-peremptory humanitarian law obligations, invoking a state of necessity to justify precluding the wrongfulness of State conduct conflicts directly with the purpose of humanitarian treaties, which seek to subordinate the immediate military objectives of belligerents to higher, humanitarian interests. Humanitarian law principles already reflect a certain equilibrium between military expediency and consideration of humanity. As such, they cannot yield to additional unilaterally perceived requirements of military necessity. Third, clauses which permit States to invoke such exceptions as urgent military necessity:

> '... apply only to the cases expressly provided for. Apart from these cases, it follows implicitly from the text of the conventions that they do not admit the possibility of invoking military necessity as a justification for State conduct not in conformity with the obligations they impose. (...) The Commission took the view that a State cannot invoke a state of necessity if that is expressly or implicitly prohibited by a conventional instrument.'[17]

State unless:

a) the act was the only means of safeguarding an essential interest of the State against a grave and imminent peril; and

b) the act did not seriously impair an essential interest of the State towards which the obligation existed.

2. In any case, a state of necessity may not be invoked by a State as a ground for precluding wrongfulness:

a) if the international obligation with which the act of the State is not in conformity arises out of a peremptory norm of general international law; or

b) if the international obligation with which the act of the State is not in conformity is laid down by a treaty which, explicitly or implicitly, excludes the possibility of invoking the state of necessity with respect to that obligation; or

c) if the State in question has contributed to the occurrence of the state of necessity.

Yb. of the ILC, II, 1980, loc. cit. n. 8, at 34.

For the ILC's discussion of humanitarian intervention, see *ibid.*, at 44-45; R. Ago, Addendum to the Eighth Report on State Responsibility, loc. cit. n. 14, at 43. See also N. Ronzitti, Rescuing Nationals Abroad through Military Coercion and Intervention on Grounds of Humanity (1985). A paper prepared in 1984 by the staff of the British Foreign and Commonwealth Office doubts whether a State has the right to have recourse to a humanitarian intervention abroad on behalf of persons who are not that State's nationals. Foreign and Commonwealth Office, 148 Foreign Policy Document, repr. in 57 BYIL 614 (1986).

16 Yb. of the ILC (1980), loc. cit. n. 8, at 46-47.

17 *Ibid.*

Thus, in interpreting humanitarian instruments, it is appropriate to resort to the principle of non-derogability on the grounds of necessity. The drafters of humanitarian agreements did not intend to permit States to invoke the customary law exception of state of necessity regarding the norms stated in those agreements. By contrast, human rights instruments, which are subject to derogations in most cases, do not share this rule of non-derogability with humanitarian law instruments. However, the ILC's position, set forth in Article 33(2,b), that a State cannot invoke a state of necessity which is expressly or implicitly prohibited by a conventional instrument, applies as well to human rights instruments. This principle is especially applicable to those instruments which contain provisions on derogations, such as the International Covenant on Civil and Political Rights (Political Covenant). The language of the Political Covenant prohibits any derogation not explicitly permitted by Article 4, thus excluding invocation of the customary law exception of state of necessity. Therefore, the Article 4 exceptions from the Covenant's obligations are both exclusive and comprehensive. Anything not expressly included among the already very broad freedoms which Article 4 grants to States Parties[18] is inherently incompatible with the primary goal of the Covenant, which is to ensure respect for human rights.[19]

An interesting question is whether, in the absence of a provision governing derogations on grounds of necessity, a State may invoke necessity to preclude the wrongfulness of its conduct which does not conform with norms stated in a human rights treaty. The answer differs with the treaty concerned. For example, did the drafters of the African Charter on Human and Peoples' Rights, which contains no provisions on derogations, intend to exclude the right of States under customary law to invoke justifications such as state of necessity? It is far from clear that the Charter's *travaux préparatoires* would support such an interpretation, although it would undoubtedly serve the cause of the effective protection of human rights. Regrettably, there is a danger that the absence of a derogations clause in the Charter will be used to infer that the Charter

---

18 For a critique of derogation clauses, see T. Meron, Human Rights Law-Making in the United Nations: A Critique of Instruments and Process 86-100 (1986).

19 This conclusion is supported by the *travaux préparatoires* of Article 4, which confirm that '... the main concern was to provide for a qualification of the kind of public emergency in which a State would be entitled to make derogations from the rights contained in the covenant which would not be open to abuse ...'. M. Bossuyt, Guide to the *'Travaux Préparatoires'* of the International Covenant on Civil and Political Rights 85-86 (1987). It was essential 'to prevent States from derogating arbitrarily from their obligations where such an action was not warranted by events'. *Ibid.*, at 87.

implicitly allows States to invoke the customary law exception of state of necessity to derogate from the rights enumerated in the Charter, without the safeguards routinely built into such clauses.[20] Hopefully, however, the African Commission on Human and Peoples' Rights will balance the various interests implicated and not allow necessity and the 'preeminence of State interest'[21] to take precedence over the human rights which are stated in the Charter. The above discussion suggests that danger persists that States will try to invoke the exception of necessity in order to derogate, in times of internal strife, from some of their customary and even conventional obligations to respect human rights. A statement of a minimum core of non-derogable rights, which must be respected in all circumstances, including national emergencies triggered by internal strife, such as the proposed declaration, would, it is hoped, serve to deter States from invoking the state of necessity exception. It is important to note that normative declarations not infrequently contain explicit prohibitions of derogations.

4.   SOME THOUGHTS ON THE CONTENT OF A DECLARATION

I shall now discuss the content of the declaration that is needed to cover abuses which are inadequately addressed by existing norms. In the space available, I shall touch only upon some of the needed normative

---

20 See U. Umozurike, *The African Charter on Human and Peoples' Rights*, 77 AJIL 902, 909-10 (1983). It is noteworthy that the African Charter contains a number of limitation clauses, *e.g.* Articles 6, 11, 12. See also B. Weston, R. Lukes, K. Hnatt, *Regional Human Rights Regimes: a Comparison and Appraisal*, 20 Vand. J. Transnat'l L. 585, 627-28 (1987).

21 B. Okere, *The Protection of Human Rights in Africa and the African Charter on Human and Peoples' Rights: A Comparative Analysis with the European and American Systems*, 6 Hum. Rts. Quarterly 141, 143 (1984). It may be noted that prior to the entry into force of the American Convention on Human Rights, the Inter-American Commission on Human Rights in its discussion of derogations resorted to the norms stated in Article 27 of the Convention as reflecting regional customary law:
'With respect to American international law -which is the normative system that the Commission must take primarily into account- it must be understood that, in the absence of conventional standards in force in this area, the "most accepted doctrine" is that which is set forth in the American Convention on Human Rights, ... which has been signed by twelve American countries (among them Chile), and whose ratification has already begun.
The Convention contains an express provision in Article 27 ....' Inter-American Commission on Human Rights, Report on the Status of Human Rights in Chile, OAS Doc. OEA/Ser.L./V/II.34 Doc. 21 corr. 1, at 2-3 (1974). See T. Buergenthal, *The Revised OAS Charter and the Protection of Human Rights*, 69 AJIL 828, 835, at n. 37 (1975).

protections. Whenever possible, the declaration should confirm and develop already existing norms, rather than create new ones. In some respects the declaration will have, however, to articulate new norms. Of course, some, indeed, many norms such as the prohibition of murder, disappearances, torture, and hostage taking can be regarded as applicable in all situations, including situations of internal strife and are not susceptible to derogations. It has to be recognized, however, that the Political Covenant and other human rights instruments simply do not contain certain essential rules necessary to protect human rights in situations of state violence, such as those relating to means and methods of combat.

4.1   Absence or abuse of judicial safeguards

Experience indicates that widespread abuse of judicial guarantees is common in situations of internal strife. The important guarantees of due process are mostly derogable in human rights instruments, *e.g.* Articles 9 and 14 of the Political Covenant. These guarantees also appear in humanitarian instruments and are thereby non-derogable. It is essential that the new declaration prohibits derogation of essential judicial guarantees, relatively and unintrusive.

Providing due process guarantees presents a strategic question. The Geneva Conventions and the Protocols contain detailed and explicit provisions on due process, while a different approach is followed in common Article 3(1,d). This provision contains only the requirement that regularly constituted courts afford 'all the judicial guarantees which are recognized as indispensable by civilized peoples.' Which approach is the better one for a declaration on internal strife? Since States are sensitive to due process issues, a less intrusive approach may be preferable. Such an approach might be based on enumerating certain essential elements of due process, such as the right to counsel (as provided by the Fourth Geneva Convention, Article 72; the Third Geneva Convention, Article 105, and in provisions concerning prosecutions for grave breaches, *e.g.* the Third Geneva Convention, Article 129), or at least requiring the extension of 'all necessary rights and means of defence' (Protocol I, Article 75(4,a), Protocol II, Article 6(2,a)) and such elementary safeguards as the right to appeal, the prohibition of retroactive penal measures, the presumption of innocence, and the right to be judged by an independent tribunal. If such a list would be difficult for States to accept, a short, general formula such as that of common Article 3(1,d) would be helpful if stated in a declaration on internal strife.

4.2   Summary and arbitrary executions, capital punishment, and murder

The question of judicial guarantees is clearly related to the protection of the right to life. Protecting the right to life from arbitrary deprivation is the first and most important of the non-derogable rights enumerated in Article 4(2) of the Political Covenant. However, because the critically important due process guarantees stated in Article 14 of the Political Covenant are derogable and the protection of the right to life under Article 6 is not absolute, there is considerable danger that some States will argue that in times of emergency, death sentences may be imposed following summary procedures, provided that the more limited guarantees stated in Article 6 itself are observed. Despite salutary efforts to establish that the procedural safeguards of Article 14 are non-derogable for the hearing of a case where the death penalty may be imposed, even during public emergency, the frequent resort to arbitrary and summary executions in situations of internal strife continues unabated.

Ways of strengthening the protection of the right to life are urgently needed. One possibility would be the 'freezing' or suspension of executions, to allow for appeal, reconsideration and foreign humanitarian intercession. It should be provided that the death penalty should not be carried out during internal strife, or at least (as provided in Article 75 of the Fourth Geneva Convention), until a stated period of time has elapsed following the entering of the final judgment.

4.3   Excessive use of force

Abusive and excessive force is frequently used against civilians and innocent bystanders in situations of internal strife *e.g.* to suppress demonstrations, enforce curfews or to intimidate the population.

The problem is exacerbated by the absence in human rights instruments of provisions aimed at humanizing violent conflict situations, such as requiring 'proportionality' between a legitimate objective and the amount of force used to achieve the objective. Most importantly, rules are needed pertaining to the regulation of the use of means and methods of combat. Such provisions are contained in international humanitarian law instruments governing international armed conflicts. But only few provisions concerning permissible use of force can be found in international humanitarian instruments governing internal armed conflicts. While it is possible to maintain that certain general principles of customary law should govern the use of force even in internal strife, efforts to humanize behaviour by invoking general principles of customary law have not proven particularly successful.

Because of the lack of clarity characterizing the applicability of rules pertaining to means and methods of combat which have been developed for international armed conflicts to non-international armed conflicts, the International Institute of Humanitarian Law (San Remo Institute) has attempted, in its 1989 Session, to elaborate a declaration of rules of international humanitarian law governing the conduct of hostilities and restrictions on the use of certain weapons in non-international armed conflicts. These rules, regarded by the Institute as a confirmation of already received or at least emergent customary principles of humanitarian law, have been arrived at through an enlightened extrapolation of existing rules. They include the principle of a distinction between combatants and civilians, the immunity of the civilian population, a prohibition of superfluous injury or unnecessary suffering, a prohibition of perfidy, a prohibition of certain weapons such as chemical and bacteriological weapons, dum dum bullets, and poison, and rules regulating use of mines, booby-traps, and incendiary weapons. Such a declaration will eventually help to generate and shape concordant practice of States.

A similar strategy is needed for internal strife, where both the lack of and the demand for rules concerning means and methods of combat is even clearer. The prohibition of the use of materials calculated to cause unnecessary or indiscriminate suffering stated in Article 23(e) of the Regulations Annexed to Hague Convention IV concerning Laws and Customs of War on Land could be reaffirmed for situations of internal strife. And, most importantly, it should be stated, that the rules governing means and methods of combat in international armed conflict are recognized as applicable in internal strife as well.

The international community has already made important attempts to develop a system of rules regulating the use of violence in internal strife, as for instance in Article 3 of the Code of Conduct for Law Enforcement Officials, adopted by the UN General Assembly on December 17, 1979 in Res. 34/169[22] and in the more recent Report, adopted at the Eight UN Congress on the Prevention of Crime and the Treatment of Offenders, on Basic Principles on the use of Force and Firearms by Law Enforcement

---

22 GA Res. 34/169 of 17 December 1979, 34 UN GAOR Supp., at 185, UN Doc. A/34/46 (1979).

Officials.[23] In accordance with the guiding ideas of these texts the declaration should attempt to curtail the use of firearms. The declaration should reflect the concept that the use of firearms constitutes an extreme measure that is simply not permitted in certain cases.

---

23 This report states, in part, as follows:

1. Governments and law enforcement agencies shall adopt and implement rules and regulations on the use of force and firearms against persons by law enforcement officials. In developing such rules and regulations, Governments and law enforcement agencies shall keep the ethical issues associated with the use of force and firearms constantly under review.

2. Governments and law enforcement agencies should develop a range of means as broad as possible and equip law enforcement officials with various types of weapons and ammunition that would allow for a differentiated use of force and firearms. These should include the development of non-lethal incapacitating weapons for use in appropriate situations, with a view to increasingly restraining the application of means capable of causing death or injury to persons. For the same purpose, it should also be possible for law enforcement officials to be equiped with self-defensive equipment such as shields, helmets, bullet-proof vests and bullet-proof means of transportation, in order to decrease the need to use weapons of any kind.

3. The development and deployment of non-lethal incapacitating weapons should be carefully evaluated in order to minimize the risk of endangering uninvolved persons and the use of such weapons should be carefully controlled.

4. Law enforcement officials, in carrying out their duty, shall, as far as possible, apply non-violent means before resorting to the use of force and firearms. They may use force and firearms only if other means remain ineffective or without any promise of achieving the intended result.

5. Whenever the lawful use of force and firearms is unavoidable, law enforcement officials shall:

a) exercise restraint in such use and act in proportion to the seriousness of the offence and the legitimate objective to be achieved;

b) minimize damage and injury, and respect and preserve human life;

c) ensure that assistance and medical aid are rendered to any injured or affected persons at the earliest possible moment;

d) ensure that relatives or close friends of the injured or affected persons are notified at the earliest possible moment.

6. Where injury or death is caused by the use of force and firearms by law enforcement officials, they shall report the incident promptly to their superiors, in accordance with principle 22.

7. Governments shall ensure that arbitrary or abusive use of force and firearms by law enforcement officials is punished as a criminal offence under their law.

8. Exceptional circumstances such as internal political instability or any other public emergency may not be invoked to justify any departure from these basic principles.

Special provisions

9. Law enforcement officials shall not use firearms against persons except in necessary self-defence or defence of others against the imminent threat of death or serious injury, to prevent the perpetration of a particularly serious crime involving grave to life, to arrest a person presenting such a danger and resisting their authority, or to prevent his or her escape, and only when less extreme means are insufficient to achieve these objectives. In any event, intentional lethal use of firearms may only be made when strictly unavoidable in order to protect life ....

4.4   Deportations, forced movement of population

Deportations and forced movements of the population which cause great
suffering and often lead to the loss of life are common in situations of
internal strife. Articles 12-13 of the Political Covenant addressing the
liberty of movement and the expulsion of aliens are derogable and subject
to limitation clauses. These Articles do not explicitly address, though they
clearly implicate, the phenomenon of mass expulsions, but the major
regional human rights instruments do expressly prohibit mass expulsions of
aliens. Although the General Comments of the Human Right Committee on
Article 13[24] are beneficial in fighting deportation abuses, it is important
that the declaration should address these phenomena explicitly for
situations of internal strife following the model of the provisions contained
in humanitarian law instruments.

4.5   Massive and prolonged administrative detentions without judicial review

Among the phenomena endemic to internal strife, massive and prolonged
administrative detentions merit special consideration because of their
frequency and the Political Covenant's lack of non-derogable provisions
guaranteeing judicial review.

A provision addressing the phenomenon of massive and prolonged
detentions (often ostensibly for preventive purposes) would, therefore, be
of great importance. Such a provision should contain minimum standards
of treatment, the right to correspond with families and the right to family
visits. A particularly difficult question concerns the extent to which the

---

Policing unlawful assemblies
12. As everyone is allowed to participate in lawful and peaceful assemblies, in accordance
with the principles embodied in the Universal Declaration of Human Rights and the
International Covenant on Civil and Political Rights, Governments and law enforcement
agencies and officials shall recognize that force and firearms may be used only in accordance
with principles 13 and 14.
13. In the dispersal of assemblies that are unlawful but non-violent, law enforcement officials
shall avoid the use of force, or, where that is not practicable, shall restrict such force to the
minimum extent necessary.
14. In the dispersal of violent assemblies, law enforcement officials may use firearms only
when less dangerous means are not practicable and only to the minimum extent necessary.
Law enforcement officials shall not use firearms in such cases, except under the conditions
stipulated in principle 9.
UN Doc. A/CONF.144/28, at 120-122 (1990).
24 41 UN GAOR Supp. (No. 40), at 117-119, UN Doc. A/41/40 (1986).

declaration should address the reasons for preventive detention. Minimally, ordering the preventive detention of an individual should be subject to at least some due process guarantees such as the right to appeal[25] and a periodic review.

In order to encourage Governments to respect the declaration without fear that its application might amount to recognition of, or grant of political status to dissidents or opposition groups it might specify that its application shall not affect the legal status of any authorities, groups, or persons involved in the situation of internal strife. Such a provision would follow the model of the last sentence of common Article 3.

The declaration might also explicitly prohibit derogation from its provisions on any grounds whatsoever, including public emergency which threatens the life of the nation.[26] The declaration would thus incorporate the principle of non-derogability on grounds of necessity or emergency, which is characteristic of humanitarian law instruments. Finally, the declaration might state that nothing in it shall be interpreted as impairing the provisions of the Geneva Conventions of 12 August 1949 for the Protection of War Victims and the Additional Protocols of 8 June 1977 and of any international human rights instruments.

4.6   Collective punishments

The prohibition of collective punishments is stated explicitly in humanitarian law instruments, but only implicitly in human rights conventions, such as the Political Covenant. Because of the relevance of this prohibition to situations of internal strife, it merits inclusion in the declaration.

---

25 See Fourth Geneva Convention, Article 78.
26 See Principle 6 of Principles of Medical Ethics relevant to the Role of Health Personnel, particularly Physicians, in the Protection of Prisoners and Detainees against Torture and Other Cruel, Inhuman or Degrading Treatment or Punishment, which was adopted by the UN General Assembly on 18 December, 1982 by Res. 37/194 and Article 4(1) of the Political Covenant. See also Report loc. cit. n. 23, at § 8.

4.7   Protection of children

In situations of internal strife, children are often mobilized and forced to participate in acts of violence. A prohibition against mobilizing children or otherwise forcing them to participate in violent activities should be included in the declaration.[27]

4.8   Protection of medical personnel; protection and care of sick and wounded; activities of humanitarian bodies and relief

In internal strife situations, medical personnel acting in accordance with the principles of medical ethics are often punished for treating guerrillas and dissidents. The Political Covenant does not provide these individuals with explicit protection, nor does the Covenant address the protection and care of the sick and wounded or the activities of humanitarian bodies and humanitarian relief. The declaration should contain provisions addressing these matters.

5.   CONCLUSIONS

The proliferation of situations of internal violence and human suffering that it entails together with the present improvement of the climate of international relations suggest that time has come to renew efforts for the adoption of a normative declaration stating the necessary norms for the protection of human rights in such situations. In this essay, I have tried to demonstrate the reasons for such a declaration and to outline its tentative content. I have not dealt with the scope of the material applicability of the declaration. The several possible approaches to material applicability were discussed in my earlier writings on the subject.[28]

One of the difficulties involved in limiting the scope of applicability of the future declaration to internal strife and violence is that it would create another layer and more thresholds of applicability, facilitating efforts at evasion. States may try to evade the norms stated in the declaration by claiming, for example, that the violence accompanying the internal strife in question is not of a collective character or is not intense enough. The focus

---

27 See Protocol I, Article 77(2,3); Protocol II, Article 4(3); 1989 UN Convention on the Rights of the Child, Article 38, §§ 2,3, GA Res. 44/25, 20 November, 1989, 44 UN GAOR Supp. (No. 49) at 166; UN Doc. A/34/46 (1990).

28 See *e.g.* Meron, op. cit. n. 1, at 145-148.

may, therefore, have to be shifted from exclusive applicability to internal strife to applicability in all situations, including internal violence. Such a declaration would constitute a safety net of minimum humanitarian norms and an 'irreducible core of human rights that must be applied at a minimum at all times'.[29]

29 Meron, *On the Inadequate Reach,* loc. cit. n. 2, at 604.

IV

ARMS AND ARMAMENTS

WHAT ONE MAY DO IN COMBAT - THEN AND NOW

LESLIE C. GREEN

1.   INTRODUCTION

In recent years, both before and since the adoption of the 1977 Protocols on Humanitarian Law in Armed Conflicts, Professor Kalshoven has devoted much of his academic writing to issues relating to the law of war, particularly those concerned with restraining cruelties in the course of conflict.[1] It is meet, therefore, that a contribution to a *Festschrift* in his honour should deal with matters close to his own interest.

During armed conflict a variety of problems regarding conduct must be settled at the highest political and military levels, and the man in the field, while subject to the law concerning war crimes and superior orders,[2]

---

1   *Cf.*, F. Kalshoven, Belligerent Reprisals (1971); F. Kalshoven, The Laws of Warfare (1973); F. Kalshoven, Constraints on the Waging of War (1987).
2   See, Y. Dinstein, The Defence of 'Obedience to Superior Orders' in International Law (1965); L.C. Green, Superior Orders in National and International Law (1976).

frequently has no option but to obey. It is not for him to decide whether he will release the gas that his Government has decided to use, nor is he free to decide whether the war is just or unjust. While in feudal times it might have been possible to state that:

> '"... in illicit matters it is not necessary to obey temporal lords, thus knights when they feel a war is unjust should not follow the standards of the prince." Stephen Langton (Archbishop of Canterbury) argued that if the King of France declared an unjust war on the King of England, a French knight should indeed obey the summons but he should abstain or withdraw at the moment of combat.'[3]

Today, however, the soldier who decides that his Government is waging an unjust war is likely to face a criminal trial with the verdict going against him.[4] On the other hand, *durante belli* he may find that the law does enjoin him from certain acts or using certain weapons. Since:

> '... war is fought with men it is also fought with implements for killing and vanquishing or for protection. Qualitatively and quantitatively these weapons are the product of the technical capacity of the society which makes them, the military habits of the people who use them and of the initiatives and reactions of individuals, communities and governing authorities. In many respects the history of war grows out of a history of techniques.'[5]

Methodology is also connected to the purpose for which war is fought. Sun Tzu stated:

> 'To capture the enemy is better than to destroy it; to take intact a battalion, a company or a five-man squad is better than to destroy them .... To subdue the enemy without fighting is the acme of skill.'[6]

Over two millenia later Clausewitz was saying much the same thing: 'to impose our will on the enemy is [the] object [of force] .... The [enemy's]

---

3 P. Contamine, *La Guerre au moyen age* (War in the Middle Ages, translated by M. Jones) 287 (1984).

4 See also *Levy* v. *Parker* (1973), repr. in 1 MLR 2130; H. Lauterpacht, *Rules of Warfare in an Unlawful War*, in G.A. Lipsky, Law and Politics in the World Community 89 (1953).

5 Contamine, op. cit. n. 3, at 175.

6 S.B. Griffith, The Art of War 77 (1963), Chapter III 'Offensive Strategy'.

fighting forces must be *destroyed*: that is they must be *put in such a condition that they no longer carry on the fight*'.[7]

2.   CLASSICAL HUMANITARIAN RESTRICTIONS

These views are in direct contrast to the purpose of war in Biblical times. Thus, during the exodus from Canaan, 'the Lord delivered up the Canaanites; and they utterly destroyed their cities,'[8] and on the fall of Jericho 'they utterly destroyed all that was in the city, both man and woman, young and old, and sheep and ass, with the edge of the sword.'[9] Yet, the Israelites were also enjoined, after conquest, to take their enemy captive.[10] Moreover:

'... when thou comest nigh unto a city to fight against it, then proclaim peace unto it. And ... if it make thee answer of peace, and open unto thee, then ... all the people that is found therein shall be tributaries unto thee.'[11]

If, however, the peace overtures are rejected, then, when the place is conquered:

'... thou shalt smite every male therof with the edge of a sword: But the women, and the little ones, and the cattle, and all that is in the city, ... thou shalt take unto thyself ....'[12]

Thus, once the object -defeat- has been achieved, some measure of humanity comes into play. But these exhortations to destruction related to operations against the heathen and idolators, and the intention was to ensure that the Israelites were not contaminated by any of the evil ways of such people. But it was made clear that complete devastation was not envisaged:

'When thou shalt beseige a city a long time, in making war against it to take it, thou shalt not destroy the trees thereof by wielding an axe against

---

7 C. von Clausewitz, *Vom Kriege* (1832), in English: M. Howard, P. Paret, eds., On War 90 (1976).

8 Numbers, 21, iii.

9 Joshua, 6, xxi.

10 Deuteronomy, 21, x.

11 *Ibid.*, at 20, x, xi.

12 *Ibid.*, at xii-xiv.

them; for thou mayest eat of them, but thou shalt not cut them down; for is the tree of the field man, that it should be beseiged of thee? Only the trees of which thou knowest that they are not trees for food, them thou mayest destroy and cut down.'[13]

The Greco-Roman attitude was somewhat similar to the Israelite approach to heathens, for:[14]

'... the rule and principles of war were considered ... to be applicable only to civilized sovereign States, properly organized and enjoying a regular constitution; and not to conglomerates of individuals living together in an irregular and precarious association .... [I]n Hellas we find remarkable oscillations of warlike policy. Brutal treatment and noble generous conduct are manifested at the same epoch, in the same war, and apparently under similar circumstances. At times ... we read narratives which emphasise the fundamental cruelty and disregard of human claims prevalent amongst the ancient races when at war with each other.'

While such conflicts of champions remind us of the encounter between David and Goliath,[15] it should not be forgotten that such single combats 'are attested throughout the history of the West down to the end of the Middle Ages',[16] and even when such combat was not resorted to casualties including those caused by accidents, frequently did not reach double figures.[17]

It is clear, therefore, that even in classical times many of what we now describe as the laws and customs of war were already recognized.

By the time of the Roman Empire changes were inevitable in view of the centralized nature of the State,[18] so that practices:

'... varied according as their wars were commenced to exact vengeance for gross violations of international law, or for deliberate acts of treachery. Their warlike usages varied also according as their adversaries were regular

13 *Ibid.*, at xix-xx. See also G.B. Roberts, *Judaic Sources of and Views on the Laws of War*, 34 MLR 221, 226-37 (1988).
14 C. Phillipson, 2, The International Law and Custom of Ancient Greece and Rome 195, 207-208 (1911).
15 1 Samuel 17.
16 Contamine, op. cit. n. 3, at 261.
17 *Ibid.*, at 256.
18 Phillipson, op. cit. n. 14, at 227-229, 232.

enemies ... or uncivilized barbarians and bands of pirates and marauders .... [Under Germanicus] Roman conduct far transcended in its civilized and humane character that of the German leader, Arminius, who is reoported to have burnt and other wise barbarously[19] slain the centurions and tribunes of the Varian legions, and nailed the skulls to trees.[20] Undoubtedly, the belligerent operations of Rome, from the point of view of introducing various mitigations in the field, and adopting a milder policy after victory, are distinctly of a progressive character. They were more regular and disciplined than those of any other ancient nation. They did not as a rule degenerate into indiscriminate slaughter, and unrestrained devastation .... The *ius belli* imposed restrictions on barbarism, and condemned all acts of treachery .... The Romans refused to countenance a criminal attempt made on the life of even a powerful foreign aggressor.'[21]

In addition, Rome invariably spared the lives of captives, although they were frequently made slaves, they could nevertheless achieve their freedom and even become Roman citizens.[22]

2.1   Use of weapons

In the epic Sanskrit poem *Mahabharata* we read that 'a King should never do such an injury to his foes as would rankle in the latter's heart'[23] and we learn that in ancient India conflict was a matter of close combat so that 'a car-warrior should fight a car-warrior. One on horse should fight one on horse. Elephant riders must fight with elephant riders, as one on foot fights a foot soldier'.[24] The striking weapons in Greece and Rome tended to be the sword, the dagger, the shield and the battering ram, with the spear,

---

19 Term used by Tacitus, Annals I, lvi.

20 Contamine states that:
'The Kriegsordnung ... of Zurich in 1444 thought it necessary to prohibit combatants from tearing out the hearts of their dead enemies and cutting up their bodies. J. Froissart attests (Oeuvres, K. de Lettenhove, ed., xv, 168 (1869)), for his part, that the Irish "never leave a man for dead until they have cut his throat like a sheep and slit open his belly to remove the heart, which they take away. Some who know their ways, say that they eat it with great relish. They take no man for ransom ...."'
Contamine, op cit. n. 3, at 291.

21 Cicero, *De officiis*, III, xxii. Churchill is reported to have rejected any proposal to assassinate Hitler.

22 Justinian, *Institutes*, Lib. I, Tit. V, s. 2.

23 Written between 200 B.C. and 200 A.D., *cf.* W.S. Armour, *Customs of Warfare in Ancient India*, 8 Transactions of the Grotius Society 81 (1922).

24 *Ibid.*, at 74.

javelin, sling or bow and arrow for distance. In more primitive societies weapons tended to be the implements used in hunting, with their striking weapons:

> '... confined to arm-, foot- or mouth propelled instruments. These include war hammers, battle-axes, and swords; thrusting spears; and missile weapons, such as the hurled spear, or javelin, the arrow propelled by arm- or foor-drawn bow, or the blowpipe. The striking edge or point of these weapons is of hard wood, stone, bone or metal, and occasionally poison is used on the tip of arrow or spear.'[25]

To a great extent, these weapons are similar to those of feudal times, particularly by and against mounted knights in armour, although there were special refinements peculiarly useful in dismounting or overthrowing men dressed in iron.[26]

In addition to a dress that was in keeping with the current technology, new weapons in the form of artillery, together with longer-range man-held weapons made this type of warfare outmoded. While the modern soldier might use his rifle as a club *in extremis*, such weapons as the mace, the broad-axe, the ball and chain, the halberd, the glaive, the partizan, the military fork and the like have fallen into desuetude, and have been out of use so long that they would now be considered unlawful. Similarly, with the disappearance of the siege of defended places, weapons like the flaming cannonball, the battering ram, and boiling oil have ceased to have any value and would almost certainly be regarded as illegal, especially since modern technology has replaced them by more sophisticated weapons which achieve the same purpose. Fire, on the other hand, 'an essential feature of medieval warfare',[27] remained in use by way of flame-throuwers, incendiary bombs, napalm and the like, until the adoption of the Protocol on Prohibitions or Restrictions on the Use of Incendiary Weapons in 1980.[28] The Protocol has not been ratified by any major Western power other than France. It does not forbid:

---

25 Q. Wright, A Study of War 81 (1965).
26 Contamine, op. cit. n. 3, at 67-74.
27 Contamine, op. cit. n. 3, at 244, n. 15.
28 D. Schindler, J. Toman eds., The Laws of Armed Conflict 190 (1988). See, W.J. Fenrick, *New Developments in the Law Concerning the Use of Conventional Weapons in Armed Conflict*, 19 Can. Y.b. Int'l Law 229, 246-50 (1981).

'... munitions which may have incidental incendiary effects ... [or] designed to combine penetration, blast or fragmentation effects with an additional incendiary effect, such as armour-piercing projectiles ... and combined-effects munitions in which the incendiary effect is not specifically designed to cause burn injury to persons, but to be used against military objectives, such as armoured vehicles, aircraft and installations or facilities.'

It would be interesting to ascertain how such incendiaries can be thought of as not 'designed to cause burn injuries to (such) persons' as tank or air crews, or the workers in a munitions factory!

As noted, weapons may become unlawful by disuetude; others may be expressly forbidden as have incendiaries, while others once forbidden may become lawful. Thus, at the time of the American Civil War it was considered unlawful to fire on sentries,[29] an argument that was still being made as late as 1908,[30] though no such contention would be put forward today, so that this customary rule has become invalid.

As early as the code of Manu[31] rules were being enunciated to forbid the use of particular weapons:

'When the king fights his foes in battle, let him not strike with weapons concealed, nor with barbed, poisoned or the points of which are blazed with fire .... These are the weapons of the wicked, ...'[32]

In 1139 the Second Lateran Council anathematised the use of the crossbow and the arc, at least against Christians, a view which coincided with those of the orders of knighthood:

'To the Church these weapons were hateful to God. To the knights they were weapons whereby men not of the knightly order could fell a knight .... Worse, they were weapons which enabled a man to strike without the risk of being struck.'[33]

Christians were also forbidden by the Church from using 'darts and catapults (in order to reduce as far as possible the engines of destructions

---

29 See *e.g.* Lieber Code, 1863 (Schindler, Toman, eds., op. cit. n. 28), Article 69.

30 G.B. Davis, Elements of International Law 297 (1908).

31 Written c. 2nd century B.C., G. Bühler, The Laws of Manu 230 (Tit. VII, 90) (1976).

32 See Hague Regulations 1907, Article 1(3); Protocol I, 1977, Article 44(3).

33 G.I.A.D. Draper, *The Interaction of Christianity and Chivalry in the Historical Development of the Law of War*, 5 Int'l Rev. of the Red Cross 3, 19 (1965).

and death), and the prohibition was enforced under pain of anathema',[34] and this too was in accord with the views of the orders of knighthood:[35]

> 'Paolo Vitelli while recognizing and using the cannon "put out the eyes and cut off the hands of the captured arquebusiers because he held it unworthy that a gallant and ... noble knight should be laid low by a common, despised foot soldier".'[36]

Despite the Church, 'from the end of the twelfth century the crossbow was widely used on land and sea, amongst horsemen as well as infantry',[37] and in 1563 Belli wrote:

> 'But today regard is so far lacking for this rule that firearms of a thousand kinds are the most common and popular implements of war; as if too few avenues of death had been discovered in the course of centuries, had not the generation of our fathers, rivalling God with his lightning, invented the means whereby, even at a single discharge, men are sent to perdition by the hundreds.'[38]

This comment, reflecting the significance of technology, exemplifies the fact that if a State believes certain weapons or methods of combat are likely to give it advantages over an enemy, especially one not so well equipped, it will maintain that its so doing is perfectly lawful. Thus, naval powers have sought to restrict limitations on maritime belligerents or the rights of maritime neutrals as much as possible,[39] while remaining content with imposing strict limits on the rights of land belligerents. A belligerent in posession of sophisticated weapons will hardly refrain from using them

---

34 *Corpus juris canonici*, 1500, Decretal V, C. Belli, *De Re Militari et Belli Tractatus*, 1563, Pars III, Cap. III, 29 (Carnegie 186, [1936]). See also, E.R.A. Sewter, The Alexiad of Anna Commena 316-317 (1969). According to Sewter:
'The crossbow is a weapon of the barbarians ... a truly diabolical machine'.

35 Draper, loc. cit. n. 33, at 18.

36 *Cf.*, view of Lenz at sinking of *The Peleus*, In re Eck (1945), UNWCC, 1 War Crimes Report 1, 3, 7; J. Cameron, The Peleus Trial 85-86, 116, 131 (1948). See also, Contamine, op. cit. n. 3, at 257: 'gentlemen were careful to avoid surrender to "commoners" (English archers, for example) because they expected no mercy from them'.

37 Contamine, op. cit. n. 3, at 72.

38 Belli, op. cit. n. 34, at 20. See also, A. Gardot, *Le Droit de la Guerre dans l'Oeuvre des Capitaines Français du XVIe Siècle*, 72 Hague Recueil 397, 416 (1948).

39 See *e.g.* Report of Brit. Inter-Deptl. Cttee, 1908; *cf.*, G. Best, Humanity in Warfare 246 (1980); C. Savage, Policy of the U.S. toward Maritime Commerce in War 1934-1936; R.W. Tucker, The Law of War and Neutrality at Sea 181-190 (1955).

against an enemy which is technologically disadvantaged. Thus Bynkershoek[40] stated bluntly: '... we may destroy an enemy though he be unarmed, and for the purpose we may employ poison, an assasin, or incendiary bombs, though he is not provided with such things'. One is tempted to refer to an animal parallel:[41] 'Cobras would advocate the banning of horses, claws and cutting teeth, but would denounce in the strongest terms a proposal to outlaw venom'. By way of contrast, in ancient India 'when the antagonist has fallen into distress he should not be struck .... Brave warriors do not shoot one whose arrows are exhausted'.[42]

2.2   Towards a principle of distinction

In feudal times military codes laid down principles regulating the conduct of armies, postulating respect for women, priests, children, the infirm and others, and forbidding pillage and the destruction of private property.[43] By the time of the American Revolution these earlier principles derived from the codes of chivalry had become ensconced in the general rules of warfare, so that by the time of the Battle of Bennington, 1777, perfidy was generally condemned.[44] During the Napoleonic campaign in Spain it was not surprising that regular troops would respond to the atrocities of the Spanish peasantry in coin. When, however, the guerrilla bands took on some semblance of organization, so that it became possible to distinguish between guerrillas and bandits, the former received some measure of protection.[45] By the time of the American Civil War, the principles regarding warfare and the behaviour of those engaged therein had hardened sufficiently for Lieber to consolidate them in his Code, which was soon

---

40 *Quaestionum Juris Publicis*, Lib. I, Cap. 1 (1737, Carnegie 1930, at 16).

41 J.W. Bishop, Justice Under Fire 270 (1974).

42 Armour, loc. cit. n. 23, at 74.

43 See *e.g.* the *Estatutz et Custumes en l'Ost*, promulgated by Richard II, Vol. I (1385) *cf.* I Black Book of the Admiralty, T. Twiss, ed., 453-454 (1841); Gardot, loc. cit. n. 38, at 452-453, 467-473. At 467 Gardot cites Baron de Taube who pointed out that it was a combination of the law of nations and these codes which formed 'le meilleur frein pratique pour imposer aux armées le respect d'un modus legitimus de mener les guerres'; see also, Gentili, *De Jure Belli*, Lib. I, Cap. XXI (1612) (Carnegie 251, 257 (1933)); Contamine, op. cit. n. 3, at 289-291; H. Bovet, L'Arbre des Batailles (1386) (translated by G.W. Coopland 185 (1949)).

44 See M.J. Clancy, *Rules of Warfare during the War of the American Revolution*, 2 World Polity 203, 245 (1960).

45 Best, op. cit. n. 39, at 116-119.

copied by other armies.[46] With the passage of time, these regulations which had originated to control conduct in a town taken by siege, developed into those principles which were embodied in the Martens Clause[47] as 'usages established among civilized peoples, from the laws of humanity and the public conscience'. However, to make assurance doubly sure, many of them are now expressly spelled out in the Hague and Geneva conventions and Protocol I.

Today's soldier may find that he is now worse off than was his predecessor in Spain, for there the guerrillas tended to be distinguishable from the 'bandits'. While the Hague Regulations required a combatant 'to have a fixed distictive emblem recognizable at a distance and to carry arms openly',[48] and while during World War II the United Nations demanded that 'resistance' forces be treated as regular units entitled to all the benefits of ordinary combatants, particularly when wearing identification marks like the Croix de Lorraine,[49] Article 44 of Protocol I requires combatants, when preparing or engaging in attack, to distinguish themselves from civilians. Conceding, however, that in some circumstances, especially during a war for self-determination, this may not be possible, they retain combatants status so long as they carry their arms openly during an engagement or when visible to an adverse party during deployment. Since compliance with these requirements will save the individual from any charge of perfidy, it follows that he need not be in any way distinguishable from the remainder of the population, other than by carrying his arms openly when about to attack.

This provision was aimed at protecting members of national liberation movements who might be 'farmers by day and soldiers by night', who, if they satisfy the arms requirement, are now entitled to be treated as prisoners of war. In practice, this apparent change may not affect the man in the field unduly. While he is entitled to treat a non-combatant indulging in warlike acts as losing his protective status, this does not entitle him to treat such person other than in accordance with the principles of humanitarian law and to hand him over for trial or other treatment by the military authorities. It is not for the soldier to decide whether his captive is protected by Article 44 or otherwise. He himself is required to wear some

---

46 Schindler, Toman, eds., op. cit. n. 28, at 3; T.E. Holland, The Laws of War on Land 72-73 (1908); R.R. Baxter, *The First Modern Codification of the Law of War*, 3 Int'l Rev. of the Red Cross 1 (1963).

47 See Preamble to IV Hague Convention.

48 Regulation 1(2), (3).

49 Best, op. cit. n. 39, at 239-244.

sort of 'uniform' or distinguishing mark, and may not 'make improper use of the national flag or of the military insignia and uniform of the enemy'.[50] However, he may wear such enemy uniform or insignia as a ruse, but it would be improper for him to continue wearing it when in combat, although he may apparently do so outside the zone of combat to collect information.[51] In sixteenth century France the wearing of enemy uniform was considered intolerable.[52]

2.3 Treatment of the dead

While the modern soldier is unlikely to treat his fallen enemy as did the Greeks and Romans on occasion, or as did the Spanish partisans, he has not always shown the same respect for his dead opponent as did his ancestors. The *Mahabharata* required burial with full military honours, for 'with death our enmity has terminated',[53] and during the latter part of the Middle Ages Christian burial and listing of the dead was expected from the victor.[54] The Geneva Conventions made provision for proper treatment of the dead,[55] but during the Vietnam War body counts were frequently proven by way of amputated ears of enemy corpses, and in 1970 the United States Department of the Army reminded military personnel that 'the mutilation of bodies is a war crime, and an order to cut off ears would therefore be illegal. Equally illegal would be permission to take as souvenirs valuables from dead bodies or from any prisoner'.[56]

As has been mentioned, Bynkershoek recognized the legality of enemy assassinations,[57] but this was condemned by Grotius[58] and Vattel[59] if done 'treacherously'. Modern treaties make no reference to the practice,

---

50 Hague Regulation 23(f).

51 Brit. Manual of Military Law, III, Law of War on Land, § 310, and nn. 2 and 3 (1958); US Dept. of the Army, The Law of Land Warfare, FM 27-10, § 54 (1956).

52 Gardot, loc. cit. 38, at 464.

53 Armour, loc. cit. n. 23, at 77.

54 See for medieval practice, Contamine, op. cit. n. 3, at 275.

55 I, Art. 17; II, Artt. 19, 20; III, Art. 120; IV, Art. 130; see also Protocol I, Artt. 33, 34.

56 Dept. of the Army, *The Geneva Convention of 1949 and the Hague Convention of 1907*, AsubjScd 27-1, (1970) - this document is discussed in L.C. Green, *Aftermath of Vietnam: War Law and the Soldier*, in R. Falk, ed., 4 The Vietnam War and International Law 147, 168-174 (1976).

57 See n. 40 *supra*.

58 H. Grotius, *De Jure Belli ac Pacis*, Lib. III, Cap. IV, s.xviii (1625) (Carnegie 654-655 [1925]).

59 E. de Vattel, *Le Droit des Gens*, Lib. II, Ch. VIII, s. 155 (1758) (Carnegie 287-288 [1916]).

but the Hague Regulations[60] forbid the 'kill[ing] or wound[ing] treacherously [of] individuals belonging to the hostile nation or army' and modern military manuals condemn such acts,[61] while recognizing that the borderline between an unlawful assassination and a legitimate killing might be somewhat narrow:

> '.... This prohibition applies only to treacherous killing. It is not forbidden to send a detachment or individual members of the armed forces to kill, by sudden attack, members or a member of the enemy armed forces. Thus, for instance, the raid by a British commando party on the headquarters of General Rommel's African Army at Beda Littoria in 1943 was not contrary to the provision of the Hague Rules. The operation was carried out by military personnel in uniform; it had as part of its objective the seizure of Rommel's operational headquarters, including his own residence, and the capture or killing of enemy personnel therein.'[62]

Furthermore, the lawfulness of the attempt would not have been affected had it been carried out at night and against a sleeping enemy.[63] This should be compared with the reaction to the killing of General Gordon by an American scout during the American Revolution, which was condemned as an 'assassination ... an indicent, illiberal, and scurrilous performance ... highly unbecoming the Character of a Soldier and a Gentleman'.[64] On the other hand, one should note the comment of a leading American professor of interntional law well-known for his pacifist and humanitarian instincts. Falk has suggested, particularly in view of the implications of nuclear war, that:

> 'Perhaps thought can be given to techniques for the assassination of the enemy's leader or its elite rather than to recourse to a characteristic nation-to-nation repsonse. The aggressive agent might be the target of response, the action being justified by the production of evidence.'[65]

---

60 Regulation 23(b).

61 See *e.g.* German Gen. Staff, Usages of War on Land, II, 1902, (tr. J.H. Morgan) The German War Book (1915). This condemns the 1815 Declaration of Outlawry Against Napoleon as 'an indirect invitation to assassination'; see *supra* n. 51, Brit. Manual, § 115; US Manual, § 31.

62 Brit. Manual § 115, n. 2; see *supra* n. 51.

63 Vattel would appear to permit this, Vattel, op. cit. n. 59. The Mahabharata, however, condemns it. See, Armour, loc. cit. n. 23, at 250-251.

64 Clancy, loc. cit. n. 44, at 250-251.

65 R. Falk, Legal Order in a Violent World 424 (1968).

2.4   Protection of women and children

One of the most common accusations against an army moving through
enemy territory, whether that territory is formally occupied or not, is that
its personnel has, regardless of treaties or regulations to the contrary,
indulged in rape of the local female population. During the sixteenth
century senior French knights adamantly protected the modesty of women
in cities that had surrendered,[66] and an Ordinance published by Coligny
made violence against women a capital offence[67] while Diez de Games
(1379-1449), forbade the taking or carrying off of any woman whether
married or free.[68] When Gentili wrote that 'to violate the honour of
women will always be held to be unjust' and supported his view by that of
Alexander: 'I am not in the habit of warring with prisoners and
women',[69] he was merely giving expression to accepted practice. The
Mahabharata prohibited the killing of those suffering from any natural,
physical or mental incapacity, and 'he is no son of the Vrishni race who
slayeth a woman, a boy or an old man',[70] and Bovet in the *Arbre des
Batailles* was emphatic:

'Whether a child should be made prisoner and put to ransom? ... I hold
firmly, according to ancient law, and according to the ancient customs of
good warriors, that it is an unworthy thing to imprison either old men
taking no part in the war, or women or innocent children. Certainly it is a
very bad custom to put them to ransom as it is common knowledge that
they can have no part in war ... and whoever does the contrary deserves
the name of pillager.'[71]

The situation is now regulated by the Civilians Convention[72] as
extended by Protocol I,[73] so that any soldier who attacks a woman in an
occupied place is liable not only to the processes of his national criminal
law, but is equally amenable to a charge arising from the treaty law of
armed conflict, and this prohibition is not limited to the period of active

66 Gardot, loc. cit. n. 38, at 452-453.
67 *Ibid.*, at 469, citing Forquereux, La Discipline Militaire (1592).
68 G. Diez de Games, El Victorial (1410), translated by J. Evans, The Unconquered Knight 313
    (1928).
69 Gentili, op. cit. n. 43, Lib. II, Cap. XXI (Garnegie 251, 257).
70 Armour, loc. cit. n. 23, at 76.
71 Bonet, op. cit. n. 43 (tr. Coopland 185).
72 Article 27.
73 Article 76.

occupation during hostilities, but continues so long as the occupation subsists. Equally, the same instruments make provision for the care of children in occupied territory.[74]

2.5   Restraint in early doctrine

Since the Hague Convention speaks of the usages of nations and has been treated by the Nuremberg Tribunal as customary law,[75] it is perhaps useful to look at the classical writers in order to ascertain the *opinio juris*. Thus Gentili:

> 'In war ... our only precaution must be not to allow every kind of craft and every cunning device; for evil is not lawful, but an enemy should be dealt with according to law. ... Necessity does not oblige us to violate the rights of our adversaries ... [but] the laws of war are not observed towards one who does not himself observe them.'[76]

However, since the 1929 Prisoners of War Convention[77] reprisals against prisoners are forbidden, and this prohibition was extended in 1949[78] to include 'all protected persons and their property',[79] and made even more extensive by Protocol I in 1977.[80] Regardless of the lack of ratification of the latter by most of the major military powers, since these provisions were adopted by consensus and are in line with the earlier stipulations, it may be contended that they merely confirm a general rule and the individual soldier would be well advised to abstain from any reprisal that he might feel inclined to resort to against an enemy that he considers to have disregarded his obligations towards him. This is the more important in view of the difficulty the man in the field may have in deciding correctly whether such an obligation has been breached and whether his response is sufficiently proportionate to qualify as a reprisal. Grotius was of the opinion that:

---

74 Civilians Convention, Article 50; Protocol I, Article 77.
75 HMSO (1946), Cmd. 6964, 75; 41 Am J. Int'l Law 172, 248-249 (1947).
76 Gentili, op. cit. n. 43, Lib. II, Cap. III, VI, XXIII (Carnegie, 143, 159, 272).
77 Schindler, Toman, eds., op. cit. n. 28, at 271; Article 2.
78 Convention I, Article 46; II, Article 47; III, Article 13.
79 Convention IV, Article 33.
80 Articles 20, 51-56. Article 51(8) specifically states:
    'any violation of these prohibitions relating to the protection of the civilian population shall not release the Parties to the conflict from their legal obligations with respect to the civilian population and civilians...'

'... by the law of nations, anything is permissible as against an enemy ... the slaughter even of infants and women is made with impunity ... not even captives are exempt from this right to inflict injury ... although [this right] is restricted, now more, now less, by the laws of states. .... Nevertheless from old times the law of nations - if not of all nations, certainly of those of the better sort - has been that it is not permissible to kill an enemy by poison [and this extends to the use of poison on weapons or in springs, but] it is not forbidden by the law of nations to pollute waters in another way .... Whoever forcibly violates chastity [of women], even, in war, should everywhere be subject to punishment. .... There is in fact a limit to vengeance and to punishment ... children should always be spared; women, unless they have been guilty of an extremely serious offence, and old men ... [and] those also should be spared whose occupations are solely religious or concerned with letters. .... [Likewise], farmers, merchants, prisoners of war and those who surrender.'[81]

He also calls for the avoidance of useless fighting and calls for moderations in laying waste, in regard to captured property and prisoners and for the exercise of good faith between enemies.[82] The man in the field is forbidden from acting as if he were engaged in a private dispute, for war is a public matter, so he may not commit warlike acts after a retreat or an armistice,[83] nor keep captured property for himself.[84] Moreover:

'... if a soldier or any other person, even in a just war, has burned houses belonging to the enemy, has devastated fields, and caused losses of this character without orders, when, furthermore, there was no necessity or just cause ... he is bound to make good the losses. ... [I]f there is such a cause he will perhaps be answerable to his own state, whose laws he has transgressed, but not likewise to the enemy, to whom he has done no legal wrong.'[85]

---

81 Grotius, op. cit. n. 58, Lib. III, Cap. IV, ss xviii, ix, x, xv, xvi, xvii, xix, Cap. XI, ss. i, ix, xi-xv (654, 649, 652-653, 657, 722, 734, 737-740). See also, Armour, loc. cit. n. 23, at 76, 74, 75.
82 *Ibid.*, Lib. III, Cap. XI, xix (743); see also, re Hindu law on conduct by an invader, treatment of the conquered and treaties of peace, Armour, loc. cit. n. 23, at 80-83.
83 *Ibid.*, Cap. XVIII, ss. i. (788-789); see also, Grumpelt (Scuttled U-Boats) Trial 13 Ann. Dig. 309 (1946).
84 *Ibid.*, at 789.
85 *Ibid.*, at ss. vi, 791.

Vattel, too, somewhat more aware of what States actually do, was also concerned with discussing restraints during conflict:

'A lawful end confers a right only to those means which are necessary to attain that end. Whatever is done in excess of such measures ... must be condemned as evil. ... [T]he belligerent who should make use of [any measure of war] without necessity, when less severe measures would have answered his purpose, would not be guiltless .... This is what constitutes the difference between what is just, proper, and irreprehensible in war, and what is merely permissible and may be done by Nations with impunity.'[86]

Gentili condemned the killing of those who surrender, denial of quarter, reprisals against prisoners, violence against women, children, the aged and the sick, ecclesiastics and men of letters, husbandmen and in general all unarmed persons, assassination, the use of poison and poisoned weapons, as well as the poisoning of streams, springs and wells.[87] However, while such activities were condemned by many of the classical writers,[88] it is Vattel who is most direct in seeking restraints upon the horrors of war:

'Nations ... should all refrain from ... whatever tends to render war more disastrous. All acts of hostility which injure the enemy without necessity ... are unjustifiable, and as such condemned .... Hence ... the voluntary Law of Nations limits itself to forbidding acts that are essentially unlawful and obnoxious, such as poisoning, assassination, treason, the massacre of an enemy who has surrendered and ... condemns every act of hostility which ... contributes nothing to the success of our arms ... [I]t is not, generally speaking, contrary to the laws of war to plunder and lay waste to a country. But if an enemy of greatly superior force should treat in this manner a town or province which he might easily have held possession of, as a means of obtaining just and advantageous terms of peace, he would be universally accused of waging war in a barbarous and uncontrolled manner.[89] The deliberate destruction of public monuments, temples, tombs, statues, pictures, etc., is, therefore, absolutely condemned even by the voluntary

---

86 Vattel, op. cit. n. 59, Vol. II, Liv. III, ch. VIII, ss. 138, 137 (Carnegie 280, 279).
87 *Ibid.*, at ss. 140, 142, 145-147, 155-157 (280-283, 287, 289).
88 *E.g.* B. Ayala, C. Belli, C. van Bynkershoek, C. Wolff, R. Zouche. Also, Armour, loc. cit. n. 23, at 74-77.
89 See also, the 13th Edict of the Emperor Asoka, 256 B.C., of which Armour states:
   'In consequence of the sufferings brought about by this campaign, Asoka thereafter foreswore warfare, and he left his descendants to rid themselves of the popular notion that conquest by war is the duty of kings.'
   Armour, loc. cit. n. 23, at 80.

Law of Nations, as being under no circumstances conducive to the lawful object of war. The pillage and destruction of towns, the devastation of the open country by fire and sword, are acts no less to be abhorred and condemned when they are committed without evident necessity or urgent reasons.'[90]

In this paragraph Vattel has condemned measures of combat that were not formally condemned by black letter international law until after World War II. While pillage has long been forbidden, the protection of cultural property during armed conflict only found its treaty basis in 1954.[91] It was not until Protocol I that similar protection was afforded to objects indispensable to the survival of the civilian population, such as foodstuffs, agricultural areas, crops, drinking water installations and the like.[92] The Protocol extends the prohibition to a method of warfare that might have such long-term effects, but would not be used by the individual soldier. Article 53 forbids any warlike action likely to damage the natural environment thereby prejudicing the health or survival of the population, and in 1976 the Convention on the Prohibition of Military or any other Hostile Use of Environmental Modification Techniques was adopted.[93]

3. RESTRICTIONS IN TREATY LAW

3.1 Means and methods

The first Treaty in which we find any of these classical humanitarian considerations solemnly embodied is the 1868 Declaration of St. Petersburg renouncing explosive projectiles of less than 400 grammes weight and which were either explosive or charged with fulminating or inflammable substances.[94] The humanitarian basis appears from the preamble, asserting that civilization demands the reduction of casualties in war, the sole purpose of which is to weaken the enemy's forces. Since this may be achieved by disablement, it would be contrary to the laws of humanity to use arms which would aggravate suffering or make death inevitable.

---

90 Vattel, op. cit. n. 59, Liv. III, Ch. VIII, s. 156, Ch. IX, ss, 172-173 (289, 294-295).
91 Schindler, Toman, eds., op. cit. n. 28, at 745, as amended by Protocol I, Article 53.
92 Article 54.
93 Schindler, Toman, eds., op. cit. n. 28, at 163.
94 *Ibid.*, at 95.

Of more direct interest to the actual conduct of hostilities as undertaken by the man in the field was the Brussels Project of an International Declaration concerning the Laws and Customs of War of 1874.[95] Having stated that 'The laws of war do not recognize in belligerents an unlimited power in the adoption of means of injuring the enemy', this went on to 'forbid' the use of poison or poisoned weapons, murder by treachery or of one who had surrendered at discretion, the denial of quarter, employment of arms, etc., 'calculated to cause unnecessary suffering', improper use of a flag of truce, of the enemy flag or military insignia or uniform, or of the Red Cross and similarly protected emblems, or the unnecessary destruction or seizure of enemy property. In addition, 'a town taken by assault ought not to be given over the pillage by the victorious troops'. These proposals found formal acceptance in the Hague Regulations of 1899 and 1907 which, as has been seen, were considered to have become part of customary law by the time of World War II. As such, they are binding on all States, including non-Parties,[96] and regardless of the fact that Article 2 of the governing Convention declared the Convention and the Regulations irrelevant in any conflict if any belligerent was not a Party thereto. Treaties relating to the law of armed conflict will always represent the highest common factor or lowest common multiple of agreement among the drafting Parties and this fact is clearly spelled out in the Convention's preamble, which is generally known as the Martens Clause, preserving the usages of civilized peoples, the laws of humanity and the requirements of public conscience. What these terms really mean can only be derived from the classical and later writings, military manuals and the laws and customs of war recognized by the majority of States at any particular time.

Perhaps one of the most significant provisions in the Regulations is the dogmatic statement[97] that: 'the right of belligerents to adopt means of injuring the enemy is not unlimited. ... [I]t is especially forbidden ... to employ arms, projectiles, or material calculated to cause unnecessary suffering'. This provision is preserved is Article 35 of Protocol I. It is probably true to say that the man in the field regards any wound he may suffer, however caused, as 'unnecessary', but the test is not subjective. As with the classical view of necessity, proportionality is the measure. What is

---

95 *Ibid.*, at 25 (italics in original).

96 It is interesting to note that as early as 1906, Holland maintained that the ban on trecherous killing -assassination- in Article 23(b) of the 1899 Regulations was 'merely an express enactment of a well-established rule of the law of nations' and of general application; T.E. Holland, Letters Upon War and Neutrality 1881-1909 51-52 (1909).

97 Articles 22, 23(e).

prohibited are 'those measures of military violence, not otherwise prohibited by international law, which are not necessary (relevant and proportionate) to the achievement of a definite military advantage'.[98] It is enough to disable an enemy. It is not necessary to kill him. Thus, it is forbidden to alter a weapon, such as a bayonet, to cause an aggravated wound almost certain to produce death.

Both the British and American Military Manuals list lances with barbed heads, irregularly shaped bullets, projectiles filled with broken glass and the use of any substance likely to inflame a wound, as well as poison and poisoned weapons as falling within the unnecessary suffering ban.[99] They state that explosives in hand grenades are not forbidden, but neither mentions claymore or similar grenades which splinter or discharge shards of sharp metal on explosion. Broadly speaking, the German War Book is to the same effect, but:

'... closely connected with the unlawful instruments of war [is] the employment of uncivilized and barbarous peoples in European wars ... [and] the transference of African and Mohammedan Turcis to a European seat of war [by the French] in the year 1870 was ... a retrogression from civilized to barbarous warfare, since these troops had and could have no conception of European-Christian culture, of respect for property, and the honour of women, etc..'[100]

Insofar as the modern soldier is concerned, he is forbidden from discriminating in any way among his enemies, whether it be on the basis of sex, race,[101] religion, political opinions, or any other similar criteria.[102] All members of an adverse party are therefore entitled to equal treatment and protection, even though Article 47 of Protocol I denies mercenaries recognition as combatants and status as prisoners of war, although there was apparently a tacit agreement at the drafting Conference that they 'would be one of the groups entitled to the protection of ... Article (75)

---

98 M. Bothe, K.J. Partsch and W.A. Solf, eds., New Rules for Victims or Armed Conflicts 195 (1982).

99 Op cit. n. 51, at §§ 110, 111, and at §§ 34, 37, resp.

100 Op. cit. n. 61, at 65-67.

101 It is unfortunate that during the Vietnam war, for example, the US media applied derogatory terms to the adverse party almost hinting that they were beneath contempt and barely human.

102 1949, I-Article 12, II-Article 12, III-Article 16, IV-Article 13, Protocol I Article 75, which also forbids discrimination on grounds of 'language, ... national or social origin, wealth, birth or other status ...'.

which established minimum standards of treatment for persons not entitled
to more favorable treatment under the Conventions and Protocol I'.[103]

3.2   Use of weapons

Among the earliest 'personal' weapons to be declared illegal was the 'dum-
dum' explosive bullet,[104] apparently invented because of the inadequacy
of ordinary bullets to stop the onrush of hordes of 'native' forces.
Whatever their value at that time, and Westlake suggests that their use in
such circumstances might not in fact be illegal,[105] there is no doubt that
it would be illegal for a modern soldier to alter his normal issue of
ammunition so as to expose its core or render it explosive on contact.
However, neither explosive nor incendiary bullets are forbidden against
tanks or aircraft,[106] and it is possible that the man in the line would have
a valid defence if these were actually issued to him.

Among weapons that the man in the field can make for himself is the
booby-trap, but here, too, he must ensure that this weapon does not affect
or endanger innocent persons, such as non-combatants and especially
children, nor cause unnecessary suffering. The punji stick -a sharpened
stake covered with excrement and placed in a camouflaged hole- is clearly
illegal, both on account of its concealment and its poisonous character.[107]
The use of booby-traps is now governed by Protocol II annexed to the
1981 Convention on Prohibitions or Restrictions on the Use of Certain
Conventional Weapons which may be Deemed to be Excessively Injurious
or to have Indiscriminate Effects.[108] A booby-trap is 'any device or
material which is designed, constructed or adapted to kill or injure and
which functions unexpectedly when a person disturbs or approaches an
apparently harmless object or performs an apparently safe act.' It is banned
only if employed as a reprisal against civilians or indiscriminately placed

---

103 Bothe, Partsch and Solf, eds., op. cit. n. 98, at 271-272; see also, L.C. Green, *The Status of
Mercenaries in International Law*, IX Essays on the Modern Law of War (1984).
104 Declaration IV, 1907, Schindler, Toman, eds., op. cit. n. 28, at 109.
105 See J. Westlake, International Law 2, War, 78 (1913); see also, Holland, op. cit. n. 46, at 53-
56.
106 See *e.g.* Hague Rules on Air Warfare (1923), Schindler, Toman, eds., op. cit. n. 28, at 147,
Article 18 -though lacking legal force- these Rules are generally considered declaratory of
existing law. *Ibid.*; see also H. Lauterpacht, Oppenheim's International Law 2, 518-524
(1952); J.M. Spaight, Air Power and War Rights 42-43, 213 (1947). See now, especially,
Protocol on Incendiary Weapons, n. 28 *supra.*
107 J.E. Bond, The Rules of Riot 142 (1974). Punji sticks were widely used during the Vietnam
War.
108 Schindler, Toman, eds., op. cit. n. 28, at 185; see Fenrick, loc. cit. n. 28, at 242-246.

so that it 'may be expected to cause incidental loss of civilian life, injury to civilians, damage to civilian objects, or a combination thereof, which would be excessive in relation to the concrete and military advantage anticipated', but there is no indication as to how this is to be measured. However, as to military personnel, Article 6 would appear to be significant:

'1)   Without prejudice to the rules of international law applicable in armed conflict relating to treachery and perfidy, it is prohibited in all circumstances to use:

a)   any booby-trap in the form of an apparently harmless portable object which is specifically designed and constructed to contain explosive material and to detonate when it is disturbed or approached, or

b)   booby-traps which are in any way attached to or associated with:

    i   internationally recognized protective emblems, signs or signals;

    ii   sick, wounded or dead persons;

    iii   burial or cremation sites or graves;

    iv   medical facilites, medical equipment, medical supplies or medical transportation;

    v   children's toys or other portable objects or products specially designed for the feeding, health, hygiene, clothing or education of children;

    vi   food or drink;

    vii   kitchen utensils or appliances except in military establishments, military locations or military supply depots;

    viii   objects clearly of a religious nature;

    ix   historic monuments, works of art or places of worship which constitute the cultural or spiritual heritage of peoples;

    x   animals or their carcases.

2)   It is prohibited in all circumstances to use any booby-trap which is designed to cause superfluous injury or unnecessary suffering.'

3.2.1   *ABC weapons*

While the weapons already considered are of primary concern to military personnel, the ordinary citizen is likely to be more interested in gas, chemical, bacteriological and nuclear warfare. These means of combat depend on policy decisions made by governmental authority, with the armed forces using such weapons if issued. There is a tendency to condemn all such weapons as falling within the ban on poison which dates from earliest times. So far as the European countries are concerned, it has

been suggested while 'for the Church poison was allied to the black arts, to
sorcery and witchcraft, to the knightly order it was but another method of
killing an opponent without personal risk'.[109] But much of the early
condemnation was, nevertheless, tied in to the thought that poison was a
'secret' and therefore 'treacherous' weapon.

At the 1899 Hague Conference a Declaration was adopted agreeing 'to
abstain from the use of projectiles the *sole* object of which is the diffusion
of asphyxiating or deleterious gases'.[110] However, the United States
maintained this was premature and refused to accede:

'... no shell emitting such gases is as yet in practical use, or has undergone
adequate experiment, consequently a vote taken now would be taken in
ignorance of the facts as to whether the result would be of a decisive
character, or whether injuries in excess of that necessary to attain the end
of warfare, the immediate disabling of the enemy would be inflicted.
The reproach of cruelty and perfidy, addressed against these supposed
shells, was equally uttered formerly against firearms and torpedoes, both of
which are now employed without scruple. Until we know the effect of such
asphyxiating shells there was no saying whether they would be more or less
merciful than missiles now permitted.[111]

Nevertheless, the United States was among those to make use of gas
bombs and cylinders during World War I.[112] The Treaty of Versailles
repeated that such use was illegal[113] and in 1925 the Geneva
Protocol[114] declared:

'... the use in war of asphyxiating, poisonous or other gases, and all
analogous liquids, materials or devices has been justly condemned by the
general opinion of the civilized world ... [their] prohibition shall be
universally accepted as part of International Law, binding alike the
consience and the practice of nations ... [and the Parties] agree to extend
this prohibition to the use of bacteriological methods of warfare.'

---

109 Draper, loc. cit. n. 33, at 19.
110 Declaration IV, Schindler, Toman, eds., op. cit. n. 28, at 109 (italics added).
111 C.C. Hyde, International Law Chiefly as Interpreted and Applied in the United States 1819
    (1947) (italics added).
112 *Ibid.*.
113 Article 171.
114 Schindler, Toman, eds., op. cit. n. 28, at 115.

The United States, however, refused to become a Party to the Protocol. This situation changed in 1975, when the United States ratified, reserving[115] the right to use such materials for riot control, to reduce civilian casualties, for rescue missions and to protect rear area convoys, as well as to control vegetation in US installations and bases or around their defensive perimeters. In fact, many of the parties have reserved their right to use gas in reply to its use against them.

During World War II there was evidence that Germany had made use of illegal medical experiments,[116] and there were allegations that Japan had resorted to these as well as chemical and bacteriological warfare,[117] In 1972 the Convention on the Prohibition of Development, Production and Stockpiling of Bacteriological (Biological) and Toxin Weapons and on their Destruction was adopted.[118] The Convention is in force and has been ratified by the major powers, but many are alleged to be continuing production, purportedly for defensive purposes. Moreover, there were allegations that Soviet forces had used such weapons in Afghanistan, while a United Nations Commission confirmed the use of gas and chemical agents during the Iran-Iraq War.[119] As to banning or controlling chemical weapons, negotiations with a view to a convention continue.

Controversy rages as to the legality of nuclear weapons. Some maintain they fall within the general ban on poison or indiscriminacy,[120] while others concede their use by way of reprisals,[121] and it has even been suggested that, although their use is contrary to the laws of humanity, they may be employed against a belligerent that has placed itself outside the ambit of civilized States.[122] There is judicial opinion that the weapon is

---

115 Reservation printed in Schindler, Toman, eds., op. cit. n. 28, at 126, is inadequate; see Presidential Statement of 22 January 1975, and Executive Order 11850 of 8 April 1975, XIV ILM 299, 794.

116 See *e.g.* Re Brandt (Doctors' Trial), 14 Ann. Dig. 296 (1947).

117 See *e.g.* USSR, Materials on the Trial of Former Servicemen of the Japanese Army Charged with Manufacturing and Employing Bacteriological Weapons (1950); P. Williams, D. Wallace, Unit 731 (1989); S. Morimura, The Devil's Feast (1982); The Times, 12 August 1985, for statements by British POW as victims of Unit 731.

118 Convention on Prohibition of Development, Production and Stockpiling of Bacteriological (Biological) and Toxin Weapons and on their Destruction, Schindler, Toman, eds., op. cit. n. 28, at 137.

119 The Times, 28 March 1984.

120 *E.g.*, N. Singh, E. McWhinney, Nuclear Weapons and Contemporary International Law 120-126, 147-152 (1989); A. Miatello, L'arme Nucléaire en Droit International 626 (1987).

121 *E.g.*, G. Schwarzenberger, The Legality of Nuclear Weapons, 58 (1958). Singh and McWhinney appear ready to accept the nuclear weapon by way of reprisal against the earlier use of such a weapon. Singh, McWhinney, op. cit. n. 120, at 103.

122 See Lauterpacht, Oppenheim, op. cit. n. 106, at 351.

so inhumane as to prevent any finding of guilt in respect of more traditional crimes by nationals of a country against which it has been used.[123] But in assessing the claims of humanity we should not overlook Kalshoven's warning:

> 'True, the use of nuclear weapons may (with some right) be regarded as uncivilized, or as contrary to the interests of humanity. Such considerations are, however, only half of the argument, the other half being the military interest involved. Put another way, the principles and standards in question all rest on the basic idea of a balance between the interests of humanity and the military interest at stake, and in this equation it cannot be simply asserted that humanity preponderates in all cases: it will depend on the peculiarities of the concrete situation which side outweighs the other.'[124]

To some extent this statement is supported by the Judgment of the Tokyo District Court which,[125] perhaps not surprisingly, held in 1963 that the atomic bombing of both Hiroshima and Nagasaki was 'an illegal act'. However, the Judgment is so worded that one may easily apply it to whatever purpose one chooses.

The British Manual of Military Law,[126] after pointing out that there is no treaty banning nuclear weapons, states that 'their use is governed, therefore, by the general principles' governing methods of warfare. The United States manual is more specific:

> 'The use of explosive "atomic weapons", whether by air, sea or land forces, cannot as such be regarded as violative of any customary rule of international law or international convention restricting their employment.'[127]

While it would seem that nuclear weapons fall within the provisions of Protocol I prohibiting indiscriminate attacks endangering the civilian population and the ban on 'methods of warfare which are intended, or may be expected, to cause widespread, long-term and severe damage to the

---

123 See Justice Pal, International Military Tribunal of the Far East: Dissenting Judgment, 620-621 (1953).

124 Kalshoven, The Law of Warfare, op. cit. n. 1, at 94-95.

125 *Shimoda et al.* v. *Japan* (1963) 8 Jap. Ann. Int'Law, 212, 234, *et seq.* (1964); 32 ILR 626, 628 *et seq.*

126 Op. cit. n. 51, at § 113.

127 Op. cit. n. 51, at § 35.

natural environment',[128] this was not the view of the major powers. Moreover, in introducing its Draft, the ICRC stated:

> '... problems relating to atomic, bacteriological and chemical weapons are subjects of international agreements or negotiations by governments, and in submitting these draft Protocols the ICRC does not intend to broach these problems, ...'

and the United Kingdom, the United States and the Soviet Union expressed concurrence in these views,[129] which are reiterated in British and American statements made at the time of signature.[130]

In the light of the ambiguities in the Shimoda Judgment, the clear statements by the ICRC and the nuclear powers at the Geneva Conference, as well as the continued manufacture, possession and testing of weapons both by Parties and non-Parties to the Test-Ban Treaty,[131] it is suggested that, regardless of long-term and perhaps indiscriminate effects, the use of the nuclear weapon during conflict is at present almost certainly not illegal.[132]

3.2.2 Disused and future weapons

As time has passed various weapons have fallen into disuetude and lengthy non-use has resulted in their becoming illegal, a point expressly made in the German War Book.[133] Today, however, the tendency is not to wait for the passage of time, but to declare such weapons unlawful. Thus, with the virtual disappearance of static and trench warfare, it became possible to adopt the 1981 Protocol limiting the use of incendiary weapons, while preserving them for tank and air warfare, where their use is still significant.[134] While it would appear that the definition of incendiary weapon ('any weapon or munition which is primarily designed to set fire ... or cause burn injury to persons through the action of flame, heat or combination thereof') clearly forbids its use against ground troops, this is not so when they are using armoured vehicles. Similarly, the ban on their

---

128 See Articles 35, 51, 52, 57.
129 Bothe, Partsch and Solf, eds., op. cit. n. 98, at 188-189.
130 Schindler, Toman, eds., op. cit. n. 28, at 717-718.
131 II ILM 889 (1963).
132 See, *e.g.*, L.C. Green, *Nuclear Weapons and the Law of Armed Conflict*, 17 Denver. J. Int'l Law and Relations 1 (1988).
133 Op. cit. n. 61, at 66.
134 See n. 28 *supra*.

use against civilians is somewhat ambiguous, if not contradictory. While it is forbidden to deliver air- or otherwise delivered incendiaries against a military objective within a concentration of civilians, it is permitted to use non-air-delivered incendiaries against military objectives within such concentrations so long as such objectives 'are clearly separated from the concentration of civilians' and all feasible precautions are taken to avoid or minimize civilian injuries resulting from their use.

When the proposal to ban gas shells was put forward in 1899 the United States, as we have seen, based its objection on the fact that they had not yet been invented. Nowadays it would appear that in such circumstances it is easy to achieve the necessary treaty ban. Thus, in 1980, it was possible to secure a Protocol[135] prohibiting the use of 'any weapon the primary effect of which is to injure by fragments which in the human body escape detection by X-rays'. This is a one-sentence Protocol agreed without difficulty, since none of the Conference participants possessed such weapons or envisaged their invention.

This illustrates the fact that difficulties arise when dealing with weapons that exist and are militarily useful, as compared with those which have not been invented, or are considered so unlikely of invention that the parties are able to appear before their publics as devoted to principles of humanitarianism. If anything is needed to prove the validity of Kalshoven's comment on humanity and military necessity, it is submitted that this does so to perfection.

4.   CONCLUDING OBSERVATIONS

Meanwhile, steps must be taken to ensure that principles of a humanitarian character receive more than mere lip-service and that proper steps are taken, particularly under the auspices of the United Nations, to ensure that especially those smaller States which appear to have illusions of grandeur, are prevented from developing weapons the effects of which are virtually uncontrollable. At the same time the developing countries must ensure that their nationals do not provide such States with the means to produce weapons which have such effects.

Now that the rivalries among the Great Powers seem to have lessened, perhaps we may hope that those who consider their self-interest to be more important than the interests of humanity and are prepared to endanger

---

135 Schindler, Toman, eds., op. cit. n. 28, at 185; Fenrick, loc. cit. n. 28, at 242.

mankind are effectively restrained. Some steps in this directions may be seen in the terms laid down by the United Nations to be observed by Iraq in accordance with the cease-fire terminating hostilities in the Gulf conflict. Perhaps the pressure of public opinion during this period of the reassertion of democratic values may be sufficient to make certain that military necessity and concepts of power and sovereign dignity are no longer permitted to prevail over humanitarian principles - even if this means having recourse to those weapons the use of which remains lawful. We should, however, always bear in mind the dictum of Edmund Burke: 'It is not what a lawyer tells me I *may* do; but what humanity, reason, and justice, tell me I ought to do'.[136]

---

136 E. Burke, *Speech on Conciliation with de Colonies*, in W.J. Bate, ed., Selected Writings of Edmund Burke 140 (1960).

LES ARMES NUCLEAIRES ET LE DROIT DE LA GUERRE

Henri Meyrowitz

1.   INTRODUCTION

Pourquoi les armes nucléaires posent-elles, au regard du droit de la guerre, un problème? La réponse à cette question s'impose d'elle-même: l'armement nucléaire n'est pas *'just another weapon'*. Il est d'une nature, d'une essence radicalement autre que les moyens destructifs 'classiques' dont l'utilisation est réglementée par le droit traditionnel de la guerre. Se pose donc dès l'abord un problème crucial, propre à désorienter le juriste, problème que des militaires clairvoyants, des politologues, des philosophes, des moralistes, ont bien discerné, sans toutefois pouvoir y trouver, dans le domaine du savoir et de l'agir qui est le leur, une solution théoriquement et pratiquement adéquate. Le fait nucléaire, a écrit le général Poirier, 'a provoqué une double coupure, praxéologique et épistémologique, dans la stratégie'.[1]

'*It is unsound to think in conventional terms about nuclear problems*', a pensé Morgenthau.[2] Et en effet, les armes nucléaires sont perçues par les peuples comme des armes d'une autre espèce, et elles sont traitées comme telles par les gouvernements. Elles font l'objet d'un certain nombre de traités conclus entre les deux superpuissances, ou de conventions multilatérales, telles le Traité de Tlatelolco sur l'interdiction des armes nucléaires en Amérique Latine, de 1967, le Traité sur la non-prolifération des armes nucléaires (TNP), de 1968, et le Traité interdisant de placer des armes nucléaires et d'autres armes de destruction massive sur le fond des mers et des océans ainsi que dans leur sous-sol, de 1971, ou de déclarations unilatérales générales de non-emploi en premier -cas de la Chine et de l'Union Soviétique-, ou d'engagements de non-utilisation d'armes nucléaires envers les Etats non dotés de ces armes et parties au Traité de Tlatelolco ou au TNP.[3] Ces traités ou engagements unilatéraux

---

1 L. Poirier, *Epistémologie de la stratégie*, 1 Anthropologie et Sociétés 79 (1983).
2 H. Morgenthau, *The Fallacy of Thinking Conventionally about Nuclear Weapons*, dans C. Schaerf, réd., Arms Control and Technological Innovation 255 (1977).
3 Dans le Traité de Tlatelolco, l'engagement des puissances nucléaires de 'ne recourir ni à l'emploi d'armes nucléaires ni à la menace de leur emploi' est stipulé à l'Article 3 du Protocole additionnel II annexé au Traité. Pour ce qui est du TNP, cet engagement résulte de déclarations unilatérales. Celles des Etats-Unis et du Royaume-Uni, qui sont conditionnelles, datent de 1978 et sont formulées à peu pres dans les mêmes termes:
'... will not use nuclear weapons against any non-nuclear-weapon State party to the NPT or any comparable internationally binding commitment not to acquire nuclear explosive devices, except in the case of an attack on the United States, its territories or armed forces, or its allies, by such a State allied to a nuclear-weapon State or associated with a nuclear-weapon State in carrying out or sustaining the attack.'
L'engagement de la France date de 1982; son libellé tient compte du fait que la France n'est pas partie au TNP:
'... n'utilisera pas d'armes nucléaires contre un Etat non doté de ces armes et qui s'est engagé à le demeurer, excepté dans le cas d'une agression menée en association ou en alliance avec un Etat doté d'armes nucléaires contre la France ou contre un Etat envers qui celle-ci a contracté un engagement de sécurité.'
La déclaration de l'Union Soviétique ne contient pas ces restrictions:
'... n'emploiera jamais des armes nucléaires contre des Etats qui renoncent à la production et à l'acquisition de ces armes et n'en possèdent pas sur leur territoire.'
La déclaration de la Chine de 1982 réunit l'engagement de non-utilisation en premier d'armes nucléaires, qui remonte à 1964, et la garantie de non-attaque nucléaire envers les Etats non

ressortissent au domaine du désarmement ou à celui de la maîtrise des armements (*arms control*). A l'exception du Traité de Tlatelolco (Article 1(1,a)), ils ne renferment pas de prohibition de l'emploi des armes atomiques, mais, au contraire, impliquent la non-illicéité, en soi, du recours à ces armes.[4]

De la constatation de la profonde altérité des armes nucléaires, de la qualité et de la démesure de leurs effets destructeurs, et de la considération des enjeux qui seraient en cause dans une guerre nucléaire, certains juristes ont cru devoir conclure que ces armes se dérobent nécessairement à l'empire du droit. La thèse de l'incompétence du droit de la guerre -voire du droit tout court- à l'égard des armes nucléaires a trouvé des partisans à la Commission du droit international des Nations Unies. Selon Quentin-Baxter, 'la guerre nucléaire ne se plie pas au droit, non plus qu'à aucune autre discipline humaine'.[5] Le regretté professeur Reuter estimait que 'l'usage des armes nucléaires échappe malheureusement au droit, voire même, avec certaines limitations, au *jus cogens*, en raison de la nature même de ces armes'.[6] Pour d'autres juristes, la prétendue incompétence du droit de réglementer l'emploi des armes nucléaires tient à la 'nature essentiellement politique' du problème posé par ces armes.[7]

L'argument du caractère politique des armes nucléaires est encore avancé dans un autre sens pour contester la compétence du *jus in bello* à leur égard. Les armes nucléaires, dit-on, sont par essence des armes politiques: le seul usage rationnel et conforme à leur nature consiste dans

---

dotés d'armes nucléaires, de 1978:

'... the Chinese Government has long declared on its own initiative and unilaterally that at no time and under no circumstances will China be the first to use nuclear weapons, and that it undertakes unconditionally not to use or threaten to use nuclear weapons against non-nuclear countries and nuclear-free zones.'

4 Sur la portée de cette non-illicéité, *infra* 3.2 - 3.4.

5 Comptes rendus analytiques des séances de la 37e session, I Annuaire de la CDI 35, § 1 (1984).

6 *Ibid.*, § 4, p. 13.

7 Sir I. Sinclair, Comptes rendus de la 38e session, I Annuaire de la CDI § 20, 112 (1986). *Cf.*, McCaffrey, *ibid.*, § 13, p. 127. McCaffrey a dit: 'Ce problème est éminemment politique et étranger au domaine du droit.' Au sein de l'Institut de droit international, E. Giraud s'était, au sujet des armes thermonucléaires, exprimé dans le même sens:

'C'est à notre avis un problème exclusivement politique qui est d'une importance capitale, mais sur lequel nous n'avons pas, en tant que juristes, d'opinions à donner.'

II Annuaire de l'IDI 115 (1967).

Voir aussi, entre autres, A. Freeman:

'The problem of the regulations of these weapons has been, from the beginning, a political one, not a legal one. It was not disposed of by the Hague IV Regulations nor by general international law, and it remains unsolved'. (ASIL, Proc. 72nd Annual Meeting 50 (1978)).

leur fonction de dissuasion, c'est-à-dire dans leur non-emploi effectif. Or, pour satisfaire aux conditions physiques et psychologiques de cette fonction primordiale, qui est mieux exprimée par le terme anglais *deterrence* que par le mot 'dissuasion', toute référence aux limitations et interdictions imposées par le droit international à l'emploi des armes classiques est, par définition et par nécessité, exclue. Il faut bien voir que sous l'aspect pragmatique de ce raisonnement se cache un dogme pseudo-juridique tenace, celui de la primauté du *jus ad bellum* sur le *jus in bello*. En maintenant la paix, objet premier et impératif du droit international, les armes nucléaires, affirme-t-on, remplissent par elles-mêmes authentiquement une fonction quasi-normative.

Parmi les autres arguments invoqués à l'appui de la thèse de l'incompétence du droit de la guerre à l'égard des armes nucléaires, nous nous bornons à en mentionner deux, qui sont d'ailleurs liés entre eux. Par leurs caractères intrinsèques, dit-on, les armes nucléaires excèdent les présupposés factuels et normatifs ainsi que l'économie du droit classique de la guerre, autrement dit, du droit de la guerre classique, droit fait pour des armes classiques, et adapté à la mesure de leur pouvoir destructif. Aussi l'emploi des armes nucléaires n'est-il imaginable que pour la défense -si tant est, la plupart des avocats de cette thèse en conviennent, que le mot 'défense' ait, dans une guerre nucléaire, un sens- d'enjeux totaux, excédant, eux aussi, le pouvoir régulateur du droit.

Pour réfuter les arguments que nous venons d'énumérer, il suffit d'invoquer un fait décisif, qui clot le débat. Ce fait, c'est la démonstration qu'il existe en droit positif un statut des armes nucléaires selon le *jus in bello*, statut qui s'impose aux puissances nucléaires, et qui n'est d'ailleurs contesté, dans son principe, par aucune d'elles.[8] Cette démonstration forme l'objet du présent article.

Dans le processus, rappelé plus loin, qui a conduit à l'éclaircissement du statut des armes nucléaires selon le droit de la guerre, la dissuasion nucléaire, la conscience de sa nécessité, a joué un rôle capital. La dissuasion dont il s'agit est celle qui existait entre les deux superpuissances, ou entre l'OTAN et la défunte organisation du Pacte de Varsovie, dissuasion dont la caractéristique essentielle consistait dans l'égalité des armes de destruction massive existant de part et d'autre, donc dans la réciprocité. Bien que les moyens physiques sur lesquels reposait cette dissuasion continuent d'exister pour l'essentiel, la mutation profonde des rapports politiques intervenue entre les deux superpuissances a produit

---

8   En ce qui concerne la position particulière de la France, *infra* 3.2.

une conjoncture nouvelle et a entraîné un changement d'optique important: de la considération de l'état de dissuasion réciproque et stable sous lequel le monde a vécu durant quarante ans, l'attention doit désormais se porter sur des situations conflictuelles nouvelles, susceptibles de mettre en présence soit des Etats nucléaires nouveaux, soit un tel Etat et un ou plusieurs Etats non dotés d'armes atomiques. C'est dans la perspective, éminemment néfaste, de la prolifération nucléaire, et à l'intention d'éventuels Etats nucléaires nouveaux, qu'il importe aujourd'hui d'exposer les règles du droit de la guerre auxquelles est soumis l'emploi des armes atomiques.

2. LA NON-INTERDICTION, EN SOI, DE L'UTILISATION DES ARMES NUCLEAIRES

2.1 La distinction et la séparation normatives entre la dissuasion nucléaire et l'emploi des armes nucléaires

Le droit international positif s'abstient de soumettre la dissuasion aux limitations et interdictions imposées par le *jus in bello* à l'emploi des armes atomiques. Aussi le principe de la distinction et de la séparation normatives entre la dissuasion nucléaire et l'emploi des armes nucléaires est-il le premier élément du statut des armes nucléaires selon le droit international positif. Considérant que par sa finalité, la dissuasion ressortit au temps et à l'ordre de la paix, au *jus ad bellum* (ou *jus contra bellum*), même si elle n'est pas réglementée par ce dernier, l'auteur a, dans des travaux précédents, employé au sujet de ce principe l'expression de 'théorie des deux ordres'. Entre les deux modes, ou stratégies, d'utilisation des armes nucléaires, la dissuasion et leur emploi guerrier, il existe une solution de légalité: liberté -sous une réserve dont il sera question plus loin- des moyens et du discours de la dissuasion, d'un côté, réglementation stricte, de l'autre.

Cette apparente dichotomie normative,[9] consistant dans la non-interdiction de l'acte de 'menacer'[10] de faire ce qui est interdit

---

9 Apparente seulement, car, à strictement parler, il ne s'agit pas de dualisme normatif, ou de contradiction normative (et logique), puisque la dissuasion est précisément caractérisée par la (quasi-)absence de normes.

10 Les guillemets encadrant le mot 'menacer' indiquent qu'à notre avis, la pertinence de la notion de *menace*, appliquée aux moyens et au discours de la dissuasion nucléaire, est sujette à caution. Ce n'est pas le lieu d'exposer les réserves que suscite le recours à cette notion.

d'accomplir, est facile à comprendre. La liberté dont bénéficie la dissuasion nucléaire est fondée sur la reconnaissance de la nécessité factuelle de celle-ci, et sur la licéité de sa finalité. Cela signifie que la non-illicéité de la dissuasion est limitée par cette finalité. Un mode d'utilisation de l'armement nucléaire à des fins de chantage, par exemple, de menace de la force au sens de l'Article 2(4) de la Charte des Nations Unies, ne serait pas couvert par la non-illicéité de la dissuasion. L'échec de la dissuasion fait automatiquement disparaître la cause de la non-illicéité, *qua* dissuasion, de ceux moyens de la 'menace' dissuasive dont la mise à exécution constituerait des violations des règles du droit de la guerre applicables à l'emploi des armes nucléaires. Dès l'instant où le dissuadant devient belligérant, ses actes sont justiciables du *jus in bello*. C'est là que réside l'importance pratique du principe de la distinction et de la séparation normatives entre la dissuasion et l'emploi des armes nucléaires: les attaques effectuées avec ces armes ne doivent pas être prédéterminées par les 'menaces' dissuasives.

L'hiatus juridique entre la dissuasion nucléaire et l'emploi des armes nucléaires trouve un tempérament dans un principe qui, lui, appartient au droit de la guerre: le principe de la 'rétroaction' des règles du *jus in bello* sur la composition, en temps de paix comme dans la guerre, de l'arsenal des Etats.[11] Ce principe a été formulé pour la première fois en 1977, à l'Article 36 du Protocole additionnel I aux Conventions de Genève de 1949:

> 'Dans l'étude, la mise au point, l'aquisition ou l'adoption d'une nouvelle arme, de nouveaux moyens ou d'une nouvelle méthode de guerre, une Haute Partie contractante a l'obligation de déterminer si l'emploi en serait interdit, dans centaines circonstances ou en toutes circonstances, par les dispositions du présent Protocole ou par toute autre règle du droit international applicable à cette Haute Partie contractante.'

Par son contenu et son but, cet article, qui exprime une règle de bon sens, doit être considéré comme applicable aussi bien aux armes conventionnelles nouvelles qu'aux armes nucléaires; malgré l'expression 'armes nouvelles', il s'applique aux armes qui existaient déjà dans les arsenaux avant 1977. La règle s'impose à tous les Etats, indépendamment

---

11 On peut parler indifféremment de 'rétroaction' ou de 'préaction' du droit de la guerre, le point de vue temporel se confondant ici avec le point de vue normatif: les règles faites pour être appliquées en temps de guerre 'rétroagissent' ou 'préagissent', en matière d'armements, sur la politique militaire des Etats en temps de paix.

de la ratification ou de la non-ratification du Protocole. Elle n'interdit pas à un Etat de se doter d'un type d'arme dont l'emploi serait interdit, 'dans certaines circonstances ou en toutes circonstances': l'acquisition de cet armement peut être justifiée, en l'espèce, par la connaissance de la possession, par un ennemi potentiel, du même type d'arme, ou d'une arme de nature ou aux effets comparables, autrement dit, par la perspective de l'emploi éventuel, licite, de l'arme en question au titre de représailles ou de réciprocité. Mais si un Etat possède un type d'arme qui, en raison de ses caractères intrinsèques, ou de ceux de ses vecteurs, ne pourrait en aucune circonstance être employé en premier sans violer les règles du droit de la guerre applicables, menacer explicitement de recourir, en cas de guerre, à l'utilisation en premier de cette arme, et se préparer en vue de cet emploi interdit, est aussi illicite que le serait la menace et la planification de l'emploi, en premier, d'armes chimiques ou biologiques. C'est dans cette 'rétroaction' du *jus in bello* sur les moyens de la dissuasion que consiste la réserve au principe de la distinction et de la séparation normatives dont nous avons parlé plus haut.

2.2 Preuve de la non-interdiction, en soi, de l'emploi des armes nucléaires

2.2.1 *La doctrine*

Un certain nombre d'internationalistes, tant américains qu'européens, continuent d'affirmer l'illégalité *de lege lata* de l'emploi des armes nucléaires en soi.[12] Pour appuyer cette thèse, ces auteurs se fondent

---

12 E. Menzel a dressé, dans *Atomwaffen und völkerrechtliches Kriegsrecht* (Les armes atomiques et le droit international de la guerre), *Abschreckung und Entspannung*, 76 Veröffentlichungen des Instituts für Internationales Recht an der Universität Kiel 148-229 (1977), une liste d'auteurs soutenant, comme lui-même, la thèse de l'illégalité de l'emploi (en premier) des armes nucléaires. Cette liste (p. 163-164) était impressionnante par le nombre des auteurs cités; mais était-elle réellement représentative, à l'epoque, de la doctrine internationale relative à un sujet dont les implications politiques incitent nombre de juristes à observer une prudente réserve? De toute façon, les opinions mentionnées sont antérieures au Protocole I de 1977. Quant aux auteurs qui se sont exprimés après 1977, ceux qui maintiennent la thèse de l'illicéité de l'emploi -en premier, ou également en second- des armes nucléaires forment, semble-t-il, toujours la majorité, et celle-ci, bien qu'étant de proportions plus faibles, soulève les mêmes réserves quant à son caractère représentatif. Nous nous bornons à en citer quelques noms.
Aussi, A. Andries, *Pour une prise en considération de la compétence des juridictions nationales à l'égard des emplois d'armes nucléaires*, Revue de droit pénal et de criminologie 31-95 (1984); F.A. Boyle, *The Relevance of International Law to the 'Paradox' of Nuclear Deterrence*, 80 Northwestern University Law Review 1407-1448 (1986); E. David, *A propos*

principalement sur une phrase du préambule de la Déclaration de Saint-Pétersbourg de 1868, proclamant illicite 'l'emploi d'armes qui aggraveraient inutilement les souffrances des hommes mis hors de combat, ou rendraient leur mort inévitable', la 'clause Martens' du préambule de la IVe Convention de La Haye de 1907, l'Article 23(a) et (e) et l'Article 25 du Règlement annexé à cette Convention, interdisant respectivement 'd'employer du poison ou des armes empoisonnées', 'd'employer des armes, des projectiles ou des matières propres à causer des maux superflus', 'd'attaquer ou de bombarder, par quelque moyen que ce soit, des villes, villages, habitations ou bâtiments qui ne sont pas défendus', le Protocole de Genève de 1925, prohibant l'emploi à la guerre de gaz asphyxiants, toxiques ou similaires, 'ainsi que tous liquides, matières ou procédés analogues', et de moyens bactériologiques, et, enfin, sur la Convention pour la prévention et la répression du génocide, de 1948.[13]

En ce qui concerne certaines de ces interdictions, dont la plupart ont d'ailleurs la qualité de règles du droit coutumier, en particulier celle visant l'emploi du poison ou d'armes empoisonnées, leur application aux armes nucléaires pouvait effectivement être défendue avec quelque plausibilité, avant que l'etablissement, à partir des années soixante-dix, d'une solide pratique internationale, appuyée par une *opinio juris* générale, n'eût définitivement confirmé la non-illicéité ou, si l'on préfère, la non-interdiction, *en soi*, de l'emploi des armes nucléaires. Les deux mots en italiques soulignent que cette non-interdiction d'emploi vise seulement les armes nucléaires *comme telles*, c'est-à-dire en leur qualité d'armes nucléaires. Elles ne s'étend pas à la manière dont ces armes sont employées: contre quelles cibles, dans quelles circonstances, selon quels procédés, avec quels effets indirects. C'est donc le contraire du cas des

---

de certaines justifications théoriques à l'emploi de l'arme nucléaire, dans C. Swinarsky, réd., Etudes et essais sur le droit international humanitaire et sur les principes de la Croix-Rouge, en l'honneur de Jean Pictet 325-342 (1984); I. Detter de Lupis, The Law of War (1987); J.H.E. Fried, *International Law Prohibits the First Use of Nuclear Weapons*, 1 RBDI 33-52 (1981); N. Grief, *The Legality of Nuclear Weapons*, dans I. Pogany, réd., Nuclear Weapons and International Law 21-52 (1987); E.L. Meyrowitz, *The Laws of War and Nuclear Weapons*, Brooklyn Journal of Int. Law 227-258 (1983); Th. Schweisfurth, *Rechtsfragen und Raketenstationierung* (Questions juridiques relatives au stationnement des missiles), NJW 1506-1509 (1984).

13 Ces arguments (à l'exception du dernier) ont également été invoqués par le Tribunal civil de Tokyo, qui a déclaré illégaux, selon le droit international en vigueur à l'époque, les deux premiers et uniques lancements de l'arme atomique, dirigés contre les villes de Hiroshima et de Nagasaki: affaire *Shimoda*, 7 décembre 1963, publ. dans 8 Japanese Annual of International Law 212-252 (1964). L'importance de ce jugement et sa valeur au point de vue doctrinal ont été exagérées par des commentateurs.

armes chimiques et biologiques, dont l'utilisation est prohibée en soi par le Protocole de Genève de 1925 et, selon la majorité de la doctrine, par le droit coutumier, quelles que puissent être les cibles, les circonstances, les modalités et les effets de leur emploi.

Puisque les arguments mentionnés continuent d'être invoqués par des juristes, malgré le démenti décisif que leur a apporté et ne cesse de leur apporter la pratique des Etats, il faut en dire brièvement un mot. La référence à la clause Martens est, en l'espèce, sans pertinence. Par son origine historique, dans le préambule de la Convention sur les lois et coutumes de la guerre sur terre de 1899, cette clause est étrangère au domaine des armes ou autres moyens de guerre. Il n'existe aucune interdiction de l'emploi d'un type déterminé d'armes ou d'autres moyens de guerre qui ne résulterait pas d'une règle spéciale conventionnelle ou coutumière, mais qui soit déduite directement de la clause Martens. La preuve la plus récente de l'absence de force régulatrice autonome de la clause, en ce qui concerne les armes ou autres moyens de guerre, se trouve dans la Convention sur l'interdiction ou la limitation de l'emploi de certaines armes classiques qui peuvent être considérées comme produisant des effets traumatiques excessifs ou comme frappant sans discrimination, de 1980. Un alinéa du préambule de cet instrument reprend, dans la formulation légèrement modifiée qu'elle a reçue à l'Article 1(2) du Protocole I de 1977, la clause Martens. Pour aboutir à la définition des armes dont l'emploi est interdit dans les trois Protocoles additionnels annexes, et, inversement, pour s'accorder sur la détermination des catégories d'armes qui sont exlues des interdictions nouvelles, il aura pourtant fallu de longues et difficiles négociations; ce qui confirme que la clause est par elle-même impuissante à interdire ou limiter l'emploi d'une catégorie d'armes déterminée.

Il en est de même en ce qui concerne l'alinéa, cité plus haut, du préambule de la Déclaration de Saint-Pétersbourg et son développement à l'Article 23(e) du Règlement de La Haye. Cette dernière règle, dans la rédaction légèrement remaniée figurant à l'Article 35(2) du Protocole I de 1977, se trouve, elle aussi, sous la qualification de 'principe', dans le préambule de la Convention de 1980, et appelle les mêmes remarques que la clause Martens. Comme cette dernière, ce principe ne possède pas de pouvoir régulateur propre, mais doit passer par la voie -difficile en raison des implications militaires et politiques- de l'élaboration de règles conventionnelles. Quant à la Convention sur le génocide, l'hypothèse ne saurait être exclue que des actes 'commis dans l'intention de détruire, en tout ou en partie, un groupe national, ethnique, racial ou religieux, comme tel' et consistant dans le meurtre ou l'atteinte grave à l'intégrité physique de membres du groupe (Article II), puissent être perpétrés au moyen d'armes nucléaires. Mais ce serait alors la commission de l'acte ou des actes constitutifs de la définition du génocide qui tomberait sous le coup de cette incrimination, non pas le recours au moyen ayant servi à la perpétration du crime.

Les défenseurs de la thèse de l'illicéité, selon le droit en vigueur, de l'emploi des armes nucléaires font aussi état d'une série de résolutions de l'Assemblée générale des Nations Unies. Outre que les résolutions dont il s'agit ne possèdent pas de force obligatoire, elles doivent être considérées comme dépourvues de valeur juridique. Le contraste est éclatant entre la légèreté avec laquelle ces textes sont généralement votés par la majorité, et le temps ainsi que les soins que mettent les services compétents de ces mêmes Etats à préparer et à élaborer une convention du droit de la guerre, comme le Protocole I de 1977, et à en proposer à leurs gouvernements la signature, puis la ratification, ou la non-ratification. La composition de la minorité formée par les Etats ayant voté contre les résolutions en question ou qui se sont abstenus, minorité qui comprend régulièrement, en dehors des trois puissances nucléaires occidentales et de leurs alliés, un certain nombre d'Etats 'non engagés', interdit de voir dans ces textes la manifestation, ni même seulement l'amorce, de la formation d'une *opinio juris*. La plupart du temps, le libellé des résolutions fait d'ailleurs apparaître qu'elles sont conçues dans la persective *de lege ferenda*. Mais il y a plus. La résolution 40/151 F du 16 décembre 1985, intitulée 'Convention sur l'interdiction de l'utilisation des armes nucléaires', réaffirme dans son préambule que 'le recours aux armes nucléaires constituerait une violation de la Charte des Nations Unies et un crime contre l'humanité', comme l'Assemblée générale l'a déclaré dans ses résolutions 1653(XVI) du 24 novembre 1961, 33/71 B du 14 décembre 1978, 34/83 G du 11 décembre 1979, 35/152 D du 12 décembre 1980 et 36/921 du 9 décembre 1981.

Cette affirmation est répétée dans le préambule du projet de Convention annexé à la résolution: 'Convaincus que toute forme d'utilisation des armes nucléaires constitue une violation de la Charte des Nations Unies et un crime contre l'humanité'. L'Article premier du projet prévoit: 'Les Etats parties à la présente Convention s'engagent solennellement à n'employer ni menacer d'employer des armes nucléaires en aucune circonstance'. Cela ne prouve sans doute pas que les auteurs du projet considèrent l'emploi des armes atomiques comme licite selon le droit en vigueur. Mais ils n'affirment pas non plus que l'utilisation des armes nucléaires est interdite *de lege lata*. L'Article 3(3) du projet, en effet, contredit de la façon la plus flagrante la thèse de l'illicéité, selon le droit positif, de l'emploi des armes nucléaires: 'La présente Convention entrera en vigueur lorsque vingt-cinq gouvernements auront déposé les instruments de ratification, y compris les gouvernements des cinq Etats dotés d'armes nucléaires (...).'[14] Ainsi, la majorité, formée par les Etats non dotés d'armes nucléaires et non alliés d'une puissance nucléaire, reconnaît que la définition du statut des armes atomiques selon le droit de la guerre n'est pas possible sans l'accord des cinq puissances.

2.2.2 *La pratique des Etats*

Envisagés sous l'angle du droit de la guerre, les traités multilatéraux ou bilatéraux d'*arms control* relatifs aux armes nucléaires relèvent de la pratique des Etats, en ce qu'ils impliquent la non-illicéité de l'emploi des armes nucléaires comme telles. Pour des raisons invoquées plus haut, les résolutions de l'Assemblée générale de l'ONU affirmant l'illicéité de l'utilisation des armes atomiques ne peuvent être regardées comme des actes de la pratique des Etats. Il n'en est autrement que de la résolution 40/151 F et des résolutions identiques postérieures, mentionnées plus haut, qui ont réellement une valeur juridique en ce que la majorité formée par les Etats non nucléaires et non alliés d'une puissance nucléaire y a admis implicitement, mais clairement, la non-interdiction de l'emploi des armes nucléaires en soi. Mais ce n'est là que la moitié du problème de la licéité de l'utilisation des armes atomiques. L'autre moitié, la question de savoir à quelles règles est soumis l'emploi de ces armes, relève jusqu'à présent entièrement, quant à la réponse de principe, de la pratique des Etats, même si, comme nous verrons, cette pratique est reliée à une convention, le Protocole I de 1977, et qu'elle renvoie au droit coutumier. Mais avant la Conférence diplomatique de 1974-1977, la question de la licéité de l'emploi des armes nucléaires, dans ses deux branches, avait déjà fait l'objet de déclarations gouvernementales qu'il faut ranger sous la rubrique des actes de la pratique des Etats. Ces déclarations se trouvent dans des manuels militaires ou règlements nationaux du droit de la guerre.

Le manuel de l'armée américaine FM 27-10, The Law of Land Warfare, de 1956, déclare au sujet des armes nucléaires: '*The use of explosive "atomic weapons", whether by air, sea, or land forces, cannot as such be regarded as violative of international law in the absence of any*

---

14 La résolution a été réitérée lors de sessions ultérieures: voir les résolutions 42/39 C du 30 novembre 1987, et 44/117 C du 15 décembre 1989. Ces deux résolutions ont été adoptées par 134 voix contre 17 (les seize Etats membres de l'OTAN moins la Grèce, plus l'Australie et la Nouvelle-Zélande) et quatre abstentions (Grèce, Irlande, Israël, Japon).

customary rule of international law or international convention restricting their employment'. (Paragraphe 35) Formule ambiguë: s'il est en effet exact qu'il n'y a pas de règle coutumière ou conventionelle (mis à part l'Article 1(1,a) du Traité de Tlatelolco) interdisant l'utilisation des armes nucléaires *'as such'*, les règles coutumières qui limitent l'emploi de toutes les catégories d'armes ne faisant pas l'objet d'une interdiction spécifique s'appliquent aussi aux armes nucléaires, règles très importantes, dont l'existence, sinon le contenu exact, a été reconnue par le gouvernement américain, notamment dans le contexte du Protocole I. Le manuel officiel de la Marine américiane, Law of Naval Warfare, de 1955,[15] ne prête pas à la même critique. Paragraphe 613: *'Nuclear Weapons. There is at present no rule of international law expressly prohibiting states from the use of nuclear weapons in warfare. In the absence of express prohibition, the use of such weapons against enemy combatants and other military objectives is permitted.'* Une note relative à ce paragraphe précise: *'The employment, however of nuclear weapons is subject to the basic principles'* énumérés dans le manuel au sujet de l'utilisation des armes classiques, à savoir le principe de nécessité militaire (au sens non pas permissif mais restrictif de la notion de nécessité militaire), le principe d'humanité, la distinction entre combattants et non-combattants, la prohibition de *'wanton destruction of cities, towns or villages, or any devastation not justified by military necessity'*, l'interdiction *'to make non-combatants the target of direct attack in the form of bombardment, such bombardment being unrelated to a military objective'*, l'interdiction du bombardement *'for the sole purpose of terrorizing the civilian population'*, l'interdiction *'to bombard a city or town that is undefended and that is open to immediate entry by own or allied forces'*, et les restrictions concernant les biens spécialement protégés. Une autre note à laquelle est fait référence énonce le principe élémentaire, applicable à toutes les armes: *'Hence, a distinction must be drawn between the legality of a weapon, irrespective of its possible use, and the legal limitations placed upon the possible use of any weapon.'* (Paragraphe 415, note 2).

Dans le même sens s'exprime le manuel de l'armée britannique, *The Law of War on Land, being Part III of the Manual of Military Law,* de 1958. Paragraphe 113: *'There is no rule of international law dealing specifically with the use of nuclear weapons. Their use, therefore, is governed by the general principles laid down in this chapter.'* Une note

---

15 Publié en annexe de l'ouvrage de R.W. Tucker, The Law of War and Neutrality at Sea (1987).

renvoie au paragraphe 107, qui rappelle que les moyens de guerre '*are restricted by international conventions and declarations, and also by the customary rules of warfare. Moreover, there are the compelling dictates of humanity, morality, civilisation and chivalry, which must not be disregarded.*' Dans la note relative à ce paragraphe, il est dit: '*In the absence of any rule of international law dealing expressly with it, the use which may be made of a particular weapon will be governed by the ordinary rules and the question of the legality of its use in any individual case will, therefore, involve merely the application of the recognized principles of international law, as to which, see Oppenheim, volume II, pp. 346-352*'. Ce renvoi à un traité de doctrine, en l'espèce L. Oppenheim, International Law, Volume II, 7th edition by H. Lauterpacht (1952),[16] peut réjouir le juriste, mais est sans doute un procédé singulier pour la rédaction d'un manuel destiné à être manié par des militaires. Mais le principal, c'est que le War Office a souscrit, en ce qui concerne les règles applicables à l'emploi des armes nucléaires, aux principes mentionnés. Dans aucun document ni aucune déclaration, le gouvernement britannique n'a exprimé une opinion qui contredirait la position énoncée dans le manuel de 1958.

La France se singularise par l'absence d'un manuel militaire ou d'un règlement du droit de la guerre. Pour ce qui est de République fédérale d'Allemagne, l'Etat non nucléaire européen le plus important, sur le territoire duquel se trouve le plus grand nombre d'armes nucléaires, destinées à être actionnées, en cas de guerre, conjointement par les forces américaines et allemandes, le règlement HDv 100/600 *Rechtsgrundlagen für die Truppenführung*, de 1975, répète, sous une forme plus simple et plus claire, la doctrine exposée dans le manuel de la Marine américaine et le manuel britannique (paragraphe 614 et 615). Très nette est en particulier la précision de la portée de la non-interdiction de l'emploi des armes nucléaires en soi: 'Cependant, l'emploi des armes nucléaires est soumis par le droit international de la guerre aux mêmes limitations que celles qui sont applicables à l'emploi des moyens de guerre utilisés jusqu'à présent.'[17]

---

16 Oppenheim était un des deux coauteurs du chapter XIV du Manual of Military Law de 1914, et H. Lauterpacht est l'auteur principal du texte de 1958.

17 §§ 614, 615. *Cf.*, identiques, ZDv 15/10, Kriegsvölkerrecht. Leitfaden für den Unterricht (Droit international de la guerre. Guide pour l'instruction) § 84 (1961) et Völkerrechtliche Grundsätze der Landkriegführung (Anhang Teil III zu HDv 100/2, Führungsgrundsätze des Heeres für die atomare Kriegführung) (Principes de droit international relatifs à la conduite de la guerre terrestre (Annexe; 3e partie à la HDV 100/2; Principes directeurs de l'Armée pour la conduite de la guerre atomique)) § 56 (1961).

En 1968, la IIIe Commission de l'Assemblée générale de l'ONU était saisie d'un projet de résolution qui reprenait textuellement les termes des quatre principes fondamentaux fomulés dans la résolution intitulée 'Protection de populations civiles contre les dangers de la guerre indiscriminée', adoptée en 1965 par la XXe Conférence internationale de la Croix-Rouge, et dont le dernier rappelait que 'les principes généraux du droit de la guerre s'appliquent aux armes nucléaires et similaires'. Le représentant de l'Union Soviétique à la Commission demanda et obtint la suppression de ce quatrième alinéa, non point parce qu'il le considérait comme erroné, mais parce, selon lui, il n'était pas compatible avec la proposition de l'Union Soviétique qui préconisait la conclusion d'une convention internationale visant à interdire l'emploi des armes nucléaires. La représentante des Etats-Unis maintenait que les quatre principes constituaient 'une réaffirmation du droit international existant' et ajouta: *'There are indeed principles of law relative to the use of weapons in warfare, and these principles apply as well to the use of nuclear and similar weapons.'* Le représentant de la France, tout en estimant que la question des armes nucléaires devait être étudiée dans le cadre du désarmement général, conclut, selon le compte rendu: 'Toutefois, sa délégation n'aurait eu aucune difficulté à voter le projet de résolution dans sa forme initiale'. La représentante de la Grande-Bretagne s'associa aux déclarations faites par les délégués des Etats-Unis et de la France.[18] La déclaration de la représentante américaine est rappelée dans l'Air Force Pamphlet AFP 110-31 *International Law - The Conduct of Armed Conflict and Air Operations*, publié en 1976 par le Department of the Air Force.[19]

Les déclarations gouvernementales juridiquement les plus pertinentes se rapportant directement à notre question sont celles qui ont été émises à l'occasion de l'élaboration, de l'adoption, de la signature ou de la ratification du Protocole I. Nous en ferons état dans la section suivante.

---

18 Doc. officiels de l'Ass. Gén., 28e session, Troisième Commission. Comptes rendus analytiques, 1633e et 1634e séances, 9 et 10 décembre 1968.

19 *Ibid.*, pp. 5-17. *Cf.*, les explication de M. Wiley, General Counsel du Département de la défence, qui se rapportent à la fois à ce qui a été dit plus haut au sujet de l'Article 36 du Protocole et à la pratique relative à la question considérée dans le texte:
'I would like to add that, as far as the legal review of new weapons program by the Defense Department is concerned, (...) it is definitely part of our Departmental Weapons Review Program to review new weapons developments which involve nuclear devices. That would not only be in the tactical field but also involving strategic nuclear weapons. (...) Nuclear weapons will come under legal review. The same underlying legal principles are applied to the extent feasible, in both the pre-engineering developments stage and in the production decision phase.'
11 The International Lawyer 127 (1977).

3.   LE PROTOCOLE ADDITIONNEL I ET LES ARMES
     NUCLEAIRES

3.1   **La définition du statut des armes nucléaires par le texte et
      le contexte du Protocole**

Ce n'est pas dans le texte du Protocole I que l'on doit chercher la
définition du statut des armes nucléaires selon le *jus in bello*: non
seulement ce texte est muet sur cette question, mais les participants à la
Conférence diplomatique sur la réaffirmation et le développement du droit
humanitaire applicable dans les conflits armés (CDDH) s'étaient interdit
d'aborder le problème de l'application à l'emploi des armes atomiques des
règles qu'ils allaient formuler. Ce silence a été, en fait, la condition même
de la réunion et de la réussite de la Conférence:[20] c'est proprement à lui
que l'on doit l'existence de la convention du droit de la guerre la plus
importante depuis les quatre Conventions de Genève de 1949 et, en ce qui
concerne les règles applicables à la conduite des hostilités sur terre, depuis
la IVe Convention de La Haye de 1907.

La majorité formée par les Etats non nucléaires n'aurait jamais consenti
à l'adoption du Protocole s'il fallait en déduire que l'ensemble des règles
énoncées dans cette convention, règles 'réaffirmées' et règles
'développées', dût être compris comme s'appliquant uniquement à l'emploi
des armes classiques. L'opinion du professeur Green, selon laquelle
'*nothing in Protocol I, whatever its form or implied content, can be taken
to nuclear weapons*',[21] est contredite par les travaux de la CDDH,
contraire au 'consensus nucléaire' et démentie par la 'clause nucléaire'.

---

20 Comme l'a écrit le professeur Kalshoven:
    '... the choice has been clear throughout the proceedings of the Diplomatic Conference: it was
    either a Protocol not bearing on the use of nuclear weapons, or no Protocol at all.'
    F. Kalshoven, *Arms, Armaments and International Law*, 191 Recueil des Cours de l'Académie
    de Droit International II, 283 (1985).
21 L. Green, dans M. Cohen, M.E. Couin, réds., Lawyers and the Nuclear Debate, Proc. of the
    Canadian Conf. on Nuclear Weapons and the Law 102 (1988). *Cf.*:
    'It should be made clear however, that throughout the negotiations relevant to Protocol I, the
    ICRC, as well as *the* participants in the Conference, were emphatic that *the* provisions of the
    Protocol only related to conventional weapons. In fact, at the time of signature, *most* of the
    NATO Powers expressed their understanding of the nature of the Protocol as excluding *any*
    application to the nuclear arm.' [italiques, HM].
    L. Green, *Aerial Considerations in the Law of Armed Conflict*, 5 Annals of Air and Space
    Law 112 (1980). Les déclarations faites lors de la signature du Protocole I aux quelles se
    réfère le passage cité émanent des Etats-Unis et du Royaume-Uni, et elles disent le contraire
    de ce qu'expose le professeur Green.

L'historique de la formation de la trinité Protocole I - 'consensus nucléaire' - 'clause nucléaire' n'a plus besoin d'être retracé. Cette trinité peut être considérée aujourd'hui comme définitivement établie. Le silence du texte du Protocole relativement à la question du régime des armes nucléaires selon le droit de la guerre a déconcerté certains des premiers commentateurs. Ils ont cru devoir conclure de ce mutisme que les dispositions de cette convention s'appliquaient intégralement et sans distinction à l'emploi des armes classiques et à celui des armes nucléaires. En réalité, le Protocole n'interdit aucune catégorie spécifique d'armes. Ses règles relatives aux méthodes ou moyens de guerre ne visent pas des catégories déterminées d'armes, mais définissent les objectifs militaires, seules cibles licites, et les autres conditions de légalité des attaques. Autrement dit, ces règles traduisent, en les concrétisant, les trois principes de base du droit de la guerre relatifs aux attaques: le principe de l'immunité de la population civile et des biens civils, le principe de discrimination et le principe de proportionnalité des pertes et dommages civils indirects. Dans quelle mesure les règles énoncées dans le Protocole sont-elles applicables à l'emploi des armes nucléaires? C'est le 'consensus nucléaires' et la 'clause nucléaire' qu'il faut interroger pour répondre à cette question capitale.

3.2   Le consensus nucléaire

Il est impossible de parler du consensus nucléaire sans évoquer la clause nucléaire. Or, cette dernière, qui rend exactement la teneur du consensus nucléaire, n'apparaît dans des documents officiels que six mois après l'adoption du Protocole: elle forme l'un des *understandings* dont les gouvernements américain et britannique ont assorti l'acte de signature du Protocole I. Cette clause est capitale pour la compréhension du statut des armes nucléaires selon le droit de la guerre; elle fournit la clé de la réponse à la question posée plus haut: dans quelle mesure les règles énoncées dans le Protocole I s'appliquent-elles à l'utilisation des armes atomiques? La clause sera analysée plus loin, mais il faut la citer ici en tant qu'expression authentique du consensus nucléaire. La clause des *understandings* des Etats-Unis est ainsi conçue: '... *that the rules established by this protocol were not intended to have any effect on and do not regulate or prohibit the use of nuclear weapons.*' La clause britannique dit: '... *that the new rules introduced by the Protocol are not intended to have any effect on and do not regulate or prohibit the use of nuclear weapons.*' L'expression '*rules established*' dans le libellé de la clause américaine doit à l'évidence être comprise comme le contraire de: règles préexistantes au Protocole, et a donc le même sens que *'rules introduced'* dans la déclaration britannique, ce que le chef de la délégation américaine a d'ailleurs confirmé dans un article publié en 1981[22] et ce qui nous autorise à parler de la clause nucléaire au singulier, en lui donnant le sens qui ressort de la clause britannique.

On a contesté la propriété, en l'espèce, de l'expression de consensus, que l'auteur de cet article a employée dès 1979. Il peut, pour justifier le maintien de ce terme, se réclamer de l'autorité du professeur Kalshoven.[23] Ce consensus résulte d'abord des déclarations faites à la CDDH par les chefs des délégations des trois puissances nucléaires occidentales, soulignant que les travaux de la Conférence ne portaient pas sur les armes nucléaires,[24] et de l'acceptation tacite de ces déclarations par les délégations des Etats non nucléaires, dont plusieurs avaient pourtant -mais sans y insister- invité la Conférence à interdire l'emploi des armes atomiques. Ces déclarations impliquent l'idée que le régime des armes nucléaires selon le droit de la guerre devait rester en l'état, ce que le chef de la délégation américaine a d'ailleurs confirmé explicitement: *'He recognized (...) that their use in warfare was governed by the present principles of international law'*.[25] Mais la preuve la plus pertinente du consensus nucléaire consiste dans les déclarations écrites des Etats-Unis et de la Grande-Bretagne -c'est la clause nucléaire de 1977, que nous venons de citer- et de ceux de leurs alliés qui ont ratifié le Protocole I en formulant des déclarations interprétatives contenant la clause nucléaire,[26] et dans le fait, juridiquement concluant, de l'absence d'objections ou de déclarations interprétatives contraires de la part des autres Etats parties. Le

---

22 Aldrich a dit: '... the fact is that the Conference, from its beginning in 1974 through the final adoption of the Protocol, operated on the understanding that the *new rules it was adopting* would not deal with nuclear weapons and their effects [italiques, HM].'
G.H. Aldrich, *New Life for the Laws of War*, 75 AJIL 781 (1981).

23 Kalshoven a dit: '... there was a consensus among the participants at the Diplomatic Conference that anything new emerging from the Conference would not apply to nuclear warfare.' ASIL, Proc. 74th Annual Meeting 203 (1980).

24 Selon l'ambassadeur Aldrich, qui fut le chef de la délégation américaine, la délégation de l'Union Soviétique, qui, pour des raisons évidentes d'opportunité, s'est abstenue de s'exprimer sur ce point, *'privately agreed with'* ces déclarations. G.H. Aldrich, *Commentary. Progressive Development in the Laws of War: A Reply to Criticisms of the 1977 Geneva Protocol I*, 26 Virginia Journal of International Law 719 (1986). Cet accord n'est plus privé depuis la ratification du Protocole par l'Union Soviétique en septembre 1989, non assortie d'une déclaration relative aux armes nucléaires.

25 VII Official Records of the Diplomatic Conference on the Reaffirmation and Development of International Humanitarian Law Applicable in Armed Conflicts, Geneva 1974-1977, § 82, at 295.

26 *Infra* 3.3.2.

consensus nucléaire qui s'est formé à la CDDH se prolonge donc et manifeste sa continuité dans les clauses nucléaires formulées six mois, ou neuf, dix, douze et treize ans après l'adoption du Protocole I. Cette continuité du consensus nucléaire et son lien historique et objectif avec la clause nucléaire ont été bien mis en lumière par la réponse du gouvernement de Bonn à une question écrite du groupe des Verts du Bundestag au sujet de la clause anglo-américaine de 1977. Cette déclaration, y lit-on, 'constitue une interprétation qui est déduite des travaux préparatoires et de l'histoire de la Conférence de Genève sur le droit humanitaire applicable dans les conflicts armés, interprétation qui est partagée par le gouvernement fédéral'.[27]

Ainsi, la centaine d'Etats parties au Protocole I ne sont pas seulement liés par les dispositions de celui-ci (compte tenu des déclarations interprétatives, *understandings* ou réserves fomulées par certains d'entre eux), mais également par la teneur du consensus nucléaire; c'est, ou ce sera, aussi le cas, en raison de leur acceptation de la clause nucléaire, de ceux des Etats parties qui n'ont pas participé à la CDDH. Un Etat nucléaire futur qui ne serait pas partie au Protocole se trouve, en ce qui concerne les règles du droit de la guerre applicables à l'utilisation des armes nucléaires, dans la même situation que les puissances nucléaires actuelles qui, comme la Chine et l'Union Soviétique, ont ratifié le Protocole sans faire de déclaration relative aux armes nucléaires, ou qui, comme c'est le cas jusqu'à présent des trois puissances nucléaires occidentales, ne sont pas parties au Protocole I et qui, si elles décident d'en devenir parties, ne manqueront pas de faire, lors de la ratification ou de l'adhésion, des déclarations comportant la clause nucléaire, ou que de futurs Etats nucléaires parties au Protocole, avec ou sans clause nucléaire. Car ce n'est pas en vertu de cette clause que les Etats nucléaires, présents ou futurs, sont tenus par les règles coutumières du droit de la guerre, auxquelles renvoie implicitement la clause, mais en vertu de ces règles elles-mêmes. Le Protocole, en effet, plus exactement: la trinité Protocole-'consensus nucléaire'-'clause nucléaire', prouve qu'il ne s'est formé ni une règle coutumière dérogatoire, ni une règle conventionnelle exemptant l'emploi des armes atomiques du droit général, coutumier, de la guerre. De même aucune des cinq puissances nucléaires n'a jamais prétendu -et ne peut ni n'osera prétendre que l'emploi des armes nucléaires fût soustrait aux règles coutumières applicables aux attaques, de même un Etat

---

27 Deutscher Bundestag, 10. Wahlperiode. Drucksache 10/445 p 11. La référence aux travaux préparatoires -et donc au lien avec le consensus nucléaire- se trouve aussi dans le texte de la clause nucléaire des déclarations interprétatives de la Belgique. *Infra* 3.3.2.

nucléaire nouveau, partie au Protocole ou non, ne pourrait revendiquer une telle licence.

On a également objecté contre la thèse du consensus nucléaire la position adoptée par la France à l'égard du Protocole I. N'ayant pas signé ce dernier et n'y ayant pas adhéré, le gouvernement français n'a pas eu à faire de déclaration sur la question de l'application de cet instrument à l'emploi des armes atomiques. Dans la 'communication' qui était jointe à l'acte d'adhésion au Protocole II, il a justifié le refus de devenir partie au Protocole I 'plus particulièrement par l'absence de consensus entre les Etats signataires du Protocole I en ce qui concerne la portée exacte des obligations assumées par eux en matière de dissuasion'.[28] La doctrine stratégique nucléaire française, très particulière, est entièrement dominée par le concept de dissuasion. Aussi le discours que les gouvernements français successifs se croient obligés de tenir à des fins de dissuasion, et uniquement à ces fins, n'est-il pas destiné à un usage et à une lecture juridiques. Il importe peu, en tout cas, que le gouvernement français rejette le consensus nucléaire dans la formulation exacte qu'il a reçue dans la clause nucléaire anglo-américaine de 1977. La France est liée par la teneur de ce consensus, parce que celui-ci n'est pas constitutif d'un lien juridique que les Etats nucléaires seraient libres d'accepter ou de refuser, mais traduit le régime objectif, de nature non contractuelle, auquel doit obéir l'emploi des armes nucléaires, régime qui est formé par les règles coutumières du droit de la guerre, préexistantes à leur réaffirmation dans le Protocole I.

3.3   La clause nucléaire

3.3.1   *La clause anglo-américaine de 1977*

La teneur de la clause nucléaire des *understandings* des Etats-Unis et de la Grande-Bretagne de 1977 comprend, comme le consensus nucléaire, deux éléments, dont seul le premier est explicitement énoncé: la non-application à l'emploi des armes nucléaires des règles nouvelles, 'introduites par le Protocole'. Son second élément, la confirmation de l'assujettissement de l'utilisation des armes atomiques aux règles préexistantes, réaffirmées par le Protocole, règles qui ont le caractère de normes du droit coutumier, est renfermé dans le premier: celui-ci n'a pas de sens, pas d'objet, sans le second.

---

28 Revue internationale de la Croix-Rouge 239 (juillet-août 1984).

Le fait que les deux puissances n'aient pas ratifié le Protocole[29] ne diminue en rien la portée juridique de la clause, en tant que déclarations gouvernementales émises à l'occasion de l'accomplissement d'un acte qui, s'il n'exprimait pas le consentement des deux Etats signataires d'être liés par le Protocole, n'en revêt pas moins un caractère juridique particulier. Celui-ci n'est pas affecté par la non-ratification du Protocole par les deux puissances pour la bonne raison que le contenu de la clause est indépendant du consentement des Etats nucléaires. Son libellé exclut d'ailleurs lui-même, logiquement, la nécessité de ratification pour celles des règles du Protocole qui ne doivent pas être considérées comme 'new rules indroduced by the Protocol', et dont les deux Etats ont reconnu, dans la clause, l'application à l'emploi des armes nucléaires. En vertu de leur caractère de normes de droit coutumier, ces règles régissent indifféremment l'emploi des armes nucléaires et des armes classiques, parce que la légalité des attaques n'est pas fonction de la nature des armes employées, mais de la nature des cibles et des modalités d'excution des attaques.

La clause rectifie ce que nous avons dit plus haut en parlant de sa conformité avec le consensus nucléaire. Celui-ci, tel qu'il pouvait être déduit des déclarations orales faites à la CDDH par les chefs des délégations des deux puissances, notamment de la déclaration du chef de la délégation américaine, citée plus haut, était imprécis en ce que ces déclarations se bornaient à constater que l'utilisation des armes nucléaires était soumise aux principes du droit de la guerre en vigueur. La clause, elle, se réfère, implicitement, mais clairement, à l'articulation et à la concrétisation de ces principes dans le texte du Protocole. Il est vrai que ce renvoi au Protocole renvoie au difficile problème de la discrimination entre les règles préexistantes à cette convention de codification et les règles 'nouvelles'. Mais il indique aussi, et cela est précieux, que, pour connaître le contenu des règles 'réaffirmées', applicables à l'utilisation des armes nucléaires, il faut partir du libellé des dispositions énoncées dans le Protocole. La référence aux simples *principes* n'est désormais plus possible.

---

29 Dans les motifs invoqués par le président Reagan à l'appui du refus de recommander au Sénat la ratification du Protocole I, la question des armes nucléaires n'est pas mentionnée. Voir *Letter of Transmittal*, reproduit dans 81 AJIL 910-912 (1987), suivi d'une réplique aux arguments exposés dans ce message, par H.-P. Gasser, conseiller juridique du Comité international de la Croix-Rouge. Quant au gouvernement britannique, il ne semble pas encore avoir arrêté sa position au sujet de la ratification du Protocole I.

3.3.2 *La clause nucléaire des déclarations interprétatives d'Etats membres de l'OTAN, parties au Protocole I*

Parmi les onze des seize Etats membres de l'OTAN qui ont ratifié le Protocole I (état des ratifications fin février 1991), cinq l'ont fait sans déclaration relative aux armes atomiques (dans l'ordre chronologique: Norvège, Danemark, Islande, Grèce, Luxembourg). Les déclarations interprétatives dont sont assortis les actes de ratification de l'Italie, de la Belgique, des Pays-Bas, de l'Espagne et de la République fédérale d'Allemagne comportent la clause nucléaire dans une rédaction qui diffère de celle de la clause anglo-américaine de 1977. La clause belge est ainsi conçue:

> 'Le Gouvernement belge, considérant les travaux préparatoires de l'instrument présentement ratifié, tient à souligner que le Protocole a été établi en vue d'élargir la protection conférée par le droit humanitaire exclusivement lors de l'usage d'armes conventionnelles dans les conflits armés, sans préjudice des dispositions de droit international relatives à l'usage d'autres types d'armement.'

Le libellé de la clause des déclarations de l'Italie, des Pays-Bas, de l'Espagne et de la Republique fédérale d'Allemagne est, à des détails de pure forme et insignifiants près, identique:

> '*It is the understanding of the Government of Italy that the rules relating to the use of weapons introduced by the Additional Protocol I were intended to apply exclusively to conventional weapons. They do not prejudice any other rules of international law applicable to other types of weapons.*'

Deux traits, liés entre eux, caractérisent ces déclarations: d'une part, l'élimination -l'évacuation, devrait-on dire- du mot 'armes nucléaires', et, d'autre part, un défaut évident de logique dans la construction de la phrase. La première moitié de celle-ci, dans la version italienne, hollandaise, espagnole et allemande, emploie la même espression-clé qui se trouve dans la clause anglo-américaine: '*rules introduced by Protocol I*', et elle déclare *ces* règles applicables uniquement à l'emploi des armes conventionnelles. Après cette constatation, qui est exacte, on attend, logiquement, une réponse à la question: *quid* des règles qui n'ont pas été '*introduced*', mais réaffirmées par le Protocole? Au lieu de cette réponse, il y a, dans les deux déclarations citées, une rupture de logique. La référence aux '*other rules of international law applicable to other types of weapons*' ne peut viser, en fait, que les armes nucléaires ... non nommées. L'expression '*any other rules of international law*' apparaît ainsi non pas comme le corrélatif de '*rules introduced by Protocol I*', c'est-à-dire comme désignant les règles réaffirmées, mais comme se rapportant à des règles obscures, non déductibles du Protocole, applicables à des types innommées d'armes non conventionnelles.

L'explication de ces défauts de la clause des cinq pays se trouve dans un motif politique: le souci des gouvernements en question d'éviter toute allusion explicite aux armes nucléaires. Mais le procédé ne trompe personne. Les destinataires, nationaux et étrangers, de la déclaration savent que la clause ne peut avoir un autre sens que son précédent: la clause anglo-américaine de 1977. La meilleure preuve de cette conformité, et en même temps de la continuité du consensus nucléaire, c'est le libellé de l'*understanding* figurant dans les déclarations dont est assorti l'acte de ratification du Protocole I par le Canada, du 20 novembre 1990, et qui reprend presque textuellement la teneur de la clause anglo-américaine de 1977:

'*It is the understanding of the Government of Canada that the rules introduced by Protocol I were intended to apply exclusively to conventional weapons. In particular, the rules so introduced do not have any effect on and do not regulate or prohibit the use of nuclear weapons.*'

3.4   Les règles applicables à l'emploi des armes nucléaires

Les armes nucléaires ne bénéficient pas d'un privilège juridique; ni leur propriétés physiques, ni le caractère métaphysique qu'on leur attribue, ne les soustraient à l'autorité du droit commun de la guerre. La difficulté, qui est très grande, de dégager des dispositions du Protocole -puisque c'est de leur libellé qu'il faut partir- la teneur des règles coutumières réaffirmées, applicables à l'emploi des armes nucléaires comme à celui des armes classiques, est la même pour les Etats parties et les Etats non parties au Protocole, et pour les puissances nucléaires comme pour les Etats non nucléaires. Mais les implications de cette difficulté sont incomparablement plus graves quand il s'agit des armes atomiques: une divergence, de bonne foi, sur la qualification d'une disposition du Protocole comme 'nouvelle, introduite' par la CDDH, ou, au contraire, comme une règle coutumière, 'réaffirmée', peut se traduire, dans le cas d'hostilités nucléaires, par une différence de centaines de milliers, voire de millions de pertes de vies humaines dans la population civile.

Cette difficulté de discriminer entre les règles préexistantes et les règles nouvelles, entre la 'réaffirmation' et le 'développement' du droit, est propre à toutes les conventions de codification, dont la caractéristique est de réunir dans un même texte, et souvent dans une même phrase, des règles de la *lex lata* et des règles relevant de la *lex ferenda*, et de laisser à la jurisprudence, à la pratique et à la doctrine le soin de déterminer ce qui appartient au droit préexistant et ce qui est du droit nouveau. Dans le cas du Protocole, celles des règles se rapportant aux attaques qui sont intégralement nouvelles sont faciles à distinguer: ce sont les interdictions de représailles formulées aux Articles 51 à 56, l'Article 49(2) qui étend l'application des dispositions réglementant les attaques au 'territoire national appartenant à une Partie au conflit mais se trouvant sous le contrôle d'une Partie adverse', l'Article 54(2) interdisant d'attaquer des biens indispensables à la survie de la population civile, et l'Article 55(2) interdisant 'd'utiliser des méthodes ou moyens de guerre conçus pour causer ou dont on peut attendre qu'il causent de tels dommages (étendus, durables et graves) à l'environnement naturel', encore que ces deux dernières dispositions renferment indubitablement un noyau de droit coutumier. Or les plus novatrices de ces règles 'developpées', les interdictions de représailles contre la population civile et des biens civils, échappent à l'effet de la clause nucléaire, sans pour autant être applicables à l'emploi des armes nucléaires; on verra plus loin pourquoi.[30] Les articles les plus importants, relativement aux interdictions ou limitations imposées à la conception et à l'exécution des attaques, les Articles 51 et 52 (et l'Article 57, qui, pour l'essentiel, traduit en mesures de précaution les interdictions énoncées aux Articles 51 et 52) se présentent sous la forme de règles mixtes, dans lesquelles des éléments de droit coutumier et des éléments 'nouveaux' se trouvent non pas juxtaposés, mais mélangés. C'est le démêlement de ces deux éléments qui est plein de difficultés et qui donnera inévitablement lieu à des controverses.

On pourrait être tenté de ressentir une certaine déception en constatant que la belle limpidité du principe posé par la clause nucléaire -dans sa version originale: celle des déclarations interprétatives américaines et britanniques de 1977- s'évanouit quand on entreprend d'appliquer au texte du Protocole la 'grille' qu'elle prescrit. Tout le profit de l'éclaircissement que l'on doit à la clause ne risque-t-il pas d'être, sinon annulé, mais fortement amoindri par la difficulté de dégager les règles applicables à l'emploi des armes nucléaires? Non. Car si grande que soit cette difficulté,

---

30 *Infra* 4.3.

elle ne saurait faire que la teneur des dispositions des Articles 51 et 52 puisse être réduite aux principes que, dès avant le Protocole, les Etats avaient reconnus applicables à l'emploi des armes nucléaires. Il est vrai que pour déterminer en quoi ces dispositions traduisent le droit coutumier et en quoi elles innovent, elles ont besoin d'être interprétées, et cette interprétation comporte toujours forcément une part de subjectivité. Mais il est vrai aussi que ces règles, par le seul fait qu'elles concrétisent le principe de l'immunité de la population civile et des biens civils et son double corollaire, le principe de discrimination et le principe de proportionnalité, constituent une barrière qui force les gouvernenments à soumettre leur choix d'armements, leur stratégie, les concepts et les plans d'emploi des armes nucléaires au test de légalité.

4.   LES CAUSES, OU PRETENDUES CAUSES, D'EXCLUSION DE L'ILLICEITE DE L'EMPLOI D'ARMES NUCLEAIRES

Le problème des circonstances, ou prétendues circonstances, exclusives de l'illicéité[31] ne se pose pas au sujet des armes nucléaires d'une façon différente qu'au sujet des armes classiques. Il faut néanmoins l'aborder, ne fût-ce que très sommairement, dans une étude relative au statut des armes nucléaires selon le droit de la guerre, car c'est à propos de ces armes -plus exactement, à propos de certaines doctrines visant l'emploi des armes nucléaires dites stratégiques- que l'existence de ces prétendues 'causes justificatives' a été défendue avec le plus de ténacité. Nous passerons brièvement en revue ces prétendues circonstances exclusives de l'illicéité: la légitime défense; l'état de nécessité; les représailles.

4.1   La légitime défense

L'argument de la légitme défense comme cause de 'justification' est étroitement liée à la thèse du primat du *jus ad bellum* sur le *jus in bello*, laquelle à son tour a pour corollaire la thèse de la discrimination, au regard du *jus in bello*, de l'Etat agresseur, c'est-à-dire la négation du principe de l'egalité des belligérants devant le droit de la guerre. Or ce

---

31 La Commmission du droit international a, dans son Projet d'articles sur la responsabilité des Etats, écarté les termes de 'faits justificatifs' ou de 'causes de justification', parce qu'elle estimait que ces mots comportent une connotation morale, qui ne correspond pas à la nature des *circonstances excluant l'illicéité* telle qu'elle a été caractérisée par la Commission. Rapport de la CDI sur les travaux de sa 31e session, II Annuaire de la CDI 2, 118 (1979).

principe est, au point de vue juridique, moral et pratique, à la base même, *la* base même, du droit de la guerre.

Le 'droit naturel de légitime défense, individuelle ou collective', contre une agression armée, confirmé par l'Article 51 de la Charte des Nations Unies, exclut l'illicéité du recours à la force armée par l'Etat victime de l'agression, mais rien de plus. Les moyens par lesquels ce droit est exercé sont soumis aux règles du droit de la guerre de la même façon que ceux par lesquels l'agresseur commet son agression. La sanction de la violation du *jus ad bellum* ne relève pas et ne peut relever du *jus in bello*. Comme le rappelle l'Instruction HDv 100/600 de la Bundeswehr, de 1975 (paragraphe 403): 'L'application du droit international de la guerre est indépendante de la question de savoir si la guerre a été déclenchée par une violation du droit international, par exemple de l'interdiction de la guerre d'agression.[32]

4.2   L'état de nécessité

La nécessité dont il est question ici n'est pas la notion de 'nécessité militaire' qui figure dans le texte de certaines règles du droit de la guerre conventionnel, où elle désigne, sous des noms variés -tels que 'nécessité', 'nécessité absolue', 'impérieuse nécessité', etc.- une circonstance exceptionnelle qui autorise un belligérant se trouvant dans cette situation à ne pas observer la règle qui contient la clause expresse de nécessité. Cette exception est limitée aux règles où elle se trouve énoncée; les manuels militaires ou instructions sur le droit de la guerre, la jurisprudence des tribunaux militaires et la doctrine sont unanimes sur ce point. Par définition, elle est inapplicable à une stratégie. Toute différente est la notion d'état de nécessité dans le droit international coutumier. Dans son rapport de 1980, la Commission du droit international a défini l'expression 'état de nécessité' comme désignant 'la situation où se trouve un Etat n'ayant absolument pas d'autres moyens de sauvegarder un intérêt essentiel menacé par un péril grave et imminent que celui d'adopter un comportement non conforme à ce qui est requis de lui par une obligation internationale envers un autre Etat'.[33]

---

32 *Cf.*, ZDv 15/10, loc. cit. n. 17, § 14, et (US) Air Force Pamphlet 110-131 (1976), loc. cit. n. 19):
   'The Law of armed conflict applies equally to all parties to an armed conflict, whether or not the international community regards any participant as the "aggressor" or "victim". Its application is not conditioned by the causes of the conflict. This principle is vitally necessary.'
33 II Annuaire de la CDI, 2, 33, § 1 (1980).

L'exclusion de l'état de nécessité dans le droit de la guerre, disent certains -ou plutôt disaient certains, avant le changement radical intervenu dans les rapports entre l'Ouest et l'Est-, est liée et limitée aux conditions matérielles et politiques de la guerre classique et aux potentialités des armes classiques. Le problème, affirme-t-on, ou affirmait-on, se pose dans des termes radicalement différents s'agissant des conditions et de l'enjeu d'un conflit où s'affronteraient l'Occident et l'empire communiste. Les armes nucléaires sont des armes extrêmes, réservées à des situations extrêmes. Il s'agit, a-t-on écrit, d'armes *in extremis*, voulant dire par là que c'est dans la perspective de situations extrêmes, et non pas simplement de situations de nécessité, que le problème de la justification des attaques nucléaires non conformes aux règles coutumières du droit de la guerre -de la guerre classique- doit être envisagé et résolu.

Or, malgré l'énorme différence qui existe au point de vue quantitatif et qualitatif entre les armes nucléaires et les armes classiques, et entre la nature, les effets, et les conséquences des effets, d'une guerre nucléaire et ceux d'une guerre classique, on ne voit pas en quoi l'introduction des armes atomiques aurait modifié les éléments du problème juridique de l'état de nécessité. Les situations de nécessité extrême, c'est-à-dire de péril non seulement de la défaite, mais de subjugation (*debellatio*) ont toujours fait partie intégrante du phénomène et de la notion de guerre. Et tout comme elle est un élément logique de la notion de guerre, la défaite est aussi un élément logique, présupposé, du droit de la guerre. Comme l'a rappelé la Commission du droit international dans le rapport mentionné, les règles conventionnelles du droit de la guerre ont été spécialement conçus pour des 'situations anormales de péril', et 'l'exclusion de la possibilité d'invoquer l'état de nécessité ressort alors implicitement, mais clairement de l'objet et du but de la règle'. Cette remarque s'applique aussi, bien entendu, aux normes coutumières du droit de la guerre. Celui-ci, de même qu'il présuppose un agresseur et un agressé, de même il implique qu'à l'issue du conflit, il y aura un vainqueur et un vaincu. Il n'a pas et ne peut avoir pour fonction de remédier aux déficiences ou défaillances du *jus ad bellum* et d'empêcher la victoire de l'agresseur.

4.3   Les représailles nucléaires

Les interdictions nouvelles de représailles, en premier lieu celles visant la population civile ou des personnes civiles (Article 51(6)) et les biens de caractère civil (Article 52(1)), sont les innovations les plus controversables, et les plus controversées, introduites par la CDDH. Les gouvernements américain et britannique, en déposant, lors de la signature du Protocole, les *understandings* contenant la clause nucléaire, étaient persuadés que celle-ci s'appliquait aux interdictions nouvelles de représailles,[34] et c'est aussi l'opinion des gouvernements belge, hollandais, espagnol et canadien, relativement à la portée de la clause nucléaire de leurs déclarations interprétatives. C'est là une erreur, que le gouvernement italien et allemand se sont gardés de commettre. Leurs déclarations contiennent, à côté de la clause nucléaire que nous avons citée, le paragraphe suivant, qui exclut l'application des interdictions nouvelles non seulement en ce qui concerne les représailles exécutées avec des armes nucléaires, mais aussi celles effectuées avec des armes classiques, interdictions que tous les autres Etats parties au Protocole ont acceptées sans restriction:

> '*Italy [The Federal Republic of Germany] will react to serious and systematic violations by an enemy of the obligations imposed by Additional Protocol I and in particular of its Articles 51 and 52 with all means admissible under international law in order to prevent any further violation.*'

Bien que cette déclaration évite d'employer le mot 'représailles', il s'agit sans équivoque d'une réserve aux interdictions nouvelles de représailles, et 'en particulier' à celles formulées aux Articles 51 et 52.

L'opinion selon laquelle la clause nucléaire s'applique aux interdictions de représailles est erronée pour deux raisons. La première, c'est que la clause, ainsi comprise, n'est pas conforme au consensus nucléaire; la seconde raison, c'est la disparité radicale entre les règles nouvelles du Protocole relatives aux attaques, interdictions effectivement couvertes par la clause, et les interdictions nouvelles de représailles.

La clause nucléaire tire sa validité de sa conformité au consensus nucléaire. Or, celui-ci est limité à l'affirmation de l'application des (seules) règles coutumières, réaffirmées par le Protocole, aux *attaques* effectuées avec des armes nucléaires. Quant au problème des représailles nucléaires,

---

34 Dans son rapport au secrétaire d'Etat, le chef de la délégation américaine, par ailleurs très critique à l'égard des interdictions nouvelles de représailles, exprimait l'avis que la clause nucléaire des *understandings* suffisait pour écarter l'application de ces interdictions à l'emploi des armes nucléaires. 72 AJIL 400 (1978). Mais voir l'opinion contraire de H.H. Almond, du National War College:
'... all prohibitions on reprisals in the 1977 protocols [*sic*] must be nullified by reservations.'
ASIL, Proc. 74th Annual Meeting, 201 (1980). *Cf.*, dans le même sens, en ce qui concerne le Protocole I: W.A. Solf, dans M. Bothe, K.J. Partsch, W.A. Solf, réds., *New Rules for Victims of Armed Conflicts*. Commentary on the Two 1977 Protocols Additional to the Geneva Conventions of 1949, 315 (1982).

il n'y a pas de consensus, mais confusion. Dans les débats à la CDDH sur cette question, on a mélangé, sans égard à leur profonde différence, les représailles à l'encontre des personnes et des biens protégés par les Conventions de Genève, dont l'interdiction n'est pas subordonnée au principe de réciprocité, et les représailles ressortissant au droit coutumier.

La fausseté de l'opinion des gouvernements belge, hollandais, espagnol et canadien sur le portée de la clause nucléaire se révèle si on analyse la clause au point de vue logique et matériel. Le poids respectif des règles nouvelles par rapport aux règles réaffirmées est très différent dans le cas des règles applicables aux attaques et dans celui des interdictions de représailles. Contrairement aux attaques interdites par les règles réaffirmées, applicables indifféremment aux attaques par armes classiques ou par armes nucléaires, les représailles dirigées contre la population civile, des personnes civiles ou des biens civils se trouvant sous le contrôle de l'ennemi sont permises, ou, si l'on préfère, non interdites, par le droit coutumier. La portée des incidences militaires directes et des implications stratégiques des règles nouvelles relatives à la protection de la population civile et des biens civils contre les attaques n'est pas comparable à l'importance stratégique que revêtent les interdictions de représailles énoncées aux Articles 51 et 52, ou qu'elles revêtiraient si elles étaient observées.

L'erreur commise par les gouvernements belge, néerlandais, espagnol et canadien, erreur qui leur a fait dire -implicitement- quelque chose qui est clairement contraire à leur intention, est, sur le plan formel, irréparable. Quant au fond, sa portée est réduite. Car les interdictions nouvelles de représailles doivent être comprises comme étant subordonnées au principe fondamental de réciprocité.[35] S'agissant d'un principe du droit coutumier, la confirmation expresse de son application aux interdictions nouvelles de représailles est, au point de vue théorique, superflue. Sous l'angle pratique, le rappel, sous la forme d'une déclaration interprétative, aurait été plus qu'opportune. L'avantage d'une telle déclaration consiste dans le fait qu'elle est plus restrictive que les contre-mesures, la 'réaction' dont parle la réserve italienne, ou celles qui seraient prévues dans toute autre formule qui chercherait à résumer les conditions et les limites des

---

35 Cette question a été traitée par l'auteur dans 'Le statut des armes nucléaires en droit international', 26 German Yearbook of International Law 161-195 (1983) et *Die Respressalienverbote des I. Zusatzprotokolls zu den Genfer Abkommen vom 12. August 1949 und das Reziprozitätsprinzip (Les interdictions de représailles du Protocole additionnel I aux Conventions de Genève du 12 août 1949 et le principe de réciprocité)*, 28 Neue Zeitschrift für Wehrrecht 177-193 (1986).

représailles et qui s'imposent avec une rigueur particulière quand il s'agit d'actes de violence frappant la population civile. Plus restrictive, principalement, en ce que la riposte, outre qu'elle serait soumise aux mêmes conditions et limites et aurait la même finalité que les représailles, serait strictement *in kind*: seules des attaques graves contre la population civile pourraient justifier le recours à des actions nucléaires contre la population civile ennemie. Que l'on range cette réaction exceptionnelle et limitée sous le titre de représailles ou sous celui de réciprocité, il est évident qu'elle ne peut jamais s'appliquer à une *stratégie*, arrêtée en temps de paix et que l'Etat en question est décidé et préparé à mettre en oeuvre sans aucun égard au comportement réel de l'ennemi.

5.   CONCLUSION

Nous sommes partis de la constatation que l'arme nucléaire n'est pas 'une arme comme les autres', et que ce qui la distingue des armes classiques, dont l'emploi fait l'objet des règles du droit de la guerre, ce n'est pas simplement une différence de degré de la puissance destructrice, mais une différence de nature. Et cependant, nous avons vu que le droit international positif ne tient pas compte de cette différence, mais qu'il soumet l'emploi des armes nucléaires aux mêmes règles que l'emploi des armes classiques, règles qui ont été réaffirmées par le Protocole additionnel I aux Conventions de Genève. Ces règles ayant le caractère de normes du droit coutumier, le fait que les trois puissances nucléaires occidentales aient refusé, jusqu'à présent, de devenir parties au Protocole I ne les soustrait pas à la force obligatoire de ces règles, en ce qui concerne l'emploi des armes classiques aussi bien que des armes nucléaires. Le recours en premier à des armes nucléaires n'est pas, en soi, interdit par le droit international général. La riposte nucléaire à un premier emploi ne constitue donc pas un acte de représailles, mais obéit aux mêmes limites que l'emploi en premier. Quant aux représailles nucléaires, elles sont soumises aux mêmes conditions, interprétées restrictivement, que les représailles exécutées par des armes classiques.

En conclusion, le droit international en vigueur, loin de conférer à l'emploi des armes nucléaires un statut privilégié, assujettit cet emploi à des règles qui lui tracent des limites étroites, limites qui se situent très au-dessous des potentialités de ces armes.

THE CHANGING ROLE OF INTERNATIONAL LAW IN THE NUCLEAR AGE: FROM FREEDOM OF THE HIGH SEAS TO NUCLEAR-FREE ZONES

Hisakazu Fujita

1.   Introduction

2.   Nuclear deployment in ambiguous situations between peace and war

3.   Efforts for 'peaceful enclosure' of the seas

4.   Perfect or imperfect denuclearization of nuclear-free zones in the Pacific Ocean region

5.   Conclusion

1.   INTRODUCTION

In his lecture to the Hague Academy, Professor Kalshoven gave the following warning: 'it is beyond doubt that the present level of armaments does not only threaten world peace -as weapons have always done- but the survival of mankind as well'.[1]

Nuclear weapons are certainly to be numbered among such armaments; indeed they are Janus-faced, one face showing a formidable instrument threatening the human race itself, while the other offers, in the eyes of many at least, an ultimate means of defence against aggression - two views that contradict each other. The former is supported principally by peace movements and anti-nuclear trends in the public opinion, and the latter by nuclear strategists. How should we, scholars of international law, treat this problem?

First of all, many authorities in this field have expressed doubt as to whether contemporary international law possesses principles or rules sufficient to the regulation of nuclear weapons; and on this point we encounter certain difficulties. One of these concerns the multi-

---

1   F. Kalshoven, *Arms, Armament and International Law*, 191 Recueil des Cours 203 (1985 II).

dimensionality of the military utilization of nuclear weapons, presenting such diverse problems of regulation as those concerning testing, production, deposit, deployment, and use of such weapons as part of nuclear weapons systems. Another difficulty concerns international law itself.

The system of international law, especially during the period following the promulgation of the UN Charter in 1945, has lost all clear distinction between international law applying to peace time and that applicable during periods of war. In a sense, contemporary international law governs only in peace time, because, in international relations, war, or the use or threat of use of force, has now been prohibited (Article 2(4) of the UN Charter). As a consequence, it does not give really serious consideration to the regulation of nuclear weapons under conditions whose development it has outlawed, namely, those of war.

On the other hand, international law concerning peace time may without any internal contradiction regulate the testing, production, deposit, etc., of nuclear weapons, these matters belonging to the problem of disarmament, which also includes the concept of arms control. The division between the problem of use of nuclear weapons in war and that of nuclear disarmament therefore reflects a characteristic and fundamental trend in contemporary international law.

In reality, international humanitarian law, or the law of war conceived in traditional terms, may only regulate the use of nuclear weapons in armed conflicts. However, international lawyers are far from unanimous in their opinions relating to the legality or illegality of the use of nuclear weapons; and, while international law concerning disarmament may regulate the production, possession, etc. of nuclear weapons, this new field of international law has not so far succeeded in bringing about true nuclear disarmament. In fact, when judged in the light of the goal of the total regulation of the global nuclear weapons system, the results so far gained in the dichotomous situation that the present author has outlined above, must be judged quite insufficient.

This problem is both subtle and very complicated. While, with the exception of cases of forcible measures authorized by the United Nations, contemporary international law prohibits all use of force, even condemning any State initiating its use as *prima facie* aggressor, it permits certain exceptional uses of force in the self-defence of individual States. Therefore, the justification for stockpiling nuclear weapons in the arsenals of individual States, and their deployment in military basis and/or in the seas, is derived from their usefulness in self-defence. All nuclear strategies such as nuclear deterrence and even first stike (or use) of nuclear weapons ultimately rest on the legal concept of self-defence.

This, however, raises an important problem: is the premise of the concept of self-defence the condition of peace, or that of war? And what of cases of feigned self-defence? Is the concept of self-defence to be allowed to afford legality to all aspects of nuclear armament, including not only the use of nuclear weapons but also their production, possession, and deployment? Why, in particular, should their stockpiling and deployment be permitted not only within the territorial boundaries of both nuclear weapon-possessing States and non-possessing States, but also in the sea (in particular the high seas)?

Indeed, contemporary international law has tried, however inadequately, to regulate some of these aspects of nuclear armament; and this study will consider some of the efforts that have been made to regulate nuclear weapons in the field of the law of the sea and nuclear-free zones.

2. NUCLEAR DEPLOYMENT IN AMBIGUOUS SITUATIONS BETWEEN PEACE AND WAR

Most international lawyers consider that States are not prohibited from testing, producing, and stockpiling nuclear weapons, with the exception of the restrictions stipulated in certain disarmament treaties such as the Partial Test Ban Treaty of 1963. They have argued that States may lawfully deploy nuclear weapons in self-defence. And further, even those lawyers who consider the military use of nuclear weapons illegal, do acknowledge the legality of their use in measures of reprisal. And strategists, on the other hand, utilise the premise of the legality of self-defence in such strategies as nuclear deterrence, and the first strike doctrine.

It is therefore important to give more precise consideration to this question of the use of nuclear arms in self-defence situations. When such use is made, is the condition created by their use still that of peace, or does it thereby become one of war? Or should it be regarded as somewhere between the two? While the concept of self-defence was certainly a peace time one until World War I, both the appearance on the international scene of nuclear weapons and the establishment of the United Nations have since rendered the situation ambiguous.

We shall not embark upon a consideration of either the controversial question of whether Article 51 of the UN Charter restricting self-defence to the condition, 'if an armed attack occurs', is constitutive of the right of self-defence, or the question of whether it has left the customary right of so-called anticipatory self-defence unimpaired.[2] We can, however, observe that, whatever the contemporary interpretation of self-defence may be, the existence of nuclear weapons and their world-wide deployment have paralyzed the peace-time situation, while nuclear strategies have in turn brought about changes in the situation originally established concerning self-defence.

It has been proposed that a State wishing to defend itself against a nuclear (ballistic missile) attack must initiate protective measures before the attack has been launched, a proposition that has been defended not only by strategists but also by a number of international lawyers. It presupposes that a nuclear attack involving ICBMs, or other strategic nuclear weapons, could occur at the very inception of an armed attack. Once an armed attack has occurred, a nuclear attack assumes the character of forcible reprisals in war time rather than that of anticipatory self-defence. While civilian analysists generally believe that neither Superpower would use its strategic nuclear arsenal at the inception of an armed conflict, because of the risk of nuclear retaliation, military strategists instinctively favour the immediate use of nuclear weapons, as soon as an armed conflict seems inescapable.[3] As early as 1946, the United States was already contending that 'an "armed attack" is now something entirely different from what it was prior to the discovery of atomic weapons'; and that it includes 'not simply the actual dropping of an atomic bomb, but also certain stages in themselves preliminary to such action'.[4] And the subsequent development of nuclear technology has further broadened this interpretation: it has promoted the application of the doctrine of anticipatory self-defence to conflicts involving the use of nuclear weapons.

What is important here is not the question of the applicability of this doctrine of anticipatory nuclear self-defence, but the preparation for a nuclear attack, that is, the stockpiling of nuclear armaments, and the

---

2   In the *Case concerning Military and Paramilitary Acitvities in and against Nicaragua* the ICJ
    referred to pre-existing customary self-defence:
    '... [t]his reference to customary law is contained in the actual text of Article 51 ....
    Moreover, a definition of the "armed attack" which, if found to exist, authorizes the exercise
    of the "inherent right" of self-defence, is not provided in the Charter, and is not part of treaty
    law. It cannot therefore be held that Article 51 is a provision which "subsumes and
    supervenes" customary international law.'
    ICJ Reports 1986, § 176, at 94.
3   I. Pogany, ed., Nuclear Weapons and International Law 65 (1987).
4   *International Control of Atomic Energy: Growth of a Policy*, US Department of State,
    Publication No. 2702, 164 (1946). Repr. in P. Jessup, A Modern Law of Nations 166-167
    (1952). This interpretation broadly permits nuclear self-defence in the context of a possible
    nuclear attack in peace-time.

deployment of nuclear weapons systems backed up by nuclear strategies, in particular by the Superpowers. Some manner of nuclear deployment -for example, the presence and navigation of nuclear submarines equipped with submarine-launched ballistic missiles (SLBMs) or sea-launched cruise missiles (SLCMs) in the high seas as well as in the territorial seas of a coastal State- may easily offer nuclear attack against not only a potential enemy, but against almost any country or people in the world. In this sense, there may be no country, no section of mankind itself, to the safety of which a world-wide nuclear deployment does not constitute some sort of threat, and in international relations may eventually provoke exactly the sort of 'threat of force' prohibited in Article 2(4) of the UN Charter.

Humanitarian law does not regulate ambiguous situations of this sort, arising from nuclear deployment or threat; and as long as complete nuclear disarmament remains unachieved in the world, the development of regional (oceanic) nuclear regulation and of nuclear-free zones are indispensable for the security of mankind.

3.   EFFORTS FOR 'PEACEFUL ENCLOSURE' OF THE SEAS

More than two thirds of the earth's surface is covered by sea, and over two thirds of the global population live within 300 kilometers of a sea coast. While land territories are in general under the sovereignty of territorial States, and their use is the internal affair of each State, a large part of the seas, that is, the high seas, are not under the territorial control of any State. The sea, however, is not therefore an area free from regulation under international law. This law has a number of principles and rules and, since the era of Grotius, the most important among these has been what is known as the 'freedom of the seas'.

This freedom of the seas has been advantageously exploited by the sea powers. They have utilized the seas for fishing and trading purposes in peace time and for their military activities in war time. According to O'Connell, until the prohibition by the UN Charter of the use of force, the high seas were the arena of naval conflict, wherein belligerents gained rights not only with respect to each other but also with respect to neutrals.[5]

Since World War II, the United States has controlled the oceans through its Pax Americana and since the nineteen-sixties the Pax Russo-

---

5   *Cf.*, D.P. O'Connell, The Influence of Law on Sea Power 114 (1975).

Americana has continued under circumstances of peaceful co-existence and detente. Since the Truman Proclamation in 1945 declaring jurisdiction and control over the natural resources of the contiguous continental shelf of the United States, its definition of territory has been taken as a model by other States, resulting in the four Geneva Conventions on the Law of the Sea in 1958. These, however, made no direct reference to military uses of the seas.

Of these four Conventions, those that we are here concerned with are the Convention on the Territorial Sea and the Contiguous Zone, and the Convention on the High Seas. The former confirms, *inter alia*, and regulates what is more or less a right of innocent passage of foreign ships through the territorial seas of coastal States as well as the non-suspendible right of passage through straits used in international navigation (Articles 14-23).

The latter Convention proclaims the freedom of the seas in somewhat absolute, though not limitative, terms, that is, by listing four specific freedoms (of navigation, of fishing, of laying submarine cables and pipelines, and of overflight) and adding that these 'and others which are recognized by the general principles of international law' must be exercised by all States with reasonable regard to the interests of other States in the exercise of the freedom of the high seas (Article 2). These 'others' may, for example, include the execution of military manoeuvres and of nuclear weapon tests, as well as the deployment and emplacement of nuclear armaments.

The Seabed Treaty of 1971, however, prohibits emplanting or emplacing on the seabed, on the ocean floor, and in the subsoil thereof, beyond the outer limit of a seabed zone (that is, twelve-mile outer limit of the zone referred to in part II of the Convention on the Territorial Sea, and the Contiguous Zone) any nuclear weapons or any other types of weapon of mass destruction (Article 1).[6]

The Geneva Conventions of 1958 presuppose principally peacetime application under the UN system,[7] and are not so importantly affected by

---

6 See detailed analysis of this Treaty by T. Treves, *Military Installations, Structures and Devices on the Seabed*, 74 AJIL 808-890 (1980).

7 In O'Connells words:
   '... [t]he pressures of the international community to confine disputes to the territories with which they are connected, and hence to insulate the high seas from belligerent operations, are evident in the cases of limited war from the Spanish Civil War to Vietnam.'
   O'Connell, loc. cit. n. 5, at 115, 122. He also posed the question of whether the confining of hostilities to the territorial sea is a matter of exigency or whether it reflects *per medium* of State practice a modern rule of international law derived from the prohibition of the use of

naval strategy, including nuclear strategy, with the exception of the controversial concept of innocent passage.[8]

The Third UN Conference on the Law of the Sea (UNCLOS III) of 1974-1982 was held during an epoch in which the structure of the international community underwent considerable change. Following their struggle for decolonization and independence a number of new States appeared in the international community. Since 1960, 'The Year of Africa', these developing countries have begun to occupy a majority position in the UN membership as well as at diplomatic conferences.

This epoch was, moreover, marked by an acceleration in the nuclear arms race between the United States and the Soviet Union, consequent upon successive technological developments. This arms race has particularly developed concerning the oceans, because nuclear-powered submarines equipped with SLBMs or SLCMs were considered by nuclear strategists as least vulnerable in the eventuality of nuclear attack by an adversary.

UNCLOS III has, however, ignored, military and naval issues. The UN Convention on the Law of the Sea (LOSC) of 1982, which resulted from UNCLOS III, does not include any provision treating military issues or nuclear disarmament. Its silence concerning this area was in fact intentional on the part of the participating States, in particular the naval powers concerned in UNCLOS III. The Convention stresses in its Preamble the importance of contributing to 'the maintenance of peace ... for all peoples of the world', and of promoting the 'peaceful uses of the seas and oceans'. And it made specific provisions regulating the use of warships, including

---

force in the UN Charter; a rule that the high seas are free from belligerency. *Ibid.*

8 At the Geneva Conference in 1958 neither the Western naval powers nor the Soviet Union were successful in gaining acceptance of their own arguments on the right of innocent passage for warships. As a consequence, the text of the Geneva Convention was left open to interpretation. On the one hand, the Western naval powers could point to the fact that the Convention's articles on innocent passage referred to 'ships', meaning 'all ships', and that the rump provision left after the excision of the Article on warships allowed for the regulation of their passage by the coastal State; on the other hand, the Soviet Union could point out that there was no text expressly allowing for the pasage of warships, and that the power to regulate necessarily includes the power to exclude. *Ibid.*, at 140.
At the time of ratification of the Convention, the Soviet Union made a reservation, according to which the Soviet Government considered that a coastal State has the right to establish an authorization procedure for the passage of foreign warships through its territorial waters. W.E. Butler, The Law of Soviet Territorial Waters 140 (1967). Also, W.E. Butler, *The Legal Regime of Russian Territorial Waters*, 62 AJIL 51-77 (1968). The Soviet legislation of 1960 specifically provided for such authorization. See, Butler, loc. cit., at 111-125, 126-132. Some States Parties to this Convention insist that the passage of warships including submarines requires either notification or prior consent.

nuclear ones, in territorial waters and international straits, besides other
povisions that included what has come to be known as the 'peaceful
purposes' clauses.

As to the regulation of the use of nuclear weapons in the seas, the
provisions for the regime of innocent passage through territorial seas up to
a breadth of twelve miles from the shore, and for that of transit passage
through straits used in international navigation, must be noted. The
meaning of innocent passage 'so long as it is not prejudicial to the peace,
good order, or security of the coastal State' is somewhat clarified by
Article 19, which lists twelve non-innocent activities, many of which are
military or quasi-military. This list does not, however, include certain
kinds of ships, such as nuclear-powered ones.[9] Ships and aircraft of any
kind whatsoever may exercise this new right of transit passage solely for
the purpose of continuous and expeditious transit (Article 38).

After the adoption at Montego Bay of the new LOSC, the Soviet Union
changed its previous interpretation of the term 'innocent passage'. And, in
1989, the United States and the Soviet Union issued a joint statement on
uniform interpretation of the term 'innocent passage'. According to this
interpretation: 'all ships, including warships, regardless of cargo,
armament or means of propulsion, enjoy the right of innocent passage
through territorial sea in accordance with international law, for which
neither prior notification nor authorization is required' and 'Article 19 of
the Convention of 1982 sets out in paragraph 2 an exhaustive list of
activities that would render passage not innocent. A ship passing through
the territorial sea that does not engage in any of those activities is in
innocent passage'.[10]

---

9   The list is as follows: a) any threat or use of force against the sovereignty, territorial integrity
    or political independence of the coastal State, or in any manner in violation of the principles of
    international law embodied in the Charter of the United Nations; b) any exercise or practice
    with weapons of any kind; c) any act aimed at collecting information to the prejudice of the
    defence of security of the coastal State; d) any act of propaganda aimed at affecting the
    defence or security of the coastal State; e) the launching, landing or taking on board of any
    aircraft; f) the launching, landing or taking on board of any military device; g) the loading or
    unloading of any commodity, currency or person contrary to the customs, fiscal, immigration
    or sanitary laws and regulations of the coastal State; h) any act of wilful and serious pollution
    contrary to this Convention; i) any fishing activities; j) the carrying out of research or survey
    activities; k) any act aimed at interfering with any systems of communication or any other
    facilities or installations of the coastal State; l) any other activity not having a direct bearing on
    passage.
10 The Decree of the Soviet Council of Ministers promulgated a set of rules for the navigation of
    foreign warships in Soviet territorial seas, which contained a number of elements of this
    Convention and did not require prior authorization for innocent passage by warships. XXIV

The regime of innocent passage and of transit passage established in the new LOSC do not, therefore, provide full and sufficient regulation of activities of nuclear warships or submarines.

While these texts concern only the territorial sea of States and limited international straits, the peaceful purposes clauses apply principally to the oceans as a whole, or the high seas. Nuclear deployment in the seas as part of the nuclear strategies of the Superpowers presupposes the freedom of the seas as it was broadly interpreted up to World War II. Is any military use (of nuclear warships) on the basis of this freedom restricted by the provisions of the Convention?

The Convention of 1982 contains a number of provisions with peaceful purposes clauses.[11] The inclusion of such clauses in the Convention here occurs for the first time in the history of the law of the sea, although some antecedents to this inclusion may be seen in the Antarctic Treaty, the Outer Space and Moon Treaties, and the Seabed Treaty.

The most fundamental and general provision is Article 301 entitled 'Peaceful uses of the seas', which reads:

'In exercising their rights and performing their duties under this Convention, States Parties shall refrain from any threat or use of force against the territorial integrity or political independence of any State, or in any other manner inconsistent with the principles of international law embodied in the Charter of the United Nations.'[12]

Although this provision does not make any direct mention of the peaceful purposes clause, it does, however, reflect its original and general meaning, being undoubtedly derived from the UN Charter formula laid down in Article 2(4). This means that under this Convention the rights and duties of the States Parties must be applied or exercised in conformity with

---

ILM 1715-1722 (1985). On 23 September 1989 the US-Soviet joint statement was issued with attached uniform interpretation of rules of international law governing innocent passage. XXVIII ILM 1444-1447 (1985). *Cf.*, L. Juda, *Innocent Passage by Warships in the Territorial Seas of the Soviet Union: Changing Doctrine*, 21 ODILA 111-116 (1990).

11 They are the Preamble, Articles 58(2), 88, 141, 240(a), 242(1), 246(3) and 301.

12 This provision originated in an informal proposal made by Costa Rica, Ecuador, El Salvador, Pakistan, Peru, the Philippines, Portugal, Senegal, Somalia, and Uruguay. Doc. GP/1 of 21 March 1980. Repr. in R. Platzoder, ed., 12 Third United Nations Conference on the Law of the Sea: Documents 297 (1987). The sponsors initially wanted the proposal added to Article 88. See, Doc. A/CONF.62/L.53/Add. 1, 1 April 1980. Supplementary Report of the President on the Work of the Informal Plenary Meeting of the Conference on the Law of the Sea. Also B.H. Oxman, *The Third United Nations Conference on the Law of the Sea: The Ninth Session (1980)*, 75 AJIL 211, 227-238 (1981).

the fundamental principle of the prohibition of the threat or use of force in international relations; and it is here, therefore, that the difficulties of interpretation of this fundamental principle still lie. This Article 301 is not to be dismissed as making no new contribution.[13]

Other provisions having peaceful purposes clauses presuppose the content of this Article 301, which means that the interpretation of provisos concerning peaceful purposes must be strengthened or supplemented by the application of the fundamental principle of the prohibition of the threat or use of force.

While Article 87 reconfirms that the high seas are open to all States, and specifies five freedoms, namely: navigation, overflight, the laying of submarine cables and pipelines, the construction of artificial islands and other installations, and fishing and scientific research, Article 88 briefly lays down that 'the high seas shall be reserved for peaceful purposes'. Does this latter Article challenge traditional freedoms of the high seas, including their military utilization, as reconfirmed in the former Article?

It is well known that the concept of 'peaceful purposes' was originally introduced by Ambassador Pardo of Malta, and subsequently crystallized in the Declaration of Principles governing the Seabed of 1970 (GA Res. 2749(XXV)). And naturally, in the debates of UNCLOS III, the meaning of the peaceful purposes clause was discussed. Again, Pardo's concept led to a dichotomy of views, one side favouring a 'non-aggressive' interpretation, and the other a wholly 'non-military' one.

Of these two interpretations, the former deposes that use for peaceful purposes means use that is consistent with the law of the UN Charter proscribing threat or use of force; and therefore that, while military activities based on the right of self-defence are to be regarded as peaceful, aggressive activities alone are to be regarded as not peaceful. This argument was advanced by the United States and other Western States.[14]

The latter interpretation, being urged by Ecuador, argues that 'peaceful purposes' require complete demilitarization, and that all military uses whatsoever are to be assumed to be non-peaceful. This follows the precedent of the Antarctic Treaty, Article 1 of which prohibits any

---

13 *Cf.*, B.A. Boczek, *Peaceful Purposes Provisions of the United Nations Convention on the Law of the Sea*, 20 ODILA 370 (1989).

14 The United States delegate stated:
'The term "peaceful purposes" did not, of course preclude military activity generally ... the conduct of military activities for peaceful purposes was in full accord with the Charter of the United Nations and with the principles of international law. Any specific limitation on military activities would require the negotiation of a detailed arms control agreement.'
Repr. in 5 Off. Rec. UNCLOS III 62 (1976).

activities of a military nature, reserving Antarctica for 'peaceful purposes'.[15]

It can also be observed that, with the exception of Ecuador, even Third World delegates at UNCLOS III interpreted the term 'peaceful purposes' as not inevitably banning all military activity from the oceans.[16]

Further, it must be noted that the Soviet Union, changing its previous attitude to this concept, described this problem as being beyond the scope of the work facing UNCLOS III.[17]

Some attempts were made to agree upon the fundamental elements of this vague concept, such as establishing zones of peace and nuclear-free zones, and banning military exercises on the high seas, and especially in the EEZ of foreign countries.[18] This debate could not, however, clarify the term 'peaceful purpose'; and the concept remains vague and ambiguous.

It is true that the peaceful purposes clauses of the Convention impose apparently far-reaching limitations upon military activities, especially on and in the high seas. But from the above debate and different arguments on this issue, we can see that at least some military activities on the high seas seem to be regarded by many as a routine use of the sea, and, as such, not to be prohibited. And among these may be included some that are listed as non-innocent activities for coastal States in Article 19.[19]

It is certainly difficult to regard the peaceful purposes clauses as somehow transcending the obligation of States, as stipulated in Article 301 of the Convention, to refrain, in accordance with the UN Charter, from the threat or use of force. So, do these clauses have no significance, or else some legal effect other than that of Article 301? The following argument, proposed by Boczek, characterising them as *soft law* may be helpful:

'[I]n recent years the concept of soft law has emerged in international legal docrine, referring, in general, to intentionally vague provisions adopted in order to overcome deadlock in international negotiations, but which in

---

15 The Ecuadorian delegate said that 'the use of the ocean space for exclusively peaceful purposes must mean complete demilitarization, the exclusion from it of all military activities'. Repr. in 5 Off. Rec. UNCLOS III 56 (1976).

16 For example, the Philippines, 5 Off. Rec. UNCLOS III, 65 (1976); Tunesia, *ibid.*, at 67.

17 5 Off. Rec. UNCLOS III, 59 (1976). *Cf.*, P. Birnie, *Law of the Sea and Nuclear Weapons: Legal Aspects*, in Pogany, ed., loc. cit. n. 3, at 142, 164 (1987).

18 5 Off. Rec. UNCLOS III, 57-68 (1976).

19 *Cf.*, Boczek, loc. cit. n. 13, at 371-372. It goes without saying, however, that freedom of the high seas, including military activities such as nuclear deployment, must be exercised subject to 'due regard for the interests of other States' (Article 87).

principle are expected to be respected by the parties in whatever way they may interpret the soft law's injunctions. It is noteworthy that while fitting the concept of soft law, the peaceful purposes clauses in the 1982 Convention are not couched in less binding verbal phrasing, such as "may" or "should" or "endeavour"; all are introduced by the mandatory "shall" formula. (...)

Thus, however "soft" the reservation may be, it will provide a legal base for efforts at restricting military uses of the oceans. Combined with the growing realization of the need for genuine arms control, these efforts may eventually succeed in operationalizing the soft concept of peaceful purposes of the Convention into a firmer rule of law.'[20]

For the seabed, 'one must finally resume that mandate of Article V of the Seabed Arms Control Treaty[21] to continue negotiations concerning further measures in the field of disarmament for the prevention of an arms race in the deep seabed area'. To the high seas, the latter Article 88 of the 1982 Convention presents an even more serious challenge:

'Realistically, the reservation of the high seas for peaceful purposes cannot be operationalized in terms of complete demilitarization. In view of the seemingly brighter prospects for arms control today, however, a mutual balanced reduction of the nuclear strategic submarine forces is within the reach of possibility. Also, as demonstrated by the Rarotonga Treaty, the establishment of nuclear-free zones is also possible.'[22]

For the time being, this agenda may certainly be seen as unrealistic, except with regard to the establishment of nuclear-free zones (which will be analyzed in the following section). Yet, he confirms that:

'... in the long term, the trend of the law of the sea, initiated by the innovative but vague reservation, may eventually reverse the process of militarization of the oceans. Thus it may contribute to making them more "peaceful" in the sense of being "non-military" rather than merely "non-

---

20 Boczek, loc. cit. n. 13, at 379-380. According to his explication of this soft law concept, the agenda for such law making would in general concern two subjects: the seabed and the high seas.

21 Treaty on the Prohibition of the Emplacement of Nuclear Weapons and other Weapons of Mass Destruction on the Seabed and the Ocean Floor and in the Subsoil thereof, signed on 11 February 1971, entered into force on 18 May 1972. Repr. in 955 UNTS, at 115.

22 Boczek, loc. cit. n. 13, at 380.

agressive", yet permitting virtually unlimited use of the seas for military purposes.'[23]

4. PERFECT OR IMPERFECT DENUCLEARIZATION OF NUCLEAR-FREE ZONES IN THE PACIFIC OCEAN REGION

The concept of a Nuclear-Free Zone (NFZ) projects a designated area within which the testing, use, production and stockpiling of nuclear weapons are prohibited, thereby excluding from its boundaries all nuclear-weapon systems. The idea of the NFZ is based upon the need to preserve some zone that will not be directly involved, and thus remains fairly secure, in the eventuality of nuclear war. This concept is more precise and positive than that of the above-mentioned reservation of the sea for 'peaceful purposes'.

Concerning this issue, and with the exception of the Antarctic Treaty, only two regional treaties have so far been successfully elaborated: namely, the Treaty for the Prohibition of Nuclear Weapons in Latin America (Treaty of Tlatelolco) of 1967[24] and the South Pacific Nuclear-Free Zone Treaty (Treaty of Rarotonga) of 1985.[25] While both treaties offer many interesting points for analysis, we shall here take up only two.

One of these is the question of the 'transit' (or port-call) permissibility of nuclear-equipped ships and aircraft of nuclear-weapon States within the zone in question; the other is that of guarantees given by the nuclear-weapon States that they will respect the NFZ, and their undertaking not to use or threaten to use nuclear weapons against it. Analysis of these points, which seem to be crucial to security interests of nuclear-weapon States, will reveal not only the limitations of the significance of the NFZ but also its inherent vulnerability in the face of the strategic manoeuvres of the nuclear Superpowers.

The Treaty of Tlatelolco was elaborated upon initiatives from the Latin American States in reaction to the Cuban missile crisis of 1962. Its first Article stipulates in detail the obligations of the contracting Parties (the Latin American States) to use their nuclear material and facilities for exlusively peaceful purposes, and to keep their territories forever free of nuclear weapons. Furthermore, the term 'territory' includes territorial sea, air space, and any other space over which the State exercises sovereignty

---

23 *Ibid.*, at 380-381.
24 634 UNTS, at 281.
25 XXIV ILM, at 1440.

in accordance with its own legislation (Article 3). This Treaty is applicable to the entirety of all of the territories for which the Treaty is in force (Article 4(1)). Moreover, upon fulfillment of certain requirements, the zone of application 'shall also be that which is situated in the Western Hemisphere', within the limits provided for in Article 4(2).

On the other hand, the United States, which had been invited to participate in the Preparatory Commission for the Denuclearization of Latin America, issued in 1966 its official comments on the Draft proposals for the Latin American Denuclearization Treaty. In these comments, concerning Article 1, the United States assumes that:

'... the proposed treaty would impose no prohibition that would restrict the freedom of transit within the Western Hemisphere. The US policy on freedom of transit is based on our national security needs and the vital security interests of the Hemisphere, and we do not believe a nuclear-free zone need, or should, compromise this freedom. We therefore assume that the language of Article 1, as finally agreed, will not in any way impair the freedom of transit now enjoyed by all powers.'[26]

In fact, Article 1 of the adopted Treaty makes no reference to this issue. But at the Preparatory Commission there were discussions on the permissibility of transit or transport in question.[27]

The Final Act of the Fourth Session of the Preparatory Commission contained the following specific statement regarding transit and transport:

'The Commission deemed it unnecessary to include the term "transport" in Article 1, concerning "obligations" for the following reasons:
1) If the carrier is one of the Contracting Parties, transport is covered by the prohibitions expressly laid down in the remaining provisions of Article 1 and there is no need to mention it expressly, ...
2) If the carrier is a state not a party to the Treaty, transport is identical with "transit", which, in the absence of any provision in the Treaty, must

---

26 Documents on Disarmament (1966), United States Arms Control and Disarmament Agency Publication 43 (1967).

27 At the Third Session of the Preparatory Commission, one of the alternative texts prohibited the Contracting Parties from permitting 'transport' of nuclear weapons in their respective territories. Mexico submitted an alternative text that did not include any reference to 'transport'. At the Fourth Session of the Preparatory Commission, Argentina submitted that it desired a prohibition against transit and transport to be included in the Treaty. The Commission, however, refused to adopt the Argentinian position. Treaty of Tlatelolco, Hearing before the Committee on Foreign Relations, US Senate 95th Congress, Second Session 18 (1978).

be understood to be governed by the principles and rules of international law; according to these principles and rules it is for the territorial state, in the free exercise of its sovereignty, to grant or deny permission for such transit, in each individual case, upon application by the state interested in effecting the transit unless some other arrangement has been reached in a treaty between such states.'[28]

While the Contracting States have undertaken obligations to eschew nuclear armament done upon their own authority, they are not therefore under any obligation to keep their territories free from nuclear weapons belonging to a State not a Party to the Treaty. The expression, 'the principles and rules of international law', invoked in the above statement, signifies no more than the exercise of territorial sovereignty of a State which is not yet restricted by the nuclear-free obligation.

The Latin American States dit not contest the above interpretation on transit when they signed or ratified the Treaty. For example, Nicaragua deposited its instrument of ratification to the Treaty on 5 November 1968, and made a declaration in which it stated that 'in signing this Treaty, Nicaragua does so reserving its sovereign right to use nuclear energy for peaceful purposes at its own discretion ... as well as permitting the transit of atomic materials through its territory'.[29] Panama, a Party to the Treaty, saw no conflict between its Treaty obligations and the Treaty Concerning the Permanent Neutrality and Operation of the Panama Canal, Article III (1,e) of which commits Panama to permit 'vessels of war ... of all nations ... to transit the Canal, irrespective their armament'.[30]

The nuclear-weapon States, and in particular the United States and the Soviet Union, though not Parties to the Treaty, are Parties to its Additional Protocol II (to respect the Statute of Denuclearization of Latin America) and each made some reference to the above interpretation in their respective declarations on signing or ratification of this Protocol.

In its own declaration made at the time of ratification of Additional Protocol II, the United States Government took note of the Preparatory Commission's interpretation of the Treaty, and relied on the interpretation of 'transit' contained in the above statement: '... each of the contracting parties retains exclusive power and legal competence, unaffected by the

---

28 *Ibid.*, at 18-19.
29 *Ibid.*, at 48.
30 *Ibid.*, at 49.

terms of the treaty, to grant or deny non-contracting parties transit and transport privileges'.[31]

According to the United States interpretation, both the statement in the Final Act and the United States statement preserve for the United States the right of innocent passage through the territorial sea (this being one effect of the phrase previously noted, 'governed by the principles and rules of international law'). This statement in the Final Act, and the United States statement, also preserve for the United States the privilege, if granted by the relevant Party, of port visits and overflights incidental to transit. The Final Act statement provides assurance that the continuation of present United States policies and practice with respect to the transport or transit of nuclear weapons will not be inconsistent with United States undertakings under Additional Protocol II to fully respect the 'Statute of Denuclearization' and not to contribute to violations of Article 1 of the Treaty.[32] When regarded, however, from the point of view of the essential definition of a NFZ, this interpretation, in particular concerning port visits and overflights incidental to transit, must raise some doubts.[33]

This interpretation of the Final Act, as well as that asserted by the United States, has been contested principally by another Superpower, the Soviet Union. In signing Additional Protocol II to the Tlateloco Treaty on 18 May 1978, the Soviet Union issued a statement in which it reaffirmed that:

'... transit authorization for nuclear weapons in any form would be contrary to the purposes of the Treaty, according to which, as specifically stated in the Preamble, Latin America must be completely free from nuclear

---

31 United States Treaties and Other International Agreements 754-761 (1971) and XXVIII ILM 1422-1423 (1989). In signing the Protocol I on 26 May 1977, the United States made a similar declaration of understanding.

32 Additional Protocol II to the Latin American Nuclear Free Zone Treaty, Hearings before the Committee on Foreign Relations United States Senate, 91st Congress, Second Session, 92nd Congress, First Session 24 (1971).

33 The territories affected by United States adherence to Protocol I will include Puerto Rico, the Virgin Islands, the Canal zone, and the US military base at Guantanamo. In a hearing before the Committee on Foreign Relations US Senate, a governmental official responded thus:
'... the US retains rights under the protocol to visit ports in the above-mentioned places with vessels carrying nuclear weapons in ports in these places, and she has the right to off-load nuclear weapons from vessels in port in these places in the event of emergency requirements but not for the purposes for deployment or storage.'
Treaty of Tlatelolco, Hearing (1978) loc. cit. n. 25, at 26. See also the understandings issued at the time (on 13 November 1981) of ratification of Additional Protocol I by the United States Senate Resolution in ILM, loc. cit. n. 31, at 1410.

weapons, and would be incompatible with the statute of denuclearization of
the States Party to the Treaty and with their obligations laid down in Article
1 of the Treaty.'[34]

The Soviet interpretation has not been supported by other nuclear
powers. The United Kingdom made no express statement on this issue, her
silence indicating that Britain supports the United States interpretation.[35]
France issued a statement on 15 April 1974 in connection with its
ratification of Additional Protocol II, in which she took note of the
Preparatory Commission's interpretation of the Treaty.[36]
The People's Republic of China's statement, issued in connection with
signing the Additional Protocol on 21 August 1973, declared China would
not 'test, manufacture, produce, stockpile, install or deploy nuclear
weapons in these countries or in this zone, or send her means of
transportation and delivery carrying nuclear weapons to cross the territory,
territorial sea or air space of Latin American countries'[37] and further
called upon all nuclear countries, and particularly the Superpowers, to take
the following additional steps: (1) dismantling all foreign military bases in
Latin America, and refraining from setting up any new foreign millitary
bases in that region, and (2) prohibiting the passage of all carriers of
nuclear weapons through the territory, the territorial sea, or the air space
of Latin America.[38]

---

34 Treaty of Tlatelolco, Hearing (1978), loc. cit. n. 27, at 50 and ILM, loc. cit. n. 31, at 1418.
The Soviet Union did not expressly reiterate this statement upon ratification. It did, however,
give a communication (on 14 April 1982) to the Government of Mexico, regarding the
understanding made by the United States Government upon deposit of the instrument of
ratification of Additional Protocol I of the Treaty. In this communication, it reaffirmed the
position set forth in the Soviet statements issued at the times of the signature and the
ratification of Additional Protocol II, and further stated as follows:
'In particular, the Soviet side deems it necessary to reemphasize that transportation of nuclear
weapons is covered by the prohibitions stipulated in Article 1 of the Treaty, and that
permitting transit of nuclear weapons in any form through the Treaty zone would be at
variance with the objectives of the Treaty, under which (as its Preamble explicitly states) Latin
America must be completely free of nuclear weapons, and would be incompatible with the
non-nuclear status of the signatories to the Treaty and with their obligations set forth in Article
1 of the Treaty.'
Repr. in ILM, loc. cit. n. 31, at 1412-1413.
35 Treaty of Tlatelolco, Hearing (1978), loc. cit. n. 27, at 49.
36 *Ibid.*, at 38. Repr. in ILM, loc. cit. n. 31, at 1415.
37 *Ibid.*, at 1415.
38 Treaty of Tlatelolco, Hearing (1978), loc. cit. n. 27, at 49. In the American Legal Adviser's
opinion 'this statement clearly demonstrates Chinese recognition that a prohibition against
transit had not been established by the present Treaty'. *Ibid.*, at 49.

344 *H. Fujita*

In fact, the United States interpretation must be indispensable to what is called its 'neither confirm nor deny' policy on clarification concerning the presence of nuclear weapons aboard its naval vessels and military aircraft - a policy dating from before the Treaty of Tlatelolco. And, in the words of the United States Legal Advisor:

'[I]n recent years, U.S. military aircraft have routinely overflown and landed in the territory of Parties to the Treaty, and U.S. naval vessels have visited their ports and passed through their territorial waters. In no case have such transit and transport privileges been denied on the basis of the Treaty, even though, because of the "neither confirm nor deny" policy, the State granting those privileges was necessary unaware of whether the U.S. vessel or aircraft carried nuclear weapons. Nor are we aware of any case where this question has ever been raised with respect to the ships or aircraft of any other nuclear-weapon State.'[39]

This policy has been not only maintained by the United States but also adopted by other nuclear-weapon States.[40]

Efforts of non-nuclear-weapon States to establish a NFZ in a given region have always met with one inevitable obstacle to their gaining the co-operation of nuclear-weapon States with regard to respect for the basic status of a NFZ: namely, the problem of transit carried out according to this policy.

In elaborating their own NFZ, the South Pacific countries attempted to clarify this point. They also discussed this issue in the process of drafting the Treaty of Rarotonga. The Working Group on a South Pacific Nuclear Free Zone considered the problem of the prevention of stationing of nuclear explosive devices, meaning any nuclear weapon or other explosive device capable of releasing nuclear energy (irrespective of the purpose for which it could be used). It was accepted that the definition should be rigorous, and should cover the emplantation, emplacement, transport on

---

39 *Ibid.*.
40 For example, during the Falklands (Malvinas) conflict in 1982, a serious allegation was made in press reports, according to which some British ships, frigates and destroyers engaged off the Falkland (Malvinas) Islands, were carrying nuclear weapons designed for anti-submarine warfare. *Cf.*, The Times, 3 November 1982. The British Government did not, however, disclose the whereabouts of its nuclear weapons, and refused to confirm or deny reports regarding the presence of these weapons in the area in question. SIPRI Yearbook 1973, 480-482 (1973).

either land or internal waters, stockpiling, storage, installation and deployment of nuclear explosive devices in the territories of the Parties.[41]

The Treaty of Rarotonga applies to territories within the South Pacific Nuclear Free Zone (described in Annex 1), while nothing in this Treaty prejudices or in any way affects the rights, or the exercise of the rights, of any State under international law with regard to freedom of the seas (Article 2(1)). It gives to the term 'stationing' an identical definition, and prohibits all acts of this nature within the territory of each Party (Articles 1(d), 5(1)). While this is more explicit than the corresponding provision in the Treaty of Tlatelolco, it is also accompanied by a broad exception to this prohibition of stationing.

Article 5(2) of the Treaty of Rarotonga acknowledges the right of the Parties to choose whether or not to allow visits or transits by foreign nuclear-armed ships or aircrafts in the following terms:

'... each Party in the exercise of its sovereign rights remains free to decide for itself whether to allow visits by foreign ships and aircraft to its ports and airfields, transit of its airspace by foreign aircraft, and navigation by foreign ships in its territorial sea or archipelagic waters in a manner not covered by the rights of innocent passage, archipelagic sea lane passage or transit passage of straits.'

Strangely enough, while mentioning foreign ships and aircraft, this passage contains no reference to 'nuclear explosive devices', although the former could easily be nuclear-armed. It is moreover certain that the visits of such to the ports and airfields of the Parties, as well as their transit of the airspace, are permitted if these Parties freely decide for themsleves to give permission.

Both such visits and transit may be regarded as in a sense tantamount to stationing since, for the purposes of the Treaty, the latter term implies 'transportation on land or inland waters'. In considering the definition of stationing, the Working Group addressed such issues as whether it should include a time element to cover, for example, the duration or pattern of port visits:

'[I]t was noted that the principles adopted by Forum Heads of Government had explicitly stated that the sovereign right of a country to decide on port access was unqualified. Moreover, the utility of such a time frame was

---

41 Report by the Chair of the Working Group on the South Pacific Nuclear Free Zone (SPNFZ), § 35.

questioned since the circumstances of port visits varied considerably. It was also noted that should any party have doubts or questions concerning the duration or pattern of visits it would be open to it to resort to the consultation provisions of the draft Treaty in order to seek clarification.[42]

The Working Group considered the possibility of an emergency affecting a ship or aircraft (*e.g.* a ship which has run aground) resulting in a nuclear weapon being on the territory of a Party. It was agreed that while such a situation was extremely unlikely to occur, if it should, the Party would not be in breach of the Treaty provided it took effective steps to ensure the earliest practicable removal of the device from its territory.[43]

In signing Protocols 2 and 3 to the Rarotonga Treaty, the Soviet Union stated the view that admission of transit of nuclear weapons or other nuclear explosive devices by any means, as well as visits by foreign military ships and aircraft with nuclear explosive devices on board, to the ports and airfields within the nuclear-free zone would contradict the aims of the Treaty of Rarotonga, and would be inconsistent with the status of the zone.[44]

While the prevention of stationing or of port-calls of nuclear-armed ships has been much discussed with regard to the case of the Treaty of Rarotonga, some Forum States, in particular New Zealand, have pursued their own anti-nuclear policies. New Zealand's policy was adopted by the Labour Government in 1984. In 1985, Prime Minister Lange refused to allow the *USS Buchanan* to visit a New Zealand port during an ANZUS exercise, because the United States would not confirm that it would not be nuclear-armed. In thus putting its anti-nuclear policy into practice, the Government presented an act entitled the New Zealand Nuclear Free Zone, Disarmament, and Arms Control Act, 1985.[45] The zone specified therein comprises: a) all of the land, territory, and inland waters within the territorial limits of New Zealand; b) its internal waters; c) its territorial sea; and the airspace above the areas specified at a) to c). According to the act, no person shall emplant, emplace, transport on land or inland water,

42 *Ibid.*, § 36.
43 *Ibid.*, § 38.
44 SIPRI Yearbook 1989 503 (1989).
45 The Parliament of New Zealand adopted this Act by a 39-0-29 vote, on 4 June 1987.

stockpile, store, install, or deploy any nuclear explosive device in the zone.[46]

On the other hand, the nuclear-weapon States have given some guarantee to respect the NFZ by legal commitments annexed to the basic Treaties concluded by the Contracting non-nuclear-weapon States in the given regions.

In Latin America, Additional Protocol II, annexed to the Treaty of Tlatelolco, and intended for signature and ratification by nuclear-weapon States, provides that the statute of denuclearization of Latin America in respect of warlike purposes, as defined, delimited and set forth in the Treaty, shall be fully respected by them in all its express aims and provisions (Article 1); and that they also undertake not to use or threaten to use nuclear weapons against the Contracting Parties of the Treaty (Article 3). These provisions are very important from the view-point of the basic concept of a NFZ. In concluding the Treaty, the Latin American States have gained a negative security from nuclear-weapon States, the most significant result of their efforts to create a NFZ.

On the occasion of their respective signatures or ratifications of this Protocol, the nuclear-weapon States have, however, made some important declarations of understanding or announced reservations on this issue of no use and no threat of use of nuclear weapons against the Contracting Parties to the Treaty.

In its declaration and understandings made on the occasion of its ratification of Additional Protocol II in 1971, the United States stated that: 'as regards the undertaking not to use or threaten to use nuclear weapons against the parties, the U.S. would consider that an armed attack by a party, in which it was assisted by a nuclear-weapon State, would be incompatible with the party's obligations under Article 1 of the Treaty'.

With the exception of China,[47] other nuclear-weapon States more or less followed the United States formula.[48] These understandings mean that

---

46 *Cf.*, S. McMillan, Neither Confirm Nor Deny - The Nuclear Ships Dispute between New Zealand and the United States (1987). See also Freedom from Nuclear Weapons Act, enacted by the Senate of the Philippines and pending at the House of Representatives.

47 On signing Protocol II, China stated that she would never use or threaten to use nuclear weapons against non-nuclear Latin American countries and the Latin American nuclear-free zone.

48 The United Kingdom's declarations of understanding of 1969 says:
    '[S]hould a party to the Treaty carry out any act of aggression with the support of a nuclear weapon state, the UK would be free to reconsider the extent to which it could be regarded as committed by the provisions of Protocol II.'

the guarantee not to use or threaten to use nuclear weapons against the Latin American States Parties to the Treaty is not absolute but qualified, and that in some cases the nuclear-weapon States with the exception of China may eventually even have occasion to use nuclear weapons in the nuclear-weapon-free zone defined in the Treaty.

Thus, the security interests of the non-nuclear-weapon States establishing the NFZ may conflict with the strategic interests of the nuclear-weapon States.

The Treaty of Rarotonga follows a similar pattern. Article 2 of its Additional Protocol 2 provides that each Party *inter alia* undertakes not to use or threaten to use any nuclear explosive device against: a) Parties to the Treaty; or b) any territory within the South Pacific Nuclear-Free Zone for which a State that has become a Party to Additional Protocol 1 of the Treaty of Rarotonga is internationally responsible.

This Additional Protocol is open to signature by five nuclear-weapon States. The Soviet Union signed it in 1986, as did China in 1987, but gave similar statements of reservation concerning non-use of nuclear weapons against the Contracting Parties to the Treaty.

In signing Additional Protocols 2 and 3, the Soviet Union warned that, in case of action taken by a Party or Parties violating their major commitments connected with the nuclear-free status of the zone, as well as in case of aggression committed by one or several Parties to the Treaty, supported by a nuclear-weapon State, or together with it, with the use by such a State of the territory, airspace, territorial sea or archipelagic waters of the Parties for visits by nuclear weapon-carrying ships and aircraft, or for transit of nuclear weapons, it will have the right to consider itself free of its non-use commitments assumed under Additional Protocol 2. But in ratifying these Protocols in 1988, the Soviet Union made no reference to the conditions included in its statement issued at the time of signature.

The French statement issued on signing Additional Protocol II in 1974 interprets the undertaking contained in Article 3 of the Protocol to mean that it presents no obstacle to the full exercise of the right of self-defence enshrined in Article 51 of the UN Charter. The Soviet statement issued on signing and ratifying Additional Protocol II in 1979 *inter alia* stated:

'Any actions undertaken by a state or states parties to the Treaty which are not incompatible with their non-nuclear status, and also the commission by one or more states parties to the Treaty of an act of aggression with the support of a state which is in possession of nuclear weapons or together with such a state, will be regarded by the USSR as incompatible with the obligations of those countries under the Treaty. In such cases the USSR reserves the right to reconsider its obligations under Protocol II. It further reserves the right to reconsider its attitude to this Protocol in the event of any actions on the part of other states possessing nuclear weapons which are incompatible with their obligations under the said Protocol.'

In signing Protocols 2 and 3 to the Rarotonga Treaty, China declared that it respected the status of the South Pacific nuclear-free zone, and would neither make use or threat of use of nuclear weapons against the zone nor test nuclear weapons in the region. However, China reserved its right to reconsider its obligations under the Protocols, if other nuclear-weapon States or the Contracting Parties to the Treaty should take any action in 'gross' violation of the Treaty and the Protocols, thus changing the status of the zone and endangering China's own security interests.

The United States and Great Britain, however, after making remarks indicative of hesitation, decided not to sign; and France rejected this whole Treaty system because the Treaty prohibits nuclears in the South Pacific region. Due, therefore, to such attitudes on the part of nuclear-weapon States, the negative security of the Parties to the Treaty of Rarotonga is weaker than that of the Latin American States.

Be these matters as they may, it remains true that, consequent upon the Treaty of Tlatelolco, a vast nuclear-free zone has been realized in the South Pacific region. An extensive area of the Pacific Ocean, including that comprised within the Antarctic region, has become a more or less denuclearized zone. This realization depends essentially upon the intention of the peoples of the region in question, while the co-operation of nuclear-weapon States affords a condition favourable to the respect of the status of this area as a NFZ. One may criticize this arrangement arguing that these Treaties will not change any existing weapon involvement in these zones; nevertheless, the Treaties may still have a preventive role, because there are as yet probably no nuclear weapons on any territory in these zones.[49]

5.   CONCLUSION

It goes without saying that nuclear disarmament on a global scale is the ultimate solution to the problem of the prevention of nuclear war, and of the peaceful settlement of international disputes. Pending the realization of global nuclear disarmament, regional disarmament must be recognised, not simply as a mere collateral measure, but as one that in a nuclear-threatened world is very useful during our present period of neither war nor peace.

---

49 Holding this point in high esteem, Fry says:
   '[I]t is significant to move to effectively ban home-basing in the South Pacific for the nuclear-armed ships or aircraft of either superpower. This puts an obstacle in the way of competitive base development in the South Pacific.'
   G.E. Frey, SIPRI Yearbook 1986, 506 (1986).

Even now, after the realization of a new epoch in Europe promoted by Gorbachev's *perestroika* and the reunification of Germany, the Pacific region still remains the arena of an 'old-fashioned' cold war situation between the nuclear Superpowers. It is therefore in this vast region that nuclear-weapon tests have been repeated, and the dumping of radioactive wastes has been planned. It is in this very Pacific Ocean, which may ironically be called a 'nuclear lake', that the navigation of nuclear warships and submarines most frequently takes place; and there may always be an eventual nuclear confrontation or conflict.

Of course, the establishment of a NFZ represents the initiatives and efforts of the peoples living in this nuclear-victimized region. Although, in the face of international politics and the nuclear strategies of the Superpowers, the treaties concerning NFZs have been forced to include some compromising provisions, through these legal instruments, the States or countries of this region may decide their future by exercising their sovereignty in a manner that keeps their territories nuclear-weapon free.

Finally, we take up the words of Professor Kalshoven: 'no matter how tremendous the difficulties ahead, we should never abandon the hope of developing and improving the twin bodies of disarmament and humanitarian law.' On one occasion the Professor strikingly characterized them as 'these laws which protect man from his own folly'.[50]

---

50 Kalshoven, loc. cit. n. 1, at 326.

IMPLEMENTATION MEASURES AND INTERNATIONAL LAW OF ARMS CONTROL

BERNHARD GRAEFRATH

1.   INTRODUCTION

International humanitarian law has many roots and its connections go far beyond human rights and the law of warfare. In his lecture at The Hague Kalshoven has drawn our attention to the close relationship that exists between international humanitarian law and the law of disarmament or arms control.[1] Normally when 'the close functional connection'[2] or the 'interplay between disarmament and humanitarian law'[3] is referred to reference is made to Articles 35, 36, 51 and 55 of Protocol I Additional to the Geneva Conventions. But this relationship is much broader. In his last publication Frei has called for a 'proper consideration of the manifold

---

1   F. Kalshoven, *Arms, Armaments and International Law*, 191 Recueil des Cours, II, 187 (1985); F. Kalshoven, Constraints on the Waging of War (1987).

2   K. Ipsen, *International Law Preventing Armed Conflicts and International Law of Armed Conflict - a Combined Functional Approach*, in C. Swinarski, ed., Studies and Essays on International Humanitarian Law and Red Cross Principles in Honour of Jean Pictet 349, 356 (1984).

3   A. Rosas, P. Steinbäck, *The Frontiers of International Humanitarian Law*, 24 Journal of Peace Research 219, 231 (1987).

interconnections existing between' these branches of international law.[4] Defining the purposes of arms control he points to four aspects:
- reducing the likelihood of war,
- reducing the suffering and damage in the event of war,
- reducing expenditure on armaments,
- 'contributing to conflict management by providing a framework for negotiation between opposite sides, by reducing suspicion and by generally contributing to an atmosphere conducive to relaxation of tensions'.[5]

He had no difficulty finding 'that what has been achieved by international humanitarian law ... conforms perfectly well to that definition'[6] and reached the conclusion that 'international humanitarian law just can be seen as part of the arms control process'.[7] We would like to concentrate on the fourth aspect because it has led to a promising development of implementation measures. This is a process we also witness in international humanitarian law where we have seen in Protocol I the emergence of procedures 'to consider general problems concerning the application of the Conventions and the Protocol' (Article 7) and the establishment of an international fact-finding Commission (Article 90) which allows enquiry into any facts alleged to be a grave breach or other serious violation of the Conventions or the Protocol.[8] This, together with reporting obligations, the system of protecting powers and an obligation to enact penal laws, points to a system of implementation measures which covers the whole process of complying with the obligations undertaken by ratifying the Conventions and the Protocol. This can also be understood as part of a conflict management process which is of general importance for international relations and is something that international humanitarian law and the law of arms control have in common. It has even been stated that 'it seems justified to say that the ICRC represents *mutatis mutandis* a verification institution that goes far beyond the mandate and efficiency of

---

4   D. Frei, *International Humanitarian Law and Arms Control*, 28 International Review of the Red Cross 491-492 (1988).
5   *Ibid.*, at 494, 499.
6   *Ibid.*, at 494.
7   *Ibid.*, at 503.
8   *Cf.*, Y. Sandoz, C. Swinarski, B. Zimmermann, eds., Commentary on the Additional Protocols of 8 June 1977 to the Geneva Convention of 12 August 1949, 103, 1037 (1987); B. Graefrath, *Die Untersuchungskommission im Ergänzungsprotokoll zu den Genfer Abkommen vom 12.8.1949* (The International Fact-Finding Commissions in Additional Protocol I to the Geneva Conventions of 12 August 1949), in XXX Wissenschaftliche Zeitschrift der Humboldt-Universität zu Berlin, Ges.-Sprachw. 9 (1981).

any verification mechanism established so far by other disarmament and arms control accords'.[9]

2. ARMS CONTROL AND SECURITY

Despite recent progress, disarmament still lags behind the expectations of peoples and nations. Nevertheless, the international law of arms control deserves the full attention of international lawyers. The present author sees two main reasons for that:

Firstly, the international law of arms control is among the most important means of securing observance of the ban on the use of force and implementing the rule of law in international relations. This is why improvements in the field of international law of arms control always have direct and positive repercussions on international law as a whole.

Secondly, within international law of arms control there is an especially developed system of implementation measures for the purpose of supervision and enforcement of international legal obligations. This, undoubtedly, is due to the fact that in this sector of international law, measures which guarantee the implementation of the treaty necessarily at the same time also guarantee the security of the parties. We live in a period of growing awareness that State security can no longer be based anymore on military domination and that even the weaponry which is designed for defense purposes will, if used, end up destroying what was the objective of defence. Models of co-operative security are offered to replace individual security. Under such circumstances it is necessary and possible to ensure that guaranteeing the security of the parties coincides with guaranteeing the implementation of the treaty, because the treaty with its substantive and procedural rules is the instrument used by the parties to organize their common security. Implementation measures, including verification, are the means to achieve this goal provided 'the quality of the machinery' established is correspondingly adequate for this function. The present author, therefore, tends to stress the co-operative elements in the different kinds of implementation measures and their contribution to overcoming unilateral evaluation and measures which were typical of classical international law. Knowing that in case of treaty violations even today evaluation and possible reactions are often left to the State Party

---

9   Frei, loc. cit. n. 4, at 503. As to verification in general see also M. Bothe, *Verification of Facts*, in R. Bernhardt, ed., 9 Encyclopaedia of Public International Law 383 (1986).

concerned, this should not diminish what has already been achieved in the field of implementation measures but further improve instead their scope and effectiveness.[10]

3.   IMPLEMENTATION OF ARMS CONTROL AGREEMENTS

3.1   Verification

Undoubtedly, the development of implementation measures within arms control treaties has a significant impact on the overall development of international law, reaching far beyond questions of disarmament and strengthening the normativity of international legal obligations by limiting the margin of auto-interpretation by the parties. And it is certainly not by chance that means and methods to strengthen the implementation of international law are the centre of efforts recommended by GA Resolution 44/23 for the last decade of our century. This, indeed, seems utterly necessary if we want to ensure that the international legal order is enabled to cope with the global problems we have to face.

International law of arms control has -as indicated in the notion itself- not only a substantive aspect but also a conspicuous procedural component, since effective disarmament is impossible without control and a procedure for conflict management. In the first two principles of verification it is explicitly stated that:

> 'Adequate and effective verification is an essential element of all arms limitations and disarmament agreements. Verification is not an aim in itself, but an essential element in the process of achieving arms limitation and disarmament agreements.'[11]

---

10 It therefore does not seem to be an argument when Sur in relation to the mechanisms of the INF Treaty states:
'... verification emerges more as a guarantee of the security of the parties rather than as a guarantee of the implementation of the Treaty.'
S. Sur, *Verification problems of the Washington Treaty on the Elimination of Intermediate-range Missiles*, UNIDIR Research Paper 2, 17 (1988); S. Sur, *A Legal Approach to Verification in Disarmament or Arms Limitation*, UNIDIR Research Papers 1, 30 (1988). See also M. Mohr, *Völkerrechtliche Fragen der Kontrolle von Abrüstungsverträgen* (International Law Questions concerning the Control of Disarmament Treaties), 36 Staat und Recht 196 *et seq.* (1987).

11 *Cf.*, *Principles of Verification affirmed by the Disarmament Commission, 2-20 May 1988, New York*, UNIDIR Research Paper 1, loc. cit. n. 10, at 67.

Security matters have such an importance in the disarmament process that not only is the end result of the treaty strictly controlled but so also are the intermediate steps and activities. The INF Treaty certainly contains the most elaborate control system. It represents a complex system of implementation measures to monitor the whole process of eliminating intermediate-range missiles. It starts with a detailed obligation to provide and update basic data.[12] It establishes a system of at least six different types of on-site inspection (Article XI).[13] And, finally -as in the IBM Treaty- it relies in Article XII on national technical means of supervision, involving an agreement to apply mainly remote sensing technique in a manner consistent with generally recognized principles of international law and the conditions laid down in Article XII.

One of the oldest and most crucial features inherent in international law is the fact that compliance, control and implementation of international legal obligations are vested in the subjects of these very obligations. Thus, in the absence of special organs or procedures, implementation is subject to potentially divergent interpretations. This is already a disturbing factor in bilateral treaties, although it is lessened to a certain extent by the reciprocal nature of legal interests in such treaties. But in multilateral treaties, especially in those regulating so-called 'extra-State interests'[14] and possessing an integral structure of obligations[15] and an *erga omnes*

---

12 This refers to the number and location of missiles, launches, support facilities, technical characteristics and the number, type, location and date of elimination of missiles (Article IX), so as to document progress made in their elimination. To make sure that the process will not be hampered by any dispute on the kind of data envisaged, Article IX of the Memorandum of Understandings contains detailed definitions. The exchange of data is processed through national Nuclear Risk Reduction Centres which had already been set up under a treaty in 1987.

13 This refers to all missile operation bases and missile support facilities and the portals of missile production facilities. It operates for 13 years after the entry into force of the Treaty. The procedures governing the conduct of inspections are regulated in a lengthy Protocol on Verification. *Cf.* Sur, loc. cit. n. 10, at 9. M. Mohr, *Völkerrecht als Garantiefaktor: der Vertrag über die Beseitigung der Mittelstreckenraketen vom 8. Dezember 1987* (International Law as a means of guarantee: The Treaty on the Elimination of Intermediate-range Missiles), 42 Neue Justiz 166 (1988).

14 W. Riphagen, *State Responsibility: New Theories of Obligation in Interstate Relations*, in R.St.J. Macdonald, D.M. Johnston, eds., The Structure and Progress of International Law - Essays in Legal Philosophy, Doctrine and Theory 581-625 (1983).

15 K. Sachariew, *Die Rechtsstellung der betroffenen Staaten bei Verletzungen multilateraler Verträge, Fragen der Aktivlegitimation und der völkerrechtlich zugelassenen Rechtsfolgen* (The Legal Status of Injured States in Case of Multilateral Treaty Violations: The Right to Claim Legal Consequences under International Law) (1986); K. Sachariew, *State Responsibility for Multilateral Treaty Violations: Identifying the Injured State and its Legal Status* in XXXV NILR 273-289 (1988); B. Graefrath, Das Verantwortlichkeitsverhältnis im Völkerrecht und die Definition des 'verletzten Staates' (The Legal Relationship of Responsibility and the Definition

character, the inadequacy of this system becomes so evident that such treaties contain as a rule specific implementation measures and provide for competent treaty organs. Such functions as those set forth in the Principles of Verification, stating that: 'Verification should promote the implementation of arms limitation and disarmament measures, build confidence among States and ensure that agreements are observed by all Parties', are valid for all implementation measures.[16] An important goal of all control measures is to make co-operative, agreed verification of facts possible, to limit the margin and the danger of divergent interpretations by the Parties, to promote mutual confidence, to assure compliance with the obligations of a treaty and in case of dispute to determine whether an obligation has been violated. Implementation measures, therefore, not only have a deterrent effect but also help to build the confidence which breeds further co-operation.[17]

3.2   The need to control, stimulate and enforce compliance

Specific problems concerning the fulfillment and implementation of international legal obligations arise out of the absence in international law of mechanisms comparable to those in domestic administrative law and capable of controlling, stimulating and -as the case may be- enforcing compliance. This is even more so in the case of international legal obligations which are implemented in several steps or within a process extending over a relatively long period of time and requiring a certain balance of interests between the parties during the process of fulfillment. But it is especially in these instances that -due to today's political, technological, economic and military developments and to the increasing interdependence among nations- there is a growing need for mechanisms enabling the subjects of international law to control, stimulate and enforce compliance with agreed legal standards. This is especially true for those sectors of international law in which obligations are owed simultaneously to all parties and do not simply represent a bundle of bilateral

---

of 'Injured State' in International Law), in Probleme des Völkerrechts 107-138 (1987).

16 *Cf.*, Principles of Verification, 3.

17 Sur admits that: '... verification can in itself be regarded as a confidence-building measure', and '... in addition, compliance with certain confidence-building measures can be verified', but he stresses that 'confidence-building measures establish primary obligations ... whereas verification establishes a secondary obligation ... more simply put, confidence-building measures contain data, facts or situations, whereas verification concerns legal norms'.
Sur, *A Legal Approach*, loc. cit. n. 10, at 3-4. The present author is not at all sure that this strict distinction can always be upheld or is necessary.

relationships. The present author would refer to four such sectors: human rights, international humanitarian law, the protection of the environment, disarmament (and arms control).

In all four -although in some cases for different reasons- we witness the insufficiency of classical methods of State responsibility and dispute settlement in cases of disputes or alleged violations. It is simply not sufficient to provide for dispute settlement machinery to guarantee implementation or to restore implementation of an obligation breached or to enforce reparation in whatever form. What is needed is some kind of procedure which accompanies the process of compliance in order to ensure *inter alia* the observance of human rights and humanitarian law obligations, to prevent pollution and preserve the environment or to control the elimination of intermediate-range missiles. It seems that we have to distinguish between four catagories of implementation measures which may be established under treaty law or customary rules:

a) Exchange and collection of general information on the implementation of treaty obligations. Typical examples are the reporting procedures in human rights treaties.[18]

b) Procedures for the establishment of facts. Typical examples are the procedures of specified data exchange as provided for in Article IX of the INF Treaty, Article VII(5) of the Antarctic Treaty and Article 13(1b) of the ABM Treaty; some kind of on-site inspection as provided for in Article XI in the INF Treaty, Article VII(3) of the Antarctic Treaty, Article XII of the Outer Space Treaty and Article 15(1) of the Moon Treaty, and national technical means of verification.[19]

c) Legal means of establishing a violation in a (more or less) mandatory manner. Typical examples are the complaint procedures in human rights treaties;[20] challenge inspections as provided for in Article 16(1b) of the Tlatelolco Treaty; dispute settlement procedures which allow for fact-finding and legal assessment, for example, the procedure provided by Article 90 of Protocol I, or arbitration and judicial procedures.

---

18 See also the notification requirement in Article XI of the Treaty on Outer Space and Article 5 of the Moon Treaty; the reporting obligations under Article 14 of the Tlatelolco Treaty and Article 9 of the Rarotonga Treaty.

19 They were mentioned in Article XV of SALT II; Article 3(5) of the Sea-Bed Treaty; Article 12 of the ABM Treaty; Article 12 of the INF Treaty.

20 See also Annex 4 of the Rarotonga Treaty which contains several specific consultation procedures. *E.g.* Article 15(2) of the Moon Treaty; Article 10 and Annex 4 of the Rarotonga Treaty.

d) Means of ensuring proper implementation or appropriate sanctions in case of an established violation.

The procedures of the first two categories of implementation measures are applied without the suspicion of wrongful conduct or the reproach of non-implementation. They furnish information on the application of the treaty by the other party and ensure a kind of transparancy which stimulates compliance and is in itself confidence-building.

Procedures within the third category suppose a suspicion that an obligation has been violated, or are aimed at settling a dispute regarding alleged non-compliance. They are typical dispute settlement procedures.

The fourth category relates procedures and measures to enforce compliance with an obligation which has been breached. They mainly comprise legal consequences of wrongful conduct: not only the different kinds of possible countermeasures but also the conditions and procedures to apply them.

Most treaties do not provide for all four categories. It would, however, be useful if States could agree in future to distinguish clearly the different stages in the process of compliance and provide for specific implementation measures. This would, on the one hand, stimulate compliance with the obligation and, on the other, considerably facilitate the appropriate fact-finding and dispute-settlement procedures as well as enforcement measures in case of an internationally wrongful act.

3.3   Institutionalization of control bodies

A co-operative control procedure accompanying the compliance process would possess the advantage of objectivizing the establishment of facts and possibly also their legal evaluation (assessment). It would work independently of possible allegations of non-compliance. Although the scope of this procedure is limited to establishing facts, the facts to be established are selected according to parameters set out in rules or other terms of reference. It is therefore of no use to ask whether we have to deal with the establishment of facts amounting to a breach of obligation or confirming the compliance with the obligation. Putting the questions in such narrow terms produces in both cases a one-sided orientation. Frontiers between notions are flexible in this field.

The current ascertainment by the parties to a treaty that the compliance process proceeds within agreed parameters represents also a confidence-building measure giving States the security they need and providing the treaty with the stability necessary for the next steps.[21] It already goes beyond the mere establishment of facts and contains an element of legal assessment. In cases of departure from the agreed standard of behaviour this procedure allows States to react promptly, to introduce changes if necessary, to fill gaps or to clear misunderstandings. These are all measures which prevent a formal dispute, the setting in motion of a dispute settlement procedure or even unilateral sanctions based on State responsibility.

These procedures are based on the co-operation of the parties. They do not have the character of adversarial proceedings and leave room for agreed conclusions.[22] This is evidenced by the provisions of the INF Treaty. Article XI(7) provides, *inter alia*, for the possibility of inspections in the process of eliminating intermediate-range missiles, which allows for a determination that the processes have been completed. It also allows the other party (in Article XI(8)) to conduct inspections to confirm the completion of the process. In both cases there is a legal assessment of facts and the Protocol on Verification provides in both cases that the parties shall, if possible, resolve ambiguities regarding factual information. Relevant clarification shall be recorded in the report. Article 13 of the INF Treaty contains a provision similar to that in Article 13 of the ABM Treaty concerning the establishment by the Parties of a Special Verification Commission which shall meet at the request of either party and resolve questions relating to compliance with the obligation assumed, and agree upon measures necessary to improve the viability and effectiveness of the Treaty.[23]

The result of implementation procedures accompanying the compliance process and operating independently from the existence of a dispute is that they may be utilized for different purposes according to their substance and nature. They can be used simply for data-collection; they may constitute a

---

21 See Principles of Verification, 11: 'Continued confirmation of compliance is an essential ingredient to building and maintaining confidence among the parties'. It seems that this aspect is neglected by Sur. In his opinion:

'... it must be emphasized ... that verification, contrary to what is sometimes affirmed, cannot demonstrate that an agreement is being applied. It can simply lead to the conclusion that violation of an agreement has not been demonstrated and that therefore compliance is assumed (...). It must therefore be considered that an ostensible reference to verification as proof that obligations are being fulfilled properly constitutes at best a misuse of its machinery and almost a shame.'

Sur, *A Legal Approach*, loc. cit. n. 10, at 33.

22 *Ibid.*, at 15.

23 See also Annex 3 of the Rarotonga Treaty establishing a Consultative Committee.

prerequisite for setting in motion follow-up steps in the treaty process; they may lead to an agreed finding on the existence of a fact or possibly the adjustments of the treaty obligation by a competent body; they may also serve as basis of a dispute settlement procedure.

It is a peculiar feature of these procedures that they usually lead to specific institutionalization of the organs of control. This is true even for bilateral treaties. Multilateral treaties create by way of agreement relatively independent control bodies, for example, in human rights treaties, or they charge existing international organizations -for example the NPT or the Tlatelolco Treaty- while ensuring that the establishment of necessary data is as much as possible objective and not distorted by auto-interpretation. In human rights treaties this function has been conferred upon independent expert bodies and sometimes also international tribunals. The competence of these bodies depends in general on the exhaustion of local remedies. In international humanitarian law we have the institution of protecting powers and the ICRC. In international environmental law special bodies or organizations are entrusted with such functions. In the field of arms control, but not only there, an important role is played by mutual inspections or control by international inspectors. Examples may be found in the Antarctic Treaty, the NPT and INF Treaties, as well as the Tlatelolco Treaty, which entrusts the IAEA with control functions.

As soon as an international organization is involved in the process of control and establishment of facts, there is often a tendency towards a phasing of the relevant procedures in two or more stages. While the establishment of facts often lies in the hands of experts, decisions involving a legal or political assessment are taken at the political level by the competent organs of the international organization.

4.   SANCTIONS

The least developed procedures so far are sanctions in case of an established violation. The Geneva Conventions and Protocol I contain detailed provisions on grave breaches in order to create and co-ordinate national penal sanctions against individuals who have been found guilty of serious war crimes. Article 91 of Protocol I further states that a party to the conflict which violates the provisions of the Convention or the Protocol shall be liable to pay compensation. This does not seem to add anything to the general rules on State responsibility. Some arms control treaties contain a specific withdrawal clause in case 'extraordinary events, related to the subject matter of this Treaty, have jeopardized the supreme interests' of a party,[24] or in case of circumstances 'which affect its supreme interests or the peace and security of one or more Contracting Parties'.[25] Sur considers these clauses as providing for responses in the event of a violation.[26] But generally these clauses do not speak about violations. Rather, they confirm the sovereign rights of the parties in case their 'supreme interests' are affected. That may happen by a change of circumstances or anything else, which does not necessarily have to amount to a violation of treaty obligations. Sometimes the withdrawal is conditioned by a notice given three months or more in advance. This would make it difficult to understand this kind of withdrawal as a countermeasure against a serious violation. Neuhold,[27] therefore, tends to compare these withdrawal clauses with the *clausula rebus sic stantibus* as enshrined in Article 62 of the Vienna Convention on the Law of Treaties. However, Article 13 of the Rarotonga Treaty links the right of withdrawal clearly to a violation of a provision 'essential to the achievement of the objectives of the treaty or of the spirit of the treaty' and demands that notice be given twelve months in advance! Withdrawal under such conditions may not be a very effective reaction.

In some cases treaties directly refer to the Security Council of the United Nations. Thus, Article 20 of the Tlatelolco Treaty distinguishes between a violation of treaty obligations in general and a violation which might endanger peace and security. In the latter event the General Conference is duty bound to report thereon to the Security Council. The Convention on the prohibition of bacteriological weapons gives in Article 6 States Parties a right to lodge a complaint with the Security Council in case they find a Party acting in breach of obligations deriving from the provisions of the Convention.[28] This, of course, is more a complaint procedure than a reaction to a violation and it does not add much to the already existing legal situation.[29]

---

24 See *inter alia* Article IV of the Test Ban Treaty; Article X of the NPT; Article VIII of the Sea-Bed Treaty; Article 15 of the INF Treaty.
25 Article 30 of the Tlatelolco Treaty.
26 Sur, *A Legal Approach*, loc. cit. n. 10, at 29.
27 H. Neuhold, *Legal Aspects of Arms Control Agreements*, in K.-H. Böckstiegel, H.-E. Folz, J.M. Mössner, K. Zemanek, eds., Völkerrecht, Recht der Internationalen Organisationen, Weltwirtschaftsrecht. Festschrift für Ignaz Seidl-Hohenveldern (International Law, the Law of International Organizations, International Economic Law. *Festschrift* in honour of Ignaz Seidl-Hohenveldern) 427-448 (1988).
28 See also Article 3(4) of the Sea-Bed Treaty and Article 5(4) of the Convention on the Prohibition of Military or Any Other Hostile Use of Environmental Modification Techniques.
29 Sur even speaks of 'an empty gesture' which 'masks the absence of any specific regulation'. Sur, *A Legal Approach*, loc. cit. n. 10, at 25.

It seems that the international law of arms control has hitherto not developed specific rules on State responsibility or specific measures which would allow for an adequate response to a breach of an international obligation on disarmament or arms control.[30] It relies on the general rules which, of course, enable the Security Council to act within its competence in accordance with the UN Charter. It may, however, be questionable whether this is sufficient. In particular, in connection with far-reaching and ambituous multilateral conventions, the possibility of collective reaction should be considered, complementing procedures for collective verification and assessment in the case of an established violation.

Recently the ILC has discussed the proposal to draft an Article on individual penal responsibility in connection with the Draft Code of Crimes Against Peace and Security of Mankind. This Article would apply in case of the breach of treaty provisions concerning a prohibition of armaments, disarmament, restriction or limitation of armaments. But at its 41st Session the Commission could not agree on a Draft Article.[31] Even if we, eventually, get a Draft this would be only a penal sanction against the individual responsible. As is rightly stated in Article 3 of the Draft, the prosecution of an individual does not relieve a State of its responsibility. This, therefore, remains a question to be solved. Disarmament and arms control treaties are an essential instrument for implementing the prohibition of the use of force. Therefore, the development of regional security systems should also include enforcement measures to ensure implementation of provisions on disarmament and arms control and organize collective reaction against violations in order to complete the system of preventive and control measures.

5.   CONCLUSION

The development and application of implementation measures may very well become one of the most important issues international humanitarian law will face in the near future. Procedures to stimulate compliance and mechanisms for fact-finding or mediation between the parties of an armed conflict are indispensable tools to guarantee compliance with the obligations of the Geneva Conventions and the Additional Protocol. They

---

30 There is some competence within the framework of the IAEA in case of a violation of safeguard agreements.
31 See ILC Report A/44/10, at 179 (41st session). See also Report Drafting Committee ILC A/CN.4/L.455, at 2 (42nd session) and ILC Report A/45/10, §§ 89-92 (42nd session).

may allow to prevent recourse to reprisals which mostly result in an escalation of violence. Especially in our times when new weapon systems and the proliferation of weapons of mass destruction threaten human life and the existence of mankind conflict prevention and control is badly needed. It, therefore, is encouraging to state that with the rapidly disappearing of the East-West confrontation effective control systems in the area of arms control and disarmament emerge. They strengthen the relationship between this branch of international law and international humanitarian law. This development should be carefully studied, since it could have a direct bearing on the functioning of international humanitarian law.[32]

---

32 *Cf.*, Kalshoven, op. cit. n. 1, at 326.

V

NEUTRALITY
AND
NAVAL WARFARE

TRANSFORMATIONS IN THE LAW OF NEUTRALITY SINCE 1945

DIETRICH SCHINDLER

1.   INTRODUCTION: THE DECLINE OF THE LAW OF NEUTRALITY

Up to World War I and to a large extent also until World War II, the law
of neutrality had its fixed and uncontested place within the law of nations.
It was one of the chapters to be found in every treatise of international
law. At that time international law was divided between the law of peace
and the law of war. The law of neutrality was attached to the law of war
because it only became applicable when war broke out. It regulated the
relations between the belligerent States and the States remaining outside the

war. Unlike the law of war, however, the law of neutrality did not replace the law of peace but only modified it in some respects.

Since 1945 the law of neutrality has largely lost its former significance in the system of international law. Many believe that it has become irrelevant due to such causes as the UN Charter, economic interdependence, new kinds of warfare, ideological cleavages etc. Most treatises of international law no longer contain chapters on the law of neutrality and this branch of international law is now seldom taught at university. A similar situation also applied to the law of war for a considerable time after World War II.[1] However, this part of international law was revised in 1949 in the framework of the four Geneva Conventions. Furthermore it attracted new interest in the nineteen-seventies under the designation of international humanitarian law through the Diplomatic Conference on the Reaffirmation and Development of International Humanitarian Law Applicable in Armed Conflicts and the two Additional Protocols, adopted in 1977, to which Kalshoven has contributed so much. However, by way of contrast, the law of neutrality remained in a state of uncertainty.[2] The two 1907 Hague Conventions on neutrality (Conventions V and XIII) have largely fallen into oblivion. There has hardly been any discussion on the problems of the law of neutrality outside the permanently neutral States.[3] Nevertheless, States have not completely ceased to refer to the law of neutrality. Occasionally they declare themselves neutral or invoke specific rights or duties of neutrals.[4]

In the Korean War 1950-1953, for instance, the Arab States and Indonesia issued statements that they wanted to remain neutral and would not participate in UN actions.[5] In the same war even China and the Soviet Union considered themselves to be neutral. China characterized its troops fighting on the side of North Korea as volunteers who had individually crossed the frontier in accordance with Article 6 of Hague Convention V

---

1   See J.L. Kunz, *The Chaotic Status of the Laws of War and the Urgent Need for their Revision*, 45 AJIL 37-61 (1951).

2   See K. Zemanek, *The Chaotic Status of the Laws of Neutrality, in* Im Dienst an der Gemeinschaft, Festschrift für Dietrich Schindler zum 65. Geburtstag 443-454 (1989).

3   Most notable exceptions to this statement are P.M. Norton, *Between the Ideology and the Reality, the Shadow of the Law of Neutrality*, 17 Harvard International Law Journal 249-311 (1976); W.L. Williams, *Neutrality in Modern Armed Conflicts: A Survey of the Developing Law*, 90 Military Law Review 9-48 (1980); Y. Dinstein, The Laws of Neutrality, 14 Israel Yearbook of Human Rights 80-110 (1984).

4   A survey of such cases is given by Norton and Williams, loc. cit. n. 3.

5   See H.J. Taubenfeld, *International Actions and Neutrality*, 47 AJIL 392, n. 92 (1953); Norton, loc. cit. n. 3, at 267.

on Neutrality in Case of War on Land.[6] In the Indo-Pakistani War of 1965, Ceylon adopted a neutral attitude and declined the transit of war materials for the belligerents.[7] In the Yom Kippur War of 1973 between Arab States and Israel, several Western European States declared themselves neutral and refused to allow the United States to use their territories for the supply of war materials to Israel.[8] They hoped thereby to avoid the Arab oil embargo. In the Iran-Iraq War (1980-1988) many States declared themselves neutral and invoked rights of neutrality in maritime warfare.[9] In the military enforcement action against Iraq in 1991, authorized by Security Council Resolution 678 of 29 November 1990, some States, most notably Iran, declared to remain neutral. Iran affirmed that Iraqi military aircraft and pilots who had landed on its territory would be kept there until the end of the hostilities.

Not only did States which intended to remain outside armed conflicts occasionally refer to the law of neutrality but so also did belligerents who claimed belligerent rights against non-participating States. During the Vietnam War, the invasion of Cambodia in 1970 by South Vietnam and the United States was justified by some authors on the ground that Cambodia had failed in its neutral duty to prevent the use of its territory as a base for North Vietnam and the Vietcong.[10]

Belligerent rights towards non-participating States have been invoked most consistently in naval warfare. In the Arab-Israeli conflict, Egypt exercised its right of visit and search over neutral vessels in the Suez canal region. It instituted a Prize Court and seized contraband.[11] The same rights were claimed by Pakistan and India in their wars of 1965 and 1971.[12] In the Iran-Iraq conflict, Iran also made use of the right of belligerents to visit ships of non-participating States. Much more important

6	Taubenfeld, loc. cit. n. 5, at 392; Norton, loc. cit. n. 3, at 279. Also J.G. Verplaetse, *The Ius in Bello and Military Operations in Korea*, 23 ZaöRV 713, 716 (1963).
7	Norton, loc. cit. n. 3, at 262, 294.
8	Norton, loc. cit. n. 3, at 260, 295, 300; U. Beyerlin, W. Strasser, *Völkerrechtliche Praxis der Bundesrepublik Deutchland im Jahre 1973*, 35 ZaöRV 811 (1975).
9	*Infra* n. 13.
10	Norton, loc. cit. n. 3, at 268, 283. Also D. Schindler, *L'emploi de la force par un Etat belligérant sur le territoire d'un Etat non belligérant*, in Estudios de Derecho Internacional, Homenaje al Profesor Miaja de la Muela (Studies in International Law in Honour of Professor Miaja de la Muela) 847 *et seq.* (1979).
11	Norton, loc. cit. n. 3, at 258, 303-305; R. Ottmüller, Die Anwendung von Seekriegsrecht in militärischen Konflikten seit 1945 (The Application of the Law of Naval Warfare in Military Conflicts since 1945) 50 *et seq.* (1978).
12	Norton, loc. cit. n. 3, at 262, 294; Ottmüller, op. cit. n. 11, at 271; S.P. Sharma, The Indo-Pakistan Maritime Conflict 8 *et seq.* (1970).

in this war, however, were the attacks on neutral shipping which were justified partly by the establishment of exclusion zones by the belligerents and partly by asserting that neutral merchant ships were performing unneutral services. A major debate developed on the law of naval warfare in which the law of neutrality played a considerable role.[13] Interestingly, however, governments and the UN Security Council -which adopted four resolutions on neutral shipping in this war-[14] generally made no express mention of the law of neutrality.

In spite of the restraint by governments in invoking the law of neutrality, this law has continued to be extensively reproduced in manuals of military law edited by several States.[15] Most of them define the rights and duties of neutrals and belligerents according to the traditional law of neutrality.

This short survey setting out some of the attitudes adopted by States towards the law of neutrality since 1945, reveals a rather confusing situation. On the one hand, there is a strong tendency to consider this part of international law as obsolete. Yet on the other hand in certain cases governments nevertheless refer to it. For the permanently neutral States it forms the essential basis for their neutral behaviour. The present essay, in

---

13 See E. David, *La Guerre du Golfe et le droit international*, 20 Revue belge de droit international 153-183 (1987); L. Doswald-Beck, *The International Law of Naval Armed Conflicts: The Need for Reform*, 7 The Italian Yearbook of International Law 251-282 (1986-1987); W.J. Fenrick, *The Exclusion Zone Device in the Law of Naval Warfare*, 24 Canadian Yearbook of International Law 91-126 (1986); M. Jenkins, *The Legality of the Iraqi Exclusion Zone and Iranian Reprisals*, 8 Boston College International and Comparative Law Review 551-549 (1985); R. Lagoni, *Gewaltverbot, Seekriegsrecht und Schiffahrtsfreiheit im Golfkrieg* (Prohibition of the Use of Force, Law of Naval Warfare and Freedom of Navigation in the Gulf War), in W. Fürst, R, Herzog, D.C. Umbach, eds., 2 Festschrift für Wolfgang Zeidler, 1833-1867 (1987); R. Leckow, *The Iran-Iraq Conflict in the Gulf: The Law of War Zones*, 37 ICLQ 629-644 (1988); N. Ronzitti, *The Crisis of the Traditional Law Regulating International Armed Conflicts at Sea and the Need for its Revision*, in N. Ronzitti, ed., The Law of Naval Warfare 1-57 (1988); N. Ronzitti, *La Guerre du Golfe, le déminage et la circulation des navires*, 32 Annuaire français de droit international 647-661 (1987); P. Tavernier, *La Guerre du Golfe: Quelques aspects de l'application du droit des conflits armées et du droit humanitaire*, 30 Annuaire français de droit international 43-64 (1984); R.L. Weiner, *Limited Armed Conflict Causing Physical Damage to Neutral Countries: Questions of Liability*, 15 California Western International Law Journal 161-191 (1985).

14 SC Res. 540 (1983), 552 (1984), 582 (1986), 598 (1987), in Resolutions and Decisions of the Security Council, SC Off. Rec.

15 *E.g.* U.S. Field Manual, FM 27-10, Chapter 9 (1956); Law of Naval Warfare, §§ 230-233, at 443-444 (1955), in R.W. Tucker, The Law of War and Neutrality at Sea 359 *et seq.* (1957); The Commander's Handbook of Naval Operations, Naval Warfare Publications 9, Chapter 7 (1987); also in Great Britain: *The Law of War on Land*, Manual of Military Law, Chapter XV (1958).

honour of Kalshoven, is designed to bring some clarification into the problem of the present status of the law of neutrality within the system of international law. It will only consider the law of neutrality as a whole and not individual rules of this law.

2. FROM THE DUALISM NEUTRALITY - BELLIGERENCY TO A MULTIPLICITY OF INTERMEDIATE POSITIONS

2.1 The dualism neutrality - belligerency

Under classical international law, as it existed before World War I, the rule developed that in the case of war breaking out, any non-participating State should have the free choice to enter the war as a belligerent or to remain neutral and to apply the law of neutrality. War was not prohibited at that time, but when a State chose to remain outside a war it was automatically bound by the law of neutrality. International law did not recognize intermediate forms of benevolent neutrality, as they were practised in earlier periods, but only one form of neutrality, *i.e.*, strict neutrality, whose rules were codified in Hague Conventions V and XIII of 1907.

2.2 The impact of Article 2(4) of the UN Charter

Article 2(4) of the Charter abolished the right of States to resort to war. All UN Member States have to refrain in their international relations from the threat or use of force against the territorial integrity or political independence of any State. The only exceptions admitted are UN enforcement measures (Chapter VII of the Charter) and the right of individual or collective self-defence (Article 51). Actions against former enemy States provided for in Articles 53 and 107 are no longer of significance nowadays. Article 2(4) has the consequence that States, in case of an armed conflict between other States, can no longer choose freely between neutrality and belligerency. Their choice is limited by the Charter.

2.3 The impact of Chapter VII of the UN Charter

Most discussions on the impact of the UN Charter on neutrality have turned around the question whether neutrality remains possible in the system of collective security established by Chapter VII of the Charter. In fact, however, this question has proved to be of minor importance as the

Security Council has only rarely been able to decide on enforcement measures. If a decision is reached by the Security Council as to enforcement measures, those Member States bound by such decisions can no longer fully comply with the law of neutrality. In the case of non-military measures they have to deviate from the rule of impartial treatment of belligerents (Article 9 of both Conventions V and XIII). In the case of military enforcement measures -which are binding only for States which have concluded special agreements with the Security Council in accordance with Article 43 of the Charter- they can no longer fulfil their obligation not to render military assistance to a belligerent. The neutrality of States participating in UN enforcement measures is, however, not completely abolished but only reduced in some respects. One has therefore spoken of 'qualified neutrality'. Full or strict neutrality is still possible if the Security Council or the General Assembly adopt non-binding recommendations or if the Security Council, by virtue of Article 48, does not call upon all Members to carry out its decisions or, thirdly, if measures are taken against a State which is not involved in an international armed conflict (the law of neutrality being applicable only in such conflicts). The measures against Southern Rhodesia decided upon in 1966 and against South Africa in 1977 were both directed against countries not involved in international armed conflicts. Some writers maintain that the law of neutrality is conceived for traditional inter-State wars only and therefore is inapplicable to UN enforcement measures.[16] Although this opinion is theoretically defensible, it must be kept in mind that a State which participates in enforcement measures will hardly be considered as a neutral by the target State and therefore will also not be suitable for neutral functions. On the other hand, if the entire international community adopts enforcement measures against a State, it becomes practically impossible, even for a Non-Member State, to remain neutral between such unequal parties. That is the reason why Switzerland, in the case of Southern Rhodesia, decided to restrict its commerce with this country to the *courant normal* in order not to make UN trade restrictions ineffective. In the case of the economic sanctions against Iraq in 1990 Switzerland decided to participate fully as did the other permanently neutral States. In military matters, however, Switzerland decided to remain strictly neutral. It did not

---

16 In this sense Article 5 of the Resolutions of the Institut de droit international on *Conditions of Application of Rules, Other than Humanitarian Rules of Armed Conflicts to Hostilities in which United Nations Forces may be Engaged*, 56 Annuaire de l'Institut de droit international 541 (1975).

permit the overflight of its territory by military aircraft of 'belligerent' States, as did Austria, except for humanitarian purposes.

2.4   The impact of Article 51 of the UN Charter

Article 51 has influenced the law of neutrality to a greater extent than have the other Charter provisions. It states that nothing in the Charter shall impair the inherent right of individual or collective self-defence if an armed attack occurs against a Member of the United Nations, until the Security Council has taken measures necessary to maintain international peace and security. Based on the right of collective self-defence, third States may assist the victim of an armed attack by any conceivable means. They have, however, no duty to do so but may remain neutral. On the other hand, they are prohibited from assisting the aggressor State.

As to the behaviour towards the *victim of aggression*, any attitude between strict neutrality and participation in the armed conflict on the side of the victim is admissible.[17] The dualism neutrality-belligerency has thereby been abolished. States not wishing to take part in the armed conflict on the victim's side are no longer obliged to apply the law of neutrality. Benevolent neutrality or non-belligerency have become legally admitted attitudes. Neutrality has become purely optional. State practice since 1945 shows that States have in fact assumed a great variety of intermediate positions regarding armed conflicts between other States. In the Vietnam War, for instance, some States assisted South Vietnam by sending troops to it, others put air bases at its disposal or delivered war materials. In the Arab-Israeli conflict and in the Iran-Iraq War, third States behaved in a similar way. The international community has recognized such intermediate positions by introducing the term 'neutral and non-belligerent powers' in Article 122 of Geneva Convention III of 1949 and the term 'neutral and other States not parties to the conflict' in several Articles of Protocol I of 1977 (Articles 2(c), 9(2,a), 19, 22(2,a), 31, 39(1), and 64). 'Neutral' States are those which apply the law of neutrality in its entirety; 'other States not parties to the conflict' are those which assist a party without becoming themselves parties to the conflict.[18]

---

17   *Cf.*, L. Oppenheim, H. Lauterpacht, eds., II International Law 651, 7th ed. (1955); I. Brownlie, International Law and the Use of Force by States 403-404 (1963); Tucker, op. cit. n. 15, at 178.

18   *Cf.*, E. Kussbach, *Le Protocole additionnel I et les Etats neutres*, 62 Revue internationale de la Croix-Rouge 231-251 (1980); F. Kalshoven, Constraints on the Waging of War 113 (1987).

With respect to the attitude towards the *aggressor State*, any assistance to him is prohibited. Neutrality, however, remains possible for third States. As long as the Security Council has not decided on the measures to be adopted against the aggressor, third States may maintain relations with it to the extent which is admissible under the law of neutrality. In particular, they may maintain economic relations with it, with the exception that no war materials may be supplied. The law of neutrality, in other words, sets an upper limit to what is admissible action in favour of the aggressor State.[19] It may seem contradictory that the law of neutrality should apply to only one party to the conflict and not to both. Yet, this is a consequence of the fact that rules of different periods of legal development have to be applied simultaneously.

If the Security Council is not able to determine who is the aggressor -this is the situation envisaged by Article 51- third States may make use of their right of collective self-defence only if the two conditions are met as defined by the ICJ in its Nicaragua Judgment in 1986:[20] first, the State which is the victim of an armed attack must form the view and declare that it has been so attacked; secondly, the attacked State must have addressed a request to the third State. These two conditions apply, however, only to the use of force. Other forms of assistance, such as economic help (including the supply of war materials) which are generally admissible according to international law, are not subject to these conditions. There is no duty to remain neutral in the sense of the old law of neutrality.

2.5   The problem of the 'state of war'

According to classical international law, the law of neutrality became applicable only if a state of war existed between two or more States. In most international armed conflicts since 1945 no state of war has been recognized. It is generally assumed that if the parties to an armed conflict do not consider their hostilities as war, then third States are not bound by

---

19 Judge Ammoun, in his Separate Opinion in the *Namibia (South West Africa) Case* (1971), expressed the same opinion. He assumed that a state of war existed between Namibia and South Africa in which third States had to apply the law of neutrality. However, in his view, they had to discriminate between the aggressor and the victim of agrression. While they had the right to assist the victim they were bound by the rules of neutrality towards the aggressor. ICJ Reports, 1971, at 91-100.
20 ICJ Reports, 1986, §§ 195-199, at 104-105.

the law of neutrality.[21] This is a further explanation for the fact that since 1945 the law of neutrality has no longer been considered as binding for States not parties to armed conflicts. The question remains, however, whether non-participants, if a state of war has been recognized by the parties to a conflict, are still bound to apply the law of neutrality. Some writers have affirmed this question,[22] yet, as is believed, erroneously. According to Article 51 of the Charter, non-participating States have the right to assist the victims of an armed attack without any regard to a state of war. They do not have to take the law of neutrality into consideration. The Charter evidently prevails over older customary law. State practice confirms this conclusion. No State, since 1945, has ever considered itself bound by the law of neutrality in the case of a state of war recognized by parties to a conflict. Examples of this are provided in the case of the Arab-Israeli conflict, in the Indo-Pakistani War, possibly also, in the Iran-Iraq War (in which a state of war never was officially affirmed)[23] and in the enforcement action against Iraq in 1991 in which some of the participating States spoke of being at war with Iraq although they did not issue formal declarations of war.

However, it should be emphasized, that the law of neutrality may be applied in all armed conflicts even if no state of war has been recognized. States which since 1945 have referred to the law of neutrality have generally done so without regard to a possible state of war. The permanently neutral States in particular have considered the law of neutrality to be applicable to all international armed conflicts. The right to apply the law of neutrality in all international armed conflicts finds its confirmation in the Geneva Conventions of 1949. It is stated in their common Article 2 that they apply 'to all cases of declared war or of any other armed conflict which may arise between two or more of the High Contracting Parties, even if the state of war is not recognized by one of

---

21 *Cf.*, *inter alia*, P. Guggenheim, 2 Traité de droit international public 314, 510 (1954); R.L. Bindschedler, *Frieden, Krieg und Neutralität im Völkerrecht der Gegenwart* (Peace, War and Neutrality in Present Day International Law), in J. Tittel, ed., *Multitudo Legum, Ius Unum*, Essays in Honour of W. Wengler 37 (1973); D. Schindler, *State of War, Belligerency, Armed Conflict*, in A. Cassese, ed., The New Humanitarian Law of Armed Conflicts 13 (1979); J. Köpfer, Die Neutralität im Wandel der Erscheinungsformen militärischer Auseinandersetzungen (Neutrality and Changing Forms of Military Conflicts) 92, 98, 100, 103 (1975).

22 *Cf.*, Guggenheim, op. cit. n. 21, at 510; L. Kotzsch, The Concept of War in Contemporary History and International Law 143 (1956); Köpfer, op. cit. n. 21, at 96 *et seq.*

23 *Cf.*, C. Greenwood, *The Concept of War in Modern International Law*, 36 ICLQ 293-294 (1987).

them'. At the same time the Conventions confer several tasks upon neutral powers, thereby presupposing that there are neutrals even though no state of war is recognized.

It may seem that the state of war has lost any relevance to the law of neutrality. Yet, in one respect there remain some doubts. According to a widely held opinion, belligerents in maritime warfare may exercise rights over neutral merchant ships and cargoes, especially the rights of visit, search and seizure of contraband, only if the state of war is recognized. This opinion was corroborated by governments and authors in the Arab-Israeli conflict and in the Indo-Pakistani War. It played no role, however, in the Iran-Iraq War even though belligerent rights against third States were extensively exercised in this conflict. One could possibly argue that belligerents who exercise rights over neutral shipping in maritime warfare thereby implicitly assume the existence of a state of war.[24] In fact, in none of the armed conflicts in which a state of war was alleged to exist did the parties to the conflict ever issue declarations of war. If, in this way, the exercise of belligerent rights against third States is considered as an implicit recognition of a state of war and if it is assumed that the exercise of belligerent rights is the only legal consequence of a state of war, the invocation of the state of war has become futile. The Iran-Iraq conflict where belligerent rights were invoked without any formal recognition of war may be taken as a sign of this futility. In the enforcement action against Iraq the Security Council by Resolution 665 of 25 August 1990, ordered States deploying maritime forces in the Gulf to halt and inspect ships in order to enforce the economic sanctions against Iraq which had been decided upon by Resolution 661 of 6 August 1990. It was widely assumed that this 'blockade', similar to classical blockades, created a state of armed conflict or war between the blockading States and Iraq; no distinction was thereby made between armed conflict and war.

2.6   Neutrality and wars of national liberation

According to Article 1(4) of Protocol I Additional to the Geneva Conventions, armed conflicts in which peoples are fighting against colonial domination and alien occupation and against racist régimes are to be considered as international armed conflicts. It has been said that by virtue of this provision the law of neutrality had become applicable to wars of

---

24 In none of the situations referred to, was a state of war declared. It was only implicitly assumed. *Cf.*, Schindler, loc. cit. n. 21, at 8, 10-11; Greenwood, loc. cit. n. 23, at 293-294.

national liberation.[25] This is undoubtedly correct if one enlarges this statement by adding that third States, apart from permanently neutral States, have no duty to apply this law. Furthermore, it should be noticed that the situation for third States in wars of national liberation is different from the one in inter-State conflicts, insofar as Article 51 of the Charter is not applicable. The question whether third States may assist one or other party to such a conflict depends on the recognition of the right of self-determination. On the basis of UN resolutions it is generally assumed that no aid may be given to a government which denies self-determination to a people while, on the other hand, 'moral and material assistance' (but no military aid), may be rendered to peoples struggling for self-determination.[26] Liberation movements, for their part, in an armed conflict, have to respect the rights of neutral States and other States not parties to the conflict in the same way as States have to comply.

3. RIGHTS AND DUTIES OF 'STATES NOT PARTIES TO THE CONFLICT' COMPARED WITH THE RIGHTS AND DUTIES OF 'NEUTRALS'

In traditional international law the rights and duties of States not parties to an armed conflict were fixed in a uniform way. All non-participating States were bound to apply the law of neutrality. Positions of non-belligerency, as adopted by some States in World War II, were considered to be illegal.[27] Nowadays, after intermediate positions have become lawful, the question arises as to what extent the rights and duties fixed by the law of neutrality apply to 'neutrals' only and how far they are applicable to all non-participants. Apparently, it has so far been widely assumed in legal doctrine and practice that the law of neutrality formed a coherent body of norms which could only be applied as a whole. It was not realized that

25 I. Seidl-Hohenveldern, Befreiungskriege und Neutralität (Wars of National Liberation and Neutrality), in A. Giuffrè, ed., Studi in onore di Manlio Udina (Studies in Honour of Manlio Udina) 656 (1975).
26 *Cf.*, H.J. Uibopuu, *Wars of National Liberation*, in R. Bernhardt, ed., 4 Encyclopaedia of Public International Law 345 (1982); D. Schindler, *Die Grenzen des völkerrechtlichen Gewaltverbots* (Limitations of the Prohibition of the Use of Force), Berichte der Deutschen Gesellschaft für Völkerrecht (Reports of the German Association of International Law) 27-28 (1986).
27 *Cf.*, R.L. Bindschedler, *Neutrality, Concept and General Rules*, in R. Bernhardt, ed., op. cit. n. 26, at 13; A. Verdross, Völkerrecht (International law) 5th ed., 505-506 (1964); E. Castrén, The Present Law of War and Neutrality 450-452 (1954).

some of the rights and duties fixed in the law of neutrality apply to all non-participants while others apply to neutrals in the traditional sense only. Unawareness of this may explain to some extent why governments and authors have been hesitant in referring to the law of neutrality in the case of States not practising neutrality in its strict sense.

3.1   Rights and duties of all States not participating in an armed conflict

In a general way it may be stated that the so-called rights of neutrals as well as their duty to tolerate certain measures taken by belligerents apply to all States not parties to an armed conflict. The so-called rights of neutrals are in fact not rights in the proper sense. They consist, on the one hand, of the duty of the belligerents to respect neutral territory and neutral property including vessels on the High Seas (with the restrictions mentioned later), and, on the other hand, of the negation of certain duties of neutrals which might be presumed if they were not expressly denied. Concerning the respect of neutral territory, Article 1 of Hague Convention V states: 'The territory of neutral Powers is inviolable'. Originally this right could only be claimed by States which fulfilled all the duties of neutrality, *i.e.*, the truly neutral States. Today, however, the use of force against the territorial integrity of any State is prohibited by Article 2(4) of the UN Charter. Use of force against other States is lawful only if the conditions of Article 51 of the Charter are fulfilled. Article 2(4) of the Charter has thus transformed the right of neutrals to inviolability of their territory into a right of all States. Concerning those rights which are mere negations of duties, the following examples taken from Hague Convention V (neutrality in case of war on land) may be given:

'Article 6
The responsibility of a neutral Power is not engaged by the fact of persons crossing the frontier separately to offer their services to one of the belligerents.

Article 7
A neutral Power is not called upon to prevent the export or transport, on behalf of one or other of the belligerents, of arms, munitions of war, or, in general, of anything which can be of use to an army or a fleet.

(...)

Article 10
The fact of a neutral Power resisting, even by force, attempts to violate its neutrality, cannot be regarded as a hostile act.

(...)

Article 14
A neutral Power may authorize the passage over its territory of sick and wounded belonging to the belligerent armies ....'

One could add rights which are recognized by customary law only, such as the right to maintain trade relations with belligerent States or the right to maintain a free press. All these rights are not reserved to genuine neutrals. The Geneva Conventions and Protocol I also fix some rights of neutrals which obviously are rights of all States not participating in an armed conflict. Examples of this are the right of Red Cross societies of neutral countries to lend the assistance of their medical personnel and units to a party to a conflict (Article 27 of Convention I) and the right to permit military hospital ships of belligerents to remain in their ports (Article 32 of Convention II). While the 1949 Conventions generally speak of 'neutral' countries only, the 1977 Protocol I expressly speaks of 'neutral and other States not parties to the conflict'.

The duty of neutrals to tolerate certain measures of belligerents (duty of acquiescence) is also applicable to all States not parties to a conflict. Belligerents, as has already been stated, have the right in maritime warfare to visit and search neutral merchant ships on the high seas and to confiscate contraband as prize. In certain conditions they may attack and destroy neutral merchant ships. All the States not parties to an armed conflict have to tolerate such acts. Belligerents who have exercised such rights since 1945, especially in the Arab-Israeli War and the Iran-Iraq War, have never made any distinction between genuine neutrals and other States not parties to the conflict. Such measures would indeed not have any justification if they were limited to States which are genuine neutrals.

3.2 Rights and duties of 'neutral' States only

The remaining duties of neutral States, *i.e.*, all the duties other than the duty to tolerate certain measures of belligerents, are duties of neutral States only. They are generally classified into the three duties of abstention, prevention and impartiality. Abstention means that the neutral State may not provide military assistance to belligerents. In particular it may not put at their disposal troops, war materials, territory, military intelligence and credits for war purposes (*cf.*, Articles 5-8 of the Hague Convention V and Article 6, Hague Convention XIII).

Under the duty of prevention, the neutral State is obliged to prevent belligerents from using its territory for war purposes. Neutrals may not tolerate on their territory acts of belligerents which are prohibited by the law of neutrality (*cf.*, Articles 5 and 10 of the Hague Convention V, Articles 8 and 25, Hague Convention XIII).

Finally, the duty of impartiality obliges the neutral State to apply equally to all belligerents the rules set up by itself with regard to its relations with belligerents *e.g.* rules restricting the private export of war materials (*cf.*, Article 9 of both Hague Conventions V and XIII). These three duties constitute the characteristic traits of neutrality, as it is commonly understood. They alone justify the use of the word 'neutral'.

The fact that in practice the term 'neutral' is sometimes used in its strict sense and sometimes to designate all States not parties to an armed conflict, has given rise to much confusion. The Korean Armistice Agreement, for instance, set up a 'Neutral Nations Supervisory Commission'. The word 'neutral' thereby was used in the broad sense of States not parties to the Korean War. Similary, the term 'neutral countries' in the Geneva Conventions of 1949 refers to all States not parties to an armed conflict. It would be desirable to make a clear distinction in future international instruments between the rights and duties of all States not parties to armed conflicts and the rights and duties of neutral States in the strict sense.

The development which has been described reveals that the truly neutral States have to fulfil specific duties without having corresponding rights. In fact, as has been shown, all the rights of neutrals can be claimed by all the States not participating in an armed conflict. They are not dependent on the fulfilment of the particular duties of genuine neutrals. This may seem to be a one-sided burden laid upon neutral States. Originally, as has been stated, the right to inviolability of the territory of neutral powers was dependent on the fulfilment of neutral duties. Nowadays, however, Article 2(4) of the Charter prohibits the use of force against the territorial integrity of any State. Truly neutral States no longer enjoy a privileged position as they did previously. Nevertheless, strict neutrality still has some advantages, although these have a more political than a legal character. States which deviate from strict neutrality and assist a belligerent run the risk of countermeasures by the injured belligerent and of being drawn into the war, even though their assistance to a belligerent may be lawful and the countermeasures unlawful. A belligerent against whom a third State takes discriminatory measures easily finds a pretext for countermeasures against the third State. For the truly neutral State the old law of neutrality serves as a code of conduct which sets a clear line for neutral behaviour. In particular, it limits the neutral's duties and clearly shows what neutral actions are admissible.

3.3   The question of reprisals for non-compliance with rules of neutrality

Although the problem of reprisals has already been touched on, a closer look at it is necessary. As long as the law of neutrality was binding on all States not parties to an armed conflict, belligerents were authorized to take reprisals against States which violated that law to their detriment. At present, after intermediate positions between neutrality and participation in a conflict have become admissible and neutrality has become purely optional, reprisals are no longer admissible unless a State is individually obliged to respect the law of neutrality. Any actions involving the use of force against a State not party to a conflict are, moreover, prohibited by Article 2(4) of the Charter except for measures of self-defence.[28] Whereas reprisals are lawful only when directed against an internationally wrongful act, retorsions are merely unfriendly acts and do not presuppose an international delict. Retorsions such as the breaking off of economic relations, are therefore lawful countermeasures of belligerents against States which render assistance to their enemy.

In two cases since 1945, the question of countermeasures for non-compliance with the law of neutrality has been discussed. The first occasion was the invasion of Cambodia by the United States and South Vietnam in 1970.[29] These actions were justified by some authors with the argument that Cambodia had violated its neutral duty to prevent its territory from being used for war purposes by North Vietnam and the Vietcong. This argument would only have been pertinent if Cambodia had been internationally obliged to apply the law of neutrality which presumably it was not. The invasion could, however, be justified by the right of self-defence, since the use of Cambodian territory in order to

---

28 *Cf.*, in the same sense, IDI Res. of 1975, loc. cit. n. 16, Article 1; David, loc. cit. n. 13, at 172-173; Greenwood, loc. cit. n. 23, at 298. For a general discussion of the problem see Schindler, loc. cit. n. 10.

29 On the intervention in Cambodia see R. Falk, ed., 3 The Vietnam War and International Law, 23 *et seq.* (1972); D.T. Fox, ed., The Cambodian Incursion, Legal Issues (1971).

attack South Vietnam amounted to an armed attack in the sense of
Article 51 of the Charter.

The second case concerned the Arab oil embargo against European and
American States and Japan on the occasion of the Arab-Israeli War of
1973.[30] In legal doctrine it was argued that this measure could be justified
by the unneutral behaviour of these States. This opinion, however, is
untenable since the respective States were not bound by the law of
neutrality. Moreover, they probably did not even deviate from neutral
behaviour. The embargo nevertheless presumably did not conflict with
international legal duties.[31]

Various authors, as well as a number of manuals on military law
continue to reproduce the old rule of the law of neutrality which says:

'If the neutral nation is unable or unwilling to enforce effectively its right
of inviolability an aggrieved belligerent may resort to acts of hostility in
neutral territory against enemy forces, including warships and military
aircraft, making unlawful use of that territory.'[32]

As the use of force against the territory of another State is now regulated
by the UN Charter, the cited rule of the law of neutrality is no longer
applicable. The legality of armed countermeasures is to be judged on the
basis of Article 51 of the Charter, the Charter taking precedence over the
old law of neutrality. Moreover, the law of neutrality is not applicable in
this case because third States are no longer bound by it unless they have
individually assumed a respective obligation. Article 51 of the Charter
allows acts of hostility by a belligerent on the territory of a third State if
enemy forces use this territory to carry out attacks against it. Such acts of
hostility have to be restricted to enemy forces on neutral territory. Acts of
self-defence by belligerents on neutral territory are also to be considered as
lawful if such territory has been occupied by the opponent or serves as a
military base for him or is used for the permanent passage of troops.

---

30 *Cf.*, I.F.I. Shihata, *Destination Embargo of Arab Oil: Its Legality under International Law*, 68
     AJIL 614 *et seq.* (1974). Repr. in I.F.I. Shihata, The Case for the Arab Oil Embargo (1975)
     and in Paust, Blaustein, ed., The Arab Oil Weapon (1977).
31 *Cf.*, Shihata, loc. cit. n. 30, at 608 *et seq.*; D.C. Dicke, Die Intervention mit wirtschaftlichen
     Mitteln im Völkerrecht (Intervention by Military Means in International Law) 221 *et seq.*
     (1978).
32 Cited in Annotated Supplement to the Commander's Handbook on the Law of Naval
     Operations, NWP 9, (Rev. A), FMFM 1-10, Chapter 7-11 (1989). Further references in
     Schindler, loc. cit. n. 10.

Although the old law of neutrality is still cited in connection with belligerent acts of hostility on neutral territory many authors use the term 'self-defence' in this context[33] without recognizing that it is the Charter, not the law of neutrality, which is to be applied in this case.

4.   TRANSFORMATIONS IN THE LAW OF PERMANENT NEUTRALITY

Since the beginning of the nineteenth Century, a number of States have assumed the international obligation to remain permanently neutral: Switzerland in 1815, Belgium in 1831, Luxemburg in 1867 (for the two latter States permanent neutrality was abrogated by the Treaty of Versailles in 1919).[34] Of a rather ephemeral nature was the permanent neutrality of Cracow (1815-1846) and of the Congo Free State (1885-1908). The Vatican State assumed the status of permanent neutrality in 1929, Austria in 1955. Other States, such as Sweden, have acted in the same manner as permanently neutral States but are not legally bound to do so. By accepting the status of permanent neutrality, a State commits itself to remain neutral and to apply the law of neutrality in all wars involving other States. In the period of classical international law, when States still had an unrestricted right to go to war, the permanently neutral States renounced that right. In every other respect, however, their status was the same as that of all other States. In wartime permanently neutral States had exactly the same rights and duties as other States not participating in war.

The transformations in the law of neutrality which have occurred since 1945 have also affected permanent neutrality. First of all, the permanently neutral States have taken on the role of being the only States which are still bound to apply the law of neutrality. All other States are no longer under such an obligation as far as the duties of strict neutrality are concerned. They no longer consider this law as relevant. This development has obviously weakened the legal position of permanent neutrality. Secondly, the old law of neutrality has lost much of its relevance even for the permanently neutral States by the fact that the role of permanent neutrality has shifted from war to peace. Since 1945, the prevention of wars has become much more important than the determination of the rights and

---

33 See the statements made by several authors on the 'problem of the weak or unwilling neutral', in 26 Revue de Droit Pénal Militaire et de Droit de la Guerre 49-51 (1987).

34 See the survey given by R.L. Bindschedler, *Permanent Neutrality of States*, in Bernhardt, ed., op. cit. n. 26, at 133.

duties of neutrals in case of war. In the framework of the UN and other international organizations and conferences (such as the CSCE), permanently neutral States and their nationals have assumed or have been entrusted with particular functions which presuppose a certain measure of impartiality. For such functions the law of neutrality, which is applicable in case of war only, is irrelevant. It is therefore not surprising that, since 1945, no State has assumed the status of permanent neutrality based on the old law of neutrality with the one exception of Austria which took Switzerland as its model in 1955.

In two cases, however, new forms of permanent neutrality detached from the old law of neutrality, were created by international agreements.[35] In 1962, Laos was declared permanently neutral on the basis of two congruous declarations, one issued by Laos and the second by thirteen other States. Laos, following the principle of peaceful coexistence and non-alignment, agreed not to enter into any military alliance nor to allow the establishment of military bases on its territory nor to allow any country to use its territory for other military purposes. The two declarations made no mention of the law of neutrality nor of armed conflicts. In fact they were designed for the situation of cold war as had been brought about by the East-West schism. The question remained open whether or not the law of neutrality would be applicable in case of an armed conflict. The neutrality of Laos withered away within a few years. A similar kind of permanent neutrality was created for Malta in 1981. It followed the Laotian example. Two declarations were adopted by Malta and Italy which fixed the rights and duties of the two States on the lines of the Laotian declarations. No reference to the law of neutrality was made in this case either.

Even though the neutralities of Laos and Malta were of a transitional rather than of a permanent nature, they show two significant traits which may be important for future developments. First of all, they separate neutrality from war. They fix rights and duties of neutral States independently of armed conflicts. In this regard they reflect more adequately than the old law of neutrality the role which permanently neutral States have in fact assumed since 1945. Secondly, although no mention is made of the old law of neutrality, the declarations leave no

---

35 As to Laos see D. Schindler, *Aspects contemporains de la neutralité*, 121 Hague Recueil 308 et seq. (1967); as to Malta see N. Ronzitti, *Malta's Permanent Neutrality*, 5 Italian Yearbook of International Law 171 (1980-1981). Also D. Schindler, *Neue Fälle dauernder Neutralität: Malta und Costa Rica* (New Cases of Permanent Neutrality: Malta and Costa Rica), in Mélanges Georges Perrin 279 *et seq.* (1984).

doubt that in the case of armed conflicts the same fundamental rules would apply as those which are laid down in the Hague Conventions of 1907. The duty of abstention is reaffirmed in the provision that Laos and Malta may not enter into military alliances nor allow other States to use their territories for military purposes. By virtue of this prohibition any military aid to belligerents in the case of an armed conflict would be illegal. The duty of prevention finds expression in the same prohibition not to allow other States to use their territory for military purposes. This prohibition implies the duty to prevent by all means available such use by a belligerent. The Declaration of Malta even expressly refers to the right of self-defence. The duty of impartiality is, finally, so closely interwoven with the concept of neutrality that an unequal treatment of the two parties to an armed conflict would be contrary to the pledge to neutrality made in the declarations. Surprisingly therefore the declarations on the neutrality of Laos and Malta confirm the basic principles -though not necessarily each individual rule- of the old law of neutrality as laid down in the Hague Conventions.

5.   CONCLUSIONS

In all future considerations on the law of neutrality a distinction should be drawn between the rules applicable to all States not parties to an armed conflict and the rules applicable to genuine neutrals only. The fact that this distinction has not been made so far and that the two sets of rules have been considered as parts of a single and indivisible law of neutrality has given rise to much confusion. Protocol I, adopted in 1977, Additional to the Geneva Conventions now explicitly draws the distinction between neutrals and other States not parties to a conflict.

Both sets of rules keep their validity. The rules relating to all States not parties to armed conflicts still apply to the same extent as originally; *i.e.*, they continue to be relevant for all non-participants in an armed conflict. On the other hand, the rules on strict neutrality have a much more restricted applicability nowadays. They are relevant only for the permanently neutral States and for States which, in a specific armed conflict, wish to maintain the status of neutrality.

A new codification of the law of neutrality will have to take into account the distinction between the two sets of norms. It would no longer be feasible to include both of them in one regulation as was done in 1907. As to the rules applicable to all non-participants in armed conflicts, new regulations with a limited reach seem to be politically possible. Such rules, as has been mentioned, were adopted in the framework of the Geneva Conventions of 1949 and of Protocol I of 1977. Another new regulation would be conceivable and desirable for the rights and duties of belligerents and non-belligerents in naval warfare, especially with regard to commercial ships flying the flag of non-participating States. Kalshoven has made useful suggestions to this effect.[36]

The situation is different with regard to strict neutrality. A new codification of the respective rules would hardly be possible as only a very restricted number of States have been concerned with strict neutrality since 1945. A codification of these rules would also raise delicate questions. First of all, it would be necessary to determine in what situations the law of neutrality is to be applied (international armed conflicts, non-international armed conflicts, mixed conflicts, UN enforcement measures, political tensions, etc.). Secondly, all the rules of neutral behaviour in armed conflicts and possibly in peace-time would have to be fixed (duties of abstention, of prevention, of impartiality, of acquiescence). While a general codification of the law of strict neutrality cannot be envisaged for the foreseeable future, it could well be possible to fix rules of neutrality for particular States which adopt the status of permanent neutrality. The cases of Laos and Malta are examples for such individual regulations. However, as long as no new rules on neutrality and non-participation in armed conflict are set up, the old law of neutrality, especially the two Conventions of 1907, will continue to play a useful although restricted role.

---

36 F. Kalshoven, *Commentary on the 1909 London Declaration Concerning the Laws of Naval War*, in N. Ronzitti, ed., The Law of Naval Warfare 275 (1988).

NEUTRALITY IN NAVAL WARFARE

What is left of traditional
international law?

MICHAEL BOTHE

1.   INTRODUCTION: THE BASIC QUESTION

Traditionally, the sea is an important theatre of war and it has remained
so, albeit to a limited extent, in the conflicts which have taken place after
World War II.[1] The major case of a naval war was the Falkland/Malvinas
conflict. Naval operations were important during the Gulf War between

---

[1] For a concise summary on naval warfare operations which have taken place during conflicts
     after World War II, see N. Ronzitti, *The Crisis of Traditional Law Regulating International
     Armed Conflicts at Sea and the Need for its Revision*, in N. Ronzitti, ed., The Law of Naval
     Warfare 1, 4 *et seq.* (1988).

Iraq and Iran; they were so to a lesser extent during the recent Gulf War. Naval warfare also took place during the conflicts between Israel and Egypt, India and Pakistan and in Vietnam. It is obvious that naval war operations affect the navigational activities of third States. But these activities may in many respects also have an impact on the position of the belligerent powers. Over the centuries, international rules regarding the respective rights and duties of neutrals and belligerents have developed, which strike a difficult balance between the interests of both sides.[2] The basic rationale underlying this part of the law can be reduced to two principles: the neutral State should not be impaired in its normal situation; on the other hand, it should not tip the balance in favour of one of the belligerents. From these basic principles, a number of concrete rules are derived which form part of customary international law, but are in part also codified by international treaties.[3]

There are certain limitations on the sojourn of warships of the belligerent States in neutral waters. On the other hand, belligerent States have the right to prevent the transportation of goods relevant to the enemy war effort by neutral ships (contraband). They have thus a right to visit and search neutral merchant ships and may, if contraband is carried, seize ship and cargo through a prize procedure. A specific means of interdicting intercourse between the enemy and the outside world, which affects both enemy and neutral shipping, is the blockade.

In contradistinction to the rules of land warfare, there has been no update of neutrality law since the Hague Conference of 1907. It is thus necessary and legitimate to ask what the rules of neutrality in naval warfare have become since. There are three particular reasons for asking this question. The first one concerns the basic status of neutrality, what can be called the double dichotomy. Under traditional international law, there is a dichotomy between war and peace and between neutrality and belligerency. This double dichotomy has come under pressure in State practice for the last five decades at least.[4] The second reason for asking

---

2   R.L. Bindschedler, *Neutrality, Concept and General Rules*, in R. Bernhardt, ed., 4 Encyclopaedia of Public International Law 9 *et seq.* (1982); Y. Dinstein, *Neutrality in Sea Warfare*, in Bernhardt, ed., *ibid.*, at 19 *et seq.*; E. Castrén, The Present Law of War and Neutralitiy 241 *et seq.* (1954).

3   Dinstein, loc. cit. n. 2, at 19 *et seq.*; See also N. Ronzitti, in ASIL Proc. 604 (1988). The most important relevant Treaties are the 1907 Hague Convention XI Relative to Certain Restrictions with Regard to the Exercise of the Right of Capture in Naval War and Convention XIII Concerning the Rights and Duties of Neutral Powers in Naval War.

4   Bindschedler, loc. cit. n. 2.

the question is the effect of the UN Charter on the law of neutrality.[5] Has the UN Charter in any way superseded the traditional law of neutrality? Have the rules of neutrality been modified by those on the legality of the use of force? The third reason is that specific practices have developed in the field of naval warfare and new technological options have come up which may or may not have modified the traditional law of naval warfare.[6] It has to be asked whether the concept of blockade is still valid. New concepts have evolved, such as 'quarantine', 'interdiction', 'exclusion zone'. Modern technology has developed and caused new problems, in particular through the development of long-range weapons, long-range means of detection and the effect of modern weapons and attacks. The developments of modern warfare may also have an impact on traditional notions of permissible (military) targets.

2. THE PROBLEM OF THE DOUBLE DICHOTOMY:
WAR AND PEACE - NEUTRALITY AND BELLIGERENCY

There has been a long debate in doctrine and practice on the question whether an intermediate status exists between neutrality and belligerency. During World War II, certain States described their position as one of non-belligerency,[7] which meant that they supported one of the belligerents, probably in violation of the laws of neutrality, but did not want to become parties to the ongoing armed conflict. A closer analysis shows that the question of non-participation in an armed conflict which is not neutrality *stricto sensu* arises in two different contexts.

Firstly, the question of the legal status of non-participation in an armed conflict relates to the dichotomy of war and peace. The essential question in this respect is the definition of the scope of application of the law of war, the *ius in bello, ratione materiae*. Does the law of war apply only in case of a formal state of war or also in case of an armed conflict of an international character, where for one reason or another, a formal state of war does not exist? In a development of several decades, the notion of armed conflict has to a great extent replaced that of war in order to define

---

5 Bindschedler, *ibid.*, at 13; Castrén, op. cit. n. 2, at 433 *et seq.*.
6 Y. Dinstein, *Sea Warfare*, in Bernhardt, ed., loc. cit. n. 2, at 201 *et seq.*; Ronzitti, loc. cit. n. 1, at 10; Y. Dinstein, in ASIL Proc. 607 (1988).
7 Bindschedler, loc. cit. n. 2, at 13; Castrén, op. cit. n. 2, at 451 *et seq.*.

situations where the law of war applies.[8] The notion of armed conflict is expressly used by the Geneva Conventions of 1949 and Protocol I Additional thereto of 1977, in order to define their scope of application. But it is submitted that these provisions of the Geneva Conventions do not constitute exceptions, but rather reflect a rule which has developed under customary international law, at least as far as the conduct of hostilities and the protection of war victims is concerned.

Whether this development has also affected the law of neutrality is, however, doubtful. Important authors still hold the view that the application of the law of neutrality indeed requires the existence of a state of war.[9] In State practice after World War II, there are cases where States protested against certain measures taken by belligerent States against merchant ships of States which were not parties to the conflict on the ground that no formal state of war existed. Consequently, the belligerent did not have the powers of control over neutral shipping as they would have had against neutrals in the case of a formal state of war. That view, however, seems to be too formalistic and does not correspond to the requirements of situations of armed conflict. If there is actual fighting, it seems to be both unrealistic and inappropriate to deny belligerents a power of control over the flow of contraband. It seems that during the Iran-Iraq War, 'neutral' States indeed accepted a power of visit for the belligerent States and no longer raised the question of the existence of a formal state of war.[10]

The consequences of this controversy for the existence of an intermediate status between belligerency and neutrality are quite clear. If the status of neutrality only exists in the case of a formal state of war, then there must be a different kind of non-party status. These considerations seem to underlie the formula used in Protocol I Additional to the Geneva Conventions, where the State not participating in an armed conflict is described as 'neutral or other State not party to the conflict'.[11] Although these provisions remove any doubt as to the application of certain

---

8 See K.J. Partsch, *Armed Conflict*, in R. Bernhardt, ed., 3 Encyclopaedia of Public International Law 27 (1982); also W. Meng, *War*, in Bernhardt, ed., op. cit. n. 2, at 290 *et seq.*. His view is much too restrictive as to the applicability of the 'law of war' in situations where no formal state of war exists.

9 Bindschedler, loc. cit. n. 2, at 10; E. Kussbach, *L'évolution de la notion de neutralité dans les conflits armés actuels*, 17 Military Law and Law of War Review 26 (1979).

10 Bindschedler, loc. cit. n. 2, at 10; Partsch, loc. cit. n. 8, at 27; see also the practice reported by Ronzitti, op. cit. n. 1, at 7 *et seq.*

11 Articles 2(c), 9(2), 19, 31, 39, 64 of Protocol I. *Cf.*, M. Bothe, K.J. Partsch, W.A. Solf, eds., New Rules for Victims of Armed Conflicts 106 (1982).

provisions of the Protocol, there is still considerable uncertainty as to the law governing non-participation in armed conflicts in general. This is a situation which should certainly be remedied in any future revision of the law of neutrality and of naval warfare.

The use of the notion of non-belligerency mentioned above has, however, a different background. It was originally used to describe a situation where a State supported a belligerent party, probably in violation of the law of neutrality, without actually becoming a party to that conflict. This kind of involvement in the armed conflict, however, does not lead, as a matter of law, to a kind of intermediate status between neutrality and belligerency. The rendering of unneutral services is indeed a violation of the law of neutrality and may give rise to an appropriate reaction by the belligerent party which is the victim of that violation, in particular to reprisals or a declaration of war. But such a violation does not by itself lead to the cessation or exclusion of the status of neutrality.[12] That status only ends if and when the 'non-belligerent' State, as a consequence of a reaction by a belligerent State, is drawn into the armed conflict.

This last-mentioned situation raises the more general question of the effect which acts of violence occurring between a belligerent and a neutral State may have on the latter's neutral status. There may indeed be a number of situations where such acts occur or even must occur.[13] A neutral State must defend its territory where a belligerent uses it for military purposes. Such action to defend the neutral status may lead to actual fighting. If such fighting is limited to small-scale operations to repel certain intrusions, this does not change the status of a neutral State. Only if such limited fighting degenerates into a larger-scale operation, then the (former) neutral State becomes as a matter of fact a party to the conflict. It may well be that this describes the situation of the United States during certain times of the Iran-Iraq War, but this appears to be highly doubtful.

3.   THE LAW OF NEUTRALITY AND THE PROHIBITION OF THE USE OF FORCE

At first glance, it may indeed appear as if the UN Charter excludes the possibility of neutrality. All States must join against an aggressor and assist the victim. Ideally, there are just two sides, that of the aggressor and that

---

12 Bindschedler, loc. cit. n. 2, at 13.
13 Castrén, op. cit. n. 2, at 459 *et seq.*.

of the victim. This system, however, has not worked in this way because of the inability of the Security Council to fulfil its functions.[14] Only recently has it appeared that, quite surprisingly after more then forty years, the system might work as originally conceived. But until now, the more traditional situation has prevailed: there have been armed conflicts with parties and non-parties. Thus, the traditional situation of neutrality has remained unchanged. The rules of neutrality were indeed relied upon and applied in practice. States exercised a right of visit and search and other States acquiesced in it. Prize courts were instituted.[15] Thus, the traditional conflict pattern where a status of neutrality is legally and factually possible continues to exist.[16]

But this does not necessarily mean that the UN Charter and in particular the prohibition of the use of force contained therein has no bearing on the law of neutrality. Indeed the law of neutrality developed at times when resort to war was not prohibited. Thus, measures of coercion permissible under the traditional law of neutrality are not necessarily legal under current conditions. But this question forms part of a more general one, namely that of the relation between the law of war, the *ius in bello* and the prohibition of the use of force, the *ius contra bellum* (the traditional term *ius ad bellum* being really the wrong expression under modern international law).

The rules of the *ius in bello* and the *ius contra bellum* constitute two different levels of legal restraint on violence. The law of war comes into operation where the law of peace has been broken, no matter by whom. The law of war does not know or recognize the distinction between aggressor and victim, it applies in an equal manner to both sides.[17] The laws of war apply independently of any legal justification of a party's participation in a conflict under the *ius contra bellum*. The *ius ad bellum* does not justify any violation of the laws of war. But the reverse is also true. The laws of war do not justify any violation of the *ius contra bellum*. In this sense, no belligerent right exists which would justify an action illegal under the normal rule of the law of peace. An aggression fought by legal means is still an aggression, and that aggression engages the

---

14 Castrén, op. cit. n. 2, at 433 *et seq.*; Bindschedler, loc. cit. n. 2, at 13.
15 Ronzitti, loc. cit. n. 1, at 7.
16 M. Jenkins, *Air Attacks on Neutral Shipping in the Persian Gulf: The Legality of the Iraqi Exclusion Zone and Iranian Reprisals*, 8 Boston College International & Comparative Law Review 517, 525 (1985).
17 Bothe, Partsch, Solf, eds., op. cit. n. 11, at 33; for a more detailed analysis see M. Bothe, *Le droit de la guerre et les Nations Unies*, in 5 Etudes et travaux de l'institut universitaire des hautes études internationales 163 *et seq.* (1967).

responsibility of the aggressor for the armed action as a whole, even if there is no violation of the laws of war.

It must be stressed in this respect, that the legal yardstick under the *ius contra bellum* indeed is the action as a whole, not the individual single act of violence occurring within the framework of an armed conflict. Once an armed conflict has started because aggression has occurred, it is not possible to ask the question, whether there is an armed attack or a situation of self-defence, for each individual shot fired. Within the framework of an armed conflict, the legal yardstick for the individual act of violence is the law of war only, not the *ius contra bellum*. If no armed conflict exists, it is the individual action which has to be evaluated in the light of the *ius contra bellum*. There exists, thus, a principle of double scrutiny. Violence between States has to be submitted to both the legal yardstick of the *ius contra bellum* and that of the *ius in bello*. Where there is an armed conflict, however, the scrutiny under the *ius contra bellum* applies only to the armed conflict as a whole, not to the individual act of violence. Where there is an individual act of violence in a generally peaceful situation (what is often called an incident), that action has to be evaluated both under the *ius contra bellum* and the *ius in bello* (to the extent that the *ius in bello* is at all applicable in relation to an 'incident').[18]

What are the consequences of this legal situation for the law of neutrality? Where there are acts of coercion under the law of neutrality, the double scrutiny principle must also apply. The admissibility of such acts must be evaluated both under the law of neutrality and under the *ius contra bellum*. In other words, the law of neutrality, as a matter of principle, cannot justify violations of the prohibition of the use of force. But in contradistinction to the relation between belligerents, there exists no overall violent situation between a neutral and a belligerent State. Thus, the double scrutiny principle applies not to the situation as a whole, but to the individual act of violence or coercion.

In order to test and illustrate this principle, certain acts of coercion relevant under the law of neutrality may be analysed more closely. The first case in point is the right of search and visit in relation to neutral commercial shipping. If a neutral merchant ship is ordered or even forced to stop in order to facilitate a visit, this does not constitute a use of force against the flag State which would be prohibited under the Charter. Under

---

18 On the latter problem, see Bothe, op. cit. n. 17, at 149 *et seq.*

M. Bothe

the definition of aggression, adopted by the General Assembly[19] the attack on the 'marine merchant fleet' is mentioned as an example of aggression thus excluding an attack on an individual merchant ship. The right of visit and search has indeed remained unchallenged in postwar naval conflicts.[20] Whether a use of force against a merchant ship going beyond what is necessary for enforcing a right of visit and search constitutes an 'armed attack' (and thus triggers a right of self-defence) is, however, a difficult question. On the other hand, an attack on a warship certainly constitutes a forbidden attack on the 'sea forces' of a State within the meaning of Article 3(b) of the Declaration on Aggression. If neutral merchant ships are assembled as a convoy and protected by warships, an attack on them might also constitute an attack on the 'marine fleets' within the meaning of the said provision. This would buttress the traditional, but controversial view according to which the right of visit and search does not exist in relation to merchant ships travelling in convoy under the protection of neutral warships.[21] It appears that the United States relied on this rule in organizing the passage of 'neutral' tankers under the protection of United States warships through the Gulf during the Iran-Iraq War.[22]

Another traditional institution of the law of naval warfare is the blockade. A blockade aims to prevent both neutral and enemy shipping from entering or leaving a blockaded port or coast.[23] Interesting in our context is the interdiction of neutral shipping. To the extent that neutral merchant ships are prevented from going to or from the blockaded port, such action is not a violation of the prohibition of the use of force for the reasons just stated. If, however, a neutral warship is stopped, this also constitutes, for the reason just stated, a prohibited attack. There remains, however, the question whether there is an independent justification of such action under the *ius contra bellum*. If the blockading State is the aggressor, there is certainly none. But what about the case where the blockading State is acting in self-defence against the blockaded State? That use of force is certainly justified as between the blockading and the blockaded State. But the neutral State is not an aggressor. Its legal position is in no way

---

19 GA Res. 3314 (XXIX) of 14 December 1974. See M. Bothe, *Die Erklärung der Generalversammlung der Vereinten Nationen über die Definition der Aggression* (The Declaration of the General Assembly of the United Nations on the Definition of Aggression), 18 GYIL 127 (1975).

20 Ronzitti, loc. cit. n. 1, at 7 *et seq.*

21 On this controversy, see, on the other hand, Dinstein, op. cit. n. 2, at 24 *et seq.*, also R. Stödter, *Convoy*, in Bernhardt, ed., loc. cit. n. 8, at 128 *et seq.*

22 Ronzitti, op. cit. n. 1, at 9.

23 L. Weber, *Blockade*, in R. Bernhardt, ed., op. cit. n. 8, at 47.

impaired by the fact that another State has committed an aggression. Self-defence justifies the use of force against the aggressor. But it is at least difficult to construe self-defence as also having a kind of collateral effect against non-aggressors. The situation would, however, be legally different if the actions of the warship itself constitutes an act of aggression. But the mere fact that a neutral warship tries to approach a blockaded port does not constitute an act of aggression. A clear justification of a blockade enforced against a neutral warship could only be found where such action is authorized by the UN Security Council. Such authorization would render legal any action against neutral warships trying to break a blockade.[24]

The situation just described raises a more general issue, that is, the right of self-defence of the neutral State. The rights and duties of a neutral State imply to a certain extent self-defence action. As the neutral State may not allow the use of its territory by a belligerent, it is its duty to defend that territory against intrusion by belligerent forces.[25] In addition, the neutral State also possesses a right of self-defence where its warships are attacked. As is well known, this question played an important role during the Gulf War, although most of the publicity was generated by two erroneous decisions: the decision of the responsible officer of *USS Stark* not to attack an aircraft which was in reality attacking the ship, and that of the commander of *USS Vincennes* to attack an airplane which was a civilian one and not attacking the ship. The principle underlying the United States attitude is quite clear. United States ships were demonstrating their right of passage through the Gulf. According to the rule established by the International Court of Justice in the *Corfu Channel Case*, a ship which is (not unexpectedly) attacked while demonstrating and using its right of passage has the right to respond by force.[26] This general statement, however, does not solve the real problem. Self-defence in this connection also presupposes an attack by the other side. Thus, force in self-defence may only be used if it is reasonably certain that there is indeed an attack. As the examples have shown, this requires a very difficult factual judgment in conflict conditions such as those prevailing in the Gulf. Had there been an armed conflict between Iran and the United States, the situation would have been much simpler in legal terms. Under the laws of war, shooting down a military aircraft would have been legal, no matter what the mission of that aircraft was at the time of shooting. The only thing the ship's commander had to make sure was whether it was a military aircraft or not.

---

24 See also infra text accompanying note 46.
25 See B.-O. Bryde, *Self-defence*, in Bernhardt, ed., loc. cit. n. 2, at 212 *et seq.*
26 ICJ Reports 1949, at 4, in particular at 30 *et seq.*

In the framework of an armed conflict, the question of the legality of the individual action under the *ius contra bellum* does not arise. But as pointed out above, the relationship between a neutral and a belligerent is a peaceful one, not a situation of armed conflict.

The legal characterization of actions taken by a neutral State against the armed forces of a belligerent may of course vary according to the legal status of the place where they take place. Military action of the neutral State against warships belonging to a belligerent party may serve as an example. The right of sojourn of warships in neutral waters is limited. They have the right of passage and they have a limited right to stay in neutral ports (so-called 24-hours-rule).[27] If a warship does not leave a neutral port where it is not entitled to remain, the neutral power may take such action as to render the ship incapable of taking part in the war.[28] This may involve the use of force against the ship. It is a use of force authorized under the law of neutrality, and not a use of force prohibited under the *ius contra bellum*, although there may be no attack against the neutral State. But the belligerent ship, in this case, is in an area which is subject to the territorial jurisdiction of the neutral State. The exercise of such jurisdiction against the warship is not an armed attack under international law. Warding off a foreign intrusion by using force is legal even where this intrusion can not be characterized as an armed attack.[29] It is not an illegal use of force under the *ius contra bellum* if a neutral State prevents belligerent warships from using neutral waters in a manner inconsistent with their neutral status.

Having analysed situations where a neutral State may use force, certain situations involving the use of force against the neutral State may also be considered. The main problem in this respect is that of permissible reactions against violations of the law of neutrality committed by the neutral State. If a State violates the law of neutrality by rendering assistance to one of the belligerents (unneutral services), reprisals against that State are certainly permissible. Under traditional international law, it would have been legal to disregard the neutral status completely and to attack the neutral State. This, however, is no longer true. An unneutral service is not an armed attack, and it thus does not trigger a right of self-defence against the neutral State. Hence, the *ius contra bellum* excludes a reaction which would be legal under the traditional law of neutrality. Even

---

27 Article 12 of the Hague Convention XIII.
28 Article 24 of the Hague Convention XIII.
29 As to the cases of aerial intrusion, see K. Hailbronner, Der Schutz der Luftgrenzen im Frieden (The Protection of Aireal Boundaries in Peacetime) 13 *et seq.* (1972).

if an unneutral service amounts to an armed attack, which is possible where, for instance, a neutral State lends its territory to one of the belligerents and permits its use as a basis of hostile action, the legality of a response by the use of force, of course, depends on the status of the whole conflict under the *ius contra bellum*. If the belligerent party affected by that unneutral service is acting in self-defence, then it may also react in self-defence against the neutral State. If the affected party, on the other hand, is the aggressor, it does not enjoy a right of self-defence against the State which supports a self-defence action by the victim of aggression.

To sum up, the *ius contra bellum* and the law of neutrality constitute different levels of restraint concerning the use of force. As a practical matter, there are a few cases where the *ius contra bellum* prohibits actions which would be legal under traditional rules of the law of neutrality. To that very limited extent, the modern law relating to the use of force has indeed modified the traditional law of neutrality.

4. SPECIFIC TYPES OF MEASURES IN MODERN NAVAL WARFARE

4.1 Naval blockade

As already mentioned, blockade means a complete interdiction of all sea traffic to and from a particular harbour or coast. It thus affects neutral and enemy shipping alike. A traditional blockade is the so-called close blockade, which is enforced by ships in position in the vicinity of the blockaded port, but also by aircraft, mines and submarines. In modern times, the notion of long-distance blockade has been introduced. This became controversial because it was doubtful whether it could be an effective bar to access to the blockaded port, effectiveness being an essential element in the legality of a traditional blockade.[30]

The fundamental question in relation to the law of blockade, however, is not that of the long-distance blockade, but the question whether the blockade is still a valid legal concept at all. First, State practice in relation to blockade makes it doubtful whether it is still used as a means of warfare. Although there have been no formal declarations of blockade since World War II,[31] in a number of cases, access to certain coasts or

---

30 *Cf.*, W.O. Miller, *Law of Naval Warfare*, 62 US Naval War College International Law Studies 265 (1980); J. Mc Nulty, *Blockade: Evolution and Expectation, ibid.*, at 184.

31 Ronzitti, loc. cit. n. 1, at 9.

ports was indeed barred by belligerents.[32] The lack of a formal reliance on this legal concept does not necessarily mean that the concept has fallen into desuetude. Such a kind of negative practice must be accompanied by a corresponding *opinio juris*, for the traditional customary law of blockade to be changed.[33] The concept of blockade, however, seems to be very much alive. It is mentioned in the UN General Assembly's definition of aggression as a measure of warfare which may constitute an illegal aggression.[34] It is enumerated among the measures which might be considered as enforcement action under Article 42 of the UN Charter. A blockade was instituted against Iraq in the recent Gulf crisis.

The essential question, however, is whether the concept of blockade has undergone certain modifications in view of recent developments of treaty law, in particular, to what extent has it been modified by Article 23 of the Fourth Geneva Convention on the Protection of War Victims and by Article 54 and 70 of Protocol I Additional to the Geneva Conventions. Article 23 of the Fourth Convention provides for the free passage of certain relief consignments, although under very restrictive conditions. If that provision modified the traditional law of blockade, it did so only to a very limited extent. Article 54 of Protocol I prohibits starvation as a means of warfare. Article 70 provides for the passage of relief consignments, and the obligations to grant such passage go much further than those provided for in Article 23 of the Fourth Convention.[35] There are some indications that Article 54 was not meant to change the traditional law of blockade, but Article 70 certainly constitutes a serious limitation on the right of a blockading State to bar any access to a blockaded port or coast. Food, medical and other supplies essential to the survival of the civilian population must be allowed to pass a blockade. The recent UN practice in relation to Iraq seems to be inspired by the respect for that principle.

It must be stressed that the means of enforcing the blockade is to stop and seize a 'blockade runner'. The essential difference between the normal control of neutral shipping and a blockade consists in the fact that a blockade runner can be seized for the mere breach of a blockade, even if it does not carry contraband. The use of force against a blockade runner is permissible to the extent necessary to stop and seize it. A blockade does

---

32 For example, see B.A. Harlow, *The Law of Neutrality at Sea for the 80's and Beyond*, 3 Pacific Basin Law Journal 44 (1984).

33 Ronzitti, op. cit. n. 1, at 9 *et seq.*

34 GA Res. 3314 (XXIX) of 14 December 1974. *Cf.*, Bothe, loc. cit. n. 19, at 127.

35 On this question, see Bothe, Partsch, Solf, eds., op. cit. n. 11, at 336 *et seq.*; Ronzitti, op. cit. n. 1, at 35.

not give any right to destroy neutral ships where no attempt is made to stop and seize them. If a belligerent State enforces a blockade just by attacking from a distance (which was the case during the Gulf War), this amounts to the establishment of an exclusion zone which, as will be shown, is unlawful.[36]

4.2 Quarantine or interdiction

The notion of quarantine[37] was invented by the United States during the Cuban missile crisis.[38] The notion is different from that of a blockade because the so-called quarantine did not bar shipping in general from going to and from Cuba. The 'interdiction' was limited to specific shipments.[39] In terms of the law of war, such interdiction causes no problem whatsoever. In the context of an armed conflict, the shipment of materials to those affected by the quarantine could certainly be stopped by any belligerent as being war material destined for the adverse party. It is, thus, certainly inappropriate to consider quarantine as a new notion in the field of the laws of naval warfare.

The real legal problems posed by the quarantine relate to the *ius contra bellum*. To the extent that the enforcement of the quarantine constituted a use of force within the meaning of Article 2(4) of the UN Charter, it could only be justified if it was a reaction to an armed attack or if it was justified by the authorization of a competent international organisation, a question which cannot be dealt with in this connection in greater detail.

4.3 Laying mines

The practice of laying mines[40] has been quite common during conflicts since World War II. They were used in order to block access to certain ports or sea areas. Like a blockade, it is a measure which affects belligerents and neutrals alike. Laying mines is certainly an act of force against the State whose territory is affected thereby. Under the law of armed conflict, laying mines must conform to the requirements of Hague

---

36 See *infra* § 4.4.
37 L. Weber, *Cuban Quarantine*, in Bernhardt, ed., op. cit. n. 8, at 136.
38 See L.C. Meeker, *Defensive Quarantine and the Law*, 57 AJIL 515 (1963); C.Q. Christol, C.A. Davis, *Maritime Quarantine: The Naval Interdiction of Offensive Weapons and Associated Material to Cuba* 525 (1962).
39 W.O. Miller, *Belligerency and Limited War*, 62 United States Naval War College International Law Studies 170 (1980).
40 Ronzitti, loc. cit. n. 1, at 5 *et seq.*

Convention XIII of 1907. This was stressed by the International Court of Justice in the *Nicaragua Case* in relation to the mining of certain Nicaraguan harbours by the United States,[41] and also by the United States in relation to the laying of mines by Iran in the Persian Gulf.[42] The essential content of the said Convention is that it is forbidden to use contact mines in a way which may render them indiscriminate weapons. Thus, it is forbidden to lay unanchored automatic contact mines or anchored automatic contact mines which do not become harmless as soon as they have broken loose, or to use torpedos which do not become harmless when they have missed their mark. In addition, it is forbidden to lay automatic contact mines with the sole object of intercepting commercial shipping. It must be noted in this respect that these obligations apply not only to belligerent parties, but also to neutral powers using mines to protect their territorial waters.

4.4   Special zones

What became known as the 'exclusion zone' during the Falklands/ Malvinas conflict[43] resembles quite closely the notion of 'war zones' instituted by Germany around the British Isles during World War II.[44] It was a zone where any ship, neutral or belligerent, could be sunk without warning. Admiral Dönitz was not condemned for war crimes on that account, but only because the United States practised the same in the Pacific. The rule as such remained unaffected.

During the Falklands/Malvinas conflict there were really two versions of the exclusion zone. The first one was a sort of limitation of the theatre of war. It was directed only against the Argentine naval forces. If this kind of declaration poses any problem under international law, it is the question whether such a declaration creates a situation of confidence that no attack is to be expected outside that zone. A further declaration, however, extended the meaning of the exclusion zone so as to include neutral shipping, which would be considered as hostile if found in the zone and thus liable to attack. Against this extension of the exclusion zone, there

---

41 ICJ Reports 1986, at 112.
42 See the references quoted by Ronzitti, loc. cit. n. 1, at 5.
43 Ronzitti, loc. cit. n. 1, at 40; Jenkins, loc. cit. n. 16, at 526 *et seq.* A good general overview on the subject-matter of exclusion zones is given by W.J. Fenrick, *The Exclusion Zone Device in the Law of Naval Warfare*, 24 Can. Yb. of International Law 91 (1986).
44 See J. Schmitt, Die Zulässigkeit von Sperrgebieten im Seekrieg (The Admissibility of Exclusion Zones in Naval Warfare) 66 *et seq.* (1966).

were some neutral protests. In order to consider the legality of such zones, one has to stick to the old rule that neutral shipping is subject to visit and search and to be taken as a prize where contraband is found, but not to more sweeping acts of violence. It is in this sense that the sentence of the Nuremberg Tribunal has to be understood. The question thus arises whether this kind of exclusion zone has become accepted under a new development of customary law. The answer must clearly be negative. There was enough protest against the declaration to prevent British practice becoming an element of the formation of new law, at least for the time being.

The forgoing analysis of the legal situation is confirmed by the practice of the United Nations in relation to the Gulf War. When Iraq instituted a fifty-mile war zone around Kharg Island and attacked neutral ships, the practice of indiscriminate attacks on such shipping[45] was condemned several times by the UN Security Council. In this connection, it is also necessary to oppose views which are found in legal literature according to which a tanker, even a tanker flying a neutral flag, carrying oil exported from a belligerent oil-producing State, would constitute a military objective because the revenue derived from such exports is so essential to the war effort of the belligerent. Such indirect advantage can never be the basis of the military character of an objective. This view is also in contradiction to the fundamental principle of the law of neutrality that a neutral may not be impaired by the armed conflict. Again, this situation may be changed on the basis of a binding SC Resolution authorizing forceful measures against exports which would foster the war effort of an aggressor.[46] Measures against neutral shipping going beyond the traditional rights of visit and search, and of seizing contraband, would require a special enabling resolution by the Security Council.

It has thus to be concluded that so-called exclusion zones have not become a new element of the positive law of neutrality in naval warfare. Practice shows, however, a certain inclination of States to establish zones from which they want to bar all traffic. These tendencies must be viewed very critically and must be carefully restricted in any future codification.

---

45 On the illegality of these actions, see also Jenkins, loc. cit. n. 16, at 534 *et seq.*

46 It has to be noted that at the time of writing, the measures against Iraq authorized by the Security Council did not include the use of force against ships navigating or aircraft flying over, the high seas or international straits. *Cf.*, SC Res. 661 of 6 August 1990 and 670 of 25 September 1990.

5.   THE IMPACT OF THE NEW LAW OF THE SEA

Article 88 of the 1982 LOSC reads: 'The high seas shall be reserved for peaceful purposes'.

There is general agreement, however, that this Article does not really mean what it says, if taken literally. It is not meant to exclude all military activities on the high seas, it only prohibits the use of the high seas for committing acts of aggression[47]. Thus, naval warfare is not outlawed by the 1982 LOSC. However, the new Convention may have a restraining effect on naval operations which are also relevant for the law of neutrality.

The recent development of the law of the sea is characterized by a substantial expansion of the rights of a coastal State, a phenomenon which has rightly been called 'territorialization' or 'terranization'[48] of the sea. Three developments are of particular importance for the law of naval warfare, namely the status of international straits, the rights of coastal States relating to the continental shelf and the regime of the exclusive economic zone (EEZ).[49]

The regime of international straits has not only become more important because more international passages have become territorial waters due to the extension of those waters under recent developments of the law of the sea, but also because the regime of passages has been developed or at least clarified to a certain extent by the 1982 LOSC in particular, due to the distinction between innocent passage and transit passage. As is well-known, the question of the right of passage through straits presented a particular problem during the Gulf War. Generally speaking, one has to distinguish two situations: the coastal state may be neutral or may be at war. Where the coastal State is neutral, the rules of the 1982 LOSC and those relating to neutrality can be applied concurrently.[50] Transit rights under the law of the sea do not go beyond rights of transit under neutrality law. Thus, the 24-hours-rule would also apply and the waters of an

---

47 B.-O. Bryde, *Militärische und sicherheitspolitische Implikationen der neuen Seerechtskonvention* (Military and Security Policy Implications of the new Law of the Sea Convention), in J. Delbrück, ed., Das neue Seerecht. Internationale und nationale Perspektiven (The new Law of the Sea. International and National Perspectives) 162 (1984).

48 Graf Vitzthum, *Einleitung*, in Graf Vitzthum, ed., Die Plünderung der Meere (Looting the Seas) 13 (1981); Ronzitti, loc. cit. n. 1, at 28.

49 D.H.N. Johnson, *Straits*, in R. Bernhardt, ed., 11 Encyclopaedia of Public International Law 323 *et seq.* (1989); *Innocent Passage, Transit Passage*, in Bernhardt, ed., *ibid.*, at 150 *et seq.*; C.L. Rozakis, *Continental Shelf*, in Bernhardt, ed., *ibid.*, at 82 *et seq.*; L. Gündling, *Die 200 Seemeilen-Wirtschaftszone* (The 200 Miles Economic Zone) (1983).

50 On this question, see Bryde, loc. cit. n. 47, at 174 *et seq.*

international strait may not be used as a basis for maritime hostilities by the belligerent States. On the other hand, the existence of an armed conflict would not justify a neutral coastal State's barring or severely limiting military traffic through a strait if that traffic is compatible with the law of neutrality.[51]

Where the coastal State is a party to the conflict, the existence of transit rights would certainly not affect the right of control which the belligerent State possesses over neutral shipping. These rights exist as to neutral shipping on the high seas; they would *a fortiori* exist where the neutral ship is in the territorial waters of a belligerent. The essential question, however, is to what extent the belligerent coastal State has the right to exclude neutral shipping from its territorial waters forming part of an international strait. The practice during the Gulf War in this respect seems to be somewhat contradictory. In this respect, there seems to be a need for clarification *de lege ferenda*.

As to the continental shelf, it is clear that it cannot be equated with territorial waters. The rights of a coastal State in relation to the continental shelf are not comprehensive sovereign rights, but limited to the exploration and exploitation of the natural resources of the shelf. Third States are excluded from building structures on the continental shelf, but apart from economic activities, the continental shelf has to be treated like the seabed of the high seas. Thus, a neutral State has no right or duty to prevent military activities on the continental shelf, a right or duty it would have if these activities took place in its territorial waters.[52] It is an open question, however, how far the duty not to hinder economic activities being carried out by the coastal State on its continental shelf would limit the possibility of military activities.[53] A reverse question may also be put: to what extent could a belligerent State control economic activities on the continental shelf of a neutral State? Could it, for example, prohibit the production and transportation of oil from continental shelf sources where such oil is destined for export to another belligerent State? If such oil was transported on the high seas by a neutral ship, it could certainly be seized.

It is also quite clear that the EEZ cannot be equated with territorial waters. Thus, a neutral coastal State has no right or duty to exclude military activities of belligerent States in this zone. As in relation to the continental shelf, the question is how far the economic rights enjoyed by the coastal State in relation to the EEZ may limit the right of the bel-

---

51 Harlow, loc. cit. n. 32, at 50.
52 *Ibid.*, at 52.
53 Bryde, loc. cit. n. 47, at 169, 173.

ligerent States to conduct military activities, including fighting. Military activities will certainly quite often constitute a considerable risk or impediment for economic activities of the coastal State, in particular fishing. This is a question, which, it is submitted, requires some clarification *de lege ferenda*. On the other hand, the question of control of neutral economic activities just discussed in relation to the continental shelf also arises in respect of certain activities of a coastal State in the EEZ.

6.   NEW TECHNOLOGY AND THE PROTECTION OF THE ENVIRONMENT - THE QUESTION OF COLLATERAL DAMAGE

Naval war activities under modern conditions of warfare may in many respects not only affect economic activities of a neutral coastal State in the waters near to its coast, but also, more generally speaking, the marine environment of these waters and the coastal areas of the neutral States themselves. The question thus arises whether and to what extent such collateral damage to the environment and the property of the neutral State and its nationals is legally acceptable.

The fundamental principle which must underlie the answer to this question is the rule that the neutral State must not be impaired by the armed conflict. This is, in turn, the basis of the provision of Article 1 of the Fifth Hague Convention respecting the rights and duties of neutral powers and persons in case of war: the territory of neutral powers is 'inviolable'. It follows that the belligerent may not cause any damage to neutral territory as a result of hostilities. During World War II, damages were indeed paid where collateral damage had been caused to Switzerland by an attack which hit a German town.[54] The principle of proportionality which governs the admissibility of collateral damage caused to civilians or civilian objects does not apply to collateral damage caused to neutral States. It is submitted that the same holds true for damage caused to the neutral territory by military operations carried out at sea. Thus, the attack on a tanker navigating off the coast of a neutral State which leads to

---

54 G. Jaccard, *Über Neutralitätsverletzungsschäden in der Schweiz während des Zweiten Weltkriegs* (On Damages Caused by Violations of Swiss Neutrality During the Second World War), 87 Zeitschrift des Bernischen Juristenverbandes 225 *et seq.* (1951). These questions were the object of a study by a group in which both F. Kalshoven and this author took part. Unfortunately, the institution which commissioned the report has so far not given the permission to publish it.

pollution of the coastal waters and coastal areas of that State would be an illegal act in relation to the neutral State and give rise to a claim for compensation.

Whether this principle holds true where legitimate neutral activities were impaired in the EEZ or if collateral damage was caused to neutral ships navigating on the high seas in the vicinity of military activities is, however, doubtful. It would seem that at least on the high seas, neutral ships, although they may not be attacked, operate at their risk and peril when they move close to military operations.[55]

7.   CONCLUSIONS

It appears from the foregoing that the fundamental rules concerning neutrality in relation to warfare at sea which were codified in 1907 have to a large extent remained unchanged.[56] State practice is still based on, and invokes, those codifications. Certain modern developments, however, have modified these traditional rules in significant details. The main elements of these changes are the development of the concept of war and armed conflict, the prohibition of the use of force in the Charter of the United Nations; international humanitarian law codified and developed in the 1949 Geneva Conventions and the 1977 Protocols Additional thereto, the new rules of the law of the sea, and changing technological and economic environment.

Generally speaking, legal restraints on warfare have become tougher while war becomes more and more dreadful. It is, however, difficult to ascertain clearly the development of customary law in relation to maritime neutrality. The relationship between the new rules and the traditional rules of maritime neutrality is by no means always clear. The law of maritime neutrality is certainly one of the fields which deserves much thought *de lege ferenda.*

---

55 See *e.g.* the note of the 'Service juridique' of the French Ministry of Foreign Affairs concerning French ships in Chinese ports which may have been hit by accident during the Japanese attacks 21 January 1938, A. Kiss, VI Repertoire de la pratique francaise en matière de droit international public, no. 1086.

56 Miller, loc. cit. n. 30, at 265.

TOPICAL APPROACHES TOWARDS DEVELOPING THE LAWS OF ARMED CONFLICT AT SEA *

DIETER FLECK

1.   INTRODUCTION

Like many distinguished international lawyers before him, Professor Kalshoven started his career as a legal adviser in the navy. It is impressive to see, however, that he has always shown a certain reluctance when dealing with specific proposals designed to develop new rules for the law of armed conflict at sea while he has had reason to explain time and again that many principles of humanitarian law which are applicable to land warfare are likewise relevant for naval operations.[1]

---

*   Director, International Legal Affairs, Federal Ministry of Defence, Bonn. The views expressed in this contribution are those of the author and do not necessarily reflect either the policy or the opinion of the Government of the Federal Republic of Germany.

1   F. Kalshoven, *Merchant Vessels as Legitimate Military Objectives*, Paper presented to the Bochum Round Table of Experts on International Humanitarian Law Applicable to Armed Conflicts at Sea, International Institute of Humanitarian Law, Bochum, (1989). Also, F. Kalshoven, *Enemy Merchant Vessels as Legitimate Military Objectives*, Paper presented to the

A cautious approach to the law of armed conflict at sea is required for stringent policy reasons. In recent armed conflicts some common elements have become equally important to numerous maritime operations. Any reference to conventional criteria and arguments relating to the rules of the law of war at sea are regularly avoided in official comments voiced by the parties to the conflict. Instead, increasing use is being made of criteria that refer to international law as valid in peacetime or even to national police law, such as restoring public order, proportional action and sanctions. Aspects of crisis management are being stressed although they cannot claim a definite legal quality.[2] Even studies dealing with international law or political science have followed this trend, at times somewhat neglecting considerations of the law of war at sea in a more narrow sense.[3] The concept of operational law[4] as comprising both peacetime and wartime elements governing the employment of armed forces is the last but not the least important step towards transgressing traditional limits of the law of armed conflict. It underlines the great complexity of this part of international law, a complexity which stands against any effort to develop a new codification.

The law of armed conflict at sea was more or less expressly left in abeyance when negotiations were conducted on the Protocols Additional to the Geneva Conventions adopted on 8 June 1977: Article 49(3) of Protocol I stipulates that the rules on the general protection against the effects of hostilities (Articles 48-67) apply to any land, air or sea warfare which may affect the civilian population on land and to all attacks from the sea or from the air against objectives on land but do not otherwise affect the rules of international law applicable in armed conflict at sea or in the air. Therefore, the new rules of Protocol I are not applicable to combat operations between naval vessels or aircraft, nor do they apply to attacks

---

Symposium on the Law of Naval Warfare, US Naval War College (1990).

2   R. Ottmüller, *Die Anwendung von Seekriegsrecht in militärischen Konflikten seit 1945* (The Application of the Law of Naval Warfare in Military Conflicts since 1945) in: Institut für Internationale Angelegenheiten der Universität Hamburg, ed., 10 Das geltende Seekriegsrecht in Einzeldarstellungen (1978).

3   K. Booth, Law, Force and Diplomacy at Sea (1985); J. Cable, Gunboat Diplomacy: Political Applications of Limited Naval Force (1981).

4   NWP 9, The Commander's Handbook on the Law of Naval Operations (1987); see also NWP 9, Rev. A/FMFM 1-10, Annotated Supplement to the Commander's Handbook on the Law of Naval Operations (1989).

from land against ships at sea or aircraft in flight.[5] A rule which is so obviously a compromise in nature is not safe from later attempts at interpretation, the aims and methods of which would not have stood any chance during the negotiations themselves.[6] In this regard, again, a cautious approach appears to be adequate. The argument of an 'unintended' change of certain parts of the law of armed conflict at sea must be questioned even where it is based upon a detailed textual analysis of the First Additional Protocol. It not only contradicts the express intentions of the Contracting Parties, but also and likewise is opposed to their objectively determinable interests. This reveals that a mere textual interpretation, particularly in international law, will quickly reach its limits.

The aim of this contribution is to discuss some of the main legal problems which should be contemplated in any effort to reaffirm, implement and develop legal rules for naval operations. In this respect a new reflective approach to the importance of legal principles for international crisis management should deal with the limits to the prohibition of the use of force (2). A comprehensive survey should be made of the main open questions of international law applicable in an armed conflict at sea today (3). Moreover, generally acceptable proposals need to be evaluated in order to create and strengthen confidence in the validity of legal rules during armed conflicts also (4). All of these three tasks are closely related to a general problem of balance: balance between the prohibition of force and the right of self-defence; balance between the protection of war victims and military necessity; and last but not least balance between the legal aim to achieve comprehensive regulations and the operability of their implementation.

---

5   W.A. Solf, in M. Bothe, K.J. Partsch, W.A. Solf, eds., New Rules for Victims of Armed Conflicts, Commentary on the Two 1977 Protocols Additional to the Geneva Conventions of 1949, 290 (1982); C. Pilloud, J. de Preux, in Y. Sandoz, C. Swinarski, B. Zimmermann, eds., Commentary on the Additional Protocols of 8 June 1977 to the Geneva Conventions of 12 August 1949 at 1895-1898 (1987).

6   E. Rauch, *The Protocol Additional to the Geneva Conventions for the Protection of Victims of International Armed Conflicts and the United Nations Convention on the Law of the Sea: Repercussions on the Law of Naval Warfare*, 90 Veröffentlichungen des Instituts für Internationales Recht, Kiel (1984). But see H. Meyrowitz, *Le Protocole Additionel I aux Conventions de Genève de 1949 et le Droit de la Guerre Maritime*, 89 RGDIP 11-66 (1985). See also E. Rauch, *Le Droit Contemporain de la Guerre Maritime: Quelques Problèmes Créés par le Protocole Additionel I de 1977*, 89 RGDIP 958-976 (1985); *Discussion at the Xth Congress of the International Society for Military Law and the Law of War* (1985), XXVI Revue de Droit Pénal Militaire et de Droit de la Guerre 1-3, 9-181 (1987).

2.   LIMITS TO THE PROHIBITION OF FORCE

The codification of the prohibition of the use of force in Article 2(4) of the UN Charter has set a new milestone in the progressive development of international law. But there may be doubt as to whether this will be of much practical relevance for armed forces after the outbreak of hostilities.[7] The principle of proportionality inherent in the Charter system, indeed, is very similar to the principle of proportionality as part of humanitarian law applicable in armed conflicts. Yet there is much room for the direct application of the UN Charter in naval operations.[8] Such operations are normally not connected with border crossing and they are different from army and air force operations in that they may be of much greater importance outside armed conflicts, in situations where the direct applicability of humanitarian law may be a matter of dispute.

The prohibition of force has its sole limits in the right of individual and collective self-defence, as described, but not exhaustively defined in Article 51 of the UN Charter. The GA Resolution on the Definition of Aggression,[9] due to its rather general wording -with its explicitness being further reduced by a large number of restrictive clauses and the far-reaching lack of agreement between the parties to a conflict on the meaning of such clauses-, can hardly be considered a distinct decision-making aid. At the same time, self-defence may be justified also against certain activities which would not qualify as aggression under the Resolution.[10] By no means must a commander wait for the first torpedo, which might well be sufficient to sink his ship, before he can react in his defence. A certain form of anticipatory, or at least 'interceptive',[11] self-defence must be permitted after an adverse party has committed itself to an armed attack in an ostensibly irrevocable way.

The very critical question as to the circumstances and purposes which justify one country using force against another, has been raised time and

---

7   *Cf.*, C. Greenwood, *Self-Defence and the Conduct of International Armed Conflict*, in Y. Dinstein, M. Tabory, eds., International Law at a Time of Perplexity. Essays in Honour of Shabtai Rosenne 273-288 (1989).

8   R. Lagoni, *Some Effects of the Charter of the United Nations and the Modern Law of the Sea on the Law of Naval Conflicts*, Paper presented to the Bochum Round Table of Experts, loc. cit. n. 1.

9   GA Res. 3314 (XXIX) of 14 January 1975.

10 D. Fleck, *Rules of Engagement for Maritime Forces and the Limitation of the Use of Force under the UN Charter*, 31 GYIL 175-180 (1988).

11 Y. Dinstein, War, Aggression and Self-Defence 180 (1988).

again. One of the most precise, but by no means undisputed, answers supports its admissibility in the following five cases:[12]

a) when a State has been subjected to an armed attack on its territory, vessels or military forces;
b) when the imminence of an attack is so clear and the danger so great that the necessity of self-defence 'is instant (and) overwhelming';
c) when another State that has been subjected to an unlawful armed attack by a third State requests armed assistance in repelling that attack;
d) when a third State has unlawfully intervened with armed force on one side of an internal conflict and the other side has requested counter intervention in response to the illegal intervention; or
e) when its nationals in a foreign country are in imminent peril of death or grave injury and the territorial sovereign is unable or unwilling to protect them.

These cases will not be commented on here. They clearly illustrate, however, how difficult or even hopeless it would be to find a general ruling and how vital it remains to take into account in any interpretation the concrete development of a situation and its environment.

It should also be borne in mind that Article 2(4) of the UN Charter does not cover specific naval cases such as the seizure of a pirate ship or aircraft or hot pursuit. Measures to implement decisions of the Security Council to maintain or restore international peace and security in accordance with Article 39 of the UN Charter and even peacekeeping activities which are -as is presently the case- based on the consent of all Parties involved may include the use of force, without being prohibited by Article 2(4). Moreover, the latter provision expressly applies to 'international relations' and consequently does not cover force used in the exercise of sanctions against ships of one's own flag, wherever required as part of the duties of a naval commander.

Bilateral agreements on the prevention of incidents at sea, under certain circumstances even multilateral efforts for this purpose, as proposed by Sweden[13] and the German Democratic Republic,[14] could complement

---

12 O. Schachter, *The Lawful Resort to Unilateral Use of Force*, 10 Yale Journal of International Law 291-294 (1985).
13 Permanent Mission of Sweden to the United Nations, Aide-Mémoire on a Multilateral Agreement for the Prevention of Incidents at Sea, 10 May 1989.

existing crisis management efforts. The conclusion of such agreements can have confidence building effects. Quite obviously the Convention of 20 October 1972 on the International Regulations for Preventing Collisions at Sea cannot be expected to offer a sufficient basis in situations of tension. Maritime rules of engagement should be evaluated and openly consulted to provide for a balanced approach to crisis management as an important part of international confidence building.[15]

3.   STOCKTAKING OF INTERNATIONAL LAW OF MARITIME
         OPERATIONS

The major part of the law of naval warfare still in force is rather old and only imperfectly takes account of all the aspects of modern maritime operations. Where treaty arrangements do exist, they have become obsolete to such an extent as to give reason to doubt their value altogether.[16] A complete survey of international rules governing war at sea is no longer available today and it is quite realistic to doubt whether it would be at all possible in the foreseeable future to reconfirm and update comprehensively international treaty provisions.[17] In this situation, all efforts to obtain an objective description of the present status of the rules governing naval warfare must be supported. This applies as much to military regulations as to text books[18] and individual presentations.[19]

A fruitful exchange between jurists practising law and law schools could perhaps lead to a successful division of work in this field. The publication of individual studies is increasing continuously, but the task of conceiving an overall outline seems to be too venturous an undertaking for most of today's scientists. What has still not been fulfilled is the demand

---

14 Entwurf eines Abkommens für die Ostseeanliegerstaaten über die Verhinderung von Zwischenfällen auf bzw. über See außerhalb der Territorialgewässer, May 1989 (in German: Draft Convention of the Baltic Sea Coastal States on the Prevention of Incidents at and above Sea beyond Territorial Waters, May 1989).

15 Fleck, loc. cit. n. 10, at 185.

16 N. Ronzitti, ed., The Law of Naval Warfare. A Collection of Agreements and Documents with Commentaries (1988).

17 *Study on the Naval Arms Race*, UN Doc. A/40/535 of 17 September 1985, at 303.

18 C.J. Colombos, II The International Law of the Sea (1962); D.P. O'Connell, The International Law of the Sea (1984); R.W. Tucker, The Law of War and Neutrality at Sea (1957).

19 W.T. Mallison Jr., Studies in the Law of Naval Warfare: Submarines in General and Limited Wars (1968); loc. cit. n. 2. Institut für Internationale Angelegenheiten der Universität Hamburg, ed., Das geltende Seekriegsrecht in Einzeldarstellungen, 10 Vol. Hamburg 1965-1974.

by the late Professor O'Connell of a 'future analysis ... which may assist naval staff work and also diplomats and their legal auxiliaries who may have to formulate national attitudes to defence planning in the counsels of nations.'[20] The armed forces, however, cannot evade this mission. There is a clear military need for a comprehensive set of regulations dealing with the law of armed conflict at sea. Such regulations must be prepared by the defence ministries and should be co-ordinated in an international effort. It would be useful if the great number of scientific papers on individual issues of the law of naval operations as well as military manuals already existing at national level could be considered in this work and if co-operation between the experts on international law in the armed forces and at the universities could be intensified.

3.1   Merchant vessels

The question as to the conditions under which merchant vessels may qualify as military objectives is one of key importance for both systematic and operational reasons. The vessel's course, the type of cargo and also activities on board can suffice for such qualification in certain circumstances. The problem of definition lies not so much in special maritime requirements but rather in the difficulty of the general task of defining military objectives: what is an effective contribution to military action and how can such a contribution be concluded from the nature, location, purpose or use of the particular object? Legal criteria to be developed for this purpose can hardly be different in land, sea, and air warfare. An illustrative list of military objectives, as annexed to Article 7 of the 1956 New Delhi Draft Rules of the ICRC[21] might be helpful in providing practical answers. But even then the crucial question remains: under which conditions are merchant ships legitimate military objectives?

The Bochum Round Table,[22] which has provided the first international forum for an in-depth discussion of these problems in recent times, had no difficulty in defining as military objectives those ships 'which by their nature, location, purpose or use make an effective contribution to military action and whose total or partial destruction, capture or neutralization, in

---

20 D.P. O'Connell, The Influence of Law on Sea Power xv (1975).

21 ICRC, Draft Rules for the Limitation of Dangers Incurred by the Civilian Population in Time of War 72-73 (1958).

22 Bochum Round Table, loc. cit. n. 1.

the circumstances ruling at the time, offers a definite military advantage.'[23] The experts have also revoked the rule of proportionality as formulated in Article 51(5,b) of Protocol I Additional to the Geneva Conventions and the obligation to take all feasible precautions in attack as reaffirmed in its Article 57(2,a,ii). Specific rules developed at this Round Table revealed a wide congruence between the situation of enemy merchant vessels and merchant vessels of neutral and other States not party to the conflict. In both situations merchant vessels will run the risk of losing their status as civilian objects if they:

a) engage in acts of war on behalf of the enemy, e.g. laying mines, minesweeping, cutting undersea cables and pipelines, visiting neutral merchant ships or attacking other merchant ships;
b) act as an auxiliary to an enemy's armed forces, e.g. troop carrying or replenishing warships;
c) are incorporated into or assist the enemy's intelligence system;
d) sail under convoy escorted by enemy warships or military aircraft;
e) refuse an order to stop or actively resist a visit, a search or capture;
f) are armed to an extent that they could inflict damage on a warship;
g) make an effective contribution to military action, e.g. carrying military materials; or
h) engage in any other activity bringing them within the definition of a military objective.

The identical applicability of these requirements to both neutral and enemy merchant vessels reveals that there is hardly any difference between the two categories under international humanitarian law. Yet enemy merchantmen may in most cases be less successful in proving compliance with these requirements.

It should be contemplated, whether a standard code of conduct for all merchant vessels cannot be developed as a useful tool to facilitate legal protection in a given conflict. Such a code could go far beyond technical hints issued by competent transport associations during the Iran-Iraq

---

23 International Institute of Humanitarian Law, Results of the First Meeting of the Madrid Plan of Action Held in Bochum 2 (1989). This definition of military objectives may be considered as customary law. It is applicable also in armed conflicts at sea though reaffirmation of this rule by Article 52(2) of Protocol I Additional to the Geneva Conventions is confined 'to any land, air or sea warfare which may affect the civilian population, individual civilians or civilian objects on land' as well as to 'attacks from the sea or from the air against objectives on land.' *Cf.*, Article 49(3).

conflict.[24] The continuation of neutral waterborne trade was particularly urgent in the Gulf area, since an interruption would have had dramatic consequences for the price of oil, if not for the direct impact on supply. But in all armed conflicts many shipowners have taken the position that to shrink before the threat of attack would only reinforce the dangers for civilian lives and prosperity rather than solve existing problems.

A standard code of conduct for merchant shipping could consist of general rules as well as of specific rules applicable in certain areas. Such rules would be designed for shipowners and captains rather than for governments. But adherence to the rules by merchant shipping would not fail to have effects also on state practice due to the principle of reciprocity. A standard code of conduct could facilitate the distinction to be made by parties to the conflict between civilian objects and military objectives. Close co-operation between experts from the merchant navy and the military would thus not only contribute to making traffic at sea technically safer, but also to developing international law in this respect. Relevant economic organizations including insurance companies, but also governmental organizations and law institutes should be encouraged to participate in this type of co-operation.

For the purpose of such a standard code of conduct an attempt should be made to define 'unneutral services' or rather 'l'assistance hostile', to use the original French text of Articles 45-47 of the London Declaration of 1909,[25] a now old-fashioned instrument that was not ratified by any Signatory and cannot be considered complete and legally binding, though it largely corresponded to established practice in its time and was recognized by several belligerent States during World War I. A modern concept of 'l'assistance hostile' might be defined as comprising a direct and effective contribution to military action. There would, however, still be a certain amount of room for interpretation.[26] Trading with the enemy may have different effects, depending on the duration of the conflict, the type and quantity of goods concerned, and even on the economic interests of the parties to the conflict. National laws and regulations are relevant for the proper application and implementation of accepted principles and nations

---

24 General Council of British Shipping, ed., Iran-Iraq War. The Situation in the Gulf, Guidance Notes for Shipping (1988); INTERTANKO, ed., Iran-Iraq Conflict 1984-1988. The Tanker War - No End? (1988); see also *Safety Circular Letters* issued by INTERTANKO during the Iran-Iraq Conflict.

25 Declaration Concerning the Laws of Naval War, signed at London, 26 February 1909.

26 F. Kalshoven, *Commentary to the 1909 London Declaration*, in Ronzitti, ed., op. cit. n. 16, at 264-266.

have always tended to keep existing options open.[27] Nevertheless, attempts should be made to protect certain imports of belligerents and to develop principles for the protection of their exports to neutral countries.

Also, specific recommendations for the conduct of merchant vessels could be given (*e.g.* not to sail under convoy escorted by enemy warships or military aircraft, not to carry arms which could inflict damage on a warship) and additional recommendations for behaviour during visit and search could be developed. It should, however, be borne in mind that such recommendations cannot be of a mandatory character. Military escorts for merchant vessels would remain possible, but they would change the status of such vessels into military objectives.

3.2   Mine warfare

Aspects of international law regarding the laying of sea mines and countermeasures have assumed a new quality dimension in our era. The importance of sea lines of communication to allied reinforcements and the protection of resupply is significant. But technology, too, has progressed by leaps and bounds.[28] What technical precautions must be taken to protect neutral shipping? What must be the criteria to be used as a yardstick for a warning? What must be done to mark minefields and to deactivate them when hostilities are over? The Hague Convention VIII of 1907 Relative to the Laying of Automatic Contact Mines does not answer

---

27 At the beginning of World War II, German lawyers who were actively devoted to defending the rule of law and later lost their lives in the resistance against Hitler tried to implement the British experience in the field of economic warfare and considered it legitimate for a party to the conflict to a certain degree to influence the economy of neutral States, see H.J. v. Moltke, *Der englische Wirtschaftskrieg. Grundsätze - Lehren - Gegenmaßnahmen* (in German: The British Economic Warfare, Principles - Lessons - Countermeasures). Lecture held in Berlin on 23 November 1939, Bundesarchiv Freiburg. See also D. Fleck, ed., The Gladisch Committee on the Law of Naval Warfare. A German Effort to Develop International Law During World War II (1990).

28 See, W. Schücking, *Die Verwendung von Minen im Seekrieg* (The Use of Mines in Naval Warfare), in 16 Zeitschrift für internationales privat- und öffentliches Recht 121-152 (1906). Schücking pointed out that the first use of sea mines in the history of war took place in the Kiel Bay in 1848: the invention by W. v. Siemens of a 'dependent' mine, whose detonation was controlled from the shoreline had deterred the Danish Fleet which had been dispatched to punish by means of a bombardment the city of Kiel as the focal point of the revolutionary movement in Schleswig-Holstein. Today's technology has used a detour via the system of contact ignition to return, in a manner of speaking, to remotely controlled activation, with electronic devices providing for an activation over great distances. This permits the use of sea mines even in those areas where formerly legal reservation had to be made because of the problems of technical control.

these questions sufficiently. It would therefore be a sensible approach to develop a code of practice for mine warfare.

A 1988 Swedish Draft Protocol on Prohibitions or Restrictions on the Use of Naval Mines[29] includes balanced proposals for obligatory control of mines and torpedoes as well as for precautionary measures. Such proposals might be helpful in implementing existing legal principles. A detailed answer to the above mentioned open questions requires a thorough assessment of the general principle of self-defence and the rule of proportionality, combined with a full knowledge of the technical control possibilities available. Taking into consideration that decisive portions of such knowledge have already been widely published in various countries, international co-operation in the development of operating procedures for the laying of seamines should be possible and recommended within the existing alliances and even beyond.

3.3   Submarine warfare

The existing conventional rules for 'action with regard to merchant ships', to use the language of the 1936 London Protocol,[30] have undergone misinterpretations, negligence in state practice and critical observations by scholars. A systematic evaluation of the London Protocol should start with a terminological question: What does the London Protocol mean by merchant ships and what are the conditions under whch such ships would lose their status as civilian objects protected under international law? Merchant ships may only be attacked if they comply with the definition of a military objective, *i.e.*, if by their nature, location, purpose or use such ships make an effective contribution to military action and their total or partial destruction, capture or neutralization, in the circumstances ruling at the time, offers a definite military advantage.

The key problem posed by this definition is how to define an 'effective contribution to military action' and how such a contribution can be concluded from the nature, location, purpose or use of the particular object. It has correctly been argued that 'no basis will be found until the whole matter is conscientiously viewed in the context of the full emergence of the economic arm of warfare, with the annihilation of enemy maritime

---

29 UN Doc. A/CN. 10/141 of 8 may 1990.

30 Procès-Verbal Relating to the Rules of Submarine Warfare set forth in Part IV of the Treaty of London of 22 April 1930, signed at London, 6 November 1936.

commerce as a major naval objective.'[31] But legal criteria to be developed for this purpose can hardly be different in land, sea, and air warfare: the standards are uniform, even if their implementation poses specific problems in the different situations of the surface, the submarine and the airborne platform.

In some aspects these categories are more specific than the Naval Warfare Publication (NWP) 9.[32] The latter is phrased in general terms as far as military objectives are concerned.[33] It uses a very similar list of categories to define the circumstances under which enemy merchant vessels may be attacked and destroyed by surface warships. The authors suggest that these categories were modifications of the 1936 London Protocol 'in light of current technology, including satellite communications, over-the-horizon weapons, and anti-ship missile systems, as well as the customary practice of belligerents that evolved during and following World War II.'[34] But there may be doubt as to whether such a complex argument is necessary. The London Protocol reaffirmed the applicability of existing rules to submarine warfare. Such rules did not and do not include special protection for military objectives. Merchant ships which fall under one of the eight categories described earlier[35] are military objectives and cannot therefore be expected to be safe against attacks. Indeed, the London Protocol could not extend to 'warshiplike merchantmen'.[36] The prohibition of the effective use of submarines against such ships was not part of the London Protocol.[37] Attacks must, however, be confined to military objectives and they must comply with the principles of proportionality and necessity.

As far as submarine warfare is concerned, the NWP 9 states that the London Protocol, coupled with the customary practice of belligerents, imposes upon submarines the responsibility to provide for the safety of passengers, crew, and ship's papers before destroying an enemy merchant vessel, unless:

a) the enemy merchant vessel refuses to stop when summoned to do so or otherwise resists capture;

---

31 J. Stone, Legal Controls of International Conflict. A Treatise on the Dynamics of Disputes and War-Law 606 (1954).
32 NWP 9, loc. cit. n. 4.
33 *Ibid.*, at 8.1.1.
34 *Ibid.*, at 8.2.2.2.
35 *Supra.*
36 F. Kalshoven, Belligerent Reprisals 128 (1971).
37 Mallison Jr., op. cit. n. 19, at 119.

b) the enemy merchant vessel is sailing under armed convoy or is itself armed;

c) the enemy merchant vessel is assisting in any way the enemy's military intelligence system or is acting in any capacity as a naval auxiliary to the enemy's armed forces; or

d) the enemy has integrated its merchant shipping into its warfighting/war-sustaining effort and compliance with this rule would, under the circumstances of the specific encounter, subject the submarine to imminent danger or would otherwise preclude mission accomplishment.[38]

But should attacks on certain merchant ships be made dependent upon a decision that the enemy has integrated its merchant shipping in general under its war-fighting or war-sustaining effort? Should such attacks on the other hand be considered lawful in all situations where they may be deemed necessary for mission accomplishment? A thorough assessment shows that the definition of military objectives in the specific situation offers the best possible criterion for drawing the line between legal and illegal attacks at sea. Mission accomplishment is too vague a notion to allow for clear legal qualifications.

The implementation of the described categories of military objectives is still difficult enough in practice: the identification of arms may pose problems, even if we do no longer insist on the impossible investigation of whether a certain armament has been used, or is intended for use, offensively against an enemy.[39] Merchant ships involved in armed conflicts since 1945 have widely avoided armament. Effective contribution to military action is a legal term of art which requires policy decisions to be taken in practice. Such decisions are dependent upon the threat posed and the military advantage anticipated. Armed forces which adhere to the principle of damage limitation will be rather restrictive in this respect. In all circumstances the rule of proportionality requires responsible commanders to abstain from attack when seizure or capture is possible by other means.

Is it true to say that the 1936 London Protocol is of legal relevance only in a situation where the submarine can act with minimal risk on the surface, a situation which is hardly ever likely to occur?[40] A careful

---

38 NWP 9, loc. cit. n. 4, at 8.3.1.

39 Article 503(3,b) No 4 of the 1955 Law of Naval Warfare, in Tucker, op. cit. n. 18, at 397. But see Mallison Jr., op. cit. n. 19, at 120-122.

40 O'Connell, op. cit. n. 20, at 78.

evaluation of the history and text of this instrument certainly supports the conclusion that it only reaffirmed rules for situations where minimal risk for submarines was involved. The rules so interpreted have not been derogated by subsequent state practice and are still worth maintaining. The continuous reaffirmation of these rules is of political and practical importance.[41]

The remaining task is therefore not only to maintain and properly implement the 1936 London Protocol in all types of armed conflict, but also to supplement its provisions with rules that would guarantee both sufficient self-defence against attacks and co-operative action by the belligerents for the protection of civilians and civilian objects.

3.4   Zonal restrictions for the protection of civil shipping

In recent armed conflicts, the parties have repeatedly declared large sea areas exclusion zones so as to increase the deterrent effect of their forces and to warn civil shipping of the consequences of unintended attacks and collateral damage. The establishment of exclusion zones at the beginning of a crisis underlines the requirement for legal evaluation and the development of detailed rules acceptable to all parties.[42] But the rights and interests of neutral shipping should also be adequately taken into account in this context. What is still lacking is a code of practice safeguarding the free passage of neutral ships. Its development would presuppose a thorough analysis of the practical aspects of conflicts in the past.

3.5   Identification

For the identification of medical transports, other ships, and aircraft entitled to protection under the Geneva Conventions and the Additional Protocols the ICRC proposals,[43] which are based on the ICAO

---

41 See E.I. Nwogugu, *Commentary on the 1922 Washington Treaty, the 1930 London Treaty (Part IV), and the 1936 London Protocol*, in N. Ronzitti, ed., op. cit. n. 16, at 353-365 (364).

42 W.J. Fenrick, *The Exclusion Zone Device in the Law of Naval Warfare*, in 24 Can.YIL 91-126 (1986); K. Zemanek, *War Zones*, in R. Bernhardt, ed., 4 Encyclopeadia of Public International Law, 337-338 (1982).

43 ICRC, Memorandum to the High Contracting Parties to the Protocol Additional to the Geneva Conventions of 12 August 1949, and Relating to the Protection of Victims of International Armed Conflicts (Protocol I), Revision of Annex I to Protocol I (Regulations Concerning Identification), December 1989. ICRC, Report on the Meeting of Technical Experts (Geneva, 20-24 August 1990), December 1990.

Airworthiness Technical Manual (Doc. 9051), the IMO-International Code of Signals (Chapter XIV) and Resolutions of ITU Member States, should be supported and widely implemented.

The identification of merchant ships will, however, remain controversial, unless it can be accompanied by a reasonable assurance that the ship does not make an effective contribution to military action. In the absence of international scrutiny of such an assurance the Navicert system[44] was introduced in World War II. While experience from recent armed conflicts would not encourage proposals for a more active role of the UN in this respect, the necessity for appropriate solutions remains.

3.6   Sea rescue

The protection of sea rescue services under international law is impaired in most countries by the fact that airborne equipment is generally not reserved exclusively for rescue operations. Under the Geneva Conventions the protective emblem of the red cross or red crescent must not be displayed at installations and objects which are used in a dual role, both for medical purposes and for combat. It is true that the establishment of a sea and air traffic search and rescue service is in keeping with an obligation under international law,[45] and the letters SAR are internationally recognized. But hardly any country in the world can afford procuring SAR helicopters exclusively for medical tasks.

Adequate defence preparations are bound also to entail unorthodox approaches to protection and care which are rendered 'to the fullest extent possible' under Article 18 of the Second Geneva Convention and Articles 8(b) and 10 of Additional Protocol I. This includes the question of the availability of civil airborne equipment for rescue operations in the event of an armed conflict. The call for greater protection to be provided under international law can only be met if the necessary sacrifices are made in one's own country and if international co-operation functions smoothly.

---

44 D. Steinicke, *Das Navicertsystem (The Navicertsystem)*, in 3 Das geltende Seekriegsrecht in Einzeldarstellungen I-II (1966).

45 International Convention on Maritime Search and Rescue (1979); Article 25 Convention on International Civil Aviation 7 December 1944.

3.7   Limitations on environmental damage

The 1982 LOSC contains detailed provisions in Part XII on the protection
and preservation of the environment at sea. These provisions, however, are
not valid for environmental damage caused in armed conflicts. Even in
armed conflicts, the Convention on the Prohibition of Military or Any
Other Hostile Use of Environmental Modification Techniques of 18 May
1977 prohibits any environmental modification techniques having
widespread, long-lasting or severe effects. That prohibition, however, still
needs to be more clearly defined. Improved cooperation with a view to its
implementation would be as desirable as any contribution towards the
universal validity of that Convention.

4.   PROPOSALS AND CONCLUSIONS

Legal questions pertaining to the military use of the sea clearly reveal the
influence of political and military considerations. At the same time, they
are blurring the traditional line separating international law applicable in
peacetime and international law of armed conflict. A systematic
identification and assessment of the legal problems which may arise today
and in the future with a view to the various forms of a military use of the
sea is not only of scientific interest. Such an effort can also render a
service to the maritime forces in their day-to-day operations.

A balanced approach towards developing existing legal principles in this
respect must be based on the prohibition of the use of force and the right
of individual and collective self-defence, without, however, aiming at new
restrictions. This can be achieved by *inter alia* addressing and taking
account of the following legal problems:

a) the role of *incident at sea agreements* should be stressed and expanded;
b) the protection of both enemy and neutral merchant vessels as civilian
   objects should be scrutinized and the development of a standard code of
   conduct for all merchant vessels considered;
c) the principles governing *mine warfare* should be reaffirmed and further
   developed in order to enhance the control of sea mines;
d) in *submarine warfare* existing restrictions are confined to acts against
   those merchant ships which are clearly civilian objects and further
   restrictions are neither feasible nor supportive to damage limitation;
e) decisions on the establishment of *exclusive zones* should make
   allowance for safeguarding the free passage of neutral ships;

f) ICRC proposals to improve the *identification of medical transports,* other ships, and aircraft deserve support. For the identification of merchant ships, however, a reasonable assurance remains necessary that the ship is not making an effective contribution to military action;

g) for *sea rescue* new national efforts should be made and international cooperation enhanced in order to make the necessary equipment and services available and to use them exclusively for rescue operations;

h) principles and regulations designed to limit *environmental damage* in armed conflict should be further developed and implemented through international co-operation.

Convincing answers to issues of international law necessitate intensified international co-operation within existing alliances and far beyond. It is only through such co-operation that the consensus still lacking on issues concerning the military use of the seas in peacetime can be brought about. Only joint efforts are the appropriate means to implement successfully recommendations tabled to reaffirm and improve the existing international law of armed conflict at sea. While the prospects of success of such efforts may not be bright, it is nevertheless in line with both scientific and political interests that scholars and practitioners undertake great endeavours towards their realization.

THE MERCHANT VESSEL AS LEGITIMATE TARGET IN THE LAW OF NAVAL WARFARE *

WILLIAM J. FENRICK

1.   INTRODUCTORY REMARKS

One of the most important unsettled questions in the modern law of naval warfare is: when is a merchant vessel a legitimate target which may be attacked on sight during an international armed conflict? A merchant vessel can be roughly defined as a cargo carrying vessel not formally incorporated as an auxiliary vessel into an enemy's naval fleet. Any attempt to resolve this question must take account of the law as it existed prior to World War I, legal developments since World War I, in particular the London Submarine Protocol of 1936 and the war crimes cases following World War II, State practice during the two World Wars, and State practice, including national law of naval warfare manuals, since World War II.

---

* The views expressed herein are those of the writer and do not necessarily reflect either the policy or the opinion of the Canadian Government.

When an attempt is made to resolve a problem in an unsettled area of the law of naval warfare, it is important to pay due heed to both military requirements and humanitarian imperatives. In an earlier paper on a similar topic, the present author noted:

'It is not essential that international law, to be valid, should always be compatible with state practice. If, however, the law of naval warfare is to have an impact on the conduct of warfare, there should be a crude congruence between law and practice so that it is marginal, extreme conduct which is condemned, not activities which are routine operations of war.'[1]

Professor Kalshoven commented on this remark:

'This may sound plausible enough from a military point of view. The second sentence may even be read to apply to customary international law in general. For obvious reasons, customary law tends to keep fairly close to practice. On the other hand, in the case at issue it may just be an instance of begging the question. Over time, "routine operations of war" and the military thinking on which they rest may have come to deviate so completely from what can be tolerated even in war as an unavoidable enroachment of human values, that a correction of the set course is urgently required.'[2]

It is unquestionable that, to almost all persons prior to World War I, the idea of sinking merchant ships on sight without providing for the safety of passengers and crews would have been viewed as an intolerable encroachment of human values. Whether or not such conduct would generally be perceived as intolerable today, after the experiences of two World Wars, is another question. Additional Protocol I, which has minimal application to naval warfare, contains several provisions regulating aerial bombardment which reaffirm the principle of distinction and would make some of the aerial bombardment practices of World War II, particularly indiscriminate area attacks, illegal if they occured today. There have, however, been several studies of the World War II bombing offensives which criticize certain aspects of these operations as being both immoral

---

1   W.J. Fenrick, *Military Objectives in the Law of Naval Warfare*, Paper presented at the Bochum Round Table of Experts on the Military Objective and the Principle of Distinction in the Law of Naval Warfare, Bochum, at 63 (1989).
2   F. Kalshoven, *Comments for Bochum Meeting* (unpublished), loc. cit. n. 1, at 1.

and military ineffective.[3] The writer is unaware of any substantial studies of the unrestricted maritime anticommerce campaigns during the two World Wars which criticize either the general concept or the general conduct of these operations on either moral or military grounds. On the other hand, apart from the Iran-Iraq conflict, sustained anticommerce campaigns do not appear to have been waged at sea since 1945.

2.   TREATMENT OF MERCHANT VESSELS IN 'CLASSICAL' LAW

The pre-World War I law concerning the treatment of merchant vessels can be summarized briefly.[4] Any merchant vessel could be attacked without warning if it sailed under convoy of enemy warships, or engaged in acts of war on behalf of the enemy such as laying mines, minesweeping or cutting undersea cables. Enemy merchant vessels could also be attacked if they were offensively armed. Enemy merchant vessels could be captured outside neutral waters and could be attacked if they resisted visit, search or capture. Captured enemy merchant vessels could be destroyed for reasons of military necessity, provided that the passengers, crew and ship's papers were first placed in a position of safety.

Neutral merchant vessels could be stopped and searched outside neutral waters. Neutral merchant vessels could be captured if they breached or attempted to breach a validly declared blockade, carried contraband goods, operated under the orders or control of an enemy agent, operated in the exclusive employment of the enemy Government, transported enemy troops or transmitted intelligence to the enemy. Neutral merchant vessels could be attacked if they resisted visit and search and there were reasonable grounds for believing they were engaged in an activity which rendered them subject to capture. There was some discussion concerning whether or not captured neutral merchant vessels could be destroyed in any circumstances. It was, however, generally agreed that the passengers, crew and ship's papers must be placed in a position of safety before the vessel was destroyed. Neutral or belligerent vessels in the following catagories were exempt from

---

3   See M. Hastings, Bomber Command (1979); J. Terraine, The Right of the Line (1985); R. Schaffer, Wings of Judgment (1985); M.S. Sherry, The Rise of American Air Power (1987).

4   This summary is based on a similar summary in L. Doswald-Beck, *The International Law of Naval Armed Conflicts: The Need for Reform*, 7 It. Y.I.L. 252-254 (1986-1987) which, in turn, is derived from the 1909 London Declaration concerning the Laws of Naval War and the 1913 Oxford Manual on the Laws of Naval War Governing the Relations between Belligerents.

attack or capture so long as they did not take any part in hostilities: coastal fishing vessels, small boats employed in local trade, vessels charged with religious, scientific or philantropic missions, and hospital ships.[5]

3.   THE WORLD WARS

It is not practicable to provide either a history of naval warfare or a history of the development and application of the law of naval warfare during the period from 1914 to today. One may, however, make certain observations and draw certain conclusions concerning this history. Both World Wars tended to become total wars and, as each war progressed, methods of warfare which were generally viewed as abhorrent at the beginning of the conflict, became common practice by the end of the conflict. Prior to World War I, the idea that merchant ships should be sunk on sight was rejected as totally unacceptable. By 1917, Germany commenced an unrestricted submarine warfare campaign which almost brought Britain to its knees.

From a law of naval warfare perspective, World War II began where World War I left off. By October 1939, Germany was once again waging unrestricted submarine warfare in certain areas. As the war progressed, Britain waged an unrestricted submarine warfare campaign in the Skagerrak and the United States waged an extremely succesful unrestricted submarine warfare campaign against Japan in the Pacific. Further, both Axis and Allied powers also used aircraft in anti-shipping campaigns in various areas during the War. If anything, aircraft were even less able than submarines to perform the traditional roles of visit, search, and removal of crew and passengers prior to sinking merchant vessels. By the end of World War II, because of the use of aircraft and submarines in the commerce destruction role, persons of a cynical disposition might have summarized naval targeting rules as: don't sink hospital ships or clearly marked neutral vessels uninvolved in the conflict and don't attack shipwrecked survivors or their lifeboats. Even these minimal rules were occasionally infringed but no State publicly indicated infringement was a desirable policy. The British jurist, Smith, writing in the immediate aftermath of World War II, argued that in a general war there was no such thing as a belligerent private merchant vessel as all such vessels would be

---

5   Articles 3 and 4 of the 1907 Hague Convention Relative to Certain Restrictions with Regard to the Exercise of the Right of Capture in Naval War. Repr. in N. Ronzitti, ed., The Law of Naval Warfare 177-178 (1988).

controlled by the State and used by the State purely to further the war effort. In his view, all enemy merchant vessels were legitimate military objectives in a general war and could be attacked on sight.[6]

Although the use of submarines and aircraft to sink merchant vessels on sight was inconsistent with the pre-1914 law of naval warfare, there were important military reasons for such practices. As the World Wars tended toward totality, merchant shipping was incorporated into the belligerent war effort. It was reasonable to conclude that, in general, merchant vessels did not travel to and from belligerent States unless they carried cargoes which would either improve the ability of a belligerent State to make war or provide revenue to bolster the belligerent's war economy. As the submarine was a small vessel and, with the exception of torpedoes, weakly armed, it was not able to perform the traditional tasks of visit and search of merchant vessels once the opposing belligerent began to arm merchant vessels and to order them to act agressively in self defense by ramming. Further, the British tactic of using Q-ships, warships disguised as merchant vessels which would attempt to lure submarines within range of their weapons and then disclose their identity and attack, did not provide an incentive for submarines to comply with traditional practices.

During the interwar period, a number of attempts were made by Britain to abolish submarines, notably at the Washington Conference of 1921-1922 and the London Conference of 1930, but on all such occasions Britain was blocked by France, which argued that submarines were useful vessels of war, particularly for weaker powers, although they should be required to follow the same rules as surface vessels.[7] A set of rules for submarine warfare was developed at the London Naval Conference and inserted as Part IV, Article 22, in the 1930 London Treaty for the Limitation and Reduction of Naval Armaments[8] and reaffirmed in a 1936 Procès-Verbal (the London Protocol of 1936).[9] The rules are as follows:

a) In their action with regard to merchant ships, submarines must conform to the rules of international law to which surface vessels are subject.
b) In particular, except in the case of persistant refusal to stop on being duly summoned, or of active resistance to visit or search, a warship, whether surface vessel or submarine, may not sink or render incapable

---

6   H.A. Smith, The Crisis in the Law of Nations 60-62 (1947).
7   W.T. Mallison, Studies in the Law of Naval Warfare - Submarines in General and Limited Wars 36-47 (1968).
8   Ronzitti, op. cit. n. 5, at 348.
9   Ronzitti, op. cit. n. 5, at 352.

of navigation a merchant vessel without having first placed passengers, crew and ship's papers in a place of safety. For this purpose the ship's boats are not regarded as a place of safety unless the safety of the passengers and crew is assured, in the existing sea and weather conditions, by the proximity of land, or the presence of another vessel which is in a position to take them on board.

The proper interpretation of some of the above rules is by no means clear, but some assistance can be derived from the Report of the Committee of Jurists which prepared the text of the 1930 London Treaty. The Report stated in part:

> 'The Committee wish to place it on record that the expression "merchant vessel", where it is employed in the Declaration, is not to be understood as including a merchant vessel which is at the moment participating in hostilities in such a manner as to cause her to lose her right to the immunities of a merchant vessel'.[10]

Unfortunately, the Committee did not go on to explain the meaning of 'participating in hostilities'.

4.   THE FINDINGS AT NUREMBERG

Law of naval warfare issues were raised in a number of war crimes trials following World War II. Admirals Doenitz and Raeder were tried, together with the other German major war criminals before the International Military Tribunal at Nuremberg for, among other things, war crimes on the high seas. Doenitz was charged with waging unrestricted submarine warfare contrary to the London Protocol of 1936. Doenitz argued in defence that the German Navy remained within the confines of international law and of the Protocol. Initially, German submarines were ordered to attack all merchant ships in convoy, and all those which refused to stop or used their radio upon sighting a submarine. Such ships were deemed to be resisting visit and search and, therefore, under the traditional law, they were subject to attack. By 17 October 1939, when German reports indicated that British merchant ships were being used to give information by wireless, were being armed, and were attacking submarines

---

10 Documents of the London Naval Conference 1930, 443 (1930).

on sight, Doenitz ordered his submarines to attack all enemy merchant ships on sight. The Court found:

> 'Shortly after the outbreak of war the British Admiralty, in accordance with its Handbook of Instructions of 1938 to the Merchant Navy, armed its merchant vessels, in many cases convoyed them with armed escort, gave orders to send position reports upon sighting submarines, thus integrating merchant vessels into the warning network of naval intelligence. On 1st October, 1939, the British Admiralty announced British merchant ships had been ordered to ram U-boats if possible.
>
> In the actual circumstances of this case, the Tribunal is not prepared to hold Doenitz guilty for his conduct of submarine warfare against British armed merchant ships.'[11]

Although the wording of this portion of the Judgment is by no means clear, considered in context it exonerates Doenitz from responsibility for attack on all belligerent merchant vessels because of the general belligerent practice of incorporating all such vessels into the war effort. Presumably when belligerents make a general practice of arming and convoying their merchant vessels, integrating them into their intelligence networks, and ordering them to ram U-boats if possible, then such merchant vessels were considered to be participating in hostilities to such an extent as to disentitle them from the benefits of the London Protocol. Unfortunately, although the Tribunal faced the issue of compatibility of the London Protocol Rules with the demonstrated conduct of belligerent merchant shipping after a fashion, it avoided addressing the substantially similar issue of the compatibility of the London Protocol Rules with the demonstrated conduct of neutral merchant shipping when such shipping was used in a manner functionally indistinguishable from the use of belligerent merchant shipping. A partial explanation for the muddiness of the Tribunal's Judgment on submarine warfare issues is that that portion of the Judgment was drafted by Biddle, the senior American Tribunal Member, who was opposed to the conviction of Doenitz on submarine warfare charges and threatened to file a public dissent. The other Judges agreed to let him write this portion of the Judgment to forestall such a dissent.[12]

The Court then considered a charge that Doenitz deliberately ordered the killing of shipwrecked survivors but found the evidence on this charge

---

11 Judgment of the International Military Tribunal for the Trial of German Major War Criminals, (CMD 6964), 108-109 (1946).

12 B.F. Smith, Reaching Judgment at Nuremberg, 247-265 (1977).

insufficient although it did censure him for ordering that rescue operations should not be carried out:

'The evidence further shows that the rescue provisions were not carried out and that the defendant ordered that they should not be carried out. The argument of the defence is that the security of the submarine is, as the first rule of the sea, paramount to rescue and that the development of aircraft made rescue impossible. This may be so, but the Protocol is explicit. If the commander cannot rescue, then under its terms he cannot sink a merchant vessel and should allow it to pass harmless before his periscope. These orders then, prove Doenitz is guilty of a violation of the Protocol.'[13]

The charges arose as a result of the *Laconia* Order issued by Doenitz following an attack by an American aircraft on German submarines attempting to rescue survivors from the *Laconia*, a British passenger ship, which one of their number had torpedoed.[14] Following this incident, Doenitz ordered that no attempts be made to rescue survivors. This particular finding is inconsistent with the earlier finding exonerating Doenitz on a charge concerning the conduct of submarine warfare against belligerent merchant vessels. Robertson, then a naval Judge Advocate, has suggested that this finding applies exclusively to neutral merchant vessels.[15]

On a number of occasions, the German Government established exclusion or operational zones around the British Isles and announced that all ships, including neutral merchant ships would be sunk without warning in these areas. Concerning exclusion zones, the Court held:

'However, the proclamation of operational zones and the sinking of neutral merchant vessels which enter those zones present a different question. This practice was employed in the War of 1914-1918 by Germany and adopted in retaliation by Great Britain. The Washington Conference of 1922, the London Naval Agreement of 1930, and the Protocol of 1936, were entered into with full knowledge that such zones had been employed in the First World War. Yet the Protocol made no exception for the operational zones. The order of Doenitz to sink neutral ships without warning when found within these zones was, therefore, in the opinion of the Tribunal a violation of the Protocol ....

---

13 Judgment, loc. cit. n. 11, at 109.
14 L. Peillard, The Laconia Affair (1967). Also Mallison, op. cit. n. 7, at 137-139.
15 H.B. Robertson, *Submarine Warfare*, 7-25 JAG Journal (1956).

In view of all the facts proved and in particular of an order of the British Admiralty announced on the 8th May, 1940, according to which all vessels should be sunk at night in the Skagerrak, and the answers to interrogatories by Admiral Nimitz stating that unrestricted submarine warfare was carried on in the Pacific Ocean by the United States from the first day that nation entered the war, the sentence of Doenitz is not assessed on the ground of his breaches of the international law of submarine warfare.'[16]

This portion of the Judgment appears to accept the legitimacy of exclusion zones for belligerent merchant vessels but to prohibit such zones when they affect neutral merchant vessels.

The Court made the same finding against Raeder as it did against Doenitz on the charge of waging unrestricted warfare, that is, guilty of waging unrestricted submarine warfare against neutrals but no sentence imposed because of similar Allied practices.[17] The acceptance of a *tu quoque* argument in mitigation is unprecedented in the Tribunal's proceedings themselves, although it should also be noted that, at a preliminary stage, the UN War Crimes Commission declined to address the issue of offences resulting from air warfare, including aerial attacks on shipping, probably because the Allies were the major practitioners of the art.[18]

Assessing the impact of the International Military Tribunal's Judgment on the scope and applicability of the London Protocol is not a simple task. Professor O'Connell has attempted to 'cut the Gordian knot' by arguing:

'The truth is that the requirements of the London Protocol are to be observed only in the situation where the submarine can act with minimal risk on the surface. Since that situation is now an ideal hardly ever in practice to be realized, one is compelled to draw from the Doenitz trial the conclusion that submarine operations in time of war are today governed by no legal text, and that no more than lipservice is being paid in naval documents to the London Protocol.'[19]

---

16 Judgment, loc. cit. n. 11, at 109.
17 *Ibid.*, at 112.
18 See, History of the United Nations War Crime Commision 492 (1948).
19 D.P. O'Connell, *International Law and Contemporary Naval Operations*, 44 BYIL 19-85 (1970). See, A. Vanvoukos, *Termination of Treaties in International Law* 271-273 (1985), contends that the London Protocol is no longer binding but his only authorities are the Doenitz Decision and the view of O'Connell.

There is some basis for arguing that the London Protocol was drafted in favour of surface naval powers, in particular Great Britain, as a fall back position after efforts to outlaw the employment of submarines in a commerce destruction role had failed, and as an attempt to neutralize the effectiveness of the submarine in such a role. If the Protocol is intended to include a very broad definition of 'merchant vessel', it is virtually unworkable in a general war between naval powers where one side has a substantial preponderance in surface naval strength because it does not confer substantially equal benefits to both sides. The practical effectiveness of the law of war in a particular conflict is conditional upon, among other factors, a crude reciprocity and a rough equivalence of benefits.

The key to a workable interpretation of the London Protocol lies in determining the proper meaning of the undefined term 'merchant vessel' in that document. In a general war such as World War I or II, the true merchant vessel is rarely to be found because the belligerent States normally assume such a degree of control over their own vessels and neutral vessels engaged in trading with them as to convert them into *de facto* naval auxiliaries. As *de facto* naval auxiliaries, it is suggested that they should be subject to the same treatment as *de jure* naval auxiliaries, that is, they may be sunk on sight outside of neutral waters. Even in a general war, however, there may be genuine neutral traffic which is entitled to proceed unmolested. For example, in World War II, before the Soviet Union declared war on Japan in 1945, there was significant neutral merchant traffic to and from the Pacific coast of the Soviet Union which passed through the United States declared Pacific War Zone and was not molested by United States submarines.

5.   CURRENT STATE PRACTICE

In a war more limited than that of World War II, for example the Korean or the Falkland War, many merchant vessels, even those of the contending Parties, will be engaged in normal trade quite unconnected with the war effort. Such merchant vessels are clearly not *de facto* naval auxiliaries. As such they should be entitled to all of the benefits of the London Protocol.

The Iran-Iraq conflict, which finally ended in 1988, is the sole major post-World War II conflict in which a sustained maritime anti-commerce campaign was conducted. In the Iran-Iraq conflict, fighting occured in the restricted area of the Persian Gulf, one of the world's most important shipping lanes. Neither Iran nor Iraq were major naval powers but both, as a result of oil profits, were equipped with modern combat aircraft at the beginning of the conflict and Iran also had a significant navy. Iran is the only State located on the entire length of the eastern coast of the Gulf (635 nautical miles) while Iraq had a mere ten miles coast at the northern end of the Gulf. Iranian bomb attacks closed down the two Iraqi oil terminals in the Persian Gulf and blocked access to all three of Iraq's commercial ports at the start of the conflict. No commercial shipping sailed to or from Iraq during the conflict although it is reasonable to presume that some of the ships visiting the ports of Iraq's neighbours in the Persian Gulf carried goods which were eventually transported overland to Iraq.

As a general statement, prior to March 1984, Iraq attacked all vessels in a proclaimed exclusion zone at the northern end of the Gulf. From March 1984 until the end of the conflict, Iraq switched the focus of its anti-shipping campaign in an effort to attack the weak link in Iran's war economy and to arouse the world's interest in the conflict. Iraq directed most of its attacks against tankers, most of them neutral and unconvoyed, sailing to or from Kharg Island, the very heavily defended main Iranian oil terminal, located towards the northern end of the Persian Gulf. All the Iraqi attacks were delivered by shore-based aircraft and almost all involved the use of air-launched missiles. Iraq appears to have devoted minimal effort to obtaining visual identification of the target before missile launch, with the result that accidents, such as the Iraqi attack on the *USS Stark*, did occur. Iran does not appear to have begun attacking commercial shipping until Iraq commenced its anti-tanker campaign in 1984. Since there was no sea traffic with Iraq, Iran attacked neutral merchant shipping destined to and from neutral ports in the Gulf, presumably in an effort to persuade Iraq's financial backers, the other Gulf States, to dissuade Iraq from its campaign against the Kharg Island tankers. Iran's attacks on merchant shipping were less numerous than those of Iraq and, in general, less costly in lives and property damage because they were usually conducted with rockets instead of missiles. In addition, it is understood that Iran devoted more effort to target identification than did Iraq. On the other hand, Iran did not conduct its attacks in declared exclusion zones and some of its attacks were carried out in neutral territorial waters. One author summarized the maritime aspects of the conflict as follows:

'Throughout the eight year course of the Gulf War, Iran and Iraq have attacked more than 400 commercial vessels, almost all of which were neutral State flagships. Over 200 merchant seamen have lost their lives because of these attacks. In material terms, the attacks have resulted in excess of 40 million dead weight tons of damaged shipping. Thirty-one of the attacked merchants were sunk, and another 50 declared total losses. For

1987 alone, the strikes against commercial shipping numbered 178, with a resulting death toll of 108. In relative terms, by the end of 1987, write-off losses in the Gulf War stood at nearly half the tonnage of merchant shipping sent to the bottom in World War II. In all, ships flying the flags of more than 30 different countries, including each of the permanent members of the United Nations Security Council, have been subjected to attacks.'[20]

The same author observed, however, that despite the relative intensity of the tanker war, only about 1% of the ship voyages were attacked.[21] A particularly unusual aspect of the Iran-Iraq conflict was the involvement of United States ships to protect neutral rights in the final stages. This involvement culminated in the tragic incident in which the *USS Vincennes* shot down an Iranian Airbus with the loss of all on board when the Airbus was erroneously identified as an Iranian fighter demonstrating hostile intent.[22]

6.   'CLASSICAL' LAW AND MODERN WARFARE

It is a much more difficult task to state a generally agreed view of the existing law concerning the treatment of merchant vessels in an international armed conflict than it is to state a similar view of the pre-World War I law. Prior to World War I, the normal practice was to capture enemy merchant vessels and neutral merchant vessels subject to capture, because capture conferred economic benefits on the captors and because the capturing vessel was not normally exposing itself to substantial risks by so doing. Modern technology, in particular, the invention of the aircraft, the submarine, modern means of detection, modern means of

---

20 F.V. Russo, *Neutrality at Sea in Transition: State Practice in the Gulf War as Emerging Customary Law*, 19 ODILA 381-399 (1988).

21 *Ibid.*, at 397.

22 The most detailed account of the Airbus Incident is the ICAO Report with many attachments contained in ICAO Doc. C-WP 18708 of 7 November 1988. It is difficult to get an adequate grip on the fact of the naval side of the Gulf War but the US Naval Institute Proceedings for the past few years contain several useful articles. The Gulf War was a topic for discussion at two panels of the 1988 ASIL Meeting and at a Conference at Syracuse University but the proceedings have not yet been published. In addition to Russo, loc. cit. n. 20, see M. Jenkins, *Air Attacks on Neutral Shipping in the Persian Gulf: The Legality of the Iraqi Exclusion Zone and Iranian Reprisals*, 8 B.C. Int'L & Comp. L. Rev. 517-549 (1985); *Conference Report: The Persian/Arabian Gulf Tanker War*, 19 ODILA 299-321 (1988); D.B. Biller, *Policing the Persian Gulf*, 11 Loy-L.A. Int'l & Comp. L.J. 171-205 (1989).

communication, and modern long-range weapons such as missiles have rendered the seas a much more dangerous environment for warships. Today, capturing a vessel, unless the capturing power has a substantial maritime superiority, below the surface, on the surface, and in the air, is often not a practical measure of war. Further, providing an opportunity for the crew of a merchant vessel to abandon ship before the merchant vessel is attacked is often not a practical measure of war. It had been suggested by at least one writer, Doswald-Beck, that the traditional law is simply unsuitable for modern conditions and that it should be re-thought using the broad basic principles of military necessity, humanity and good faith. In particular, she suggests that the traditional practice of stop, search and capture is the exception in modern naval warfare.[23] In practice, a target is a ship which will be attacked and may be destroyed. For this reason it is desirable to confine the classification of military objectives as narrowly as possible. Certainly, in any attempt to state the law, it must be borne in mind that the crews of merchant vessels, although they may be treated as prisoners of war upon capture, are civilians and that there is an obligation which pervades the law of armed conflict to spare civilian population insofar as that is practicable.

Under the pre-World War I law, any merchant vessel could be attacked without warning if it sailed under convoy of enemy warships or if it engaged in acts of war on behalf of the enemy and enemy merchant vessels could be attacked if they were offensively armed. Intelligence gathering for the enemy by neutral merchant vessels rendered them subject to capture (enemy merchant vessels outside of neutral waters were always subject to capture in any event). A number of modern law of naval warfare manuals,[24] the United States (§§ 8.2.2.2, 8.3.1 and 8.4), the French (Article 2) and the Australian (§ 822 and Chapter 10) consider intelligence gathering as equivalent to engaging in acts of war on behalf of the enemy. The United States (§§ 8.2.2.2, 8.3.1, 8.4 and 7.5.1) and Australian (§ 822 and Chapter 10) manuals also indicate that any merchant vessel acting as a naval or military auxiliary of the enemy's armed forces is subject to attack without warning. In addition, the United States manual (§§ 8.2.2.2, 8.3.1

---

23 Doswald-Beck, loc. cit. n. 4, at 276-282.
24 The manuals reviewed were:
   a) France: Armed Forces Official Bulletin No. 102-103, *Maritime Law-Instructions on the Application of International Law in Case of War* (1965);
   b) Australia: ABR 5179 *Manual of the Law of the Sea* (1983);
   c) Canada: *Canadian Forces Law of Armed Conflict Manual* (Second Draft) (1984); and
   d) United States: *Annotated Supplement to the Commander's Handbook on the Law of Naval Operations* (Rev A) NWP 9 (1989).

and 8.4) indicates armed enemy merchant ships are subject to attack without warning. The rationale for this latter position is that, with modern weapons, it is impossible to determine whether armament on merchant ships is to be used offensively or merely defensively. It should also be noted that the United States manual (§ 8.2.3) specifies that civilian passenger vessels at sea are exempt from destruction unless they are being utilized at the time for a military purpose such as transporting troops or military cargo. The rationale for this approach is that the inevitable death of the large number of civilians normally carried in them would be clearly disproportionate to the military benefit that might be gained from the attack.

7.   A NEW APPROACH

There is a strong possibility that a modern consensus could be achieved on the following propositions. During an international armed conflict:
a) Any merchant vessel may be attacked:
    i)   if it engages in acts of war on behalf of the enemy;
    ii)   if it acts as an auxiliary to the enemy's armed forces;
    iii) if it is incorporated into or assists the enemy's intelligence system; or
    iv)   if it sails under convoy of enemy warships or military aircraft.
b) Any enemy merchant vessel may be attacked:
    i)   if it is armed to an extent that it could inflict significant damage to a warship; or
    ii)   it refuses an order to stop or actively resists visit, search or capture.
c) A neutral merchant vessel may be attacked if it is believed on reasonable and probable grounds that the vessel is carrying contraband or breaching a blockade and, after prior warning, the vessel intentionally and clearly refuses to stop or resists visit, search and capture.
d) Passenger vessels when engaged in carrying civilian passengers at sea may not be attacked.
e) Neutral or belligerent vessels in the following catagories are exempt from attack or capture so long as they do not take any part in hostilities: coastal fishing vessels, small boats employed in local trade, hospital ships, medical transports, and vessels charged with religious, philanthropic or non-military scientific missions.

The central question which remains is: when, if ever, may enemy or neutral merchant vessels which do not meet the criteria listed in the preceding paragraph be attacked on sight during an international armed conflict? Is the answer to the question going to depend on such factors as whether or not a declared war exists, the scale of the conflict, the location of a vessel inside or outside a particular zone, the function of the vessel, or whether the vessel flies the flag of a belligerent or neutral State? Declared wars are extremely rare in the UN Charter era. It has been suggested that, in the absence of a state of war, a State engaged in an international armed conflict has no entitlement to exercise belligerent rights such as seizing enemy merchant vessels or visit, search and seizure of neutral merchant vessels. Although some thoughtful work has been done on the implications of the state of war in the Charter era which support this suggestion,[25] this writer remains of the view that war is a question of fact and the application of the laws of war must be conditioned on fact if coherence is to be achieved. All of the laws of war, including those portions of the law of naval warfare affecting neutral shipping, have a prohibitive as well as a permissive character. In the words of the late Professor Baxter: 'For the purposes of an economic blockade having an impact on neutrals, it is assumed that the belligerent would resort to the use of violence against neutrals if such conduct were necessary in order to overcome the enemy. The law thus protects those neutrals by keeping coercion within the permissible limits established.'[26] The UN Charter does not constitute an insurmountable barrier prohibiting the invocation of belligerent rights against non-participants to an international armed conflict. Somewhat similarly, although the scale or intensity of an armed conflict may provide sound policy reasons for making more or less restrictive targeting decisions, using such a factor as a determinant for the legality of targeting criteria would be unwise. There would be a natural tendency for a State to view any conflict in which it was involved as a general war justifying very liberal targeting criteria while conflicts in which it was uninvolved would be limited wars requiring a restrictive approach to targeting.

---

25 Exponents of this approach include: E. Lauterpacht, *The Legal Irrelevance of the 'State of War'*, ASIL Proc. 58-68 (1968); D.P. O'Connell, The Influence of Law on Seapower (1975); C. Greenwood, *The Relationship between Jus ad Bellum and Jus in Bello*, 9 Rev. Int. Studies 221-240 (1983), *The Concept of War in Modern International Law* 36 ICLQ 283-306 (1987); *Self-Defence and the Conduct of International Armed Conflict*, in Y. Dinstein, M. Tabory, eds., International Law in a Time of Perplexity 273 (1989).

26 R.R. Baxter, *The Definition of War*, 16 Rev. Egypt. de Droit Int. 10-29 (1960).

Some writers have proposed a zonal approach whereby, once
appropriate measures have been taken to warn all concerned that presence
in an area is dangerous and to give ships and aircraft in the area time to
leave it, then a belligerent may presume anything in the area without
permission constitutes a legitimate military objective. This approach
facilitates the making of targeting decisions, but it is certainly not a part of
existing law although state practice in recent conflicts indicates some
customary law standards for exclusion zones may be emerging.[27]

The relevance of the flag the merchant vessel is entitled to fly as an
absolute criterion for targeting decisions is debatable. In *Amerada Hess* v.
Argentina Republic, the owners of the Liberian tanker *Hercules* sought
damages from Argentina for a bombing attack on the *Hercules* during the
Falklands conflict which occured outside the exclusion zones proclaimed
by Argentina and the United Kingdom. The United States Court of Appeals
(Second Circuit) which seems to have relied primarily on peace time law
of the sea treaties, although it did conduct a cursory review of older law of
naval warfare treaties, held that neutral ships had a right to free passage on
the high seas and:

'In short, it is beyond controversy that attacking a neutral ship in
international waters, without proper cause for suspicion or investigation,
violates international law. Indeed, the relative paucity of cases litigating this
customary rule of international law underscores the longstanding nature of
this aspect of freedom of the high seas. Where the attacker has refused to
compensate the neutral, such action is analogous to piracy, one of the
earliest recognized violations of international law. See Blackstone,
Commentaries 68, 72. Argentina has cited no contrary authority.'[28]

The Supreme Court of the United States reversed the decision of the Court
of Appeals, but on grounds unrelated to the Court of Appeals' finding

---

27 The zonal issue has been discussed in several recent articles. See F.C. Leiner, *Maritime
Security Zones: Prohibited yet Perpetuated*, 24 Virg. J.Int.'l L. 967-992 (1983-1984); J.
Gilliland, *Submarines and Targets: Suggestions for New Codified Rules of Submarine Warfare*,
73 Geo L.J. 975-1005 (1985); C. Weiss, *Problems of Submarine Warfare Under International
Law*, 22 Intra. L.R. of N.Y. 136-151 (1966-1967); W.J. Fenrick, *The Exclusion Zone Device
in the Law of Naval Warfare*, 24 Can. Y.B. Int'l L. 91-126 (1986). None of these articles
suggest that every object in a zone should be subject to attack, although Weiss adopts the most
robust approach to targeting.
28 *Amerada Hess* v. *Argentina Republic*, US Court of Appeals (2nd circuit) 1987, Repr. in 79
ILR 1-17.

concerning the legality of the attack on the *Hercules*.[29] The Court of Appeal appears to have held the opinion that any attack on a neutral merchant vessel without a prior request for visit and search would be unlawful. It is suggested this opinion is erroneous although it may well be that the actual attack on the *Hercules* was unlawful as the *Hercules* was not providing any support to the United Kingdom in the Falklands Conflict.

It is suggested that the primary legal criterion for determining whether or not a merchant vessel should be a legitimate military objective should be a functional one: what task is the merchant vessel employed on at the time a targeting decision is made? It is conceded that decision makers may, for political reasons such as a desire to limit a conflict, decide that neutral merchant vessels may not be attacked even when they are employed on tasks which might make them legitimate military objectives.

As indicated earlier, during the Iran-Iraq conflict, Iraq attacked tankers, most of them neutral, unconvoyed and unincorporated in the Iranian intelligence system, which were engaged in exporting oil from Iran to support the Iranian war economy. Iran attacked neutral ships enagaged in exporting or importing goods, including oil, to neutral Gulf States, some of which were engaged in providing economic support to the Iraqi war effort. It is suggested that some merchant vessels which do not meet the generally agreed criteria listed earlier (engaging in acts of war, acting as an auxiliary, incorporated in the intelligence system, or being convoyed) may, nevertheless constitute legitimate military objectives. If so, however, how are the tasks of these other vessels described? Further, would the actions of Iraq or Iran be legitimate under a modern restatement of the law of naval warfare?

The current manual of the United States Navy suggests (§§ 8.2.2.2, 8.3.1 and 8.4) that enemy merchant ships may be attacked and destroyed without warning if they are integrated into the enemy's 'war-fighting/war-sustaining effort' and compliance with the 1936 London Protocol would subject the attacking force to imminent danger or otherwise preclude mission accomplishment. The Annotation to this provision states: 'Although the term "war-sustaining" is not subject to precise definition, "effort" that indirectly but effectively supports and sustains the belligerent's war-fighting capability properly falls within the scope of the term'. Another Annotation (to § 7.4) provides as examples 'imports of raw materials used for the production of armaments and exports of products the

---

29 *Argentina Republic* v. *Amerada Hess Shipping Corp et al.*, US Supreme Court, Repr. in 28 ILM 382-390 (1989).

proceeds of which are used by the belligerent to purchase arms and armaments'. It then goes on to provide (§ 7.5.2) that neutral merchant vessels acquire the character of enemy merchant vessels, and are liable to the same treatment, when they 'operate directly under enemy control, orders, charter, employment, or direction'. On the not unreasonable assumption that the neutral tankers carrying Iranian oil exports were operating under Iranian charter or control and sailing in an area where it would not be practicable for Iraqi forces to comply with the 1936 London Protocol, it would appear that the attacks of the Iraqi forces on neutral tankers would have been lawful under the criteria in the United States manual. On the other hand, it does not appear that the Iranian actions would have been lawful because there was not a sufficient linkage between the tasks carried out by the neutral vessels it attacked and the Iraqi 'war-fighting/war-sustaining effort'.

Although the influence of the views expressed in the United States manual is difficult to overestimate, because of the place of the United States among the world's navies, and because of the level of law of naval warfare expertise in the United States Navy, it must not be presumed that a simple comparison of activities in the Iran-Iraq conflict with the criteria listed in the United States manual will provide a generally accepted assessment of legality. It has been suggested, by Professor Kalshoven,[30] among others, that criteria such as 'contribution to the war effort' or integration into the 'war-fighting/war-sustaining effort' are too broad and, potentially, allow a belligerent too much latitude for classifying maritime commerce with his enemy as a legitimate military objective. Indeed, at the 1989 Round Table at Bochum in the Federal Republic of Germany concerned with the Military Objective and the Principle of Distinction in the Law of Naval Warfare, a Draft Document was produced which suggests that perhaps the appropriate phrase to describe a residual category of merchant vessels which are legitimate military objectives would be merchant vessels which 'make an effective contribution to military action' by, for example carrying military materials. Although this phrase also leaves some scope for interpretation, it would appear that, if it applies, attacks on neutral merchant vessels carrying exports would be illegitimate.

---

30 Kalshoven, loc. cit. n. 2, at 7-8, and F. Kalshoven, *Enemy Merchant Vessels as Legitimate Military Objectives* (unpublished) 6-8 (1990).

8.   CONCLUDING REMARKS

As every lawyer concerned with the law of naval warfare knows, it is extremely difficult to provide accurate, simple, bright line legal rules concerning the targeting of merchant shipping. Although the task is difficult, there is still a professional obligation to provide as accurate an assessment of the law as possible, and to make that assessment as clear as possible for both navies and those who are involved with merchant shipping. One must go beyond a creative labelling approach whereby 'our side has merchant vessels which are exempt from attack while theirs has naval auxiliaries which we can sink on sight'. The task of developing a usable word picture to describe when the merchant ship becomes a legitimate military objective has merely been begun. The United States manual uses expressions such as 'acting in any capacity as a naval or military auxiliary' and 'integrated into war-fighting/war-sustaining effort'. The Bochum Round Table used the expression 'making an effective contribution to military effort'. Both of these expressions are useful starting points. It is essential, however, that scholars and practitioners now begin to fill in the details of this word picture.

VI

HUMANITARIAN LAW IN PRACTICE

THE TREATMENT OF REBELS IN CONFLICTS OF A DISPUTED CHARACTER: THE ANGLO-BOER WAR AND THE 'ANC-BOER WAR' COMPARED

JOHN DUGARD

1.   INTRODUCTION

Injustice repeats itself in history. Tragically the victims of injustice often forget their own sufferings when they come to power. The Israeli occupation of the West Bank and Gaza is an example of this historical truism. So is the manner in which the South African Government has treated black 'rebels' in their struggle against apartheid. A predominantly Afrikaner or 'Boer' Government, nurtured on the legacy of bitterness caused by Britain's treatment of Boers during the Anglo-Boer War of 1899-1902, has repeated many of the mistakes of the British. In particular it has failed to recall the bitterness caused by the treatment of Boer combatants, who viewed themselves as belligerents in an international conflict, as rebels who failed to qualify for the protection of humanitarian law. It is this failure to learn from the lesson of history that I shall examine in my tribute to a great humanitarian lawyer - Frits Kalshoven.

2.   REBELS, HUMANITARIAN LAW AND THE
          ANGLO-BOER WAR

The Anglo-Boer War[1] occurred at a time when humanitarian law was in
its infancy. The principal conventions in force were the 1864 Geneva
Convention on the Wounded and Sick and the 1899 Hague Convention II
Respecting the Laws and Customs of War on Land.[2] The Boer Republics
-the Orange Free State and the South African Republic (Transvaal)- were
not Parties to either of these Conventions, with the result that hostilities
were governed by customary international law.[3] Both Parties to the
conflict claimed to act in accordance with the custom and usages of the law
of war; at times both Parties accused each other of violations of these
customs;[4] and municipal courts judged many disputes, particularly relating
to the seizure and forfeiture of the property of belligerents, in accordance
with the customary laws of war.[5]

The Anglo-Boer War was not a conventional war fought between the
armies of sovereign States. In the first place, the very sovereignty of the
Transvaal was suspect as a result of conventions entered into with Britain
in 1881 and 1884 which retained Britain's 'suzerainty' over the Transvaal
and curtailed the latter's treaty-making power.[6] Britain might have argued,
on the basis of these conventions, that the 'war' with the Transvaal was
therefore nothing but an internal uprising and treated all Transvaal
combatants as ordinary rebels.[7] A second difficulty concerned the failure
of the Boer forces to wear distinctive uniforms.[8] Fortunately, Britain
raised neither of these arguments against the status of the Boer combatants.
Until the formal annexation of the Orange Free State and Transvaal, in
May and October 1900 respectively, the Boer forces were recognised by
the British as lawful belligerents, entitled to be treated as prisoners of war
on their capture.

---

1   For an account of this war, see T. Pakenham, The Boer War (1979).
2   This Convention, which was substantially repeated in the 1907 Hague Convention IV, entered
     into force on 4 September 1900.
3   T. Baty, International Law in South Africa 79 (1901).
4   For accounts of the manner in which Parties to the conflict invoked customary law, see Baty,
     ibid.. Also J.M. Spaight, War Rights on Land (1911).
5   See, *Van Deventer* v. *Hancke and Mossop*, TS 401 (1903); *Lemkuhl* v. *Kock*, TS 451 (1903);
     Olivier v. *Wessels*, TS 235 (1904); *R* v. *Louw*, 21 SC 36 (1904); *Alexander* v. *Pfau*, TS 155
     (1904); *Du Toit* v. *Kruger*, 22 SC 234 (1905); *Achterberg* v. *Glinster*, TS 326 (1903).
6   The texts of these Conventions appear in Baty, op. cit. n. 3, at 102-119.
7   *Ibid.*, at 45-68; Spaight, op. cit. n. 4, at 14-15.
8   Baty, op. cit. n. 3, at 86.

After the annexation of the Boer Republics, the Boer forces continued to wage a guerrilla war against Britain until May 1902.[9] Initially Britain's response was to categorise all guerrillas as 'rebels',[10] but this position was difficult to sustain in the light of the reality of the continuing conflict and the opposition to the notion of treating the Boer guerrillas as rebels from important quarters in Britain itself.[11] Consequently the guerrilla forces of the Boer Republics were treated as lawful belligerents, except where their conduct was classified as 'marauding', which in practice was difficult to distinguish from accepted guerrilla warfare.[12] While the Boer combatants themselves were respected as lawful belligerents, the same did not apply to their families or property. Their wives and children were forced into concentration camps, where thousands died from disease and deprivation;[13] and their farmhouses were burnt and their lands devastated.[14] The nature of the war was invoked as a justification for this action.[15] But, at the same time, it is clear that the Boer forces had undergone a diminution in belligerent status in the eyes of the British after the annexation of the Republics. In effect the devastation of their property and the detention of their families were justified on the grounds that they were 'rebels' not entitled to the full respect accorded to lawful belligerents.[16]

No such ambivalence was shown by the British towards those Boers resident in the Cape Colony and Natal who joined their kith and kin in the 'peoples' war' against the British army. Despite the fact that the arena of the war was not limited to the Orange Free State and Transvaal, and many

---

9   For a personal account of this war, see D. Reitz, Commando: A Boer Journal of the Boer War (1929).

10 On 1 June 1900, shortly after the annexation of the Orange Free State, Lord Roberts issued a Proclamation which declared that:
'Inasmuch as the Orange River Colony, formerly known as the Orange Free State, is now British territory ... all inhabitants thereof, who, after fourteen days from the date of this Proclamation may be found in arms against Her Majesty within the said colony, will be liable to be dealt with as rebels and to suffer in person and property accordingly.'
Cd. 426, at 8, quoted in Spaight op. cit. n. 4, at 330-331.

11 L. Nurick, R.W. Barrett, *Legality of Guerrilla Forces under the Laws of War*, 40 AJIL 563, 578 (1946).

12 Spaight, op. cit. n. 4, at 61-63.

13 Pakenham, op. cit. n. 1, at 493-495, 502-510, 515-520.

14 Spaight, op. cit. n. 4, at 124-125, 136-139.

15 *Ibid.*, at 62-65, 136-139, 308-310.

16 *Ibid.*, at 62-63, 303-310; Nurick, Barrett, loc. cit. n. 11, at 578.

of the military operations occurred in the Cape Colony and Natal,[17] they were treated as 'rebels', entitled to none of the rights and privileges of combatants.[18] Although 'rebels' in the Cape and Natal charged with treason before special civil courts in the early days of the war were treated leniently,[19] those brought before the military courts in the later phases of the war were often denied fair trials and some thirty-two were executed.[20] Memories of these trials and sentences still feature prominently in Afrikaner folklore.[21]

3.   THE AFRICAN NATIONAL CONGRESS AND THE
       1977 GENEVA PROTOCOLS[22]

In 1961 the African National Congress (ANC) resolved to resort to violent means to achieve the destruction of *apartheid*, after peaceful methods had been exhausted. Initially this resistance took the form of sabotage of public property but over the years the 'struggle' was transformed into a low-intensity guerrilla war. ANC insurgents operating from neighbouring territories penetrated South Africa and destroyed strategic installations, detonated bombs in busy shopping centres, and, occasionally, engaged in skirmishes with the security forces on the borders and in the major cities.

---

17 The major battles of the Anglo-Boer War before the annexation of the Orange Free State and the Transvaal were fought in the Cape Colony and Natal. During this time the Orange Free State 'practically annexed' parts of the Cape Colony and its Boer inhabitants were compelled to take up arms against the British. Spaight, op. cit. n. 4, at 330. In the final stages of the war Boer forces again penetrated deep into Cape Colony.
18 Some judicial decisions give support to the view that Cape rebels who joined the Boer forces should be treated as belligerents. See *Rebels as Belligerents*, 21 South African Law Journal 119-123, 318 (1904).
19 Sentences ranged from fines to short terms of imprisonment. See *Cape Treason Trials*, repr. in 18 South African Law Journal 164-177 (1901); *R* v. *De Jager*, 22 NLR 65 (1901); *R* v. *Boers*, 21 NLR 116 (1900); *R* v. *Gowthorpe*, 21 NLR 221 (1900); *R* v. *Venter*, 22 NLR 185 (1901).
20 Papers Relating to the Administration of Martial Law in South Africa, Cd. 981 (1902); J.H. Snyman, *Rebelle-Verhoor in Kaapland Gedurende die Tweede-Vryheidsoorlog met Spesiale Verwysing na die Militêre Howe (1899-1902)* (Rebel Trials in the Cape Colony during the Second War of Liberation [Anglo-Boer War] with Special Reference to the Military Courts [1899-1902]), 25 Archives Year Book for South African History 1-71 (1962).
21 Snyman, loc. cit. n. 20, at 3, 68.
22 The Pan Africanist Congress (PAC) is also recognised by the Organisation of African Unity (OAU) and the UN as a South African liberation movement. Obviously, the PAC should be entitled to the same benefits extended to the ANC. The ANC is singled out for special attention in this study because its members have been the focus of the debate over prisoner-of-war status for combatants belonging to national liberation movements.

External intervention was supported by sporadic internal rebellion in many parts of the country. Until 1985 the ordinary security laws of the land were invoked to combat the ANC campaign and internal unrest; but from 1985 to 1990 emergency powers were promulgated for most of the country. In addition the South African security forces launched reprisal raids against ANC bases in neighbouring territories and embarked on a policy of political 'destabilisation' of those States that gave support to the ANC. At no stage did the South African Government recognise the ANC as a lawful belligerent or acknowledge the existence of a state of war or armed conflict. Moreover the courts refused to recognise that the hostilities warranted the exercise of the common-law powers of martial law.[23]

Although this study is not concerned with the treatment of South West African Peoples Organisation (SWAPO) combatants in Namibia from 1966 to 1989, it is necessary to record that a similar situation prevailed in respect of South Africa's occupation of Namibia. Despite the fact that SWAPO forces regularly engaged the South African security forces in northern Namibia, South Africa refused to accord belligerent status to SWAPO or to recognise the conflict as 'international' - despite the international status of the territory.[24]

In 1977 two Protocols additional to the 1949 Geneva Conventions were adopted. Article 1(4) of Protocol I provided that the protective principles of the Geneva Conventions were now to cover:

> '... armed conflicts in which peoples are fighting against colonial domination and alien occupation and against racist regimes in the exercise of their right to self-determination, as enshrined in the Charter of the United Nations and the Declaration on Principles of International Law concerning Friendly Relations and Co-operation among States in accordance with the Charter of the United Nations.'

That Protocol I was intended to govern the conflict between South Africa and the ANC, as well as the Namibian conflict, was clear from the debates in the 1974-1975 Diplomatic Conference on Humanitarian Law, which produced the 1977 Protocols, and from a number of United Nations GA Resolutions calling upon South Africa to treat ANC[25] and SWAPO[26]

---

23 *End Conscription Campaign* v. *Minister of Defence*, 2 SA 180 (C) (1989).
24 See J. Dugard, *SWAPO: The Jus ad Bellum and the Jus in Bello*, 93 South African Law Journal 144 (1976).
25 *Cf.*, GA Res. 2396 (XXIII) of 2 December 1968; GA Res. 39/72A (XXIX) of 13 December 1984.

combatants as prisoners of war. Today some 92 States are Parties to Protocol I.[27] Not surprisingly neither of the two States at which Protocol I is directed -South Africa and Israel- has signed it. Clearly the South African Government is unwilling to acquiesce in the categorisation of itself as a 'racist regime' or to confer legitimacy on the ANC by recognising it as a lawful belligerent. However, in 1980, the ANC somewhat ambiguously[28] indicated its preparedness to accept the obligations contained in Protocol I when it delivered to the President of the ICRC a Declaration which states:

> 'The ANC of South Africa hereby declares that it intends to respect and be guided by the general principles of international humanitarian law applicable in armed conflicts. Wherever practically possible, the ANC will endeavour to respect the rules of the four Geneva Conventions of 1949 for the victims of armed conflicts and the 1977 additional Protocol I, relative to the protection of victims of armed conflicts.'

South Africa is a Party to all four Geneva Conventions of 1949. The refusal of the South African Government to sign the 1977 Protocols, however, enabled it to categorise both the Namibian and South African conflicts as 'internal' conflicts to which humanitarian law was inapplicable. Both SWAPO and ANC combatants were therefore treated as 'rebels' to which the ordinary law of the land applied. Over the past thirty years 'rebels' have therefore been tried and convicted on charges of treason, murder, sabotage and terrorism. The denial of prisoner-of-war status to

---

26 GA Res. 2678 (XXV) of 9 December 1970.

27 274 International Review of the Red Cross 66-69 (1990).

28 This declaration purported to have been issued in terms of Article 96 of Protocol I. However the validity of this declaration has been questioned on the grounds, first, that it was deposited with the ICRC instead of the Swiss Federal Council and, secondly, because it fails to undertake to apply the rules of the 1949 Geneva Conventions and Protocol I unconditionally, but merely agrees to respect them 'wherever practically possible'.

See A. Borrowdale, *The Law of War in Southern Africa - The Growing Debate*, 15 Comparative and International Law Journal of Southern Africa 41-42 (1982). In 1970 SWAPO made a public statement that it adhered 'strictly to the Geneva Conventions of 1949'. See I. Detter de Lupis, The Law of War 53 (1987). In 1982 the PLO filed a unilateral declaration accepting the application of the four Geneva Conventions and Protocol I. In 1989 it attempted to accede to the Geneva Conventions and the two Protocols. *Cf.*, 274 International Review of the Red Cross 64-65 (1990).

such combatants clearly enjoyed the support of whites but was vigorously contested by blacks.[29]

4. SOUTH AFRICAN COURTS AND PROTOCOL I

The status of ANC and SWAPO combatants was raised before South African courts in a number of cases. In some cases it was argued that Protocol I now reflects customary international law with the result that South African courts were barred from trying combatants belonging to national liberation movements. In other cases it was contended that, while Protocol I might not yet have attained the status of customary law, the fact that combatants might believe that it had, should be taken into account as a mitigating factor in the imposition of sentence. These two categories of arguments, and their treatment by South African courts, will be considered.

4.1 Protocol I as a bar to the jurisdiction of the courts

Two cases illustrate the manner in which Protocol I has been invoked to challenge the jurisdiction of the court.

In 1985, four ANC members arraigned on charges under the Internal Security Act[30] refused to plead, stating that they did not recognise the jurisdiction of the court. One of them, Norbert Buthelezi, read the following statement to the court:

'The courts are a loyal and faithful arm of the very government the African National Congress is fighting to destroy. We therefore contend that this court cannot adjudicate in a dispute between ourselves and the government. It is absolutely impossible for the government to be an impartial judge in its own case. We received military training in the art of warfare in the people's army 'Umkonto We Sizwe' (military wing of the ANC). In that case we regard ourselves as truly fledged soldiers of our army. The African National Congress is a signatory to the Geneva Convention. We were captured in the process of executing our historical mission of liberating our

---

29 From 1983 to 1984 I conducted a survey of attitudes among South Africans towards international law which showed a clear division of opinion on this subject along racial lines. J. Dugard, *The Conflict Between International Law and South African Law: Another Divisive Factor in South African Society*, 2 South African Journal on Human Rights 17-19 (1986).

30 Act 74 of 1982. This statute creates a number of crimes of statutory treason, such as terrorism, subversion and sabotage.

people. Under the Geneva Convention we must be accorded prisoner-of-war status. As prisoners-of-war no court of law has power over our case. The Geneva Convention recognises people who take up arms to fight against national oppression as prisoners-of-war in case of capture by the oppressor's security forces. We refuse to stand trial.'[31]

The court dismissed this plea and proceeded with the trial. The four defendants were convicted and sentenced to periods of imprisonment ranging from eight to twelve years.

In the second case, *State* v. *Petane*,[32] counsel raised a similar plea in a case in which an ANC insurgent was charged with terrorism and attempted murder arising out of his attempt to place a bomb in a shopping centre and subsequent skirmishes with the police. Defence counsel argued that State practice relating to Protocol I provided evidence of a customary rule of international law extending prisoner-of-war status to members of national liberation movements, and that this rule formed part of South African law in accordance with the common law principle that customary international law forms part of South African law.[33]

After a thorough examination of the attitudes of States towards Protocol I, Judge Conradie concluded that the provisions of Protocol I which extend prisoner-of-war status to members of national liberation movements are not part of customary international law and therefore were not incorporated into South Africa law. He proceeded with the trial and in due course convicted Petane. However, although terrorism is a capital crime, the Judge declined to sentence the defendant to death and instead imposed a cumulative sentence on all counts of 17 years imprisonment. The fact that the defendant had not caused any loss of life and, possibly, the argument that the defendant saw himself as a 'soldier' and not a criminal, may have contributed to the Judge's decision not to impose the death sentence.

In reaching his finding that Protocol I did not reflect a customary rule of international law, Judge Conradie stated:

'To my way of thinking, the trouble with the first Protocol giving rise to State practice is that its terms have not been capable of being observed by all that many States. At the end of 1977 when the treaty first lay open for

---

31 *State* v. *Mapumulo*, No CC 93/85 (Natal Provincial Division; unreported decision).

32 3 SA 51 (C) (1988).

33 This rule is clearly established in South African law; see *Nduli* v. *Minister of Justice*, 1 SA 893 (A) (1978); *Inter-Science Research and Development Services* v. *Republica Popular de Mozambique*, 2 SA 111 (T), 124 (1980).

ratification there were few States which were involved in colonial domination or the occupation of other States and there were only two, South Africa and Israel, which were considered to fall within the third category of racist regimes. Accordingly, the situation sought to be regulated by the first Protocol was one faced by few countries; too few countries, in my view, to permit any general usage in dealing with armed conflicts of the kind envisaged by Protocol to develop.

One must ... look for State practice at what States have done on the ground in the harsh climate of a tempestuous world, and not at what their representatives profess in the ideologically overheated environment of the United Nations where indignation appears frequently to be a surrogate for action.'[34]

After an examination of the slow response on the part of States to ratification of Protocol I, he concluded:

'This approach of the world community to Protocol I is, on principle, far too half hearted to justify an inference that its principles have been so widely accepted as to qualify them as rules of customary international law. The reasons for this are, I imagine, not far to seek. For those States which are contending with 'peoples' struggles for self-determination, adoption of the Protocol may prove awkward. For liberation movements who rely on strategies of urban terror for achieving their aims the terms of the Protocol, with its emphasis on the protection of civilians, may prove disastrously restrictive.'[35]

Judge Conradie's finding that wars of national liberation are not international conflicts under contemporary customary international law is open to question. In 1977 when Protocol I was adopted there was already widespread support for the view that wars of national liberation were wars of an international character to which humanitarian law is applicable.[36] Today the argument that customary international law treats wars of national liberation as international and not internal conflicts has been strengthened

---

34 *State* v. *Petane*, loc. cit. n. 32, at 61.
35 *Ibid.*, at 65.
36 G. Abi-Saab, *Wars of National Liberation in the Geneva Conventions and Protocols*, 165 Recueil des Cours 372 (1979); A. Cassese, *Wars of National Liberation and Humanitarian Law*, in C. Swinarski, ed., Studies and Essays on International Humanitarian Law and Red Cross Principles in Honour of Jean Pictet 320-323 (1984); L.R. Penna, *Customary International Law and Protocol I*, in Swinarski, at 216; K. Ginther, *Liberation Movements*, in R. Bernhardt, Encyclopaedia of Public International Law 245 (1981).

by the ratification of Protocol I by over 90 States. South Africa and Israel do, however, pose a special problem as both these target States have persistently objected to this development. Consequently it has been suggested that they qualify as 'persistent objectors' and are therefore not bound to treat wars of national liberation as international conflicts.[37] Unfortunately Judge Conradie failed to distinguish between the general status of the rule and its applicability to South Africa and Israel. Both State practice[38] and *opinio juris*[39] lend support to the view that wars of national liberation qualify as international conflicts, despite the persistent objections of Israel and South Africa. The present status of this rule therefore requires closer examination than it received in *Petane's* case.

4.2   Protocol I and mitigation of sentence

Until 1990, when the South African Government declared a moratorium on the implementation of the death penalty[40] and introduced legislation to reduce the number of executions,[41] South Africa ranked with Iran as the leading executioning State in the modern world.[42] From 1977 to 1986, 1143 persons were hanged in South Africa and in 1987 alone 164 persons were hanged.[43] The overwhelming majority of those executed in South Africa were convicted of murder unrelated to any political issue. The political offences of treason and statutory terrorism[44] do, however, carry the death penalty and, in addition, many ANC combatants have been tried for murder arising out of their guerrilla activities. Consequently, despite

---

37 A. Cassese, *The Geneva Protocols of 1977 on the Humanitarian Law of Armed Conflict and Customary International Law*, 3 UCLA Pacific Basin Law Journal 71, 103, 113-114.

38 See H.A. Wilson, International Law and the Use of Force by National Liberation Movements 151-162 (1988); H.-P. Gasser, *Agora: The US Decision not to Ratify Protocol I to the Geneva Convention on the Protection of War Victims. An Appeal for Ratification by the United States*, 81 AJIL 921-922 (1987).

39 Cassese, loc. cit. n. 36, at 320-323.

40 This moratorium was announced by State President F.W. de Klerk on 2 February 1990. See, Debates of Parliament (Hansard), cols. 7-8 (2 February 1990).

41 The Criminal Law Amendment Act 107 of 1990 seeks to reduce the number of death penalties imposed by conferring a discretion on both the trial and appeal court not to impose this penalty. Previously a court was in law obliged to impose the death penalty where a person was convicted of murder without extenuating circumstances.

42 Amnesty International, *When the State Kills ... The Death Penalty v. Human Rights* 263 (1989).

43 South African Institute of Race Relations, Race Relations Survey 1987-1988, 551 (1988).

44 In terms of the Internal Security Act 74 of 1982.

vigorous protests from the United Nations,[45] a substantial number of those executed in the past decade have been ANC combatants or persons convicted of murder arising out of political conflict.

As the crime of murder without extenuating circumstances carried a mandatory death sentence until 1990, defence counsel have been compelled to devote much of their energies to proving extenuating or mitigating circumstance in order to save their clients from the gallows. An extenuating circumstance is viewed as any 'fact associated with the crime which serves in the mind of reasonable men to diminish morally, albeit not legally, the degree of the prisoner's guilt'.[46] In cases involving ANC combatants it has frequently been argued that the prisoner's belief that he is entitled to be treated as a 'soldier' and not an ordinary criminal is reasonable in the light of the wide acceptance of Protocol I and that this should be treated as an extenuating circumstance. This argument has met with a mixed response from the courts.

In *State* v. *Sagarius*[47] the High Court of South West Africa, then a part of the South African court system, accepted the growing tendency in international law to treat members of liberation movements as prisoners-of-war as an extenuating circumstance for the purpose of sentence and imposed two sentences of nine years and one of eleven years upon three SWAPO combatants convicted of the capital crime of terrorism.

South African courts have, before 1990, refused to accept this argument. In *State* v. *Mogoerane*[48] Judge Curlewis found three members of 'Umkonto We Sizwe' guilty of murder arising out of attacks on police stations. In response to my testimony on the subject of recent developments in humanitarian law, Judge Curlewis stated:

'The interest, perhaps, of Professor Dugard's evidence is that, as he told us, the convention was passed with two organisations in mind: the PLO and the ANC. The PLO, in my view, is a bunch of thugs who kill Jews. The fact therefore that irresponsible people overseas and elsewhere praise it and give it a status and put a gloss of respectability upon it, does not seem to me to show much right thinking. Over forty years ago another bunch of

---

45 See, for example, SC Res. 533 of 7 June 1983 appealing for mercy for three ANC combatants -Simon Mogoerane, Jerry Mosololi and Marcus Motaung- convicted of treason and murder. Despite this plea they were executed.

46 *Rex* v. *Biyana* 1938 EDC 310.

47 1 SA 833 (SWA), at 836 (1983).

48 Unreported Judgment of the Transvaal Provincial Division, 6 August 1982. Repr. in 1 Lawyers for Human Rights Bulletin 118 (1983).

thugs went about killing Jews and they also had a gloss of respectability put upon them for a long time. That was called appeasement.

I do not think that any comfort can be drawn for the ANC by being joined with the PLO. However, it may be said that Professor Dugard's view, although he did not express it specifically, I think it was mooted by Mr Unterhalter (counsel for the accused), is that there may well be a move amongst academics to think that this should be regarded as custom, and thus influence this court. I have taken that into account.'

The three were sentenced to death and executed.[49]

The court in *State* v. *Mncube and Nondula*[50] was equally unsympathetic. Here two ANC combatants were charged with treason and murder arising out of the military activities of the ANC on the northern borders of South Africa. Mncube carried arms openly, wore a distinctive uniform and was subject to a military disciplinary system at the time of the confrontation with the South African security forces and thus appeared to fall within the scope of Articles 43 and 44 of Protocol I. Despite this, Judge de Villiers rejected the plea in mitigation of sentence based on compliance with Protocol I and sentenced both men to death. The appeal in this matter is still pending but it seems unlikely that they will be executed in the light of the proposed amnesty for political offenders as a pre-condition to political negotiations between the ANC and the South African Government.

In a more recent case,[51] in which ANC combatants were found guilty on several counts of murder, the members of the trial court were divided on the correct approach to be adopted. While the presiding Judge found that the fact that the accused believed that they were soldiers engaged in a just struggle reduced their moral blameworthiness and hence constituted an extenuating circumstance, the two assessors found otherwise. Consequently the Judge was obliged to impose the death sentence.[52] The appeal, heard in terms of the 1990 amendment which gives wider discretionary powers to the courts in respect of the death penalty, reversed this decision, with five Judges of appeal finding that the death sentence was not a proper sentence

---

49 See n. 45, *supra*.
50 Unreported Judgment of the Transvaal Provincial Division, 5 May 1988 (Case No. 449/87).
51 *State* v. *Masina and others*. Unreported Judgment of the Transvaal Provincial Division, 27 April 1989 (Case No. 400/88).
52 Under South African law a Judge is required to sit with two persons experienced in the administration of justice as assessors in a capital case. On questions of fact, which include the existence of extenuating circumstances, the majority finding prevails. Criminal Procedure Act 51 of 1977 (sect. 145).

to be imposed in the light of the accused's belief that they were soldiers engaged in a just struggle. Consequently sentences of 25 years imprisonment were substituted.[53]

5.   CONCLUSION

In February 1990 the armed conflict between the South African Government and the ANC was brought to an end when State President De Klerk announced the 'unbanning' of the ANC and other previously outlawed organisations and initiated a process of negotiation with the ANC aimed at creating a just and democratic society.[54] The conclusion of these 'hostilities' was given formal effect by the 'Pretoria Minute', agreed upon by the South African Government and the ANC on 6 August 1990. This 'Minute' provided in paragraph 3:

> 'In the interest of moving as speedily as possible towards a negotiated peaceful political setlement and in the context of the agreements reached, the ANC announced that it was now suspending all armed actions with immediate effect. As a result of this, no further armed actions and related activities by the ANC and its military wing Umkhonto We Sizwe will take place.'[55]

The negotiations between the ANC and the South African Government have included provisions for the release of political prisoners and the granting of immunity in respect of political offences to persons both inside and outside South Africa. A Working Group comprising members of both the Government and the ANC drafted a set of guidelines on the definitions of 'political offence' and 'political prisoners', drawn largely from the jurisprudence of extradition law.[56] These guidelines, which have been officially endorsed by the Government, have regard for the motive of the offender, the context of the offence, the political objective of the act, the gravity of the offence and the question whether the act was committed in the execution of an order from an organisation.[57] The process of releasing

---

53 *State* v. *Masina & Others*, 4 SA 709 (A) (1990).
54 Debates of Parliament (Hansard), cols. 2-16 (2 February 1990).
55 The text of the 'Pretoria Minute' is published in 6 South African Journal on Human Rights 322 (1990).
56 *Ibid.*, at 319 *et seq.*.
57 Government Notice R 2625 Government Gazette 12834 of 7 November 1990.

political prisoners and indemnifying ANC combatants has already started, although it is not being executed as speedily as was originally hoped.

Those ANC combatants who have already been executed cannot be restored to life. Like the 'rebels' of the Anglo-Boer War, their memory will haunt a *post-apartheid* society. They will be seen as martyrs who were wrongly executed and their blood will leave a stain of bitterness on the process of reconciliation. This could have been avoided had South Africa accepted Protocol I or the courts taken it into account as a mitigating circumstance. Alternatively, the South African Government could, like Israel in the West Bank and Gaza,[58] have abandoned the death penalty for ANC combatants.

Conventional wars are a rare occurrence in the modern world. Their place has been taken by ideological or ethnic conflicts within a State in which the 'rebels' receive material and moral support from sympathetic outside States. Inevitably such conflicts will be categorised as 'internal' by the incumbent regime and as 'international' by those States ideologically or ethnically linked with the rebels. The two South African case studies that form the subject of this article illustrate this truism. In the Anglo-Boer War there was strong support in Britain, Europe and, of course, the Boer Republics, for the view that the Cape and Natal rebels were part of an international conflict and therefore entitled to treatment as prisoners-of-war. Similarly, ANC combatants were categorized by most States as international combatants to which the laws of war applied. However, in neither case was the incumbent regime prepared to lend legitimacy to the rebels by according them the status of belligerents. Instead they subjected them to the ordinary law of the land and did not hesitate to invoke the ultimate penalty against them.

Neither of the South African case studies is unique. Modern history provides abundant examples of the treatment as rebels of combatants who claim to be engaged in an international conflict. The question arises whether the present rules of humanitarian law are adequate and whether there is more that might practically be done to reduce the suffering of rebels.

It is surely time to recognise that Protocol I has failed in its attempt to extend the Geneva Conventions of 1949 to certain internal conflicts. It was originally conceived as a mechanism for compelling four regimes to apply the principles of humanitarian law to their 'internal conflicts' - namely,

---

58 Order concerning local courts (Death Penalty), No 268 of 1968, 14 C.P. & O., 537. Repr. in Israel National Section of the International Commission of Jurists, *The Rule of Law in the Areas Administered by Israel* 25 (1981).

Portugal, Rhodesia, South Africa and Israel.[59] By the time Protocol I materialised Portugal had already decolonised its overseas empire; in 1980 the Smith 'racist regime' was forced to give way to an independent Zimbabwe; in 1990 Namibia attained independence; and at present negotiations are underway to bring the South African conflict to an end. Israel therefore remains the sole target of Article 1(4) of Protocol I and there seems no likelihood whatsoever that it will be prepared to classify itself as an 'alien occupier' or 'racist regime' as required by Article 1(4).

This limitation on the scope and future of Protocol I was foreseen by the Third World States which pressed for the inclusion of Article 1(4). For them Article 1(4) was to serve the purpose of condemning certain specific regimes, which they realised would be unlikely to accept Protocol I.[60] It was not intended to serve as a protection to rebels in other situations. In particular, it was not intended to apply to internal rebellions in their own territories, even where the rebels sought to exercise their right of self-determination. That Third World States were opposed to the extension of humanitarian law to such conflicts was clear from the manner in which they insisted upon the narrowing of the scope of humanitarian law in Protocol II relating to the protection of victims of non-international armed conflicts.[61]

The realities of international life suggest that little can be done to redress the present situation. Protocol I has to a large extent outlived whatever usefulness it might have had as a means of extending the 1949 Geneva Conventions to certain internal conflicts; and there is insufficient support for a revision of Protocol II.

The South African case studies do, however, highlight one issue for which there may be sufficient support to warrant another additional protocol, namely the abolition of the death penalty for rebels.

It is a fundamental principle of humanitarian law that captured combatants may not be punished for their participation in belligerent activities, unless their conduct constitutes a war crime. Consequently, such captured combatants are not exposed to trial, and possible execution, for

---

59 See Wilson, op. cit. n. 38, at 150, 168; Cassese, in Swinarski, ed., loc. cit. n. 36, at 313, 317-319; M.R. Rwelamira, *The Significance and Contribution of the Protocols Additional to the Geneva Conventions of August 1949*, in C. Swinarski, at 229, 234. Also G. Abi-Saab, *Wars of National Liberation in the Geneva Conventions and Protocols*, 165 Recueil des Cours, IV, 353 (1979).

60 G.H. Aldrich, *Some Reflections on the Origins of the 1977 Geneva Protocols*, in Swinarski, ed., op. cit. n. 59, at 129, 135-136.

61 G. Best, Humanity in Warfare 321-322 (1980); Aldrich, loc. cit. n. 60, at 136.

their actions.[62] Captured rebels in a conflict not categorised as 'international' by the incumbent regime find themselves in a completely different position. They may be tried and punished for their participation in the military actions that constitute the rebellion. Moreover, the incumbent regime is permitted to execute such persons provided that they are properly tried. Neither common Article 3[63] of the four Geneva Conventions nor Protocol II[64] prohibits such a sentence.

It is the exposure to the possibility of the death penalty that most sharply distinguishes lawful combatants from rebels. If this risk were removed the difference would be substantially reduced. The prisoner-of-war would be detained and the rebel would be imprisoned. In practice the prisoner-of-war would probably be treated better than the imprisoned rebel. But in both cases their lives would be preserved.

Today there is a growing condemnation of capital punishment and a gradual movement towards abolition,[65] which is apparent at both national and international levels. The intitial acceptance of capital punishment by the European Convention on Human Rights (1950),[66] the American Convention of Human Rights 1969)[67] and the International Covenant on Civil and Political Rights (1966)[68] has been replaced by a growing commitment to abolition, as reflected in Protocol No. 6 to the European Convention on Human Rights of 1983, and the Second Optional Protocol to the International Covenant on Civil and Political Rights of 1990, which aim to abolish the death penalty in time of peace. Moves are also afoot to produce an Optional Protocol to the American Convention which will outlaw the death penalty in times of peace and war.[69] As human rights law and humanitarian law increasingly converge[70] there is a need for

---

62 The Geneva Conventions do, however, contemplate the trial and punishment of prisoners-of-war who violate the disciplinary code that governs them. In such a case the death penalty is a possible form of punishment. See Article 100 of Geneva Convention III Relative to the Treatment of Prisoners of War.

63 Article 3(1,d) merely prohibits 'the carrying out of executions without previous judgment pronounced by a regularly constituted court affording all the judicial guarantees which are recognised as indispensable by civilised peoples'.

64 Article 6 of Protocol II prohibits the imposition of the death penalty only in the cases of persons under the age of eighteen years, pregnant women and mothers of young children.

65 See, Amnesty International, loc. cit. n. 42, at 259-261 for details of the 62 States which have abolished the death penalty either *de jure* or *de facto*.

66 Article 2(1).

67 Article 4(2).

68 Article 6(2).

69 Amnesty International, loc. cit. n. 42, at 82 *et seq*.

70 T. Meron, Human Rights in Internal Strife: Their International Protection (1987).

humanitarian law to follow the approach of human rights conventions to the death penalty. The Geneva Convention of 1949[71] and Protocols I[72] and II[73] of 1977 implicitly recognise the death penalty as a competent sentence. A major challenge facing humanitarian law in the next decade therefore is the question of the continued permissibility of the death penalty. The aim should be to secure an additional protocol, along the lines of those adopted by human rights law, that would outlaw the execution of rebels convicted of crimes committed in the course of an uprising,[74] except where the crime constitutes a serious war crime.[75] Such a protocol, it is believed, would do more to advance the cause of humanity in armed conflict than Article 1(4) of Protocol I.

---

71 Articles 100-101 in Geneva Convention III Relative to the Treatment of Prisoners of War; Articles 68 and 75 in Geneva Convention IV Relative to the Protection of Civilian Persons in Time of War.

72 Articles 76(3) and 77(5).

73 Article 6(4).

74 As Israel has already done in the case of PLO combatants in the occupied areas. See n. 58 *supra.*

75 Meron, op. cit. n. 70, at 130, 154; Conference of Government Experts on the Reaffirmation and Development of International Humanitarian Law Applicable in Armed Conflicts, VI, Rules Applicable in Guerrilla Warfare, ICRC 50, 52-53, Doc. CE/6b (1971).

SUBSCRIBING TO THE 'LAW OF GENEVA' AS MANIFESTATION OF SELF-DETERMINATION: THE CASE OF PALESTINE

PAUL J.I.M. DE WAART

1.   INTRODUCTORY REMARKS

In 1989 an attempt to deposit Palestine's instrument of ratification of the 1949 Geneva Conventions foundered on the lack of statehood. This event clearly illustrates that a people fighting in the exercise of its right to self-determination 'is not and cannot become a Party to the Conventions or the Protocol'.[1] Thus it may be argued that the 'Law of Geneva' itself implies a constraint on the struggle for development. The possibility that the Palestinian people might have addressed 'a unilateral declaration to the depositary (the Swiss Government), to the effect that it undertakes to apply the Conventions and the Protocol'[2] is little short of a palliative in that respect.

The legal status of liberation movements in a war of national liberation[3] is complex and 'has to be assessed on a case-by-case basis'.[4] Palestine offers ample opportunity to that end, being one of the two issues of particular concern to the United Nations (hereafter, UN) 'which through the years have deeply stirred the Organization'.[5] Moreover, the issue concerns two peoples, whose right to self-determination in respect of the mandated territory is beyond doubt by virtue of the Covenant of the League of Nations, in conjunction with the Palestine British Mandate of 1922 and pertinent UN Resolutions.[6] Therefore, both the Jewish and the Palestinian peoples enjoy a unique and privileged position.

The recognition of Israel by the PLO on behalf of the Palestinian people should have removed legal obstacles to the realization of the right to self-

---

1   F. Kalshoven, Constraints on the waging of war 74 (1987).

2   *Ibid.*.

3   A war of national liberation is defined as an armed conflict in which a people or nation lacking statehood, but organized within the legal framework of a national liberation movement, struggles for independence so as to achieve self-determination. See H.-J. Uibopuu, *Wars of National Liberation,* in R. Bernhardt, ed., 4 Encyclopaedia of Public International Law 343 (1982).

4   K. Ginther, *Liberation Movements,* in Bernhardt, op. cit. n. 3, Instalment 3, at 247 (1982).

5   Kalshoven, op. cit. n. 1, at 20.

6   These Resolutions include GA Res. 181 (II) of 29 November 1947 (partition), 194 (III) of 11 December 1948 (right of refugees to return), 273 (III) of 11 May 1949 (admission of Israel as Member State of the UN), 3236 (XXIX) of 22 November 1974 (right to self-determination of the Palestinian people), 43/176 of 15 December 1988 (international peace conference) and 43/177 of 15 December 1988 (replacing the designation 'Palestine Liberation Organization' for 'Palestine'; SC Res. 242 of 22 November 1967 (principles for establishing a just and lasting peace in the Middle East including withdrawal of Israeli armed forces from the 1967 Occupied Territories), 338 of 22 October 1973 (cease fire) and the Decision of 11 January 1989 (observer of Palestine). See also H. Cattan, Palestine and International Law: the Legal Aspects of the Arab-Israeli Conflict, (Appendices) 259-349 (1976).

determination of the Palestinian people through the creation of its own State and thus to Palestine's ratification of the Geneva Conventions and Protocol. This would have been in the interests of a sustainable peaceful settlement of the Palestinian question. The Palestinian Declaration of Independence of 15 November 1988[7] should have enabled the UN for the first time to treat the right to self-determination of the Palestinian people in a similar way as it did in 1949 with regard to the right to self-determination of the Jewish people.

If this opportunity is missed, the UN will have neglected its duties resulting from the mandate system. Other peoples will then be worse off even in asserting their right to self-determination. Such a situation will be all the more deplorable since recent developments in international relations, started by perestroika, tend towards establishing the primacy of international law in politics and enhancing the position of the UN in order to democratize international society.[8] In this context it is worth trying to discuss legal constraints on the struggle for self-determination embodied in the rights and duties of States and human rights prohibitions.

The theme of this contribution will be the right to development as a principle of international law in general and human rights law in particular. For according to the 1986 Declaration on the Right to Development the human right to development also implies the full realization of the right of peoples to self-determination.[9]

2. PRIMACY OF INTERNATIONAL LAW: SUPERPOWERS' VIEW

2.1 United States

The ruling of the American Supreme Court of 28 February 1990 reflects the continuing unwillingness of the United States to comply with the primacy of international law:

---

7   XVII ILM 1660-1672 (1988). See also P.J.I.M. de Waart, *Long-term Development Aspects of Humanitarian Assistance in Times of Armed Conflict*, in F. Kalshoven, Assisting the Victims of Armed Conflict and Other Disasters 74-78 (1989).

8   J.A. Carty, *Changing Models of the International System*, in W.E. Butler, ed., Perestroika and International Law 14 (1990); G.I. Tunkin, *On the Primacy of International Law in Politics, ibid.*, at 5-12.

9   GA Res. 41/128 of 4 December 1986, Article 1(2).

'Situations threatening to important American interests may arise halfway around the globe, situations which in the view of the political branches of our Government require an American response with armed force. If there are to be restrictions on searches and seizures which occur incident to such American action, they must be imposed by the political branches through diplomatic understanding, treaty or legislation.'[10]

In the words of the dissenting Justices Brennan and Marshall the American Supreme Court thus holds that:

'... although foreign nationals must abide by our laws even when in their own countries, our Government need not abide by the Fourth Amendment when it investigates them for violations of our laws.'[11]

Indeed, in the prevailing American view all politics is local politics:

'Certainly, the new international politics is local. Ours is now truly a global village. The constitutional implications will be a persistent and systematic engagement of Congress in the dominant issues of our foreign relations, however strong the new conceptual foreign policy consensus, however strong the President offers to consult and however rapid the process of *glasnost* and *perestroika*.'[12]

The United States opposition to international supervision of its domestic affairs is such that it has not yet ratified the International Covenants on Human Rights and the American Convention on Human Rights.[13] However, Americans do themselves supervise human rights practices around the world. In order for a nation to receive aid from the United States, the Department of State, in compliance with the Foreign Assistance Act of 1961, as amended, must submit a report to Congress regarding the human rights practices of that country.[14] However, all politics being local politics, it should have been even more obvious that ratification is not

---

10   *United States* v. *Rene Martin Verdugo-Urquidez*, XXIX ILM 450 (1990).

11   *Ibid.*, at 453.

12   W.D. Rogers, *The Constitution and Foreign Affairs: Two Hundred Years*, 83 AJIL 898 (1989).

13   N. Hevener Kaufman and D. Whitemenan, *Opposition to Human Rights Treaties in the United States Senate: the Legacy of the Bricker Amendment*, 10 HRG Human Rights Quarterly 309-339 (1988).

14   XXIX ILM 468 (1990).

primarily an issue of domestic policy: 'The key issue then becomes: what can ratification do for rights of Americans?'[15]

In short, the American rejection of international protection of human rights runs the risk that the boat will be missed in shaping a truly democratic international society. This will be the more regrettable as the Soviet Union is now embarking on a promising course in that respect.[16]

2.2   Soviet Union

The Soviet Union is a Party to the International Covenants on Human Rights. However, like the United States it opposed international supervision of human rights. As late as 1984 Tunkin did not consider national movements, non-governmental international organizations, private corporations, etc., as components of the international system, although they 'exercise considerable influence on it'.[17] Under the impact of *perestroika* Soviet legal science is carefully reconsidering its traditionally categorical negation of human beings as juristic persons under international law. Tunkin now rejects as an obsolete and dangerous anachronism the 'conceptual model of an inter-State system according to which the relations between sovereign States, above which there is no supreme authority, are built or may be built on force, above all armed force'.[18]

Soviet legal science has been emphasizing that international treaties on human rights impose the duty upon the State Party to guarantee the rights and freedoms set forth in those treaties. In doing so, it expressed the opinion time and again that human beings did not themselves derive any rights from those treaties.[19] Times are changing now. It is said that human rights treaties not only impose duties on a State Party towards other States Parties but also towards its own citizens.[20]

In September 1989 the All-Union Juridical Correspondence Institute at Moscow launched the first special course for law students on human rights

---

15 P. Alston, *U.S. Ratification of the Covenant on Economic, Social and Cultural Rights: the Need for an Entirely New Strategy*, 84 AJIL 393 (1990).

16 J. Quigley, *Perestroika and International Law*, 82 AJIL 796-797 (1988).

17 G.I. Tunkin, *A New Dimension of International Law: Normative Model of Global International System*, Soviet Association of International Law 5 (1984).

18 Tunkin, op. cit. n. 8, at 8.

19 V.S. Vereschetin, R.A. Mullerson, *Het Primaat van het Internationale Recht in de Wereldpolitiek* (The Primacy of International Law in World Politics), 7 Sovetskoe Gosudarstvo i Pravo (Soviet State and Law), 3-11 (1989). The references to this article are based on the Dutch translation by R.C.R. Siekmann.

20 *Ibid.*.

in socialist legal systems.[21] The course deals with human rights as 'an expression of the legal views of the individual and class, of man and society, of citizen and individual'.[22] The syllabus explicitly links human rights with the concept of democracy and major State law phenomena and concepts such as humanitarian law, the interconnection of which with the system of human rights as an independent branch of law is considered to give rise to controversial issues.[23] The system of human rights in developing countries is discussed from the perspective of national liberation and democratic movements in developing countries as allies of world socialism in the struggle for human rights.[24]

In the new political thinking of *perestroika* the individual is in the limelight.[25] It is said that the consolidation of the primacy of international law implies an expanding role for international and national social movements and organisations.[26] In other words, *perestroika* will enable public opinion to make its democratic influence increasingly felt. Moreover, guided by the interests of strengthening the international legal order and ensuring the primacy of international law, the Soviet Union accepted without reservation in 1989 the compulsory jurisdiction of the

---

21 W.E. Butler, *Perestroika and the Teaching of Human Rights in the USSR*, in Butler, op. cit. n. 8, at 297.

22 *Ibid.*, at 299.

23 *Ibid.*, at 300-302. The syllabus consists of five sections, *i.e.*, introduction to the theory of human rights (I); history of human rights (II); basic orientations of the theory and practice of twentieth century human rights (III); contemporary problems of guaranteeing human rights (IV); international co-operation in the domain of human rights (V). The -twenty-seven- topics include democracy and human rights, shaping of a system of human rights in developing countries, legislation as the basis for legal machinery for ensuring human rights, internationalisation of human rights and principal ideological contradictions of modern co-operation in the domain of human rights.

24 *Ibid.*, at 306. The pertinent topic reads:
    'Problem of human rights and choice of paths of development of liberated countries. Differences of principle of approaches to conceptions of human rights in developing countries of a socialist and capitalist orientation. Struggle in the world for the right to freedom from exploitation comprising the basis of all other rights of the individual. Human rights, shaping the system thereof in the constitutions of two groups of developing countries (of socialist and capitalist orientation). Regional organisations and institutions for human rights. Role of customs, traditions, and religious norms in human rights systems and peculiarities of their realisation in liberated countries. Supra-class and nationalistic views of human rights in those countries.'

25 R.A. Tuzmukhamedov, *The Humanization of International Law*, 11 Sovjetskoie Gosudarsvto i Pravo 114-122 (1988).

26 See V.S. Vereschetin, R.A. Mullerson, loc. cit. n. 19. See also R.A. Mullerson, *Sources of International Law: New Tendencies in Soviet Thinking*, 83 AJIL 512 (1989).

International Court of Justice (hereafter, the Court) for six human rights conventions.[27]

In an even more general sense, the Soviet Union apparently has dropped its traditional opposition towards international supervision, albeit on a basis of reciprocity only. In its opinion the search by all States for ways and means to enhance the effectiveness of the UN:

'... should be aimed at the full and unselective implementation of the provisions of the Charter, active use of its machinery and procedures, and promotion of the ability to take effective preventive measures to avert international crises and conflicts.'[28]

These ways and means should include, amongst others, special provisions envisaging adjudication of disputes by the Court resulting from the interpretation and application of international agreements, to be developed under the auspices of the UN. Moreover, the:

'General Assembly and the Security Council could ask it more often advisory opinions on outstanding international legal matters. The mandatory jurisdiction of the International Court of Justice must be recognized by everybody on mutually agreed terms.'[29]

The Soviet Union's espousal of the concept of a democratic society, both nationally and internationally, has increasingly encouraged its republics to appeal to their right to self-determination. This whim of fate raises the question of the correlation between the democratic quality of the (inter)national society and the right to self-determination once more.

---

27 G.G. Shinkaretskaia, *International Adjudication Today in the View of a Soviet International Lawyer*, in Butler, op. cit. n. 8, at 257. See also Th.M. Franck, *Soviet Initiatives: U.S. Responses - New Opportunities for Reviving the United Nations System*, 83 AJIL 539 (1989). The six conventions are: Convention on the Prevention and Punishment of Genocide (1948); Convention for the Suppression of the Traffic in Persons and of the Exploitation of the Prostitution of Others (1949); Convention on the Political Rights of Women (1952); International Convention on the Elimination of All Forms of Racial Discrimination (1965); Convention on the Elimination of All Forms of Discrimination Against Women (1979); Convention Against Torture and Other Cruel, Inhuman or Degrading Treatment or Punishment (1984).

28 UN Doc. A/43/629 of 22 September 1988, *Towards Comprehensive Security Through the Enhancement of the Role of the United Nations*, at 2.

29 *Ibid.*, at 5-6.

3.   INTERNATIONAL DEMOCRATIC SOCIETY ON
        THE WAY UP

3.1   **Respect for human rights as a measure of democracy**

International legal instruments tend to use keys like people, State,
democracy without defining them. As for democracy or democratic society
one looks for them in vain in otherwise authoritative manuals of
international law. The legal profession apparently reconciles itself to
international law as offering States shelter for sovereignty and from
intervention. The Court observed in that respect:

> '... adherence by a State to any particular doctrine does not constitute a
> violation of international customary law; to hold otherwise would make
> nonsense of the fundamental principle of State sovereignty, on which the
> whole of international law rests, and the freedom of choice of the political,
> social, economic and cultural system of a State .... The Court cannot
> contemplate the creation of a new rule opening up a right of intervention by
> one State against another on the ground that the latter has opted for some
> particular ideology or political system.'[30]

It is even argued that there certainly is 'no indication in the UN Charter
that its members must be pluralist democracies'.[31] Admittedly, the
Charter does not refer to democracy explicitly.[32] However, implicitly, it
underlies its purpose of promoting and encouraging respect for human
rights and fundamental freedoms for all without distinction as to race, sex,
language or religion.[33] The 1986 Limburg Principles on the
Implementation of the International Covenant on Economic, Social and
Cultural Rights rightly state:

> 'While there is no single model of a democratic society, a society which
> recognizes and respects the human rights set forth in the United Nations

---

30 ICJ Reports, 1986, at 133. See M.T. Kamminga, Interstate Accountability for Violations of
    Human Rights 123-124 (1990). But see H. Hohmann, P.J.I.M. de Waart, *Compulsory
    Jurisdiction and the Use of Force as a Legal Issue: the Epoch-Making Judgment of the Court
    in Nicaragua v. United States of America*, NILR 186-187 (1987).
31 Kamminga, op. cit. n. 30, at 98.
32 Democracy is no entry in commentaries on the UN Charter. See, for instance, J.-P. Cot, A.
    Pellet, eds., *La charte des Nations Unies: commentaire article par article* (1985).
33 UN Charter, Article 1(3). See also Articles 55 and 56.

Charter and the Universal Declaration of Human Rights may be viewed as meeting this definition.'[34]

Whatever the differences in economic, political, social and cultural systems may be, it is now acknowledged to be beyond doubt that:

'A State in which democracy and legality predominate and respect for human rights is ensured can be expected to respect international law in the international arena more than a State in which arbitrariness predominates.'[35]

In the context of the Universal Declaration of Human Rights international order should be a democratic society itself for its Article 28 reads:

'Everyone is entitled to a social and international order in which the rights and freedoms set forth in this Declaration can be fully realized.'[36]

One may wonder whether this can be the case in the Vattelian concept of international law, which denies the possibility of international protection of human rights against one's own State.[37] Both Superpowers have adhered to this concept, as appears from their persistent rejection of such protection. However, unlike the United States the Soviet Union has recently shown its willingness to reconsider its position.

3.2 Decolonization

The Global Consultation on the Realization of the Right to Development as a Human Right held in Geneva (8-12 January 1990),[38] stressed that

---

34 9 HRQ 128-129, 143 (1987).

35 Tunkin, op. cit. n. 8, at 9.

36 But see Chr. Tomuschat, *The Universal Declaration of Human Rights of 1948: Does It Need Any Updating?*, 9 SIM Special (1989). He doubts whether Article 28 should be kept, for the human rights idea reaches in that Article 'an almost ecstatic climax'. *Ibid.*, at 79.

37 P.R. Remec, The Position of the Individual in International Law According to Grotius and Vattel 243 (1960).

38 The Third World initially raised the issue of the right to development in the context of State rights only. However, when in 1975 entry into force of the 1966 International Covenants came into sight the the UN Commission on Human Rights (CHR) decided to consider henceforth as a standing agenda-item with high priority the question of realization of the economic, social and cultural rights set forth in the Universal Declaration of Human Rights and in the International Covenant on Economic, Social and Cultural Rights, with special reference to

democracy at all levels (local, national and international) and in all spheres is essential to true development:

> 'A major goal of democracy is to achieve a just social order. To be fully effective, democracy itself depends upon the existence of a just and democratic social order, including a fair distribution of economic and political power among all sectors of national society and among all States and peoples and on the employment of such rights as freedoms of expression, freedom of association and of free elections.'[39]

Peoples subjected to alien subjugation, domination or exploitation inevitably do not live in a democratic society. Such a subjection:

> '... constitutes a denial of fundamental human rights, is contrary to the Charter of the United Nations and is an impediment to the promotion of world peace and co-operation.'[40]

In this context decolonization has been closely connected with the process of democratization 'itself based on the principle of equality'.[41] The 1960 Declaration on the Granting of Independence to Colonial Countries and Peoples declared that all peoples have the right to self-determination, by virtue of which they freely determine their political status and freely pursue their economic, social and cultural development.[42]

The mandate system of the League of Nations owed its creation to the already prevalent anti-colonial position of the United States, which elaborated 'European ideas of a trust for colonial countries'.[43] According to Article 77 of the UN Charter the trusteeship system was intended to be applied to territories held under mandate, albeit by means of trusteeship agreements only. Apart from that, the UN has also succeeded to the

---

human rights in developing countries. Partly due to the fact that the CHR by definition deals with human rights only, the attention shifted to the right to development as a human right.

39 UN Doc. E/CN.4/1990/9 (Part III) of 6 February 1990, Report prepared by the Secretary-General pursuant to Commission on Human Rights Resolution 1990/45, VII: *Conclusions and Recommendations Emerging from the Consultation*, at 4.

40 GA Res. 1514 (XV) of 14 December 1960, Declaration on the Granting of Independence to Colonial Countries and Peoples, § 1.

41 A. Bleckmann, *Decolonization*, in Bernhardt, op. cit. n. 3, Instalment 10, at 75 (1987).

42 GA Res. 1514, loc. cit. n. 40, § 2.

43 D. Rauschning, *Mandates*, in Bernhardt, op. cit. n. 3, Instalment 10, at 288 (1987).

League of Nations' responsibilities under the mandate system.[44] The colonial era having passed, the right of peoples to self-determination challenges both national and international society to be truly democratic.

3.3 The right to development

Both the 1986 Declaration on the progressive development of principles of public international law relating to a New International Economic Order (hereafter, Seoul Declaration) of the International Law Association (hereafter, ILA) and the Declaration on the Right to Development (hereafter, Development Declaration)[45] relate development to the right of peoples to self-determination.

The right to self-determination is not vested in a Government but in the people concerned.[46] Self-determination includes the right of a people to choose its own route to development, albeit with due regard for the relevant provisions of both International Covenants on Human Rights.[47] In doing so, peoples should implement their right to self-determination in such a way that it will not cause substantial harm to the right to development of other peoples.[48] The same holds true for States. They may not dispose of natural wealth and resources to the detriment of other States. According to Principle 3(2) of the Seoul Declaration:

'(...) In the legitimate exercise of their economic sovereignty, they should seek to avoid any measure which causes substantial injury to other States, in particular to the interests of developing States and their peoples.'

Principle 3(3) of the Development Declaration reads:

'States have the duty to co-operate with each other in ensuring development and eliminating obstacles to development. States should fulfil their rights and duties in such a manner as to promote a new international economic order based on sovereign equality, inter-dependence, mutual interest and co-operation among all States, as well as to encourage the observance and realization of human rights.'

---

44 International Status of South-West Africa, Advisory Opinion, ICJ Reports, 1950, at 137. See also *Dynamics of Self-Determination, Proceedings of the International Academic Conference on the Middle East* (Amsterdam 16-18 June 1988) 80-81 (1988).
45 GA Res. 41/128 of 4 December 1986.
46 J. Crawford, ed., The Right of Peoples 164-165 (1988).
47 *Ibid.*, at 84-87.
48 De Waart, op. cit. n. 7, at 70-71.

As a principle of international law in general and human rights law in particular[49] the right to development affects the right to self-determination. The latter right involves not only the establishment of States by peoples but also the operation of States once they have been established:

'The mere formation of a State does not in itself fully realize the right to self-determination, unless its citizens and constituent peoples continue to enjoy the right to their own cultural identity and to determine their own economic, social and political system through democratic institutions and actions, and the State genuinely enjoys continuing freedom of choice, within the bounds of international law.'[50]

According to the Declaration on the Right to Development, States:

'... should encourage popular participation in all spheres as an important factor in development and in the full realization of all human rights.'[51]

The right to self-determination in the context of development as a human right and as a State right reminds the Government of a pluralist State of its constant duty to conduct itself in compliance with the principle of equal rights and self-determination and *thus* to represent the whole people belonging to the territory, without distinction as to race, creed or colour.[52] In other words, in any society, pluralist or otherwise, a Government should represent all peoples belonging to its territory. As long as this is the case no people in such a territory may claim by virtue of the right to development the right to self-determination and proceed to the use of armed force to dismember or impair, totally or in part, the territorial integrity or political unity of sovereign and independent States.[53] For that

---

49 The Seoul Declaration brought the right to development to the fore as a principle of both international law and human rights law. In the former case the right to development relates to States; in the latter to collectivities other than States, in particular to peoples.

50 UN Doc. E/CN.4/1990/9, loc. cit. n. 39.

51 GA Res. 41/128 of 4 December 1986, Article 8(2).

52 GA Res. 2625 (XXV) of 24 October 1970, Declaration on Principles of International Law Concerning Friendly Relations and Co-operation Among States in Accordance with the UN Charter.

53 GA Res. 2625 (XXV) of 24 October 1970, Principle of Equal Rights and Self-Determination of Peoples, § 2:
'Nothing in the foregoing paragraphs shall be construed as authorizing or encouraging any action which could dismember or impair, totally or in part, the territorial integrity or political unity of sovereign and independent States conducting themselves in compliance with the principle of equal rights and self-determination as described above and thus possessed of a

reason the international community did not support the right to self-determination of, for example, the peoples of **Katanga** and **Biafra**.[54] However, the intended partition of the Palestine Mandate in an Arab and a Jewish State is a different matter.[55]

4.   LEGAL INSECURITIES FRUSTRATING SELF-DETERMINATION: THE QUESTION OF PALESTINE

4.1   The definition of people

The Palestine British Mandate spoke only of 'existing non-Jewish communities in Palestine'. A Draft Resolution on the 1948 Progress Report of the UN Mediator on Palestine submitted by the late Count Folke Bernadotte endorsed the recommendations contained in that report concerning 'the disposition of the territory of Palestine not included within the boundaries of the Jewish State or the City of Jerusalem, and instructs the Conciliation Commission, in full consultation with the inhabitants of Arab Palestine ...'. However the final Resolution -194 (III)- contained no such reference. It only resolved that the freest possible access should be accorded to 'all inhabitants of Palestine' and the right of 'refugees' to return.[56] The UN Relief and Work Agency for Palestine Refugees in the Middle East (UNRWA) was established to prevent:

'... conditions of starvation and distress among them (the Palestine refugees) and to further conditions of peace and stability ....'[57]

Not until 1969 did the UN unambiguously recognize that 'the problem of the Palestine Arab refugees has arisen from the denial of their inalienable human rights under the UN Charter and the Universal Declaration of Human Rights' and reaffirm the 'inalienable rights of the people of Palestine'.[58] In 1973 the General Assembly condemned all Governments 'which do not recognize the right to self-determination and

---

government representing the whole people belonging to the territory without distinction as to race, creed or colour.'

54   Thürer, *Self-Determination*, in Bernhardt, op. cit. n. 3, Instalment 8, 474 (1985).
55   See *infra* 5.1.
56   De Waart, op. cit. n. 7, at 77.
57   GA Res. 303 (IV) of 8 December 1949.
58   GA Res. 2535 A (XXIV) of 10 December 1969.

independence of peoples, notably the peoples of Africa still under colonial domination and the Palestinian people'.[59]

The Covenant of the League of Nations included Palestine in the so-called A-Mandates, which had already reached a stage of development where their existence as independent States could be provisionally recognized. This qualification concerned the Arab population at that time. It certainly applies to the present Palestinian population. It is a true test case for the international community in general and the UN in particular to guarantee effectively not only the territorial integrity and independence of Israel but also the realization of the right to self-determination of the Palestinian people within the Occupied Territories.

4.2   Definition of terrorism

The prevention of terrorism has become a great worry to the international community, partly under the influence of the question of Palestine. Opinions on the definition of terrorism differ widely. Western States especially have taken a strong interest in international co-operation to condemn and suppress it. Developing countries have stressed the necessity to distinguish between terrorism and the struggle of oppressed peoples against foreign occupation and racist regimes. In 1985 the General Assembly succeeded in accommodating these differences of opinion by stating unanimously that it:

'1. *Unequivocally condemns*, as criminal, all acts, methods and practices of terrorism wherever and by whomever committed, including those which jeopardize friendly relations among States and their security; ...
9. *Further urges* all States, unilaterally and in co-operation with other States, as well as relevant United Nations organs, to contribute to the progressive elimination of the causes underlying international terrorism and to pay special attention to all situations, including colonialism, racism, and situations involving mass and flagrant violations of human rights and fundamental freedoms and those involving alien occupation, that may give rise to international terrorism and may endanger international peace and security; ....'[60]

---

59 GA Res. 3070 (XXVIII) of 30 November 1973. See also H. Cobban, The Palestine Liberation
    Organisation: People, Power and Politics 261 (1984).
60 GA Res. 40/61 of 9 December 1985. See also SC Res. 579 of 18 December 1985.

In 1987 Israel and the United States broke the consensus by voting against an otherwise widely supported resolution which confirmed the previous one but added a paragraph which considered that:

'... nothing in the present resolution could in any way prejudice the right to self-determination, freedom and independence as derived from the Charter of the United Nations, of peoples forcibly deprived of that right referred to in the Declaration of Principles of International Law concerning Friendly Relations and Co-operation among States in accordance with the Charter of the United Nations, particularly peoples under colonial and racist regimes and foreign occupation or other forms of colonial domination, nor, in accordance with the principles of the Charter and in conformity with the above-mentioned Declaration, the right of these peoples to struggle to this end and to seek and receive support; ....'[61]

In 1989 consensus was restored in a resolution containing the same paragraph but stating in the very first paragraph the unequivocal condemnation of terrorism not only as criminal but also as 'not justifiable'.[62] This development must be applauded. The distinction between terrorism and the struggle of oppressed peoples cannot be overlooked.

According to the Global Consultation on the Right to Development as a Human Right universal respect for the principle of the non-use of force is a fundamental condition for the full realization of the right to development.[63] Nevertheless, the crux of the matter in respect of the right to self-determination is the latter's close linkage not only to development but also to armed conflicts against foreign occupation and racist regimes. The reference to alien occupation, racist regimes and the exercise of the right to self-determination in Protocol I to the Geneva Conventions of 1949:

'... clearly aims to limit the scope of the provision: it was definitely not the intention of the authors that henceforth any conflict which a group of self-styled "freedom-fighters" might choose to designate as a "liberation war", would thereby fall in the category of international armed conflicts.'[64]

---

61 GA Res. 42/159 of 7 December 1987, § 14.
62 GA Res. 44/29 of 4 December 1989.
63 UN Doc. E/CN.4/1990/9, loc. cit. n. 39, at 4.
64 Kalshoven, op. cit. n. 1, at 73-74.

However, the struggle of subject peoples:

'... for the implementation of their right to self-determination and independence is legitimate and in full accordance with the principles of international law ....'[65]

The definition of aggression does not in any way prejudice:

'... the right to self-determination, freedom and independence, as derived from the Charter, of peoples forcibly deprived of that right ...; nor the right of these peoples to struggle to that end and to seek and to receive support ....'[66]

The right to development completes the picture of the connection between self-determination, the struggle of liberation movements and development by stating:

'States shall take resolute steps to eliminate the massive and flagrant violations of the human rights of peoples and human beings affected by situations such as those resulting from *apartheid*, all forms of racism and racial discrimination, colonialism, foreign domination and occupation, aggression, foreign interference and threats against national sovereignty, national unity and territorial integrity, threats of war and refusal to recognize the fundamental right of peoples to self-determination.'[67]

The representative of the PLO called the 1985 Resolution on terrorism a milestone in the struggle against terrorism. In doing so he declared that his Organisation would continue to distinguish between criminal terrorism and the legitimate exercise of the right to self-determination. The struggle of the Palestinian people against the Israeli occupation came under the latter category.[68] In his press conference of 14 December 1988 in Geneva PLO-chairman Arafat paved the way for discussions between the PLO and the United States by distancing himself from terrorism:

---

65 GA Res. 3103 (XXVIII) of 12 December 1973, Basic Principles of the Legal Status of the Combatants Struggling Against Colonial and Alien Domination and Racist Régimes, § 1.
66 GA Res. 3314 (XXIX) of 14 December 1974, Article 7.
67 GA Res. 41/128 of 4 December 1986, Declaration on the Right to Development, Article 5.
68 Ministerie van Buitenlandse Zaken 138, Algemene Vergadering der Verenigde Naties, veertigste zitting 208-209 (1986). (Ministry of Foreign Affairs, General Assembly of the United Nations, 40th session).

'As for terrorism, I renounced it yesterday in no uncertain terms and yet I repeat, if for the record, that we totally and absolutely renounce all forms of terrorism, including individual, group and state terrorism.'[69]

In all fairness it has to be admitted that the Israeli-Palestinian conflict has not been characterized by acts of terrorism of Palestinians only. According to objective observers Jewish terrorist groups also have been active in the struggle of the Jewish people to establish the State of Israel.[70]

4.3   Status of the Occupied Territories

4.3.1   *Validity of the Palestine Mandate*

Up to World War I conquest had been an important and generally accepted mode of acquisition of territory.[71] It was only definitely outlawed by the Covenant of the League of Nations as a means of acquiring territory by force. States now refuse to recognize territorial changes based on the title of conquest. The right to self-determination implies that territorial changes may only be carried out with the consent of the population concerned.[72] In respect of peoples in colonies and territories which as a consequence of World War I had ceased to be under the sovereignty of the States which formerly governed them, Article 22 of the Covenant of the League of Nations gave practical effect to the principle that the well-being and development of such peoples form 'a sacred trust of civilization'. Nevertheless, there was no complete rupture with former times when:

'... new States were called into being by an international conference acting as a kind of supreme directing authority in European or even world affairs, such as: ... the Peace Conference of Versailles - St. German - Neuilly - Trianon - Sèvres of 1919/1929 ...: the establishment of ..., in particular the A-Mandates of the League of Nations in the Near and Middle East: Syria,

---

69 147 I&P (Israel & Palestine Political Report) 6 (1988). See also Z. Schiff, E. Ya'ari, Intifada: the Palestinian Uprising - Israel's Third Front 302-305 (1986).

70 A. Gerson, Israel, the West Bank & International Law 47, 55 (1978). See also B. Morris, The Birth of the Palestinian Refugee Problem, 1947-1949, 6, 113-115, 151 (1978).

71 I. Brownlie, Principles of Public International Law, 4th ed., 131 (1990). *Cf.*, P.J.I.M. de Waart, *Discussion Paper on International Law as a Framework for a Peaceful Solution of the Dispute Between Arab States and Israel*, in Dynamics of Self-Determination, op. cit. n. 44 at 78-79.

72 E. Kussbach, *Conquest*, in Bernhardt, ed., op. cit. n. 3, Instalment 3, 119-122 (1982).

the Lebanon, Palestine and Iraq, which emerged as a novel group of new prospective sovereign States *in fieri*.'[73]

In the aftermath of World War I, it was still open to the victorious Powers to assume for themselves the power to create spheres of interest.[74] The spirit of the age also explains how the League of Nations:

'... had no real choice as to the selection of a mandatory, because the mandated territories were already under the military occupation of the later mandatories and the decision to allocate the mandates had been made by the supreme War Council of the allied Powers prior to the creation of the League.'[75]

The mandate system was clearly devised as 'a compromise solution between the ideal of self-determination and the interest of the occupying power'.[76] Given the genesis of the mandate system,[77] Cattan's position on the invalidity of the Palestine Mandate is legally untenable.[78] True, it is deplorable, that the UN in 1947 failed to ask for an Advisory Opinion of the Court on the validity of the Palestine Mandate, as proposed by the Arab States.[79] A clarification of the legal status of the British Palestine Mandate might have prevented the UN stirring up a hornets' nest. Be that as it may, the UN should not make the same mistake now. The legal status of the West Bank, the Gaza Strip and East Jerusalem - the Palestinian Occupied Territories - should be referred to the Court for an Advisory Opinion.[80]

---

73 J.H. Verzijl, International Law in Historical Perspective, II, 97-98 (1969). The new international system of mandates was based on seven principles, *i.e.*, non-annexation, tutelage by advanced nations, open door, military non-exploitation, consultation, self-government and international supervision. See G. Schwarzenberger, Power Politics: a Study of World Society, 3rd ed. 469-473 (1964).

74 *Cf.*, the 1916 Sykes-Picot Agreement in connection with the 1917 Tripartite (St. Jean de Maurienne) Agreement for the partition of the Ottoman Empire by Britain, France and Italy.

75 Rauschning, op. cit. n. 43, at 292.

76 Thürer, op. cit. n. 54, at 471.

77 Verzijl, op. cit. n. 73, at 545-573.

78 Cattan, op. cit. n. 6, at 65-69. This also holds true for the 1968 Palestinian National Charter which deemed 'the Balfour Declaration, the mandate for Palestine and everything that has been based upon them', null and void.

79 Cattan, op. cit. n. 6, at 20.

80 See *infra* 5.2.

4.3.2   *Continuing existence of the Palestine Mandate*

As a British commitment to the Zionist movement,[81] the much disputed and ambiguous[82] 1917 Balfour Declaration should be considered as an example of the transition from acquisition of territory by victorious States to an international trusteeship system. According to this Declaration Great Britain viewed with favour the establishment in Palestine of a national home for the Jewish people without prejudice to the civil and political rights of existing non-Jewish communities.[83]

The unilateral decision of the United Kingdom to end the Mandate according to Section 1 of the Palestine Act of 1948 did not terminate the international status of the Occupied Territories. The United Kingdom was not the competent authority to take such a decision. It would be contrary to the international status of a mandate that the mere statement of the time limit of 1 August 1948 would be sufficient to terminate the international status of the Occupied Territories without the creation of the independent Arab State.

The 1947 Partition Resolution postulated the creation of independent Arab and Jewish States and an international regime for Jerusalem. The failure of the UN to create an independent Arab State and to realize an international regime for Jerusalem made the decision that the Palestine Mandate 'shall terminate as soon as possible but in any case not later than 1 August 1948', null and void for the Occupied Territories. Whether it likes it or not, the UN General Assembly still has to discharge itself of its task as the only competent body to decide upon the status of the Occupied Territories. With an interruption of the period 1953-1974 the issue has come up for discussion as 'the Question of Palestine' in the General Assembly indeed. Between 1953 and 1974 the General Assembly dealt quite improperly with the issue under the agenda item of 'Palestinian refugees'.

The seventh General Assembly was unable to cut the knot. It appeared to be impossible to get the support of a two-thirds majority for a solution of the Palestinian question. The General Assembly then decided to

---

81   G.E. Perry, *Arab - Israeli Wars*, in E. Laszlo *et al.*, eds., World Encyclopedia of Peace, 1, 50 (1986).

82   Cattan, op. cit. n. 6, at 51-63.

83   This condition was effectively disregarded when the United Kingdom by the Palestine Act of 29 April 1948 unilaterally decided to terminate its Palestine Mandate as from 15 May 1948 at the latest. In doing so it left to the UN a situation which was rapidly getting out of hand. Verzijl rightly doubted the legality of this step. Verzijl, op. cit. n. 57, at 564.

postpone the discussion indefinitely leaving the matter to the Parties themselves or the superpowers.[84] At the Arab States' request the issue has been listed again as the separate agenda item 'the question of Palestine' since the twenty-ninth General Assembly. This request was closely connected with the invitation of the PLO:

> '... the representative of the Palestinian people, to participate in the deliberations of the General Assembly on the question of Palestine in plenary meetings.'[85]

4.4   The Fourth Geneva Convention

4.4.1   *Scope of applicability*

Egypt, Israel and Jordan are Parties to the 1949 Fourth Convention Relative to the Protection of Civilian Persons in Time of War.[86] Only Jordan is a Party to the 1977 Protocols.[87] According to the Security Council and the General Assembly the latter Convention is applicable to the Arab territories occupied by Israel since 1967, including Jerusalem.[88] The opponents of this position have a point that the UN never raised the issue between 1948 and 1967 when the Gaza Strip and the West Bank were administered by Egypt and Jordan respectively.[89] In explanation it may be stated that the Palestinian people might have considered this administration as a transitional period on the way to the creation of an Arab State in the

---

84 Ministerie van Buitenlandse Zaken 32, *Verslag over het Eerste Gedeelte van de Zevende Algemene Vergadering van de Verenigde Naties* (Dutch Ministry of Foreign Affairs, Report on the First Part of the Seventh UN General Assembly), 45 (1953).

85 GA Res. 3210 (XXIX) of 14 October 1974.

86 This Convention came into force for Jordan on 29 November 1951, for Israel on 17 June 1952 and for Egypt on 10 May 1953.

87 Protocols I and II Additional to the Conventions of 12 August 1949 and relating to the Protection of Victims of International Armed Conflicts and of Non-International Armed Conflicts respectively of 12 December 1977.

88 SC Res. 35/465 (1980) of 1 March 1980 and most recently GA Res. 44/48 B of 8 December 1989.

89 See E.H. Braam, *De Volkenrechtelijke Positie van de Palestijnse Bewoners van de West Oever en de Gazastrook: het Vraagstuk van de Toepasselijkheid van de Vierde Geneefse Conventie* (The International Legal Position of Palestinians in the West Bank and the Gazastrip: the Problem of the Applicability of the Fourth Geneva Convention), undergraduate thesis, University of Amsterdam, 37 (1988).

whole of the mandated territory.[90] However, that does not alter the fact that legally speaking the Gaza Strip and the West Bank were occupied territories in those days as well, taking into account their international status. Apart from that, its alleged indecision at that time has not stopped the UN from instructing Israel to abide by its obligations under the Fourth Convention. In 1967 the General Assembly decided to leave the matter of the Israeli occupation of territories to the Security Council. In its Resolution 242 of 22 November 1967 the Security Council spoke of 'territories *occupied* in the recent conflict' (emphasis added).[91]

It is said that Israel cannot be regarded as an occupying power in the West Bank and the Gaza Strip in the meaning of the Fourth Geneva Convention. On this view the international law of belligerent occupation is meant to protect the rights of the sovereign from the occupant. In the Occupied Territories:

'... the circumstances envisioned by the Fourth Geneva Red Cross Convention do not exist because the situation here is not one in which a legitimate sovereign and an occupying power are confronting one another.'[92]

The Fourth Convention applies to:

---

90 However, the relations between Jordan and the West Bank have never been friendly. See B. Rubin, The Arab States & the Palestine Conflict 205-216 (1981). See also E. Mendelsohn, ed., A Compensionate Peace: a Future for Israel, Palestine, and the Middle East 73 (1989).

91 It is said that in the formulation 'territories occupied' the article 'the' was deliberately deleted. In doing so Res. 242 would not oblige Israel to withdraw, for instance, from East Jerusalem. See E.V. Rostow, *The Illegality of the Arab Attack on Israel of October 6, 1973*, 69 AJIL 283-284 (1975). The use of this kind of legal cleverness urges, in my opinion, the UN to ask the ICJ for an Advisory Opinion on the legal status of the West Bank, the Gaza Strip and East Jerusalem. Since the Resolution restricted the withdrawal to territories 'occupied in the recent conflict' it might be argued that the Palestinian territories occupied by Israel between 1947 and 1967 in addition to the territory, allocated to Israel by the Partition Resolution, fall outside its scope. The Palestinian acceptance of Res. 242 in 1988 may be understood as indicating the willingness of the Palestinian people to reconcile itself with that situation. Unfortunately, Israel and the United States seem to overlook the significance of this willingness for a sustainable peaceful solution.

92 Testimony of Y.Z. Blum, Professor of international law, Hebrew University. Hearing before the Subcommittee Immigration and Naturalization of the Committee on the Judiciary, United States Senate 95th Congress, 1st Session on the Question of the West Bank Settlements and the Treatment of Arabs in the Israeli-Occupied Territories, October 17 and 18 1977, at 26. But see A. Roberts, *Prolonged Military Occupation: the Israeli-Occupied Territories Since 1967*, 84 AJIL 64-65 (1990).

'... all cases of partial or total occupation of the territory of the High Contracting Party, even if the said occupation meets with no armed resistance.'[93]

The Convention does not define territory. However the nature of State authority over a mandated territory is not describable in terms of sovereignty.[94] Admittedly, Egypt and Jordan were not legitimate sovereigns because they could not unilaterally change the international status of the West Bank, the Gaza Strip and East Jerusalem, the remaining parts of the mandated territory. Be this as it may, the Palestinian people did not need protection against Egypt and Jordan as occupying powers, probably because there was no 'time of war' between these Parties. Had that been the case, then the UN should have had the obligation to act through a member State, Party to the Fourth Convention. The UN could have called upon the United Kingdom to that end to act on its behalf as the (former) Mandatory Power.

4.4.2   De facto v. de jure

The mainstream in international legal thinking is that Israel should apply the Fourth Geneva Convention not only *de facto* but also *de jure*. The applicability of the Geneva Convention to the West Bank and the Gaza Strip has been affirmed by the UN, the ICRC, and most States.[95] The Palestinians have invoked protection under the Fourth Convention after the Israeli occupation. It is said that:

'Israel's policy of balancing security measures with economic, cultural, social and civil liberties can be taken as a paradigm for future occupations. It is important to keep in mind that belligerent occupation is not peacetime democracy.'[96]

---

93 Article 2(3).
94 Brownlie, op. cit. n. 71, at 118, 178-179.
95 See E.R. Cohen, Human Rights in the Israeli-Occupied Territories 1967-1982, 35-65 (1985); J.J. Paust, G. von Glahn, G. Woratsch, *Inquiry into the Israeli Military Court System in the Occupied West Bank and Gaza*, Report of a Mission of the International Commission of Jurists 9-12 (1989). See also the joint publication by the Labour Middle East Council and the Conservative Middle East Council, *Towards a Strategy for the Enforcement of Human Rights in the Israeli Occupied West Bank and Gaza* (1989).
96 Cohen, op. cit. n. 95, at 289.

The 1987 uprising (*intifada*) has made that conclusion outdated. Israel has failed to preserve humanity in the face of the reality of war as appears from the rebellion of 'the enraged proletariat'.[97] The testimony of the rioters themselves:

'... leads almost inexorably to the conclusion that the rebellion was kindled by the depressing conditions in which Israel kept the inhabitants of the territories.'[98]

Israel's tenacious rejection of the PLO as a negotiating partner in the peace process apparently has not been dictated by an otherwise wholly justified aversion to terrorism but by an ostrich-like attitude. The Palestinians 'simply did not exist in the political consciousness of most Israelis' as a factor in the Middle East equation.[99] With regard to self-determination, after the Camp David Accords even 'the moderate faction was opposed to the creation of an independent Palestinian State' although 'it seemed genuinely committed to making autonomy something, to offering the Palestinians an autonomy that involved land as well as people and gave them control over their own affairs in at least some important areas'.[100] From that perspective it is hardly surprising -albeit improperly- that Israel, has chosen to leave open the question of *de jure* applicability of the Fourth Geneva Convention to its occupation but to observe it only *de facto*.[101]

5.   CREATION OF PALESTINE

5.1   Conditions of statehood

Transjordan -since 1946 officially known as the Hashemite Kingdom of Jordan-, Lebanon and Syria owe their creation as States both to the mandatory States and the new idea of a 'sacred trust of civilization'. The pertinent Mandates were terminated by France and Great Britain without

---

97 Schiff, Ya'ari, op. cit. n. 69, at 79-101.
98 *Ibid.*, at 80-81. See also E. Ben-Rafael, *Israel - Palestine: a Guerrilla Conflict in International Politics* 59-61 (1987).
99 Schiff, Ya'ari, op. cit. n. 69, at 41.
100 A.M. Lesch and M. Tessler, Israel, Egypt, and the Palestinians: From Camp David to Intifada 146 (1989).
101 Gerson, op. cit. n. 70, at 114.

the consent of the appropriate organ of the League of Nations, *i.e.*, the Council. Nevertheless the League Assembly at its Final Session welcomed the termination of the mandated status of Syria, Lebanon, and Transjordan. Lebanon and Syria even became original Members of the UN.[102] The statehood of Palestine is under discussion now.[103]

By recognizing Israel in 1988 the Palestinian people has reconciled itself to the situation of partition. Palestine now fulfils two of the three classical criteria for statehood, *i.e.*, defined territory (the Occupied Territories) and a permanent people (the Palestinian People). As for the third criterion -effective Government-, the Palestinian National Council has appointed PLO-chairman Arafat as provisional president. Moreover the *intifada* has already ended in 'a limited degree of Palestinian self-rule, a state of crude autonomy' and has produced 'cohabitation between two inimical systems of rule': the Israeli Civil Administration and the Palestinian popular committees.[104]

5.1.1   *UN membership*

Legally speaking the 1917 Balfour Declaration did not found the claim of the Jewish people on part of the mandated territory of Palestine. This claim emerged from the 1922 Palestine Mandate, which endorsed the Balfour Declaration. The acceptance of the 'Partition Resolution' 181 (II) by the Jewish people in its unilateral Declaration of Independence paved the way for the UN to admit Israel as a Member State. By adopting Resolution 273 (III) of 11 May 1949 the General Assembly ended the international status of the pertinent part of the mandated territory. In other words, Israel's statehood resulted from this Resolution. The same will hold true for the statehood of Palestine. The Palestinian Declaration of Independence stated that GA Resolution 181 continues to guarantee the Palestinian people the right to sovereignty and national independence. Moreover the Political Communique has accepted SC Resolution 242 of 22 November 1967 and 338 of 1973 as the basis of the final settlement of the Palestinian question. Thus Palestine's territory covers in any case the Palestinian territories which Israel has occupied since 1967.

Unlike its specialized agencies the General Assembly cannot consider the Israeli occupation (annexation) of Palestine's territory as an obstacle to

---

102 Crawford, op. cit. n. 46, at 337-341.
103 F.L. Kirgis Jr, *Admission of 'Palestine' as a Member of a Specialized Agency and Withholding the Payment of Assessments in Response*, 84 AJIL 230 (1990).
104 Schiff, Ya'ari, op. cit. n. 69, at 264.

UN membership. For it has defined Palestine's territory itself by virtue of its responsibility under the mandate system. Unlike individual States, the UN will not be in a position to question Palestine's statehood. According to its Declaration of Independence, the State of Palestine declared its commitment to the purposes and principles of the UN, the Universal Declaration of Human Rights and the principles of peaceful coexistence for the achievement 'of a lasting peace based on justice and respect for right, under which the human potential for constructive activity may flourish ...'.[105] Moreover, like the Israeli Declaration of Independence of 14 May 1948, the Palestinian Declaration refers to the 1947 UN Partition Resolution, which included the drafting of a democratic constitution for the intended Arab and Jewish States among the steps preparatory to independence.[106]

The mere fact of discussing seriously within the UN the membership of Palestine will confirm that any bilateral negotiations between Israel and Palestine under the auspices of Superpowers and Arab States, whether or not within the framework of Camp David, can only take place on an equal footing between the provisional Government of Palestine and the Government of Israel. Apart from that it would be contrary to the letter and spirit of the mandate system that Palestine's statehood should depend on the outcome of bilateral negotiations only.

5.1.2   Subscribing to the 'Law of Geneva'

The 1970 UN Declaration on Principles of International Law concerning Friendly Relations and Co-operation among States does not recognize a right of secession. This might explain the remarkable detachment of the international community towards the right to self-determination of, for example, the Baltic and Kurdish peoples. It is quite something, indeed, to determine that a Government in a pluralist State is not conducting itself in compliance with the principle of equal rights and self-determination of peoples. Supervision should not deteriorate into intervention in matters

---

105 XXVII ILM 1670 (1988).
106 See n. 6, *supra*. The Palestinian Declaration of Independence considered that the Partitition Resolution despite:
'... the historical injustice done to the Palestinian Arab people in its deplacement and in being deprived of the right to self-determination (...) nevertheless continues to attach conditions to international legitimacy that guarantee the Palestinian Arab people the right to sovereignty and national independence.'
ILM 1669 (1988).

which are essentially within the domestic jurisdiction of States. However, the creation of the State of Palestine has nothing to do with secession.

In the case of Palestine the prohibition of secession does not apply as a constraint to self-determination. The creation of a pluralist State appeared to be impossible due to the initial ambiguity of the international community in recognizing the Arab inhabitants of the Palestine Mandate as the Palestinian people with the right to self-determination, and the contradictory views of the Palestinian and Jewish peoples on the validity of the Palestine Mandate and the powers of the UN to divide the territory of Palestine. As a result both peoples claimed the whole territory of the Palestine Mandate by virtue of their right to self-determination. Unfortunately, it thus became a classic example of a liberation war.[107]

More than ninety States have already recognized the Palestinian State. Apart from that the creation of Palestine is based on too solid a legal foundation to leave the implementation to the interplay of military and political forces only. As for the military forces, 'the Israeli-Palestinian conflict can hardly find a definitive solution *manu militari'*.[108] Humanitarian law does not prolong war.[109] As for the political forces, they should be more aware of the fact that a permanent end to the conflict 'can be achieved only through compromise'.[110]

Be this as it may, the international community should take seriously Palestine's application to have the Fourth Geneva Convention ratified. Palestine's subscribing to the 'Law of Geneva' may have a moderating impact. Such a subscription will contribute to peace in the Middle East, for it underlines the rejection of terrorism. It thus enhances the duty of the PLO to control Palestinian factions. Palestine should be considered as a State in the meaning of the Fourth Geneva Convention. For the humanitarian law of armed conflict does not constitute a means to the end of protecting the rights of the sovereign but to 'the preservation of humanity in the face of the reality of war.'[111] The UN could facilitate such a solution by taking Palestine's membership into consideration, or at least by asking the Court for an Advisory Opinion.

---

107 Kalshoven, op. cit. n. 1, at 20.
108 Ben-Rafael, op. cit. n. 98, at 163.
109 Kalshoven, op. cit. n. 1, at 3.
110 Ben-Rafael, op. cit. n. 98, at 163. See also Schiff, Ya'ari, op. cit. n. 69, at 288-289.
111 Kalshoven, op. cit. n. 1, at 159. See also the testimony of W.T. Mallison, Professor of Law and Director of the International and Comparative Law Center Program, George Washington University, loc. cit. n. 92, at 47.

5.2   Advisory opinion

5.2.1   *Parallel with South-West Africa*

The Court's Advisory Opinions and Judgments in respect of the mandated territory South-West Africa (Namibia) apparently intend to be much wider in scope. In 1962 the Court indicated that the Mandate for South-West Africa, 'like practically all other similar Mandates' instituted a novel international regime.[112] In 1971 the Court also recalled its 1962 Judgment which stated as applying to all categories of mandate:

'The rights of the Mandatory in relation to the mandated territory and the inhabitants have their foundation in the obligations of the Mandatory and they are, so to speak, mere tools given to enable it to fulfil its obligations.'[113]

Moreover the Court put in general terms that it:

'... would not be correct to assume that, because the General Assembly is in principle vested with recommendatory powers, it is debarred from adopting, in specific cases within the framework of its competence, resolutions which make determinations or have operative design.'[114]

It made clear that Article 24 of the Charter:

'... vests in the Security Council the necessary authority to take action such as taken in the present case [Namibia]. The reference in paragraph 2 of this Article to specific powers of the Security Council under certain chapters of the Charter does not exclude the existence of general powers to discharge the responsibilities conferred in paragraph 1.'[115]

These considerations imply, in respect of the division of responsibilities between the General Assembly and the Security Council, that the responsibilities of the Security Council in respect of mandates do not exclude GA Resolutions which make determinations or have an operative design. However, the General Assembly needs the co-operation of the

---

112 ICJ Reports, 1962, at 331. See also ICJ Reports, 1971, at 46.
113 ICJ Reports, 1971, at 32.
114 ICJ Reports, 1971, at 50.
115 ICJ Reports, 1971, at 52.

Security Council to enforce compliance with its resolutions. In doing so the Security Council may not infringe on the General Assembly's powers.

5.2.2 *Question of Palestine ready for the Court*

It may be argued that the Court's statements on the international status of South-West Africa, the obligations of the Mandatory and the powers of the General Assembly hold true for the Palestine Mandate as well.[116] The inevitable conclusion is that the Occupied Territories still have their international status.[117]

An Advisory Opinion of the Court may be very helpful in the present situation in clarifying the powers of both the General Assembly and the Security Council in respect of admitting Palestine as a UN Member and/or its ability to ratify the Fourth Geneva Convention. The General Assembly is now in the fortunate position that an Advisory Opinion of the Court may be sufficient thanks to the acceptance of Resolutios 181 (II), 242 (1967) and 338 (1973) by the PLO and Arab States.[118]

The Court has been able to deliver Advisory Opinions within less than a year, the average time being six months. According to Article 103 of its Rules the General Assembly may inform the Court that its request necessitates an urgent answer or the Court itself may find that an early

---

116 The ICJ was of the opinion that:
'... the international rules regulating the Mandate constituted an international status for the territory recognized by the members of the League of Nations, including the Union of South Africa.'
ICJ Reports, 1950, at 132.

117 But see E.V. Rostow, *Palestinian Self-Determination: Possible Futures for the Unallocated Territories of the Palestine Mandate*, 5 Yale Studies in World Public Order 147-173 (1979). Rostow speaks of an extraordinary parallel between the problems of the Palestine and South-West Africa Mandates (at 158). However, he argues that:
'... the only possible geographic, demographic and political definition of Palestine is that of the Mandate, which included what are now Israel and Jordan as well as the West Bank and the Gaza Strip.'
Rostow, at 153. This definition of the Palestine Mandate drives him to the conclusion that only 'Jordan and Israel can solve the Palestinian problem; they are the Palestinian states, and they speak for the Palestinian people' (at 171). Legally speaking, the definition is contestable and with that the conclusion. The Balfour Declaration did not apply to (Trans)Jordan.

118 The GA might think of the following questions:
(1) What are the legal consequences for the United Nations of the continued presence of Israel in the Palestine territory occupied since 1967, notwithstanding SC Res. 242 and 338 and GA Res. 43/176 and 43/177?;
(2) More specifically, can Palestine become a Party to the 'Law of Geneva' and a Member-State of the UN, notwithstanding the Israeli occupation of its territory?

answer will be desirable. The question of Palestine has already created interest in the legal intricacies involved. It lends itself to an advisory opinion of the Court. The important Advisory Opinion on Namibia of 1971 'stands as a reminder that the Court can play a role in clarifying certain legal questions in a prolonged occupation'.[119] There will also be less risk that the United States will threaten to terminate its UN membership because of the mere fact that the General Assembly may decide to request an Advisory Opinion on the UN membership of Palestine.

6. CONCLUDING REMARKS

The question of Palestine has already burdened international relations much too long. This is contrary to the letter and spirit of the mandate system, which supports the right to self-determination of both the Jewish and Palestinian peoples. The UN should not beg the question anymore. It cannot be tolerated for Israel or Palestine to disregard about its decisions at the expense of each other's legitimate rights.

The Palestinian people has acted wisely by recognizing Israel. Whether it likes it or not, it is not good for peace in the Middle East if Israel now continues to be blind for the apparent statehood of Palestine:

'The Israelis negotiated agreements even with the Germans just a few years after Nazi Germany had sought the life of every last Jew within its sphere of control. The fact that atrocities have been committed by Palestinians does not justify denying the rights of the Palestinian people, just as complaints about callousness and cruelty on the part of Israelis is no excuse for refusing to engage in negotiations.'[120]

The international community, particularly the UN, should assist both Israel and Palestine to overcome the deadlock in negotiation.

Raising the question of Palestine's UN membership in the appropriate UN organs, including the Court, could be the prime mover in that respect. There is every reason to do so because these days, international law and the Court do attract much of attention of both the United States and Soviet Union. A lasting peaceful solution of the Israeli - Palestinian conflict through international law is there for the asking since Palestine's recognition of Israel and willingness to subscribe to the 'Law of Geneva'.

---

119 Roberts, loc. cit. n. 92, at 101.
120 Schiff, Ya'ari, op. cit. n. 69, at 329. See also Mendelsohn, op. cit. n. 90, at 244-245.

The UN should set an example in promoting acceptance of and respect for the principles of international law in order to settle the conflict peacefully. Otherwise it runs the risk that its decision to declare the period 1990-2000 as the United Nations Decade of International Law will become an empty gesture. Raising the question of Palestine's UN membership in the appropriate UN organs, including the Court, could be the prime mover in that respect. There is every reason to do so because of attention of both the United States and Soviet Union administrations. Thanks to this positive development the Security Council could take firm action against Iraq after its illegal invasion and annexation of Kuwait in August 1990.[121] The General Assembly should be encouraged by this state of affairs to prove that it still bears the responsibility for the administration of the Occupied Territories by virtue of the Palestine Mandate. In doing so it should invoke the co-operation of the Security Council to ensure the withdrawal of Israel from the Occupied Territories.

---

121 SC Res. 660-662 (1990), 664-667 (1990) and 669-670 (1990).

RELIANCE ON NORMS OF HUMANITARIAN LAW BY UNITED NATIONS' ORGANS

THEO C. VAN BOVEN

1.   INTRODUCTION

There is a growing tendency by UN organs to use norms of humanitarian law as a yardstick in the examination of situations of armed conflict. As a political organization the United Nations is increasingly confronted with situations of armed conflict, most of them of a non-international character. The Security Council has been invested with primary responsibility and with powers for dealing with situations affecting international peace and security. The General Assembly discusses many questions relating to situations which are characterized by patterns of serious violence. The Secretary-General is called upon to lend his good offices in conflict situations. The ICJ is seized with disputes which occasionally give rise to questions relating to the laws of armed conflict.

While it is the principal role of the United Nations to bring about or to facilitate peaceful solutions, the Organization cannot remain indifferent in the face of serious breaches of humanitarian standards and gross violations of human rights which often occur on a large scale in conflict situations. UN policy organs entrusted to deal with situations revealing a consistent pattern of gross violations of human rights, notably the General Assembly and the Commission on Human Rights, have to take into account a complexity of factors. These pertain *inter alia* to the root causes of a conflict, the resort to indiscriminate violence on the side of the parties to the conflict and intense human suffering inflicted upon a population. A comprehensive peace approach cannot ignore any of these factors.

Therefore, a UN policy organ dealing with a conflict situation involving gross violations of human rights, cannot effectively approach the human rights problem without addressing itself to the conflict situation as such. Humanizing the conflict and providing relief and protection to actual or potential victims are important immediate necessities but these immediate concerns cannot be separated from the ultimate goal of ending the conflict. Conversely, efforts to attain a peaceful solution should not thwart or put off immediate humanitarian and human rights concerns. Political action and respect for humanitarian law should go hand in hand. As Veuthey quite correctly stated: 'The convergence of interest between humanitarian law and political action must be emphasized now, at a time when the law alone is not sufficient to ensure respect for humanity and when humanitarianism cannot on its own make up for political deficiencies.'[1]

The awareness that the question of violations of human rights in situations of armed conflict cannot be tackled in a separate or isolated manner, prompted UN human rights organs, when dealing with such situations, to regard the conflict situation as one context in which gross violations of human rights occur. It is from this wider perspective that these UN organs are progressively relying upon and applying, in addition to human rights norms, basic standards of humanitarian law. The thrust of this paper is to analyze this development, in fact this development coincides with a growing convergence of human rights law and humanitarian law.

Before discussing in more detail some aspects of the relevant practice of the United Nations, with special reference to the role of humanitarian law in human rights monitoring and human rights decision-making, and before analyzing the factors that favoured this development, we will have to identify the place and the nature of this practice against the background of

---

1   M. Veuthey, *The Global Reach of International Humanitarian Law*, in R.C. Hingorani, ed., Humanitarian Law 39 (1987).

UN human rights procedures and mechanisms pertaining to violations of human rights. We will also have to recall the different origin and the different setting which marked the development of humanitarian law and human rights law before these two areas of law became subject to convergence.

As this paper will deal with UN practice concerning the application of humanitarian law, attention will be paid to two policy organs with human rights responsibilities: the UN General Assembly and the UN Commission on Human Rights. It should be kept in mind that other UN organs refer occasionally to humanitarian law standards as well. A well-known example is the recent judgment of the ICJ in the case of *Nicaragua* v. *the United States of America* where the Court invoked standards of humanitarian law and ruled that the United States is under an obligation not to encourage persons or groups engaged in the conflict in Nicaragua to act in violation of the provisions of Article 3 common to the four Geneva Conventions.[2]

Most remarkable are the many references to norms and principles of international humanitarian law by the Security Council in the series of resolutions it adopted since early August 1990 in response to *the invasion and occupation of Kuwait by Iraq*. The Council repeatedly reaffirmed that the Fourth Geneva Convention applied to Kuwait and that Iraq as a High Contracting Party to the Convention is bound to comply fully with all its terms and is in particular liable under the Convention in respect to grave breaches committed by it, as are individuals who commit or order the commission of grave breaches.[3] More in particular, with regard to third-State nationals, Iraq was requested and demanded to permit and facilitate their immediate departure and cease and desist forthwith from taking them hostage in violation of the Fourth Geneva Convention and other norms of international law.[4] Equally, Iraq was demanded to stop immediately the mistreatment and oppression of Kuwaiti and third-State nationals.[5] Furthermore, it was on the basis of international humanitarian law that the Security Council exempted from the embargo against Iraq supplies intended strictly for medical purposes, and, in humanitarian circumstances,

---

2   Military and Paramilitary Activities in and against Nicaragua (*Nicaragua* v. *United States of America*), Merits, Judgment, 1986 ICJ Report 14, § 220. See T. Meron, Human Rights and Humanitarian Norms as Customary Law 25-37 (1989).

3   SC Res. 670 of 25 September 1990, oper. § 13, and Res. 674 of 29 October 1990, preamb. § 5 and oper. § 1.

4   SC Res. 664 of 18 August 1990, oper. § 1, Res. 666 of 13 September 1990, preamb. § 5 and oper. § 2, Res. 674 of 29 October 1990, oper. § 1.

5   SC Res. 674 of 29 October 1990, oper. § 1.

foodstuffs.[6] The Council also demanded Iraq to ensure the immediate access to food, water and basic services necessary to the protection and well-being of Kuwaiti nationals and of nationals of third States in Kuwait and Iraq, including the personnel of diplomatic and consular missions in Kuwait.[7]

2.   CONSISTENT PATTERNS OF GROSS VIOLATIONS OF
        HUMAN RIGHTS

Whereas in the early years of the UN, human rights activities mainly concentrated on standard-setting, it was in the mid and late sixties -after an influx of many countries of the Third World- that the human rights programme was mobilized as a suitable means for concerted action against colonialism and racism. Thus, in 1965, the Special Committee on the Situation with regard to the Implementation of the Declaration on the Granting of Independence to Colonial Countries and Peoples drew the attention of the Commission on Human Rights to evidence submitted by petitioners concerning violations of human rights committed in the then territories under Portuguese Administration and also in what was called South West Africa and Southern Rhodesia.

This action, energetically sponsored by African and Asian countries, resulted in a request by the Economic and Social Council to the Commission on Human Rights to treat as an important and urgent matter the 'question of the violation of human rights and fundamental freedoms, including policies of racial discrimination and segregation and of *apartheid* in all countries, with special reference to colonial and other dependent countries and territories', and to submit to the Council its recommendation on measures to halt those violations.[8] This request eventually led to a permanent mandate of the Commission, laid down in ECOSOC Resolution 1235 (XLII) of 6 June 1967, to give annual consideration to this question which at that time had clearly anti-colonial and anti-racial overtones and responded to widespread political concerns in the United Nations.

It was in the same period that the Commission on Human Rights established the *Ad Hoc* Working Group of Experts[9] whose mandate was to 'investigate and study the policies and practices which violate human rights

---

6   SC Res. 661 of 6 August 1990, oper. § 3(c), Res. 666 of 13 September 1990, oper. § 8.
7   SC Res. 674 of 29 October 1990, oper. § 5.
8   ECOSOC Res. 1102 (XL) of 4 March 1966.
9   Res. 2 (XXIII) of 6 March 1967 of the Commission on Human Rights.

in South Africa and Namibia' and 'in co-operation with the Special Committee against Apartheid and other investigatory and monitoring bodies, to continue to investigate cases of torture and ill-treatment of detainees and the deaths of detainees in South Africa.' It should be noted that the *Ad Hoc* Working Group has regularly indicated the standards applicable to its work. In this respect it listed a broad range of human rights instruments but also 'the relevant provisions of the four Geneva Conventions of 12 August 1949.'[10] Similarly, the Special Committee to Investigate Israeli Practices Affecting the Human Rights of the Population of the Occupied Territories, initially established by GA Resolution 2443 (XXIII) of 19 December 1968 and still in operation, has relied both on human rights instruments and on instruments of humanitarian law. Since its inception the following instruments have been cited by the Special Committee for the interpretation and the carrying out of its mandate:

a) The Charter of the United Nations;
b) The Universal Declaration of Human Rights;
c) The Geneva Conventions relative to the Protection of Civilian Persons in Time of War, of 12 August 1949;
d) The Geneva Conventions relative to the Treatment of Prisoners of War, of 12 August 1949;
e) The Hague Convention for the Protection of Cultural Property in the Event of Armed Conflict, of 14 May 1954;
f) The Hague Conventions of 1899 and 1907 respecting the Laws and Customs of War on Land; and
g) The International Covenant on Civil and Political Rights, and the International Covenant on Economic, Social and Cultural Rights.[11]

In the nineteen-seventies and eighties, starting with the situation in Chile, the Commission on Human Rights widened the interpretation of its mandate under ECOSOC Resolution 1235 (XLII) of 6 June 1967 and moved from the anti-colonial and anti-racial context, where it had done valuable work, to a broad range of human rights concerns in numerous countries. Thus, the Commission on Human Rights developed a whole range of tools and mechanisms to deal with consistent patterns of gross violations of human rights in such countries as El Salvador, Bolivia, Guatemala, Haiti, Cuba, Equatorial Guinea, the Central African Republic,

---

10 B.G. Ramcharan, International Law and Fact-Finding in the Field of Human Rights 35 (1982).
11 Ramcharan, op. cit. n. 10, at 36.

Uganda, Iran, Afghanistan, Sri Lanka, Poland, Rumania, Albania etc..[12] In this connection fact-finding groups were established, special rapporteurs appointed, the Secretary-General was requested to report and use his good offices. Visits on the spot were made, hearings were granted to numerous witnesses, non-governmental organizations were mobilized to submit information and pressures were exerted on Governments to remedy situations and observe fundamental human rights.

All these activities were part of a political process. The Commission on Human Rights is essentially a political body, composed of representatives of Governments. Many of the situations, referred to above, are dealt with successively and in a concerted manner by the Commission and the General Assembly. The decision by one or both of these bodies to take up a specific country situation is basically political in nature and depends on a voting majority. This implies that the concerns thus expressed are selective, though it cannot be argued that these expressions of political concern are unrelated to the gravity of the situations in terms of breaches of basic human rights and humanitarian standards. Equally, the wording of resolutions adopted is the result of political negotiations, but again it should be emphasized that the political process is not fully oblivious of genuine human rights and humanitarian concerns.

It is submitted that many situations which in themselves constitute or generate consistent patterns of gross violations of human rights are characterized by phenomena identified in the landmark Resolution 32/130 of 16 December 1977 of the General Assembly, sponsored and supported by Third World countries. Paragraph 1(e) of this resolution reads:

'In approaching human rights questions within the United Nations system, the international community should accord, or continue to accord, priority to the search for solutions to the mass and flagrant violations of human rights of peoples and persons affected by situations such as those resulting from *apartheid*, from all forms of racial discrimination, from colonialism, from foreign domination and occupation, from aggression and threats against national sovereignty, national unity and territorial integrity, as well as from the refusal to recognize the fundamental rights of peoples to self-determination and of every nation to the exercise of full sovereignty over its wealth and natural resources.'

---

12 See also M.J. Bossuyt, *The Development of Special Procedures of the United Nations Commission on Human Rights*, 6 Human Rights Law Journal 179-210 (1985).

While the language just quoted is reminiscent of the days of strong politicization of the human rights discourse and echoes some of the notions included in Article 1(4) of Protocol I Additional to the Geneva Conventions of 12 August 1949,[13] it cannot be denied that the type of situations just referred to are potential and actual sources of grave conflicts involving large-scale violations of human rights and often taking on the nature of international or non-international armed conflicts.

Moreover, it is evident -and this element is deliberately ignored in the text of GA Resolution 32/130 which concentrated on 'external' dimensions- that to an increasing extent peoples, groups of persons and individual persons become the victims of gross violations of human rights as a result of ethnic and group conflicts generating 'internal' violence. While the latter type of conflict may be characterized by what is broadly termed 'internal disturbances and tensions', several amount to non-international armed conflicts under common Article 3 of the Geneva Conventions or even to non-international armed conflicts under Protocol II Additional to the Geneva Conventions. Whenever consistent patterns of gross violations of human rights occur in situations of armed conflict, this implies that, in addition to human rights law, standards of humanitarian law are applicable and must be observed in these situations. One of the purposes of this paper is to review how UN human rights organs -as well as their fact-finding mechanisms- invoke and apply in appropriate cases norms of humanitarian law. However, before carrying out such review, it is useful to distinguish various types of armed conflicts.

3.   VARIOUS TYPES OF ARMED CONFLICTS;
      THE MINIMUM YARDSTICK

In an enlightening essay Weissbrodt observes that international humanitarian law distinguishes four types of armed conflicts, with different legal principles and instruments applicable to each of them.[14] These four types of armed conflicts are:

---

13 This paragraph brought under the scope of Protocol I: '... armed conflicts in which peoples are fighting against colonial domination and alien occupation and against racist régimes in the exercise of their right to self-determination, as enshrined in the Charter of the United Nations and the Declaration on Principles of International Law concerning Friendly Relations and Co-operation among States in accordance with the Charter of the United Nations.'

14 D. Weissbrodt, *Ways International Organizations Can Improve Their Implementation of Human Rights and Humanitarian Law in Situations of Armed Conflict*, in E.L. Lutz, H. Hannum, K.J. Burke, eds., New Directions in Human Rights 72-75 (1989).

a) international armed conflicts to which the four Geneva Conventions of 1949, Additional Protocol I of 1977, the Hague rules and other principles apply;
b) wars of liberation or self-determination, which are principally defined by and made subject to Additional Protocol I of 1977;
c) non-international armed conflicts which are subject to the regulation of common Article 3 of the four Geneva Conventions and some customary norms; and
d) non-international armed conflicts which are narrowly defined and regulated by Additional Protocol II of 1977.

For the purpose of this paper there is no compelling reason to make neat legal classifications in order to determine with precision which category applies to a given concrete situation. When UN political organs refer to norms of humanitarian law, this is usually not done in order to identify primary sources of the applicable law but rather by way of reference to the most basic, minimum standards of conduct for Governments.[15] In this connection it must be emphasized that -whatever the nature or the classification of the conflict situation, whether international, non-international armed conflict, or 'merely' internal disturbances and tensions, such as riots, isolated and sporadic acts of violence which are not considered armed conflicts in the sense of Protocol II- UN political bodies are on perfectly good ground in invoking common Article 3 to the Geneva Conventions of 1949 as a minimum standard of humanitarian law *to be respected under all circumstances*.

Legal opinion still differs as to whether Article 3 has become part of customary law. The Legal Adviser to the Directorate of the ICRC, Gasser, gives as his personal view that: '... it has been generally recognized that the substance of Article 3, based on customary law, is part of *ius cogens*, and therefore binding on all states.'[16] In this context he referred to the Judgment of the ICJ in the case of *Nicaragua* v. *the United States of America* where the Court reached the conclusion that Article 3, as part of customary law, constituted a 'minimum yardstick' applicable to all armed conflicts.[17] And Gasser adds: 'This "minimum standard" of international humanitarian law, contained in Article 3, largely corresponds to the body of guarantees from which Governments cannot derogate, even in

---

15 Weissbrodt, loc. cit. n. 14, at 78.
16 H.-P. Gasser, *A Measure of Humanity in Internal Disturbances and Tensions: Proposal for a Code of Conduct*, 262 International Review of the Red Cross 44 (1988).
17 1986 ICJ Rep. 14, loc. cit. n. 2, § 218.

emergency situations. These rules are binding in armed conflicts, including non-international armed conflicts, and hence also logically in internal disturbances and tensions.'[18] It would appear that this view finds support in the Commentary on the Geneva Conventions of 12 August 1949. The 1958 Commentary on the Fourth Geneva Convention states with respect to Article 3: 'It merely demands respect for certain rules, which were already recognized as essential in all civilized countries, and embodied in the municipal law of the States in question, long before the Convention was signed. What Government would dare to claim before the world, in case of civil disturbances which could justly be described as mere acts of banditry, that, Article 3 not being applicable, it was entitled to leave the wounded uncared for, to torture and mutilate prisoners and take hostages?'[19]

On the other hand, Meron takes a more circumspect approach in his discussion of the customary law character of Acticle 3 of the Geneva Conventions. While arguing that: 'Article 3 may well express the quintessence of humanitarian rules found in other substantive provisions of the Geneva Conventions', he is not so sure that the rules of Article 3 have necessarily attained the character of customary rules of international law.[20] He also notes that the ICJ in the *Nicaragua Case* completely failed to inquire whether *opinio juris* and practice support the crystallization of Article 3 into customary law.[21]

In the context of the present paper it does not matter a great deal whether the provisions of Article 3 have reached in their entirety the consecrated status of customary international law or whether they express the quintessence or the core of humanitarian rules. Courts of law may consider such a distinction highly relevant in order to establish legal rights and obligations. However, political organs of the United Nations are obviously not courts of law and, in assessing the policies and actions of Governments or of any other relevant entities, they can base themselves on the premise that governments and other actors must comply with basic standards of humanitarian behaviour. It is on this ground that as a minimum the provisions of Article 3 of the Geneva Conventions, and in appropriate cases other rules of humanitarian law also, are most pertinent in situations where the United Nations is involved and such situations entail a consistent pattern of gross violations of human rights. The question now arises why human rights standards do not provide sufficient and adequate

18 Gasser, loc. cit. n. 16, at 45.
19 J.S. Pictet, ed., Commentary on the Geneva Convention IV, 36 under Article 3 (1958).
20 Meron, op. cit. n. 2, at 33.
21 *Ibid.*, at 36.

guidance and why standards of humanitarian law should also be relied upon. We will revert to this question but first some cases and situations should be reviewed where UN bodies did invoke norms of humanitarian law.

4.   SITUATIONS REQUIRING EXPLICIT REFERENCE TO STANDARDS OF HUMANITARIAN LAW

4.1   Introduction

In paragraph 2 above, a range of country situations were mentioned which at one time or another were identified and selected in public proceedings of UN policy organs involving consistent patterns of gross violations of human rights. Several of these situations became a regular feature for many years on the agenda of these organs in the absence of any fundamental improvement. At least one situation, the territories under Israeli occupation, comprising the Golan Heights, the West Bank (including East Jerusalem) and the Gaza Strip, has been under constant UN scrutiny for more than two decades. Two other situations, those pertaining to Afghanistan and El Salvador, have been quasi-permanent features on the agenda of the United Nations for some ten years. Another situation, which relates to Sri Lanka, is also a matter of serious and long-standing concern but UN action has been limited in scope and time. These four situations will be briefly reviewed inasmuch as the United Nations has chosen in relation to them to rely on standards of humanitarian law.

4.2   Territories under Israeli occupation

More than in any other situation the United Nations has relied on humanitarian law with regard to these territories. Since its establishment by GA Resolution 2443 (XXIII) of 19 December 1968, the Special Committee to Investigate Israeli Practices Affecting the Human Rights of the Population of the Occupied Territories has cited instruments of humanitarian law for interpreting and carrying out its mandate. In particular the Fourth Geneva Convention relative to the Protection of Civilian Persons in Time of War, which contains a special section on the status and treatment of protected persons in occupied territories (Articles 47-78) has been from the very beginning the main and substantial yardstick for critical assessment of the behaviour and the actions of the Israeli authorities. While the Government of Israel has consistently failed to acknowledge the applicability of the said Convention to the territories it has occupied since 1967, virtually all States of the international community have, in numerous resolutions, reaffirmed that the Convention is applicable to the situation.[22]

In other resolutions adopted by the General Assembly and the Commission on Human Rights the long series of specific Israeli policies and practices which violate the Fourth Geneva Convention and other applicable international instruments are strongly condemned, in particular those violations which the Convention designates as 'grave breaches' thereof. The Special Committee is also requested to consult, as appropriate, the ICRC in order to ensure the safeguarding of the welfare and human rights of the population in the occupied territories. Particular concern is further expressed about the continuing deportation of Palestinians from the occupied territories in violation of Article 49 of the Fourth Geneva Convention. The General Assembly and the Commission on Human Rights also continue to highlight the relevance of common Article 1 of the Geneva Conventions, under which the High Contracting Parties undertake to respect and to ensure respect for the Conventions in all circumstances. This reference to common Article 1 is of special significance because the undertaking to *ensure respect* is generally interpreted to mean 'that in the event of a Power failing to fulfil its obligations, the other Contracting Parties may, and should, endeavour to bring it back to an attitude of respect for the Conventions'.[23] In this respect the activities of the United Nations with regard to the territories occupied by Israel may well be qualified as an expression of collective responsibility implied in the undertaking to *ensure respect*.[24]

4.3   Afghanistan

In his early Reports to the Commission on Human Rights and the General Assembly the Special Rapporteur on the Situation of Human Rights in

---

22 Recently GA Res. 44/48B, adopted on 8 December 1989 by 149 votes in favour, one against (Israel) and two abstentions (Dominica and the United States).

23 J.S. Pictet, ed., op. cit. n. 19, under Article 1 (1958 and 1960).

24 See in particular with respect to the Israeli occupied territories the Report of the UN Secretary-General submitted to the Security Council in accordance with SC Res. 672 of 12 October 1990, in which the Secretary-General suggested that 'given the special responsibility of the High Contracting Parties for insuring respect for the Convention, the Security Council might wish to call for a meeting of the High Contracting Parties to discuss possible measures that might be taken by them under the Convention.' (UN Doc. 5/21919, dated 31 October 1990, § 24).

Afghanistan, Ermacora, stated that all parties to the conflict are at least bound by common Article 3 of the Geneva Conventions, regardless of whether the conflict is considered as international or non-international. He concluded that in spite of this, the following practices have taken place:

a) the use of anti-personnel mines and of so-called toy bombs;
b) the indiscriminate mass killings of civilians, particularly women and children;
c) the growing use of heavy weapons with most destructive effects;
d) the systematic discrimination against persons not adhering to the People's Democratic Party of Afghanistan; and
e) the non-acceptance of members of the Afghan opposition movements as prisoners of war.[25]

In later reports the Special Rapporteur consistently and repeatedly insisted that humanitarian law should be respected by all parties to the conflict; that captured members of the resistance should be treated as prisoners of war under the Geneva Conventions; that the use of weapons against the civilian population must be halted and that any such use must be qualified as terrorism. The Special Rapporteur also recommended that the ICRC should be given full access to any prisoner, prison or place of detention under the control of the resistance movements and that the Government should conclude an agreement with ICRC as soon as possible allowing the Organization to carry out regular inspection of prisons and places of detention and to meet prisoners on a regular basis, in accordance with its established criteria.[26]

Recent resolutions of the General Assembly and the Commission on Human Rights continue to reflect the findings and the concerns contained in the Reports of the Special Rapporteur. Thus, the General Assembly recognized that a situation of armed conflict continues to exist in Afghanistan, leaving large numbers of victims without protection or assistance, and called upon all the parties to the conflict, in order to alleviate the suffering of the people of Afghanistan, to apply fully the principles and rules of international humanitarian law and to cooperate fully and effectively with international humanitarian organizations, in particular to facilitate the protection activities of the ICRC.[27] The General Assembly also urged that all parties to the conflict respect the Geneva

---

25   UN doc. A/40/843, § 128.
26   UN doc. A/42/667, § 123, and A/44/669, § 107.
27   GA Res. 43/139 of 8 December 1988.

Conventions of 1949 and their Additional Protocols of 1977, to halt the use of weapons against the civilian population, to transmit to humanitarian organizations and, in particular, to the ICRC, the names of all political prisoners and detained Afghan soldiers, as well as to allow the ICRC to visit all prisoners in accordance with its established criteria. The General Assembly further urged all parties to the conflict to release all prisoners of war in accordance with the internationally recognized principles of humanitarian law and urged all parties to the conflict to treat all prisoners in their custody in accordance with the internationally recognized principles of humanitarian law and to protect them from all acts of reprisal and violence, including ill-treatment, torture and summary execution.[28]

4.4   El Salvador

Since the appointment in 1981 of the Special Representative of the Commission on Human Rights, Pastor Ridruejo, to examine the situation of human rights and fundamental freedoms in El Salvador, the Special Representative has presented Reports on that situation twice a year: an Interim Report to the General Assembly and a Final Report to the Commission on Human Rights. The Special Representative noted that El Salvador is a Party to the Geneva Conventions and to the Additional Protocols. He emphasized the importance of common Article 3, which requires in particular respect for the life of non-combatants and combatants who are *hors de combat.*[29]

In his Reports the Special Representative referred to information concerning the indiscriminate killing of thousands of non-combatants by bombardment from the air, shelling, and ground sweeps. He had also received reports on the use by the Air Force of fragmentation bombs with fuse extenders, napalm-like incendiary bombs and white phosphorous. He stated he was convinced that the Salvadorian Army's military operations resulted in unwarranted civilian casualties.[30] He also criticized the guerrilla organizations for the forced recruitment of young civilians, for planting contact mines killing or seriously maiming non-combatants and for attacking the economic infrastructure of El Salvador.[31]

Over the years UN resolutions have addressed many facts and features in El Salvador which make up a consistent pattern of gross violations of

---

28   GA Res. 44/161 of 15 December 1989.
29   UN doc. A/36/608, § 10.
30   UN doc. A/39/636, §§ 105 *et seq..*
31   UN doc. A/42/641, §§ 66 *et seq..*

human rights, including questions of humanitarian law in armed conflicts and violations of such law. The General Assembly and the Commission on Human Rights considered that in El Salvador an armed conflict of a non-international character continues to exist in which the parties involved are under an obligation to apply the minimum standards of protection of human rights and humanitarian treatment provided for in Article 3 common to the Geneva Convention and in Additional Protocol II. The General Assembly requested that the Government of El Salvador and all the authorities, courts and political forces of the country, including the *Frente Farabundo Marti para la Liberación Nacional-Frente Democrático Revolucionario*, should adopt appropriate measures to eliminate attacks on the lives and integrity of persons, independently of, during and as a result of combat situations, as well as attacks on the economic infrastructure and, in general, all types of actions constituting a violation of the fundamental rights and freedoms of the Salvadorian people.[32] The General Assembly also requested the parties to the conflict to guarantee respect for the international standards applicable to an armed conflict of a non-international character, in particular the protection of the civilian population and the war-wounded and war-injured, whether civilians or combatants, in order that they might receive the medical care they need and, furthermore, to co-operate with humanitarian organizations working to alleviate the suffering of the civilian population in any part of the country in which such organizations are operating and the General Assembly further requested that medical and health personnel shall under no circumstances be penalized for carrying out their activities.[33]

4.5   Sri Lanka

The conflict situation in Sri Lanka only once prompted a UN policy organ to adopt a resolution addressing that situation. The moderately phrased resolution adopted by the Commission on Human Rights was largely couched in terms of humanitarian law. In the resolution the Commission called upon all parties and groups to respect fully the universally accepted rules of humanitarian law, to renounce the use of force and acts of violence and to pursue a negotiated political solution, based on principles of respect for human rights and fundamental freedoms. Further the Commission invited the Government of Sri Lanka to intensify its co-

---

32   GA Res. 43/145 of 8 December 1988.
33   GA Res. 44/165 of 15 December 1989.

operation with the ICRC in the fields of dissemination and promotion of international humanitarian law and to consider favourably the offer of the services of the ICRC to fulfil its functions of protection of humanitarian standards, including the provision of assistance and protection to victims of all affected parties.[34]

5.   CONVERGING TENDENCIES

The development of law to be respected in armed conflicts started from different assumptions and other premises than the development of the law of human rights. The law of war was largely influenced by the tension between military necessity and humanitarian restraints. The principle of reciprocity was a major factor in enhancing the efficacy of the operation of the law of war between belligerents.[35] In humanitarian law the inter-State obligations prevail. On the other hand, human rights law primarily entails obligations for the State with respect to 'all individuals within its territory and subject to its jurisdiction'.[36] As was correctly stated:

'... the observance of human rights is not based on reciprocal interests of States, but on the broader goal of States to establish orderly and enlightened international and national legal orders. In human rights instruments, the contractual (inter-State) elements are far less important than those which are objective and normative.'[37]

However, with growing emphasis on the prescriptions for upholding the values of humanity and in view of the fact that the principle of reciprocity does not operate effectively in domestic situations, humanitarian law and human rights law have become the subject of converging tendencies, both with regard to the substance of the law and as to the protected persons. It is clear that the two 1977 Protocols Additional to the Geneva Conventions, in particular Protocol II, were strongly influenced by basic human rights standards elaborated in the United Nations. As the authoritative Commentary on the Additional Protocols states:

---

34 Commission on Human Rights Res. 1987/61 of 12 March 1987.
35 T. Meron, *On the Inadequate Reach of Humanitarian and Human Rights Law and the Need for a New Instrument*, 77 AJIL 592-593 (1983).
36 Article 2, § 1 of the International Covenant on Civil and Political Rights.
37 Meron, op. cit. n. 2, at 100.

> 'Protocol II contains virtually all the irreducible rights of the Covenant on Civil and Political Rights .... These rights are based on rules of universal validity to which States can be held, even in the absence of any treaty obligation or any explicit commitment on their part. It may be accepted that they form part of *jus cogens.*'[38]

These converging tendencies are not only evident from the orientation and the normative content of humanitarian law and human rights law but they are also confirmed in recent practice of the United Nations as discussed above in connection with the situations in the territories under Israeli occupation, Afghanistan, El Salvador and Sri Lanka. And these situations are by no means the only ones where UN bodies are relying upon standards of humanitarian law. It is claimed that the wider acceptance of the norms of humanitarian law constitutes an important reason why international human rights organizations may feel on stronger grounds when they rely on humanitarian law.[39] Indeed, as of 1 January 1990 the four Geneva Conventions of 1949 had each received 166 ratifications (Additional Protocols I and II respectively 92 and 82 ratifications) and the International Covenant on Civil and Political Rights and the International Covenant on Economic, Social and Cultural Rights were on that same date ratified by 89 and 94 States Parties.[40] The status of ratifications certainly has significance for the purpose of establishing accountability of States, but as far as UN policy organs are concerned, their preferred frame of reference is internationally recognized standards of conduct (which in addition to conventions may include important declarations and resolutions) rather than strictly legal norms. In this regard the special procedures instituted by UN resolutions which address States as responsible members of the organized international community should be distinguished from treaty based procedures, whose inherent delimitations and definitions are governed by the legal scope of such treaties.

A more compelling argument for citing norms of humanitarian law can be inferred from the nature and the exigencies of many conflict situations. In such situations there are usually several parties, of which at least one is not a governmental authority. In order to tackle the urgent needs of such situations, human rights and humanitarian bodies have to address all parties

---

38 Commentary on the Additional Protocols of 8 June 1977 to the Geneva Conventions of 12 August 1949, ICRC 1340 (1987).

39 Weissbrodt, loc. cit. n. 14, at 68; see also Meron, loc. cit. n. 34, at 590.

40 J.-B. Marie, *International Instruments relating to Human Rights, Classification and Chart showing ratifications as of 1 January 1990*, 11 Human Rights Law Journal 175-202 (1990).

in the conflict and not only the governmental authority. In this respect human rights instruments, which are largely regarded as defining relationships between State power and persons under the jurisdiction of the State, are inadequate for use against parties in a conflict who are not invested with governmental authority.[41] However, this problem does not arise under international humanitarian law: its rules are addressed to all parties to an armed conflict. Fully consistent with this approach, the UN General Assembly and the Commission on Human Rights, in citing principles and norms of international humanitarian law, have appealed, as noted before, to all parties to the conflict.

It was argued by some commentators, particularly in connection with the activities of the United Nations *vis-à-vis* the territories under Israeli occupation, that the UN went beyond its competence and should have confined itself to relying upon the law of human rights. According to this view the UN was mistaken in applying the 1949 Geneva Conventions and the Protocols additional to these Conventions because the latter instruments fell outside the terms of reference of the United Nations. The ICRC as an independent and impartial body would be the appropriate body to control the application of international humanitarian law rather than the United Nations which as a political organization could offer no guarantees of independence and impartiality.[42]

In fact, the practical involvement of the United Nations with norms of international humanitarian law did not stop with the situation in the territories under Israeli occupation. In dealing with the situations in Afghanistan, El Salvador and Sri Lanka, UN policy organs -and this applies equally to their fact-finding tools- could not possibly split up their mandate into a human rights sector which would properly belong to the United Nations and a humanitarian law sector which would fall under the competence of the ICRC. Such a division in the applicable standards and in respective competences does not correspond to the realities of the situation and is simply not feasible. This division is artificial and based on the mistaken assumption that the United Nations and the ICRC are in rival positions.

It is true that human rights bodies, including those of the United Nations, and humanitarian organizations such as the ICRC have their own distinct roles to play and that they have to protect their respective

---

41 See Gasser, loc. cit., n. 16, at 46.
42 A.S. Calogeropoulos-Stratis, Droit humanitaire et droits de l'homme; La protection de la personne en période de conflit armé 198-199 (1980).

identities.[43] Their methods of work are diverse but in actual fact, and with due respect for the specific characteristics of each organization,[44] their actions are complementary. It is on the basis of this awareness and in this spirit that, as we have seen, UN bodies have repeatedly urged parties to the conflict to co-operate with and make use of the humanitarian services of the ICRC and to respect the established criteria of the Red Cross (in cases of visits to prisoners). In sum, the tendency of the international law to converge is combined with the complementarity of the international actors.

6.   CONCLUDING OBSERVATIONS

As the UN Secretary-General aptly observed in his Report of September 1990 on the work of the Organization: 'Today, in a growing number of cases, threats to national and international security are no longer as neatly seperable as they were before. In not a few countries, civil strife takes a heavy toll of human life and has repercussions beyond national borders'.[45] In the contemporary political setting inter-State wars are on the decline but intra-State conflicts, generated by ethnic and religious tensions, economic and social disparities and repressive governmental practices, are increasingly rampant. Some of these intra-State conflicts have reached a level that Additional Protocol II is applicable. Many other conflicts have not attained that threshold but are no less violent and cause large-scale suffering, notably also when they are characterized in terms of internal disturbances and tensions. Basic human rights standards have to be respected under all circumstances and, with regard to humanitarian law, common Article 3 of the Geneva Conventions constitutes a minimum standard which is to be respected equally under all circumstances by all who are involved in the conflict. We strongly favour that this minimum standard containing fundamental rules of humanity be restated and re-enforced. Various proposals to that effect, notably the Draft Model Declaration on Internal Strife elaborated by Meron[46] and the Draft Code

---

43 Weissbrodt, loc. cit. n. 14, at 86.
44 Veuthey, loc. cit. n. 1, at 42.
45 UN doc. A/45/1, section IV.
46 T. Meron, *Draft Model Declaration on Internal Strife*, 262 International Review of the Red Cross 59-76 (1988).

of Conduct in the Event of Internal Disturbances and Tensions presented by Gasser[47], deserve an energetic and concerted follow-up.

It has been the main thrust of this essay that the protection of human rights standards and the protection of humanitarian norms are not separate efforts but joint and concerted goals and concerns. Political, legal and humanitarian action is carried out under the responsibility of diverse and distinct actors but essentially their actions are complementary. The present author fully supports the Report of the Independent Commission on International Humanitarian Issues in its plea for better observance of humanitarian norms:

'States have undertaken not only to observe humanitarian norms but also, more importantly, to ensure their implementation and, thus, in the face of serious breaches, to act individually or collectively. This kind of collective control could be effective if it were used more frequently. It is in the interest of States [and of all others concerned] to combine political and humanitarian concerns. Far from being incompatible, they condition and complement one another.'[48]

The challenge facing the international community is to bring about a firmer and broader acceptance and observance of basic human rights and humanitarian standards. At the same time the awareness is growing that preventive action and anticipatory diplomacy are urgently required in order to stop imminent conflict situations from reaching catastrophic levels. In this respect, new potentials are within sight and within reach. The Charter of Paris for a New Europe, signed on 21 November 1990, in the framework of the Conference on Security and Cooperation in Europe, embodies challenging prospects which will hopefully stretch beyond the boundaries of Europe and gain a global momentum.

47 H.-P. Gasser, *Code of Conduct in the Event of Internal Disturbances and Tensions*, 262 International Review of the Red Cross 51-58 (1988).
48 Report of the Independent Commission on International Humanitarian Issues, *Winning the Human Race?* 75 (1988).

INTERNATIONAL HUMANITARIAN LAW AND THE SECURITY COUNCIL RESOLUTIONS ON THE 1990-1991 GULF CONFLICT *

ERIK SUY

1.   INTRODUCTION

That international humanitarian law becomes applicable in every international conflict from the moment that armed force is used is obvious to every lawyer. Politicians and, in their wake, the military, are primarily concerned, however, to achieve victory over the opposition with minimum casualties among their own forces.

In the Gulf Conflict, international humanitarian law came into effect on 2 August 1990 when Iraqi armed forces invaded Kuwait. Both States are Parties to the four Geneva Conventions.[1] Kuwait is also a Party to both Additional Protocols, which have not been ratified by Iraq.

The UN Security Council, as is well-known, reacted immediately to the invasion of Kuwait by Iraq and, in the period from 2 August to 29 November 1990, adopted twelve Resolutions relating to the matter. The

---

* This contribution is an edited version of a speech delivered by Professor Dr. Erik Suy on 29 January 1991 at The Hague, on the occasion of the Closing Ceremony of the Humanitarian Law-Essay Contest, organized by the Flemish and Netherlands' Red Cross Societies.

1   Iraq ratified the Conventions on 14 February 1956, Kuwait on 2 September 1967.

issue that arises here has rather a restricted scope, namely, examination of those aspects of international humanitarian law that are evident in the involvement of the Security Council in this affair.

2.   SC RESOLUTIONS AND THE HUMANITARIAN *ISSUE*

Upon reviewing these twelve Resolutions one can distinguish between:

a) the resolutions that condemn the invasion and annexation;[2]
b) the sanctions resolutions that impose and extend economic sanctions;[3]
c) the resolutions that condemn certain actions by Iraq in respect of protected persons;[4]
d) SC Resolution 678 on the use of all necessary means;[5]
e) SC Resolution 669 taken under Article 50 of the UN Charter.[6]

Each Resolution has an effect on the application of international humanitarian law, but that does not mean that this issue was always evident in the discussions and present in the minds of the initiators of proposals and the Members of the Security Council.

The recognition and condemnation of the invasion of Kuwait by Iraq and the demand for immediate and unconditional withdrawal of the Iraqi troops confirms the existence of an international armed conflict and implies the applicability of international humanitarian law even though there was no subsequent reference thereto.[7]

SC Resolution 662, which declared the annexation of Kuwait by Iraq void and contrary to law, refers to the occupation of Kuwait by Iraq[8] and consequently implies that the provisions of international humanitarian law, and particularly Convention IV, relating to occupied territories are applicable. But here also there is no express reference to humanitarian law in the text of the Resolution.

---

2   SC Res. 660 of 2 August 1990 and SC Res. 662 of 9 August 1990.
3   SC Res. 661 of 6 August 1990; SC Res. 665 of 25 August 1990; SC Res. 666 of 13 September 1990 and SC Res. 670 of 25 September 1990.
4   SC Res. 664 of 18 August 1990; SC Res. 667 of 16 September 1990; SC Res. 674 of 29 October 1990 and SC Res. 677 of 28 November 1990.
5   SC Res. 678 of 29 November 1990.
6   SC Res. 669 of 24 September 1990.
7   SC Res. 660 of 2 August 1990.
8   Preamble, § 4.

The humanitarian *issue* was increasingly more clearly stated in the second category of Resolutions, the sanctions Resolutions, although an explicit reference to international humanitarian *law* was conspicuously absent.

The basic sanctions Resolution (SC Resolution 661) imposed in the first place a *trading embargo* with and to Iraq and the occupied territory of Kuwait. The Resolution laid down that all States must prevent all trade with those territories, 'not including supplies intended strictly for medical purposes, and in *humanitarian circumstances*, foodstuffs ...'. The question that may here immediately be asked is, how is one to interpret the phrase '*humanitarian circumstances*'. The *Sanctions Committee* set up by the Security Council was almost immediately confronted with the problem of supplies to the foreigners in the occupied territories of what for them were essential foodstuffs.[9] When the *Sanctions Committee* was unable to take a decision on this the Security Council itself, in SC Resolution 666, took a decision that deserves further attention on a number of grounds.

SC Resolution 666 certainly provides a clear interpretation to the sanctions SC Resolution 661. The interpretation rests on the following elements:

a) The Council assumes that it may be necessary, in certain circumstances, to supply foodstuffs to the civilian population 'in order to relieve human suffering', but emphasises that only the Council or the Committee is empowered to determine if such humanitarian circumstances exist - a most important determination!;

b) The *Sanctions Committee* must assess the levels of food stocks but Iraq must remain responsible for the nationals of third States (foreigners) in conformity with *international humanitarian law* including, 'where applicable, the Fourth Geneva Convention'. It should be noted that it was only on 13 September 1990 that, for the first time, a reference to international law appears!;

c) To determine the need for food supplies the Secretary-General was requested to obtain reliable information from, amongst others, 'appropriate humanitarian agencies';

d) Any decisions concerning food aid must be taken by the United Nations '... in co-operation with the International Committee of the Red Cross or other appropriate humanitarian agencies and distributed by them or

---

9 A shipment of tea from India and Sri Lanka.

under their supervision in order to ensure that they reach the intended beneficiaries'.

One should pause at this SC Resolution 666, which should be read with SC Resolution 661, and consider the issue of the extent to which the provisions of this Resolution may have influenced international humanitarian law. The question that immediately presents itself here relates to the possibility of 'humanitarian agencies' (not only the ICRC but also the League and its members, and the other humanitarian agencies) supplying food aid.

The SC Resolutions refer repeatedly to the nationals of third States.[10] Does this mean that the State's own nationals are neglected? In actual fact, was the Security Council, which condemned the invasion and annexation of Kuwait, stating that it had consideration only for the foreigners, the 'nationals of third countries'? This problem needs to be resolved before continuing.

2.1   Protection of foreigners

Whoever reads SC Resolution 664 will be struck by the fact that the Security Council demonstrates its concern for the 'Safety and well-being of third State nationals in Iraq and Kuwait',[11] and requests that Iraq should permit and facilitate 'the immediate departure from Kuwait and Iraq of the nationals of third countries' and that Iraq should not engage in any activity that would endanger the 'safety, security or health of such nationals'.[12] The Council referred to Iraq's obligations under international law but did not go any further.

This Resolution relates to the measures taken by the Iraqi Government prohibiting *foreigners*, whether located in Iraq or in Kuwait, from leaving the country and regarding them as 'guests', which in fact amounted to their being hostages. Although the obligations of Iraq under international law were not further elaborated it is quite clear that what is at issue here are obligations based on international humanitarian law and in particular Convention IV of 1949, Article 35 of which expressly concerns the right of aliens to leave the territory of the Parties to the conflict. Article 48 accords that right also to aliens in the occupied territories.

---

10   *Cf.*, SC Res. 664 of 18 August 1990 and SC Res. 666 of 13 September 1990.
11   Preamble, § 2.
12   Operative §§ 1-2.

This was stated more precisely only one month later in SC Resolution 666, operative paragraph 2 of which 'confirms that Iraq is fully responsible for the welfare of nationals of third countries according to international humanitarian law including, where applicable, the Fourth Convention of Geneva'.[13]

2.2   Protection of the Kuwaiti civilian population

It was on 25 September 1990, in SC Resolution 670, that the Security Council concerned itself with the fate of the Kuwaitis. The Council condemned the treatment of the Kuwaitis by the Iraqi armed forces, including the measures compelling them to leave the country and the mistreatment of persons and property. The Resolution here made reference to international law.[14] Why was there no reference here to international *humanitarian* law, as was done in Preamble paragraph 2 where Iraq was once again condemned for detaining foreigners against their will? This step was taken in operative paragraph 13 of the Resolution where the Security Council 'reaffirms that the Fourth Geneva Convention applies to Kuwait and that as a High Contracting Party to the Convention Iraq is bound to comply fully with all its terms ...'. The Council added immediately that Iraq, according to the Convention, is responsible for the 'grave breaches committed by it, as are individuals who commit or order the commission of grave breaches', a clear reference to Articles 146 and 147 of Convention IV.

This is confirmed again in SC Resolution 674, which was adopted after the Council had obtained fresh evidence of the actions undertaken by Iraq in occupied Kuwait, although a careful study of this Resolution once again creates the impression that the Council's principal concern was for the foreigners. These reprehensible Iraqi actions are summarized in the Preamble to the Resolution but in the operative part the Kuwaitis fare rather badly. Operative paragraph 1 requests that Iraq should desist from 'mistreating and oppressing Kuwaiti and third-State nationals and any other actions reported to the Security Council and described above ...', with a reference to Convention IV. Paragraph 5 demands that Iraq shall grant immediate 'access to food, water and basic services necessary to the protection and well-being of Kuwaiti nationals ...'.

---

13 See also Preamble, § 5.
14 Preamble, § 3.

2.3   Humanitarian circumstances

Let us return to SC Resolutions 661 and 666 which state *inter alia*: a) that food aid is permitted only in 'humanitarian circumstances', and b) that the existence of such circumstances is to be determined by the Security Council or its Sanctions Committee. Difficult problems exist here for humanitarian organizations such as the ICRC, and the association of national Red Cross societies, problems which are related to the following Resolutions of the Security Council.

It is laid down in SC Resolution 661 (paragraph 3,c), that States must prevent:

> 'the ... supply by their nationals or from their territories ... of any commodities or products ... but not including supplies intended strictly for medical purposes and, in humanitarian circumstances, foodstuffs, to any person or body in Iraq or Kuwait ...'.

SC Resolution 666 provides that what constitute 'humanitarian circumstances' can be determined only by the Security Council, and that the provision of permitted foodstuff supplies must be done through the United Nations, the ICRC or other appropriate humanitarian organizations.

The Resolutions concerning economic sanctions were adopted in the context of Article 41 of the UN Charter, which implies the existence of a breach of the peace or an act of aggression, that is, a situation in which international humanitarian law is applicable.

Geneva Convention IV contains a whole series of provisions concerning care for the population of occupied territories, in particular Articles 59 *et seq*. Article 59 provides that 'the Occupying Power shall agree to relief schemes ...' and that such activities may be undertaken by States or by impartial humanitarian organizations such as the ICRC and 'shall consist, in particular, of the provision or the consignment of foodstuffs, medical supplies and clothing'.

2.4   Is there room for humanitarian organizations?

The key question here is whether these provisions can be squared with the decisions of the Security Council whereby the existence of humanitarian circumstances is determined exclusively by the Council or by its Sanctions Committee. Do the decisions of the Council impose restrictions on humanitarian organizations such as the ICRC? It is the first time since 1949 and the Geneva Conventions that this question has been posed.

There is no easy answer to this question. Any answer must proceed from the important consideration that international humanitarian law is accepted as positive law in time of war (as was certainly the case from 2 August 1990) and that no departure therefrom by the parties to an armed conflict is permitted. International humanitarian law is *jus cogens* or mandatory law.

The UN Charter provides, in no less mandatory manner, that decisions of the Security Council are binding on all Member States. SC Resolution 661 addresses *all* States with the result that non-Member States, to the extent that they accept it, are also bound by the Resolution.

In this situation, the issue is to determine which of these legal norms has priority, and the frame of reference here is Article 103 of the Charter, which provides that obligations under the Charter have priority over obligations deriving from other international agreements.

SC Resolution 666 offers a way out. One may recall that this is the first Resolution in which the Security Council signifies its awareness of the role and significance of international humanitarian law. The central role of the Council and its Sanctions Committee in determining what constitutes 'humanitarian circumstances' permitting the supply of food is emphasized in this Resolution.

The Resolution shows that the Sanctions Committee, although exclusively competent to determine 'humanitarian circumstances'[15] nevertheless must rely on external information. Operative paragraph 3 provides that the Secretary-General of the UN must urgently and continuously gather information from, amongst others, 'appropriate humanitarian agencies and all other sources on the availability of food in Iraq and Kuwait' and that such information must be passed to the Sanctions Committee. The Security Council instructed the Sanctions Committee further that any deliveries of foodstuffs must take place through the agency of the United Nations in co-operation with the ICRC or other humanitarian bodies and must be distributed by them or under their supervision in order to ensure that the food reaches those persons for whom it is intended.[16]

By means of this process of co-operation among the Secretary-General, the organizations for humanitarian assistance, including the ICRC, and the Security Council, the provisions of the Fourth Convention concerning supply of foodstuffs in occupied territories can actually be implemented ... provided, naturally, that the occupying power permits it.

---

15 Preamble, § 4.
16 Operative § 6.

Whether such a reconcilable interpretation of the two texts referred to has actually been achieved will have to be judged in the light of the activities of the Sanctions Committee, work that is as yet not amenable to review, and of the information still lacking from the ICRC. Nonetheless, it is still very questionable whether the activities of the ICRC or other humanitarian bodies can be restricted by decisions of the Security Council and placed under its care and control.

The ICRC is exclusively a Swiss organization, and the Swiss Government is entitled to decide, upon answering the call by the Security Council to all States, that it does not wish to act to curtail the activities of the ICRC.

For the *national* Red Cross societies in the Member States of the UN it can be a very different situation. Here the question that must be posed is whether the decisions of the Security Council, and in particular SC Resolution 661, are binding not only for but also within these Member States. This requires an examination of national statutes and decrees implementing the Resolution and the Regulation of the Council of the European Communities.[17]

Article 3 of the Regulation provides that the prohibition on export does apply to 'any foodstuff intended for humanitarian purposes as part of emergency aid operations'. An identical provision appears in the *Netherlands* Sanctions Decision on trade, air and sea transport with Iraq and Kuwait 1990.[18] I have a number of thoughts on the question how this national and European legislation fits within SC Resolution 666 which refers every decision on humanitarian circumstances to the Security Council.

The Belgian implementation decrees, in particular the Ministerial Decree 90-1986 of 8 August 1990[19] provides in Article 2: 'the export to Iraq or Kuwait of any products from or originating in the European Community is subject to the issuance of a licence'. Here 'humanitarian circumstances' are not even mentioned. Rather it may be presumed that the Belgian and Netherlands Governments submit every request for permission to export foodstuffs for humanitarian purposes to the Sanctions Committee of the Security Council which, as provided in SC Resolution 666, shall work closely with the appropriate humanitarian organizations.

---

17 Regulation No. 2340/90.
18 *Sanctie-beschikking handelsverkeer, luchtvaart en scheepvaart Irak en Koeweit 1990.* *Staatscourant*, Friday 10 August 1990, at 4.
19 Belgian *Staatsblad*, 9 August 1990, 15539-15540.

It may be recalled that SC Resolution 661 did not subject the provision of medical supplies to the embargo, but SC Resolution 666 'strongly recommends' that such supplies should be exported 'under the strict supervision of the Government of the exporting State or by appropriate humanitarian agencies'. When the Belgian Red Cross sent a shipment of medicine to Baghdad in December 1990 the Sanctions Committee instructed the UN representative in Brussels to be present when the medicines were loaded on board.

SC Resolution 677, which charged the Secretary-General of the UN to take a copy of Kuwait's registers of births, deaths and marriages into safekeeping, was a condemnation by the Security Council of Iraq's attempt to alter the demographic composition of Kuwait. In a number of meetings of the Legal Advisers to the Security Council this practice was also branded a violation of the Fourth Convention, yet the Resolution contained no reference to international humanitarian law.

2.5   International humanitarian law after 15 January 1991

SC Resolution 678 permitted States after 15 January 1991 'to use all means to uphold and implement' all previous Resolutions of the Security Council. This implied the use of force, which has since occurred, and created an entirely new legal situation whose contours have not yet been clearly traced.

The Geneva Conventions also became applicable to the relationships between Iraq and the so-called 'coalition partners'. As of 20 January 1991 this problem was dramatically demonstrated when Iraqi television transmitted pictures of captured American, British and Italian pilots. The problem of the treatment of prisoners of war had already been acutely presented during the war between Iraq and Iran and, in the light of that experience, on 17 January 1991 I warned on Belgian radio and television of possible breaches of the Conventions and urged greater vigilance by the Security Council in respect of compliance with international obligations, thereby supporting the tasks undertaken by the ICRC.

The Third Geneva Convention Relative to the Treatment of Prisoners of War was clearly violated by Iraq when it paraded captured pilots through the streets of Baghdad and showed those scenes on television. This was a flagrant breach of Article 13 of the Convention which lays down that prisoners of war must be protected 'against insults and public curiosity'. The threat by Iraq to use prisoners of war as human shields at possible military targets was contrary to the provisions of Article 19 and 23 of the Convention which, on the one hand, provide for the evacuation of prisoners of war to camps situated in an area far enough away from the combat zone for them to be out of danger -'prisoners of war shall not be unnecessarily exposed to danger'- and, on the other, prohibit the use of the presence of prisoners of war to render certain objectives or areas immune from military operations. These provisions must naturally be related to other applicable provisions of the law of war which prohibit attacks on non-military objectives, the torture or other mistreatment of prisoners of war, etc. The proposition by Iraq that only some of the prisoners of war recognised by the enemy had a right to treatment in conformity with Convention III is likewise contrary to the clear provisions of Articles 4 and 5.

The ICRC has not neglected to draw attention to these provisions, as have also the Governments of the prisoners of war concerned. Their actions must be politically supported by appropriate condemnation by the Security Council which, in such manner and in furtherance of the twelve Resolutions which preceded military intervention based on SC Resolution 678, would thereby demonstrate that it also supports international humanitarian law.

There exist unmapped contours relating to the following problem: the continuation of the economic sanctions and the application of Protocol I of 1977. It was seen above that Article 41 of the UN Charter provides that economic sanctions may be imposed and the problems relating to the supply of food in humanitarian circumstances were examined: supervision by the UN Sanctions Committee in co-operation with the humanitarian organizations. What is the situation when the threshold of Article 41 has been crossed?

2.6   Economic sanctions

Are economic sanctions to be continued if military action commences? A negative answer would place the system provided for by the Charter in jeopardy. Military intervention as permitted by SC Resolution 678, even if, strictly speaking, it is not entirely on all fours with Article 42 and should rather be seen as a sort of Article 42(A), does not mean that economic sanctions cease, with all the consequences which were discussed above.

A new element exists in relation to prisoners of war when considering the application of Section V of Convention III which deals with 'Relations of prisoners of war with the exterior'. These are detailed provisions concerning the right to correspondence between prisoners of war and members of their families. But Article 72 of the Convention also provides that prisoners of war are entitled personally or collectively to receive parcels containing, in particular, foodstuffs and other things. The remaining articles lay down the procedures concerning such deliveries. It is not unimaginable that the detaining Government shall decline to permit such deliveries while food shipments, except in humanitarian circumstances, fall within the scope of the sanctions resolutions. The Security Council and/or its Sanctions Committee should have taken a decision on this in order to emphasize the applicability of international humanitarian law. Furthermore the Security Council should have adopted another Resolution in which the Resolutions concerning the economic and trade embargo would be adapted in the light of the specific humanitarian circumstances deriving from application of Convention III (and, in fact, of all the Geneva Conventions).

3.   CONCLUDING OBSERVATIONS

A final observation concerns the applicability of Additional Protocol I. The provisions of this Protocol contain a mixture of the Hague and the Geneva laws and refine the rules of the four Geneva Conventions in the light of more recent experience. The Parties to the present armed conflict have not ratified but only signed this Protocol which contains, *inter alia*, provisions on the protection of civilian objectives such as 'works or installations containing dangerous forces, namely dams, dykes and nuclear electrical generating stations' (Article 56). Another provision, Article 55, concerns the protection of the natural environment.

Here one may recall the provisions of the Vienna Convention 1969 on the Law of Treaties which expressly stipulates that the signatory to a treaty may not act in contravention of the aims of the treaty in the period between signing the treaty and its entry into force.

What is happening at present in the Gulf Conflict, including the attacks on oil and nuclear installations, by either side, does not square with the provisions of Protocol I. Here also the Security Council could have called on the parties to the conflict to remind them of their international obligations in the interests of mankind. These topics and issues addressed above lead to the following conclusions:

a) During the initial phase of the Gulf Conflict the Security Council, albeit tardily, recognized the importance of international humanitarian law;

b) It may be taken that the intervention by the humanitarian organizations, and in particular the ICRC, with the Members of the Council played its part in emphasizing the role of international law;

c) The Security Council must (and should have), under the continued impulse generated by the humanitarian organisations concerned, and with the actual support of the Members of the Council, including Belgium, ensure that international humanitarian law is respected in the Gulf conflict and thus provide the necessary backing for the activities of the ICRC and other humanitarian bodies and organisations.

DE LA GUERRE D'OCTOBRE 1973 AU CONFLIT DU GOLFE 1991: LES APPELS DU CICR POUR LA PROTECTION DE LA POPULATION CIVILE *

MICHEL VEUTHEY

1.   INTRODUCTION

La population civile est, aujourd'hui plus que jamais, la catégorie de personnes la plus menacée dans les conflits armés.[1]

Les Protocoles additionnels de 1977 aux Conventions de Genève du 12 août 1949, en codifiant de nombreuses règles coutumières relatives au respect de la population civile dans les conflits armés,[2] et en ajoutant de nouvelles limitations aux moyens de nuire à l'ennemi comme l'interdiction

---

*   Les opinions exprimées sont celles de l'auteur et ne représentent pas nécessairement la position officielle du CICR.

1   Voir, pour un exposé juridique sur les attaques aériennes de la Tripolitaine en 1911 au Vietnam en 1973, C. Rousseau, Le droit des conflits armés 354-367 (1983). Pour un exposé historique, voir S. Hartigan, Richard, The Forgotten Victim: A History of the Civilian (1982).

2   Particulièrement le Titre IV du Protocole I.

M. Veuthey

des représailles,[3] ont apporté une contribution remarquable au droit humanitaire contemporain,[4] dans le but d'ancrer dans le droit écrit des règles actualisées sur la protection des civils contre les hostilités.[5]

La valeur de ces dispositions humanitaires, qui a déjà été démontrée en 1973, alors qu'elles n'en étaient qu'à l'état de propositions du CICR, mérite d'être soulignée aujourd'hui: leur application entre Etats Parties à ces Protocoles, voire leur mise en vigueur par voie d'accords spéciaux, entre belligérants qui ne seraient pas tous encore Parties à ces Protocoles, ou tout simplement le rappel du caractère coutumier des principes qui sont à leur base, est d'une impérieuse actualité.

2.   L'APPEL D'OCTOBRE 1973

Le 6 octobre 1973, à deux heures du matin, l'Egypte et la Syrie attaquent Israël par surprise sur deux fronts. Les hostilités vont durer, pour l'essentiel, dix-huit jours, jusqu'au 24 octobre.[6] Les deux parties au conflit

---

3   Les représailles sont interdites dans plusieurs articles du Protocole I:
    Article 20 (Interdiction des représailles); Article 52 (Protection générale des biens de caractère civil); Article 53 (Protection des biens culturels et des lieux de culte); Article 54 (Protection des biens indispensables à la survie de la population civile); Article 55 (Protection de l'environnement naturel); Article 56 (Protection des ouvrages et installations contenant des forces dangereuses).
    Ces interdictions de représailles contre les personnes civiles et les biens de caractère civil sont d'autant plus importantes que, lors de la Seconde Guerre mondiale, les parties au conflit, alléguant qu'ils agissaient à titre de représailles, ont finalement pratiquement mené une guerre indiscriminée. Voir, CICR, Commentaire des Protocoles additionels du 8 juin 1977 aux Conventions de Genève du 12 août 1949, p. 596 (1986). Voir aussi F. Kalshoven, Belligerent Reprisals (1971).

4   Voir notamment à ce sujet F. Kalshoven, Constraints on the Waging of War 87-109 (1987); B. Graefrath, *Die Bedeutung des Ergänzungsprotokolls für den Schutz der Zivilbevölkerung* (L'importance du Protocole additionnel pour la protection de la population civile), dans C. Swinarski, réd., Etudes et essais sur le droit international humanitaire et sur les principes de la Croix-Rouge en l'honneur de Jean Pictet 169-179 (1984); L. Doswald-Beck, *The Value of the 1977 Geneva Protocols for the Protection of Civilians,* dans M.A. Meyer, réd., Armed Conflict and the New Law: Aspects of the 1977 Geneva Protocols and the 1981 Weapons Convention 137-172 (1989).

5   Jusqu'aux Protocoles additionnels de 1977, la protection de la population civile contre les hostilités ne faisait l'objet, en droit écrit, que de l'Article 23, alinéa 1, lettre g, et des Articles 25 à 28 du Règlement de La Haye de 1907 sur les lois et coutumes de la guerre sur terre interdisant d'attaquer des villes, des villages, des habitations et des bâtiments qui ne sont pas défendus, et respect de certains édifices voués à la science et à la charité; CICR, Commentaire des Protocoles de 1977, § 1827, p. 596, et des Articles 1 et 2 de la IXe Convention de La Haye de 1907 concernant le bombardement par des forces navales en temps de guerre.

6   Voir notamment J.R. Gainsborough, The Arab-Israeli Conflict 182 *et seq.* (1986).

lancent des attaques aériennes qui font des victimes civiles.[7] Dans la nuit du 8 au 9 octobre, à New York, le Conseil de sécurité des Nations Unies ajourne ses travaux sans avoir pu adopter une résolution demandant un cessez-le-feu.[8]

Le 9 octobre 1973, le CICR lançait un appel en faveur des populations civiles au Moyen-Orient:

'Le Comité international de la Croix-Rouge est extrêmement préoccupé par l'ampleur qu'a prise la guerre au Moyen-Orient, en particulier son extension à des zones urbaines peuplées. Cette évolution dramatique, qui lui a été confirmée par des informations contrôlées et qui se reflète dans les protestations que lui ont transmises diverses Parties au conflit, amène le CICR à réitérer les démarches pressantes qu'il a effectuées il y a 24 heures auprès des Gouvernements concernés pour que soient respectées les quatre Conventions de Genève de 1949. Il lance en outre un appel solennel pour qu'en toutes circonstances, les populations civiles soient épargnées par les belligérants.'[9]

Deux jours plus tard, le 11 octobre 1973, le CICR allait plus loin que cet appel général en faisant des propositions concrètes pour la sauvegarde des populations civiles au Moyen-Orient:

'Suite à son appel du 9 octobre 1973, et devant les nouvelles alarmantes qui lui parviennent au sujet du sort des populations civiles, le Comité international de la Croix-Rouge (CICR) vient de proposer à tous les belligérants, par l'intermédiaire de leurs Missions permanentes à Genève, de respecter d'ores et déjà les dispositions du Titre IV ('Populations civiles') du projet de Protocole additionnel aux quatre Conventions du 12

---

7 A. Decker, B. Nicolas, De la guerre du Yom Kippour à la Conférence de Genève 30, 40, 45 (1973). Decker et Nicolas citent ainsi des raids israéliens sur Damas, visant l'Etat-Major de l'Armée et la radio, mais qui atteignent des civils et même un hôpital; ils citent le fait que des sources israéliennes justifient ces bombardements comme représailles à des attaques par missiles sol-sol syriens sur des villages israéliens.

8 Decker, Nicolas, op. cit. n. 7, p. 40. Le Conseil de sécurité siègera encore deux fois avant d'ajourner ses séances jusqu'au 21 octobre. P. Rondot, Le Proche-Orient à la recherche de la paix. 1973-1982, p. 29 (1982). Rondot ajoute que la résolution 338 (1973), comme la résolution 339 (1973) ne seront pas suivies d'effet, et que ce n'est que la résolution 340 (1973) qui sera effectivement appliquée, car entérinant un accord américano-soviétique: 'Le Conseil de sécurité devient une chambre d'enregistrement, priée de transformer en hâte des accords secrets et bilatéraux en décisions publiques et multilatérales'. *Ibid.*, p. 27.

9 Appel rendu public par le communiqué de presse 1170 du 9 octobre 1973 et publié dans la Revue internationale de la Croix-Rouge de novembre 1973, p. 664, 667.

août 1949 relatif à la protection des victimes des conflits armés internationaux, en particulier les articles 46 ('Protection de la population civile'), 47 ('Protection générale des biens de caractère civil') et 50 ('Précautions dans l'attaque'), dont le texte est donné en annexe.

Le CICR, soucieux de contribuer à atténuer les souffrances engendrées par ce conflit, a demandé à toutes les Parties intéressées de se prononcer formellement et rapidement à l'égard de cette proposition. Il prendra acte des accords qui lui seront signifiés par les Parties à ce conflit et procédera aux notifications nécessaires.'[10]

Les trois projets d'articles[11] que le CICR proposait de mettre en vigueur etaient:
- le projet d'article 46, devenu l'Article 51 ('Protection de la population civile') du Protocole I, selon le Commentaire du Protocole I, édité par le CICR, 'l'un des plus importants du Protocole', qui 'confirme expressément la règle selon laquelle les civils inoffensifs doivent être tenus autant que possible en dehors des hostilités et bénéficier d'une protection générale contre les hostilités';[12]
- le projet d'article 47, devenu l'Article 52 ('Protection générale des biens de caractère civil');
- et le projet d'article 50, devenu l'Article 57 ('Précautions dans l'attaque').

3.   LES REPONSES DES BELLIGERANTS AU CICR

Les réponses à cet appel furent échelonnées dans le temps et, bien qu'en principe toutes positives, ont été nuancées dans leurs termes:
- la Syrie faisait connaître, le 12 octobre 1973, lendemain de l'appel du CICR, son acceptation totale des propositions du CICR, par l'intermédiaire de sa mission permanente à Genève.[13] Le CICR a pris note avec satisfaction de cette réponse et l'a transmise au Gouvernement d'Israël;
- l'Irak a accepté cette proposition du CICR le 13 octobre 1974. Le CICR, soulignant l'importance d'un accord rapide de toutes les parties

---

10 Ces propositions seront rendues publiques le même jour par un communiqué de presse 1171 du 11 octobre 1973.
11 Le texte de ces projets d'articles figure en annexe au communiqué de presse 1171 du CICR.
12 CICR, loc. cit. n. 5, § 1923, p. 629.
13 Réponse rendue publique par le communiqué de presse du CICR 1173 du 12 octobre 1973.

intéressées, fit savoir dans le même communiqué de presse qu'il attendait maintenant les réponses d'Israël et de l'Egypte;[14]
- l'Egypte, dont le Président Anouar al-Sadate avait, la veille, le 16 octobre 1973, menacé d'utiliser des fusées sol-sol,[15] a donné, le 17 octobre, une réponse positive sous condition de réciprocité de la part d'Israël. Dans le même communiqué de presse rendant publique la réponse égyptienne, le CICR lançait aussi un appel pour une réponse rapide d'Israël;[16]
- Israël fit connaître le 19 octobre 1973 sa réponse dans les termes suivants:

'En réponse à l'appel du CICR, le Gouvernement d'Israël déclare qu'il a strictement respecté et qu'il continuera à respecter les dispositions du droit international public qui interdisent les attaques contre les civils et les objectifs civils.'

Cette réponse fut, sur le moment, jugée insatisfaisante par le CICR, qui, dans son communiqué de presse 1176 du 20 octobre 1973, déclara:

'Le CICR considère que cette communication du Gouvernement d'Israël équivaut à une réponse négative à sa proposition. Le CICR le déplore d'autant plus vivement que son initiative visait justement à assurer aux populations civiles du Moyen-Orient une protection plus efficace que celle accordée par le droit international en vigueur, lequel, en cette matière dans sa forme écrite, date de 1907 et, par conséquent, n'est pas adapté aux conditions des guerres modernes.'

Le Gouvernement d'Israël, par l'intermédiaire de M. R. Kidron, Conseiller politique du Ministre des affaires étrangères, a complété sa réponse, le 1er novembre 1973, de la manière suivante:

'...[A]insi que vous le savez, à la suite des entretiens étendus que nous avons eus les 30 et 31 octobre, le Gouvernement d'Israël a été à la fois surpris et déçu de la réaction négative du CICR à sa déclaration. J'ai expliqué que la proposition du CICR avait été examinée à Jérusalem avec le plus grand sérieux et la plus grande attention, et que la déclaration reproduite ci-dessus a été formulée après une étude approfondie.

---

14 Communiqué de presse du CICR 1174 du 16 octobre 1973.
15 Rondot, op. cit. n. 8, p. 30.
16 Communiqué de presse 1175, du 20 octobre 1973.

(...).

Toutefois, afin de dissiper tous les doutes quant à son attitude en cette matière, j'ai reçu instruction de faire savoir que l'opinion du Gouvernement d'Israël est que la déclaration relative à sa position, communiquée au CICR le 19 octobre 1973, comprend les obligations découlant des articles 46, 47 et 50 du projet de protocole additionnel mentionnées dans la note du CICR du 11 octobre 1973 et qu'elle va bien au-delà, par le fait qu'elle englobe l'ensemble du droit international public, tant écrit que coutumier, relatif à la protection des civils et des objets civils contre les attaques lors de conflits armés internationaux.

(...).

J'espère que le CICR acceptera, dans l'esprit positif qui l'a inspirée, cette explication de l'attitude adoptée par mon Gouvernement, et qu'il en prendra acte dans le sens indiqué.'[17]

L'appel du CICR du 11 octobre 1973 sur la protection des populations civiles fut donc accepté par toutes les Parties à ce conflit.

4.   L'APPLICATION DES CONVENTIONS DE 1949

Dans le cadre du même conflit, le CICR avait, dès le début des hostilités, rappelé à toutes les Parties leurs obligations résultant des quatre Conventions de Genève de 1949[18] - une pratique qui est courante de la part du CICR lors de chaque conflit.

Le 23 octobre 1973, le CICR réaffirmait cet appel dans un communiqué se terminant ainsi:

'Le CICR a rappelé à plusieurs reprises à toutes les parties qu'elles se sont engagées, vis-à-vis de l'ensemble de la communauté internationale, à appliquer les Conventions de Genève sans réserve. Par conséquent, il déplore que des hommes blessés ou prisonniers soient privés de la protection et de l'assistance que leur accordent ces Conventions, lesquelles ne sont pas soumises à la condition de réciprocité et prohibent toute mesure de représailles à l'égard de personnes protégées.

(...).

En conséquence, le CICR a demandé aux belligérants de placer les principes d'humanité au-dessus de toutes autres considérations et de mettre

---

17 RICR, Novembre 1973, p. 667-668.
18 Ibid., p. 664.

en pratique sans restriction et sans tarder les engagements qu'ils ont pris pour le respect et la sauvegarde de la personne humaine.'[19]

Le 2 novembre 1973, le CICR apportait, dans un communiqué, la précision suivante:

'Devant diverses prises de position récentes des parties au conflit du Moyen-Orient, le CICR tient à rappeler que l'application des Conventions de Genève n'est pas soumise à la condition de réciprocité. En effet, elles visent à la protection des droits fondamentaux des personnes protégées civiles et militaires.'[20]

Quelques jours plus tard, le CICR lançait un nouveau communiqué, faisant l'inventaire des demandes adressées à l'Egypte, à Israël et à la Syrie pour l'application inconditionnelle des Conventions de Genève de 1949.[21]

Le 15 novembre, le CICR signalait le début, puis la fin des rapatriements des prisonniers de guerre entre l'Egypte et Israël.

Enfin, le 12 décembre 1973, pour faire face aux graves accusations que l'Egypte, Israël et la Syrie ont porté les uns à l'égard des autres quant à des violations des Conventions de 1949, le CICR proposait la création de Commissions d'enquête au Moyen-Orient:

'Le CICR, dans une note identique remise en date du 12 décembre aux trois Gouvernements intéressés, se déclare disposé à prêter ses bons offices pour établir, sous ses auspices ou sous ceux d'une autre autorité agréée par les parties, une procédure ad hoc prévoyant la création de commissions bipartites chargées d'enquêter sur les cas de violations alléguées. Le mandat de ces commissions consisterait à établir la matérialité des faits de violations alléguées ou à préciser l'interprétation d'une disposition des Conventions sur laquelle les Parties seraient en désaccord. Les conclusions auxquelles aboutiraient les commissions seraient communiquées aux Gouvernements intéressés.
(...).
Chaque commission serait constituée de trois membres, dont deux désignés par chacune des Parties intéressées; le troisième membre serait une personnalité ressortissante d'un pays neutre à désigner par le CICR ou par toute autre instance agréée par les Parties. Au cas où le CICR serait appelé

---

19 Communiqué de presse 1180, du 23 octobre 1973.
20 Communiqué de presse 1181, du 2 novembre 1973.
21 Communiqué de presse 1182.

à choisir cette personnalité, ce serait, conformément à sa pratique et à sa doctrine, une personne en dehors de son sein. En effet, le CICR ne procède pas lui-même à des enquêtes, car cela sort de sa mission telle que prévue par les Conventions de Genève.'[22]

A relever que l'Article 90 ('Commission internationale d'établissement des faits') du Protocole I reprend cette idée, qui correspond à la position du CICR: le CICR ne se considère en effet pas comme un organisme d'enquête publiant ses constatations et rapportant sur les violations.[23]

Cette Commission internationale d'établissement des faits devrait être établie en 1991, vu que les 20 Hautes Parties contractantes au Protocole I nécessaires à sa constitution en ont accepté la compétence.[24]

5.   L'IMPACT DE L'APPEL DU CICR DE 1973

Ces démarches publiques du CICR ont certainement eu plusieurs conséquences:
- des conséquences immédiates, en mettant chaque Partie au conflit publiquement devant ses responsabilités (ces démarches publiques ayant été précédées de notifications discrètes à chaque Partie, par la voie diplomatique à Genève et par les délégations du CICR dans les capitales);
- à plus long terme, en contribuant à réaffirmer la valeur des Conventions de Genève de 1949 et du caractère absolu, non soumis à réciprocité, de leurs obligations;
- en mettant enfin en vigueur ponctuellement, en recueillant l'accord des Parties au conflit, trois dispositions essentielles des projets de Protocoles additionnels sur un point fondamental, non couvert par les Conventions du 12 août 1949, la protection des populations civiles contre les hostilités;
- en montrant l'interdépendance entre le respect des diverses parties du droit humanitaire, dont les Protocoles additionnels de 1977 ont marqué

---

22 Communiqué de presse du CICR 1189 du 13 décembre 1973.
23 Voir le Commentaire des Protocoles du CICR, loc. cit. n. 5, § 3602, p. 1064; et, pour la position officielle du CICR, *Les démarches du CICR en cas de violations du droit international humanitaire*, RICR 79-86 (1981).
24 Sur les mécanismes d'enquête des Conventions de 1949 et sur l'Article 90 du Protocole I, voir notamment l'étude de S. Ihrai, *Les mécanismes d'établissement des faits dans les Conventions de Genève de 1949 et dans le Protocole I de 1977,* dans F. Kalshoven, Y. Sandoz, réd., Mise en oeuvre du droit international humanitaire 153-168 (1989).

l'intégration effective, entre 'droit de Genève', protecteur des victimes hors de combat, et 'droit de La Haye', régulateur des méthodes et moyens de combat.

6. AUTRES APPELS ULTERIEURS DU CICR EN FAVEUR DES CIVILS

Le CICR a, dans son histoire récente, lancé plusieurs appels publics pour l'application des règles et principes humanitaires en faveur des civils, dont:
- deux appels dans le conflit Rhodésie/Zimbabwe, le premier le 14 janvier 1977, le second le 19 mars 1979;[25]
- quatre appels pour la population civile au Liban en 1982;[26]
- trois appels dans le conflit Iraq/Iran, le premier le 7 mai 1983, le deuxième le 15 octobre 1983, le troisième le 10 février 1984, tous trois

---

25 Communiqué de presse du CICR 1288 du 28 janvier 1977, Rapport annuel du CICR 1979, p. 13-14. Ce second appel, à la différence de la plupart des autres, n'avait pas fait l'objet d'un communiqué de presse. Le CICR lui a néammoins donné une large publicité: outre les principaux intéressés, à savoir les Autorités de Salisbury, la ZANU et la ZAPU, l'appel a été adressé aux pays de 'première ligne' (Angola, Botswana, Mozambique, Tanzanie et Zambie), dont plusieurs se déclarèrent prêts à soutenir les efforts du CICR. L'appel a également été transmis au Secrétaire général des Nations Unies, qui lui a accordé son appui dans une déclaration publique, au Président du Conseil de sécurité des Nations Unies et au Secrétaire général de l'OUA, ainsi qu'aux 145 Etats alors Parties aux Conventions de Genève de 1949, dont le Royaume-Uni. Enfin, le Président du CICR en avait fait l'objet d'une conférence de presse à Genève le 20 mars 1979.

26 Communiqué de presse 1444 du 11 juin 1982; Communiqué de presse 1446 du 4 juillet 1982: 'Le CICR renouvelle son appel du 9 juin en raison du climat de tension qui règne à Beyrouth et risque à tout moment de causer des souffrances répétées et intolérables à de nombreux civils, femmes et enfants notamment. Le CICR exprime sa profonde préoccupation devant la situation au Liban, en particulier à Beyrouth.

En conséquence, le CICR, en vertu de son devoir humanitaire et du mandat qui lui est conféré par le droit international humanitaire, adresse un appel solennel à toutes les parties au conflit du Liban et aux autorités concernées, afin qu'elles garantissent que nulle souffrance supplémentaire ne sera infligée à la population civile de Beyrouth et prennent immédiatement les mesures nécessaires en vue de garantir la sécurité et la protection des civils, particulièrement des femmes et des enfants.'

Le 27 juillet 1982, dans son communiqué de presse 1447, le CICR terminait son appel par ce paragraphe sur les civils:

'Vivement préoccupé par cette atteinte à l'emblème protecteur de la croix rouge, le CICR rappelle à toutes les parties au conflit l'obligation absolue qu'elles ont de respecter toutes les installations et le personnel sanitaires dument signalisés et d'épargner les populations civiles ne prenant aucune part aux combats.'

Le quatrième appel surviendra après les massacres de Sabra et Chatila, dans le communiqué de presse 1450, du 18 septembre 1982.

rendus publics quelques jours après avoir été remis aux parties au conflit et à l'ensemble des Etats Parties aux Conventions de Genève de 1949;[27]
- un appel pour le Sud-Soudan, le 19 septembre 1986.[28]

Dans aucun de ces appels, le CICR n'a mentionné les Protocoles additionnels de 1977, vu qu'aucune des Parties à ces conflits n'étaient liées par ces instruments.

7.   LE CONFLIT DU GOLFE (2 AOUT 1990 - 28 FEVRIER 1991)

L'appel du CICR d'octobre 1973 reste toujours d'actualité, et dans la même région du monde en particulier, où les Parties à deux conflits, le conflit israélo-palestinien et la crise du Golfe (Irak/Koweït) démontrent ce double besoin:
- d'une application fidèle des Conventions de Genève du 12 août 1949, notamment pour ce qui est du traitement des prisonniers de guerre (Troisième Convention) et des personnes civiles dans des territoires occupés (Quatrième Convention);
- du respect du droit -coutumier et écrit- sur la protection des populations civiles contre les hostilités.

Depuis 1973, les deux Protocoles additionnels aux Conventions de Genève du 12 août 1949 ont été adoptés à Genève le 8 juin 1977. Plus de cent Etats ont ratifié le Protocole I, relatif à la protection des victimes des conflits armés internationaux. Plusieurs Etats engagés dans cette crise du Moyen-Orient depuis l'intervention irakienne au Koweït le 2 août 1990, sont formellement liés par cet instrument du droit international humanitaire (ainsi l'Arabie séoudite, le Bahrein, les Emirats arabes unis, la Jordanie, le Koweït, Oman, Qatar, la Syrie, sans parler de l'Algérie, de l'Allemagne,

---

27 Communiqués de presse du CICR 1462 du 11 mai 1983, 1480 du 15 février 1984. Le 15 octobre 1983, dans son communiqué 1479, le CICR faisait un appel aux belligérants pour qu'ils cessent leurs attaques contre les civils.

28 Communiqué de presse 1522, dans lequel le CICR déclarait notamment:

'Le CICR tient à exprimer son extrême préoccupation quant au sort des populations civiles affectées par les opérations militaires au Sud-Soudan, qu'elles se trouvent dans certaines villes actuellement totalement isolées ou dans les campagnes. Les règles et l'esprit du droit international humanitaire, et notamment le principe fondamental d'Humanité, imposent aux belligérants d'épargner les non-combattants et de tout mettre en oeuvre pour leur assurer les moyens essentiels à leur survie.

Le CICR en appelle donc solennellement au parties concernées afin qu'elles lui accordent toutes les garanties de sécurité et facilités nécessaires à l'accomplissement de sa mission en faveur des victimes de la situation conflictuelle.'

de la Belgique, du Danemark, de l'Italie, des Pays-Bas, de l'Union Soviétique et du Yémen).

En revanche, ni les Etats-Unis, ni la France ni le Royaume-Uni, ni Israël, ni l'Irak n'ont ratifié ce Protocole I.

Toutefois, les Etats-Unis, qui, comme Israël, ont fait savoir qu'ils ne ratifieraient pas le Protocole I, ont laissé officieusement entendre qu'ils en respecteraient toutes les dispositions qui ont un caractère coutumier.

La question reste donc de savoir si et quand le CICR aurait pu lancer un appel similaire à celui du 11 octobre 1973 dans le cadre de cette nouvelle crise qui a frappé le Moyen-Orient depuis le 2 août 1990.

La nécessité d'obtenir un accord clair des Parties sur des dispositions précises relative à la protection des personnes civiles contre les hostilités semble évidente.

L'existence de textes de droit positif devrait faciliter, espérons-le, l'acceptation d'un éventuel nouvel appel du CICR, dont l'opportunité politique devrait être jugée selon le développement de la crise: lançant son appel trop tôt, le CICR apparaîtrait comme alarmiste; trop tardif, l'appel interviendrait au moment où l'irréparable aurait déjà pu être commis, et le cycle des représailles entamé. C'est ainsi que le CICR a envisagé un appel à toutes les Parties engagées dans la crise du Moyen-Orient, demandant à toutes les Parties de respecter les dispositions suivantes du Protocole additionnel I de 1977, qui correspondent aux projets d'articles dont le CICR avait proposé l'application en 1973: l'Article 48 ('Règle fondamentale'); l'Article 51 ('Protection de la population civile'); l'Article 52 ('Protection générale des biens de caractère civil'); l'Article 57 ('Précautions dans l'attaque'); les Articles 53 ('Protection des biens culturels et des lieux de culte'), 54 ('Protection des biens indispensables à la survie de la population civile'), 55 ('Protection de l'environnement naturel'), 56 ('Protection des ouvrages et installations contenant des forces dangereuses').

En décembre 1990 et janvier 1991, le CICR a soulevé ces questions en s'adressant aux parties à ce conflit du Moyen-Orient d'une manière analogue mais pas similaire à celle de l'appel d'octobre 1973.

Le CICR a déclaré les quatre Conventions de Genève de 1949 applicables dès le 2 août 1990, date de l'entrée au Koweït des troupes irakiennes[29].

---

29 Communiqué de presse du CICR 1640 du 2 août 1990. Une note verbale pour transmission aux Ministères des Affaires étrangères avait été remise auparavant aux Missions permanentes de l'Irak et du Koweït à Genève rappelant l'applicabilité des Conventions de 1949, l'obligation des Parties au conflit de prendre les mesures nécessaires de mise en oeuvre et en particulier de

Le CICR a remis, début décembre 1990, à un certain nombre de Gouvernements directement impliqués dans la crise, un Mémorandum sur l'applicabilité du droit international humanitaire dans la région du Golfe[30] mentionnant les quatre Conventions de 1949, les règles contenues dans les Conventions de La Haye de 1899 et 1907, en soulignant le fait que la plupart de ces règles ont acquis une valeur coutumière. Le CICR relevait aussi que ces règles ont été réaffirmées et, pour certaines, développées, dans le Protocole I de 1977. Sans faire de référence explicite aux dispositions mentionnées plus haut du Protocole I, le CICR rappelait dans ce Mémorandum certaines 'règles générales reconnues obligatoires pour toute Partie à un conflit armé' en particulier sur la protection de la population civile[31] et sur l'usage d'armes particulières;[32] y compris les armes de destruction massive:

'Par ailleurs, le CICR rappelle que l'usage d'armes, en particulier d'armes de destruction massive, est subordonné au respect des règles générales du droit international humanitaire et en particulier du principe fondamental de

---

laisser le CICR remplir son mandat humanitaire en vertu de ces Conventions.
30 En date du 3 décembre 1990, ce Mémorandum comportait cinq parties: I. Protection des personnes ne participant pas ou plus aux hostilités; II. Conduite des hostilités; III. Respect de l'emblème et de la mission médicale; IV. Diffusion du droit international humanitaire; V. Action du CICR et obligation des Etats.
31 Relevons les deux paragraphes suivants de ce Mémorandum du CICR du 3 décembre 1990:
'- Une distinction doit être faite en toutes circonstances entre les combattants et objectifs militaires, d'une part, et les personnes et biens civils d'autre part. Il est interdit de diriger des attaques contre des personnes ou biens civils ou de procéder à des attaques indiscriminées.
- Toutes les précautions pratiquement possibles seront prises pour éviter des pertes ou dommages à la population ou aux biens civils et l'on renoncera aux attaques dont on peut prévoir qu'elles causeront incidemment des pertes en vies humaines ou des dommages qui seraient excessifs par rapport à l'avantage militaire concret et direct attendu'.
32 Le Mémorandum du CICR rappelait les règles suivantes: Interdiction de l'emploi de gaz asphyxiants, toxiques ou similaires et de moyens bactériologiques (Protocole de Genève de 1925); Interdiction de la mise au point, de la fabrication et du stockage des armes bactériologiques (biologiques) ou à toxines (Convention de 1972); Interdiction de l'emploi de balles qui s'épanouissent ou s'aplatissent facilement dans le corps humain (comme par exemple les balles dum dum (Déclaration de La Haye de 1899); Interdiction de certains projectiles explosifs (Déclaration de Saint-Pétersbourg de 1868); Limitation de l'emploi de mines maritimes (Convention de La Haye de 1907); Interdiction ou limitation de l'emploi de certaines armes classiques qui peuvent être considérées comme produisant des effets traumatiques excessifs ou comme frappant sans discrimination (Convention de 1980, avec ses Protocoles I (relatifs aux éclats non localisables), II (sur l'interdiction ou la limitation de l'emploi de mines, pièges et autres dispositifs) et III (sur l'interdiction ou la limitation de l'emploi des armes incendiaires)).

la distinction entre combattants et civils et de l'immunité de la population civile.'

Le CICR terminait cette partie de son Mémorandum du 3 décembre 1990 par une invitation aux Etats non Parties au Protocole I à en respecter certaines dispositions:

> 'Le CICR invite les Etats non Parties au Protocole I de 1977 à respecter, en cas de conflit armé, les articles suivants de ce Protocole qui découlent du principe fondamental de l'immunité de la population civile:
> - Article 54: Protection des biens indispensables à la survie de la population civile;
> - Article 55: Protection de l'environnement naturel;
> - Article 56: Protection des ouvrages et installations contenant des forces dangereuses.'

A noter que cette invitation du CICR à ces Etats non Parties au Protocole I d'en respecter certaines dispositions ne demandait pas de réponse formelle, à la différence de l'appel d'octobre 1973: le CICR était bien conscient de la position très réservée de certaines Parties à ce conflit -en particulier les Etats-Unis et la France- à l'égard d'un engagement formel de respecter des dispositions de ce Protocole I. Il n'en a pas moins fait référence à des règles qu'il estimait coutumières[33] ou du moins essentielles à la protection de la population civile dans ce conflit.

Le 17 janvier 1991, avec le commencement des hostilités aériennes de la part de la coalition, le CICR rappelait à toutes les Parties au conflit leurs engagements en vertu des Conventions de Genève de 1949, mettant notamment l'accent sur la protection de la population civile:

> 'Un tel engagement de la part des Etats impliqués est particulièrement requis et attendu dans un contexte où des développements dramatiques pour la popultion civile peuvent être redoutés; en effet, les hostilités se déroulent dans un environnement rendant très périlleuse une réelle protection des civils exposés aux actes de guerre.

---

33 Relevons ainsi ce passage d'un document rédigé par la Division juridique du CICR, mis au point à l'attention des Sociétés nationales de la Croix-Rouge et du Croissant-Rouge (analyse provisoire des aspects juridiques relatifs au conflit du Golfe (qui) ne devrait pas être considérée comme la position officielle du CICR):
'L'Irak, les Etats-Unis, la Grande-Bretagne et la France n'ont pas ratifié le Protocole I additionnel aux Conventions de Genève du 12 août 1949; en conséquence, les dispositions de ce Protocole ne sont pas obligatoires, à moins qu'elles ne codifient des lois coutumières.'

Compte tenu des circonstances, le CICR a insité auprès des Etats impliqués, dans une note verbale remise ce jour,[34] sur l'absolue nécessité de prendre la conduite des hostilités, toutes les précautions visant à épargner les populations civiles.

(...).

De plus, le CICR réitère aux Parties l'interdiction, réglée par le droit international humanitaire, d'utiliser des armes chimiques et bactériologiques et leur enjoint de ne pas avoir recours à l'arme atomique, incompatible avec ce droit. De manière générale, les armes de destruction massive frappant sans discrimination causent des ravages irréparables au sein de la population civile, qui doit être tenue à l'écart des combats.'[35]

Le 1er février 1991,[36] le Président du CICR lançait un appel préventif pour l'application du droit humanitaire aux victimes civiles et militaires du conflit au Moyen-Orient;

Le 18 février 1991, devant l'imminence d'une attaque terrestre alliée, le CICR lançait un appel à toutes les Puissances concernées[37] pour exprimer sa préoccupation devant le sort de la population civile enfermée au Koweït, rappeler une nouvelle fois aux Etats leurs responsabilités et obligations en matière de protection des civils, en faisant mention des Conventions de La Haye de 1899 et de 1907, des Conventions de Genève de 1949 comme de leur Protocole I additionnel de 1977, et rappelant que le CICR était prêt à offrir ses services pour faciliter la mise en oeuvre du droit international humanitaire visant à protéger les civils contre les effets des hostilités. Le CICR ajoutait qu'il était, en tant qu'intermédiaire neutre, disposé à faciliter les négociations visant à créer des zones sanitaires ou des zones neutralisées, à faciliter l'évacuation de civils d'une zone dangereuse vers une zone protégée, à faciliter l'acheminement de secours pour la population civile en général et pour celle pouvant se trouver dans les zones

---

34 Cette note a été remise le matin du jeudi 17 janvier 1991 aux Missions permanentes à Genève et à New York des pays suivants: Arabie saoudite, Argentine, Australie, Bahrein, Belgique, Bangladesh, Canada, Danemark, Egypte, Emirats Arabes Unis, Espagne, Etats-Unis, France, Grèce, Irak, Italie, Koweït, Maroc, Niger, Norvège, Oman, Pakistan, Pays-Bas, Qatar, Royaume-Uni, Sénégal, Syrie.

35 Communiqué de presse du CICR 1658 du 17 janvier 1991.

36 Communiqué de presse 1659. Cet appel, traduit notamment en arabe, anglais, allemand et espagnol, a été volontairement rédigé de manière générale et non juridique pour avoir une dimension morale.

37 Cette terminologie de 'Puissances concernées', qui comporte la liste des Etats mentionnés plus haut en note 34, répondait à la susceptibilité exprimée par certains Gouvernements de ne pas apparaître comme Parties à ce conflit devant leur propre opinion publique, même si ces mêmes Gouvernements avaient envoyé des troupes en Arabie saoudite.

protégées. Cette démarche s'effectuait à nouveau en deux temps: remise d'une note verbale détaillée, avec une Annexe énumérant les règles de base -extraites ou paraphrasées des Articles 48, 51, 57 et 58 du Protocole I, sans qu'il ne soit fait mention explicite du Protocole I- protégeant les personnes et les biens civils contre les effets des hostilités,[38] aux Missions permanentes à Genève de ces Etats engagés dans ce conflit pour

---

38 Cette Annexe mentionnait le Protocole I et, sans mentionner ses Articles spécifiquement, énumérait plusieurs 'règles générales considérées comme obligatoires pour toute Partie à un conflit armé international' (les citations des Articles correspondants du Protocole I ne figurent pas dans le texte de cette Annexe et sont ici ajoutées par l'auteur à titre indicatif et comparatif):
'- une distinction doit être faite en toute circonstance entre les combattants et objectifs militaires, d'une part, et les personnes et biens civils, d'autre part. Il est interdit de diriger des attaques contre des personnes ou biens civils ou de procéder à des attaques indiscriminées; [paraphrase de l'Article 48]
- les attaques dirigées à titre de représailles contre la population ou les personnes civiles sont interdites; [Article 51, (6)]
- sont interdits les actes ou menaces de violence dont le but principal est de répandre la terreur parmi la population civile; [Article 51, (2)]
- toutes les précautions pratiquement possibles seront prises pour éviter des pertes ou dommages à la population ou aux biens civils et l'on renoncera aux attaques dont on peut prévoir qu'elles causeront incidemment des pertes en vies humaines ou des dommages qui seraient excessifs par rapport à l'avantage militaire concret et direct attendu; [Article 51, (5, b)]
- lorsque le choix est possible entre plusieurs objectifs militaires pour obtenir un avantage militaire équivalent, ce choix doit porter sur l'objectif dont on peut penser que l'attaque présente le moins de danger pour les personnes civiles ou pour les biens de caractère civil; [Article 57, (3)]
- dans le cas d'attaques pouvant affecter la population civile, un avertissement doit être donné en temps utile et par des moyens efficaces, à moins que les circonstances ne le permettent pas; [Article 57, (2, c)]
- les parties au conflit éviteront de placer des objectifs militaires à l'intérieur de cités ou d'autres zones fortement peuplées; [Article 58, (b)]
- la population civile et les personnes civiles ne doivent pas être utilisées ou, le cas échéant, déplacées pour mettre des objectifs militaires à l'abri des attaques;[Article 51, (7)]
- au contraire, les parties au conflit feront tout ce qui est pratiquement possible pour éloigner ou évacuer la population et les personnes civiles des objectifs militaires et des zones où se déroulent les combats; [Paraphrase de l'Article 58, (a)]
- les parties au conflit prendront toutes autres précautions nécessaires pour protéger la population, les personnes et les biens civils; [Paraphrase de l'Article 51, (1)]
- les biens culturels, notamment les monuments historiques et les lieux de culte qui constituent le patrimoine culturel ou spirituel des peuples bénéficient d'une protection spéciale contre tout acte d'hostilité. Il est prohibé d'utiliser ces biens à l'appui de l'effort militaire. [Paraphrase de l'Article 53].'
A relever à ce sujet que l'UNESCO a fait, en 1991, quatre déclarations sur la protection des biens culturels dans ce conflit: une le 7 janvier, une le 14 janvier, une le 7 février, une enfin le 13 février 1991.

transmission à leurs Ministères des Affaires étrangères dans les capitales et publication d'une brève communication à la presse reprenant l'essentiel de cette démarche auprès des Gouvernements;[39]

Enfin, le 24 février 1991, jour du déclenchement de l'offensive terrestre alliée, le CICR lançait un nouvel appel, aussitôt rendu public par un communiqué de presse.[40]

8.   CONCLUSION

D'octobre 1973 à février 1991, le CICR a ainsi poursuivi ses appels en faveur de la population civile. En 1973, le CICR, se fondant sur des projets d'articles des projets de protocoles, avait obtenu un accord formel des Parties en conflit; en 1991, les Protocoles additionnels de 1977 en vigueur, le CICR procède de manière plus informelle; il en rappelle l'applicabilité aux Etats qui les ont ratifiés; ne voulant pas s'attirer une réponse négative des belligérants qui ne les ont pas ratifiés, il ne leur

---

39 Communication à la presse 91/10 du 18 février 1991.
40 Communiqué de presse 1661 du 24 février 1991, dont voici le texte intégral:
    'Genève (CICR) - Le CICR lance aujourd'hui, au nom de toutes les victimes civiles et militaires, un nouvel appel à tous les belligérants pour que les dispositions prévues par le Droit international humanitaire soient entièrement respectées et appliquées.
    Dans les combats terrestres qui font rage depuis plusieurs heures au Moyen-Orient, le nombre des soldats tués ou blessés et de combattants tombés en mains ennemies s'accroît rapidement. Face à l'intensité toujours croissante des hostilités en cours et aux effets dévastateurs qu'elles ont sur la population civile, le CICR se doit de rappeler aux Etats Parties au conflit leurs responsabilités et obligations en matière de protection de toutes les victimes - militaires et civiles.
    Les soldats blessés, malades ou naufragés -à quelque partie qu'ils appartiennent- doivent être recueillis, respectés et protégés en toutes circonstances.
    Les soldats qui se rendent doivent être épargnés. Ils ont droit au respect des belligérants et seront traités avec humanité. En outre, ils seront évacués du front et éloignés des combats vers un lieu où leur sécurité pourra être garantie.
    Toutes les précautions doivent être prises pour épargner les populations civiles. Les Parties au conflit doivent prendre des mesures pratiques en vue de protéger la population civile contre les effets des combats. Les belligérants sont invités à conclure des accords en vue d'établir des zones neutralisées. Si les combats risquent d'affecter la population civile, les Parties au conflit doivent permettre l'évacuation des non-combattants et surtout des catégories de personnes particulièrement vulnérables, telles que les blessés, les malades, les enfants et les personnes âgées. Finalement, les Parties au conflit doivent permettre l'acheminement des biens essentiels à la survie de la population civile.
    Conformément à son mandat, le CICR, en tant qu'intermédiaire neutre, renouvelle ses offres de services pour faciliter la mise en oeuvre de ces dispositions visant à protéger les victimes civiles et militaires.'

adresse pas, comme il l'avait fait en 1973, un appel formel pour leur demander de s'engager à respecter certaines dispositions de ce Protocole I: par des démarches discrètes, qui ne trouvent qu'un écho limité dans ses prises de position publiques, le CICR réaffirme le caractère coutumier de certaines dispositions de ces Protocoles additionnels.

D'un fil ténu entre des belligérants, certaines dispositions essentielles des Protocoles sur la protection de la population civile sont ainsi devenues des points d'ancrage fondamentaux du droit internationale humanitaire universel.

Il n'en reste pas moins que la ratification des deux Protocoles tant par les Puissances de la coalition que par l'Irak aurait très certainement rendu plus claires les obligations de toutes les parties à ce conflit pour la protection de la population civile. Cette leçon mérite d'être retenue pour une protection efficace des populations civiles dans d'autres conflits en cours ou à venir.

REPORTING MECHANISM FOR SUPERVISION OF NATIONAL LEGISLATION IMPLEMENTING INTERNATIONAL HUMANITARIAN LAW

KRZYSZTOF DRZEWICKI

1.   INTRODUCTION

This paper tends to address an issue of reporting mechanism for supervision of the implementation of international humanitarian law in its national legislative dimension. However, for the pragmatic achievement of this objective it seems indispensable to approach the whole issue of reporting mechanism from a view-point that has more to do with its 'operationalization' than a theoretical discussion of legal niceties.

It is both an appropriate place and time to do so in a collection of essays in honour of Professor Kalshoven who contributed so invaluably in his scholarly and promotional activity to the cause of both development and implementation of international humanitarian law. His exceptionally competent and pragmatic way of dealing with humanitarian law stems largely from a unique combination of military experience and a comprehensive and thorough legal expertise.

More specifically, it is an appropriate place to examine the issue in this collection of essays, since Professor Kalshoven was essentially behind my research project on a supervisory mechanism for national legislative implementation of international humanitarian law and also became a main driving force behind promotional endeavours to put the project's conclusions into operation.[1] After the completion of my research project, which also included a draft resolution for the International Conference of the Red Cross, I approached the Netherlands Red Cross and the Norwegian Red Cross Societies with a request to submit and formally sponsor this draft resolution. The idea was to give promotional momentum to conclusions of the research project as an individual private initiative and to submit it to an official standard-setting process.[2] Both National Red Cross Societies accepted the idea and decided to present the Explanatory Memorandum with the draft resolution to the XXV International Conference of the Red Cross which took place in Geneva from 23 to 31 October 1986.

At the International Conference, the Dutch-Norwegian draft was considered together with a draft resolution on the same subject submitted by the International Committee of the Red Cross.[3] Both drafts were transmitted to Commission I dealing with international humanitarian law which established a small working group with the task of attempting to merge both drafts. The working group recognized the Dutch-Norwegian text as going further and hence took it as the point of departure. Following suggestions put forward by experts of the Netherlands Red Cross (Professor Kalshoven) and of the Norwegian Red Cross (Trosdahl Oraug), certain elements of the ICRC's draft were adapted to the Dutch-Norwegian

---

1   It was in 1986 when, as a participant of the Centre for Studies and Research in International Law and International Relations of the Hague Academy of International Law, I was able to conduct my research project within a study group under the directorship of Professor Kalshoven. He accepted tolerantly though not uncritically my concept of establishing a reporting procedure for national implementation of international humanitarian law. His thought-provoking remarks helped me to improve significantly the final outcome of my research. For the final version of the research project see K. Drzewicki, *National Legislation as a Measure for Implementation of International Humanitarian Law*, in F. Kalshoven, Y. Sandoz, eds., Implementation of International Humanitarian Law. Research Papers by participants in the 1986 Session of the Centre for Studies and Research in International Law and International Relations of the Hague Academy of International Law 109-131 (1989).
2   For those promotional needs I drafted an 'Explanatory Memorandum to the Draft Resolution of the XXV International Conference of the Red Cross on National Implementation of Humanitarian Law' which constituted a reflection of final conclusions of the research project.
3   Respect for International Humanitarian Law. National Measures to Implement the Geneva Conventions and their Additional Protocols in Peacetime. ICRC, Doc. C.1/2.4/2 (1986).

version. This solution caused the ICRC to accept and co-sponsor the Dutch-Norwegian draft resolution. Co-sponsorship of the draft was also undertaken by the Red Cross of Yugoslavia and the Egyptian Governmental delegation. Finally, the draft resolution was adopted in Commission I by consensus and transmitted to the plenary session of the Conference which adopted it as Resolution V on 31 October, also by consensus.[4]

As mentioned above, it is not only an appropriate place but also an appropriate time to attempt a further examination of a modest reporting mechanism instituted by virtue of Resolution V for supervising the national legislation implementing humanitarian law. The time is ripe to do so, since the first reporting cycle is approaching its completion and the next International Conference of the Red Cross and Red Crescent scheduled for December 1991 is to assess results and potential improvements of the whole procedure. It is thus extremely desirable to discuss substantive and procedural issues of the reporting mechanism well in advance so to identify its imperfections and failures, and to suggest feasible improvements for its more viable operation in the future.

2. REPORTING EXPERIENCE AND HUMANITARIAN LAW

With the adoption by the XXV International Conference of the Red Cross (Geneva, 31 October 1986) of Resolution V on 'National Measures to Implement International Humanitarian Law' a fundamental breakthrough was achieved for the potential strengthening of the national legislative dimension of implementation of international humanitarian law. Its significance cannot be overlooked and its 'dormant' potentials should not be underestimated. This appears to be so because under Resolution V the ICRC received a wide mandate for arrangement of national reporting with an international procedure for regular assessment of legislative information. This mandate is a preliminary though important step towards establishing effective machinery for regular supervision of domestic legislation implementing humanitarian law. The problem is rather how to

---

4 But see Annual Report 1986. ICRC 86 (1987), which inaccurately describes Resolution V by claiming that the ICRC proposed to the Conference a Resolution on 'National measures to implement international humanitarian law' which was adopted. Regrettably, there was no mention that Resolution V was adopted as a result of merger of two drafts and that the ICRC accepted a co-sponsorship of the revised Dutch-Norwegian draft.

make use of this potential for significant improvement in implementation of humanitarian law.

Resolution V offers an opportunity for more organized and continuous supervision in an apparent contrast to earlier standards and practice. Of the endeavours undertaken and experience to date in instituting reporting procedures prior to the adoption of Resolution V a brief account should be made of the status of humanitarian law provisions on the one hand, and of extra-conventional attempts arranged within the Red Cross movement in this respect.

The Geneva Conventions of 1949 and Additional Protocols of 1977 do not provide for any reporting system. On several occasions a preference for a kind of reporting obligation by States Parties was proposed and discussed in official statements and debates, like those at the Diplomatic Conference on the Reaffirmation and Development of International Humanitarian Law Applicable in Armed Conflicts (Geneva 1974-1977). Surprisingly strong opposition on the part of some Governments ensured that such a solution, though worded as a modest obligation, had to be abandoned.[5] However, instruments of international humanitarian law contain provisions revealing certain elements of a reporting-like duty. This is the case of treaty obligation of the States Parties to communicate to one another, through the depositary and, as appropriate, through the Protecting Powers, their official translations of the Conventions and Protocols as well as the laws and regulations adopted to ensure their application.[6] Although some trace-elements of reporting appear to be inherent in that treaty obligation, this arrangement can better be described as submission of information through specified intermediaries than as a reporting mechanism *proprio sensu*. In practice, States Parties largely ignored their duty to transmit the texts of required instruments, and the depositary, due to its very technical and passive functions, has been unable to undertake any

---

5   This was the experience with a proposal on regular reporting about dissemination as provided for by Article 72(3) of the 1973 ICRC's Draft Additional Protocols to the Geneva Conventions of 12 August 1949. Drzewicki, loc. cit. n. 1, at 115-116.

6   See Article 48 Geneva Convention I, Article 49 Geneva Convention II, Article 128 Geneva Convention III, Article 145 Geneva Convention IV and Article 84 of Additional Protocol I. On the desirable impact of humanitarian law on uniformity of national legislation see F. Kalshoven, *The Netherlands and International Humanitarian Law Applicable in Armed Conflicts*, in H.F. van Panhuys *et al.*, ed., III International Law in the Netherlands 327-335 (1980).

corrective measures against conduct of states failing to fulfil the obligations in question.[7]

On the other hand, the International Red Cross, and particularly the ICRC, have worked out in the course of years quite remarkable and diversified reporting procedures. They examined national measures on, *inter alia*, repression of violations of the Geneva Conventions (1963-1969), the use and protection of the emblem (1977-1981) and dissemination activities (since the nineteen sixties).[8] However, it was only reporting on dissemination activities that evolved to become a permanent and regular pattern of information about national measures taken for implementation of that fundamental treaty obligation, while other procedures were deliberately designed as *ad hoc* endeavours pursuant to resolutions of the Red Cross bodies which had initiated them. More importantly, none of these procedures developed or generated even a modest verification mechanism on a regular basis. Yet, such limited actions were not without positive results. They all brought about an extensive, though still insufficient, body of information on the current status of legislative implementation. Unlike the 1963-1969 reporting procedure on repression of violations of the Geneva Conventions, the 1977-1981 report on the use of the emblem was extended to follow-up action by the ICRC entailing, *inter alia*, preparation of 'explanatory guidelines for national regulations on the use and protection of the emblem'.[9]

All in all, these procedures produced certain valuable experience from which many conclusions may be drawn for the process of further implementation of Resolution V. They were introduced on an extra-conventional basis and operated mainly (with the exception of reporting on dissemination) as single ventures, but lacked any follow-up assessment of the information submitted or proper feedback between the States Parties and report-receiving body.

Against the background of these earlier reporting procedures, Resolution V distinguishes itself as a nucleus for a fully-fledged but flexible reporting mechanism in the field of humanitarian law, and thus deserves further comment here.

---

7 An alarming degree of failure by States to fulfil that obligation was reported by the ICRC in its document of 1986. Supra n. 3.

8 For more detailed examination of those procedures see Drzewicki, loc. cit. n. 1, at 117-119.

9 See, *Use and Protection of the Emblem. Explanatory Guide* (item 5.1 of the provisional agenda of Commission I). Report submitted by the ICRC, Doc. CPA/5.1/1, II, at 1-21 (1981).

3.   REPORTING ARRANGEMENT UNDER RESOLUTION V

3.1   Background of Resolution V

There are two basic and widely shared considerations that led to the adoption of Resolution V on national measures to implement international humanitarian law. Firstly, the legal status of the obligation to implement binding instruments of humanitarian law leaves no doubt of its unequivocal and strongly imperative nature. The respective general rules of the Geneva Conventions and Additional Protocols spell out the implementation duties of the States Parties to undertake 'to respect and to ensure respect for' these instruments 'in all circumstances' and consequently to take 'without delay ... all necessary measures' for their execution, including 'orders and instructions' to be issued for ensuring their observance and supervision of their execution.[10] The adoption of adequate national legislation and other regulations to implement international humanitarian law forms just part of these categorial executive obligations. More importantly, the duty to adopt or supplement the relevant legislation is widely assumed to be more than an *international obligation of conduct*, that is an obligation requiring of States Parties to adopt a particular course of conduct in conformity with a treaty rule. It is also an *international obligation of result*, *i.e.*, an obligation requiring the achievement of a specified result as an outcome of a required conduct.[11] The question is in fact much more complicated because the instruments of international humanitarian law specify in some of their provisions an explicit duty to adopt appropriate legislation, while in others this obligation is merely implied. However, even in the latter case the freedom of choice of measures, be they legislative or otherwise, to be taken for ensuring the respect for humanitarian law does not absolve States Parties from achieving an accurate observance of its rules as a specified result.[12]

---

10 See Article 1 common to the four Geneva Conventions of 1949 and Article 80 of Protocol I of 1977. For more on the nature of those executive obligations see L. Condorelli, L. Boisson de Chazournes, *Quelques remarques à propos de l'obligation des Etats de 'respecter et faire respecter' le droit international humanitaire 'en toutes circonstances'*, in C. Swinarski, ed., Studies and Essays on International Humanitarian Law and Red Cross Principles in Honour of Jean Pictet (1984); also N. Levrat, *Les conséquences de l'engagement pris par les Hautes Parties contractantes de 'faire respecter' les Conventions humanitaires*, in Kalshoven, Sandoz, eds., op. cit. n. 1, at 263.
11 See II Yb ILC, 2, § 88, at 77, 80 (1979).
12 See also on the distinction between positive and negative duties of States with respect to national legislation, K. Drzewicki, *The Status of International Human Rights Instruments in*

Secondly, there is an ample practical evidence that in a majority of States Parties the degree of conformity of the existing national legislation implementing international humanitarian law is highly unsatisfactory.[13] Realistically, domestic legislation constitutes only one of several factors determining the proper implementation of humanitarian law. But there should be no doubt that without the effective integration of humanitarian law into domestic legal systems a proper observance of its rules is exposed to heavy risk. In the words of paragraph 5 of the preambular part of Resolution V the '... very applicability of international humanitarian law depends largely upon the adoption of appropriate national legislation'. The wide failure of humanitarian law to take desirable effect within domestic legal systems as confronted with imperative obligations to adopt the necessary legislative measures exerted self-evidently a strong pressure on the International Red Cross to undertake remedial means, one of the most recent of them being the adoption of Resolution V in 1986.

3.2   Substantive content of Resolution V

The operative part of Resolution V is composed of four paragraphs. To achieve its main objective, that is to assign a mandate to the ICRC with respect to arranging a flexible reporting mechanism, Resolution V starts with reminding the Governments of States Parties to the Geneva Conventions and, as the case may be, to the Additional Protocols about their contractual obligations.

Thus, in paragraph 1 it urges the Governments: '... to fulfil entirely their obligation to adopt or supplement the relevant national legislation, as well as to inform one another, as stated above, of the measures taken or under consideration for this purpose'. The second part of paragraph 1 refers, by wording 'as stated above', to the preambular paragraph 3 of Resolution V which recalls the duty of the: 'States Parties to communicate to one another, through the depositary and, during hostilities, through the Protecting Powers, the official translations of the Conventions and the Additional Protocols, as well as the laws and regulations they may adopt to ensure their application.

Domestic Law, in A. Rosas, ed., International Human Rights Norms in Domestic Law. Finnish and Polish Perspectives 1-3 (1990).

13 See presentations and discussion on that issue, Yearbook, International Institute of Humanitarian Law (1986-1987).

This formulation is a virtually reworded version of Article 84 of Additional Protocol I. Since the sole intention of paragraph 1 was to remind the States Parties of their valid obligations, it was a proper framework to refer to duties regarding both the adoption of necessary legislation and its mutual intergovernmental communication and exchange.[14]

Paragraph 2 of Resolution V invites 'National Societies to assist and co-operate with their own governments in fulfilling their obligation in this respect'. The idea behind this paragraph was to encourage the National Societies of the Red Cross and Red Crescent both to assist and co-operate with their Governments in adopting any domestic legislation necessary to implement humanitarian law. This was not meant to reduce the treaty responsibility of the States Parties for ensuring the adoption of relevant legislation. It rather tends to stress the position of National Societies as lobbies exerting pressure on their Governments to enact appropriate legislation. No less significant is that part of the domestic legislation to be adopted is of direct concern of the National Societies, most notably legislation on the use and protection of Red Cross and Red Crescent emblems. It is a well-established practice that irrespective of national legislation on the use of emblems the National Societies issue their own regulations in this respect in conformity with, and sometimes under direct authorization of statutory provisions. It is thus in this context that the role of National Societies was emphasized so boldly in paragraph 2.

The core of Resolution V are its paragraphs 3 and 4. The former appeals to: '… governments and National Societies to give the ICRC their full support and the information to enable it to follow up the progress achieved in legislative and other measures taken for the implementation of international humanitarian law'.

The latter paragraph of Resolution V requests the ICRC to gather and assess the said information and to report regularly to the International Conferences of the Red Cross and Red Crescent on the follow-up to the present Resolution.

Despite cautious formulations of paragraphs 3 and 4 they are sufficiently clear and consistent to construe them as a procedural

---

14 As a matter of fact, the inclusion of formulations of Article 84 was a result of compromise achieved during the XXV International Conference between the ICRC's and Dutch-Norwegian draft proposals. The former tended to make the ICRC a report-recipient in addition to the Swiss Federal Council as a depositary. This way the ICRC would have been receiving reports only as an extension of the depositary. As it would put the ICRC in a position of indirect and thus weaker report-recipient, this option was rightly rejected.

framework for a reporting mechanism according to the original concept of the initiators of Resolution V. Both paragraphs concerned require further comment.

It is specified unequivocally in paragraph 3 that both Governments and National Societies are to assume the position of report-senders on domestic legislation. They are expected to give the ICRC their full support and information in this respect. Although the term 'report' is not mentioned in paragraph 3, there should be no doubt that an appeal for 'full support and the information' is tantamount to a request to submit reports with the relevant information. For tactical rather than legal reasons, the intention behind both drafts discussed at the XXV International Conference was deliberately to avoid resort to such terms as 'report' or 'reporting' with regard to States since it might have prejudiced some Governments against giving their consent to Resolution V. It was also felt that a statement like 'full support and the information' corresponds more adequately to the non-binding nature of Resolution V than the term 'report' typical of treaty-based reporting obligations, *e.g.*, under international human rights conventions.[15]

Paragraph 3 is not confined solely to defining who is to take the position of report-sender, or information-sender, but also specifies what the information is to be about and what purposes it is to serve. As far as the substantive content of requested information is concerned, the original idea (in the Dutch-Norwegian draft) was to receive reports on legislative implementation measures. On its part, Resolution V has resorted to an apparently wider formulation of 'legislative and other measures taken for the implementation of international humanitarian law'. It was a common understanding in the Commission I of the International Conference in 1986 that such a wide formula was not to be meant as implying anything more than the adoption of required legislation properly speaking, and of 'other measures taken', that is non-legislative domestic instruments. In any case, however, the formula 'other measures' was not intended to mean the application process of international humanitarian law. Otherwise, Resolution V would have encroached upon the sensitive issue of violations, and thus have most likely met with a strong opposition. In fact, this confusion about the proper meaning of 'other measures' could have been

---

15 Resolution V refers, however, to the term 'report' (paragraph 4) but with regard to reports to be submitted by the ICRC to the International Conferences. It is thus a reflection of the relationship between the bodies of the International Red Cross and Red Crescent Movement.

avoided by reference to 'legislative measures' alone whose wide definition seems to be well recognized in modern international law.[16]

The main idea behind Resolution V, the establishment of reporting mechanism, has been reflected in references to the purpose of report-submission (paragraphs 3 and 4). While appealing to Governments and National Societies for 'full support' and submission of relevant information, Resolution V made it clear that it aimed at enabling the ICRC 'to follow up the progress achieved' in legislative implementation. It goes without saying that such stipulations imply a regular assessment by the ICRC of the legislative information received in a sort of continuous dialogue with report-senders. This purpose was more precisely declared in paragraph 4 requesting the 'ICRC to gather and assess the said information and to report regularly to the International Conferences of the Red Cross and Red Crescent on the follow-up to the present resolution'. It is thus a mechanism that has to be established not only on regular basis but also its regularity has been specified by reference to reporting by the ICRC on the follow-up to the International Conferences. The deliberate resort to 'plural' wording cannot be overlooked in this context. It also implies that reporting cycles are in principle determined by the statutory term of the International Conference. Under Article 11 of the Statutes of the International Red Cross and Red Crescent Movement, the Conference meets every four years, unless it decides otherwise.[17] What has been settled in this way is a cycle of reporting by the ICRC to the International Conferences and this only indirectly affects cycles for reporting by the Governments and National Societies, thus leaving a certain degree of flexibility for practical arrangements.

An important feature of the reporting mechanism in question is that the ICRC may not confine itself to gathering solely legislative information, but should also extend its conduct to a kind of assessment procedure. For obvious reasons, Resolution V, as merely a starting-point in setting up a whole reporting system, is silent on several other procedural issues which require proper attention from practical point of view. Before attempting to address some of them, one should briefly analyse steps that have already been taken by the ICRC to implement Resolution V.

---

16 For instance, the ILC defined the term legislation as 'the constitutions of States, the enactments of their legislative organs, and the regulations and declarations promulgated by executive and administrative bodies.' II Yb ILC, § 60, at 370 (1950).

17 For the text of the Statutes, see 256 International Review of the Red Cross 25-44 (1987).

4.   FOLLOW-UP TO RESOLUTION V

It took some time, perhaps too much, for the ICRC to reflect upon a more concrete *modus operandi* to be adopted for following up Resolution V.[18] After one year and a half, the ICRC eventually contacted, by letters of 28 April 1988, the States Parties to the Geneva Conventions and, separately, the National Societies. While reminding them of the substantive content of the ICRC's mandate generally, and specifically under Resolution V, the letters contained a request to submit the relevant information on national legislative measures to implement international humanitarian law, the information whose more detailed scope was defined in some of the Annexes enclosed to the letter (*i.e.*, Annex 2 - Memorandum, and indicative list of measures of implementation contained in Annex 3).[19] Replies were requested to be received within six months, thus approximately about the end of 1988.

On 15 August 1989, the ICRC issued an 'Interim Report' on the follow-up action taken to implement Resolution V in which both information on a number of received replies and preliminary outline of their content was offered. It regretted that 'very few answers' had been received by the ICRC since the letter had been transmitted to the Governments and National Societies more than a year previously. The ICRC reported that by 30 June 1989 only twenty six replies from States Parties and fifteen from the National Societies. The preliminary examination of the replies by the ICRC indicated quite poor quality compared with what had been requested. The 'Interim Report' concluded with a justified warning stressing that the ICRC:

'... will not be able to submit a substantive report to the next International Conference of the Red Cross and Red Crescent - and above all will not be able to provide any useful services to States in the long term - unless the States entirely fulfil their obligations relative to the implementation of the Conventions and, as appropriate, the Additional Protocols.'[20]

---

18 Irrespective of follow-up action taken by the ICRC later on, the President of the League of Red Cross and Red Crescent Societies and the Chairman of the Standing Commission of the Red Cross and Red Crescent in their letters to, respectively, the National Societies (on 18 June 1987) and Governments (on 25 June 1987) brought to their attention Resolution V, together with other resolutions adopted at the XXV International Conference.

19 Both letters with Annexes are reproduced in 263 IRRC 121-140 (1988).

20 Interim Report, CICR, 15 August 1989, at 6.

By the middle of 1990 the ICRC was able to report some increase in the number of reports submitted. At that time thirty seven reports of Governments and twenty six reports of the National Societies had been registered by the ICRC. This has slightly improved the quantitative results of reporting but scarcely its quality. Despite the relatively poor results of the first cycle of reporting, it should not prevent the ICRC from drafting and submitting its report to the XXVI International Conference. The results achieved should rather serve the ICRC as an incentive for a thorough analysis and identification of the reasons for the failure to report and for the insufficient quality of reports in order to improve the whole mechanism in the course of the next reporting cycles. It is not only negligence or lack of will by the Governments and National Societies that lies behind the unsatisfactory outcome of reporting. It may also be submitted that part of the failure stems from the way in which the ICRC dealt with the initial arrangements for the reporting mechanism. Certainly, the issues involved are much more complex and thus need to be examined carefully by the ICRC and International Conference. Some tentative suggestions to that end may already at this stage be submitted for discussion.

5.   POTENTIAL IMPROVEMENTS OF REPORTING MECHANISM

The XXVI International Conference of the Red Cross and Red Crescent is to be held in early December 1991 in Budapest. Within an agenda item on implementation of international humanitarian law, part of a discussion will be devoted to the follow-up of Resolution V of 1986, a discussion that may decisively affect the whole concept of a reporting mechanism. It is therefore of vital importance that representatives of all delegations to the International Conference will be given an opportunity to consider that issue based on a thorough preparatory document submitted by the ICRC and possibly by other delegations. Conference diplomacy is rarely able to work out detailed arrangements without concrete analytical study and tentative proposals drafted well in advance. What should thus be avoided is a submission of a report containing purely factual references and speaking in generalities. In other words, a more concrete set of proposals, providing preferably for alternative options, should be submitted to the International Conference.

5.1   Organizational arrangements

Pursuant to Resolution V it is the mandate of the ICRC to 'gather and assess' reports submitted by Governments and National Societies, and subsequently to report regularly on the follow-up to the International Conferences. However, the designation of the ICRC as report-recipient and of the International Conference as a supreme 'supervisory' body does not exhaust all aspects of the structural framework for the reporting mechanism.

There is also a need to identify an appropriate 'structure' to be specifically in charge of a thorough and regular examination of reports for the International Committee itself. It must be considered which body, whether one already existing or one to be set up, should be responsible for performing such a task for the ICRC. The former option has already become an accomplished fact in the course of the first reporting cycle due to involvement in the procedure by the ICRC's Legal Commission and Legal Division, with the latter being responsible for administration of reporting. But this solution does not seem to correspond adequately to the emerging needs of a reporting mechanism, and should be modified for the needs of future reporting cycles. What largely supports this conclusion is the discernible overburden of the ICRC's bodies, and particularly of its Legal Division, in charge of diverse legal duties performed by a relatively small staff whose members, in addition, travel a great deal in official missions. Both units might have thus difficulties in devoting sufficient attention to a detailed examination of reports. Moreover, in addition to the examination of reports, the whole reporting mechanism is expected to provide an extensive scheme for advisory services, an expectation that can hardly be satisfied by experts of the ICRC themselves.

For these and other reasons, the second option, of a body to be set up, seems to be much more attractive. Above all, it may ensure that such a body will be a specialized organ concentrating exclusively on questions of national reporting on legislative implementation. As far as the composition formula of the body under discussion is concerned, it should provide for a reasonably high degree of participation by independent experts in addition to those of the ICRC, the League, Red Cross and Red Crescent Societies and the depositary. It should also be taken into account that when dealing with reports a body might achieve better results if its members represented diversified legal systems and cultures. A preference for such an option corresponds in addition to recently re-emerging ideas of a limited internationalization of the ICRC.[21] It is particularly at the level of experts that such ideas may prove to be feasible and workable.

The submission then is that the International Conference invites the ICRC to establish a Commission of Experts with a mandate to study national reports and draft its own report with comments and recommendations both of a general nature and those addressed to individual States Parties and National Societies. Such a report might then be transmitted by the ICRC to the International Conference. An essential feature of the proposed arrangement is that it facilitates a more equitable division of labour and strengthens feedback between national and international actors responsible for implementation of humanitarian law.

Beyond doubt, there is much in the conceptual framework for a reporting mechanism that may be borrowed from the pragmatic reporting system elaborated by the ILO. This applies not only to the proposed Commission of Experts whose structural and functional settings might potentially be modelled on those of the Committee of Experts on the Application of Conventions and Recommendations of the ILO. It extends equally to the whole tripartite relationship which proved its efficiency in the process of supervising implementation of labour standards within domestic legislation. A similar relationship, though not identical to that of the ILO, has evolved between the non-governmental organisations constituting component parts of the International Red Cross and Red Crescent Movement on the one hand, and the Governments of States Parties to humanitarian law instruments on the other. Within this relationship the three parties are the ICRC, National Red Cross and Red Crescent Societies together with their international federation, the League, and the Governments of States Parties to the Geneva Conventions and Additional Protocols. They all share, in their respective parts, a responsibility for a proper implementation of humanitarian law, and interaction between them may improve the results of implementation. Once a Commission of Experts drafts its report and the ICRC presents it to the International Conference a tripartite interaction is set in motion at both plenary debates of the Conference and Commission I dealing with humanitarian law.[22] This structural scheme reflects the actual division of

---

21 *Cf.*, D.D. Tansley, *Final Report: An Agenda for Red Cross* 113-114 (1975); K. Obradovic, *Que faire face aux violations du droit humanitaire? - Quelques réflexions sur le rôle possible du CICR*, in Swinarski, ed., op. cit. n. 10, at 493-494.

22 An important aspect of such a framework, as has been proved by the ILO, is that a substantive report prepared by experts becomes then a subject of discussion and conclusions by tripartite bodies.

responsibility of all actors bound to implement international humanitarian law.

5.2   Procedural Arrangements

According to Resolution V, Governments and National Societies were called on to give the ICRC their full support and the information on legislative and other measures taken to implement international humanitarian law (paragraph 3). In addition, paragraph 2 invites National Societies to assist and co-operate with their own Governments in fulfilling their obligations concerning legislative implementation. All these stipulations imply who is to assume the responsibility of a report-sender, but they do not wholly solve the question. In its follow-up, the ICRC sent letters requesting information on legislative measures to both Governments and National Societies. Without going into details, there are several sound arguments for maintaining this solution in the future. What may be found as its drawback, namely a dual and parallel reporting on the same national legislation, may be outweighed by some of its advantages.

To a large extent, that weakness can be diminished once Governments and National Societies co-operate more closely and regularly on a national level, an idea already promoted vigorously on several other occasions, including practical suggestions by the ICRC made, *inter alia*, for the needs of implementation of Resolution V.[23] Legally speaking, Resolution V is not an obstacle to submission of a joint report by Government and National Society from the same country. But this would require the National Society to enjoy a fairly high degree of autonomy from its Government. Otherwise, a joint report might reflect the views of Government rather than of the National Society, while there should always be space for separate opinions by the latter, if any, about the status of national legislation. This does not mean that each joint report would necessarily have to reflect a predominantly pro-governmental stand and ignore the opinions of the National Society. The argument is merely that such a risk exists and that the other option, namely dual reporting, seems to ensure more pluralism and autonomy for both report-senders.

Regardless of its drawbacks, dual and parallel reporting may then prove its advantages also. It equally encourages co-operation of both report-senders on the national level and may generate even more interaction between them. Furthermore, such a system allows National Societies as

---

23   See Interim Report, loc. cit. n. 20, at 4-5.

non-governmental organizations to be a more significant pressure group towards Governments and to play this role not only domestically but also internationally by submitting their own reports independently of government. Moreover, from the viewpoint of the report-recipient, it will be of greater value to receive two national reports potentially reflecting different perspectives and evaluation of national legislation. Another reason for this system is that it gives an opportunity to have at least one national report if the other report-sender from the same country fails to submit requested information. It also keeps the 'two-way avenue' for exerting pressure on report-senders failing to report or submitting incomplete information.[24] That all speaks in favour of the solution provided for by Resolution V.

A further procedural issue deserving comment is that of reporting cycles. As mentioned above, paragraph 4 of Resolution V sets out only reporting cycles by the ICRC to the International Conference, cycles being tantamount to terms of the Conference (in principle a four year cycle under the Statute, but since 1981 actually a five-year term). In any case, a more frequent reporting cycle to the ICRC by Governments and National Societies is not precluded. The problems, however, is whether it is desirable to shorten cycles for report-senders to 2-3 years periods or to maintain 4-5 years cycle corresponding to that of the ICRC towards the International Conference. The answer to this question is largely dependent upon the *modus operandi* adopted for dealing with reports. If the ICRC as the report-recipient and the Commission of Experts engage in a substantive dialogue with Governments and National Societies on the issues covered by their reports, then a 4-5 years cycle is the most suitable solution.

One of the most crucial elements of the reporting system is the identification of substantive scope of reporting. It should first be made clear that, unlike the majority of human rights treaties, most of the provisions of Geneva Conventions and Additional Protocols are of a self-executing nature.[25] Thus, the substantive content of reports should be

---

24 One should, however, bear in mind that from some countries solely governmental reports may be received due to the still greater number of States Parties to Geneva Conventions (164) than internationally recognized National Societies (147) as of 1 January 1991.

25 Also, Drzewicki, loc. cit. n. 1, at 111. It has been submitted that the high degree of textual determinacy, which is characteristic of self-executing rules, goes together with a high degree of rule-conforming State behavior rules. See, T.M. Franck, *Legitimacy in the International System*, 82 AJIL 713-719 (1988). However, as far as humanitarian law is concerned, determinate rules may not be identified, as Franck did, only in the area of treatment of war prisoners, since they prevail in the all four Geneva Conventions and their Additional Protocols.

referred to those provisions of humanitarian law which require legislative action. However, such a statement defines only a point of departure for a precise identification of provisions calling for domestic legislative implementation.

From the perspective of national legal systems, it will have to be defined what is meant by the term legislation. A general trend has emerged to accept the widest possible interpretation of the notion of legislation, but its more thorough specification seems to be indispensable with regard to specific content and needs of humanitarian law.[26] On the other hand, from the perspective of international humanitarian law instruments, it appears fairly easy to identify explicit obligations in the provisions stipulating *expressis verbis* the adoption of legislative measures (*e.g.* provisions concerning the repression of abuses and infractions), but it is harder to point out which provisions imply the adoption of national legislative instruments in the absence of an explicitly formulated treaty-duty to do so. Despite that difficulty, it should be assumed that legislative measures which are to be reported ought to concern all non-self-executing provisions, which either explicitly or implicitly, may be deemed to require legislative intervention.[27]

In a follow-up to Resolution V, the ICRC addressed the issue of substantive content of requested reports by reference, in an Annex 3 to its letter of 28 April 1988, to 'Measures of Implementation (Indicative List)'. Article by Article of the Geneva Conventions and Additional Protocols, the list commendably reflects a wide notion of both domestic legislation (including also administrative regulations) and non-self-executing provisions. But this naturally made the indicative list very extensive and thus impractical as guidelines for report-senders. And it is in this sense, as pointed out above, that the ICRC partly contributed to the failure of the first reporting cycle by leaving report-senders with the indicative list solely. Instead, the ICRC should, in addition to the indicative list, have facilitated the task of report-senders with a well-structured questionnaire containing questions concentrated around groups of related issues requiring replies about domestic legislation. However, it is not implied here that the

---

26 A point of departure for defining legislation for those needs may be that one elaborated by the ILC, loc. cit. n. 16.

27 On the necessity to enact necessary criminal legislation see M. Bothe, *Prevention and Repression of Breaches of International Humanitarian Law*, Yearbook. International Institute of Humanitarian Law 117 *et seq.* (1986-1987).

system of so-called partial reporting should be introduced as a remedy for failure of the first-cycle reporting.[28]

It should rather be a system based on the deliberate assumption of comprehensive reports setting priorities to the most important non-self executing rules by formulating questions in a proper way and proportion. It would then be for the following cycles to request further legislative information to fulfil gaps and omissions of earlier reports. A major focus should be centred on legislation to implement provisions regarding repression of violations of humanitarian law, provisions concerning protection of personnel and emblems of Red Cross and Red Crescent and other recognized aid Societies and of medical units, provisions related to dissemination, and other executive provisions. Thus, a model questionnaire appears to be a key instrument that may generate more encouraging results for an assessment stage of the reports submitted and follow-up actions. Probably, there is no better technical measure determining satisfactory answers than a well-drafted questionnaire requiring specific answers to specific questions. Leaving to report-senders virtually entire liberty as to what is to be answered within a wide range of issues, such as those contained in the indicative list, would inevitably produce such obstructive results as it did.

There are several other procedural aspects of the reporting mechanism that will have to be considered in the course of discussions on making Resolution V a more workable and efficient device for improvement of domestic legislative implementation of international law. Without going into more detailed examination of these questions, it should suffice to emphasize certain basic features for the whole reporting mechanism. As has already been pointed out, the basic assumption for the reporting system should be an adequate share of responsibility for implementation of international humanitarian law by all the actors brought together by International Red Cross and Red Crescent Conferences. Within this interaction, the role and mandate of the ICRC ought to be strengthened by establishment of a specialized body -a Commission of Experts- to deal with substantive assessment of submitted reports. The reporting mechanism should first and foremost be non-political in its nature, based on a

---

28 After years of unsatisfactory experience with partial reporting under the International Covenant on Economic, Social and Cultural Rights it was decided to resort to global reports upon the recommendation of the Committee on Economic, Social and Cultural Rights endorsed by ECOSOC Res. 1988/4 of 24 May 1988, Committee on Economic, Social and Cultural Rights. Report on the Fourth Session (15 January-2 February 1990), 3 Off. Rec. E/C.12/1990/3 94-102 (1990).

predominantly pragmatic approach to assessment of national legislation and thus avoid encroaching upon the application of humanitarian law, and be oriented towards dialogue with and, if necessary, assistance to report-senders (*e.g.* offering them advisory legal services or drafting model legislative acts).

6. CONCLUDING REMARKS

It should be emphasized that Resolution V established a uniquely favourable framework for the arrangement of regular mechanism of reporting on national legislation implementing international humanitarian law. Obviously, it is not simply for its own sake that a reporting mechanism was instituted. It has been designed to achieve essential improvement in the implementation of humanitarian law within national legal orders. Since there are sound and large-scale symptoms of perilous failure in enacting national legislation for implementation of humanitarian law, an urgent need to remedy this undesirable situation has become self-evident. But Resolution V is merely a dormant opportunity. The very first years of its operation have brought about quite disappointing results so far.

One may assume that there is a wide consensus about the need to ensure compatibility of national legislation with international humanitarian law. If so, there should also be a conducive climate for making Resolution V a viable arrangement through a constructive dialogue. Otherwise, yet another opportunity for strengthening the national legislative implementation of international humanitarian law may be wasted. Among potential obstacles to operationalization of the reporting system one should identify first of all attitudes of Governments and components of the International Red Cross and Red Crescent Movement. However, since the adoption of Resolution V in 1986 many States, notably in Eastern and Central Europe, have changed fundamentally their traditionally reluctant attitudes to any mechanisms of international monitoring and supervision. National Societies in those countries have undergone thorough transformations towards securing their more independent and autonomous status.

All that will obviously reduce the impact of previously strong political considerations towards accepting international supervisory procedures by Governments and National Societies of those countries. The International Committee of the Red Cross should, on its part, be more open to accept essential reform of the *modus operandi* for Resolution V, including particularly the establishment of a Commission of Experts. Such a reform hardly constitutes a threat of re-definition of the ICRC's mandate in the field of humanitarian law but, more importantly, it may significantly contribute to more effective accomplishment of this mandate. It may then be legitimately expected that improvements in the reporting mechanism under Resolution V will now find much wider support than in 1986.

A few critical comments on structural and procedural arrangements for reporting mechanism and tentative suggestions for its fundamental improvement offered in this paper may hopefully constitute an invitation to further discussion before initiation of a decision-making process by the XXVI International Conference of the Red Cross and Red Crescent.

VII

RELATED ISSUES

HOW MUCH HUMANITY DO TERRORISTS DESERVE?

TORSTEN STEIN

1.   INTRODUCTION

The rules of international humanitarian law applicable in armed conflicts are rules that apply under exceptional, if not extreme, circumstances. So, the 'disturbing decline in the respect of international humanitarian law', noted during the XXVth International Conference of the Red Cross in autumn 1986[1] is, deplorable though it may be, perhaps not that surprising. Unlike offences under peace-time criminal law, which in most cases are committed deliberately after calculating the risks, violations of the rules of international humanitarian law can often be attributed, it is assumed, to chaotic situations on the battlefield, to the absence of responsible military leaders or to the lack of discipline or adequate training. Deliberate

---

1   See XXVth ICRC, Plenary Meeting, Report of the International Humanitarian Law Commission (I), Annex 1, Resolution adopted by consensus on Respect for International Humanitarian Law in Armed Conflicts and Action by the ICRC for Persons Protected by the Geneva Conventions, 6th preambular paragraph.

violations resulting from a misinterpretation of the *necessité de guerre* or based on the outlawed maxim *Kriegsräson geht vor Kriegsmanier* seem to be the exceptions, although every war since the coming into force of the 1949 Geneva Conventions may possibly provide some examples for these exceptions.

But even in extreme times, as in war, when the very violence inherent in such a situation blurs the view of law in general,[2] and even under chaotic circumstances, there are a number of strong incentives for respecting the rules of international humanitarian law. One may be the somewhat chivalrous feeling among professional soldiers that even during an armed conflict there are some rules of the game one is bound to respect. Another incentive may be the related feeling that civilians or other persons who take no active part in the hostilities, have no part in that 'game'. But doubtless the strongest incentive is 'positive reciprocity',[3] *i.e.*, the conviction that one may only expect to benefit from the rules of international humanitarian law if one is prepared to obey these rules oneself. And an adversary who shows respect for these rules will remain an adversary and not become an 'enemy' or even an 'outlaw'. Adversaries have a claim to humane treatment.

But to what extent do terrorists deserve humane treatment, humane in the widest possible sense, provided that they are a distinguishable category? Terrorists commit their crimes deliberately, in cold blood, and after carefully calculating the risk; 'kamikazes' are the exception. Terrorists do not abide by any 'rules of the game'. Terrorists do not spare 'civilians', but apply violence indiscriminately and without any concern whatsoever for persons who are foreign to the motives behind the act of terrorism. Terrorists, when apprehended, often claim all possible privileges, such as, *e.g.* prisoner-of-war status, the political offence exception to extradition, or at least to be held together in the same prison block; but they never offer reciprocity of any kind. In reaction, an emotionalized public opinion, after a spectacular terrorist act, not infrequently categorically demands not only that the law be applied in all its rigour, but to return like for like and to make short work of terrorists. Although there should not be the slightest doubt that a State which decides, in the fight against terrorism, to leave the path dictated by the rule of law, would do exactly what terrorists want it to do, it seems nevertheless to be

---

2   See also F. Kalshoven, *The Present State of Research Carried out by the English-Speaking Section of the Centre for Studies and Research: the Application of Humanitarian Law*, Hague Academy of International Law 70, 73 (1986).

3   *Ibid.*.

a legitimate question whether terrorists should necessarily benefit from all those rules of international (and national) law which find their origin in humanitarian considerations for the person concerned. Or do democratic States, which subscribe to the rule of law and human rights, get inevitably caught in their own rules if it comes to fighting terrorism?

2.   DEFINITION OF TERRORISM

Certainly, exceptions to legal rules, otherwise applicable, for a specific category or group of persons, do have as a prerequisite that this group or category can be sufficiently delineated or defined. Does this mean that one has to prove an accepted, if not binding, definition of terrorism before one could consider exceptions to the applicability of rules of humanitarian law to terrorists? It is rather commonplace that all efforts to find a definition of terrorism which would be acceptable to the community of nations, have, so far, failed.[4] No less than 109 different definitions of the term 'terrorism' are said to have been advanced between 1936 and 1981,[5] prominent examples including the 1937 Convention for the Prevention and Punishment of Terrorism,[6] which only received one ratification (India), and the 1972 US Draft Convention for the Prevention and Punishment of Certain Acts of International Terrorism,[7] which was never even put to a vote in the UN *Ad Hoc* Committee on Terrorism.[8] The 1971 OAS Convention to Prevent and Punish the Acts of Terrorism Taking the Form of Crimes against Persons and Related Extortion that are of International Significance[9] uses the term 'acts of terrorism', but abstains from defining it and gives only an example ('especially kidnapping, murder and other

---

4   *Cf.*, J.F. Murphy, State Support of International Terrorism 3 (1989).

5   W. Laqueur, *Reflections on Terrorism*, 65 Foreign Affairs 86-100 (1986).

6   M.O. Hudson, VII International Legislation 499, 862 (1935-1937). The Convention defines acts of terrorism as: 'criminal acts directed against a State and intended or calculated to create a state of terror in the minds of particular persons, or a group of persons or the general public.'

7   UN Doc. A/C.6/L.850. Repr. in XI ILM 1382 (1972). The Draft Convention intended to cover, within a rather narrow framework of 'international significance', only: 'any person who unlawfully kills, causes serious bodily harm or kidnaps another person'.

8   For details see S. Kaye, *The United Nations Effort to Draft a Convention on the Taking of Hostages*, 27 American University Law Review 433-487 (1978); J.F. Murphy, *Protected Persons and Diplomatic Facilities*, in A. Evans, J.F. Murphy, eds., Legal Aspects of International Terrorism 277-339 (1978).

9   27 U.S.T. 3949.

assaults against ... [diplomats]').[10] Finally, the 1977 European Convention on the Suppression of Terrorism[11] uses the term 'terrorism' in its title and Preamble, but not in the operative Articles. Resignation seems to be the only result of those 109 attempts to define terrorism.

But this does not necessarily rule out every possibility of applying some special rules of law to terrorism or of making exceptions from otherwise generally applicable rules with regard to terrorists. Also the 110th attempt to define terrorism in an all-embracing manner will inevitably fail, on the one hand due to the resistance of those States which expect some political benefit for themselves from so-called 'wars of national liberation', or which still believe in the old cliché[12] according to which 'one man's terrorist is another man's freedom fighter', and on the other hand because there are, admittedly, some 'gray areas' to which a uniform definition of terrorism will not in all cases do justice. But there are certain acts which -according to the maxim 'we know one when we see one'- undoubtedly are 'acts of terrorism', and the fact that there remain uncertainties at the outer edges of the term is no reason not to apply special rules to acts which are clearly grouped in its centre.

The ILA's International Committee on Legal Problems of Extradition in Relation to Terrorist Offences took this into account, when it described (not: 'defined') in its Final Committee Report[13] acts of international terrorism as being those 'which create a collective danger to the life, physical integrity or liberty of persons, and affect persons foreign to the motives behind them.'[14] Whatever violent acts the Red Army Faction (RAF) in Germany, the *Action Directe* in France or the *Brigate Rosse* in Italy commit, come under that description, whether one is prepared to include the Provisional IRA or not.

---

10 The original Draft did contain a rather comprehensive definition; *cf.*, OEA/Documentos Oficiales/Ser.G.,CP/ACTA 30/70 of 9 December 1970, at 71.
11 XV ILM 1272 (1976).
12 See Murphy, op. cit. n. 4, at 3.
13 ILA Committee Report, Part II, Draft Articles on Extradition in Relation to Terrorist Offences, Article I, *Report of the Sixty-Third Conference* 1032 (1988).
14 J.A. Carillo Salcedo, J.A. Frowein have stated in their *Corpus of Principles Relative to the Attitude of States towards International Terrorism*: 'Terrorist acts in the sense of the present principles are, among others, attacks on or threats to life or personal integrity, affecting people in an indiscriminate way or using heinous methods condemned by the international community if these acts contain an international element.' The Legal Aspects of International Terrorism 17 (1988).

What are then, without claiming completeness, the major areas of international humanitarian law (in its widest sense) which may not apply in their entirety to terrorists?

3. THE LAWS OF ARMED CONFLICT

Some years ago one could witness an intensive -and sometimes almost heated-[15] debate on whether the laws of war could be applied, by analogy, to acts of terrorism.[16] This debate, in some instances, indeed gave rise to confusion: it is one question whether acts of terrorism, which have nothing whatsoever to do with armed conflicts, can be better suppressed and punished by making analogies to the laws of war. It is another, quite different, question what the laws of war provide for acts of terrorism committed during armed conflicts; and both questions should be clearly kept apart.

3.1 Law of war applicable?

To start with the first question, it is a legitimate as well as long established[17] maxim that no one should be allowed to commit acts in peace-time which would be illegal even if committed in times of war by a soldier engaged in an international armed conflict. So, the Fourth Interim Report of the ILA's Committee on International Terrorism was probably less innovative than it had intended to be: '[N]o person shall be permitted to escape trial or extradition on the ground of his political motivation who, if he performed the same act as a soldier engaged in an international armed

---

15 *Cf.*, the Dissenting Statement by L.C. Green and J. Lador-Lederer to the Fourth Interim Report of ILA's Committee on International Terrorism, *Report of the Sixtieth Conference*, 354-357 (1982), which summarized the critique by stating:'We agree that acts of terrorism should be suppressed and punished, but we are of opinion that the attempt to compare such acts with those forbidden during armed conflict is unwarranted and confusing.'

16 *Cf.*, J.J. Paust, *Terrorism and the International Law of War*, 64 Military Law Review 1-36 (1974); P.A. Tharp, *The Laws of War as a Potential Legal Regime for the Control of Terrorist Activities*, 32 Journal of International Affairs 91-100 (1978); A.P. Rubin, *Terrrorism and the Laws of War*, 12 Denver Journal of International Law and Policy 219-235 (1983); A.P. Rubin, *Should the Laws of War Apply to Terrorists?*, 79 ASIL Proc. 109-112 (1985).

17 *Cf.*, Article 5(2) of the French Extradition Statute of 1927:'En ce qui concerne les actes commis au cours d'une insurrection ou d'une guerre civile, par l'un ou l'autre des parties engagés dans la lutte et dans l'intérêt de sa cause, ils ne pourront donner lieu à l'extradition que s'ils constituent des actes de barbarie odieuse et de vandalisme défendus suivant les lois de la guerre ....'

conflict, would be subject to trial or extradition.'[18] The disadvantages connected with that approach manifestly outweighed its advantages, if it had any, taking into account that this not-so-new maxim had never been regarded as being sufficient to prevent the abuse by terrorists of the 'political offence' exception to extradition.[19] The ILA Report was honest enough to point to the weak spot itself when it explained that 'general international law already contains rules which fix a limit to politically-motivated behaviour by authorized public officials, including soldiers ...', and that '... no reason is perceived why other *equally well-motivated*[20] individuals or groups should be legally insulated by their political ideals from the punishment to which officials or soldiers are subjected for the same atrocities.'[21]

Terrorists may have strong motives, but they are not 'well-motivated'. And it is not only so that '... not all acts that might be "war crimes" or "grave breaches" are directly pertinent to the legal regime appropriate to international terrorism.'[22] It is also true that quite a number of acts which can be labelled as 'acts of terrorism' would not qualify as 'war crimes' or 'grave breaches'. Situations of internal disturbances and tensions, such as riots, isolated and sporadic acts of violence and other acts of a similar nature are not governed by the laws of armed conflict,[23] because they are not armed conflicts. Any analogy to the laws of war in connection with peace-time acts of terrorism would insinuate that although terrorists could never get away with acts which are forbidden in war-time, they might well do what regular soldiers may do. Regular soldiers in an armed conflict may use violence against the soldiers of the other belligerent State and against military installations, and under such an analogy it would be for the terrorists to choose their 'soldier-counterparts' (probably members of the government or other public figures) and to decide on what they regard as targets from the 'military-industrial-complex'. Moreover, the application of the laws of war to peace-time terrorism, even by analogy, would not be possible without conceding terrorists a combatant status, and thus giving

---

18 ILA, *Report of the Sixtieth Conference* 349-354 (1982).
19 One needs only to cite the notorious 'attentat-clause'. *Cf.*, C. van den Wyngaert, The Political Offence Exception to Extradition 136 *et seq.* (1980).
20 Italics added by the author.
21 ILA Report, loc. cit. n. 18, § 20.
22 *Ibid.*, at 354.
23 *Cf.*, Article 1(2) of the 1977 Protocol II Additional to the Geneva Conventions. *Cf.*, also H.P. Gasser, *Genfer Abkommen und Terrorismusverbot*, in Völkerrecht im Dienste des Menschen, Festschrift für Hans Haug (Geneva Conventions and the Prohibition of Terrorism) 69-80 (1986).

them title to prisoner-of-war status. The entire system of the laws of war is founded on the basic distinction between combatants and civilians, between lawful acts of combatancy and punishable war crimes. Without accepting these basic categories, the whole system becomes unworkable.[24] Consequently, the humanitarian law applicable in armed conflicts cannot apply, even by analogy, to peace-time terrrorism. ILA's reinstituted Committee rightly abandoned this approach.[25]

3.2   Terrorism during armed conflicts

On the other hand, the rules concerning acts of terrorism committed during armed conflicts, contained in the 1949 Geneva Conventions and the 1977 Additional Protocols, are unambiguous as to their applicability as well as to their content. Acts of terrorism during an international or non-international armed conflict are primarily those acts of violence which, although committed by combatants, do not acknowledge that certain groups of persons are protected even in times of war, and which therefore violate the rules of behaviour imposed by humanitarian law. Article 33(1) of the Fourth Geneva Convention Relative to the Protection of Civilian Persons prohibits 'all measures of intimidation or of terrorism'. This is reinforced by Article 51(2) of the 1977 Protocol I Additional to the Geneva Conventions, which provides: '[A]cts or threats of violence the primary purpose of which is to spread terror among the civilian population are prohibited'. The same prohibition is laid down, for non-international armed conflicts, in Article 13(2) of Protocol II, which, in addition, lists among the 'Fundamental Guarantees' under Article 4(2) the prohibition of 'acts of terrorism', at 'any time and in any place whatsoever'. As far as penal sanctions for the violation of these prohibitions ('grave breaches') are concerned, the Geneva Conventions and Additional Protocols refer to the laws of the High Contracting Parties,[26] subject to certain safeguards of fair trial by which even the perpetrators of 'grave breaches' shall benefit.[27] Since these rules are explicitly made also for those 'grave breaches' which may be characterized as 'acts of terrorism', any deviation from these safeguards *vis-à-vis* terrorists would not be admissible.

---

24 *Cf.*, S. Oeter, *Terrorism and 'Wars of National Liberation' from a Law of War Perspective. Traditional Patterns and Recent Trends'*, 49 ZaöRV 445 *et seq.* (1989).
25 See ILA Committee Report, loc. cit. n. 13.
26 *Cf.*, Article 146 of the Fourth Geneva Convention and Articles 85-88 of Protocol I.
27 *Cf.*, Article 146(4) of the Fourth Geneva Convention. Also Article 6 of Additional Protocol II.

One could also consider as acts of terrorism *ratione personae* those acts of violence which are committed by non-combatants or combatants who fail to meet the minimum requirements set forth in Article 44(3) of Additional Protocol I.[28] One may assume that only the latter category might pose problems in practice, although it is, for the purpose of this essay, not necessary to take up the debate on whether Article 1(4) and Article 44(3) of Additional Protocol I in combination might result in what has been called a 're-barbarization of war', because regular combatants could never be sure whether the 'civilian' on the side-walk across the street will not in the next moment pull out a weapon and launch an attack.[29] It suffices to draw attention to the fact that even in such a case Article 44(4) of Additional Protocol I accords 'protections equivalent in all respects to those accorded to prisoners of war ...'[30] to those which have failed to meet the requirements laid down in Article 44(3) of Additional Protocol I. These are, again, specific rules which allow no deviation. The laws of war, in sum, do not seem to permit sufficient distinction in the treatment of lawful combatants on the one hand and 'terrorists' on the other, and are, therefore, not much of an incentive for terrorists to abide by the rules of humanitarian law applicable in armed conflicts.

4.   EXTRADITION LAW

Terrorist acts, whether committed in peace-time or in the course of an armed conflict, are crimes which, in principle, may give rise to extradition. Again, general extradition law laid down in treaties or

---

28 See Gasser, loc. cit. n. 23, at 71 *et seq.*.

29 See K. Doehring, *Verfassungsrecht und Kriegsvölkerrecht* (Constitutional Law and the Law of War), in: Festschrift für Friedrich Berber 145 (1973). More recently D.J. Feith, *Protocol I: Moving Humanitarian Law Backwards*, 19 Akron Law Review 531-535 (1986) and the response by W.A. Solf, 20 Akron Law Review 261-289 (1986). Also F. Kalshoven, *Reaffirmation and Development of International Humanitarian Law Applicable in Armed Conflicts*, 8 NYIL 107-135 (1977). It is rather doubtful whether the declarations made on signature of Protocol I by *e.g.* the United Kingdom and the United States in relation to Article 44 or envisaged by the Federal Republic of Germany for the time of ratification (*cf.*, Bundesrat, Drucksache 64/90 of 2 February 1990, Annex 3), will be a sufficient remedy. For the declarations see D. Schindler, J. Toman, eds., The Laws of Armed Conflict 633-636 (1981).

30 The degree to which Additional Protocol I is a political rather than a humanitarian document becomes apparent if one notes that under Article 47 (extensively defined) mercenaries shall not have the right to be a combatant or prisoner-of-war, even if they obey all rules of the law of war.

domestic statutes makes no distinction between ordinary (capital)crimes and terrorist acts. But general extradition law does not, on the other hand, explicitly provide that terrorists have, in all instances, a claim to the same treatment as ordinary criminals. The provision, contained in almost all general extradition treaties and statutes (including the most recent ones, which should have known better)[31] and which in far too many extradition cases benefitted terrorists, is the 'political offence exception'. This exception was originally motivated by humanitarian concern for the fugitive on the one hand and on the other by the politically rooted unwillingness of the requested State to become involved in the political affairs of the requesting State. But the common wording of the political offence exception mixes both motives behind the rule inseparably, does not require the necessary differentiation between those two motives and, therefore, gives rise to manifold errors.[32] The literature on the political offence exception and its application to terrorists has become legion,[33] and the problems connected with the extradition of presumed terrorists are well known and need not be repeated. Suffice it to recall that by mere interpretation of the political offence exception, Governments and courts of law do have the possibility to withhold the 'political privilege' from terrorists, because there is no general or uniform, let alone binding, definition of the 'political offence'. It is possible to limit the political offence exception to 'absolute' or 'purely' political offences. It is also possible to make the recognition of a political offence contingent on the relationship between the political aspects and the offence charged; this 'proportionality' or 'predominance' test requires consideration of such factors as the seriousness of the offence or its consequences, the indiscriminate use of violence against innocent victims and the futility of the attempt to further the political object claimed for the offence. Not one of these considerations is, however, as such binding under international law.

---

31 *Cf.*, *e.g.* the Extradition Treaty between the Netherlands and Canada of 13 October 1989. Repr. in 169 Tractatenblad (1989), the Extradition Treaty between France and Canada of 17 November 1988. Repr. in Journal officiel de la République française 226 (1990), the Extradition Treaty between France and Australia of 31 August 1988. Repr. in Journal officiel de la République française 15639 (1989). Also the treaty between the Federal Republic of Germany and Australia of 14 April 1987, II BGBl 110 (1990).

32 *Cf.*, the analysis of some 150 -in part unpublished- court decisions in T. Stein, Die Auslieferungsausnahme bei politischen Delikten (The Political Offence Exception to Extradition) 180-334 (1983).

33 See, *e.g.* P. Felchlin, Das politische Delikt (The Political Offence) (1979); Stein, op. cit. n. 32; C. van den Wyngaert, op. cit. n. 19.

Since the maxim *aut dedere aut judicare*, laid down in a number of multilateral conventions,[34] has not produced satisfactory results, there have also been attempts to 'depoliticize' certain serious crimes which are generally characterized as 'terrorist acts', by explicitly providing that, for the purposes of extradition, none of these crimes shall be regarded as a political offence.[35] The most recent and most comprehensive attempt in this context are the 'Draft Articles on Extradition in Relation to Terrorist Offences', submitted by ILA's International Committee on Legal Problems of Extradition in Relation to Terrorist Offences at the 1988 Warsaw Conference.[36] Although it should be generally acceptable that no political considerations whatsoever (which are one motive behind the political offence exception) can justify refusal of extradition for terrorist acts, while there are other ways to safeguard humanitarian concerns for the fugitive, it is not to be expected that this approach will be more promising than previous attempts. It is nevertheless maintained that it would be not only in the interest of justice, but also in the interest of those fugitive offenders which are in need of asylum, to abandon the political offence exception in extradition law altogether and to replace it by a clause which takes care of the humanitarian motive behind the existing, ambiguous, exception.[37]

5.   RIGHT OF ASYLUM

Article V(A,2) of ILA's 'Draft Articles on Extradition in Relation to Terrorist Offences'[38] provides that:

'Extradition may be refused when ... the requested State has reasonable and substantial grounds to believe that the requested person, if extradited, would

---

34 In particular the Convention for the Suppression of Unlawful Acts Against the Safety of Civil Aviation (The Hague 1970, Montreal 1971); the Convention on the Prevention and Punishment of Crimes against Internationally Protected Persons, including Diplomatic Agents (1973) and the International Convention Against the Taking of Hostages (1979).

35 The only true examples are the 1948 Genocide Convention and the 1977 European Convention on the Suppression of Terrorism. As to the latter, see T. Stein, *Die Europäische Konvention zur Bekämpfung des Terrorismus* (The European Convention on the Suppression of Terrorism) 37 ZaöRV 668 *et seq.* (1977); recently O. Lagodny, *The European Convention on the Suppression of Terrorism: A Substantial Step to Combat Terrorism?*, 60 University of Colorado Law Review 583-600 (1989).

36 See ILA Committee Report, loc. cit. n. 13.

37 *Cf.*, the proposal made by Stein, op. cit. n. 32, at 356 *et seq.*.

38 See ILA Committee Report, loc. cit. n. 13.

be persecuted on account of his race, religion, nationality, membership of a particular social group or political opinion.'[39]

In other words: even the terrorist who has committed the most horrible atrocities will not be returned to a State in which he will be subject not only to criminal prosecution, but also to political persecution.[40] Territorial asylum may also be claimed by a (former) terrorist who does not face extradition, but deportation.[41] All this is expression of the conviction, deeply rooted in the rule of law and in humanitarian principles, that no civilized society should let itself be carried away and return like with like.

But there are limits to this principle, both under international law and domestic law: Article 33(2) of the 1951 Convention Relating to the Status of Refugees provides that:

'... the benefit of the ... (non-refoulement principle) may not ... be claimed by a refugee whom there are reasonable grounds for regarding as a danger to the security of the country in which he is, or who, having been convicted by a final judgment of a particular serious crime, constitutes a danger to the community of that country.'

The German Federal Constitutional Court recently had the opportunity to apply the rationale which underlies Article 33(2) of the Refugee Convention to Article 16(2) of the German Basic Law, which guarantees an enforceable fundamental right of asylum to every person persecuted on political grounds.[42] The case concerned a Turkish Kurd who had in Turkey advocated the secession of Kurdistan and had supported -and actively participated in- violent and terrorist actions, and who had been confined to prison several times, where he claimed to have been tortured and treated in a degrading manner. In 1980 he came to Germany, joined a militant separatist group and was convicted for causing serious bodily

---

39 If extradition is refused on that ground, the requested State is under the obligation to prosecute the fugitive (Article V(B) in connection with Article XI of the Draft Articles).
40 Since Article 16(2) of the Constitution of the Federal Republic of Germany contains an enforceable individual fundamental right of asylum, there is ample case law as to the circumstances under which criminal prosecution turns into political persecution, in particular in States which try to preserve its existence by fighting separatist movements which, themselves, commit terrorist acts. *Cf.*, *e.g.* the Decision of the Federal Constitutional Court of 10 July 1989. Repr. in BVerfGE 80, 315-353 (concerning Sri Lanka).
41 Also see T. Stein, *Rendition of Terrorists: Extradition versus Deportation*, 19 Israel Yearbook on Human Rights 281-295 (1989).
42 Decision of 20 December 1989, BVerfGE 81, 142.

injury to other Turks who did not share his political beliefs. His request for asylum was rejected and his deportation ordered. The Constitutional Court, called upon by way of a constitutional complaint, held: although the criminal prosecution which the appellant would have to face in Turkey after deportation would probably amount to political persecution, his request for asylum must fail because it is beyond the scope of asylum, if a refugee only looks for a new battlefield from which he continues to support, or participate in, terrorist activities. Asylum is only granted to those refugees who are prepared to end the political fight which threatened their very life and existence, and to live in peace in the country of refuge. The Court was convinced that the appellant had continued his political fight from his safe haven not only by making use of his freedom of expression, but by actively supporting terrorist activities. Since the expulsion order allowed for unconditional deportation, the Court reminded the Immigration Office that, in view of Article 3 of the European Convention on Human Rights and Fundamental Freedoms, sufficient guarantees might have to be obtained that the appellant, if deported, would not be subject to torture or to inhuman or degrading treatment.[43] This leads us to our last point:

6.   HUMAN RIGHTS AND FUNDAMENTAL FREEDOMS

Article V(A,1) of ILA's Draft Articles[44] also provide that extradition may be refused when:

> 'The requested State is not satisfied that the requesting State is able and willing to apply, or, in case of a convicted person, has applied, before, during and after the trial the fair trial standards required by applicable rules of international law, and to refrain from subjecting the accused or convicted person to torture or to cruel, inhuman or degrading treatment or punishment.'

Carillo Salcedo and Frowein have stated in their 'Corpus of Principles'[45] that: '[s]uspected terrorists must always be treated with respect for their

---

43 It is established case-law in Germany that even if a fugitive does not qualify for 'political asylum', he will nevertheless be granted 'humanitarian asylum' in cases where there is an imminent danger of torture in his country of origin. Torture, according to the courts, amounts to political persecution only when it is politically motivated. *Cf.*, Federal Administrative Court, 27 May 1986, Informationsbrief Ausländerrecht 265 (1986).

44 See ILA Committee Report, loc. cit. n. 13.

45 Carillo Salcedo, Frowein, loc. cit. n. 14, at 5.4.

human rights. Torture can never be justified. An effective defence must be guaranteed during the investigation and the trial.' This, again, gives expression to the fact that it is one, if not the, strength of a State governed by the rule of law, to stick to these rules even under extreme circumstances; not to 'turn the other cheek', but also not to 'take an eye for an eye'.

It should not be too difficult for a State governed by the rule of law, under 'normal' conditions, to treat suspected terrorists with respect for their human rights and to guarantee an effective defence. However, in 1977 Germany witnessed a situation which was anything but normal. There were reasonable and substantial grounds to believe that some of the defence counsel for (suspected) terrorists held in pre-trial confinement or serving their sentences, had sided with their clients and helped to exchange messages between those imprisoned in different penal institutions or between those imprisoned and their accomplices outside. At the same time the president of the German Employer's Association had been kidnapped by terrorists who threatened to kill him if the imprisoned terrorists were not released and given the opportunity to travel to a country of their choice. There were strong suspicions that the entire operation was guided, if not from inside the prison than at least in co-ordination with those imprisoned. In this situation the German authorities decided to cut off temporarily all links between the imprisoned terrorists themselves and between them and the outside world, including any oral or written communication with their defence counsel. These measures were initially taken on the basis of an executive order and shortly afterwards based on a law[46] which limited those measures in time, made them subject to judicial control and stayed all proceedings and the corresponding prescriptive times with respect to those affected by those measures. The law was later upheld by the Constitutional Court as being constitutional under the prevailing circumstances.[47]

The case as such apparently never reached the Commission in Strasbourg, but one could imagine an application claiming the violation of the right to an effective defence, taking into account that Article 6 of the European Convention on Human Rights does not provide for exceptions 'in accordance with the law and necessary in a democratic society', and taking furthermore into account that the conditions for derogation under Article

---

46 Law of 2 October 1977, I BGBl 1877 (1977).
47 BVerfGE 49, 24 (1 August 1978).

15 of the Convention were certainly not fulfilled.[48] Although Article 6 of the European Convention might require constant and uninterrupted contact between an accused and his defence counsel under normal circumstances, it is rather inconceivable that the Commission or the Court would have found the *Kontaktsperre-Gesetz* and the measures taken thereunder to be in violation of the European Convention on Human Rights, although it has become clear from the decisions taken in comparable cases that the Commission and the Court are determined to uphold a high standard of protection also for terrorists.[49]

It is sometimes debated, fortunately on a rather theoretical level, whether extreme terrorist threats could justify extreme counter-measures, in particular whether it would be admissible to use torture during the interrogation of a terrorist who knows where the bomb is hidden which could kill hundreds of innocent bystanders. The question comes up whenever the possibility is discussed that terrorists one day might even use 'special weapons' (nuclear, chemical or biological). Although it might sound to those responsible for the protection of public security as saying 'we can't say it is legal, but we hope somebody will do it if need be', the legal answer is clear: there is no justification whatsoever for torture. The prohibition of torture, whether or not it is part of *ius cogens*,[50] is 'emergency-resistant' under all existing human rights instruments in the sense that even in an emergency the prohibition of torture cannot be derogated from.[51] Whether analogies to 'distress' or 'necessity'[52] could preclude the criminal responsibility of those who apply torture in a situation as described above, is a different question.

---

48 But see European Court of Human Rights, *Ireland* v. *United Kingdom*, 25 Publications of the European Court of Human Rights, Ser. A, where the Court accepted that, under the existing emergency in Northern Ireland, extra-judicial measures of deprivation of liberty could reasonably be considered as being strictly required for the protection of public security. For a general survey on derogations from human rights guarantees see T. Stein, *Derogations from Guarantees laid down in Human Rights Instruments*, in I. Maier, ed., Protection of Human Rights in Europe, Proceedings of the Fifth International Colloque about the European Convention on Human Rights 123 *et seq.* (1982).

49 See the Decision of the Commission in the *Case* of *McVeigh*, 25 Decisions and Reports, 15. The decision of the Court in the *Case* of *Brogan and Others*, 152 Publications of the European Court of Human Rights, Ser. A, and the Decision of the Commission in the *Case* of *Kröcher-Möller* v. *Switzerland*, 34 Decisions and Reports, 52 *et seq.*

50 *Cf.*, J.A. Frowein, R. Kühner, *Drohende Folterung als Asylgrund und Grenze für Auslieferung und Ausweisung* (The Threat of Torture and its Consequences for the Law of Asylum, Extradition and Expulsion), 43 ZaöRV 537-565 (1983).

51 *Cf.*, Stein, loc. cit. n. 48.

52 *Cf.*, Articles. 32-33 of the ILC's Draft Articles on State Responsibility (Part I).

7.   CONCLUSION

Terrorist acts are attacks on the most fundamental human rights, but the neglect terrorists show for human rights is irrelevant for the question, how much human rights terrorists deserve themselves.[53] Since human rights bind State organs and not individuals (although in recent decades it has been implicitly or explicitly accepted that organized or semi-organized political groups engaged in insurgency may be responsible for violation of human rights),[54] human rights cannot be forfeited by terrorists. Terrorists may not 'deserve' respect for their human rights in the proper sense of the word, but it is, after all, perhaps not so much with regard to the individual terrorist that human rights are respected, but with regard to the democratic States themselves which have to maintain the credibility of the rule of law and of human rights every day and under all circumstances, even if they have to do it sometimes with their fists clenched in their pockets. The lawful possibilities for restricting the protection of human rights for terrorists are, as our (necessarily incomplete) survey has shown, rather limited themselves.

Terrorism will continue to be a challenge for our societies and legal systems for the years ahead, and the way in which terrorists, when apprehended, are treated, will, therefore, remain to be a challenge for humanitarian law and its respect.

---

53 See Carillo Salcedo, Frowein, loc. cit. n. 14, at 86.
54 See T. Meron, *When do Acts of Terrorism Violate Human Rights*, 19 Israel Yearbook on Human Rights 275 (1989).

THE OBLIGATION TO INTERVENE IN THE DOMESTIC AFFAIRS OF STATES *

HENRY G. SCHERMERS

1. INTRODUCTION

One of the challenges of humanitarian law in the years to come is the problem of enforcement. The rules of humanitarian law are useful for those who want to follow them. They specify and clarify their obligations. But for those who do not want to follow them the rules of humanitarian law are no less important. The most fundamental rules of humanitarian law should be generally applied independent of any willingness to do so. This means that there must be a possibility to enforce them.

The international community has insufficient powers to enforce rules of law. The real powers are with the sovereign States. May, should, or must these States enforce the rules of international humanitarian law? There is a rule of international law prohibiting intervention in the domestic affairs of

---

* The manuscript was finished June 1990.

foreign States.[1] If there is another rule obliging States to enforce international humanitarian law, then we are faced with a conflict of obligations. Should priority be given to humanitarian law or to the obligation of non-interference? In this essay the present author wants to reconsider the strength of the prohibition to interfere and the need for its change or mitigation.

2.   THE PROHIBITION OF INTERVENTION

Traditionally, international law was a separate legal system with its own particular rules aimed only at relations *between* States. The relations *within* States, both those between citizens and their Governments and those between citizens mutually, fell outside international law. They were governed solely by the national legal system concerned. In this conception it is clear that international legal rules applying directly to citizens were *ultra vires*.

Governments of States cherished this restricted role of international law. It left them free to order their national affairs without outside supervision and without having to account for whatever they did. The theory of unlimited national sovereignty meant in fact uncontrolled power for the domestic Governments.

In this conception the prohibition of intervention fitted well. Each State was full master of its own internal affairs. Other Sates were not entitled to intervene, unless their own citizens or national interests were involved.

In the early twentieth century it became clear that it was no longer possible to regard States as completely sovereign. Some interstate organization became necessary, and international organizations were established. Though their competence was limited, their power to discuss international affairs to a very small extent restricted the monopoly of States in international relations. The effect on national sovereignty was small, only its external aspects being open for debate, but it was the beginning of a process of ever growing 'internationalization'. The internal sovereignty was carefully protected at first, expressed, for example in the first part of Article 2(7) of the Charter of the United Nations, which reads:

---

1   For a thorough study of humanitarian intervention under international law and for references to further literature, see W.D. Verwey, Humanitarian Intervention under International Law, 32 NILR 357-418 (1985).

'7. Nothing contained in the present Charter shall authorize the United Nations to intervene in matters which are essentially within the domestic jurisdiction of any state or shall require the Members to submit such matters to settlement under the present Charter.'

A comparable provision existed between the two World Wars in Article 15(8) of the Statute of the League of Nations. But in the UN Charter an exception was added in the last part of Article 2(7) for threats to the peace, breaches of the peace or acts of aggression:

'... but this principle shall not prejudice the application of enforcement measures under Chapter VII.'

Also, after the admission of the newly independent States, the United Nations underlined the full sovereignty of States to act within their domestic affairs as they pleased. The General Assembly adopted Resolution 2131 (XX) of 21 December 1965, which provided *inter alia* in its Preamble:

'The General Assembly,
(...)
    Reaffirming the principle of non-intervention, proclaimed in the Charters of the Organization of American States, the League of Arab States and the Organization of African Unity and affirmed at the conferences held at Montevideo, Buenos Aires, Chapultepec and Bogotá, as well as in the decisions of the Asian-African Conference at Bandung, the First Conference of Heads of State or Government of Non-Aligned Countries at Belgrade, in the Programme for Peace and International Co-operation adopted at the end of the Second Conference of Heads of State of Government of Non-Aligned Countries at Cairo, and in the Declaration on Subversion adopted at Accra by the Heads of State and Government of the African States,
    Recognizing that full observance of the principle of non-intervention of States in the internal and external affairs of other States is essential to the fulfilment of the purposes and principles of the United Nations,
(...)
    Mindful that violation of the principle of non-intervention poses a threat to the independence, freedom and normal political, economic, social and cultural development of countries, particularly those which have freed themselves from colonialism, and can pose a serious threat to the maintenance of peace,
    Fully aware of the imperative need to create appropriate conditions which would enable all States, and in particular the developing countries, to

choose without duress or coercion their own political, economic and social institutions.'

In the light of these considerations the General Assembly subsequently solemnly declared, *inter alia*:

'1. No State has the right to intervene, directly or indirectly, for any reason whatever, in the internal or external affairs of any other State. Consequently, armed intervention and all other forms of interference or attempted threats against the personality of the State or against its political, economic and cultural elements, are condemned.'

In October 1970 the General Assembly of the UN adopted the Declaration on Principles of International Law concerning Friendly Relations and Co-operation among States in Accordance with the Charter of the United Nations.[2] In the Preamble of this Declaration it considered *inter alia*:

'(...)
    Convinced that the strict observance by States of the obligation not to intervene in the affairs of any other State is an essential condition to ensure that nations live together in peace with one another, since the practice of any form of intervention not only violates the spirit and the letter of the Charter, but also leads to the creation of situations which threaten international peace and security,
(...)
    Considering that the progressive development and codification of the following principles:
        (...)
        (c)   The duty not to intervene in matters within the domestic jurisdiction of any State, in accordance with the Charter,
        (...)
so as to secure their more effective application within the international community, would promote the realization of the purposes of the United Nations.'

In the Declaration itself the General Assembly proclaimed a number of principles, among which the principle concerning the duty not to intervene in matters within the domestic jurisdiction of any State, in accordance with the Charter. Under this principle it held:

---

2   GA Res. 2625 (XXV) of 24 October 1970.

'No State or group of States has the right to intervene, directly or indirectly, for any reason whatever, in the internal or external affairs of any other State. Consequently, armed intervention and all other forms of interference or attempted threats against the personality or against its political, economic or cultural elements, are in violation of international law.'

In 1975 the principle of non-intervention was underlined in the Final Act of the Conference on Security and Co-operation in Europe (the Helsinki Act). The sixth principle to which the participating States adhered reads:

'The participating States will refrain from any intervention, direct or indirect, individual or collective, in the internal or external affairs falling within the domestic jurisdiction of another participating State, regardless of their mutual relations.

They will accordingly refrain from any form of armed intervention or threat of such intervention against another participating State.

They will likewise in all circumstances refrain from any other act of military, or of political, economic or other coercion designed to subordinate to their own interest the exercise by another participating State of the rights inherent in its sovereignty and thus to secure advantages of any kind.

Accordingly, they will, *inter alia*, refrain from direct or indirect assistance to terrorist activities, or to subversive or other activities directed towards the violent overthrow of the regime of another participating State.'

3.   GOVERNMENTS' RIGHT TO STAY IN POWER

Apart from the general principle of non-intervention, present international law contains another rule for the protection of the Governments of States. This rule is expressed in the two most important Resolutions of the General Assembly of the UN on non-intervention (GA Resolution 2131 (XX) and 2625 (XXV)). They both contain the following provision:

'Every State has an inalienable right to choose its political, economic, social and cultural systems, without interference in any form by another State.'

This means that neither the international community, nor any other State is entitled to overthrow the Government of a State. Whether a Government is really chosen and whether it is supported by the population or not is irrelevant. The phrase means to say: 'Every Government which has full control over a State has the right to stay in power, however bad its activities may be.'

The acceptance of this rule as a part of international law clearly indicates that the provisions of international law -and in particular those codified in GA Resolutions- are made by Governments rather than by courts or by parliaments representing the population. In the way it is meant to be interpreted it is a clear rule of self-protection.

This does not mean that the prohibition of intervention and the inalienable right to choose one's own political system do not create a useful rule. Allowing other States to impose a Government upon a State would meet with grave objections. It is only the interpretation of the rule which makes it a rule of non-intervention. If it meant: '[e]very people has the right to choose its Government', it could at the same time mean that the international community has the obligation to replace a Government which is not supported by the people of the State concerned. Such a rule would be difficult to realize (how can one establish the wishes of a population without co-operation of the Government of the State concerned?), but it would not be part of the prohibition of intervention.

4.   THE NEED FOR CHANGE

From the above, it may be clear that the principle of non-intervention is strongly embedded in international law. Should that remain so? It is a general phenomenon of the law that the rules of today are based on needs and experiences of yesterday. The rule of non-intervention is based on the principle of full sovereignty of States, a principle which has dominated international law for a long time. But that principle is rapidly weakening. States are no longer fully sovereign and international law is no longer a legal system applicable only to the relations between States. With increasing speed international law creates rules for others besides States, for companies as well as for private citizens. These are rules on navigation in the air and on the seas, codes of conduct for multinational companies, rules on war crimes and on the environment.

Often such rules are codified in international treaties. That means that under international law they are binding only for the States which have ratified them. But next to these traditional rules of international treaty law, binding rules of world law develop to an increasing extent as international *jus cogens*, binding on mankind in general. Nowadays nobody will consider torture, slave-trading, racial discrimination or genocide lawful for those countries which have not ratified the treaties prohibiting them. Factual circumstances compel air companies to respect the international rules for air navigation over the high seas and postal services follow the requirements which the UPU has made for transnational mail. The rules of the UPU which require ratification by the participating States are generally applied long before the ratifications (if they ever come) are received.

In order to be effective law must be enforced. International law is no exception. The more important its rules become, the more important also is their enforcement. In many cases the sheer necessity of co-operation is strong enough to guarantee application of the law. The international rules on air-navigation, international mail or telecommunications hardly need an enforcement mechanism. In other cases the national Governments, who still claim full authority over their subjects, are able to enforce the rules of international law. They can fight slave-trading and control codes of conduct. But many international rules urgently need stronger co-operation since they cannot properly be executed by national Governments alone. The rules of international law concerning the protection of human rights especially are directed against national Governments. To an ever increasing extent international law obliges Governments to act in a particular way, orders them to respect particular minimum rights of the persons within their jurisdiction and prohibits particular kinds of behaviour. In such cases enforcement is insufficiently possible. New methods must be developed.

It may be true that under traditional international law the community could not act nor be held responsible when a State murdered a racial or religious minority on its territory. That was a domestic affair, solely within the jurisdiction of the State concerned. That was at a time when human rights were a purely domestic matter. Now, the world community has accepted responsibility for the protection of human rights, which means that severe violations cannot be tolerated, that the community must act against Governments which violate the rules. Since international law has expanded to protect fundamental human rights, neither the total prohibition of intervention, nor the unlimited right for a Government to stay in power can be maintained. In extreme cases, such as existed in Amin's Uganda and in the last years of Ceaucescu's Rumania, the international community is obliged to intervene, to set aside a dictator who is unwilling to respect the fundamental rights of his subjects. The world may not tolerate groups of people being tortured or killed. International law on the protection of human rights has developed to such an extent that it now necessarily entails international solidarity and an international obligation to enforce the law.

The prohibition of intervention and the right of a Government to stay in power are outdated. Under modern international law Governments operate under legal obligations and must be corrected when their obligations are infringed. In particular situations there may be an international obligation to interfere.

5.   NEW PROBLEMS

This confronts us with the immense problem of how to legally determine when a situation within a particular State requires intervention. Were the United States interventions in Grenada and Panama and the Soviet Union's interventions in Hungary, Czechoslovakia and Afghanistan needed? Or were they perhaps not absolutely necessary but sufficiently needed to be justified? Or were they not necessary for humanitarian reasons and only the consequence of power politics? How can it be established that the domestic situation in a State is such that intervention is required?

Fifty years ago, under traditional international law, the answer to this question was simple: 'It is impossible to establish when intervention is justified; therefore all intervention should be prohibited.' But since 1945 international law has developed in many ways and the available instruments have enormously increased. Now it should be possible to establish when international intervention is needed. The question is certainly not an easy one, as three obstacles must be overcome:

a) no intervention should be permitted for the sole reason that a State changes its Government or that it no longer fits in the block to which it used to belong;
b) no intervention should be permitted which -under whatever pretext- serves the power politics of another State; and
c) it should be objectively established that the domestic situation in the country concerned is contrary to the rules of international law.

Though still weak and undeveloped our present society has the institutions which can overcome these obstacles. The General Assembly of the UN, in which all blocks are represented, should be able to decide whether a change of Government actually means an infringement of fundamental human rights or not. It may be necessary to provide for a special majority for this kind of decisions. The Security Council must be able to condemn intervention as an aspect of power politics. The ICJ is sufficiently objective and familiar with international law to establish, with the help of counsel, whether a particular situation is an infringement of international (humanitarian) law. Certainly, these tasks will not be easy. When the local

Government resists the establishment of the facts, this alone may cause grave problems. But when the co-operation of the General Assembly, the Security Council and the ICJ are required there may be sufficient protection against unjustified intervention. However, obtaining the approval of those three institutions necessarily requires much time. When human rights are badly infringed speedy action may be required. Speedy intervention is dangerous intervention. When the situation in a country is unclear the press may easily spread the impression that serious infringements of the law are part of government policy. For a justified intervention a well-founded decision is needed. Perhaps we must accept that justified intervention is necessarily slow. Better a slow correction than no correction at all.

It should be clear that international law on intervention meets many problems. Because of the long lasting prohibition no rules on intervention have been developed. As any possibility of intervention will restrict the freedom of national Governments, Governmental initiatives, even Governmental co-operation cannot yet be expected. The academic world and non-governmental organizations will have to develop this new branch of international law.

6. METHODS OF INTERVENTION

International intervention should be possible against a particular national Government for the sake of the population which is oppressed by that Government. This means that methods should be used which pressurize the Government without harming the population. Is that at all possible?

There is a great interdependence in our modern world. This means that many international sanctions are available apart from the use of force. For each specific case it should be decided which sanction is the most appropriate. Effective intervention, in particular in urgent cases, may well mean military intervention. Also in this respect we have experience which was not available in the beginning of our century. UN troops have operated in several parts of the world. Even if their military experience is limited, logistical improvements have been made and the availability of UN soldiers is not a major problem. With some effort it should be possible to mobilize an active military UN force in any part of the world.

Each possible sanction meets with objections. It may be that innocent people must suffer harm or that the total economy of a State is badly damaged. For each possible sanction rules will be needed to limit these objections to a minimum. It is not the intention to develop rules in the present essay, but it may be justifiable in a book in honour of Professor Kalshoven to pay at least some attention to the rules of warfare. Are international forces bound by these rules when intervening in a State to terminate or prevent infringements of human rights? Or should such forces be completely free to act in order to reach their aim as quickly as possible? Is it relevant that the UN is not a party to the important treaties on warfare? May forces be used from States which are not parties to such treaties?

Treaties are no longer the sole sources of modern international law. Humanitarian law has gradually developed into generally binding world law. It is part of *jus cogens*.[3] The answer to the above questions, therefore, is easy: 'All troops are bound by laws on warfare'. Even if those laws harm the effective functioning of international forces, they should be respected. Respect for the law must prevail in any legitimate action.

But the *jus cogens*, the general principles of the laws on warfare are vague and undefined. In practice, UN regulations and agreements on peacekeeping forces consistently refer to the 'principles and spirit' of the Conventions on international humanitarian law, never to any binding force of the Conventions themselves. This makes the law unclear and pleads for clarification.[4]

7. CONCLUSIONS

The following conclusions can be drawn:

a) The protection of fundamental human rights is no longer a matter solely within the jurisdiction of each individual State. The international community bears responsibility.

b) The international responsibility entails a right, in extreme cases even a duty, to intervene when States severely infringe human rights.

c) As any intervention has long been prohibited under international law, the necessary legal rules on intervention are underdeveloped.

---

3 On the *jus cogens* character of international humanitarian law, see G. Abi-Saab, *The Specifications of Humanitarian Law*, in C. Swinarski, ed., Studies and Essays on International Humanitarian Law and Red Cross Principles in Honour of Jean Pictet 265-280 (1984); G. Perrin, *La nécessité et les dangers du jus cogens, ibid.*, at 751-759.

4 See D. Schindler, *United Nations Forces and International Humanitarian Law*, loc. cit. n. 3, at 521-530.

d) Governments being the natural enemy of intervention, such rules must be developed in non-governmental fora. There is a task for the academic community and especially for the many former students of Professor Kalshoven.

JUS AD BELLUM AND JUS COGENS:
IS IMMORALITY ILLEGAL?

ALFRED P. RUBIN

1.   INTRODUCTION

Kalshoven is one of the most eloquent and knowledgeable scholars of international humanitarian law of our generation. This essay, raising some fundamental questions regarding past attempts to translate humanitarian principles into positive law, can come as no surprise to him.

It sets out some of the reasons why I believe the successes of codification and progressive development have been limited in our time; reasons which in no way deny the importance of the past work, but which suggest the possible utility of beginning to move in a different direction to implement the ideals so ably urged by Kalshoven and his many friends and colleagues.

The legislators of the international legal order have tried for millenia to restrict recourse to violence aimed against each other by the legal orders, the States,[1] that are the primary units of the system. An analogy can be made to statesmen in municipal legal orders trying to remove the spectre of violence beyond what the cohesion of the State requires from the burdens their subjects must carry. Immediately, it becomes apparent that the cohesion of the State is the higher good; violence in enforcing the criminal law within the State is permissible to authorized persons, both police in many (but not all) circumstances, and individuals in some circumstances (as to defend themselves or to stop the commission of some felonies). Personal violence is not the deepest evil in either the virtue-based or positive morality of Government; the problem is to determine under what conditions it ought to be permitted, who ought to be authorized to commit it, and who ought to be authorized to determine what results should flow within the legal order after it has been committed. In a strictly positivist framework, it is even possible to suggest that violence as a tool to maintain an authority structure based on divine law or historical tradition, or even common law, is a part of the legal order. It is the purpose of this essay to consider whether the international legal order can forbid recourse to force in any meaningful way; whether some uses of force are inherent in the order itself, and, if so, what that might mean to attempts to further restrict the use of force in international affairs by using the tools of codification and progressive development of the positive law.

2.   THE FAILURE OF POSITIVE LAW

Historically, there have been numerous utopian proposals to abolish recourse to the use of force in matters of governance, and more practical but tension-ridden proposals by 'universal' organizations, like the Roman Catholic Church or the Muslim Caliphate which would impose a violence-free society as a reward for voluntary submission to an organization. But with the triumph of secular approaches to the 'international' legal order by

---

1   The separation of legal orders, not necessarily based on religious or ethnic divisions, into the fundamental units of an 'international' legal order can be traced back to biblical and pre-biblical days despite periods of history in which theories of universal authority dominated the literature that has survived. See *Joshua* 9:1-27; *The Voyage of Wen-Amon*, in J.B. Pritchard, 1 The Ancient Near East 16-24 (1958).

the time of the Peace of Westphalia in Europe, the dream failed of creating an over-arching order with the authority in some institution to enforce prohibitions on the use of force without the consent of the alleged malefactor itself.

2.1   The League of Nations Covenant

It is not necessary to review all the various organizational accommodations from 1648 to today. The immediate ancestor of the current international organization which, by agreement of States within the Westphalian constitution, has had some authority to react institutionally to some uses of force was the League of Nations. In its Covenant, the Members of the League undertook:

> '... to respect and preserve as against external aggression the territorial integrity and existing political independence of all Members of the League. In case of any such aggression or in case of any threat or danger of such aggression the Council shall advise upon the means by which this obligation shall be fulfilled' (Article 10).

The Covenant then sets out a complex set of procedures to be followed in cases of war, threat of war, or, indeed, any 'dispute likely to lead to a rupture' between Members (Articles 11 and 12). Should there be a resort to war by a League Member in disregard of these procedures, legal results flowed automatically. The other Members of the League were obliged immediately to sever all trade or financial relations, prohibit intercourse between their nationals and the nationals of the Covenant-breaking State, and prevent all 'financial, commercial or personal intercourse between the nationals of the Covenant-breaking State and the nationals of any other State, whether a Member of the League or not' (Article 16).

With regard to disputes involving non-Members, the League Council was authorized to 'take such measures and make such recommendations as will prevent hostilities and will result in the settlement of the dispute' (Article 17(4)).

There are no express exceptions for self-defense or 'just wars' or any other basis for Members of the League to resort to force, but there is a provision requiring Members of the League to submit their disputes to arbitration, or judicial settlement or inquiry by the League Council. If the path of inquiry is chosen, and the Council cannot decide the matter unanimously except for the vote of a contending Party, then the Members 'reserve to themselves the right to take such action as they shall consider necessary for the maintenance of right and justice' (Article 15(7)).

In this context, there is no institution able to make a definitive interpretation, leaving each State to self-enforce its own interpretations. Thus, where automatic sanctions are not fixed by objective criteria, the imposition of sanctions under this Article depends on national discretion in categorizing matters about which reasonable people notoriously disagree: 'right and justice'.

2.2   The Kellogg-Briand Pact

This 'lacuna' in the Covenant, made wider by the possibility of a League Member renouncing its Membership and leaving the League and its obligations, a possibility unstated in the Covenant but exercised in practice, was purportedly closed by the conclusion in 1928 of the Kellogg-Briand Pact. In the two substantive Articles of that multilateral Treaty States Parties condemned 'recourse to war' and renounced it as an instrument of national policy in their relations with one another (Article 1), and agreed that disputes among them should be settled only 'by peaceful means' (Article 2). The United States Senate advised and consented to ratification only after being formally assured that the commitment did not hinder military action that might be taken by the United States in 'self-defense'.[2] Senator Glass of Virginia called it, 'this worthless, but perfectly harmless peace treaty'.[3]

2.3   The United Nations Charter

The United Nations Charter took a very different approach. Promises that had exceptions as wide as the ingenuity of statesmen interpreting vague words could make them, and no institutions in the legal order to encourage compliance with community expectations, like the promises in the Kellogg-Briand Pact, were still considered important politically and perhaps in the moral sphere; but without results in the legal order to flow from violation, such promises were seen not to be an adequate basis for establishing legal relationships on which real lives and property could be risked.[4] Automatic

---

2   R.H. Ferrell, Peace in Their Time 250 (1952) n. 35.

3   *Ibid.*, at 251.

4   The Kellogg-Briand Pact was in fact used as a basis for the victorious Allies finding the leaders of Nazi-Germany and Imperial Japan guilty of war crimes in planning and initiating World War II. But the same rules were not applied to the Soviet Union and Italy, and have not

sanctions of the sort contained in the League Covenant had failed to avert World War II. They were abandoned. Collective political discretion was tried in their place.

Under the terms of the Charter, the Security Council was supposed to determine if there were a 'threat to the peace, breach of the peace, or act of aggression' and then make recommendations 'or decide what measures shall be taken ... to maintain or restore international peace and security' (Article 39). These Security Council 'decisions' are binding on the Members (Article 25).[5] If somehow the Security Council had not acted in time to avoid an 'armed attack', Article 51 of the Charter reserves to the members the 'inherent right of self defense ... until the Security Council has taken measures necessary to maintain international peace and security ...'. As the willingness of the Members of the Security Council to find a 'threat to the peace' has receded in practice, the threshold for 'self-defense' action under Article 51 has been conceived to expand, and States now argue self-defense in the context of the Charter to justify military actions in situations far removed from the 'imminent, overwhelming' necessity threshold of the classical 'Caroline Case' formulation of the international law of self-defense[6] and the qualifying phrase 'if an armed attack occurs' has as a practical matter been deleted from the Article.

---

been applied in practice since, although frequently appearing in polemical writings. In retrospect, the argument seems more hypocritical than convincing. *Cf.*, J. Stone, Legal Control of International Conflicts 324-329 (1959).

5　There is a substantial question whether such decisions are binding if they do not involve the sort of action contemplated by Articles 41 or 42 of the Charter, which were specifically mentioned in Article 39. There is also some question about the relationship of Articles 48 and 49 to Articles 24 and 25 of the Charter. *Cf.*, Advisory Opinion on the Legal Consequences for States of Continued Presence of South Africa in Namibia, ICJ Rep., 1971, §§ 113-116, with Dissenting Opinion by Judge Gros, §§ 34-36.

6　J.B. Moore, Digest of International Law 412 (1906); 30 Br. & For. State Papers (1842-1843) § 193, at 201. For an example of arguing self-defense in a context far removed from both the Caroline and 'armed attack' criteria but brought within them by ingenuity and the apparent political conclusion of the Security Council that for purposes of this particular use of force the technical consistency of the justification in terms of Article 51 was not vital, see the Security Council debate on Israel's Entebbe (Uganda) raid briefed in 13 UN Chronicle 15-21, 67-76 (1976) and J. Sheehan, *The Entebbe Raid*, 1(2) The Fletcher Forum 135-153 (1977). Sheehan suggests that a different rule of international law, which he calls 'rectification', was at play, authorizing a State to perform the legal obligation of another State when the failure of the second State creates irremediable damage to the first. He bases this on analogy to parallel rules in municipal legal orders. *Cf.*, American Law Institute, *Restatement of the Law of Restitution* §§ 114-115 (1937). *Cf.*, the British argument to support action against 'pirates' in Turkish territory referred to in A.D. McNair, 1 Law Officers' Opinions 275 *et seq.* (1956).

3.   POSITIVE LAW AND MORALITY

To those who see the rules of international common law as those rules
implicit in the structure of society and reflecting its ultimate values, this
evolution confirms the moral 'virtue' of some uses of force in international
affairs in a context far removed from the 'human rights' arguments that
seem to dominate discussions of the moral content of international common
law. 'Morality' in this model of the structure of the international legal
order is 'positive morality', the *mores* of society perceived by practice
accepted as law rather than the rules asserted to reflect ultimate value
judgments confined to notions of virtuous behavior or 'the good'. Those
who accept positive morality as part of the 'moral' underpinning of the
legal order see the codification of the sources of law in Article 38 of the
Statute of the ICJ as essentially free of preconceptions of 'virtue-morality'.
To those whose concept of 'morality' is inextricably tied to notions of
virtue and humane values, this positive morality is not 'moral' at all. The
system itself must seem to them to be amoral.

   But Article 38 of the Statute of the ICJ does not directly refer to virtue
or to morality in any particular sense. Instead, Article 38(1,a) refers to
treaty rules whatever they might be, accepted by the Parties to a legal
dispute; Article 38(1,b) refers to 'international custom, as evidence of a
general practice accepted as law'; Article 38(1,c) refers to 'the general
principles of law recognized by civilized nations'; and only in
Article 38(1,d) is there a reference to the opinions of 'the most highly
qualified publicists', and then only as 'subsidiary means for the
determination of rules of law'.

   The fact is that none of these provisions prescribes a virtue content to
rules as a threshold in the translation from practice or assertion to
bindingness. The ICJ is permitted to reach decisions on the basis of moral
argument, '*ex aequo et bono*', but only when the Parties agree to that in a
submission different from their submission to the jurisdiction of the Court
to apply public international law.

   Now, it is entirely possible to argue that this model is not the only
model that can be adopted by statesmen or publicists as the abstraction of
the legal order best reflecting reality or a pattern of interaction that
statesmen in their own national interest may, or in fact do, try to create. It
can also be argued that the Statute of the ICJ can be interpreted differently
to include decisions *ex aequo et bono* in the general authority of the Court
to determine 'any question of international law' (Article 36(2,b) of the
Statute). But for any such arguments to be persuasive, it would have to be
shown to reflect the realities of the existing international legal and political

order and not merely the notions of good-hearted and virtuous publicists as to which values they would like the order to enhance. It is an awkward but, in my opinion, undeniable fact that the first concern of any statesman is the well-being of his or her constituencies; that whatever other notions of virtue or morality exist, the defense of the legal order represented by that statesman is his or her first responsibility under the law of the order from which the statesman derives his or her authority.

4.   THE INHERENT RIGHT OF SELF-DEFENSE

What that means in moral argument is that self-defense of the municipal legal order is the highest value the system protects. It can be no other way. Even if a treaty must be interpreted out of any rational meaning or violated, no legal results flow against the State acting in self-defense.[7]

It also means that self-defense must be defined in the natural order, not restricted to the high threshold of the Caroline correspondence, but to take account of the legal structure by which States exist as legal orders independent of each other and select their own officials and representatives. This has so many implications for the international legal order that only a few can be set forth here. They all seem to be amply supported by any objective view of actual State practice and distinguishable from rules of general international law under Article 38(1,b) of the Statute of the ICJ only by presupposing models of the international legal order that are far more complex and require an elaborate system of assumptions, exceptions and sub-exceptions. The burden must be on those who prefer to posit different models to show conformity to Occam's Razor, the fundamental rule of philosophical and scientific inquiry that 'essences', assumptions of fact or order, must be kept to a minimum.[8]

---

7   *Cf.*, A.P. Rubin, *Self Defense at Sea*, 7 Thesaurus Acroasium 101-139 (1977), pointing out that Gidel's argument for a rule of exclusive flag State jurisdiction on the high seas in time of peace, which, he asserts made an act of self-defense against a merchant vessel a 'violation of principle, which is clear but in practice excusable', was based on an unnecessary legal fiction: the existence of a legal wrong with no legal consequences. The quotation is from G. Gidel, 1 Le Droit International Public de la Mer 354 (1932). In the words of Gidel: '... *la violation, certaine mais pratiquement excusable, du principe*'.

8   *Essentia non sunt multiplicanda, praeter necessitatem.* 19 Encyclopedia Britannica 965-966 (11th ed., 1911) ('Occam, William of'). Also, 20 Encyclopedia Britannica 868 (1911) ('Parsimony, Law of').

602 A. P. Rubin

4.1   Self-defense and *jus cogens*

The first among the corollaries of assuming the defense of a municipal
legal order is the highest duty of a statesmen in case of conflict is a
reconsideration of the notion of *jus cogens*, the assumption that there is an
international public policy that will render void treaties that are
inconsistent with that policy.

Many, if not all, muncipal legal orders posit the existence of 'illegal'
contracts which the system rejects. The notion that the international legal
order has an equivalent rule seems to rest either on mere virtue-moral
argumentation, which presumes that some moral values are necessarily also
legal values, or on a reading of Article 38(1,c) of the Statute of the ICJ
and its general law analogue to permit municipal systems' general
principles to be transferred directly to the international legal order as
general principles. The first seems to presume an equivalence between
virtue-morality and legal principle that has little if any practice to support
it and seems fundamentally inconsistent with the notion of 'law' as a
community rule rather than an individual rule of conscience. The second
appears to rest on logic which was effectively destroyed by Suarez about
four hundred years ago[9] (a more recent analysis by a 'naturalist' jurist of
towering reputation comes to the same conclusion as Suarez on the basis of
a more complex but more superficial analysis[10]). There seems little point
to reviewing either argument here.

This leads to the unexpected conclusion that if there is any content to
the category *jus cogens* formally adopted by the ILC and the Parties to the

---

9   F. Suarez, *De Legibus Ac Deo Legislatore*, II, XIX, §§ 2, 6, 8; XX § 1 (1612). The original
   texts were translated by G.L. Williams, A. Brown, J. Waldron, eng. text (1944):
   'The main points are that the *jus gentium* differs fundamentally from natural law first because
   the *jus gentium* is perceived in the parallel laws of different legal orders, thus is not
   necessarily derived from reason or the nature of the case, but from other sources, principally
   positive legislation or custom; second, because the *jus gentium* being the positive law of many
   different communities remains mutable at the discretion of each community's legislator; and
   third, because no single precept of the *jus gentium* has been found to be universal.'
10 H. Lauterpacht, Private Law Sources and Analogies of International Law 81-87 (1927).
   Lauterpacht strongly supports the fundamental naturalist notion that the same basic principles
   apply equally to States as units in the legal order, and to individuals in a natural law system.
   But the transferrence of natural law-based municipal rules to the international order rests on
   showing the circumstances surrounding the application of the rule in both systems to be near
   enough to identical to support an argument based on analogy, not identity.

1969 Vienna Convention on the Law of Treaties[11] it makes unenforceable as contrary to international public policy treaties that purport to limit the inherent right of a State to defend itself. The legal search then must be for the limits to that 'inherent right', a matter considered in the Caroline correspondence and resolved there without regard for the authority of an international collective policy decision or a need for a prior armed attack. Of course, nothing in this argument removes the possibility that there might be other peremptory rules of the legal order than the rule authorizing the use of force in self-defense, but that search for normative guidance is beyond the scope of this paper.

4.2   Self-defense and governing elites

Another implication of accepting the integrity of 'States' as the basic units of the Westphalian legal order is that Governments receiving assistance to suppress those with whom there is a dispute over authority under the national legal order cannot represent the 'State' whose constitution is in fact being challenged. Belligerents and perhaps other non-State actors disrupting the normal relations among States in the order might be, indeed, by some theoretical frameworks, are undoubtedly, directly part of the international legal order, with authority and substantive rights and obligations under that order. But only within the context of the State system. What this means is that those outside the State who perceive some elite group as the 'lawful' or 'legitimate' or proper holders of the authority to speak for the State in international affairs exceed their authority under the Westphalian constitution if they act on their perception in disregard of the facts within the State undergoing disruption. The result of this excess in the real world, the world of affairs, is to ally the struggling elite or rebel group with its foreign supporters and undermine the conceptions of law or tradition on which either depends for its internal authority. This is not to say that support for the struggling elite or rebel group will inevitably cause that elite or group to fail; in the short run, it might even be the only

---

11 UN Doc. A/CONF.39/27 (1969). *Cf.*, Article 53:
'A treaty is void if, at the time of its conclusion, it conflicts with a peremptory norm of general international law. For the purposes of the present Convention, a peremptory norm of general international law is a norm accepted and recognized by the international community of States as a whole as a norm from which no derogation is permitted and which can be modified only by a subsequent norm of general international law having the same character.'
Also Article 64:
'If a new peremptory norm of general international law emerges, any existing treaty which is in conflict with that norm becomes void and terminates.'

way for an elite to retain authority in its State or a rebel group to establish itself as a political actor in the local struggle for authority. But in the long run the effect of outside support in matters of authority is devastating. A legal order that depends on outside military aid to maintain its authority confuses military power with legal power and finds the expenses of the first nullify the advantages of the second. Even where the expenses of the first are bearable to the elite or its outside supporters, the usual result in the middle term is an unproductive, restive, sullen community, and in the long run either economic or political collapse of the legal order held together by outside force, or both.

4.2.1   *The naturalist perspective*

From this point of view, it is also possible to categorize from a natural law perspective the international legal implications of a revolution rather more easily than has been done by most modern studies. A revolution is by definition a change in the distribution of authority, a rupture of the constitution, of a State. For an outside power to take sides is not so much a breach of neutral obligations as an intervention in the internal affairs of a legal order which has the absolute right to determine its own constitution and to defend itself against all foreign attempts to influence that determination. It thus makes no difference in law whether the threshold of 'belligerency' has been crossed, whether there is an 'armed conflict', and, if there is, whether it is or is not of 'international character'.[12]

In the international legal order, a State or other actor can respond to any other's uses of force to affect the distribution of authority, whether in the international legal order or a national legal order that is a component of the international system, by either involvement or abstention. Involvement can be on many different levels, from formal participation as a co-belligerent in a declared war, to economic or political support that might or might not amount to 'unneutral' service. In any case, the laws of war

---

12 These categories are taken from Articles 2 and 3 common to the four Geneva Conventions of 1949 Relative to the Protection of the Victims of War. An argument that the positive law as developed through those Conventions is inconsistent with the underlying distribution of authority and structure of the international legal order is American Branch of the ILA, Proceedings and Committee Reports 1979-1980, *Report of the Committee on Armed Conflict* 38-54 (1979-1980). See also A.P. Rubin, *Terrorism and the Laws of War*, 12 Den. J. Int'l L. & Policy 219-235 (1983).

apply to govern neutral obligations and belligerent reprisals and belligerency itself.[13]

Where abstention is required by the structure of the legal order, as where the struggle is for authority within another legal order, another State, then the outsider still has obligations of neutrality under the laws of war if it wants to be free of the legal results of unneutral service. Failure to obey the natural law rule results in natural law consequences: involvement in an expensive and probably losing struggle, as the faction being supported is undercut in its claim to municipal legal authority by the very fact of outside support. In all cases, the natural laws of war apply.

This has even further implications. If there is no threshold of duration, intensity, organization etc. for the categorization in law of an 'armed conflict', but only military means and a struggle for authority within a legal order to bring into play the laws of war, as seems to be the case from a natural law point of view, then the laws of war should apply even to relations between 'terrorist' bands (even individuals) and the legal orders affected by their activities. In fact, despite constant denials by defending elites that this is the case, it does seem to provide a framework for categorizing those relations that fits what actually happens in the real world better than any other.

4.2.2 *The positivist perspective*

From a positivist point of view the same result flows. Each legal order, each State or other international actor, attaches the legal labels to the situation that best suits its policy. Defending elites with the titles of 'Government' call their rebels 'criminals' (as, of course, they are under the laws of the legal order whose constitution is under attack) and treat them as such, although usually with modifications that let criminal punishment seem very close to prisoner of war treatment for those not involved in 'war crimes'. Third States maintaining neutrality in the internal struggle typically refuse extradition of these 'criminals' ostensibly on the basis of a 'political offense' exception to their extradition obligations or the authority of their executive officials to hand over the fleeing 'criminal' to their opposite numbers in the requesting State. Third States in whose jurisdiction (territory or vessels or aircraft) 'terrorist' incidents occur treat the captured 'terrorists' as they would soldiers in a wartime situation: trying them under

---

13 The subject is too complex for simple summary. See A.P. Rubin, *The Concept of Neutrality in International Law*, in A.T. Leonhard, ed., Neutrality; Changing Concepts and Practices 9 (1988).

municipal law for whatever 'crimes' they have committed under that law as
they would apply municipal law to punish those committing 'war crimes'
against their nationals or in their territory while they are neutral in the
conflict; holding to non-belligerent behavior under municipal legislation
those who have acted within what are considered by that State to be
soldiers' privileges, but not punishing them for 'terrorist' acts against
foreigners done elsewhere, even if not 'war crimes', and not extraditing
them for acts within soldiers' privileges committed elsewhere. Negotiations
on a diplomatic level (usually denied in public, but in fact occurring) take
place to bargain for the release of persons or property wrongly seized by
the rebels.

Typically, the third State involved does not proclaim neutrality; there is
no need to. Indeed, it may silently or in harmless contexts even agree with
the defending elite's legal categorization of events under the law of that
legal order or its interpretation of international law. But in fact the natural
law result almost always flows. The third State either acts as a neutral
would under the laws of war, or acts unneutrally and becomes itself the
object of reprisal or other belligerent action by the rebels, either
encouraging it to withdraw from its 'unneutral' involvement in the struggle
among others for authority elsewhere, or slowly involving it in assistance
to a troubled elite with long range legal and political consequences it then
usually comes to regret. From this point of view, the American
involvement in Viet Nam followed a predictable course. The Americans'
refusal to become involved in the troubles in Northern Ireland has annoyed
their British allies, but encouraged a true neutrality that in fact helps them.
American assistance to Israel has involved the United States in events in
the Middle East it cannot control militarily and encouraged the taking of
American hostages. The taking is illegal under the laws of war, but seems
justifiable as reprisals to the militias which feel themselves prejudiced by
the American activities, and the United States seems not to have been able
to bring itself to use the legal categories necessary to clarify its activities
and gain the co-operation of the Governments in the area to treat the
hostage-taking as war crimes, 'grave breaches', illegal reprisals or
otherwise impermissible by the laws of war. The legal results of those
violations by the respective militias have therefore not flowed.

Nothing in what precedes should be taken to indicate any notion of the
inevitability of rebel victory. The fact that a governing elite in trouble
accepts foreign help is a sign it needs such help, and might be some
indication of its weakening base. But occasionally governing elites on their
own do re-establish their authority. It should never be forgotten in
discussions of the laws of war as applied during internal conflicts that the

paradigmatic conflict was the United States Civil War of 1861-1865. That conflict was won by the Union forces, the Government purporting to rule the entire country when in practice its authority was denied by the 'rebel' components of the Union. But throughout that struggle, the Union received little foreign help and it was the rebelling confederacy that sought it. The Union never declared war or conceded that the laws of war applied except as a concession to the confederate soldiers, made as a policy choice by the Union. It was the struggle that created the Lieber Code, the great codification of the laws of war issued as General Orders to the Union Armies in the Field by President Lincoln, that became the source of the codifications of 1899 and 1907 and is still regarded as the basic document of modern research into the laws of war.

4.3   Wars of national liberation

It is thus argued that it is the fact of military activity in a struggle for authority that determines the application of the laws of war, and those laws apply to all skirmishes regardless of 'recognition' by anybody, although a defending elite and an attacking rebel force may each insist that its municipal law applies to the other side and no third State has the standing to challenge that local categorization. From this point of view, discussions of the *jus ad bellum* as if pertinent to a determination of the application of the laws of war are fundamentally inconsistent with the structure of the international legal order as well as being inconsistent with the principal focus of the laws of war: the protection of war's victims in such a way as not to prejudice the outcome of the struggle. Thus the intrusion of qualifications regarding national liberation, racist regimes and other 'just war' terms reflecting political objects and virtue-moral judgments are not only irrelevant to the legal issues, but are antithetical to the objects of the law itself and presume the dominance of a virtue-based moral order in the world that is not visible in any analysis of fact. It is very hard to see such assertions improving the virtue of the world because they are based on falsity, and a moral order based on falsity is unlikely to encourage virtuous behaviour as much as it encourages more falsity.

5.   PUBLICISTS

It is easy to be mistaken for original when presenting an argument that is merely inconsistent with the current trend of legal writing. The writings confusing the *jus ad bellum* with the *jus in bello* abound not only in the

1949 Geneva Conventions and their 1977 Protocols, but in major writings
currently popular.[14] In fact, as the mention of the Lieber Code above
indicates, the views expressed here are not new; only neglected as the
dominance of natural law logic in the law of war has made various natural
law theories based on virtue-morality *seem* more persuasive on statesmen
than they in fact have ever been or are ever likely to be.

5.1   Grotius

The distinctions between the application of the natural laws of war to local
skirmishes and the application of the positive laws of war as a matter of
discretion were apparent in the Westphalian order from its very
beginnings. Grotius himself, after writing that: 'It is also necessary ... that
it [war] should be publicly declared' in order that it be legal,[15] went on to
say:

> 'To understand the foregoing passages, and others dealing with the
> declaration of war, we must carefully distinguish what is due according to
> the law of nature, and what is not due by nature but is honourable; what is
> required by the law of nations to secure the effects peculiar to this law, and
> what, in addition, is derived from the particular institutions of certain
> peoples. In a case where either an attack is being warded off, or a penalty
> is demanded from the very person who has done wrong, no declaration is
> required by the law of nature.'[16]

A more precise appreciation of Grotius's distinctions among what was
required by precisely which orders of law or morality and in precisely
what circumstances goes beyond the scope of this study, but the approach
is clear.

---

14 *Cf.*, H. Wilson, International Law and the Use of Force by National Liberation Movements
    (1988); T. Meron, Human Rights and Humanitarian Norms as Customary Law (1989). The
    first of these won the Paul Reuter Prize of the ICRC as a major work in the field of
    humanitarian law.

15 H. Grotius, *De Iure Belli ac Pacis* (1646), III, iii, 5. In the original Latin:
    '*Sed ut iustum hoc significatu bellum sit, non sufficit inter summas utrinque potestates geri:
    sed oportet, ut audivimus, ut et publice decretum sit ....*'

16 *Ibid.*, at III, iii, 6:
    '*Quae loca et alia de belli promulgatione agentia ut intelligantur, accurate distinguenda sunt
    quae iure naturae debentur, quae natura non debentur sed honesta sunt, quae iure gentium
    requiruntur ad effectus iuris gentium proprios, et quae praeterea ex peculiaribus populorum
    quorundam institutis veniunt. Naturali iure ubi aut vis illata arcetur, aut ab eo ipso qui
    deliquit poena deposcitus, nulla requiritur denuntiatio.*'

5.2   John Marshall and the United States Supreme Court

Grotius's complex but neat categorizations of legal and moral orders were overborne in the 18th and 19th centuries by doctrinal developments which did not bring greater clarity to legal analysis as much as they reflected a struggle for intellectual dominance between lawyers on the one side and statesmen on the other. The lawyers seemed constantly to try to find reasons why statesmen were bound to follow the rules propounded by the lawyers; the statesmen continued to act in disregard of legal advice except when, by national traditions or reasons of international policy decided by themselves, particular issues were shifted to an arena in which lawyers could dominate the discussion, such as an arbitral or judicial tribunal.

The United States legal accommodation was found early. In 1801 an issue arose over the neutral rights of Mr Seeman, the owner of a Hamburg vessel captured by France during a war between France and England and 'recaptured' by an American naval vessel, the *USS Constitution*. The American Congress had authorized such recaptures, but had not declared war against France. Captain Talbot of the *Constitution* wanted the vessel to be considered French, thus his prize; Seeman claimed title subject only to paying salvage, if any, for the return of his vessel from an illegal capture. Chief Justice John Marshall for the United States Supreme Court first considered whether the belligerent law of prize applied at all. He (for the Court) wrote: '[C]ongress may authorize general hostilities, in which case the general laws of war apply to our situation; or partial hostilities, in which case the laws of war, so far as they actually apply to our situation, must be noticed.' Since Congress had not authorized the recapture of neutral vessels, the owner was given his ship back on payment only of salvage to Captain Talbot.[17] The quoted language was not really necessary to the decision, but has been often repeated and is usually regarded as fixing the legal approach of the United States to the application in practice of the laws of war.

5.3   The American Civil War; Richard Henry Dana

By 1866 modern *positivism* had developed a framework of thought that accommodated both the ultimate discretion of statesmen to attach legal labels according to their perceptions of national interest, and the ultimate

---

17 *Talbot* v. *Seeman*, 5 US 5, at 28 (1801). The case involved various constitutional issues as well which are too complex to explain in this place.

need of lawyers to maintain a theory of law that could at least guide, if not compel, the application of rules to a reality that the inconsistent labels of statesmen had made seem anarchic.

The clearest statement of the relationship of the natural laws of war to the positive law for modern times, like so much else in the laws of war, comes out of the American Civil War. Dana in his 1866 edition of the classical legal text by Wheaton offered a series of propositions as suggestions of principle in the light of inconsistent political and legal analyses. Basically, he found that each legal order decides for itself and applies through its own Courts whatever legal labels its officials determine to be the ones its legal order prefers:

'The courts of a State must treat rebellion against the State as a crime. ... If the acts are depredations on commerce protected by the State, they may be adjudged piracy *jure gentium* by the courts of the State. It is a political and not a legal question, whether the right to so treat them shall be exercised .... The fact that the State has actually treated its prisoners as prisoners of war ..., or has claimed and exercised the powers and privileges of war against neutrals, does not change the abstract rule of law, in the Court. ... Where a rebellion has attained such dimensions and organization as to be a State *de facto*, and its acts reach the dimensions of war *de facto*, and the parent State is obliged to exercise powers of war to suppress it, and especially if against neutral interests, it is now the custom for the State to yield to the rebellion such belligerent privileges as policy and humanity require .... Yet this is a matter of internal State policy only, changeable at any time.'[18]

6.   CONCLUSION

It is now possible to suggest that attempts to use the tools of the positive law, treaties, to diminish the authority of national officials to attach the legal labels each feels it within his or her authority to determine under the municipal law granting that authority, must fail. The reason for this inevitable failure lies in the fundamental distribution of authority among States (and some other actors) in the international legal order, which preserves as *jus cogens* the authority of each constituent legal order to select for itself a repository of the capacity to represent the order abroad.

---

18 R.H. Dana, ed., of H. Wheaton, *Elements of International Law* (1866), Carnegie Endowment ed. of 1936 with commentary by G.G. Wilson, at 164, n. 84 by Dana, at 168.

The 'right' of each constituent legal order within the international legal order to select its own 'Government' is inalienable. It cannot be given away by treaty. It includes the capacity to attach legal labels for the purposes of its own legal order to events both internal to that order and abroad. As applied to circumstances pertinent to the international legal order, however, it is restricted by the equal authority of the other constituent bodies of that order; it is a right of auto-interpretation only, not a power to determine legal categories for others.

The implications of this analysis of one fundamental rule of the international legal order are many. Some have been indicated. Others include difficulties in extradition, which involves the meshing of criminal law categories in different municipal legal orders, and the failure of repeated and vigorous attempts to create an international criminal court based on some notion of individual responsibility to a legal order beyond the municipal order.[19]

It can be suggested, in conclusion, that time and effort would be better spent in trying to build legal institutions capable of achieving virtue-moral goals within the fundamental constitution of the Westphalian system than in trying to alter the system by disregarding authority structures built by positive morality, history and municipal legal structures that are implicit in the international system itself.

---

19 The most recent working out of this approach to legal problems of extradition is the *Final Report of the ILA Committee on Legal Problems of Extradition in Relation to Terrorist Offences*, presented at Warsaw in August 1988. The full Proceedings including the Report and the debate that led to its adoption by the Association are printed in 11 Terrorism 511-529 (1989). Application of an identical model of the international legal order to encourage approaches to the growing problem of international environmental degradation and spoliation better attuned to political and legal reality than the usual assertion of natural law 'obligations' is J. Sette-Camara, *Pollution of International Rivers*, 186 Hague Recueil 117-217 (III, 1984). A similar approach is taken by M. Bedjaoui, *Problèmes récents de succession d'états dans les états nouveaux*, 130 Hague Recueil 457-505 (II, 1970), to uphold expropriation by States too poor to pay just compensation. But, since his fundamental value, national self-determination, is in reality not the highest value in the international legal order, and the integrity of a territorial sovereign is not threatened by the existence of an international claim which can be satisfied by many other means than military action, his argument seems more polemical than convincing. He does not actually take the approach recommended here for consistency with the order, but a naturalist variation raising a different value to the position of highest without any evidence in State practice or diplomatic correspondence that his views are shared by statesmen other than those whose constituents would clearly receive advantages by adopting them.

SLAVERY: THE PAST AND THE PRESENT

Manfred Lachs

1.   INTRODUCTION

In this Collection of Essays in Honour of Frits Kalshoven, the contributors are expected to deal mainly with humanitarian law, protection of life in time of war, and human rights in general. I propose to dwell on a closely related problem which is mainly of historical interest, yet serious and disquieting traces of it remain today: slavery.

Among the very many definitions which have been made of that institution the most pertinent seems to be that by Davis, who saw a slave as a 'human being who is legally owned, used, sold or otherwise disposed of as if he or she were a domestic animal'.[1] The Slavery Convention of 1926 defined as a slave a man in a position where 'any or all of the rights of ownership are exercised over him'. One might have thought that this institution had completely disappeared. Its abolition on an international level by means of legal instrument began in 1815 at the Congress of Vienna; was *inter alia* reflected in the General Act of Berlin in 1885 and of Brussels in 1890 and in several other conventions. It is outlawed by more recent instruments of a universal character: the Geneva Convention of 25 September, the Protocol of 7 December 1953 and the additional

---

1   D.B. Davis, Slavery and Human Progress (1984). See also D.B. Davis, The Problem of Slavery in Western Culture (1966); D.B. Davis, The Problem of Slavery in the Age of the Revolution, 1770-1823 (1975).

Convention on the Abolition of Slavery and Slave Trade and Institutions and Practices similar to Slavery (Geneva; 14 December 1956), and the Convention for the Suppression of the Traffic in Persons and of the Exploration of the Prostitution of Others (1949). Unfortunately, evidence has continuously surfaced of practices which challenge this prohibition.

For example, in some countries of Asia and Africa men, women and children are still bought and sold, to work in very harsh conditions (sometimes even up to 16 hours a day), and are exposed to brutality and physical punishment; children are being sold into forced labour, even shops are kept in some cities in which children are exhibited on sale. A particular phenomenon is still bondage on tropical plantations, a form of domination through indenture and other kinds of servitude. While in these situations in law, any or all of the rights of ownership by man over man have been abolished, in practice there has not always been an end to such bondage. The issues have been investigated and pursued within the framework of the United Nations, particularly the Commission on Human Rights and the Working Group on Slavery and the Slave Trade in all their practices and manifestations.

The Working Group on Slavery discovered such practices some years ago in certain countries of Africa and on sugar plantations in Latin America.[2] Recently it found instances of children adopted for commercial purposes, child prostitution and debt bondage.[3] In the circumstances, the greatest danger of having these prohibited practices continue lies in connivance. Very frequently Governments and the public seem to forget or ignore them, yet only recently they were re-discovered in some North African countries: quasi slaves, descendants of Moors from the north and black girls from the south. Again it was found that they get no pay, minimal clothing and only the husks of pounded millet to eat. In some cases they are reduced to the status of animals.[4] It has also been discovered that an institution of part-slaves has developed, covering those who have obtained a measure of freedom by favour or by paying money. They are still condemned to very hard work but at least they receive some

---

2 *Cf.*, The Times, 2 November 1983.

3 *Cf.*, Report Commissions of Human Rights, Sub-commission on Prevention of Discrimination and Protection of Minorities, E/CN.4/sub.2/1989/39 of 28 August 1989.

4 According to Le Monde of 23 October 1990: 'Esclaves oubliés, si le nombre d'affranchis a augmenté, l'esclavage, en depit des proclamations est loin d'avoir disparu en Mauritanie'. And: 'Aujourd'hui beaucoup d'affranchis sont economiquement independants. Mais socialement et psychologiquement, ils restent dans la categorie des esclaves'.

payment.[5] Similar in practice is the situation of some aborigines who are exposed to hardship, frequently imprisoned and kept in custody, some of them dying in detention or found hanging in their cells. This is also a subject which calls for urgent attention.[6]

Finally there is a phenomenon of a particularly dangerous dimension which has yet to be recognized for the slavery it represents. I refer to the use of children in the armed forces. According to recent reports about 200,000 children under the age of 15 are in military service. In some countries they 'enlist' in order to earn a living, in others they are 'persuaded' to do it by their parents or neighbours. In one country (Uganda) orphans or abandoned children are recruited into the army. It is estimated that about 12 countries resort to such practices. It is to be recalled that, in accordance with the Protocols Additional to the 1977 Geneva Conventions, the lowest age for military service is 15. This standard has also been adopted in Article 38 of the Convention on the Rights of the Child of 1989.[7]

2.   A BRIEF HISTORICAL SURVEY

2.1   Early period

Having reviewed the present situation regarding slavery it may be useful to enquire into its past. The roots of that institution are to be found in the early pages of history. Greece and Rome considered the institution an

---

5   An interesting incident occured several years ago in London. A woman appeared in Court on a charge of shoplifting. It was a minor offence but it was revealed that she was an orphan and was given to her employer who was posted as a diplomat: she was not paid, was alleged to be treated a 'a member of the family' and received only a present once a year. *Cf.*, The Times, 2 August 1983. *Cf.*, also the maiden speech of Lord Maughan in the House of Lords and his book: The slaves of Timbuktu (1970).

6   *Cf.*, Report of the Royal Commission Enquiry into Aboriginal Deaths in Plice Custody, The Times, 29 December 1988. *Cf.*, also the extremely useful work done on the subject by the International Commission on Humanitarian Issues established in Geneva which prepared a report and submitted it to the Sub-commission on Prevention of Discrimination and Protection of Minorities of the Human Rights Commission of the UN, Geneva, 1987.

7   In this respect it is interesting to mention that the problem of child-soldiers is also under consideration in the UN Working Group on contemporary forms of slavery. See Res. 1989/42 on Contemporary forms of slavery of the Sub-Commission on Prevention of Discrimination and Protection of Minorities, E/CN.4/Sub.2/1989/L.11/Add.6 of 1 September 1989. In this Resolution the participation of children in military training and hostilities is considered as a contemporary form of slavery.

integral part of their system. Hence the surprise of all those contemporary writers who studied the issue that countries of high culture and civilization could accept slavery as a natural phenomenon. How did it come that even religion did not affect the institution? There is of course the purely economic approach: a child of the economic interpretation of history. But slavery in fact cannot be detached from the system in which it has existed and flourished. This is even valid for the contemporary forms of slavery I have referred to above. Thus, it has rightly been stressed that it is much more correct to speak of slave society than of slavery as such. There is, on the other hand, some indication that to pay men for their services and work was felt to be degrading. There are of course historians who claim that slavery was an element of a primitive type of economy. However, the element of *mores* cannot be ignore.

Slavery has in fact been part and parcel of almost every civilization in all parts of our globe. The history of slavery in England itself makes fascinating reading. The *London Advertiser* carried in 1756 an advertisement for the sale of a 14-year-old negro boy guaranteed free from any disease. Lord Mansfield estimated the value of slaves in his time at £700,000 sterling. It has been argued that anti-slavery in Britain was connected with the concern over social control, factory discipline and the contradiction of admitting the existence of slaves abroad while deploring lack of welfare at home. The consciousness of this wrong is said to have been shared by Whigs and Tories, Anglicans, Evangelicals and Quakers alike. To recall Lord Mansfield:

'The power of a master over his slave has been extremely different in different countries. The state of slavery is of such a nature that it is incapable of being introduced on any reasons, moral or political, but only by positive law, which preserves its force long after the reasons, occasion, and time itself from whence it was ever created is erased from memory. It is so odious that nothing can support it but positive law.'[8]

It cannot be left unsaid that it was most probably the oldest and most typical reported discrimination against the human person. It has been claimed that:

'Forces fundamental to Hellenism succeeded in wresting the miraculous creation of the polis and its civilization from the poverty of the land, the

---

8   *Cf.*, *The Negro Case*, 20 repr. in Howell's State Trials, at 82 (1771).

inclemency of the climate and the opposition of a hostile world. Slavery and its attendant loss of humanity are part of the sacrifice which had to be paid for the achievements.'[9]

This is a very doubtful thesis, rightly contested by most writers on the subject. The trade in negroes flourished in the Middle East, by the Red Sea and up the Nile: the Phoenicians supplied slaves to the East and to Greece bringing them from remote countries and colonies around the Mediteranen. Evidence is available that there were slave nursemaids, tutors and doctors, there were slaves in the liberal arts in Rome. Some justification of it is found in Aristophanes and Euripides. But it cannot be denied, as Professor Finley has suggested, that: '[u]nmitigated evil remains an evil'.

Historically there were two particular sources of slavery: conquest and piracy. Those taken prisoners were transformed into slaves. But not all prisoners were made slaves, only those who were barbarians. Identity of faith prevented a man from becoming a slave. A different faith and barbary were thus identical.[10]

The period of Byzantium is another chapter in the development of slavery. Byzantium was frequently engaged in war and many prisoners were taken. It was then that Christians were sometimes taken, but mostly Turks, and both were consigned to the status of slaves. Not infrequently prisoners were given their freedom or exchanged. Finally, there was also the sale of prisoners into slavery which was ferquently practised by Turks and by the Byzantines themselves. Freedom was frequently bought for Christian prisoners.[11] This was the continuation of a practice well known in Antiquity and taken over by feudal society. The other special source of slaves was piracy, an institution well known in the Ancient and Mediaeval World. Pirates robbed ships on the high seas or even close to the coast and took the crews prisoner. They then proceeded to the sale of both booty and men.

However, the main channel for the acquisition of slaves was trade. The slave trade was known and developed in the Ancient World; such markets as Chios or Delos offered considerable numbers of slaves for sale. A characteristic feature of that period was the fact that the Greeks were the main slave traders in the Eastern Mediterranean and one has to take into account that the phenomenon was changing with changes in the

---

9 See J. Vogt, Ancient Slavery and the Ideal of Man 32 (1975).
10 See J. Juthner, Hellenen und Barbaren (Helleens and Barbarians) 113 (1923).
11 *Cf.*, A. Aziz Suryal, The Crusade of Nicopolis 110-112, 155 (1934).

sociological structure of societies.[12] With the dawn of feudalism in the Middle Ages, the demand for slaves declined; only with the growing trade between Italian cities and the Near East did the slave trade again begin to flourish. Traders from Venice and Genoa exported slaves not only to Egypt but also to Constantinople, one of the main markets notwithstanding several laws prohibiting that trade (876, 945 and 960 and the *Pactum Lotharii* of 840 AD). At a certain period the biggest traders were the Turks, who acquired a considerable number of prisoners by war or piracy, crews who were then sold in slavery. Thus, as in Antiquity, late Byzantium featured an imprtant slave trade. The phenomenon flourished where two cultures met: that of the East and the West.[13]

2.2   Seventeenth and eighteenth century

In more recent times, however, one of the basic demands for slaves came from the sugar plantations, most of them in, what was called at that time, the New World - not only in North-America but also in Brazil and the British West-Indies. The import of slaves grew apace from the seventeenth century. In Barbados, for instance, about 18,000 whites would be found in 1643 and only 5,000 negroes. About a century and an half later there were 20,000 whites and 46,000 slaves. In the British colonies, hereditary slavery continued. Apparantly, there was only one exception: when in 1733 General Oglethorpe established the new colony of Georgia, he barred slavery. This interdiction lasted, however, only seventeen years. The various journeys across the Atlantic have enhanced the slave trade. Strangely enough, notwithstanding Bacon, Newton and Locke the enlightenment, the slave trade continued. Earlier, Queen Elizabeth expressed her detestation of the trade but, as reported, Charles II and James II profited from it. Moral authorities from the Bible onwards were cited in querying that institution, yet notwithstanding individual protests the trade in slaves went on. Even Bartholomé de Las Casas, the Apostle to the Indies, in his desire to protect them defended negro labour as more fitted for hard work. Attention should be drawn also to the fact that the Portuguese were the first to organize a serious trade. They brought negroes from Spain and had them sold to the 'New World'. Thus, there was an abundance of negroes in the Spanish colonies in America until the

---

12 M.I. Finley, Economy and Society in Ancient Greece (1981); also M.I. Finley, ed., The Legacy of Greece, A New Appraisal (1981).

13 *Cf.*, A. Epeling, Die Sklaverei von den altesten Zeiten bis auf die Gegenwart (Slavery From the Early Times Until the Present) (1889).

Governor of San Domingo, Nicolas de Ovano, prohibited the entry of slaves and required the conversion to Christianity of those already present. At the same time, Sir John Hawkins and Sir Water Raleigh engaged in the negro trade. It is reported that by the time of the French Revolution, 14 English, 15 Dutch and 4 Portuguese as well as French and Danish centres in Africa were dealing in slaves.[14] The first trade in negroes in Mexico began with the *Conquistadores*: Cortez had some negroes at his disposal. From Mexico they were taken to other areas in Latin America, to Peru and Guatemala. They were transported on ships of the Spanish Armada. Negroes were imported into the 'New World' for three centuries. Meanwhile trading continued from the Guinea Coast to the Indian Ocean. A very interesting development was the transport of negro slaves across the Pacific Ocean. In respect of Africa it was claimed that slavery would never be abolished while that continent consisted of 'a prodigious number of small, independent states, perpetually at variance and under no restraining form of government'.[15] In some treaties concluded with African States, European powers protected their subjects form being made slaves.[16] It may be argued that the fact that African labour was black, was incidental. The essential point was that the 'Negro had survival value'.[17]

---

14 *Cf.*, I. Marques Rodiles, The Slave Trade with America, Negroes in Mexico 36-52, 296 *et seq.* (1961-1962).

15 This claim was made by H. Trevor-Roper (as he then was). *Cf.*, The New Statesman, 3 November 1968. He argued that:
    'In the mid-19th century British governments reluctantly admitted that slavery was the effect of African independence. So at last they moved directly into the Dark Continent. With the defeat of the Southern States in America and the British and French occupation of the slaving coasts, the unique history of African wrong came to an end, and the blindspot of civilization would lie elsewhere'.

16 *Cf.*: 'No subjects of His said Majesty shall be bought or sold, or made slaves in any part of the Kingdom of Algiers upon any pretence whatsoever.' (Art. XII, at 61). 'That no merchants being His Majesty's subjects, and residing in, or trading to the City and Kingdom of Algiers, shall be obliged to buy any merchandise against their wills; but it shall be free for them to buy such commodities as they shall think fit ...' (Art. XVI, at 62); Treaty between Great Britain and Algiers signed at Algiers, 10 April 1682, renewed 18.III.1729 (Hertslet, A Complete Collection of the Treaties and Conventions between Great Britain and Foreign Powers, VI (1820)).

17 F. Tannenbaum, *A Note on the Economic Intepretation of History*, Political Science Quarterly 248 (1946). And he adds:
    'Historically speaking the Negro has inherited the Tropics because he could inherit them. He had the competence he needed for the effort. The white man was merely a temporary instrument in making the achievement possible. But he has to admit that the great migratory movement was initiated under duress. The duress under which it began has long since passed away, but the immigrant and his children have remained. In the sum total of it all, the Negro race has been given an additional large share of the faith of the globe for its own.'

In the seventeenth and eighteenth century slavery did not reflect solely economic factors but was conditioned by prevalent sociological attitudes and institutions on both sides of the Atlantic. On the other hand, in the European 'Old World', even a philosopher like Hume felt blacks to be inferior to whites.

An important step in the fight against slavery in the nineteenth century was Beecher Stowe's *Uncle Tom's Cabin*.[18] Though nowadays decried as patronizing, this work compelled a wave of sympathy for the slave which permanently changed many an attitude for the better. While discussing the issue today, special mention should be made of the important work carried on by the Anti-Slavery Society, founded on 19 April 1839. It recently celebrated its 150th anniversary and has an unrivalled record of achievements in the field of combatting these shameful practices.[19]

3.   EFFORTS AT A NATIONAL LEVEL TO ABANDON
      SLAVERY

The descendants of some slaves were known as Creoles originating in Spain or Portugal; later they were the offsprings of thousands of settlers in Latin America. This brought about the creation of a caste system which was entirely different from that practised by the indigenous people. Inter-marriage produced a new and pejorative vocabulary: a *mulatto* was the child of a negro and a white, while *zmbaigo* was the child of a negro and

---

It is true that certain areas of the world can be inherited only by people used to that climat but this is a geographical and climatical condition. However the way the inhabitants of these areas were treated was obviously contrary to all laws of humanity and contrary to the basic premises of human decency. Tannenbaum admits that: 'Negro slavery was a fact and a tragedy'. *Ibid.*, at 251. See also F. Tannenbaum, Slave and Citizen, The Negro in the Americas (1947).

18 Published in the National Era in a serial form in 1851.

19 It is worth recalling that the society was established under Queen Victoria's reign thanks mainly to Wilberforce. It continued with its campaign and though it has a small membership of about 1,200, is active in 30 countries and supported by a series of other organizations like Amnesty International. Its co-ordinator expressed the attitude towards slavery by bureaucrats in the following way:

'Since the abuses which we highlight are forbidden through the UN Charter, international law and various conventions, it follows that they are illegal in all nations which are signatories to such agreements. Therefore in the minds of the bureaucrats, these things cannot be taking place, and since they are not taking place it follows that there is no problem to be soved.'

A. Whittaker, The Times, 14 April 1988. *Cf.*, also a publication of the Anti-Slavery Society, A Pattern of Slavery (1910).

an Indian.[20] Slavery in Latin America was the source of frequent rebellions which spread to Indians who were carrying on their own struggle to throw off the colonial yoke. The struggle for that independence united all of them into one family. In fact some of its leaders were eminent negroes: Don Miguel Hidalgo y Castilla was a Creole, and it was he who is alleged in 1810 to have proclaimed the abolition of slavery. There were also the so-called Pintos, who were mainly of negro origin, in the State of Carrero who headed the Revolution of 1854. In Mexico, Juarez was supported by important leaders of negro origin: so was Zapata and his revolution of 1910.[21]

The proces of liberation and the road to racial co-operation were entirely different in Brazil. The roots of the institution were particularly deep, and it took a long time for Brazil to abolish slavery. In this the role of Britain was of no mean importance. The British Parliament passed a law making it illegal for British subjects to engage in the slave trade after 1 May 1808; Brazil's Declaration of 1830 was not enforced for 20 years. During these years it is estimated that at least half a million Africans were imported in slavery. Britain's efforts led to the enactment which qualified the slave-trade as piracy, and Britain intercepted various vessels carrying slaves. It is reported that during the period 1845 - 1850 about 400 vessels were so intercepted.[22]

As for slave-ownership in the Caribbean, it seems erroneous to assume that the abolition of the trade was completed in 1806 and 1807. The abolition, and the emancipation of 1833, 'occurred when [they] did because of fortunate concatenation of interest, ideas and extraneous events'.[23]

One chapter in the abolition of the trade which is usually neglected in the writings of the subject concerns developments in Haiti. Here again was an example of slavery on sugar plantations. It was an area where colonialism continued, but slavery was abolished in the British West-Indies

---

20 Statistics of the early period are very instructive. By the year 1570 there were 20,569 negroes and 6,464 Europeans in Mexico, but almost two centuries later the numbers of both negroes and whites had seriously declined. Yet the confrontation remained serious. *Cf.*, I. Marques Rodeles, op. cit. n. 14, at 46.

21 *Ibid.*, at 52.

22 *Cf.*, A.K. Manchester, British Pre-eminence in Brazil: Its Rise and Decline (1933); L. Bethell, The Abolition of Brazilian Slave Trade (1970).

23 M. Craton, Sinews of Empire (1974). An element which is probably under-estimated by the writer is the importance of the Anti-Slavery Movement in both England and Scotland. An interesting early work on the subject came from the German writer F. Hochstetter, Die wirtschaftlichen und politischen Motive für die Abschaffung des britischen Sklavenhandels im Jahre 1806 und 1807 (The Economical and Political Motive for the Termination of the British Slave Trade in 1806 and 1807) (1905).

in 1838. An exception was Cuba, where colonialism and slavery continued to the end of the nineteenth century.[24] Altogether, the riches of the Caribbean area played an important part in the slave trade. For instance, Jamaica grew very wealthy part thanks to black slaves, both African and Creole, continuously supplied in ever bigger numbers. The planters not only developed exceptionally good businesses in primary products but expanded their activities to all fields where their wealth could be invested. Here again, one has to acknowledge not only the fact of outside assistance but also that slaves themselves fought for their emancipation. Attention has been drawn, and rightly so, to the function of the missionaries, and to the Jamaican slave revolt known as the Baptist War in December 1831 and its severe repression. It was finally brought to an end by an Act of Parliament in 1832.[25]

Economic factors were bolstered and parallelled by racism, activated by deep-seated prejudice against blacks. It is interesting to note that in a certain period slaves constituted 85% of the population of the Caribbean sugar colonies, 40% in the tobacco and rice colonies of North America, and 35% in the sugar and gold mining colony of Brazil. Some writers even see a link between the American Revolution and the abolition of slavery in Europe. France played a role here: for instance in San Domingo the slave revolt of 1791-1804 created the Republic of Haiti, led by what some saw as the black Jacobins.

However, mention must be made of another sad chapter on the subject. It is the so-called 'Code Noir' signed by Louis XIV in March 1685.[26] It is declared: *'Les esclaves être meubles'* equal to *'autres choses mobilieres'*.[27] They were subject to sale, seizure and inheritance.[28] Thus it was said that a slave was a *'res'*. It was claimed that slavery was

---

24 *Cf.*, R. Blackburn, The Overthrow of Colonial Slavery, 1776-1848 (1987). For a somehow simplified presentation of the history of slavery see A. Cassese, International Law in a Divided World 52-54 (1986).

25 *Cf.*, M. Turner, Slaves and Missionaries. Disintegration of Jamaican Slave Society, 1787-1834 (1983).

26 It was elaborated by Colbert and intended for the Antilles, later to Guyana (1704) and also the the Island of Bourbon (1723).

27 Articles 44 and 46.

28 It was rightly claimed that the code relied on roman law and applied it to human beings in the relationship between master and slave. *Cf.*, A. Gisler, C.S.S.P. L'Esclavage aux Antilles Françaises 20 *et seq.* (1965).

intended to 'punish the mischief makers and protect the just'.[29] The Code was amended in 1724, harsher measures were introduced for Louisiana; suspended in 1794 it was reintroduced in 1802. It will be completely abolished only in 1848[30] over half a century after the French Revolution.

4.   SOME OBSERVATIONS ON CONTEMPORARY DEVELOPMENTS

We are still awaiting a full explanation of a phenomenon that contaminated every page of human history. Or to use the words of Davis: 'Slavery [is] a deadly virus which twisted and distorted intellectual processes, social attitudes, and philosophy'. It is of course most deplorable that, even while we are preparing consecutive generations of human rights, slavery in one form or another is still being practised. The work of the UN in this field is, although encouraging, highly inadequate.[31]

It seems appropriate, therefore, to say something about these current developments as they occur within, *inter alia*, UNICEF, the Working Group on Contemporary Forms of Slavery of the Sub-Commission on Prevention of Discrimination and Protection of Minorities (of the Commission on Human Rights) and the latter Sub-Commission itself.[32]

In the most recent Draft Resolution of the Commission on Human Rights, contained in the Report of the Sub-Commission on Prevention of Discrimination and Protection of Minorities (42nd session) of 28 February 1991,[33] the Working Group on Contemporary Forms of Slavery noted the

---

29 Though the master was barred from treating slaves in a barbarous or inhumane way, evidence presented by them was of no legal value (Articles 30, 31 of the Code). It may be recalled that Rousseau's Social Contract speaks only of Europeans in case they were subjected to absolute rules but refrained from mentioning Africans and the inhabitants of the Antilles.

30 It was accepted by the Sovereign Council of San Domingo on 6 May 1687. *Cf.*, L. Sala-Molins, Le code noire, au le calvaire de Canaan (1987).

31 *Cf.*, the World Summit for Children -UNICEF- in which heads of States and Governments took part. The summit approved a 'plan of action' to support the world's two billion children and protect them against abuse and hunger. The Times, 1 October 1990.

32 See, *e.g.*, the Report of the Working Group on Contemporary Forms of Slavery, repr. in E/CN.4/Sub.2/1990/44 and Sub-Commission Res. 1987/31 and 1987/32 of 4 September 1987; 1988/31 of 1 September 1988; 1989/41 of 1 September 1989; 1990/30 of 31 August 1990. Also its Res. 1982/20 of 10 March 1982 on the question of slavery and the slave trade in all their practices and manifestations; ECOSOC Res. 1982/20 of 4 May 1982; ECOSOC Res. 1983/30 of 26 May 1983 on the suppression of the traffic in persons and of the exploitation or the prostitution of others.

33 Repr. in E/CN.4/1991/L.76.

inadequacy of the provisions of the Slavery Convention of 1926, the Supplementary Convention on the Abolition of Slavery, the Slave Trade and Institutions and Practices Similar to Slavery of 1956 and the Convention for the Suppression of the Traffic in Persons and of the Exploitation or the Prostitution of Others (1949). The Working Group asked the Commission on Human Rights to qualify contemporary forms of slavery as representing some of the gravest violations of human rights.[34] Furthermore, the Secretary-General of the UN is invited to stimulate the establishment of effective reporting mechanisms. In the opinion of the Working Group/Sub-Commission the Center for Human Rights should be designated as the focal point for the co-ordination of UN-activities concerning the suppression of contemporary forms of slavery. In order to improve co-operation within the framework of the UN, the Special Rapporteur on the sale of children, child prostitution and child pornography is asked to participate in the meetings of the Working Group.[35] Particular emphasis is put on the adherence to Articles 32, 34-36 of the Convention on the Right of the Child with a view to combating contemporary forms of slavery. In a Draft Resolution on the status of this Convention,[36] the Commission on Human Rights expressed its deep concern about 'the exploitation of children in its various manifestations', including 'the exploitation of child labour'. In this light it was noted that the draft programme of action for prevention of sale of children needed to be amended by the Sub-Commission so that it could be adopted at the 48th Session of the Commission on Human Rights. In this respect the ILO initiative to implement a new programme on the elimination of child labour was welcomed; at the same time Res. 1990/VII relating to the 'Programme of Action for the Elimination of the Exploitation of Child Labour' was endorsed.[37]

In Res. 1991/52 of 6 March 1991[38] the Commission on Human Rights expressed its profound concern with respect to, *inter alia*, the exploitation of children in many parts of the world, despite the succesful conclusion of the World Summit for Children (New York, 29-30 September 1990) and

---

34 *Ibid.*, at 2.
35 See, *inter alia*, E/CN.4/1991/L.74/Rev.1 of 4 March 1991 concerning the Report of the Special Rapporteur on the Sale of Children, Child Prostitution and Child Pornography (Agenda item 24 (b)).
36 Repr. in E/CN.4/1991/L.78.
37 *Ibid.*, at 3. States Parties to the ILO were asked to support the ILO initiative and the ensure adequate funding for the programme.
38 Repr. in E/CN.4/1991/L.11/Add.4 of 6 March 1991 (Draft Report of the Commission), at 3-5.

the entry into force of the Convention on the Rights of the Child on 2 September 1990.[39] The Committee urged 'the importance of the strictest compliance by States Parties with their obligations under the Convention'.[40]

It is obvious, therefore, that, in the light of contemporary development, the Conventions of 1926, 1956 and of 1949 require serious revisions, in particular in the field of international control of the implementation of their provisions. Only then will slavery, the sad heritage of the past hanging like a heavy cloud over the humanity of today, disappear. Four centuries ago an English court declared: 'The air of England is too free for a slave to breath', yet slavery continued. It is time that the air of the globe be declared too free for any man to be a slave, to serve or live out his life in bondage.

---

39 See, *e.g.*, with respect to the Convention on the Rights of the Child, the statement made by Martenson on 26 January 1990: 'the Convention on the Rights of the Child, more than any other instrument in this field, incorporates the whole spectrum of human rights -civil, political, economic, social and cultural- and provides that respect and protection of all the children's rights are the starting point for full development of the potential of the individual in an atmosphere of freedom, dignity and justice.'
40 Op. cit. n. 36, at 4. See also Draft Report of The Comission by Rapporteur M. Tanchi. Repr. in E/CN.4/1991/L.10/Add.1 of 7 March 1991.

APPENDICES

LIST OF CONTRIBUTORS

Georges ABI-SAAB
Professor of International Law, Graduate Institute of International Studies, Geneva; Member of the Institute of International Law.

Rosemary ABI-SAAB
Chargée d'enseignement, University of Geneva.

George H. ALDRICH
Member of the Iran-US Claims Tribunal; Professor of International Humanitarian Law, University of Leiden.

Geoffrey BEST
Senior Associate Member of St. Antony's College and the International Relations Teaching Group, University of Oxford; Formerly Professor of History, University of Sussex.

Michael BOTHE
Professor of Public Law, Johann-Wolfgang Goethe University, Frankfurt.

Theo C. VAN BOVEN
Professor of Public International Law, University of Limburg; Member of the UN Sub-Commission on Prevention of Discrimination and Protection of Minorities.

Astrid J.M. DELISSEN
Associate Professor of International and Humanitarian Law, University of Leiden.

Yoram DINSTEIN
Professor of Law, Chair of Human Rights, Tel Aviv University.

Krzysztof DRZEWICKI
Professor of Public International Law, University of Gdańsk.

John DUGARD
Professor of Law, University of Witwatersrand, Johannesburg.

René-Jean DUPUY
Professor at the *Collège de France*; Former Member of the European Commission on Human Rights.

William J. FENRICK
Director of International Law, Department of National Defence, Ottawa.

Dieter FLECK
Director International Legal Affairs, Federal Ministry of Defence, Bonn.

Hisakazu FUJITA
Professor of Law, University of Tokyo.

Hans-Peter GASSER
Legal Adviser to the Directorate, International Committee of the Red Cross.

Bernhard GRAEFRATH
Professor of International Law, Berlin; Member of the International Law Commission.

Leslie C. GREEN
University Professor, Honorary Professor of Law, University of Alberta.

Christopher J. GREENWOOD
Fellow, Magdalene College, Cambridge; Lecturer in Law, University of Cambridge.

Peter H. KOOIJMANS
Professor of Public International Law, University of Leiden; UN Special Rapporteur on Questions Relevant to Torture.

Manfred LACHS
Judge and former President of the International Court of Justice.

Theodor MERON
Professor of Law at the New York University School of Law and the Graduate Institute of International Studies in Geneva.

Henri MEYROWITZ
Doctor of Law; *Avocat honoraire* at the *Cour d'Appel de Paris*.

Stanislaw E. NAHLIK
Emeritus Professor of International Law, Jagellonian University.

Jean PICTET
Honorary Vice-President of the International Committee of the Red Cross.

Alfred P. RUBIN
Professor of International Law, The Fletcher School of Law and
Diplomacy, Tufts University, Medford.

Yves SANDOZ
Director Doctrine, Law and Relations with the Movement, International
Committee of the Red Cross.

Henry G. SCHERMERS
F.B.A., Professor of Law, University of Leiden; Member of the European
Commission on Human Rights.

Dietrich SCHINDLER
Emeritus Professor of International and Constitutional Law, University of
Zürich; Member of the International Committee of the Red Cross.

Julian J.E. SCHUTTE
Legal Adviser at the Ministry of Justice, The Hague; Professor in the Law
of European Co-operation in Criminal Matters; Member of the UN
Committee on Crime Prevention and Control.

Torsten STEIN
Professor of European and Comparative European Public Law, Director of
the *Europa-Institut*, University of Saarland, Saarbrücken.

Erik SUY
Professor of Public International Law and Law of International
Organisations, Catholic University of Leuven.

Gerard J. TANJA
Member of the Office of the Legal Adviser, Netherlands Ministry of
Foreign Affairs.

Michel VEUTHEY
Head of the International Organisations Division, International Committee of the Red Cross.

Paul J.I.M. DE WAART
Professor of Public International Law, Free University of Amsterdam.

Jan J. VAN DER WEEL
President of the Netherlands' Red Cross Society.

René-Jean WILHELM
Former Deputy Director of the General Affairs Division, International Committee of the Red Cross.

Christine VAN DEN WYNGAERT
Professor of Law, University of Antwerp.

SELECT BIBLIOGRAPHY *

HUMANITARIAN LAW IN GENERAL

ABI-SAAB G., *The Specificities of Humanitarian Law*, in C. Swinarski, ed., Studies and Essays on International Humanitarian Law and Red Cross Principles in Honour of Jean Pictet (1984).

ABI-SAAB G., *The Implementation of Humanitarian Law*, in A. Cassese, ed., The New Humanitarian Law of Armed Conflict (1979).

ABI-SAAB R., *The 'General Principles' of Humanitarian Law According to the International Court of Justice*, International Review of the Red Cross (1987).

ALDRICH G.H., *New Life for the Laws of War*, 75 AJIL (1981).

BAXTER R.R., *The First Modern Codification of the Law of War*, 3 International Review of the Red Cross (1963).

BELLO E., African Customary Humanitarian Law (1980).

BEST G., Humanity in Warfare, The Modern History of the International Law of Armed Conflicts (1980).

BINDSCHEDLER-ROBERT D., A Reconsideration of the Law of Armed Conflict; the Law of Armed Conflict (1969).

BOISSER P., Histoire du comité international de la Croix-Rouge, De Solférino à Tsoushima (1963).

BOTHE M., *Le droit de la guerre et les Nations Unies*, 5 Etudes et travaux de l'institut universitaire des hautes études internationales (1967).

CASSESE A., ed., The New Humanitarian Law of Armed Conflict (1979).

CONDORELLI L., *Le droit international humanitaire en tant qu'atelier d'expérimentation juridique*, dans W. Haller, A. Kölz, G. Müller, D. Thürer, réd., Im Dienst an der Gemeinschaft, Festschrift für Dietrich Schindler zum 65. Geburtstag (Au service de la communauté, Mélanges offerts en l'honneur du Professeur Dietrich Schindler pour son 65e anniversaire) (1989).

---

* *The entries in this bibliography are selected from the references made by the authors in their contributions to this book. Its purpose is to provide a selective list of literature for further study. This bibliography was compiled by E. Blanco and M. Brus.*

DAVID E., *'L'excuse de l'ordre supérieur et l'etat de nécessité'*, XIV Revue belge de droit international (1978-1979).

DETTER DE LUPIS I., The Law of War (1987).

DINSTEIN Y., The Defense of Superior Orders in International Law (1965).

DURAND A., Histoire du comité international de la Croix-Rouge, De Sarajevo à Hiroshima (1978).

FRIEDMAN L., ed., The Laws of War. A Documentary History (1972).

GASSER H.-P., *Prohibition of Terrorist Acts in International Humanitarian Law*, International Review of the Red Cross (1986).

GENTILI, De Jure Belli, Lib. I (1612).

GREENWOOD C., *The Relationship between Jus ad Bellum and Jus in Bello*, 9 Rev. Int. Studies (1983).

GREENWOOD C., *The Concept of War in Modern International Law*, 36 ICLQ (1987).

GREENWOOD C., *The Twilight of the Law of Belligerent Reprisals*, 20 NYIL (1989).

GROTIUS H., De Jure Belli ac Pacis, Lib. III (1625).

HARTIGAN R.S., Lieber's Code and the Law of War (1983).

HINGORANI R.C., ed., Humanitarian Law (1987).

KALSHOVEN F., Belligerent Reprisals (1971).

KALSHOVEN F., Constraints on the Waging of War (1987).

KUNZ J.L., *The Chaotic Status of the Laws of War and the Urgent Need for their Revision*, 45 AJIL (1951).

MARTENS F. DE, La paix et la guerre (1901).

NAHLIK S.E., *Droit dit de Genève et droit dit de La Haye*, Annuaire français de droit international (1978).

PICTET J., Les principes du droit international humanitaire (1966).

POST H.H.G., DEKKER I.F., eds., The Gulf War of 1980-1988, The Iran-Iraq War in International Perspective (Forthcoming).

ROBERTS A., GUELFF R., Documents on the Laws of War (1989).

ROSAS A., STEINBÄCK P., *The Frontiers of International Humanitarian Law*, 24 Journal of Peace Research (1987).

ROSENBLAD E., International Humanitarian Law of Armed Conflict (1979).

SANDOZ Y., SWINARSKI C., ZIMMERMANN B., eds., Commentary on the Additional Protocols of 8 June 1977 to the Geneva Convention of 12 August 1949 (1987).

SCHINDLER D., *State of War, Belligerency, Armed Conflict*, in A. Cassese, ed., The New Humanitarian Law of Armed Conflicts (1979).

SCHINDLER D., *Die Grenzen des völkerrechtlichen Gewaltverbots* (Limitations of the Prohibition of the Use of Force), Berichte der Deutschen Gesellschaft für Völkerrecht (Reports of the German Association of International Law) (1986).

SCHINDLER D., TOMAN J., eds., The Laws of Armed Conflicts; A Collection of Conventions, Resolutions and Other Documents, 3rd rev. ed., (1988).

STONE J., Legal Controls of International Conflict. A Treatise on the Dynamics of Disputes and War Law (1954).

SWINARSKI C., ed., Studies and Essays on International Humanitarian Law and Red Cross Principles in Honour of Jean Pictet; Etudes et essais sur le droit international humanitaire et sur les principes de la Croix-Rouge en l'honneur de Jean Pictet (1984).

SWINARSKI C., Introducción al derecho internacional humanitario (Introduction to International Humanitarian Law) (1984).

UNESCO, International Dimensions of Humanitarian Law (1988).

VATTEL E. DE, Le droit des Gens, Lib. II (1758).

VEUTHEY M., *The Global Reach of International Humanitarian Law*, in R.C. Hingorani, ed., Humanitarian Law (1987).

MEANS AND METHODS OF WARFARE

BLIX H., Means and Methods of Combat. International Dimensions of Humanitarian Law (1988).

DAVID E., *A propos de certaines justifications théoriques à l'emploi de l'arme nucléaire*, dans C. Swinarsky, réd., Etudes et essais sur le droit international humanitaire et sur les principes de la Croix-Rouge en l'honneur de Jean Pictet (1984).

FENRICK W.J., *New Developments in the Law Concerning the Use of Conventional Weapons in Armed Conflict*, 19 Can. Y.b. Int'l Law (1981).

GRIEF N., *The Legality of Nuclear Weapons*, in I. Pogany, ed., Nuclear Weapons and International Law (1987).

HARTIGAN R.S., Lieber's Code and the Law of War (1983).

HOWARD M., Restraints in War: Studies in the Limitation of Armed Conflict (1979).

HUBER M., Die kriegsrechtlichen Verträge und die Kriegsraison (The Laws and Customs of War in Relation to Military Necessity), Zeitschrift für Völkerrecht (1913).

KALSHOVEN F., The Laws of Warfare (1973).

KALSHOVEN F., *Arms, Armaments and International Law*, 191 Recueil des Cours de l'Académie de Droit International, II (1985).

KALSHOVEN F., *Conventional Weaponry: The Law from St. Petersburg to Lucerne and Beyond*, in M.A. Meyer, Armed Conflict and the New Law: Aspects of the 1977 Geneva Protocols and the 1981 Weapons Convention (1989).

LIEBER F., Instructions for the Government of Armies of the United States in the Field, rev. ed. (1863).

MEYROWITZ E.L., *The Laws of War and Nuclear Weapons*, Brooklyn Journal of Int. Law (1983).

MUDGE G.A., *Starvation as a Means of Warfare*, 4 International Lawyer (1969-1970).

NURICK L., *The Distinction between Combatant and Noncombatant in the Law of War*, 39 AJIL (1945).

ROSENBLAD E., International Humanitarian Law of Armed Conflict (1979).

PROTECTION OF VICTIMS OF ARMED CONFLICT

BEST G., Humanity in Warfare (1980).

BETTARI M., KOUCHNER B., Le devoir d'ingérence (1987).

BOTHE M., PARTSCH K.J., SOLF W.A., eds., New Rules for Victims of Armed Conflicts (1982).

CALOGEROPOULOS-STRATIS A.S., Droit humanitaire et droits de l'homme; La protection de la personne en période de conflit armé (1980).

DOSWALD-BECK L., *The Value of the 1977 Geneva Protocols for the Protection of Civilians*, in M.A. Meyer, Armed Conflict and the New Law: Aspects of the 1977 Geneva Protocols and the 1981 Weapons Convention (1989).

GRAEFRATH B., *Die Bedeutung des Ergänzungsprotokolls für den Schutz der Zivilbevölkerung* (L'importance du Protocole additionnel pour la protection de la population civile), dans C. Swinarski, réd., Etudes et essais sur le droit international humanitaire et sur les principes de la Croix-Rouge en l'honneur de Jean Pictet (1984).

KALSHOVEN F., Assisting the Victims of Armed Conflict and Other Disasters (1989).

MANN H., *International Law and the Child Soldier*, 36 ICLQ (1987).

PEIRCE B., *Humanitarian Protection for the Victims of War: The System of Protecting Powers and the Role of the ICRC*, 90 Military Law Review (1980).

PICTET J.S., Commentary, the Geneva Conventions of 12 August 1949, vol. I (1952), vol. II (1960), vol. III (1960), vol. IV (1958).

PICTET J.S., Le droit humanitaire et la protection des victimes de la guerre (1973).

PILLOUD C., *Les réserves aux Conventions de Genève de 1949*, Revue internationale de la Croix-Rouge (1976).

ROBERTS A., *Prolonged Military Occupation: the Israeli-Occupied Territories Since 1967*, 84 AJIL (1990).

SCHUTTE J.J.E., *The Applicability of the Geneva Conventions on the Protection of War Victims and Protocol I to the Relation between a Contracting Party and Its Own Nationals*, 33 Österreichische Zeitschrift für öffentliches Recht und Völkerrecht (1982).

VERWEY W.D., *Humanitarian Intervention under International Law*, 32 NILR (1985).

WAART P.J.I.M. DE, *Long-term Development Aspects of Humanitarian Assistance in Times of Armed Conflict*, in F. Kalshoven, Assisting the Victims of Armed Conflict and Other Disasters (1989).

DIFFERENT TYPES OF ARMED CONFLICTS

ABI-SAAB G., *Wars of National Liberation and the Laws of War*, 3 Annales d'etudes internationales (1972).

ABI-SAAB G., *Wars of National Liberation in the Geneva Conventions and Protocols*, 165 Recueil des Cours de l'Académie de Droit International, IV (1979).

ABI-SAAB R., Droit humanitaire et conflits internes. Origines et évolution de la réglementation internationale (1986).

BEN-RAFAEL E., Israel - Palestine: a Guerrilla Conflict in International Politics (1987).

CASSESE A., *Wars of National Liberation and Humanitarian Law*, in C. Swinarski, ed., Studies and Essays on International Humanitarian Law and Red Cross Principles in Honour of Jean Pictet (1984).

FORSYTHE D., *Legal Management of Internal War: The 1977 Protocol on Non-International Armed Conflicts*, 72 AJIL (1978).

GASSER H.-P., *International Non-International Armed Conflicts: Case Studies of Afghanistan, Kampuchea, and Lebanon*, 31 American University Law Review (1982).

GASSER H.-P., *Genfer Abkommen und Terrorismusverbot (Geneva Conventions and the Prohibition of Terrorism)*, in Völkerrecht im Dienste des Menschen, Festschrift für Hans Haug (1986).

GASSER H.-P., *A Measure of Humanity in Internal Disturbances and Tensions: Proposal for a Code of Conduct*, International Review of the Red Cross (1988).

GASSER H.-P., *Code of Conduct in the Event of Internal Disturbances and Tensions*, International Review of the Red Cross (1988).

GASSER H.-P., *Armed Conflict within the Territory of a State*, in W. Haller, A. Kölz, G. Müller, D. Thürer, eds., Im Dienst an der Gemeinschaft, Festschrift für D. Schindler (1989).

GREENWOOD C., *Self-Defence and the Conduct of International Armed Conflict*, in Y. Dinstein, M. Tabory, eds., International Law at a Time of Perplexity. Essays in Honour of Shabtai Rosenne (1989).

KALSHOVEN F., *'Guerilla' and 'Terrorism' in Internal Armed Conflict*, 33 Am. Univ. Law Review (1983).

MERON T., *Towards a Humanitarian Declaration on Internal Strife*, 78 AJIL (1984).

MERON T., *Draft Model Declaration on Internal Strife*, International Review of the Red Cross (1988).

MYREN R.S., *Applying International Laws of War to Non-international Armed Conflicts: Past Attempts, Future Strategies*, 37 NILR (1990).

NURICK L., BARRETT R.W., *Legality of Guerrilla Forces under the Laws of War*, 40 AJIL (1946).

OETER S., *Terrorism and 'Wars of National Liberation' from a Law of War Perspective. Traditional Patterns and Recent Trends*, 49 ZaöRV (1989).

PARTSCH K.J., *Regeln für den Aufstand*, Neue Zeitschrift für Wehrrecht (1989).

PAUST J.J., *Terrorism and the International Law of War*, 64 Military Law Review (1974).

RUBIN A.P., *Terrorism and the Laws of War*, 12 Denver J. Int'l Law and Politics (1983).

RUBIN A.P., *Should the Laws of War Apply to Terrorists?*, 79 ASIL Proc. (1985).

STONE J., Legal Controls of International Conflict. A Treatise on the Dynamics of Disputes and War Law (1954).

THARP P.A., *The Laws of War as a Potential Legal Regime for the Control of Terrorist Activities*, 32 Journal of International Affairs (1978).

WILSON H.A., International Law and the Use of Force by National Liberation Movements (1988).

THE 1977 ADDITIONAL PROTOCOLS

ABI-SAAB R., *Le degré d'acceptation des Protocoles de 1977 après 10 ans: ratifications, adhésions, réserves, décisions de ne pas en devenir partie*, dans Colloque sur les Protocoles de 1977 additionnels aux Conventions de 1949: Dix ans après (1987).

ALDRICH G.H., *New Life for the Laws of War*, 75 AJIL (1981).

ALDRICH G.H., *Some reflections on the origins of the 1977 Geneva Protocols*, in C. Swinarski, réd., Etudes et essais sur le droit international humanitaire et sur les principes de la Croix-Rouge en l'honneur de Jean Pictet (1984).

ALDRICH G.H., *Progressive Development in the Laws of War: A Reply to Criticisms of the 1977 Geneva Protocol I*, 26 Virginia Journal of International Law (1986).

ANDRIES A., *La répression nationale des infractions graves au droit humanitaire - aspects criminologiques*, XI Congress International Society of Military Law and the Laws of War (1988), 1-2 Revue internationale de droit pénal militaire et du droit de la guerre 1990.

BOTHE M., PARTSCH K.J., SOLF W.A., eds., New Rules for Victims of Armed Conflicts (1982).

BREUCKER J. DE, *La répression des infractions graves aux dispositions du premier Protocole additionnel aux quatre Conventions de Genève du 12 août 1949*, XVI Revue de droit pénal militaire et de droit de la guerre (1977).

CASSESE A., *The Geneva Protocols of 1977 on the Humanitarian Law of Armed Conflict and Customary International Law*, 3 UCLA Pacific Basin Law Journal (1984).

DINSTEIN Y., *The New Geneva Protocols: A Step Forward or Backward?*, 33 Yb. of World Affairs (1979).

DOSWALD-BECK L., *The Value of the 1977 Geneva Protocols for the Protection of Civilians*, in M.A. Meyer, Armed Conflict and the New Law: Aspects of the 1977 Geneva Protocols and the 1981 Weapons Convention (1989).

DOUCET G., *La qualification des infractions graves au droit international humanitaire*, in F. Kalshoven, Y. Sandoz, eds., Implementation of International Law (1989).

DUTLI M.T., *Captured Child Combatants*, International Review of the Red Cross (1990).

FORSYTHE D., *Legal Management of Internal War: The 1977 Protocol on Non-International Armed Conflicts*, 72 AJIL (1978).

GRAEFRATH B., *Die Bedeutung des Ergänzungsprotokolls für den Schutz der Zivilbevölkerung* (L'importance du Protocole additionnel pour la protection de la population civile), dans C. Swinarski, réd., Etudes et essais sur le droit international humanitaire et sur les principes de la Croix-Rouge en l'honneur de Jean Pictet (1984).

GREENWOOD C., *Reprisals and Reciprocity in the New Law of Armed Conflict*, in M.A. Meyer, Armed Conflict and the New Law: Aspects of the 1977 Geneva Protocols and the 1981 Weapons Convention (1989).

IHRAI S., *Les mécanismes d'établissement des faits dans les Conventions de Genève de 1949 et dans le Protocole I de 1977,* dans F. Kalshoven, Y. Sandoz, réd., Mise en oeuvre du droit international humanitaire (1989).

KALSHOVEN F., *Reaffirmation and Development of Humanitarian Law Applicable in Armed Conflicts, the Diplomatic Conference, 1974-1977*, Part I, 8 NYIL (1977), Part II, 9 NYIL (1978).

KALSHOVEN F., *The Belligerent Reprisals in the Light of the 1977 Geneva Protocols*, 1979 European Seminar on Humanitarian Law, ICRC (1988).

KUSSBACH E., *Le Protocole additionnel I et les Etats neutres*, 62 Revue internationale de la Croix-Rouge (1980).

MANN H., *International Law and the Child Soldier*, 36 ICLQ (1987).

MEYROWITZ H., *Le Protocole additionel I aux Conventions de Genève de 1949 et le droit de la guerre maritime*, 89 RGDIP (1985).

OBRADOVIC K., *Les Protocoles de 1977 dix ans après: bilan et perspectives pour l'avenir*, dans Colloque sur les Protocoles de 1977 additionnels aux Conventions de 1949: Dix ans après (1987).

PENNA L.R., *Customary International Law and Protocol I*, in C. Swinarski, ed., Studies and Essays on International Humanitarian Law and Red Cross Principles in Honour of Jean Pictet (1984).

ROBERTS G.B., *The New Rules for Waging War: The Case against Ratification of Additional Protocol I*, 26 Virginia Journal of International Law (1985-1986).

ROSENBLAD E., *Starvation as a Method of Warfare - Conditions for Regulation by Convention*, 7 International Lawyer (1973).

ROUSSEAU C., Le droit des conflits armés (1983).

SANDOZ Y., SWINARSKI C., ZIMMERMAN B., eds., Commentary on the Additional Protocols of 8 June 1977 to the Geneva Conventions of 12 August 1949 (1987).

SCHUTTE J.J.E., *The Applicability of the Geneva Conventions on the Protection of War Victims and Protocol I to the Relation Between a Contracting Party and Its Own Nationals*, 33 Österreichische Zeitschrift für öffentliches Recht und Völkerrecht (1982).

WORKSHOP on Customary International Law and the 1977 Protocols, 2 Am. U.J. Int. L. & Pol'y. (1987).

NEUTRALITY AND NAVAL WARFARE

BINDSCHEDLER R.L., *Frieden, Krieg und Neutralität im Völkerrecht der Gegenwart* (Peace, War and Neutrality in Present Day International Law), in J. Tittel, ed., Multitudo Legum, Ius Unum, Essays in Honour of W. Wengler (1973).

CASTRÉN E., The Present Law of War and Neutrality (1954).

DINSTEIN Y., The Laws of Neutrality, 14 Israel Yearbook of Human Rights (1984).

DOSWALD-BECK L., *The International Law of Naval Armed Conflicts: The Need for Reform*, 7 The Italian Yearbook of International Law (1986-1987).

FENRICK W.J., *The Exclusion Zone Device in the Law of Naval Warfare*, 24 Canadian Yearbook of International Law (1986).

JENKINS M., *Air Attacks on Neutral Shipping in the Persian Gulf: The Legality of the Iraqi Exclusion Zone and Iranian Reprisals*, 8 B.C. Int'L & Comp. L. Rev. (1985).

KALSHOVEN F., *Enemy Merchant Vessels as Legitimate Military Objectives*, Paper presented to the Symposium on the Law of Naval Warfare, US Naval War College (1990).

KUSSBACH E., *Le Protocole additionnel I et les Etats neutres*, 62 Revue internationale de la Croix-Rouge (1980).

LAGONI R., *Gewaltverbot, Seekriegsrecht und Schiffahrtsfreiheit im Golfkrieg* (Prohibition of the Use of Force, Law of Naval Warfare and Freedom of Navigation in the Gulf War), in W. Fürst, R, Herzog, D.C. Umbach, eds., 2 Festschrift für Wolfgang Zeidler (1987).

MEYROWITZ H., *Le Protocole additionel I aux Conventions de Genève de 1949 et le droit de la guerre maritime*, 89 RGDIP (1985).

OTTMÜLLER R., *Die Anwendung von Seekriegsrecht in militärischen Konflikten seit 1945* (The Application of the Law of Naval Warfare in Military Conflicts since 1945), in Institut für Internationale Angelegenheiten der Universität Hamburg, ed., 10 Das geltende Seekriegsrecht in Einzeldarstellungen (1978).

RAUCH E., *Le droit contemporain de la guerre maritime: Quelques problèmes créés par le Protocole additionel I de 1977*, 89 RGDIP (1985).

RONZITTI N., ed., The Law of Naval Warfare. A Collection of Agreements and Documents with Commentaries (1988).

RONZITTI N., *The Crisis of the Traditional Law Regulating International Armed Conflicts at Sea and the Need for its Revision*, in N. Ronzitti, ed., The Law of Naval Warfare (1988).

RUBIN A.P., *The Concept of Neutrality in International Law*, in A.T. Leonhard, ed., Neutrality; Changing Concepts and Practices (1988).

RUSSO F.V., *Neutrality at Sea in Transition: State Practice in the Gulf War as Emerging Customary Law*, 19 ODILA (1988).

SCHINDLER D., *Aspects contemporains de la neutralité*, 121 Recueil des Cours de l'Académie de Droit International, II (1967).

TUCKER R.W., The Law of War and Neutrality at Sea (1957).

WILLIAMS W.L., *Neutrality in Modern Armed Conflicts: A Survey of the Developing Law*, 90 Military Law Review (1980).

ZEMANEK K., *The Chaotic Status of the Laws of Neutrality*, in Im Dienst an der Gemeinschaft, Festschrift für Dietrich Schindler (1989).

HUMANITARIAN LAW AND HUMAN RIGHTS LAW

CALOGEROPOULOS-STRATIS A.S., Droit humanitaire et droits de l'homme; La protection de la personne en période de conflit armé (1980).

DRZEWICKI K., *The Status of International Human Rights Instruments in Domestic Law*, in A. Rosas, ed., International Human Rights Norms in Domestic Law. Finnish and Polish Perspectives (1990).

MERON T., Human Rights in Internal Strife: Their International Protection (Hersch Lauterpacht Memorial Lectures, Cambridge) (1987).

MERON T., Human Rights and Humanitarian Norms as Customary Law (1989).

QUESTIAUX N., Study of the Implications for Human Rights of Recent Developments Concerning Situations Known as States of Siege or Emergency, UN Doc. E/CN.4/Sub. 2/1982/15.

STEIN T., *Derogations from Guarantees Laid Down in Human Rights Instruments*, in I. Maier, ed., Protection of Human Rights in Europe, Proceedings of the Fifth International Colloque about the European Convention on Human Rights (1982).

WYNGAERT C. VAN DEN, The Political Offence Exception to Extradition. The Delicate Problem of Balancing the Rights of the Individual and the International Public Order (1980).

WEISSBRODT D., *Ways International Organizations Can Improve Their Implementation of Human Rights and Humanitarian Law in Situations of Armed Conflict*, in E.L. Lutz, H. Hannum, K.J. Burke, eds., New Directions in Human Rights (1989).

HUMANITARIAN LAW IN PRACTICE

BEN-RAFAEL E., Israel - Palestine: a Guerrilla Conflict in International Politics (1987).

BOTHE M., *Prevention and Repression of Breaches of International Humanitarian Law*, Yearbook, International Institute of Humanitarian Law (1986-1987).

CATTAN H., Palestine and International Law: the Legal Aspects of the Arab-Israeli Conflict (1976).

DAVID E., *La Guerre du Golfe et le droit international*, 20 Revue belge de droit international (1987).

DRZEWICKI K., *National Legislation as a Measure for Implementation of International Humanitarian Law*, in F. Kalshoven, Y. Sandoz, eds., Implementation of International Humanitarian Law (1989).

DUGARD J., *SWAPO: The Jus ad Bellum and the Jus in Bello*, 93 South African Law Journal (1976).

FALK R., ed., 3 The Vietnam War and International Law (1972).

GASSER H.-P., *International Non-International Armed Conflicts: Case Studies of Afghanistan, Kampuchea, and Lebanon*, 31 American University Law Review (1982).

GERSON A., Israel, the West Bank & International Law (1978).

HENTSCH T., Face au blocus: La Croix-Rouge internationale dans le Nigéria en guerre (1967-1970) (1973).

JENKINS M., *Air Attacks on Neutral Shipping in the Persian Gulf: The Legality of the Iraqi Exclusion Zone and Iranian Reprisals*, 8 B.C. Int'L & Comp. L. Rev. (1985).

KALSHOVEN F., *The Netherlands and International Humanitarian Law Applicable in Armed Conflicts*, in H.F. van Panhuys *et al.*, ed., III International Law in the Netherlands (1980).

KALSHOVEN F., The Present State of Research Carried out by the English-Speaking Section of the Centre for Studies and Research: The Application of Humanitarian Law, Hague Academy of International Law (1986).

KALSHOVEN F., SANDOZ Y., eds., Implementation of International Humanitarian Law. Research Papers by Participants in the 1986 Session of the Centre for Studies and Research in International Law and International Relations of the Hague Academy of International Law; Mise en oeuvre du droit international humanitaire. Traveaux de recherche des participants à la session de 1986 du Centre d'etude et de recherche de droit international et de relations internationales de l'Académie de droit international de la Haye (1989).

LAGONI R., *Gewaltverbot, Seekriegsrecht und Schiffahrtsfreiheit im Golfkrieg* (Prohibition of the Use of Force, Law of Naval Warfare and Freedom of Navigation in the Gulf War), in W. Fürst, R, Herzog, D.C. Umbach, eds., 2 Festschrift für Wolfgang Zeidler (1987).

MURRAY C., *The 1977 Protocols and Conflict in South Africa*, 33 ICLQ (1984).

O'BRIEN W.V., *The Law of War, Command Responsibility and Vietnam*, 60 Georgetown Law Journal (1972).

OTTMÜLLER R., *Die Anwendung von Seekriegsrecht in militärischen Konflikten seit 1945* (The Application of the Law of Naval Warfare in Military Conflicts since 1945), in Institut für Internationale Angelegenheiten der Universität Hamburg, ed., 10 Das geltende Seekriegsrecht in Einzeldarstellungen (1978).

ROBERTS A., *Prolonged Military Occupation: The Israeli-Occupied Territories Since 1967*, 84 AJIL (1990).

RUBIN B., The Arab States & the Palestine Conflict (1981).

RUSSO F.V., *Neutrality at Sea in Transition: State Practice in the Gulf War as Emerging Customary Law*, 19 ODILA (1988).

SCHIFF Z., YA'ARI E., Intifada: The Palestinian Uprising - Israel's Third Front (1986).

SCHINDLER D., *United Nations Forces and International Humanitarian Law*, in C. Swinarski, ed., Studies and Essays on International Humanitarian Law and Red Cross Principles in Honour of Jean Pictet (1984).

TAVERNIER P., *La Guerre du Golfe: Quelques aspects de l'application du droit des conflits armés et du droit humanitaire*, 30 Ann. français de droit international (1984).

ARMS CONTROL AND DISARMAMENT

FREI D., *International Humanitarian Law and Arms Control*, 28 International Review of the Red Cross (1988).

MOHR M., *Völkerrechtliche Fragen der Kontrolle von Abrüstungsverträgen* (International Law Questions concerning the Control of Disarmament Treaties), 36 Staat und Recht (1987).

NEUHOLD H., *Legal Aspects of Arms Control Agreements*, in K.-H. Böckstiegel, H.-E. Folz, J.M. Mössner, K. Zemanek, eds., Völkerrecht, Recht der Internationalen Organisationen, Weltwirtschaftsrecht (International Law, the Law of International Organizations, International Economic Law), Festschrift für Ignaz Seidl-Hohenveldern (1988).

SUR S., *A Legal Approach to Verification in Disarmament or Arms Limitation*, UNIDIR Research Papers (1988).

grave breaches 100, 102, 110, 188, 190, 199
in occupied territories 48, 137, 138, 142, 180, 182, 188, 193, 520, 536
immunity 312, 320, 539
internment 48, 49, 167
labour 167
mistreatment 519
prohibition of attack against 82, 85-86, 100, 101, 168, 190, 219, 308, 531
prohibition of reprisal against 101, 168, 319, 322, 324, 528
prohibition of the use of civilians as a human shield 100, 109, 132
protection of civilians from the effects of hostilities 97, 108-111, 130, 139, 188, 189, 408, 528, 531, 534, 536, 539, 540, 541
repatriation 193

Civilians and combatants *see:* Combatants and non-combatants

CLAUSEWITZ, K. v. 5, 270-271

Clausula si omnes 43, 47, 48,

Code of Conduct for Law Enforcement Officials (1979) 261

Code of Manu 275

Collateral damage 144, 404-405, 420

Colonial and racist regimes 136, 230, 455, 479

Colonialism 478, 480, 498, 622

Combat
law 180
means and methods of 44, 82, 213, 219, 245, 259, 261
operations 408
See also: Law of the Hague, Warfare

Combatants 17, 88, 102, 146, 179, 217, 218, 221, 308, 447, 450, 460, 461, 508, 573, 574
child-combatants *see:* Children
definition 25, 138
denial, loss of POW-status 139, 453
duties, obligations of 138, 139, 140, 232, 278
guerilla *see:* Guerilla
hors de combat 17, 86, 106, 243, 304, 507 *see also:* Personnel
irregular 107, 132, 137-141
obligation to distinguish themselves from civilians 139-141, 143
protection 82, 132, 214, 243
rebel *see:* Rebel forces
recognition 287
status 35, 82-83, 85, 88, 103, 107-108, 138, 140, 213, 214, 218, 278, 453, 573
treatment 447, 461, 574
unlawful 102
See also: Belligerents

Combatants and non-combatants 71, 507
distinction 51, 82, 107, 108, 132, 167, 244, 261, 278, 308, 539, 572

Concentration camps 167, 449

Conference on Security and Cooperation in Europe 384, 513, 587

Conflict *see:* Armed conflict

Convention on the Elimination of All Forms of Racial Discrimination (1965) 222

Convention on the Prohibition of Development, Production and Stockpiling of Bacteriological (Biological) and Toxin Weapons (1972) 291, 361

Convention on the Prohibition of Military or any other Hostile Use of

as ground for derogation 237, 239, 252, 253, 254 *see also:* Derogation
powers 451
public 222, 239, 250, 255, 260, 264
situations 69, 222, 240, 503
state of 172, 237, 238, 244, 252, 254, 258, 260

Environment 588
environmental damage 101, 104, 285, 292-293, 319, 404-405, 421-422, 423
protection 110, 168, 357, 525, 537, 539
targets *see:* Target
See also: Attacks, Convention on the Prohibition of Military or any other Hostile Use of Environmental Modification Techniques (1976)

European Convention on Human Rights and Fundamental Freedoms (1950) 237, 246, 462, 578, 579-580

Exclusive zones *see:* Zones

Extradition 175, 202-205, 449, 568, 572, 574-576, 578, 605, 611
nationality exception 203, 204
political offence exception 203, 568, 572, 575, 576

Fair trial, principles of 195, 196, 200, 238, 239, 243, 246, 450, 573, 578
See also: Judicial guarantees

Falklands/Malvinas conflict 59, 65, 387-388, 400, 434, 440-441

First strike 329

Flag of truce
improper use 186

Force *see:* Use of force

Forces *see:* Armed forces

Franco-Prussian War (1870) 41-45

FREI, D. 351-352

GASSER, H.-P. 61, 241-242, 246, 502, 513

Geneva Conventions
of 1864
Convention for the Amelioration of the Conditions of the Wounded in Armies in the Field 17, 40, 44, 448
of 1929 41, 46, 47, 48, 49
Convention II on Prisoners of War 98, 282
of 1949 28, 41, 46 ff., 94, 98, 100, 120, 135, 141, 174, 198, 200, 203, 209-210, 228, 234, 240, 242, 264, 278, 279, 282, 311, 362, 375-376, 379, 380, 390, 405, 420, 421, 452, 463, 507, 510, 525, 548
application 228, 230, 484-487, 523, 529, 532-534, 536, 537
common article 3 49, 54, 66, 83, 84, 85, 98, 113, 213, 214, 215-217, 222, 223, 227-229, 231, 233, 234, 242, 244, 245, 259, 264, 462, 497, 501, 502-503, 505, 507-508, 512
Convention II 379, 421
Convention III 52, 106, 107, 192, 260, 373, 523-525, 536
Convention IV 49, 100, 111, 147-148, 167, 174, 175, 192, 255, 259, 281, 398, 484-486, 497, 503, 504-505, 516 ff., 536, 573
derogation 255, 502
grave breaches 174, 178-185, 201, 260, 519
judicial guarantees 259, 260
protecting powers 181, 182, 548
ratification 242, 245, 467
repression of breaches 549

376, 425, 432, 438, 439, 447, 455-
456, 502, 505, 516, 532, 571
  laws applicable 82, 83, 211, 232,
    233, 244, 261, 389 *see also:*
    Geneva Conventions (1949),
    Protocols (1977)

International Commission of Law 321,
322

International Committee of the Red
Cross 24, 30, 31, 32, 35, 37, 38, 41,
44 ff., 68, 71, 83, 100, 101, 131, 156,
166, 211, 212, 217, 218, 221, 229,
228, 231, 234, 250, 252, 293, 352,
360, 413, 420, 422, 486, 505, 507,
509, 511, 512, 517, 520-522, 524,
525, 528 ff., 546, 549 ff.
  right of initiative 215, 220
  protection, treatment of detainees
    31, 37, 252, 507

International Conference on Human
Rights (Teheran, 1968) 52-55

International Convention on the
Suppression and Punishment of the
Crime of Apartheid 194

International Court of Justice 60, 68,
98, 99, 100, 121, 122, 123, 124-125,
176, 222, 229, 234, 235, 395, 400,
470, 471, 472, 482, 491-494, 495,
497, 590-591, 600, 601, 602

International Covenants
  of Civil and Political Rights (1966)
    118, 222, 237, 239, 252, 257 ff.,
    462, 468, 469, 475, 510
  on Economic, Social and Cultural
    Rights (1966) 118, 222, 469, 470,
    472-473, 475, 510

International customary law *see:*
Customary law

International Fact-Finding Commission
33, 63, 133, 143, 175, 352, 357, 534

International humanitarian law *see:*
Humanitarian law

International Institute of Humanitarian
Law (San Remo) 66, 261

International law 9, 16, 28, 49, 56,
68, 84, 113, 117, 119, 120, 121, 122,
125, 177 ff., 211, 220, 223, 254, 308,
317, 325, 328-329, 355, 356, 367,
368, 383, 467 ff., 497, 532, 575, 584
ff.

International Law Association 570,
571-573, 576, 578

International law of armed conflicts
see: Humanitarian law

International Law Commission 254-
257, 362

International Military Tribunal
  at Nuremberg 87, 98, 116-117, 121,
    146-147, 176, 201, 205, 282, 401,
    430-434
    London Agreement of 8 August
      1945 and Annexed Charter 173,
      174, 180, 188, 189, 199, 205
  at Tokyo 121, 205

International Red Cross Conferences
see: Red Cross

Intervention 74, 411, 451, 472, 489,
604
  external, foreign 135, 213, 216,
    221, 451, 480
  by humanitarian institutions 35, 38,
    68, 211
  methods 591-593
  military 524, 591
  obligation to intervene 583-593

Nuclear-free zone *see:* zones

Nulla poena sine praevia lege 181, 182, 222, 237, 302

Nuremberg Principles
Principles of International Law recognized in the Charter of the Nuremberg Tribunal and in the Judgment of the Tribunal (1950) 188
See also: International Military Tribunal

Objects indispensable to the survival of civilians 149, 168, 188, 219, 319, 398, 537, 539
See also: Destruction

Occupation 21, 131, 182, 186, 447, 455, 482, 485, 486, 487, 489, 493, 516
foreign, alien 134, 136, 230, 478, 479, 480
Israeli 480, 485, 486, 488

Occupied territory (-ies) 52, 131, 137, 140, 143, 154, 180, 182, 188, 485, 504, 517, 521
Israeli 193, 478 ff., 499, 10-11, 17
aliens, third-state nationals in 518-519
See also: Civilians

Occupied power 186

Occupying power 53, 138, 141, 180, 181, 182, 186, 193, 199, 482, 485, 486, 520, 521

Operations 108, 137, 391, 462
airforce 410
army 410
maritime, naval 387, 402, 404, 407 ff.
rescue 421, 423, 432

Palestine 136, 465-494
Palestinian Declaration of Independence of 15 November 1988 467, 488-489

Palestine Liberation Organization 112, 134, 141, 457, 466, 481, 486, 487-488, 490, 492

Peace Conference of Versailles 481

Peace Conferences of the Hague *see:* Hague Conferences of 1899 and 1907

Peaceful settlement of disputes 13, 349, 357, 358, 359, 360, 494, 597-598
arbitration *see:* Arbitration
inquiry 597-598
judicial 597-598

Penal law
enforcement for violations of humanitarian law 139, 140, 177-178, 185, 187, 198 ff., 352, 360, 573
principle of non-retro-activity *see:* Nulla poena sine praevia lege

Penal responsibility 184, 580
individual 138, 173-176, 188, 196

Perestroika 73, 350, 468, 469, 470, 471

Perfidy, prohibition of 86, 103, 105, 192, 261,277, 278, 289

Personnel
hors de combat 41, 46, 82, 132, 192, 217, 304, 517, 535
medical 147, 179, 187, 219, 265, 379, 508, (3)5,
military 141, 279, 280, 281, 289, 533 *see also:* Combatants
religious 187